Encyclopedia of Human Emotions

Editors

David Levinson
Berkshire Reference Works, Great Barrington, Mass.

James J. Ponzetti, Jr.
Warner Pacific College

Peter F. Jorgensen
Western Illinois University

Editorial and Production Staff

Brian Kinsey
Project Editor

William Kavanah
Copy Editor

Greg Teague
Proofreader

Carol Donley
Hiram College
Literature Consultant

Cynthia Crippen
AEIOU, Inc.
Indexer

Richard Hollick
Production Manager

Impressions Book and Journal Services, Inc.
Compositor

MACMILLAN REFERENCE USA
Elly Dickason, *Publisher*
Toni Scaramuzzo, *Managing Editor*

ENCYCLOPEDIA OF HUMAN EMOTIONS

Edited by

DAVID LEVINSON

JAMES J. PONZETTI, JR.

PETER F. JORGENSEN

Volume 1

MACMILLAN REFERENCE USA
New York

Copyright © 1999 by Macmillan Reference USA

Macmillan Library Reference USA
1633 Broadway
New York, NY 10019

Printed in the United States of America

Printing Number
1 2 3 4 5 6 7 8 9 10

Library of Congress Cataloging-in-Publication Data

Encyclopedia of Human Emotions
   edited by David Levinson, James J. Ponzetti, Jr., Peter F. Jorgensen
     p. cm.
   Includes bibliographical references and index.
   ISBN 0-02-864766-1 (set) — ISBN 0-02-864768-8 (v. 1) —
     ISBN 0-02-864767-X (v. 2)
   1. Emotions—Encyclopedias.   2. Affect (Psychology)—Encyclopedias.
     3. Mood (Psychology)—Encyclopedias.
   I. Levinson, David.   II. Ponzetti, James J.   III. Jorgensen, Peter F.
   BF531.E55   1999
   152.4′03—dc21
                                           99-31198
                                           CIP

This paper meets the requirements of ANSI-NISO Z39.48-1992 (Permanence of Paper).

CONTENTS

Preface   vii

List of Articles   ix

List of Contributors   xiii

Encyclopedia of Human Emotions   **1**

Bibliography Index   685

Subject Index   707

PREFACE

Emotions, or what most people call "feelings" and scientists call "affect," are the essence of being human. Feelings can make life rich and rewarding as well as difficult and painful. Individuals vary in how they experience and express their emotions. Some celebrate and share their feelings openly while other people try to deny, hide, or redefine theirs. In addition, there are differences across social groups in how emotions are experienced and expressed; for example, between adults and children, between men and women, and between people in different cultures. Emotions are so much a part of being human that they have been intensively studied by psychologists, psychiatrists, sociologists, anthropologists, biologists, communication researchers, and others and are central to the work of social workers, clinical psychologists, psychiatrists, and other therapists. Emotions have also been a major element of the creative process for artists, novelists, poets, dancers, musicians, and theologians.

The purpose of the *Encyclopedia of Human Emotions* is to bring together information from these and other perspectives in order to summarize what we know about the nature, causes, expression, and societal role of emotions—today, in the past, and across cultures. The entries in the Encyclopedia are written by experts, most of whom are active researchers who study human emotion or are involved in the treatment of emotional problems. An important strength of this Encyclopedia is that it is interdisciplinary, with all views and information about emotions carefully presented. Although the bulk of the information comes from the field of psychology, there are also contributions from the fields of psychiatry, sociology, anthropology, biology, medicine, history, communication, and the arts.

The study of emotion in the Western world goes back to the Greek philosophers Aristotle and Plato. However, the modern study of emotions is to a great extent the product of psychoanalysis in Europe at the close of the nineteenth century. Throughout most of the twentieth century, the study of emotions remained outside the mainstream of the social and behavioral sciences. Since the 1970s, however, many aspects of emotions have been the object of intensive and extensive study, not just in the social and behavioral sciences but in the biological, medical, and physical sciences as well.

Despite the relative lack of scholarly attention given to emotion (compared, for example, to the study of intelligence or motivation) until fairly recently, the study of emotion has been guided by five general models (what scientists call paradigms) of human emotion that have been developed during the past one hundred years. The first was the psychoanalytic model, in which emotion is seen as an inner drive that is channeled and brought under control by external forces and processes. The psychoanalytic approach to explaining and studying emotion and treating emotional problems was controversial when first proposed by Sigmund Freud and remains so today. The second model, the psychological or psychodynamic model, evolved from the psychoanalytic one. The emphasis shifted, however, from inner states and drives to a consideration of interpersonal relationships, the role of social situation in emotional expression, and emotional development over the life cycle. The third model, the behavioral model, set aside the study of inner states of emotion and instead focused on behavior and behavioral expressions of emotion. The fourth, which emerged in the 1970s, is the cognitive model in which emotions are seen as a means, along with rational thought, of evaluating the situation and making decisions about what actions to take. It remains a major model followed today by psychologists in research and (along with the psychoanalytic and psychodynamic models) in the treatment of emotional problems. The final model—and the most recent one—is the biological model, which is more accurately described as a number of related models that look at the anatomy, physiology, genetics, and chemistry of the human nervous and endocrine systems for an understanding of emotion. Although proponents of the five models sometimes argue for the primacy of their respective models and criticize the other models, all five continue to guide scholars and clinicians involved in the study of human emotion, and all five perspectives are represented in this Encyclopedia.

The 146 entries cover four general topics:

1. specific emotions and specific behavioral expressions of emotions,
2. conceptual, thematic, and theoretical issues that cut across emotions,
3. emotions in society and in the human experience, and
4. biographies.

The goal of the first category is to cover as many emotions and behavioral expressions as possible—that is, all those that have been the subject of scientific study. The purpose of the second category is to cover broad issues such as the five major models mentioned above, emotions throughout the life course, the historical study of emotions, and the universality of emotional expression. The third category is intended to provide discussion of the use of emotions in communication and the expression of emotions in various cultural milieu, such as religion, music, dance, and poetry. The inclusion of these topics is an important and unique feature of the Encyclopedia as they are often ignored in discussions of emotion. In addition, they add a strongly humanistic perspective to balance the scientific perspective of many of the other entries. The purpose of the fourth category is to recognize individuals—psychologists, philosophers, sociologists, and others—who have played a seminal role in the study of emotion.

The *Encyclopedia of Human Emotions* is a reference resource meant for people who want full, up-to-date, trustworthy information about all aspects of human emotions. This includes readers who want more information about the latest "hot" emotion or trend they read about in the popular literature or hear about on television. What, for example, is "emotional intelligence"? What are "mood disorders"? How does one reach an "altered state of consciousness"? The Encyclopedia will also be useful to people who are confronting emotional issues in their lives and want background information from experts on topics such as psychotherapy, emotional abuse, or loneliness. High school and college students who need material for class discussions and papers for courses in psychology, sociology, and communication will be able to turn to the Encyclopedia for relevant information. Finally, it will be of use to scholars, who can consult it as a handy state-of-the-art review about topics on which they are not expert. Although we have made every effort to keep the material as accessible to the general public as possible, some entries, because of the very nature of the topics, must and will contain technical information based on laboratory and medical research.

There are a number of individuals who deserve to be mentioned for their contributions to this project. First, we want to thank Elly Dickason, publisher at Macmillan Reference, for her support for and ideas about the project. We want to thank Brian Kinsey, also at Macmillan, for his thoughtful and typically diligent project and editorial management. Second, thanks go to the contributors for their clear, full, and thoughtful articles that make up this Encyclopedia. Third, we want to express our appreciation to Frank Salamone, Janet Madigan, and Jack Miller, who helped us identify and locate contributors. Finally, we want to thank our families for their encouragement and support.

David Levinson
James J. Ponzetti, Jr.
Peter F. Jorgensen

LIST OF ARTICLES

Abandonment
Yvonne Kellar-Guenther

Acceptance and Rejection
Ronald P. Rohner

Achievement Motivation
Hallgeir Halvari
Sven Svebak

Advertising
Mark A. Callister
Lesa A. Stern

Aggression
James T. Tedeschi

Altered States of Consciousness
Michael Winkelman

Ambivalence
Laura A. King
Christie K. Napa

Anger
Daniel J. Canary
Beth A. Semic

Annoyance
Denis G. Sukhodolsky
Howard Kassinove

Anthropology of Emotions
Donald Pollock

Anxiety
Mark E. Comadena

Anxiety Disorders
Mark R. Dadds

Aristotle
David Levinson

Attachment
Russell A. Isabella

Attachment to Animals
John Archer

Attitudes
Peter F. Jorgensen

Attractiveness
Shealy Thompson

Attribution
Shealy Thompson

Augustine
David Levinson
Ben Manning

Biochemistry of Emotions
Andrew Baum
John Paul Garofalo

Body Movement, Gesture,
and Display
Lisa E. Allspach
Judee K. Burgoon

Boredom
Paul Wink

Bowlby, John
David Levinson

Cattell, Raymond Bernard
David Levinson

Cognitive Perspective
Tim Dalgleish
Jessica Bramham

Color
Ralph B. Hupka

Commitment
Jeffrey M. Adams

Communication
Peter Alex Andersen

Conflict
Yvonne Kellar-Guenther

Consciousness
Alfred W. Kaszniak

Creativity
Cheryl A. Wright

Cross-Cultural Patterns
Klaus R. Scherer

Crying
Randolph R. Cornelius

Culture
Jeanne L. Tsai

Culture-Bound Syndromes
Robert L. Winzeler

Dance
Judith Lynne Hanna

Darwin, Charles Robert
Paul Ekman

Defense Mechanisms
Phebe Cramer

Descartes, René
David Levinson
Ben Manning

Desire
Ellen Berscheid
Matthew Heller

Disgust
Paul Rozin
Jonathan Haidt
Clark R. McCauley

Drama and Theater
David Booth

Education and Teaching
David L. Wodrich
Glenn D. Reeder

Embarrassment
Sandra Petronio

Emerson, Ralph Waldo
Ben Manning

Emotional Abuse: Women
Ileana Arias

Emotional Abuse: Children
Kieran O'Hagan

Emotional Abuse: Siblings
Vernon R. Wiehe

Emotional Abuse: Men
Richard J. Gelles

Emotional Intelligence
Peter Salovey

Emotion Experience and
Expression
Krystyna Strzyzewski Aune
R. Kelly Aune

Emotion Suppression
Heather J. Miles
James J. Gross

Empathic Accuracy
William Ickes

Empathy
Anita P. Barbee

Envy
Ralph B. Hupka

Erikson, Erik Homburger
Ben Manning
David Levinson

Eysenck, Hans Jurgen
David Levinson

Facial Expression
Lesa A. Stern
Mark A. Callister

Fear and Phobias
Andrew C. Page

Flirtation
Antonia Abbey
Tina Zawacki

Folk Theories of Emotion
Mario Mikulincer

Food and Eating
Paul Rozin

Forgiveness
Robert D. Enright

Freud, Anna
David Levinson

Freud, Sigmund
David Levinson

Friendship
William K. Rawlins

Gender and Emotions
Leslie R. Brody

Genetics
Frances H. Gabbay

Gift Giving
Aafke Elisabeth Komter

Grief
Paul C. Rosenblatt

Guilt
Tamara J. Ferguson

Happiness
Richard P. Bagozzi

Hate
Jack Levin
Monte Paulsen

Hate Crimes
Jack Levin
Jack McDevitt

Health and Illness
Barbara L. Irvin

Helplessness
Christopher Peterson

Historical Study of Emotions
Peter N. Stearns

Hope
Kimberley A. Babb
Linda J. Levine

Hopelessness
Regan A. R. Gurung

Horney, Karen
Ben Manning
David Levinson

Horror
Deirdre D. Johnston
Elissa M. Wickmann

Human Development: Overview
Tracy L. Spinrad
Nancy Eisenberg

Human Development: Infancy
Linda A. Camras

Human Development: Childhood
Barbara Rybski Beaver

Human Development:
Adolescence
Roger Kobak

Human Development: Adulthood
Fredda Blanchard-Fields

Human Development:
Old Age
Lillian E. Troll
Karen Fingerman

Hume, David
Ben Manning
David Levinson

Hurt
Mark A. Fine
Adriana J. Umana

Infatuation
Scott A. Thompson
Joel A. Gold

Intimacy
Laura K. Guerrero

James, William
David Levinson

Jealousy
Don J. Sharpsteen

Kant, Immanuel
David Levinson
Ben Manning

Literature
Douglas Arrowsmith

Loneliness
Chris Segrin
Lisa E. Allspach

Love
Robert J. Sternberg

Lust
Sandra Metts

Mind-Body Dichotomy
Steven L. Dubovsky

Mood
Norbert Schwarz
Piotr Winkielman

Mood Disorders
Lawrence N. Rossi

Motivation
Ross Buck

Music
Frank A. Salamone

Neural Systems: From Animals
to Humans
Jaak Panksepp

Neurobiology of Emotions
Howard Eichenbaum

Nietzsche, Friedrich Wilhelm
David Levinson
Ben Manning

Oratory
Ken Hawkinson

Pain
Stuart W. G. Derbyshire

Personality
Lawrence A. Pervin

Persuasion
Steven J. Breckler

Philosophy
Robert C. Solomon

Plato
David Levinson
Ben Manning

Pleasure
Nick Haslam
Louis Rothschild

Poetry
Norman Finkelstein

Post-Traumatic Stress Disorder
Charles R. Figley

Prejudice
Thomas F. Pettigrew

Propaganda
Anthony R. Pratkanis

Psychoanalytic Perspective
Robert A. Murphy

Psychological Assessment
Andrew J. Tomarken
Gabriel S. Dichter
J. Cara Pendergrass

Psychology of Emotions
Donald K. Fromme

Psychophysiology of Emotions
Kirsten M. Poehlmann
John M. Ernst
John T. Cacioppo

Psychotherapy
Susan L. Sandel
Joseph Forscher

Relationships
Sandra Metts
William R. Cupach

Rogers, Carl Ransom
David Levinson

Sadness
Tracy M. Laulhere
Linda J. Levine

Sartre, Jean-Paul
David Levinson

Satisfaction
Walter R. Schumm

Seasonal Affective Disorder
Toru Sato

Self-Esteem
Michael H. Kernis
Brian N. Goldman

Sensation Seeking and Risk
Taking
Kjell Erik Rudestam
Elissa Slanger

Shame
Anita L. Vangelisti
Stacy L. Young

Shyness
Holly M. Hendin
Jonathan M. Cheek

Sin
Randy Michael

Smiling
Karen Caplovitz Barrett

Sociology of Emotions
Lynn Smith-Lovin

Spinoza, Baruch
David Levinson
Ben Manning

Sports
Robin S. Vealey

Stress
Carolyn M. Aldwin
Loriena A. Yancura

Sullivan, Harry Stack
David Levinson

Surprise
Julie A. Hadwin

Sympathy
Candace Clark

Temperament
Maria Amy Gartstein
Mary Klevjord Rothbart

Trust
Laurie L. Couch

Universality of Emotional
Expression
Klaus R. Scherer

Visual Arts
Franklin Sirmans

Xenophobia
Meredith W. Watts

LIST OF CONTRIBUTORS

Antonia Abbey
Wayne State University
Flirtation

Jeffrey M. Adams
High Point University
Commitment

Carolyn M. Aldwin
University of California, Davis
Stress

Lisa E. Allspach
University of Arizona
Body Movement, Gesture, and Display
Loneliness

Peter Alex Andersen
San Diego State University
Communication

John Archer
University of Central Lancashire, Preston, England
Attachment to Animals

Ileana Arias
University of Georgia
Emotional Abuse: Women

Douglas Arrowsmith
York University, Toronto, Canada
Literature

Krystyna Strzyzewski Aune
University of Hawaii, Manoa
Emotion Experience and Expression

R. Kelly Aune
University of Hawaii, Manoa
Emotion Experience and Expression

Kimberley A. Babb
University of California, Irvine
Hope

Richard P. Bagozzi
University of Michigan, Ann Arbor
Happiness

Anita P. Barbee
University of Louisville
Empathy

Karen Caplovitz Barrett
Colorado State University
Smiling

Andrew Baum
University of Pittsburgh Cancer Institute
Biochemistry of Emotions

Barbara Rybski Beaver
University of Wisconsin, Whitewater
Human Development: Childhood

Ellen Berscheid
University of Minnesota
Desire

Fredda Blanchard-Fields
Georgia Institute of Technology
Human Development: Adulthood

David Booth
Ontario Institute for Studies in Education, Toronto, Canada
Drama and Theater

Jessica Bramham
Medical Research Council, Cambridge, England
Cognitive Perspective

Steven J. Breckler
Baltimore, MD
Persuasion

Leslie R. Brody
Boston University
Gender and Emotions

Ross Buck
University of Connecticut
Motivation

Judee K. Burgoon
University of Arizona
Body Movement, Gesture, and Display

John T. Cacioppo
University of Chicago
Psychophysiology of Emotions

Mark A. Callister
Western Illinois University
Advertising
Facial Expression

Linda A. Camras
DePaul University
Human Development: Infancy

Daniel J. Canary
Pennsylvania State University
Anger

Jonathan M. Cheek
Wellesley College
Shyness

Candace Clark
Montclair State University
Sympathy

Mark E. Comadena
Illinois State University
Anxiety

Randolph R. Cornelius
Vassar College
Crying

Laurie L. Couch
Morehead State University
Trust

Phebe Cramer
Williams College
Defense Mechanisms

William R. Cupach
Illinois State University
Relationships

Mark R. Dadds
Griffith University, Australia
Anxiety Disorders

Tim Dalgleish
Medical Research Council, Cambridge, England
Cognitive Perspective

Stuart W. G. Derbyshire
University of California, Los Angeles
Pain

Gabriel S. Dichter
Vanderbilt University
Psychological Assessment

Steven L. Dubovsky
University of Colorado Health Sciences Center
Mind-Body Dichotomy

Howard Eichenbaum
Boston University
Neurobiology of Emotions

Nancy Eisenberg
Arizona State University
Human Development: Overview

Paul Ekman
University of California, San Francisco
Darwin, Charles Robert

Robert D. Enright
University of Wisconsin, Madison
Forgiveness

John M. Ernst
Illinois Wesleyan University
Psychophysiology of Emotions

Tamara J. Ferguson
Utah State University
Guilt

Charles R. Figley
Florida State University
Post-Traumatic Stress Disorder

Mark A. Fine
University of Missouri, Columbia
Hurt

Karen Fingerman
Pennsylvania State University
Human Development: Old Age

Norman Finkelstein
Xavier University
Poetry

Joseph Forscher
MidState Behavioral Health System, Meriden, CT
Psychotherapy

Donald K. Fromme
Pacific University
Psychology of Emotions

Frances H. Gabbay
*Uniformed Services University of
the Health Sciences, Bethesda, MD*
Genetics

John Paul Garofalo
University of Pittsburgh Cancer Institute
Biochemistry of Emotions

Maria Amy Gartstein
University of Oregon
Temperament

Richard J. Gelles
University of Pennsylvania
Emotional Abuse: Men

Joel A. Gold
University of Maine, Orono
Infatuation

Brian N. Goldman
University of Georgia
Self-Esteem

James J. Gross
Stanford University
Emotion Suppression

Laura K. Guerrero
Arizona State University
Intimacy

Regan A. R. Gurung
University of California, Los Angeles
Hopelessness

Julie A. Hadwin
University of Southampton, England
Surprise

Jonathan Haidt
University of Virginia
Disgust

Hallgeir Halvari
Buskerud College, Hønefoss, Norway
Achievement Motivation

Judith Lynne Hanna
University of Maryland, College Park
Dance

Nick Haslam
New School for Social Research, New York City
Pleasure

Ken Hawkinson
Western Illinois University
Oratory

Matthew Heller
University of Minnesota
Desire

Holly M. Hendin
University of California, Davis
Shyness

Ralph B. Hupka
California State University, Long Beach
Color
Envy

William Ickes
University of Texas, Arlington
Empathic Accuracy

Barbara L. Irvin
*Oregon Health Sciences University,
Southern Oregon Campus*
Health and Illness

Russell A. Isabella
University of Utah
Attachment

Deirdre D. Johnston
Hope College
Horror

Peter F. Jorgensen
Western Illinois University
Attitudes

Howard Kassinove
Hofstra University
Annoyance

Alfred W. Kaszniak
University of Arizona
Consciousness

Yvonne Kellar-Guenther
Western Illinois University
Abandonment
Conflict

Michael H. Kernis
University of Georgia
Self-Esteem

Laura A. King
Southern Methodist University
Ambivalence

Roger Kobak
University of Delaware
Human Development: Adolescence

Aafke Elisabeth Komter
Utrecht University, The Netherlands
Gift Giving

Tracy M. Laulhere
University of California, Irvine
Sadness

Jack Levin
Northeastern University
Hate
Hate Crimes

Linda J. Levine
University of California, Irvine
Hope
Sadness

David Levinson
Berkshire Reference Works, Great Barrington, MA
Aristotle
Augustine
Bowlby, John
Cattell, Raymond Bernard
Descartes, René
Erikson, Erik Homburger
Eysenck, Hans Jurgen
Freud, Anna
Freud, Sigmund
Horney, Karen
Hume, David
James, William
Kant, Immanuel
Nietzsche, Friedrich Wilhelm
Plato
Rogers, Carl Ransom
Sartre, Jean-Paul
Spinoza, Baruch
Sullivan, Harry Stack

Ben Manning
Berkshire Reference Works, Great Barrington, MA
Augustine
Descartes, René
Emerson, Ralph Waldo
Erikson, Erik Homburger
Horney, Karen
Hume, David
Kant, Immanuel
Nietzsche, Friedrich Wilhelm
Plato
Spinoza, Baruch

Clark R. McCauley
Bryn Mawr College
Disgust

Jack McDevitt
Northeastern University
Hate Crimes

Sandra Metts
Illinois State University
Lust
Relationships

Randy Michael
George Fox University, Portland Center
Sin

Mario Mikulincer
Bar-Ilan University, Israel
Folk Theories of Emotion

Heather J. Miles
Stanford University
Emotion Suppression

Robert A. Murphy
Yale Child Study Center, New Haven, CT
Psychoanalytic Perspective

Christie K. Napa
Southern Methodist University
Ambivalence

Kieran O'Hagan
The Queen's University, Belfast
Emotional Abuse: Children

Andrew C. Page
University of Western Australia, Perth
Fear and Phobias

Jaak Panksepp
Bowling Green State University
Neural Systems: From Animals
to Humans

Monte Paulsen
Washington, D.C.
Hate

J. Cara Pendergrass
Vanderbilt University
Psychological Assessment

Lawrence A. Pervin
Rutgers University
Personality

Christopher Peterson
University of Michigan, Ann Arbor
Helplessness

Sandra Petronio
Arizona State University
Embarrassment

Thomas F. Pettigrew
University of California, Santa Cruz
Prejudice

Kirsten M. Poehlmann
University of Houston
Psychophysiology of Emotions

Donald Pollock
State University of New York, Buffalo
Anthropology of Emotions

Anthony R. Pratkanis
University of California, Santa Cruz
Propaganda

William K. Rawlins
Purdue University
Friendship

Glenn D. Reeder
Illinois State University
Education and Teaching

Ronald P. Rohner
University of Connecticut
Acceptance and Rejection

Paul C. Rosenblatt
University of Minnesota
Grief

Lawrence N. Rossi
Midstate Behavioral Health System, Meriden, CT
Mood Disorders

Mary Klevjord Rothbart
University of Oregon
Temperament

Louis Rothschild
New School for Social Research, New York City
Pleasure

Paul Rozin
University of Pennsylvania, Philadelphia
Disgust
Food and Eating

Kjell Erik Rudestam
The Fielding Institute, Santa Barbara, CA
Sensation Seeking and Risk Taking

Frank A. Salamone
Iona College
Music

Peter Salovey
Yale University
Emotional Intelligence

Susan L. Sandel
MidState Behavioral Health System, Meriden, CT
Psychotherapy

Toru Sato
Morehead State University
Seasonal Affective Disorder

Klaus R. Scherer
University of Geneva, Switzerland
Cross-Cultural Patterns
Universality of Emotional Expression

Walter R. Schumm
Kansas State University
Satisfaction

Norbert Schwarz
University of Michigan, Ann Arbor
Mood

Chris Segrin
University of Arizona
Loneliness

Beth A. Semic
Pennsylvania State University
Anger

Don J. Sharpsteen
University of Missouri, Rolla
Jealousy

Franklin Sirmans
New York City
Visual Arts

Elissa Slanger
Tahoe City, CA
Sensation Seeking and Risk Taking

Lynn Smith-Lovin
University of Arizona
Sociology of Emotions

Robert C. Solomon
University of Texas, Austin
Philosophy

Tracy L. Spinrad
Arizona State University
Human Development: Overview

Peter N. Stearns
Carnegie-Mellon University
Historical Study of Emotions

Lesa A. Stern
Southern Illinois University, Edwardsville
Advertising
Facial Expression

Robert J. Sternberg
Yale University
Love

Denis G. Sukhodolsky
Hofstra University
Annoyance

Sven Svebak
*Norwegian University of Science
and Technology, Trondheim*
Achievement Motivation

James T. Tedeschi
State University of New York, Albany
Aggression

Scott A. Thompson
Boston College
Infatuation

Shealy Thompson
North Carolina State University
Attractiveness
Attribution

Andrew J. Tomarken
Vanderbilt University
Psychological Assessment

Lillian E. Troll
University of California, San Francisco
Human Development: Old Age

Jeanne L. Tsai
University of Minnesota, Twin Cities Campus
Culture

Adriana J. Umana
University of Missouri, Columbia
Hurt

Anita L. Vangelisti
University of Texas, Austin
Shame

Robin S. Vealey
Miami University
Sports

Meredith W. Watts
University of Wisconsin, Milwaukee
Xenophobia

Elissa M. Wickmann
Hope College
Horror

Vernon R. Wiehe
University of Kentucky
Emotional Abuse: Siblings

Paul Wink
Wellesley College
Boredom

Michael Winkelman
Arizona State University
Altered States of Consciousness

Piotr Winkielman
University of Denver
Mood

Robert L. Winzeler
University of Nevada, Reno
Culture-Bound Syndromes

David L. Wodrich
Illinois State University
Education and Teaching

Cheryl A. Wright
University of Utah
Creativity

Loriena A. Yancura
University of California, Davis
Stress

Stacy L. Young
University of Texas, Austin
Shame

Tina Zawacki
Wayne State University
Flirtation

A

ABANDONMENT

Many moviegoers may have experienced feelings of disbelief as they watched the scenes in the movie *Titanic* (1997) where the ship was sinking. They may have felt anguish at watching the families break up as the women and children were rowed off to safety, leaving the men behind. Feelings of sorrow may have been experienced as the viewers watched people choose to die together rather than be separated as the ship sank. The people aboard the real *Titanic* in 1912, the women specifically, faced a huge dilemma: Should they abandon the ones they loved in order to save themselves? Some parents aboard the *Titanic* even had to decide if they should "abandon" a child to save that child's life (by putting the child in a lifeboat and then waiting to die themselves, leaving the child an orphan). Although the sinking of the *Titanic* is an extreme case of abandonment, the associated feelings are the same feelings that many people must confront in their everyday lives.

Feeling Abandoned

The word *abandonment* has a negative connotation; it conjures up feelings of being rejected and left alone. The psychiatrist Daniel Shreeve (1990) discussed Alan, a seventeen-year-old boy who felt that he was "alone with God in the universe; all the people around him were 'robots sent by God' to torture him." Alan was in therapy because he felt that after his parents became divorced and his father remarried, his father no longer needed or wanted to be around him. In

essence, he felt abandoned by his father. Alan's belief that God was torturing him exemplifies the emotional effect of feeling abandoned. Often individuals who believe they have been abandoned feel that they are alone in the world and unworthy of affection.

Abandonment is defined in many ways in the research literature. Most often abandonment is defined using Sigmund Freud's definition: a fear or anxiety of losing someone or something that is loved, or the fear that someone who is loved will not love in return. It is interesting to note that Freud does not really define the emotion of abandonment; instead, he focuses on the fear that abandonment will happen and what events lead to the feeling that one has been abandoned.

Other scholars have linked the sensation of abandonment to the feeling of being rejected and, as a result, believing one is unworthy. Abandonment is also closely tied to the feeling of being lonely. While abandonment can be a precursor to these emotions, individuals can only feel abandoned if they believe another has physically or emotionally withdrawn from them. In Alan's case, he felt abandoned when his father physically moved out of the house and then psychologically left his first family by getting remarried.

Feeling abandoned does not, however, require that someone physically leave. People can also feel abandoned if they believe that a loved one has emotionally left. This is illustrated in country singer Shania Twain's song "Home Ain't Where His Heart Is," in which she sings "And he may still come home, but I live here alone; the love that built these walls is gone. Home ain't where his heart is anymore." The husband in this

A period painting shows women being forced to choose between staying aboard the sinking Titanic *and abandoning their husbands to save themselves.* (Corbis/Bettmann)

song has emotionally abandoned his wife. Another example of feeling abandoned even though the loved one has not physically left comes from a case recorded by psychiatrist Deborah Steiner (1986), who recalls a case where a son felt abandoned by his mother when a new child was born. The boy felt that his sibling replaced him in his mother's eyes; he was no longer the object of his mother's affection. This fits with Freud's definition. The boy had lost someone he loved, his mother, and he believed his mother no longer returned his love. This boy was not physically left by his mother, he just felt that his mother had emotionally abandoned him. All these examples show that the feeling of abandonment is strongly tied to an external condition—the other leaving—and can only occur after a person thinks that a loved one has left, either physically or emotionally, and will not return.

However, as Freud and many other psychologists point out, the act of abandonment is so negative that people may experience a fear that they will be abandoned, even if they never are. This is why scholars often study the fear of abandonment, another emotion tied to abandonment. Fear, according to the American Psychiatric Association (1994), is an emotion that occurs due to a recognizable external threat.

Causes of Feeling or Fearing Abandonment

Most people have experienced the feeling of being abandoned at one time or another. Fear of abandonment can, in fact, occur to anyone at any time. The majority of researchers have found no gender difference with regard to fear of abandonment. Neither have they been able to establish a link between fear of abandonment and age. Robert Kastenbaum, in his book *Death, Society, and Human Experience* (1977), states that every age is sensitive to separation and abandonment. Researchers have identified some of the events that cause people to feel abandoned or fear being abandoned. These events include, but are not limited to, the ending of a romantic relationship or friendship; a terminal illness and/or death; a child growing up, becoming an adult, and leaving the parents; and a parent emotionally withdrawing from a child.

Most people feel abandoned when relational partners break off the relationship. This theme is reflected in many songs, especially country songs. For example, George Strait, in his song "Rockin' in the Arms of Your Memory" relays his heartache of being left by a love when he sings, "I'm living, but I'm dying. I'm laughing but crying, Somebody tell me it will be alright." This song conveys a sense of being alone and rejected, both of which are emotional responses to feeling abandoned. Perhaps what hurts so much about being left is the perception that the loved one has *chosen* to leave. This action sends the signal that the person being left is unworthy of love, a thought expressed by Alan, the seventeen-year-old boy who was in therapy because he felt abandoned by his father.

It is important to note, however, that people can feel abandoned even if they believe the person who left had no control over the decision to leave. Kastenbaum (1977) reports that family members often feel abandoned when a relative is dying, a situation depicted in the movie *Kolya* (1996), where a little boy is left with his stepfather after his grandmother, who raised him, dies. In one scene, the boy pretends he is talking on the telephone with his dead grandmother; he is crying and asking her why she left. Family members are not the only ones to fear abandonment due to death. Kastenbaum states that individuals who are terminally ill also fear being abandoned during their last hours. Freud, in his book *The Psychology of Everyday Life* (1901), argues that individuals fear they will be abandoned after they die. Freud argues that people fear being abandoned just before and after they die because individuals cannot fear death. He argues that people cannot fear the unknown and no one has actually died before. As a result, people instead fear issues associated with death, such as being abandoned.

Fearing a child will abandon the family is similar to death in that it is considered to be a natural part of the life cycle. According to Raymond Montemayor (1983), many parents report that they fear they will no longer be needed when their children become teenagers. Because adolescence is the transition period from being a child to becoming an adult, early adolescence is often the period where children try to change their relationships with their parents from complementary (i.e., I need you and you provide for me) to symmetrical (i.e., I need you and you need me). To become more equal, an adolescent must lessen his or her dependency on the family. This change takes place when a child begins looking outside the family for interpersonal need fulfillment. Margaret Mahler (1971) argues that while separation from one's family is a normal part of the growth cycle, some parents experience difficulty enabling their children to become more autonomous. These parents often report that they feel their children are abandoning them in favor of their peer friends.

A parent who is unable to cope with a child's emerging autonomy (referred to as separation-individuation) will withdraw the emotional support the child needs to engage in this process. As a response to this emotional abandonment, the child will revert back to the complementary relationship with the parent. The

In Jack London's "The Law of Life" (1900), the old blind and lame chief of the Eskimo tribe understands that the group must abandon him to die because he cannot travel the long journey they must make for hunting. As he sits alone beside his dwindling fire, the chief thinks of an old moose killed by wolves when it could not keep up with the herd.

child then begins to fear separation. So fear of abandonment, or separation anxiety as it is sometimes called, can be learned by interacting with one's family. Freud actually states that people will develop separation anxiety in childhood and that fear will continue into adulthood.

John Bowlby, the author of attachment theory (which was introduced in the late 1970s and explains the relationship between childhood experiences and adult behavior), states that parents' behaviors can influence whether individuals fear that they will be abandoned by loved ones. According to Bowlby, individuals can have one of three types of attachment: secure, avoidant, or anxious/ambivalent. Which attachment pattern individuals form depends on their beliefs about the trustworthiness and likability of themselves, their significant others, and others in general; the degree of interpersonal closeness they desire with others; and their expectations about how people should behave when distressed. The anxious/ambivalent attachment style, which is the least frequent of the three styles, deals specifically with abandonment.

People who are labeled as anxious/ambivalent feel that others are reluctant to get as close as they would like, worry that their romantic partners do not really love them or will not want to stay with them, and fear that their desire to merge completely with another person scares people away. Bowlby, like Freud, argues that children typically form attachment patterns based on how the significant others around them behave and that these patterns become set and influence how they related to others when they become adults. Incidents during childhood, then, like death or separation from a parent, may not only result in a feeling of abandonment at the time the event occurs but may also result in the child forming an anxious/ambivalent attachment style. As a result, these individuals will constantly fear during their adulthood that others will abandon them.

Why Are Humans Prone to Feeling or Fearing Abandonment?

Knowing why one may feel or fear abandonment does not explain why humans are so prone to this emotion. What is it about being human that makes people vulnerable to the feeling or fear of being abandoned? Most scholars would answer this question by stating that to be human, one must interact with others. In fact, there are several theories that state humans are social creatures who get their needs met through contact with others and that identity is defined by symbolic interaction with others.

Humans need to feel affection and a sense of belonging. Fulfillment of these interpersonal needs are met by interacting with others. Harry Sullivan, in his book *The Interpersonal Theory of Psychiatry* (1953), expands on this concept by explaining that interpersonal needs are summative. In other words, in addition to existing needs, new ones emerge when individuals reach a new stage of development. For example, all that infants need is tenderness, but by early adolescence, the fifth and final stage of Sullivan's model, there are a total of five interpersonal needs: tenderness, companionship, acceptance, intimacy, and sexuality. In addition to identifying interpersonal needs, Sullivan discusses which interpersonal relationships fulfill these needs. Up until six years of age, families provide the majority of children's interpersonal needs. This is the group with which children spend a majority of their day and, as a result, this is the primary group with which they interact. Once children start going to school, their peers start providing some of their interpersonal needs. Sullivan argues that while parents provide tenderness and companionship, peers provide companionship and acceptance. By the time individuals reach pre-adolescence (nine to twelve years) their peers provide a majority of their interpersonal needs. During this stage, parents provide only tenderness and companionship, while friends provide tenderness, companionship, acceptance, and intimacy. By the time individuals reach early adolescence (twelve to sixteen years), their friends and romantic partners provide for almost all of their interpersonal needs.

Contact with others, moreover, provides individuals with their sense of personal identity. According to George Herbert Meade, in the book *Mind, Self, and Society* (1934), people base their sense of identity on how others interact with them. This concept refers to the looking-glass self. A looking glass is a mirror; people reflect an individual's identity back to him or her based on how they react to that individual. For example, if others surround a person and want to be with him or her, that individual may self-identify as being desirable and likable. However, if others abandon that person, he or she may self-identify as being unlovable. Research has, in fact, shown that individuals who are fearful that others will leave them typically believe that they are not likable.

These theories of need fulfillment explain why humans fear abandonment. Loved ones play a prominent role in helping individuals achieve their interpersonal needs. When individuals are abandoned, there is a chance that they will not have their needs met. Furthermore, because people who are abandoned feel that they are unworthy or not likable, they may not be *willing* to have their needs met; they may feel they are not deserving of such.

Results of Abandonment

The unwillingness to have interpersonal needs met is one probable reaction for those who feel abandoned or fear abandonment. Researchers have identified several typical responses for those individuals who feel or fear abandonment. These reactions range from leaving others to suicide attempts.

E. Virginia Lapham and Lisa Ehrhart (1986) report that one of the reactions common to those who fear being abandoned is that they often abandon their loved ones. For example, as mentioned earlier, parents who fear their adolescent children will abandon them often emotionally withdraw from their children to lessen the hurt they expect to feel. This concept is also illustrated in a scene between the characters Lelaina and Vickie in the movie *Reality Bites* (1994). Vickie makes a comment about how the men she dates are constantly leaving her. Upon hearing this, Lelaina looks shocked and reminds Vickie that she is usually the first to leave the men, not the other way around. Vickie responds by saying "I'm just beating them to the punch." In other words, Vickie believes these men will leave, so she leaves them first.

Another possible response to fear of abandonment is the development of a clingy possessive relationship. As was stated earlier, individuals who are labeled anxious/avoidant (the attachment style that indicates these individuals fear abandonment) have low self-esteem. Nancy Collins and Stephen Read (1990) found that, as a result, these individuals rely on their relational partners for higher self-esteem and other rewards. This, in turn, makes the relationship extremely

> William Carlos Williams's "Jean Beicke" (1938) takes place in a children's hospital in New Jersey during the depression. The physician-narrator wonders if the many infants and children in the hospital, who were abandoned by their parents who could not or would not care for them, might not be better off dying than being given medical treatment to save them for what he assumes will be a life of misery.

important because these individuals need the significant other in order to feel good about themselves. Consequently, anxious/ambivalent individuals experience high levels of jealousy in their romantic relationships. The combination of high jealousy and low self-esteem can result in these individuals acting out their distress in a negative fashion. For example, there is a scene in the movie *Parenthood* (1989) when Gary (a young boy living with his single-parent mother) calls his father to ask if he can go live with his father and his father's "new" family. Gary's father tells him that he does not think having Gary live with him is a good idea. That night, Gary breaks into his father's office and vandalizes it. Another example is Alan, the seventeen-year-old boy who was in therapy. Alan was first identified as needing counseling because he tried to commit suicide, a reaction to feeling abandoned by his father.

Suicide is actually a common response for those who feel abandoned. Nancy Wade (1987) found that adolescent girls who had actually attempted suicide suffered more from separation anxiety than those who were not suicidal or who had threatened suicide but had not actually attempted it. One reason being abandoned or the fear of being abandoned may be so strongly connected with suicide is that they are both strongly linked with feeling depressed. Furthermore, Cindy Hazan and Phillip Shaver (1987) found that individuals who are anxious-ambivalent report more feelings of loneliness than do individuals from either of the other two attachment styles). Natalie Merchant, in her song "My Beloved Wife," highlights the connection between feeling abandoned, feeling lonely, and wanting to commit suicide. In this song, a husbands mourns the loss of his wife of fifty years, a loss that makes him feel sad and lonely. He tries to find a reason to go on living without his wife, who was the "very best part" of him, but at the end of the song, he does not appear to have found a reason to continue living.

Another typical response to feeling abandoned, one which is less permanent than suicide, is a decrease in performance. Phillip, a twelve-year-old boy, was in counseling because his parents had gotten divorced and his mother often threatened to abandon him whenever he disappointed her. Phillip's feelings of abandonment in this situation manifested themselves in failing grades, despite evidence that he was incredibly bright.

Children may also respond to feelings of abandonment by acting pseudomature (i.e., overserious, excessively solemn, formal, and earnest, with a strict devotion to duty, self-control, and responsibility). An example of this behavior is Hope, a seven-year-old girl who, when her parents divorced, went to live with her mother. Hope's mother, however, became chemically dependent and, as a result, was incapable of fulfilling Hope's interpersonal needs. Hope's father was also somewhat unreliable. He took drugs and beat his new fiancée in front of Hope. In this situation, Hope felt that she had been abandoned by both of her parents. At school, Hope did not play at all, she befriended her teachers and other adults who were present. Children who become pseudomature do so because they, like adolescents, want to minimize their dependency on adults by being seen as "equals."

Conclusion

Overall, abandonment and the fear of abandonment are considered to be negative emotions. When a loved one leaves, either physically or emotionally, the person left behind no longer has someone to fulfill interpersonal needs. As a result, he or she may feel unworthy and unlovable, and this low self-image can result in negative behaviors. Many of these individuals, however, are left simply trying to answer one overwhelming question: Why has thou forsaken me?

See also: ACCEPTANCE AND REJECTION; ATTACHMENT; BOWLBY, JOHN; FEAR AND PHOBIAS; FREUD, SIGMUND; LONELINESS; RELATIONSHIPS; SELF-ESTEEM; SULLIVAN, HARRY STACK

Bibliography

American Psychiatric Association. (1994). *Diagnostic and Statistical Manual of Mental Disorders,* 4th ed. Washington, DC: American Psychiatric Association.

Bowlby, John. (1982a). "Attachment and Loss: Retrospect and Prospect." *American Journal of Orthopsychiatry* 52:664–678.

Bowlby, John. (1982b). *Attachment and Loss: Vol. 1. Attachment,* 2nd ed. New York: Basic Books.

Bowlby, John. (1988). "Defensive Processes in Response to Stressful Separation in Early Life." In *Yearbook of the International Association for Child and Adolescent Psychiatry and Allied Professions, Vol. 8: The Child in His Family,* ed. Anthony E. James and Colette Chiland. New York: Wiley.

Brenner, Charles. (1973). *An Elementary Textbook of Psychoanalysis.* New York: Schocken Books.

Collins, Nancy L., and Read, Stephen J. (1990). "Adult Attachment, Working Models, and Relationship Quality in Dating Couples." *Journal of Personality and Social Psychology* 9:5–20.

Freud, Sigmund. (1901). *The Psychology of Everyday Life.* New York: Macmillan.

Hazan, Cindy, and Shaver, Phillip. (1987). "Romantic Love Conceptualized as an Attachment Process." *Journal of Personality and Social Psychology* 52:511–524.

Kastenbaum, Robert J. (1977). *Death, Society, and Human Experience.* St. Louis, MO: C.V. Mosby.

Lapham, E. Virginia, and Ehrhart, Lisa S. (1986). "Young Adulthood: Establishing Intimacy." In *The Impact of Chronic Illness on Psychosocial Stages of Human Development,* ed. E. Virginia

Lapham and Kathleen M. Shevlin. Washington, DC: National Center for Education in Maternal and Child Health.

Mahler, Margaret. (1971). "A Study of the Separation-Individuation Process and Its Possible Application to Borderline Phenomena in the Psychoanalytic Situation." *Psychoanalytic Study of the Child* 26:403–424.

Maslow, Abraham H. (1943). "A Theory of Human Motivation." *Psychological Review* 50:370–396.

Meade, George H. (1934). *Mind, Self, and Society.* Chicago: University of Chicago Press.

Montemayor, Raymond. (1983). "Parents and Adolescents in Conflict: All Families Some of the Time, Some Families Most of the Time." *Journal of Early Adolescence* 5:22–30.

Schutz, William C. (1958). *FIRO: A Three-Dimensional Theory of Interpersonal Behavior.* New York: Rinehart.

Shreeve, Daniel F. (1990). "Pseudomaturity in the Developmental Line of Object Relations." *American Journal of Psychotherapy* 44:536–551.

Steiner, Deborah. (1986). "Secrecy Surrounding a Pregnancy and Its Effect on the Treatment of a Seven-Year-Old Child." *Journal of Child Psychotherapy* 12:99–107.

Stevens, Gwendolyn, and Gardner, Sheldon. (1994). *Separation Anxiety and the Dread of Abandonment in Adult Males.* Westport, CT: Praeger.

Sullivan, Harry S. (1953). *The Interpersonal Theory of Psychiatry.* New York: W. W. Norton.

Wade, Nancy L. (1987). "Suicide as a Resolution of Separation-Individuation among Adolescent Girls." *Adolescence* 22:169–177.

Yvonne Kellar-Guenther

ABUSE

See Emotional Abuse

ACCEPTANCE AND REJECTION

The extent to which children experience or fail to experience parental acceptance and rejection may have a greater influence on them than any other single experience. Parental acceptance and rejection have been shown in the United States and in cross-cultural research, for example, to affect the emotional, behavioral, and social-cognitive development of children, as well as their psychological functioning and well-being as adults. Beyond these personal effects, differences in the form, frequency, duration, and severity of parental acceptance and rejection tend to be associated in predictable ways with the artistic traditions of different populations around the world, with people's religious beliefs, and with other expressive behaviors and institutions. Parental acceptance and rejection also tend to be reliably predicted by specific forms of family structure, household organization, and even subsistence economy.

The Warmth Dimension of Parenting

Together, parental acceptance and rejection form the warmth dimension of parenting. This is a dimension or continuum on which all humans can be placed because everyone has experienced in childhood more or less love at the hands of major caregivers. Thus, the warmth dimension has to do with the quality of the affectional bond between parents and their children and with the physical and verbal behaviors parents use to express these feelings. One end of the continuum is marked by parental acceptance, which refers to the warmth, affection, care, comfort, concern, nurturance, support, or simply love that parents can feel and express toward their children. The other end of the continuum is marked by parental rejection, which refers to the absence or significant withdrawal of these feelings and behaviors and the presence of a variety of physically and psychologically hurtful behaviors and affects. Parental rejection can be shown by any combination of four principal modes of expression: (1) cold and unaffectionate, the opposite of being warm and affectionate, (2) hostile and aggressive, (3) indifferent and neglecting, and (4) undifferentiated rejecting. Undifferentiated rejection refers to individuals' belief that their parents do not really care about them or love them, even though there might not be any clear behavioral indicators that the parents are neglecting, unaffectionate, or aggressive toward them. In discussing parental acceptance and rejection, the terms *warmth, hostility,* and *indifference* refer to the internal, psychological feelings of the parents. That is, parents may feel warm (or cold and unloving) toward their children or they may feel hostile, angry, bitter, resentful, irritable, impatient, or antagonistic toward them. Alternatively, parents may be indifferent toward their children, feel unconcerned and uncaring about them, or have a restricted interest in their overall well being. The terms *affection, aggression,* and *neglect* refer to behaviors that result when parents act on these emotions. Thus when parents act on their feelings of love they are likely to be affectionate. This parental affection can be shown either physically (e.g., hugging, kissing, caressing, comforting) or verbally (e.g., praising, complimenting, saying nice things to or about the child). These and many other caring, nurturing, supportive, loving behaviors help define the behavioral expressions of parental acceptance.

Some children have never experienced any of the feelings and behaviors of parental love. Rather, they know only the cold, unaffectionate expressions of parental hostility and aggression, indifference and neglect, or undifferentiated rejection. British novelist George Eliot (1896, p. 265) captured much of the essence of rejection when she wrote:

A child forsaken, waking suddenly,
Whose gaze afeard on all things round doth rove,
And seeth only that it cannot see
The meeting eyes of love.

When parents act on feelings of hostility, anger, resentment, or enmity, the resulting behavior is generally called aggression. Aggression is any behavior where there is the intention of hurting someone, something, or oneself. Parents may be physically aggressive (e.g., hitting, pushing, throwing things, pinching, using hurtful symbolic gestures) and verbally aggressive (e.g., sarcastic, cursing, mocking, shouting, saying thoughtless, humiliating or disparaging things to or about the child).

The connection between indifference as an internal motivator and neglect as a behavioral response is not as direct as the connection between hostility and aggression. This is true because parents may neglect their children for many reasons that have nothing to do with indifference. For example, parents may neglect their children as a way of trying to cope with their anger toward them. The following case illustrates this:

> A mother was charged by protective services with child neglect because she tried to ignore her six-year-old son as much as she could—she failed to feed him regularly, dress him properly, or monitor his whereabouts. When asked why she did this, she explained that she felt such rage toward him that she was afraid she might kill him if she spent time with him. Eventually, through therapy, the mother realized that the rage she felt was inappropriately displaced onto the boy because he reminded her of his father who had walked out on her when she was pregnant, leaving her and her newborn penniless and with huge debts.

Neglect is not simply a matter of failing to provide for the material and physical needs of children, however; it also pertains to parents' failure to attend appropriately to children's social and emotional needs. Often, for example, neglecting parents pay little attention to children's needs for comfort, solace, help, or attention; they may also remain physically as well as psychologically unresponsive or even unavailable or inaccessible.

All of these behaviors—individually and collectively—are likely to induce children to feel unloved or rejected. Even in warm and loving families, however, children are likely to experience—at least occasionally—a few of these hurtful emotions and behaviors. Thus, it is important to be aware that parental acceptance and rejection can be viewed and studied from either of two perspectives: (1) as subjectively perceived or experienced by the individual, the phenomenological perspective, or (2) as reported by a second person, the behavioral perspective. Usually, but not always, the two perspectives lead to similar conclusions. Research suggests, however, that if there are discrepancies between the conclusions, one should probably place more trust in the information derived from the phenomenological perspective. This is true because a child may feel unloved (as in undifferentiated rejection), but outside observers may not detect many or any of the indicators of parental rejection described above. Alternatively, observers may report a significant amount of parental aggression or neglect, but the child may not feel rejected; this occurs with some regularity in reports of child abuse and neglect. Thus, there is a problematic relationship between official reports of abuse and neglect on the one hand and children's perceptions of parental acceptance and rejection on the other. As Jerome Kagan (1978, p. 57) put it, "parental rejection is not a specific set of actions by parents but a belief held by the child."

In effect, much of parental acceptance and rejection is symbolic. Therefore, to understand why rejection has consistent effects, one must understand its symbolic nature. Certainly in the context of ethnic and cross-cultural studies one must be sensitive to people's symbolic, culturally-based interpretations of parents' love-related behaviors. That is, even though parents everywhere express, to some degree, acceptance (warmth, affection, care, concern) and rejection (coldness, lack of affection, hostility, aggression, indifference, neglect), the way they do it is highly variable and saturated with cultural or sometimes idiosyncratic meaning. For example, parents anywhere might praise or compliment their children, but the way in which they do it in one sociocultural setting might have no meaning (or might have a totally different meaning) in a second setting. This is illustrated in the following situation presented by Ronald Rohner and Manjusri Chaki-Sircar (1988):

> A high caste Hindu woman was being questioned about family matters in India. The interviewer was distracted by another woman seated nearby. The second woman quietly and carefully peeled an orange and then removed the seeds from each segment. Her nine-year-old daughter became increasingly animated as her mother progressed. Later, the Bengali interpreter asked if the interviewer had noticed what the woman was doing. He answered that he had noticed but had not paid much attention to it. "Should I have?" "Well," she answered, "you want to know about parental love and affection in West Bengal, so you should know. . . ." The interpreter went on to explain that when a Bengali mother wants to praise her child—to show approval and affection for her child—she might give the child a peeled and seeded orange. Bengali children understand completely that their mothers have done something special for them, even though mothers may not use words of praise—for to do so would be unseemly, much like praising themselves.

In everyday American English, the word *rejection* implies bad parenting and perhaps even bad people. In cross-cultural and ethnic research, however, one must attempt to view the words as being descriptive of parents' behaviors, not judgmental or evaluative. This is so because parents in about 25 percent of the world's societies behave in ways that are consistent with the definition of rejection given here, but in the great majority of cases—including historically in the United States—these parents behave toward their children in the way they believe good, responsible parents should behave, as defined by their cultural norms. Therefore, in the context of worldwide research on parental acceptance and rejection, a major goal is to determine whether children and adults everywhere respond the same way when they see themselves as having been accepted or rejected as children—regardless of cultural, racial, ethnic, gender, or social class differences, or other such defining conditions.

Parental Acceptance-Rejection Theory

Parental Acceptance-Rejection Theory (PARTheory) is a theory of socialization that attempts to predict and explain major causes, consequences, and correlates of parental acceptance and rejection within the United States and worldwide. It attempts to answer five classes of questions divided into three subtheories: personality theory (1, 2), coping theory (3), and sociocultural systems theory (4, 5):

1. What happens to children who perceive themselves to be loved or unloved by their parents? More specifically, is it true, as the theory postulates, that children everywhere—in different sociocultural systems, racial or ethnic groups, genders, and the like—respond in essentially the same way when they perceive themselves to be accepted or rejected?
2. What are adults like who were accepted or rejected in childhood? That is, to what degree do the effects of childhood rejection extend into adulthood and old age?
3. What gives some children and adults the resilience to cope more effectively than others with the experiences of childhood rejection?
4. Why are some parents warm and loving and others cold, aggressive, neglecting—rejecting? It is true, for example—as PARTheory predicts—that specific psychological, familial, community, and societal factors tend to be reliably associated the world over with specific variations in parental acceptance and rejection?
5. In what way is the total fabric of society, as well as the behavior and beliefs of individuals within

society, affected by the fact that most parents in that society tend to either accept or reject their children? For example, is it true, as PARTheory predicts, that a people's religious beliefs, artistic preferences, and other expressive beliefs and behaviors tend to be universally associated with their childhood experiences of parental love and love withdrawal?

PARTheory has several distinctive features guiding its attempts to answer questions such as these. First, it draws extensively from worldwide, cross-cultural evidence as well as from every major ethnic group in the United States. Additionally, it draws from literary and historical insights as far back as two thousand years. And, which is very important, it draws from and helps provide a conceptual framework for integrating more than one thousand empirical studies on issues of parental acceptance and rejection published (mostly within the United States) since the turn of the twentieth century. From these sources the theory attempts to formulate a life span—womb to tomb—developmental perspective on issues surrounding parental acceptance and rejection. Much of this life span perspective is incorporated in PARTheory's personality theory.

PARTheory's Personality Theory

PARTheory's personality theory attempts to predict and explain major personality or psychological consequences (especially those related to mental health) of perceived parental acceptance and rejection. The theory begins with the probably untestable assumption that humans have developed the enduring, biologically-based emotional need for positive response from the people who are most important to them. The need for positive response includes an emotional wish, desire, or yearning (whether consciously recognized or not) for comfort, support, care, concern, nurturance, and the like. In adulthood, the need becomes more complex and differentiated to include the wish (recognized or unrecognized) for positive regard from people whose opinions are considered to be of value. People who can best satisfy this need for infants and children are typically parents, but the source for adolescents and adults expands to include significant others. From the global perspective emphasized in PARTheory, a parent is any person who has more or less long-term, primary caregiving responsibility for a child. This person may be a mother, father, grandparent, other relative, or even a non-kinsperson such as a foster parent or parent surrogate in an institutional setting. A significant other, on the other hand, is any person with whom a child or adult has a relatively long-lasting emotional tie, who is uniquely important to the individual, and who is interchangeable with no one else. In this sense, parents are generally significant others, but parents also tend to have one additional quality not shared by most significant others. That is, children's sense of emotional security and comfort tends to be dependent on their relationship with their parents. Because of that, parents are usually the kind of significant other called attachment figures in attachment theory. Parents are thus uniquely important to children because the security and other emotional and psychological states of offspring are dependent on the quality of their relationships with their parents. It is for this reason that parental acceptance and rejection is postulated in PARTheory to have unparalleled influence in shaping children's personality development over time. The concept *personality* is defined in PARTheory as an individual's more or less stable set

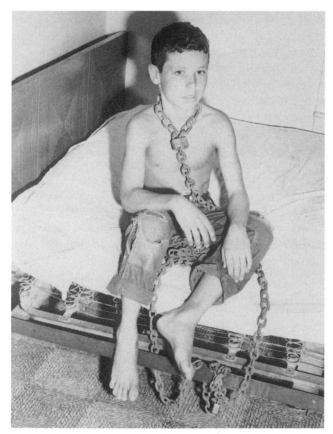

In an extreme case of parental rejection that was discovered in August 1954, eleven-year-old Joe Roach was found chained to a bed in his home in Houston, Texas. The boy said that he had spent the night before his discovery sleeping in the doghouse in his backyard rather than going into the house to be mistreated. His parents were charged in domestic relations court with contributing to the dependency of a minor. (Corbis/Bettmann)

of predispositions to respond (i.e., affective, cognitive, perceptual, and motivational dispositions) and actual modes of responding (i.e., observable behaviors) in various life situations or contexts. This definition recognizes that behavior is influenced by external (i.e., environmental) as well as internal (e.g., emotional, biological, and learning) factors and usually has regularity or orderliness about it across time and space.

PARTheory's personality theory postulates that the emotional need for positive response from significant others is a powerful motivator, and when children do not get this need satisfied adequately by their parents, they are predisposed to respond emotionally and behaviorally in specific ways. In particular—according to the theory—rejected children are likely to feel anxious and insecure. In an attempt to allay these feelings and to satisfy the need for positive response, rejected children often increase their bids for positive response, but only up to a point. That is, they tend to become more dependent. The term *dependence* refers to the internal, psychologically-felt wish or yearning for emotional (as opposed to instrumental or task-oriented) support, care, comfort, attention, nurturance, and similar parental behaviors. The term, as used in PARTheory, also refers to the actual behavioral bids children make for such responsiveness. For young children, these bids may include clinging to parents, whining or crying when parents unexpectedly depart, and seeking physical proximity with the parents when they return. Older children and adults may express their need for positive response in a more symbolic manner—especially in times of distress—by seeking reassurance, approval, or support, as well as comfort, affection, or solace from people who are important to them—particularly from parents for youths and from non-parental significant others for adults.

Dependence in PARTheory is construed as a continuum, with independence defining one end of the continuum and dependence the other. Independent people are those who have their need for positive response met sufficiently well so that they are free from frequent or intense yearning or behavioral bids for succor from significant others. Very dependent people, on the other hand, are those who have a frequent and intense desire for positive response and are likely to make many bids for response. As with all the personality dispositions studied in PARTheory, humans everywhere can be placed somewhere along the continuum of being more or less dependent or independent. According to the theory, much of the variation in dependence among children is contingent on the extent to which they perceive themselves to be accepted or rejected: Many rejected children and adults constantly feel the need for reassurance and emotional support.

According to PARTheory's personality theory, parental rejection also leads to other personality outcomes, in addition to dependence. These include (1) hostility, aggression, passive aggression, or psychological problems with the management of hostility and aggression; (2) emotional unresponsiveness; (3) immature dependence or defensive independence, depending on the form, frequency, duration, and intensity of perceived rejection and parental control; (4) impaired self-esteem; (5) impaired self-adequacy; (6) emotional instability; and (7) negative worldview. Theoretically, these dispositions are expected to emerge because of the intense psychological pain produced by parental rejection. More specifically, beyond a certain point—a point that varies from individual to individual—children who experience significant rejection are likely to feel ever-increasing anger, resentment, and other destructive emotions that may become intensely painful. As a result, many rejected children close off emotionally in an effort to protect themselves from the hurt of further rejection. That is, they become less emotionally responsive. In so doing, they often have problems being able or willing to express love and in knowing how or being capable of accepting it from others.

Because of all this psychological hurt, some rejected children—especially in adolescence—become defensively independent. Defensive independence is like healthy independence in that individuals make relatively few behavioral bids for positive response. It is unlike healthy independence, however, in that defensively independent people continue to crave emotional warmth and support—positive response—though they sometimes do not recognize it. Indeed, because of the overlay of anger, distrust, and other negative emotions generated by chronic rejection, they often positively deny this need, saying in effect, "To Hell with you! I don't need you. I don't need anybody!" Defensive independence with its associated emotions and behaviors sometimes leads in adolescence to a process of counter rejection, where rejected youths reject the rejecting parent(s). Not surprisingly, this process sometimes escalates into a cycle of family violence.

In addition to dependence or defensive independence, rejected children are predicted in PARTheory to develop impaired feelings of self-esteem and self-adequacy. This comes about because children tend to view themselves as they think their parents view them. Thus, insofar as children feel their parents do not love them, children are likely to start feeling they are unlovable, perhaps even unworthy of being loved. British psychiatrist Ronald Laing (1970, p. 9) masterfully captured the essence of self-esteem and related self-feelings that swirl around parental acceptance and rejection when he wrote,

> My mother loves me.
> I feel good.
> I feel good because she loves me.
> I am good because I feel good.
> I feel good because I am good.
> My mother loves me because I am good.
>
> My mother does not love me.
> I feel bad.
> I feel bad because she does not love me.
> I am bad because I feel bad.
> I feel bad because I am bad.
> I am bad because she does not love me.
> She does not love me because I am bad.

Whereas self-esteem pertains to individuals' feelings of self-worth or value, self-adequacy pertains to their feelings of competence or mastery to perform daily tasks adequately and to satisfy their own instrumental (task-oriented) needs. Insofar as individuals feel they are not very good people, they are also apt to feel they are not very good at satisfying their needs. Or alternatively, insofar as people feel they are no good at satisfying their personal needs, they often come to think less well of themselves more globally.

Anger, negative self-feelings, and the other consequences of perceived rejection tend to diminish rejected children's and adults' capacity to deal effectively with stress. Because of this they tend to be less emotionally stable than accepted people. They often become emotionally upset—perhaps tearful or angry—when confronted with stressful situations that accepted (loved) people are able to handle with greater emotional equanimity.

All these acutely painful feelings associated with parental rejection tend to induce children and adults to develop a negative worldview. That is, according to PARTheory, rejected people are likely to develop a view of the world—of life and the very nature of human existence—as being hostile, unfriendly, emotionally unsafe, threatening, or dangerous. These feelings and associated thoughts often extend to people's beliefs about the nature of the supernatural world (i.e., God, the gods, and other religious beliefs).

Negative worldview, negative self-esteem, negative self-adequacy, and some of the other personality dispositions described above are important elements in the social-cognitive or mental representations of rejected children. The concept *mental representation* in PARTheory refers to an individual's more or less coherent but usually implicit theory of reality. The theory consists largely of generalizations about self, others, and the experiential world constructed from emotionally significant past and current experiences.

Mental representations about a specific domain (e.g., beliefs and expectations about oneself, significant others, or interpersonal relationships) fall along at least three continua: (1) from being consciously recognized to being wholly unconscious, (2) from being internally consistent and organized to being inconsistent and perhaps chaotic, and (3) from being loosely or flexibly scripted to being tightly or rigidly ruled. Along with one's emotional state—which both influences and is influenced by one's theory of reality—mental representations tend to shape the way in which individuals perceive, construe, and react to new experiences, including interpersonal relationships. Mental representations also influence what individuals store in their memories and how they remember experiences. Once created, individuals' mental representations of self, of significant others, and of the world around them tend to induce them to seek or to avoid certain situations and kinds of people. In effect, the way individuals think about themselves and their world shapes the way they live their lives.

This is notably true of rejected children and adults. For example, many rejected people have a tendency to perceive hostility where there is none or to devalue their sense of personal worth in the face of strong counter-information. Moreover, rejected children are likely to seek, create, interpret, or perceive experiences, situations, and relationships in ways that are consistent with their distorted mental representations. They often tend to avoid or mentally reinterpret situations that are inconsistent with these representations. Additionally, rejected children and adults often construct mental images of personal relationships as being unpredictable, untrustworthy, and perhaps hurtful. This mental representation may be carried forward into new relationships where rejected individuals find it difficult to trust others emotionally, or where they may become hypervigilant and hypersensitive to any slights or signs of emotional undependability. Because of all this selective attention or perception, faulty styles of causal attribution, and distorted cognitive information processing, rejected children are likely to propel themselves along developmental pathways that are qualitatively different from those followed by accepted or loved children. Parental rejection effectively compromises the likelihood of healthy social-emotional development for many children.

Because of all the emotional, behavioral, and social-cognitive damage potentially induced by parental rejection, it is no surprise that perceived rejection appears to be associated worldwide with a variety of mental-health issues. In addition to the constellation of personality dispositions explicitly contained in PARTheory's personality theory, empirical evidence strongly supports the likelihood that rejection is universally associated with depression and depressed affect, conduct or behavior problems, and substance (drug and alcohol) abuse. Additionally, parental rejection has been implicated in numerous other developmental problems, including borderline personality disorder and other psychiatric problems; delinquency; psychophysiological reactions such as hypertension and asthma; problems with academic and intellectual performance; and troubled personal relationships. Many of these emotions and behaviors are merely symptoms of the underlying unresolved hurt associated with perceived parental rejection. Of course, parental rejection is only one class of factors—albeit a singularly important one—in a complex matrix of interacting developmental factors that must be considered in addressing the issue of why some rejected children and adults manifest this hurt in one way and others in a totally different way.

As a counterpoint to the litany of troubles associated with rejection, it should be noted that perceived parental acceptance (love) is associated directly and indirectly with a long list of positive developmental outcomes. It is, for example, associated with pro-social behavior in childhood, including the development of generosity, helpfulness, and empathy; positive peer relations in adolescence; as well as overall physical and emotional well-being in adulthood, including lowered psychological distress, a sense of happiness, and overall life-satisfaction. In addition, parental acceptance has been shown to be an effective buffer against the development of many forms of behaviors associated with rejection, such as depression, substance abuse, conduct problems, and delinquency.

Not all accepted children and adults develop so favorably, of course. Indeed, some develop emotional and behavioral problems similar to those of rejected people but for reasons having nothing to do with parental acceptance and rejection per se. And some rejected people are able to remain fairly healthy—emotionally and behaviorally—despite having to live with parental rejection. In PARTheory, individuals in the latter group are called copers.

PARTheory's Coping Theory

PARTheory's coping theory is concerned with the following question: What gives some people the resilience to withstand the corrosive influence of parental rejection without having their emotional or mental health damaged to the extent typical of most rejected people? In response to this questions, PARTheory's postulates that, within a band of individual variation, the status of the mental health of children and adults is likely to become impaired in direct proportion to the frequency, severity, and duration of rejection experienced.

Studies in the United States and around the world consistently show that about 80 percent of the children and adults measured so far respond as personality theory predicts. In PARTheory, some of the individuals who do not respond as predicted are called "troubled." These troubled individuals are those people who experience parental acceptance but whose mental health is nonetheless impaired. PARTheory researchers have spent little time studying these individuals because it is widely recognized that people can be psychologically disturbed for reasons having nothing to do with parental acceptance and rejection.

Affective copers (the primary concern of coping theory) are those people whose emotional and overall mental health is reasonably good despite their having been raised in seriously rejecting families. Instrumental copers, on the other hand, are rejected people who do well in their professions or occupations and other task-oriented activities but whose emotional and mental health is impaired. Instrumental copers maintain high levels of task competence and occupational performance despite serious rejection. Russian novelist Maxim Gorky's (1915, p. 152) autobiography vividly describes the troubled childhood of one instrumental coper:

> I was seldom allowed on the street, from which I invariably returned scarred; for fighting was my chief, in fact my sole, diversion, into which I threw all my energy. Mama strapped me, but punishment only provoked me to fight next time with greater fury, which brought me greater punishment. And so it went until the day I threatened to bite her hand next time, and escape to the fields to die by freezing. In astonishment she pushed me away, and pacing the room, panting, said in an exhausted voice, "You've turned wild as an animal!"
>
> Denied love, I yielded to more frequent outbursts of resentment, which discharged like smoky, bluish flame, and a choking irritation smoldered in my breast, a sense of being abandoned, alone, in that drab, senseless existence.

Clearly, Gorky was a psychologically disturbed man. But despite his emotional turmoil (or perhaps, in part, because of it) he rose to an international pinnacle of success in his writing. As an instrumental coper, Gorky appears to have responded emotionally to rejection the way most people do. Affective copers, on the other hand, are able to escape the most damaging effects of rejection. It is not that they are unscathed by rejection—they are definitely not invulnerable—but they do tend to be fairly emotionally healthy, often high functioning individuals.

Theoretically and empirically, the coping process is the least well-developed portion of PARTheory. Little is yet known with confidence about the mechanisms and processes that allow some individuals to cope more effectively than others with perceived rejection. Nonetheless, according to PARTheory's coping theory, in order to understand the coping process—indeed the entire acceptance-rejection process—one must adopt a multivariate, person-in-context perspective. This perspective has three elements: self, other, and context. Specifically, the multivariate model of behavior employed in PARTheory states that the behavior of the individual (e.g., coping with perceived rejection) is a function of the interaction between self, other, and context. "Self" characteristics include the child's mental representations along with the other internal and external (personality) characteristics discussed earlier. "Other" characteristics include the personal characteristics of the rejecting parent(s), along with the form, frequency, duration, and severity of rejection. "Context" characteristics include significant others in the child's life, along with social-situational characteristics of the child's environment. A specific research hypothesis coming from this perspective states that, all other things being equal, the likelihood of rejected children being able to cope is enhanced by the presence of a warm, supportive, alternate caregiver or significant other.

Over time, from childhood into adulthood, all but the most severely rejected and psychologically damaged individuals are likely to have enough positive experiences outside their families to help moderate many of the emotional, cognitive, and behavioral effects of rejection. Thus, through successful therapy, positive work experiences, satisfying marital relations, and other such gratifying processes and outcomes, adults who had been rejected as children are often better adjusted emotionally and psychologically than they were while still under the direct influence of rejecting parents—though they tend not to have as positive a sense of well-being as adults who felt loved all along. Important elements of rejection are apt to linger into adulthood, placing people who were rejected as children at a somewhat greater risk for social and emotional problems throughout life than people who were loved continuously. One of the common but un-

> George Bernard Shaw points out in Pygmalion (1913) how superficial the discriminations are that cause one social class to reject another. Professor Henry Higgins can transform Eliza Doolittle from a raggedy Cockney flower girl into an aristocratic lady by teaching her how to speak properly. What separates the classes is not any inherent quality of blood or breeding but merely education and opportunity.

fortunate consequences of childhood rejection—even for affective copers—is for it to be perpetuated onto the next generation.

PARTheory's Sociocultural Systems Theory

PARTheory's sociocultural systems theory attempts to predict and explain worldwide causes of parental acceptance and rejection. This portion of the theory also attempts to predict and explain expressive sociocultural correlates of acceptance and rejection. For example, PARTheory predicts, and substantial cross-cultural evidence confirms, that in societies where children tend to be rejected, cultural beliefs about the supernatural world (i.e., God, gods, and the spirit world) usually portray supernatural beings as malevolent forces (i.e., hostile, treacherous, unpredictable, capricious, destructive, or negative in some other way). However, the supernatural world is usually thought to be benevolent (i.e., warm, supportive, generous, protective, or kindly in some other way) in societies where most children are raised with loving acceptance. No doubt these cultural differences are the result of aggregated individual differences in the mental representations of accepted versus rejected people within these two different kinds of societies.

Parental acceptance and rejection are also known to be associated worldwide with many other expressive sociocultural correlates such as the artistic traditions characteristic of individual societies, as well as the artistic preferences of individuals within these societies. Additionally, evidence suggests that the occupational choices adults make cross-culturally (where individual choice is possible) may be associated with childhood experiences of acceptance and rejection. All these and other expressive behaviors and beliefs appear to be by-products of the emotional and social-cognitive effects of parental acceptance-rejection discussed earlier.

Why do parents in most societies tend to be warm and loving, and parents in about 25 percent of the world's societies tend to be mildly to severely rejecting? What factors account for these societal differences and for individual variations in parenting within societies? Questions such as these guide the second portion of PARTheory's sociocultural systems theory. There is no single or simple answer to these questions, but specific factors do appear to be reliably associated with societal and intrasocietal variations in parental rejection. Principal among these are conditions that promote the breakdown of primary emotional relationships and social supports. Thus, single parents (most often mothers) in social isolation without social and emotional supports, especially if the parents are economically deprived, appear universally to be at greatest risk for withdrawing love and affection from their children. It is useful to note, however, that poverty by itself is not necessarily associated with increased rejection. Rather, it is poverty in association with these other social and emotional conditions that place children at greatest risk. Indeed, much of humanity is now and always has been in a state of relative poverty. But despite this, most parents around the world raise their children with loving care.

According to sociocultural systems theory, parental rejection may be a fairly recent phenomenon in human history. Evidence for this belief revolves around the fact that people who live in hunting societies tend universally to raise their children with considerable love (acceptance)—though they may be strict disciplinarians. Children living in all other kinds of economic systems are sometimes rejected. But because all humanity survived in a hunting and gathering state for about 99.7 percent of its evolutionary history—until about twelve thousand years ago—it seems reasonable to speculate that parental rejection may date from that time or more recently. This speculation is enhanced when one considers that the effects of parental acceptance probably gave the offspring of loving hunters a significant selective advantage (in a Darwinian sense) over the offspring of rejecting hunters. That is, such personality dispositions as emotional stability, positive self-adequacy, and a sense of self-determination—all of which are associated with parental acceptance—were no doubt more adaptive for the perpetuation of the hunting way of life than were their contraries. Thus, people with these personality dispositions were probably more willing than people without them to leave the security of the campsite to forage for food in an uncertain, demanding, and sometimes hostile environment. Insofar as they were successful, their families were able to thrive, and their children thereby reached reproductive age. These children then had children of their own to raise in the way they had been raised, with love and affection. On the other hand, hunters who had been seriously rejected, if any existed, probably did not have this constellation of adaptive characteristics. Accordingly, they were probably less successful as hunters. As a result, their families would have fared less well over time than families of accepted hunters. As the generations passed, according to sociocultural systems theory, fewer and fewer of these rejected people would have survived to perpetuate the cycle onto the next generation. The net effect is—if rejecting hunters ever existed at all—they have now vanished in favor of the more adaptive "accepting" style of parenting.

See also: ABANDONMENT; ATTACHMENT; ATTRIBUTION; EMOTIONAL ABUSE; PERSONALITY; SELF-ESTEEM

Bibliography

Ainsworth, Mary D. S. (1989). "Attachment Beyond Infancy." *American Psychologist* 44:709–716.

Baldwin, Mark W. (1992). "Relational Schemas and the Processing of Social Information." *Psychological Bulletin* 112:461–484.

Bowlby, John. (1982). *Attachment and Loss, Vol. 1: Attachment*, 2nd ed. New York: Basic Books.

Clausen, John A. (1972). "The Life Course of Individuals." In *Aging in Society, Vol. 3*, ed. Matilda W. Riley, Marilyn Johnson, and Anne Foner. New York: Russell Sage Foundation.

Colin, Virginia L. (1996). *Human Attachment.* New York: McGraw-Hill.

Crick, Nicki R., and Dodge, Kenneth A. (1994). "A Review and Reformulation of Social Information-Processing Mechanisms in Children's Social Adjustment." *Psychological Bulletin* 115:74–101.

Eliot, George. (1896). *Middlemarch: A Study of Provincial Life.* New York: Croseup and Company.

Epstein, Seymour. (1994). "Integration of the Cognitive and the Psychodynamic Unconscious." *American Psychologist* 49:709–724.

Gorky, Maxim. ([1915] 1953). *Autobiography of Maxim Gorky: My Childhood. In the World. My Universities*, tr. Isidor Schneider. London: Elek Books.

Kagan, Jerome. (1978). *The Growth of the Child: Reflections on Human Development.* New York: W.W. Norton.

Laing, Ronald D. (1970). *Knots.* New York: Pantheon Books.

Rohner, Ronald P. (1975). *They Love Me, They Love Me Not: A Worldwide Study of the Effects of Parental Acceptance and Rejection.* New Haven, CT: HRAF Press.

Rohner, Ronald P. (1986). *The Warmth Dimension: Foundations of Parental Acceptance-Rejection Theory.* Newbury Park, CA: Sage Publications.

Rohner, Ronald P. (1990). *Handbook for the Study of Parental Acceptance and Rejection.* Center for the Study of Parental Acceptance and Rejection, University of Connecticut at Storrs.

Rohner, Ronald P. (1994). "Patterns of Parenting: The Warmth Dimension in Cross-Cultural Perspective." In *Readings in Psychology and Culture*, ed. Walter J. Lonner and Roy S. Malpass. Needham Heights, MA: Allyn & Bacon.

Rohner, Ronald P., and Chaki-Sircar, Manjusri. (1988). *Women and Children in a Bengali Village.* Hanover, NH: University Press of New England.

Rohner, Ronald P., and Nielsen, Caroline C. (1978). *Parental Acceptance and Rejection: A Review and Annotated Bibliography of Research and Theory.* New Haven, CT: HRAFlex Books.

Rohner, Ronald P., and Rohner, Evelyn C., eds. (1980). "Worldwide Tests of Parental Acceptance-Rejection Theory." *Behavior Science Research* 15:Special Issue.

Ronald P. Rohner

ACHIEVEMENT MOTIVATION

All kinds of intended human accomplishments involve some kind of motivation to achieve. It is reflected in competitive athletics, the development of perceptual-motor skills, academic and interpersonal competence, art production of all kinds, scientific progress, and even in play (where often skills are developed just for the intrinsic enjoyment of the activities themselves). Achievement motivation may be a strong element in persistent efforts to accomplish some goal, whether this goal is acknowledged publicly by others or only personally by the individual. Even with failure (as seen by the individual and/or by others), motivation to respond successfully to some kind of challenge, demand, or threat (as seen by the individual) involves achievement motivation. In this way, the concept of achievement motivation relates to the concept of coping, where efforts invested to cope with stressors may or may not be successful. Emotions are involved both in successful coping and in failure to cope.

The term *achievement* refers to accomplishing something that is difficult and doing it as rapidly and as independently as possible. Achievement is regulated by motivation, so the expression of emotions and the subjective experience of emotions (both of which affect motivation) are important determinants of achievement.

Achievement motivation consists of two global underlying motives: the drive to succeed and the fear of failure. The motive to succeed is related to a personal disposition that expects positive affects or emotions when one is performing a challenging task, whereas the fear of failure motive is related to a personal disposition that expects negative affects or emotions when one is performing a challenging task. Situational uncertainty or challenge, as perceived by the individual, is supposed to be responsible for emotional arousal of the achievement motives. This uncertainty may occur when the achievement task is new, unknown, and somewhat difficult, requiring the use of ability, talent, and effort. In such situations, the individual is not at once sure how to solve the task, does not know how a particular approach will be evaluated, and is uncertain about what the consequence of a behavior will be.

A person who has a strong motive to succeed and is involved in tasks with moderate probability of success is likely to experience some kind of positive emotion—interest, pleasure, liking of the task, excitement, or pride. Conversely, a person who has a strong fear of failure motive and is exposed to the same situation is likely to experience unpleasant emotions—fear, anxiety, disliking of the task, shame, or humiliation. Thus, the relative strength of the two underlying achievement motives influences energy mobilization and direction of behavior. Positive emotional arousal implies that energy is directed toward a performance that helps achieve goals (approach motivation). Conversely, negative emotional arousal implies that energy is directed away from a performance and goals (avoidance motivation).

The Achievement Motives Scale is one instrument used by researchers, including Torgrim Gjesme (1981), to study behavioral dispositions and test the achievement motivation theory. Sample items related to the motive to succeed include "I enjoy doing things that I am not quite certain that I can handle," "I enjoy trying new, unknown things even if it is not useful," "I wish to succeed with things I am doing, even if nobody gets to know about it." Sample items related to the fear of failure motive include "I dislike working with things when I am uncertain about the outcome," and "I feel anxious when I am going to work in new situations, even if nobody gets to know what I am doing."

Energy Release and Performance

According to John Atkinson's (1957) classic achievement motivation theory, the arousal of achievement motives increases when there is a moderate probability of success (for the motive to succeed) or there is a high perceived risk of failure (for the fear of failure motive). The corresponding conclusion, according to Gjesme's (1981) more elaborate theory, is that the arousal of motives increases as the distance in time to the test (or goal) decreases.

To test these theories, Hallgeir Halvari (1991a, 1991b) studied individuals who were between sixteen and nineteen years of age. Some weeks before they performed a 1,500-meter run, their achievement motives were measured and their maximal oxygen uptake was measured so that their energy release during the run could be estimated. In addition, blood tests were taken before and after the run and analyzed for lactate concentrations. Blood lactate concentration (premeasure minus post-measures) is an indicator of the intensity of effort expended during work. In the performance situation, the individuals were randomly assigned to one of three experimental conditions by being told that the run was a one-time event, that the run was training for a test that would take place one month from that day, or that the run was training for a test that would take place one year from that day. The results with regard to heart rate, energy release, and blood lactate concentration during the run showed that among individuals who had a dominant motive to succeed, the scores on all three of these variables were lowest for individuals who were performing under the one-year training condition and highest for the individuals who were performing under the one-time test condition. Conversely, among the individuals who were negatively motivated by fear of failure, the scores were lowest for the individuals who were performing under the one-time test condition and highest for individuals who were performing under the one-year training condition. In general, in the one-time test, the individuals who had a dominant motivation to succeed worked with a higher heart rate, released relatively more energy, and had a higher blood lactate concentration than those who had a dominant fear of failure motivation.

Thus, this experiment demonstrated that achievement motives do influence the energy-related parameters and the quality of performance, which validates the work of both Atkinson and Gjesme. These same patterns have been shown by Gjesme (1974) and Halvari (1991c) to hold true with the execution of school work and the display of motor skills.

Goals and Performance

Many personality theorists have portrayed goals or goal concepts to be representations of global motive dispositions. According to David McClelland (1995, p. 595), the motive to succeed represents "a recurrent concern about the goal state of doing something better," which is an approach toward performance goals. Conversely, the fear of failure represents worry about performing well, leading to avoidance of setting performance goals. In this way, the achievement motives can be conceived as being both emotion- and competence-related entities.

Since the early 1990s, researchers have worked to develop a hierarchical model of approach and avoidance achievement motivation that integrates classic achievement motivation and goal theory. Results based on a model developed by Andrew Elliot and Marcy Church (1997) have supported the conclusion that performance avoidance (i.e., worry and rumination about possible performance outcomes) is the effect of a global fear of failure motive. Among both university students and Olympic athletes, the stronger the fear of failure, the more they set performance avoidance goals; the more the individuals become oriented to setting performance avoidance goals, the more their performances suffer.

On the other hand, performance approach goals (i.e., demonstration of competence relative to others) are shown to be regulated by both the motive to succeed and the fear of failure. These goals tend to improve performance, both in academics and athletics. From a related field of research, so-called mastery goals (i.e., self-referenced comparisons of ableness) predict the level of intrinsic personal motivation, but they tend not to predict performance quality for Olympic athletes or university students.

Other performance approach goal characteristics defined in different theories include goal-proximity, goal-clarity, instrumentality or future orientation (i.e., the importance of present activities for future personal goals), and the importance of the goal itself. Research by Gjesme (1981, 1996) and Joel Raynor (1969) indicates that all these goal concepts are related to achievement motivation. Moreover, the more goals are perceived to be closer, clearer, instrumental, and important, the more they influence motive arousal and individual differences in performance. For example, Halvari (1991d) has found that goal distance (i.e., having a goal at some distance in the future) implies that individuals who have a strong motive to succeed start to prepare earlier and devote more time in preparing than do individuals who have a strong fear of failure. In addition, Halvari (1991a, 1991b) has found that among individuals who are in a goal or test situation, those individuals who have a strong motive to succeed perform better than individuals who are dominated by the fear of failure motive.

The capacity individuals have to foresee and structure future performance goals and events, or the experience of the performance situation itself, implies that positive and/or negative emotions are aroused in relation to these perceived or actual situations. The strength of this arousal depends on the relative dominance of the simultaneously operating achievement motives. Experiencing positive emotions in imagined and/or actual situations is supposed to encourage approach motivation and foster good performance. Conversely, experiencing negative emotions as a result of motive arousal is supposed to encourage avoidance goals and undermine the quality of the performance.

Beyond Achievement Motivation Theory

Other theoretical approaches have emerged since McClelland and Atkinson made their pioneering contributions to the field of achievement motive research during the 1950s. Some of these approaches focus less on emotions and more on the interplay of mental goals, outcome expectancies, and causal attribution in success and failure. In this approach, negative mood is assumed to diminish perceived self-efficacy (i.e., the ability to perform behaviors that are relevant to a specific task or situation), whereas positive mood enhances perceived self-efficacy. Scientific support for this position was first given by David Kavanagh and Gordon Bower in 1985.

The so-called reversal theory, a radically different theory of motivation, emotions, and behavior, was presented by Michael Apter in 1989. In place of the motive to succeed and the fear of failure, Apter proposed a set of four pairs of opposite motivational states: arousal avoiding versus arousal seeking, conformist versus negativist, mastery versus sympathy, and other-focused versus self-focused. Apter asserts that humans tend to move back and forth across the distinction between states within a pair over time. Goals are intrinsically given by the four states in operation (one from each pair) at any particular moment in time. Therefore, this theory is ideally suited for exploring the often dramatic dynamics that take place in the experience of achievement situations with high investment of effort. For example, when in the negativist state, pleasure comes from the experience of successfully failing to conform to social norms and expectations of others. John Kerr (1997) has extensively applied

Motivated by the desire to become the first person to run the mile in less than four minutes, Roger Bannister, a twenty-five-year-old English medical student, achieved his goal by completing a mile race at Oxford in 3 minutes 59.4 seconds on May 6, 1954. (Corbis/ Bettmann)

this approach to the understanding of motivational and emotional processes in competitive athletics.

More in tune with traditional achievement motivation research, Ted Thompson, Helen Davis, and John Davidson (1998) investigated the attributional and affective responses of students to academic success and failure in a two (feedback: success, failure) by two (impostor fears: high, low) model. High impostors were characterized by an intense feeling of intellectual phoniness despite the fact that many of them were high-achieving individuals. They had doubts about their own abilities, which they believed to be over-estimated by others, and they feared that others would find out that they were not truly intelligent—that they were, in fact, impostors. Results showed that impostors reported a great amount of negative emotions and a tendency to attribute failure internally. They also tended to overgeneralize a single failure to their overall self-concept.

Achievement

In order to stimulate individuals to perform as well as possible, the educational environment should offer learning situations and tasks that are well adapted to the ability level of individuals, thereby fostering expectations of success. A positive interpersonal emotional climate should characterize the relationship between teachers and students so that positive emotions can strengthen the motive to succeed and weaken the fear of failure. Mastery goals or individual reference norms for ableness, at the expense of performance goals, may be used initially, in particular among students who have a strong fear of failure or a low motive to succeed. This type of goal may help produce pleasant success experiences and, thus, increase intrinsic motivation (as well as reduce the fear of failure and the performance avoidance goals). However, mastery goals should be gradually changed over time to performance approach goals, which are more positively related to performance.

Goals should be realistic. Because goals and performance outcomes are related to attribution (perceived internal and/or external causes of the outcome), individuals may also learn to explain their successes and failures in a way that strengthens their motive to succeed and weakens their fear of failure. In addition, research by Halvari (1997) indicates that an emphasis on effort, rather than on ability, as the cause of performance outcomes is probably more important for younger individuals than for older ones.

See also: ATTRIBUTION; MOTIVATION; SELF-ESTEEM; SPORTS

Bibliography

Apter, Michael J. (1989). *Reversal Theory: Motivation, Emotion, and Personality.* London: Routledge.
Atkinson, John W. (1957). "Motivational Determinants of Risk-Taking Behavior." *Psychological Review* 64:359–372.
Elliot, Andrew J., and Church, Marcy A. (1997). "A Hierarchical Model of Approach and Avoidance Achievement Motivation." *Journal of Personality and Social Psychology* 72:218–232.
Gjesme, Torgrim. (1974). "Goal Distance in Time and Its Effects on the Relations between Achievement Motives and Performance." *Journal of Research in Personality* 8:161–171.
Gjesme, Torgrim. (1981). "Is There Any Future in Achievement Motivation?" *Motivation and Emotion* 5:115–137.
Gjesme, Torgrim. (1996). "Future-Time Orientation and Motivation." In *Advances in Motivation,* ed. Torgrim Gjesme and Roald Nygård. Oslo: Scandinavian University Press.
Halvari, Hallgeir. (1991a). "Achievement Motivation, Physiological Responses, and Achievement-Related Activities." Ph.D. thesis, University of Oslo.
Halvari, Hallgeir. (1991b). "Effects of Goal Distance in Time on Relations between Achievement Motives and Energy Consumption by Aerobic Processes during 1500 m Running." *Perceptual and Motor Skills* 72:1143–1165.
Halvari, Hallgeir. (1991c). "Goal Distance in Time and Its Effects on the Relations between Achievement Motives, Future-Time Orientation, and Motor Performance among Girls and Boys." *Perceptual and Motor Skills* 72:675–697.
Halvari, Hallgeir. (1991d). "Perception of Goal Proximity, La-tency, and Duration of Action Plans, and Worry in Relation to Goal Distance in Time and Personality Characteristics." *Perceptual and Motor Skills* 72:707–738.
Halvari, Hallgeir. (1997). "Moderator Effects of Age on the Relation between Achievement Motives and Performance." *Journal of Research in Personality* 31:303–318.
Kavanagh, David H., and Bower, Gordon H. (1985). "Mood and Self-Efficacy: Impact of Joy and Sadness on Perceived Capabilities." *Cognitive Therapy and Research* 9: 507–525.
Kerr, John H. (1997). *Motivation and Emotion in Sport.* London: Psychology Press.
McClelland, David C. (1951). *Personality.* New York: Dryden.
McClelland, David C. (1995). *Human Motivation.* Cambridge, Eng.: Cambridge University Press.
Raynor, Joel O. (1969). "Future Orientation and Motivation of Immediate Activity: An Elaboration of the Theory of Achievement Motivation." *Psychological Review* 76:606–610.
Thompson, Ted; Davis, Helen; and Davidson, John. (1998). "Attributional and Affective Responses of Impostors to Academic Success and Failure Outcomes." *Personality and Individual Differences* 25:381–396.

Hallgeir Halvari
Sven Svebak

ACTUALIZATION

See Achievement Motivation; Motivation; Self-Esteem

ADOLESCENTS AND EMOTIONS

See Human Development: Adolescence

ADULTS AND EMOTIONS

See Human Development: Adulthood

ADVERTISING

Emotion plays a vital role in the success of almost any persuasive endeavor. Consider a politician's impassioned speech, a preacher's soul-stirring sermon, a student's fiery protest, a lover's stinging rebuke, or a defendant's desperate pleas for mercy. In each case, a play to emotions is used. Nowhere is this more apparent than in the realm of advertising.

A newspaper columnist wrote in 1915, according to James Twitchell (1996), that at the conclusion of the twentieth century, as historians look back and search for the appropriate subtitle to capture the spirit of the period, they may well settle on the name "The Age of Advertising." How right that columnist was. According to some estimates, individuals see approximately three thousand advertisements a day. True, they may have only processed a small fraction of those advertisements, but at some level of awareness the contact was made. One can barely move without brushing up against them. On the radio, billboards, magazines, newspapers, television, airports, bathrooms, classrooms, T-shirts, elevators, and telephones while on hold (to name just a few), advertisements permeate people's very lives.

Consumers are not the only ones frustrated with advertising clutter—advertisers are frustrated as well. In fact, according to David Moore and William Harris (1996), one of the largest concerns advertisers express regarding television advertising is that such advertising is having less persuasive effect because of "increasing clutter in the media environment." To add to this frustration, advertisers are finding that as competition grows in almost every sector of the economy it is increasingly difficult to distinguish their products and services from those of their competitors. The old advertising strategy of highlighting product information that distinguishes a product from its rivals is changing. In some cases, advertisers are now presenting a feeling of what the world is like, hoping that if a consumer identifies with that feeling they will also identify with the product.

Traditional models of advertising effects underscored the importance of the cognition (thought) factor in the success of advertising. More recently, however, practitioners and academicians have realized that emotional responses to advertisements play a critical role in the persuasion process. Always searching for new, creative ways to grab and hold attention, to break through the advertising clutter, and to make appeals more distinctive and thus more persuasive, advertisers are turning in ever-increasing numbers to emotional strategies. Their goal is often to shock consumers and make them think.

Affect, Emotion, and Mood

Marketing and advertising research of the past seems to use the terms *emotion, affect,* and *mood* interchangeably. However, expanding interest in emotions has led to greater efforts in clarifying and distinguishing these related terms. According to Joel Cohen and Charles Areni (1991), the affect concept subsumes the other two and is widely accepted as a "valenced feeling state." Emotions and moods, on the other hand, are thought of as specific examples of these feeling states. Emotions are considered to be more intense than moods and are more closely tied to a stimulus. Emotions cause people to focus attention on the emotion-producing stimulus. In addition, emotions generally occur as a reaction to events that are viewed as self-relevant. Imagine an individual watching an advertisement for film. The television commercial features short clips from a typical family reunion. A grandfather embraces his daughter, a puppy licks a child,

and the family plays lawn games and barbecues. All of these homey, nostalgic images placed in a country setting and combined with folksy music create positive feelings within the person, feelings of which he or she is aware. The resulting emotions are related to and directed toward the experience of watching the advertisement. Further, imagine that the individual's attention now shifts away from viewing television to some pressing yard work. The person continues to feel a residue of the earlier emotion generated by the advertisement, but the feeling is less intense and there is no awareness of any relationship between the feeling and the earlier advertisement. The positive affect experienced as the individual watched the advertisement was an emotional response, perhaps classified as the emotion happiness. When the intensity of the emotion lessened and its connection to the specific advertisement weakened, the positive affect was more accurately defined as a mood.

Relationship of Emotions to Executional Elements

The above example points to some of the elements in an advertisement that are responsible for triggering or influencing emotional responses. The executional cues are numerous and varied and may include such factors as words, picture motion, music, sound effects, source characteristics, voice tones, number of cuts, color, length, brightness, screen size, viewing distance, visual images, content, or themes. The two elements music and visual images serve as good examples of the effect these cues have on emotion.

Music

The prominence of music in most commercials and its ability to evoke emotional responses by arousing emotion-laden memories make music an important executional cue. People often associate music with certain emotional experiences in their lives. In the language of classical conditioning, music becomes the conditioned stimulus for many experiences, and the resulting emotions serve as the conditioned response. The music, once paired or associated with an emotional experience, can later trigger similar emotions, much like in Ivan Pavlov's experiments where the ringing of the bell, once paired with meat, could cause a dog to salivate even when there was no meat present. Consider the many people whose Christmas traditions involve playing Christmas carols. The repeated pairing over the years of the music with the positive emotions of happiness, joy, and love may create a condition in which merely hearing the music can elicit emotional responses. Many advertisers, capitalizing on these associations, include these popular tunes in their advertisements with the hope that consumers will associate the positive emotions elicited by these tunes with, say, their juicer, vodka, or camera. Their hope is that the music will evoke positive emotions that may then be transferred to their products, referred to as "affect transfer." Many songs that are selected for commercials are strategically selected because they can evoke powerful connotative meanings and emotional reactions.

Even when the music is unfamiliar to the consumer, it can still augment the words, add "color" to the picture, and provide another form of energy. This is especially true when the music is in some way related to other elements or themes in the advertisement. For example, a McDonalds commercial may show a father with his little daughter playing in the park and sharing french fries, accompanied by the gentle notes of a violin. The musical arrangement, although unfamiliar, nevertheless adds to the effect and enhances the tender quality of the experience. The key for most advertisers is to select music that will produce the desired emotional response.

Visual Image

Visual images—whether still images in a print advertisement or more dynamic ones from a television commercial—can evoke emotional reactions. Advertisers carefully select images that often resonate with viewers' past experiences in such a way that similar emotions are evoked. Advertisers hope that the positive affect generated by these images will be transferred to their products. The image of the grimacing man painfully clutching his aching head reminds the viewer of his or her last headache and the accompanying frustrations and discomfort. The man's joy and relief after taking an extra-strength pain reliever resonates with the viewer's once having experienced happiness in being similarly relieved.

Conventional advertising wisdom states that advertisements featuring babies, puppies, and kittens will guarantee positive feelings toward a product. One may sometimes wonder what a baby has to do with car tires, video rentals, orange juice, and minivans or what a dog has to do with tacos, beer, and jeep sales. Perhaps very little. But such "warm" images featured alongside an advertised product have much to do with the viewer and how he or she typically responds to them. Images provide sensory data that connect in meaningful ways to familiar personal experiences, prompting emotional reactions that persuasively relate to consumers' purchasing motives.

Influence of External Factors on Emotional Responses

Executional cues are not the only factors affecting emotional responses. External factors also play a role

Joe Camel, the R. J. Reynolds cigarette advertising mascot shown here on a billboard, was controversial because, opponents said, he appealed to underage smokers. (Corbis/Joel W. Rogers)

in how people respond to emotional appeals. Consider the following scenario. Cindy receives a telephone call from her friend Jordan. During the course of the conversation, Jordan discloses how a thirty-second coffee commercial surprisingly brought him to tears. The advertisement features a man returning home from service in the armed forces. Upon entering his home in the early morning hours, the man warmly embraces his surprised younger brother and slumbering parents. Although watching a different channel, Cindy had just seen the same commercial but without the same reaction; she barely recalled the advertised product and why the young man was hugging his family. Now, there may be a host of explanations why these two friends had such different reactions to the same advertisement, but two possible explanations are the contextual factors and the individual factors.

Context

Assume that at the time the commercial aired Jordan had been watching a comedy and was in a cheerful mood. Cindy, on the other hand, was watching a documentary on the devastation of the rainforest. What does that have to do with their different reactions? Surprisingly, quite a bit. Emotional responses are thought to result not only from the execution of the advertisement, but also from the context in which it is embedded. The context may refer to the television program, magazine articles, or other advertisements preceding the advertisement in question. Many practitioners prefer programmatic material that creates positive feelings rather than negative feelings that might encourage a critical response. Researchers Marvin Goldberg and Gerald Gorn (1987) and Alice Isen (1984) have embedded emotional advertisements in either happy/positive or sad/negative television programs and found that those people viewing the happier shows evaluated the commercials as more effective, showed greater recall of commercial material, reported feeling happier watching the emotional commercials, and expressed a greater intention to purchase the products than those watching the sad television programs. However, John Murry, John Lastovicka, and Surendra Singh (1992) qualify these findings somewhat by observing that when viewers enjoyed negatively emotional programs and perceived that the emotion was not real, the more "positive" programs did not have an advantage over the "negative" programs.

Mark Pavelchak, John Antil, and James Munch (1988) point out that viewers recall less material in commercials that follow programs that create intense emotional reactions. Most likely, such intensely emotional programs may be mentally distracting for many viewers who find themselves during the commercial break pondering over what they previously viewed on the program. Cindy's concern for the destruction of the rainforest may have preoccupied her mind during the commercial, thus inhibiting her processing of the advertisement.

Finally, the advertisements preceding the coffee commercial may have had a differential effect on Cindy and Jordan. Research by David Aaker, Douglas Stayman, and Michael Hagerty (1986) has shown that warmth advertisements that immediately follow a humorous advertisement are more effective, possibly due to the positive mood prompted by the humorous commercial. The humorous advertisement may make viewers more open and positive toward other succeeding appeals. If Jordan found himself laughing at frogs and lizards in a beer commercial just prior to seeing the coffee commercial, such exposure to humor followed by the coffee commercial's warmth appeal may have made him more open and susceptible to an emotional experience.

Individual Factors

What does the individual bring to the emotional experience? Moore and Harris (1996) argue that certain individuals are predisposed to respond with greater emotional intensity when exposed to emotional appeals. They describe a trait called "affect intensity," which simply means that some individuals exposed to emotional stimuli will consistently respond with high levels of emotional intensity while others respond with lower levels of intensity. These responses seem to hold for both negative and positive emotional appeals. Returning to the coffee commercial example, Jordan, by nature, may be classified as high in affect intensity, thus experiencing strong emotions on a regular basis. Conversely, Cindy may be moderate to low in affect intensity and therefore not as inclined to experience strong emotions when exposed to emotion-eliciting stimuli.

Another individual factor that may explain why people respond differently to advertisements deals with involvement. This is an area of advertising and marketing research that has been studied extensively over the years. Involvement is understood by the degree of personal relevance or importance a product holds for an individual. People who find aspects of an advertisement (e.g., the product and/or dramatic elements) personally relevant or important will invest more time and effort in processing the information. Perhaps Jordan has an older brother living away from home; the issue of sibling relationships, therefore, is very important to him and increased his level of involvement. Or perhaps as a connoisseur of coffee, Jordan was highly involved.

Beyond the levels of involvement, the types of involvement can also help further understanding of information processing. C. Whan Park and S. Mark Young (1986) identify two motives that underlie levels of involvement. A utilitarian motive places emphasis on the product's functional performance (e.g., the attributes and benefits that make the product better than the other brands). In contrast, a commercial may be highly involving because it targets consumers' value-expressive motives that appeal more to the emotions, focusing on people's desires to express an actual or ideal image of self to others. These researchers note that utilitarian motives lead to cognitive involvement that engages the mind in processing the advertisement's message content, whereas value-expressive motives lead to affective involvement in which a viewer concerned about image might be high in involvement if aspects of the advertisement appeal to those motives. For example, a consumer in the market for a new watch and possessing strong utilitarian motives may show low levels of involvement for an advertisement that merely shows an elegant woman wearing the product, surrounded by fawning men. With little in the way of product information, this advertisement does not attract the same attention for this consumer as would a more informative advertisement discussing the product's warranty, water- and scratch-proof design, and digital display features. However, a consumer possessing strong value-expressive motives would manifest high levels of involvement for the former advertisement.

Consider Nissan car commercials. Nissan's research on car buyers shows that consumers are tired of hearing about dual-side airbags and wishbone suspension. Thomas Petty, the advertising executive who headed up the Nissan car account, explained to Joshua Levine (1996) that since most cars these days are very similar, the real difference is in how consumers perceive the brand image and how it relates to their own image of self. This observation speaks to a shift from car buyers' traditional utilitarian motives to more value-expressive motives. Understanding this shift might explain the advertising strategies Nissan and other car companies use in increasing viewer involvement in their advertisements. Jim Schroer, executive director of new marketing strategy and the brand management office at Ford, said that rather than basing an advertisement on demographics, "it is smarter to think about emotions and attitudes, which all go under the term *psychographics*—those things that can transcend demographic groups." By doing this, Schroer believes that car marketers can do a better job of marrying car assets and consumer self-image.

Products like beer, chips, and clothing are generally considered low-involvement items in terms of utilitarian motives. That is, there is not a lot of "rational decision making" where people weigh the pros and cons of each product and come to a decision. Many of the purchase decisions for these products are based on factors such as personal preference and image (value-expressive motives), making them ideal for emotional appeals.

Implementing Fear and Humor

When advertisers decide to use rational, cognitive appeals, they operate under the assumption that the consumer is a rational being who is able, motivated, and has the opportunity to process the advertisement's message. However, consumers do not always live in a rational, cognitive world, and such appeals often go ignored. In many situations, consumers respond more to emotional appeals. Two of the most popular appeals among advertisers and academicians are fear appeals and humor appeals.

Fear Appeals

Studies on emotion in advertising often categorize emotions into one of two categories, positive or negative. However, within each category are emotions that may have differential effects on how people process an advertisement. To draw generalized conclusions for an entire category may overlook important relationships unique to a particular emotion. For example, negative emotions may include anger, insecurity, shame, regret, fear, guilt, and envy. Each emotion may lead to different information processing outcomes. It is important, therefore, for researchers to examine some of these emotions separately. Fear appeals are perhaps the most widely studied of the emotional persuasive appeals.

Research on fear appeals in advertising has investigated both physical and social threats to the receiver. Physical fear would include harm to the body; social fear is fear of disapproval by peers or other associates of some action or characteristic possessed by the receiver of the message (e.g., bad breath or ring around the collar). The persuasion literature indicates that with highly educated, motivated, and involved audiences, fear appeals are not as persuasive as objective and rational appeals. Yet, a combined approach that includes emotional/fearful appeals tied to factual information may be relatively persuasive. Overall, moderate fear appeals seem to be the most effective. High fear appeals are less persuasive because people may feel overwhelmed or manipulated.

Fear is used to motivate people to buy the product or service in order to avoid negative consequences. Political advertising often links an opponent to a depressed economy, higher taxes, and less "real" income. Even though the public has a negative attitude toward these attack advertisements, they are highly effective in influencing the candidate's numbers where it matters—in the polls. Indeed, fear appeals and competitor attacks are often more effective than promoting the product itself.

Evidence from highly controlled experiments examining the efficacy of fear appeals are mixed. That is, experimental methods have found that sometimes fear is persuasive, and sometimes it is not. Research by Kim Witte (1992) in the area of fear appeals, however, has found some promising findings in models that underscore the importance of response efficacy and self-efficacy. Response efficacy deals with people's perception that the recommended response will help avoid or overcome the negative consequences or threat. Self-efficacy is the perception that people have the power or ability to execute a response. These two concepts have proven to be very important in developing effective fear appeals. It is not enough merely to convince people that a threat is severe and that they are susceptible; an advertiser must also persuade consumers that the recommended response will work and that they can execute the response. For example, if advertisers using fear appeals to get teenagers to stop smoking only succeed in scaring teenagers by showing the harmful effects of smoking, the fear appeal may backfire, leading to an actual increase in the targeted behavior in some cases. If, on the other hand, the fear appeal goes beyond scaring and persuades them that they have the power to overcome and that a support group can be effective, the fear appeal has a much better chance of producing positive results.

Public service announcements often attempt to evoke fear in order to persuade people to live more healthy lifestyles. Examples of such campaigns include advertisements aimed to decrease/eliminate drug and alcohol use, smoking, and unsafe sex, as well as campaigns to promote seat belt and helmet use and well-baby and breast exams. The campaigns aimed at discouraging teenagers from smoking and having unprotected sex are prime examples. The teenagers often know all the negative health effects and risks involved in engaging in these activities. The advertisements providing rational claims as to the consequences of such behavior have not been highly effective. Fear appeal advertisements attempting to scare teenagers with the reality that bad things do happen to people their age may be a little more effective because they personalize the message. Other advertisements, such as linking smoking to looking "uncool" (which could lead to social rejection), may be more effective for teenagers. These fear appeal advertisements may hit at the heart of teenagers' priorities for peer group acceptance.

Similarly, advertisers are recognizing that brands have implicit—if not explicit—emotional promises to their customers. For example, mutual fund advertisements create emotional promises for financial security during retirement. Conversely, they may link fear appeals to their competitors so that competing mutual funds are perceived as risky, lacking security, faceless, and untrustworthy. Lou Rubin (1997) suggests that although a few mutual funds have name recognition, they need to create an "image" so that people can emotionally connect with the company.

Humor

Although research has yet to establish a direct link between humor and sales, it is often used to gain and maintain attention as well as promote a positive attitude toward the advertisement, the product, and the company. The hope is that this positive attitude translates into purchasing behavior. An entertaining, humorous advertisement may also be remembered more and facilitate comprehension, thus creating a greater probability of brand name recall when the consumer is actually at the store. Research by Thomas Madden and Mark Weinberger (1984) does show that using humor is most effective when the humor is directly re-

lated to the theme or main points of the advertisement. In addition, humor should not be used for sensitive products or issues. One television commercial aired in a localized area attempted to use humor in persuading people to choose a certain funeral home. In another advertisement, a prominent athletic shoe company featured two bungee jumpers, one of which had pump shoes. The young man wearing the pumps successfully jumped and sprang back, but his friend did not. The empty bungee noose implied that the jumper slipped out of his shoes because they were not pumps. This type of inappropriate juxtaposition of humor and death can backfire and damage a company's image.

As mentioned, the link between humor and persuasion is an indirect one. For products such as Budweiser beer that already own a substantial part of their market, humor may be used to maintain the positive relationship between the consumer and product, as well as to reinforce the brand name and image. However, although people enjoy these humorous advertisements and are more likely to remember and talk about them, the link to actual purchasing behavior—the bottom line—is still unclear. More controlled studies into the effects of humor and its effectiveness when combined with other strategies need to be conducted.

Emotions and Information Processing

The ultimate goal for most advertising is change—changing consumers' attitudes, beliefs, and/or behaviors. However, advertisers recognize that such goals are best realized through careful attention to a number of preliminary goals. These antecedent goals may include gaining and maintaining attention, enhancing memory, and creating a positive attitude toward the advertisements.

Attention

Advertising is a lot like fishing in an ocean. Particularly with the national networks and large newspapers, advertisers are promoting their product to a large audience. And yet, through market research, they have narrowed their "buying audience" considerably. The buying audience consists of those people who are most likely to purchase the product and to whom the advertisement is tailored. The necessary first step for advertisers is to cast their product line into this ocean, hoping to "hook" the buying audience's attention. An advertisement cannot be effective if it is not seen, heard, or read. Successful attention-gaining strategies are varied—some advertisements grab attention by exposing a fear, causing laughter, or by linking the product to a need or desire.

With the high volume of information disseminated through television, print, radio, internet, and other media, grabbing the consumers' attention is not an easy feat. Television commercials are seen by the viewer as an opportunity to channel surf other programs (called "zapping") or grab some food. Many people videotape their programs so that they can fast-forward (called "zipping") through the commercials and watch the program in forty-four minutes rather than sixty minutes. With all of these competing demands upon people's attention, advertisements must have some kind of gimmick or "hook" that gets the viewers to pay attention to the advertisement.

Certain companies link themselves with a personality or certain types of gimmicks. For example, Snapple advertisements are known for their bizarre use of humor. Taco Bell's advertisements use the absurd talking Chihuahua. And the Budweiser frogs and lizard advertisements have certainly captured viewers attention and affection. Emotional manipulations can therefore be used to gain and keep the audience's attention. Emotional responses produce arousal and, consequently, an orienting response to the stimuli.

The intensity of the emotion also plays an important role in attention. Esther Thorson (1991) found that emotional intensity has a positive effect on attention. The higher the intensity, the greater the amount of attention paid to the advertisement. Practitioners often attempt to "crank" the emotional intensity to avoid zapping and zipping and ultimately break through the consumers' perceptual screens.

Memory

Advertisers struggle with the challenge of not just getting consumers to notice their advertisements but to remember them. Marketers want the person who views the various product brands on the store shelf to have their specific product stored in his or her mind, and they want that information to be readily available. Strong evidence shows that emotional commercials are superior to neutral ones in terms of this kind of recall. According to Thorson and Marian Friestad (1988), when consumers are exposed to an advertisement, elements of the commercial (referred to as the "trace") are stored in memory. The trace may contain such elements as the brand name, product claims, and executional elements (e.g., music and sound effects). Emotional responses experienced during the viewing of the advertisement may also be stored in the trace. Any one of the elements stored in the trace can reactivate the entire trace. Thus, creating an emotional response can be advantageous for an advertiser because successful recall of the emotions one felt while watching an advertisement can activate the entire trace of the commercial. For a teenager faced with the decision about whether to join his or her drunk friends on a joyride downtown, the emotions of fear and apprehension may be instrumental in helping the teenager to recall a commercial featuring drunken teenagers in an automobile accident. The emotions experienced when he or she first viewed the commercial were stored in the memory trace, and when reactivated, they helped in the recall of other aspects of the advertisement.

What some practitioners fail to realize is that increased attention does not necessarily translate into increased brand recognition, information recall, and positive brand attitudes. Highly intense advertisements, although they may initially gain attention, may prove more a distraction than a facilitator. An intense negative emotion, for example, may cause a viewer to feel stress, anxiety, fear, or even anger. Future avoidance of the intense material may result. Moreover, intense material may direct the viewers' attention away from processing important information as they direct it more toward the intense material. Thorson's (1991) research has shown that low to moderate levels of emotional intensity can produce positive effects with regard to recognition and recall of the brand and brand information. However, the more extreme levels of emotional intensity result in a decline in information recall.

Attitudes

Strong evidence presented by Robert Zajonc (1980) shows that individual choices (e.g., what product to purchase, what cause to support, what idea to adopt) can be based on affective or emotional as well as rational factors. This has popularized the "attitude toward the ad" stream of research, which argues that one's attitude toward an *advertisement* may mediate the effects of the advertising message on *brand* attitudes and preferences. If a viewer experiences feelings of warmth and amusement during an advertisement, those feelings will affect the way the viewer reacts to the commercial itself. Those positive feelings toward the advertisement are then likely to be transferred to the brand itself. Stayman and Aaker (1988) revealed an additional—more direct—link between the emotions consumers experience when viewing an advertisement and their feelings toward the brand. In other words, the feelings of warmth and amusement may directly affect their feelings toward the product, regardless of whether they necessarily liked the advertisement.

Conclusion

Dramatic progress has been made in the study of emotions in advertising. As a result, practitioners and academicians alike have gained an increased appreciation and understanding for its critical role in advertising effectiveness. Practitioners are turning more and more to emotional appeals as a means of differentiating their products from others, forging relationships with and between consumers, and creating positive feelings toward their products. Academicians have shifted more attention away from cognitive research toward constructing models that include emotion as a key factor in information processing and decision making. The role of emotion in advertising is a rich area of research, and there is still an enormous amount to be learned.

See also: ATTITUDES; MOOD; PERSUASION; PROPAGANDA

Bibliography

Aaker, David A.; Stayman, Douglas M.; and Hagerty, Michael R. (1986). "Warmth in Advertising: Measurement, Impact, and Sequence Effects." *Journal of Consumer Research* 12:356–381.

Cohen, Joel B., and Areni, Charles S. (1991). "Affect and Consumer Behavior." In *Handbook of Consumer Behavior*, ed. Thomas S. Robertson and Harold H. Kassarjian. Englewood Cliffs, NJ: Prentice-Hall.

Cooper, Martha, and Nothstine, William L. (1996). *Power Persuasion*. Greenwood, IN: Educational Video Group.

Edell, Julie A., and Burke, Marian Chapman. (1987). "The Power of Feelings in Understanding Advertising Effects." *Journal of Consumer Research* 14:421–433.

Erevelles, Sunil. (1998). The Role of Affect in Marketing." *Journal of Business Research* 42:199–215.

Garfield, Bob. (1998). "Perspicacious Pooch Scores for Taco Bell." *Advertising Age*, March 9, p. 53.

Goldberg, Marvin E., and Gorn, Gerald J. (1987). "Happy and Sad TV Programs: How They Affect Reactions to Commercials. " *Journal of Consumer Research* 14:387–403.

Hecker, Sidney. (1984). "Music for Advertising Effect." *Psychology and Marketing* 1:3–8.

Isen, Alice M. (1984). "Toward Understanding the Role of Affect in Cognition." In *Handbook of Social Cognition, Vol. 3,* ed. Robert S. Wyer and Thomas K. Srull. Hillsdale, NJ: Lawrence Erlbaum.

Levine, Joshua. (1996). "Brands with Feeling." *Forbes* 158(14): 292–294.

MacInnis, Deborah J., and Park, C. Whan. (1991). "The Differential Role of Characteristics of Music on High- and Low-Involvement Consumers' Processing of Ads." *Journal of Consumer Research* 18:161–173.

Madden, Thomas J., and Weinberger, Mark B. (1984). "Humor in Advertising: A Practitioner View." *Journal of Advertising Research* 24:23–29.

Moore, David J. (1989). "Advertising that Makes the Brain Itch." *MBA Update, Bureau of Business Practice*. Old Lyme, CT: Simon & Schuster.

Moore, David J., and Harris, William D. (1996). "Affect Intensity and the Consumer's Attitude Toward Impact Emotional Appeals." *Journal of Advertising* 25(2):37–48.

Morgan, Carol, and Levy, Doron. (1997). "Why We Kick the Tires." *Brandweek*, September 29, p. 25.

Murry, John P., Jr.; and Dacin, Peter A. (1996). "Cognitive Moderators of Negative-Emotion Effects: Implications for Understanding Media Context." *Journal of Consumer Research* 22: 439–447.

Murry, John P., Jr.; Lastovicka, John L.; and Singh, Surendra N. (1992). "Feeling and Liking Responses to Television Programs: An Examination of Two Explanations for Media-Context Effects." *Journal of Consumer Research* 18:441–451.

Park, C. Whan, and Young, S. Mark. (1986). "Consumer Response to Television Commercials: The Impact of Involvement and Background Music on Brand Attitude Formation." *Journal of Marketing Research* 23(2):11–24.

Pavelchak, Mark A.; Antil, John, H.; and Munch, James M. (1988). "The Super Bowl: An Investigation into the Relationship among Program Context, Emotional Experience, and Ad Recall." *Journal of Consumer Research* 15:360–367.

Rubin, Lou. (1997). "Feeling Isn't Mutual." *Brandweek*, September 15, pp. 36–38.

Stayman, Douglas M., and Aaker, David A. (1988). "Are All the Effects of Ad-Induced Feelings Mediated by Aad?" *Journal of Consumer Research* 15:368–373.

Thorson, Esther. (1991). "Emotional Flows during Commercials." In *Tears, Cheers, and Fears: The Role of Emotions in Advertising*, ed. Carolyn Yoon. Cambridge, MA: Marketing Science Institute Conference Report.

Thorson, Esther, and Friestad, Marian. (1988). "The Effects of Emotion of Episodic Memory for Television Commercials." In *Cognitive and Affective Responses to Advertising*, ed. Patricia Cafferata and Alice M. Tybout. Lexington, MA: Lexington Books.

Twitchell, James B. (1996). *Adcult USA*. New York: Columbia University Press.

Witte, Kim. (1992). "Putting the Fear Back into Fear Appeals: The Extended Parallel Process Model." *Communication Monographs* 59:329–349.

Zajonc, Robert B. (1980). "Feeling and Thinking: Preferences Need No Inferences." *American Psychologist* 35(February): 151–175.

Mark A. Callister
Lesa A. Stern

AFFECT DISORDERS

See Mood Disorders

AGGRESSION

The relationship of emotional experience to aggressive behavior is not well understood. There is no general agreement about the nature of emotions, and there are problems with the concept of aggression. Theories of aggression that explicitly consider the relationship of emotions to aggressive behavior propose all possibilities: (1) emotions cause aggressive behavior, (2) emotions are parallel to but do not cause aggressive behavior; (3) emotions *may* indirectly cause aggressive behavior. Unfortunately, only limited laboratory research using less than a handful of research models has been done to evaluate the available theories. Most of this research has focused on the relationship of anger and aggression. However, there is some data that can be used to evaluate the relationships between a number of other emotions and aggressive behavior.

Conceptual Issues

Aggression is a descriptive concept and refers to a set of behaviors that are in some way similar to one another but different from other classes of behavior. A perfect definition would allow classification of all aggression into a set of behaviors—the set would not include behaviors that are not aggressive, and no aggressive behavior would be excluded from the set. Psychologists have historically proposed two different definitions of aggression: behavioristic and attributional.

Behavioristic Definition

Arnold Buss (1961) proposed a behavioristic definition that said aggression was any response that delivers noxious stimuli to another organism. Punching, kicking, stabbing, and shooting another person are examples of responses that deliver noxious stimuli to others. Behaviorists wanted to avoid using concepts that referred to internal states of the organism, such as emotions and cognitions. The philosophical issues can be avoided by examining whether the behavioristic definition adequately captures the set of responses one wants to identify as aggressive.

The behavioristic definition appears to include behaviors, such as accidents and mistakes, that are not aggressive, and it excludes behaviors where actors try but fail to harm another person. In the case of accidents, such as when a hunter shoots a passerby, the outcome is not foreseen and is not under the control of the actor. Presumably, the causal processes that explain intentional behavior and accidental behavior are quite different, and thus no theorist would choose to classify accidents, mistakes, and involuntary behaviors as being aggressive. Furthermore, the requirement that aggressive behaviors be successful in delivering harm appears too stringent. What about snipers who misfire or terrorists whose bombs fail to explode? Such failed actions are not included in the set of behaviors defined as aggressive by behaviorists.

Attributional Definition

Most theorists have adopted an attributional definition that identifies aggression as any act that is intended to harm another person. This definition eliminates accidents, mistakes, and unanticipated harmful outcomes from the set of aggressive acts, and it includes acts that are intended to do harm but fail. Intent is seldom defined, but it apparently refers to the goal of the actor. Unfortunately, observers often confuse their attributions regarding the intentions of actors with the actors' own views of their intentions. Consider a robbery. Obviously, a robbery harms the victim. But is it the primary goal of the robber to harm the victim? Perhaps in a few cases it is. It is more typical that a robber's goal is to take the victim's valuables and get away without being caught by the police. If the victim is compliant, there is seldom physical harm involved. Presumably, most robbers have no concern for the welfare of the victim and do not experience guilt about taking the victim's money or causing fear or trauma to the victim. The conceptual problem for the attribution theorist is that although the robber harms the victim (financially, psychologically, and perhaps physically) his intent is to get compliance from the victim and enrich himself. Should then armed robbery be included in the set of acts labeled as being aggressive?

Emotional and Instrumental Aggression

One strategy that has been adopted to handle this conceptual problem posed by the attributional definition is to distinguish between emotional and instrumental aggression. Emotional aggression refers to acts that are primarily motivated by a desire to harm the victim, whereas instrumental aggression refers to acts that harm the victim but only in the process of obtaining other goals. This distinction raises additional conceptual issues. For example, it can always be asked why the actor wanted to harm the victim. This is a question that refers to motives, which are reasons for actions. Intent refers to proximal goals of acts, while motives refer to terminal goals. The proximal goal of a robber is to gain compliance, and he wants compliance in order to acquire the valuables from the victim. Thus, the robber's intent is to gain compliance, and his motive is to enrich himself. The category of emotional aggression refers to motiveless acts. It assumes that people intentionally harm others for no reason—there is no goal other than to hurt the victim. This view was first proposed by the frustration-aggression theory of John Dollard and his colleagues (1939), but it has been championed by Leonard Berkowitz (1993) in a neo-associationist theory since the 1960s. Laboratory research on human aggression in social psychology has focused on emotional aggression and has largely neglected the study of instrumental aggression. This research seldom examines the intentions and motives of experimental participants, and interpretation of the results relies more on the theoretical presumptions of the researchers than on the motives or lack of motives of the participants.

The classification of instrumental aggression implicitly requires a subjective value judgment by researchers. Consider a parent who punishes a child for misbehavior. The type of punishment could include deprivation of freedom or allowance, a tepid spanking, or a verbal rebuke. The goal of the parent, in most such instances, is to change the behavior of the child, that is, to deter a possible repeat performance of the misbehavior. Since the parent intentionally harms the child and has a motive of deterrence (the terminal goal), this parental action fits the definition of instrumental aggression. However, most people, including social scientists, do not classify such parental actions as being aggressive. As social control agents, responsible parents are expected to punish their children in some way to discourage deviant, antisocial behavior or self-destructive behavior. A reasonable parental punishment is classified as legitimate aggression. This example reveals a value judgment made by researchers, who need to distinguish between legitimate and illegitimate forms of instrumental aggression. Unfortunately, there is no universal value system that can serve as a background for reliable classification of all instrumental aggression by all of the world's social scientists. The result is that considerable ambiguity exists about which acts to classify as illegitimate aggression. For example, in Scandinavian countries, corporal punishment of children is prohibited by law and presumably would be labeled as being illegitimate aggression, while in the United States, where a large majority of parents approve of and have carried out the spanking of their children, such actions must be classified as legitimate aggression.

Coercive Actions

James Tedeschi and Richard Felson (1994) rejected aggression as a useful scientific concept. They proposed instead a scheme of coercive actions that includes threats, punishments, and bodily force. Threats are communications from a source indicating that she or he will perform future harmful actions. If the future harmful action is contingent upon noncompliance by the target to some demand by the source, the intent is to gain compliance. A noncontingent threat amounts to a prior announcement for a harm-doing act and has the intent of inspiring fear and anxiety in the target person (a form of harm). Punitive acts are accompanied by an intent to harm a target person, where the harm can be a physical or social/emotional injury or a deprivation. Bodily force involves the use of the actor's body (or extensions by use of tools) to force compliance on a target person. While the target person may experience the actor's use of bodily force as being harmful, the intent of the actor is not to do harm but to gain compliance. If a parent picks up a child who is reluctant to go to bed and places the child in the bed, the child may feel humiliated, controlled,

and disapproved, but the parent may have no intent other than to gain compliance. It is noteworthy that most aggression research focuses on direct physical harm and seldom examines threats, bodily force, or the other types of harm. Indeed, since contingent threats do not have the intent to do harm, they are seldom discussed by aggression theorists.

Emotions

There are numerous views of what emotions are, what arouses them, and what effects they have. Controversies rage regarding the proper level of analysis of emotions. Are they the products of biological evolution, encoded in genes and automatically triggered by species-specific perceptual mechanisms? If so, the proper way to study emotions is primarily through research on physiological mechanisms. Perhaps there is some primitive level of emotional reaction, such as flight-or-fight dispositions, that is enriched, interpreted, and guided by cognitive mechanisms. If so, primary analysis requires consideration of language, attributions, and appraisals. Another approach, one that focuses on sociological and anthropological research, considers that social norms provide the basis for interpreting and expressing emotions. Eclectic approaches combine each of these levels of analysis, giving more or less weight to one or another of the processes. In considering the relationship of emotions to aggressive (or coercive) actions, the emphasis in this entry will be placed on the phenomenological experience of emotions, the motives that are generated, and the conditions under which aggressive actions are likely to occur.

Anger and Aggression

The individual's experience of anger may or may not be accompanied by a display of anger. A person may display anger for tactical purposes but experience no anger. For example, a negotiator may feign anger as a ploy to convey commitment to a particular position to an opponent. On the other hand, a person who experiences anger may not express it publicly. Jean Briggs (1970) reports that Utku Eskimos seldom express anger and are taught as children to isolate themselves from others when they experience anger. This distinction between experience and expression is important because some theorists combine the two aspects in defining anger, and others describe the expression of anger as aggression.

The experience of anger has been linked to frustration, attributions of blame, and a failure of control or power over events. Frustration-aggression theory proposed that interference with attempts by an organism to achieve a goal causes arousal of aggressive energy or drive. This drive state has been interpreted as anger, or more generally as arousal. Anger generated by frustration leads directly to aggressive behavior unless all alternative aggressive responses are inhibited. Which aggressive response the organism will perform depends on prior learning experiences, particularly with regard to rewards and punishments. Performing an aggressive response is self-reinforcing because it reduces the aggressive drive (or anger), a process that is referred to as catharsis. The aggressive behavior may remove the source of frustration, which is also reinforcing. An aggressive behavior is strengthened by such reinforcements and is more likely to occur the next time the organism is frustrated. Punishments inhibit and weaken particular aggressive behaviors, but they do not reduce anger. As a consequence, the individual is likely to engage in some other form of aggressive behavior.

Critics have noted that frustration does not always lead to anger. Learned helplessness and depression are associated with repeated failure. Golfers and mountain climbers view the obstacles and hurdles that interfere with their goals as being challenges to overcome. Furthermore, research has shown that aggression is not a typical way of responding to anger. James Averill (1983) found that about 60 percent of the anger episodes experienced by college students produced nonaggressive responses, such as calming activities and attempts to talk the incident over with the other person. Thus, while some forms of frustration may sometimes lead to anger and aggressive behavior, it is not an invariable or even a typical process.

Berkowitz (1993) has argued that there are two types of aggression, and they represent distinctly different processes. Emotional aggression is the more basic and primitive system, presumably based on the evolutionary history of the species, while instrumental aggression is learned. People are biologically constructed to experience negative affect when exposed to some types of physical events (i.e., aversive stimuli). Negative affect, which is a state of feeling bad or unpleasant, may not represent differentiated emotion until cognitive processes come into play. It is assumed that there is a genetically pre-wired association between negative affect and an anger/aggression syndrome involving specific feelings, physiological reactions, motor responses, and interconnected thoughts and memories. While the links between these components of the anger/aggression emotional syndrome may vary in strength, negative affect tends to evoke all of its components. People who feel bad for whatever reason are likely to feel angry, experience autonomic arousal, have hostile thoughts, and develop a *want* to hurt others. Conversely, people who feel bad are likely to experience hostile thoughts, which might make them experience even more negative affect and a stronger desire to hurt someone. This *want* to hurt directly leads to aggressive behavior when a suitable target is available, unless the organism is experienced and has learned inhibition. Anger and aggression are considered to be parallel processes because they are elements of the same syndrome and are produced by the same antecedent condition—aversive stimuli. Thus, anger does not cause aggression, although sometimes they occur together.

Berkowitz has pointed to evidential bases for his assumption that emotional aggression is a built-in reaction to experiences of negative affect. Some research has shown that animals respond to electrical shock by attacking other members of their species, a phenomenon referred to as reflex fighting. However, there is controversy regarding this evidence and how to interpret it. Berkowitz has carried out an enormous amount of research since the 1960s to show that exposure to aversive stimuli, such as loud noises, cold water, insults, and violent films, cause research participants to deliver more noxious stimuli (in the form of electric shocks) to other participants. This evidence does not, however, support a direct relationship between exposure to aversive stimuli and aggression. Aversive stimuli have no effect on aggression unless another person first attacks the actor. This pattern suggests that aversive stimuli facilitate or enhance aggressiveness when the actor is otherwise caused to be aggressive, but they do not instigate or directly cause the actor to be aggressive.

Dolf Zillmann (1983) has proposed that provocation or endangerment induce arousal and learned patterns of behavior that are associated with such situations and that these behaviors are guided by the monitoring of higher cognitive processes. Arousal energizes and intensifies behavior, but the behavior that occurs is not caused by the arousal. Thus, unlike Berkowitz, who views negative affect (or negative arousal) as being an instigation to aggression, Zillmann views arousal as being a facilitator or amplifier of aggression. The primary emotion associated with aggression is anger, and anything that increases the intensity of anger is likely to increase aggression, if that is the kind of

---

In William Carlos Williams's "Use of Force" (1938), the physician-narrator loses his patience with a young child who, out of fear and stubbornness, refuses to open her mouth so he can examine her throat. The doctor brutally forces her mouth open and even admits that he enjoyed assaulting her. Later, he realizes that he behaved irrationally and lost control.

behavior that occurs. Zillmann proposed a mechanism of excitation transfer, which allows arousal induced by one stimulus to combine with arousal induced by a subsequent stimulus. When arousal peeks, it then begins to dissipate, and at a low level of residual arousal, the individual is no longer aware of its presence. At this stage of dissipation, if the individual experiences arousal from another stimulus, the residual arousal will combine with the new source of arousal, so that the emotion experienced in the presence of the new stimulus will be more intense than it would have been had the residual arousal not been present. If the person has learned to respond to anger by aggressing against the person who provoked it, and if the greater the anger, the stronger the aggressive response, then excitation transfer is a facilitating process.

According to Zillmann, a high level of arousal interferes with cognitive functioning. When cognitive monitoring is decreased or eliminated, the individual is less apt to consider the consequences of behavior and more apt to engage in scripted actions. Thus, when arousal is high, actions will be more impulsive and less regulated by appraisals or consideration of costs. Excitation transfer, because it contributes to the intensity of arousal, is an important process associated with impulsive and intense aggressive behavior.

In their social interactionist theory of coercive actions Tedeschi and Felson (1994) adopted Averill's (1983) view that anger is a reaction to an appraisal of injustice. They agreed with Zillmann that arousal is a facilitator and interferes with cognitive functioning. In addition, Tedeschi and Felson proposed that anger induces a justice motive (or grievance). People become angry because of an experience of injustice, and because of prior socialization, they believe that justice should be restored. Among the alternative means of restoring justice are restitution by the perpetrator for harm done, apology by the harm-doer and forgiveness by the victim, or punishment of the perpetrator. Punitive action is typically designed to make the punishment fit the crime—the goal of the grievant is to get even. Restoration of justice produces a cathartic-like reduction in anger or resentment. If none of these justice-restoring alternatives occurs, usually because the victim is inhibited from acting, the aggrieved party will maintain resentment toward the perpetrator and will be ready to engage in justice-restoring action if an opportunity arises. According to Tedeschi and Felson, grievances can accumulate across incidents with the same perpetrator or across incidents with different perpetrators (a general feeling of an unjust world). Accumulated grievances may overcome inhibitions and lead to punitive action by a person who feels victimized.

It would be fair to say that the relationship between anger and aggression has only begun to be scientifically examined. While evidence has been produced to support all of the above theories, many irregular findings have also been obtained. There is not yet enough evidence available to allow for a fair evaluation of the relationships between anger and aggression that are specified by the frustration-aggression, emotional aggression, excitation transfer, or social interactionist theories.

Rage, Resentment, and Hostility

Anger varies in frequency, intensity, and duration. Low-intensity anger has sometimes been referred to as annoyance or irritation, and an extremely high level of anger has been referred to as rage. The physiological arousal that accompanies the experience of anger cannot be maintained indefinitely, so it eventually dissipates. However, if nothing is done to resolve the conflict, the individual does not simply forget about the incident. Indeed, Jennings Bryant and Zillmann (1979) found that students who were angered by a rude guest instructor provided negative evaluations of him eight days after the encounter. This lingering feeling of having been wronged by the other person is referred to as resentment. Tedeschi and Felson (1994) proposed that under specific conditions resentment may be converted into anger and may cumulate to create greater anger with new transgressions committed by the other person.

Rage has sometimes been equated with intense anger. However, Michael Lewis (1992) has argued that there are important differences between anger and rage. He indicates that anger is a restricted, focused response, while rage is diffused and unbounded. Furthermore, an angered person feels self-righteous or justified, but a person who is in a rage feels powerless. According to Lewis, the etiology of anger and rage are also different. Anger is a reaction to interference with goals, and rage is a response to humiliation and shame. While Lewis has pointed out some useful distinctions, there is an apparent confluence between the individual's experience and behavior. It might be more useful to consider intense anger (under some circumstances and in some people) as being a factor in producing aggressive behavior that has the proximal goal of injury or destruction.

Several social theorists, including Erving Goffman (1955), David Luckenbill (1982), and Tedeschi and Felson (1994), explicitly propose that insults, lack of respect, interference with autonomy, and other impolite actions of others spoil the identity of the target person, causing that person to expect or experience a loss of power and humiliation. Theodore Kemper (1978) and Thomas Scheff (1988) have asserted that

During the November 22, 1998, gang fight eruption in a commercial district of Jakarta, Indonesia, a man is attacked in a physical act of aggression. The conflict ultimately resulted in six deaths and the burning of a church and gambling hall. (Corbis/AFP)

the humiliation and shame that the person experiences, when believed to lack justification, gives rise to strong or intense anger. According to social interactionist theory, humiliation creates a motive to restore lost honor or to maintain a positive identity and to restore status and power. Anger often accompanies humiliation. Multiple motives are associated with strong responses. Anger may activate a justice motive. A humiliated person may believe that doing nothing in response to the provocation would be construed as an acceptance of the loss of face and status, contributing to an impression that the person is weak and an appeaser. A counterattack shows that the person is neither weak nor an appeaser, that she or he has honor and pride and can deter others from showing disrespect. The person is able to put her- or himself up by putting the other person down. The counterattack humiliates the other person and motivates a counter-counterattack. Whereas a person with justice motivation wants to get even, a humiliated person wants to win. The tendency for this form of "character" contest

is to escalate in intensity, and often one or both parties can be physically injured. Information provided by Felson and Henry Steadman (1983) and Luckenbill (1977) of physical assaults and homicide in the United States indicates that they frequently occur during character contests. In some cultures character contests are ritualized. For example, E. Adamson Hoebel (1954) reported that among the Eskimos living in the Arctic, disputes may lead to song duels involving insulting lyrics. The winner of the dispute is the one gaining the most applause from onlookers.

Theory and evidence, then, suggest that both the causes and consequences of anger and rage are different and are associated with different motives. Anger leads the individual to try to get even, while rage provides a motive to overcome or harm the other person (i.e., to win). This type of analysis would seem to support Berkowitz's view that emotional aggression is differentiated from instrumental aggression. Anger-instigated aggression could be interpreted as being instrumental because it is associated with the goal of achieving or restoring justice, while rage could be interpreted as being emotional aggression because its goal would be to harm the other person. However, if the reason the person wants to harm the other person is to restore face, status, and power, then the harm-doing would be instrumental and not emotional aggression.

Hostility is usually defined as being a personality disposition, representing a stable style of cognitive appraisals, experiences, and expressions of anger. A person high in hostility is not in a perpetual state of anger but rather is more easily angered and more likely to express it aggressively than a person who is low in hostility. A number of studies, such as that conducted by Kenneth Dodge and Joseph Newman (1981), have shown that hostile individuals are more likely to interpret ambiguous circumstances as being provocative and are more apt to respond aggressively to perceived provocations. A number of scales have been developed to measure hostility, but they have been shown to have only modest success in predicting aggressive behavior.

Hatred represents a desire to harm, induce suffering, or dominate the target person. There is a total lack of empathy for the other person. Indeed, there is a tendency to dehumanize the target. Other than some clinical observations and speculations, primarily from psychoanalysts, the sources of hatred are not well understood. It is not a motive that has been empirically studied.

Fear and Anxiety

Scientists who have a biological orientation to their work have long referred to a tendency of organisms to react to endangerment either by fleeing or resisting as the flight-or-fight reaction. It is assumed that these two response options have fear and anger as their underlying emotions. Such tendencies clearly exist in lower organisms, and they probably exist in some measure in humans. Babies show startle reactions, move away from visual cliffs, and cry when dropped. They also display what has been interpreted as being expressions of anger when held down or restrained. Furthermore, there is evidence from cross-cultural research to support the notion of universal facial expressions that are associated with experiencing the primary emotions of fear and anger.

When an animal is endangered, the response associated with the stronger emotion is expected to occur. An exception to this rule is that a cornered animal may fight to save its life. This rule is exemplified in a study by Luckenbill (1982). He found that active resistance to a robber who possessed a lethal weapon occurred when the robber demanded compliance from a male victim who was not able to comply. When threatened in this way, the victim had a choice either to remain passive and be harmed, or to resist and per-

haps save himself (although he might not succeed). In all seventeen cases where the victim had this choice between the lesser of two evils, all seventeen individuals actively opposed the robber. Thus, when a person experiences high fear and is unable to escape the danger, and when it is perceived that aggressive action against the source of danger may succeed in removing it, the actor may initiate a preemptive attack. The legitimacy of such action is at issue when battered women kill the men who abuse them. There is reason to believe that people cannot live in perpetual fear without experiencing psychological disturbance or taking some desperate action to eliminate or escape the source of fear.

While studies have shown some degree of association between anxiety and aggression, the *nature* of the relationship remains unclear. Anxiety and aggression are common symptoms in various personality disorders, including some forms of depression. Anxiety represents an apprehension based on anticipation of risks, where the individual has no coping behavior available. An experience of negative affect is aroused by such expectations. According to Berkowitz's theory, negative affect is an instigator to aggression, and hence it might be predicted that anxiety would be associated with aggressive behavior. However, the relationship is inconsistent across studies and weak enough to raise questions about any causal link. Zillmann's theory of excitation transfer might also account for why sometimes anxiety is related to aggression. If an individual combines anxiety-generated arousal with the arousal associated with anger, and anger leads to aggressive behavior, then the behavior will be more intense than it would have been in a non-anxious person. Such interpretations have not received scientific evaluation.

Aaron Beck (1974) has reported that people suffering from depression have low self-esteem and a negative view of their world and their future. They have a tendency to attribute negative outcomes to their own shortcomings and any positive outcomes to luck or chance. As a result they have reduced motivation to act in situations where they could control their outcomes. Often they have inwardly directed anger, which may be accompanied by outwardly directed anger. Depressive patients are known to have a different style of processing information and of making attributions. The combination of cognitive, affective, and behavioral aspects of the diagnostic category of depression has made it difficult to determine what, if any, effect such a neurosis has on aggressive behavior.

Shame, Guilt, and Embarrassment

A group of self-directed emotions have received very little attention by aggression theorists. There is evidence that these are distinct but related emotional states. All of these emotions are based on negative evaluations of one's own actions or on the evaluation of a defective self. Tedeschi and Felson (1994) proposed that humiliation is associated with identity-threatening actions performed by others, actions which one may be bound in some cultures to avenge in order to restore honor. They draw a distinction between humiliation and embarrassment, with the former involving identity-threatening actions by others and the latter referring to gaffes attributed to the self. Apart from these speculations, it is not clear what the implications are when the person accepts that she or he has done something untoward or wrong (guilt) or when the person lowers the evaluation of the self (shame). June Tangney and her colleagues (1996) suggest that guilt may motivate conciliatory actions, such as apologies and restitution, toward a harmed other and that shame may motivate withdrawal or attempts to escape shame by attributing blame to others.

Empathy and Humor

The cognitive aspect of empathy is the ability to take the perspective of another person, and the affective component is the vicarious experiencing of the emotion felt by the other person. The more one understands the reasons for another person's actions, the more understanding and tolerance there is. If a person has good perspective-taking skills or there are situational factors that induce them, she or he is apt to react less aggressively. Similarly, if a person experiences the other person's distress or pain, she or he may be motivated to relieve the distress of both the other and the self by undertaking some prosocial action. Thus, both cognitive and affective components of empathy should be associated with reduced aggressiveness.

Deborah Richardson and her colleagues (1994) found that perspective taking induced by role-taking instructions induced more tolerance and less aggression toward another person but only when the actor has not been first provoked or attacked by the other person. A review by Ken-ichi Ohbuchi (1988) indicated similar findings in studies of affective empathy. The latter studies have primarily focused on pain cues emitted by the target of the actor's aversive actions. When the actor has been provoked, pain cues appear to be positively experienced by the harm-doer, but when the actor has not been provoked, pain cues serve to reduce the amount of aggression. While these effects are consistent with theoretical expectations, the exact mechanisms for them have not been thoroughly explored.

Humor may also serve to inhibit aggression. When two persons are at the beginning of a character contest, humor introduced by a third party implies that the matter is not serious and can be dismissed without either party losing face. Humor may also induce a good mood in a person, which is incompatible with aggressive behavior. While there is evidence to support these hypotheses, it has also been found that aggressive humor does not inhibit aggressiveness, and in some cases increases it.

Jealousy and Envy

Jealousy has been defined by Eugene Mathes (1992) as being the negative emotion that results from the actual or threatened loss of love to a rival. Many people deliberately induce jealousy in their partners as a way of punishing them for various perceived slights or misbehaviors. The jealous individual may react in any number of ways, including withdrawal and depression, confronting or attacking the partner or suitor, and stalking the partner. Jealousy is the basis of many cases of physical abuse of dating and marriage partners. Such punitive acts are performed to punish the partner and to deter future dalliances.

Envy is a negative emotion associated with coveting something that is possessed by another person. Clinical observation led Melanie Klein (1957) to speculate that envy is often converted into hatred and a desire to destroy the coveted object. Envy could also create the motivation to remove or take the coveted object from whomever possesses or controls it. There is little or no research investigating whether there is a relationship between envy and aggressive behavior.

Conclusion

Any emotion may, under special circumstances, be associated with aggressive behavior. Emotions may affect subsequent appraisals and attributions, create motives for aggressive behavior, facilitate and intensify aggressive behavior, or inhibit or disinhibit aggressive behavior. However, the circumstances under which these effects can occur are not well understood. Increasing interest has been shown in these relationships, and it can therefore be anticipated that a great deal will be learned about them in the future.

See also: ANGER; ANNOYANCE; ANXIETY; EMBARRASSMENT; EMPATHY; ENVY; FEAR AND PHOBIAS; GUILT; HATE; HURT; JEALOUSY; SHAME; SPORTS; XENOPHOBIA

Bibliography

Averill, James R. (1983). "Studies on Anger and Aggression: Implications for Theories of Emotion." *American Psychologist* 38: 1145–1160.

Beck, Aaron T. (1974). "The Development of Depression: A Cognitive Model." In *The Psychology of Depression,* ed. Raymond J. Friedman and Martin M. Katz. Washington, DC: V. H. Winston.

Berkowitz, Leonard. (1993). *Aggression: Its Causes, Consequences, and Control.* New York: McGraw-Hill.

Briggs, Jean L. (1970). *Never in Anger: Portrait of an Eskimo Family.* Cambridge, MA: Harvard University Press.

Bryant, Jennings, and Zillmann, Dolf. (1979). "Effect of Intensification of Annoyance through Unrelated Residual Excitation on Substantially Delayed Hostile Behavior." *Journal of Experimental Social Psychology* 15:470–480.

Buss, Arnold H. (1961). *The Psychology of Aggression.* New York: Wiley.

Dodge, Kenneth A., and Newman, Joseph P. (1981). "Biased Decision-Making Processes in Aggressive Boys." *Journal of Abnormal Psychology* 90:375–379.

Dollard, John; Doob, Leonard; Miller, Neal E.; Mowrer, O. H.; and Sears, Robert R. (1939). *Frustration and Aggression.* New Haven, CT: Yale University Press.

Felson, Richard B., and Steadman, Henry J. (1983). "Situational Factors in Disputes Leading to Criminal Violence." *Criminology* 21:59–74.

Goffman, Erving. (1955). "On Face-Work: An Analysis of Ritual Elements in Social Interaction." *Psychiatry* 18:213–231.

Hoebel, E. Adamson. (1954). *The Law of Primitive Man.* Cambridge, MA: Harvard University Press.

Kemper, Theodore D. (1978). *A Social Interactional Theory of Emotions.* New York: Wiley.

Klein, Melanie. (1957). *Envy and Gratitude: A Study of Unconscious Sources.* New York: Basic Books.

Lewis, Michael. (1992). *Shame: The Exposed Self.* New York: Free Press.

Luckenbill, David F. (1977). "Criminal Homicide As a Situated Transaction." *Social Problems* 25:176–186.

Luckenbill, David F. (1982). "Compliance Under Threat of Severe Punishment." *Social Forces* 60:810–825.

Mathes, Eugene W. (1992). *Jealousy: The Psychological Data.* Lanham, MD: University Press of America.

Ohbuchi, Ken-ichi. (1988). "Arousal of Empathy and Aggression." *Psychologia* 31:177–186.

Richardson, Deborah R.; Hammock, Georgina S.; Smith, Stephen M.; and Gardner, W. I. (1994). "Empathy As a Cognitive Inhibitor of Interpersonal Aggression." *Aggressive Behavior* 20:275–289.

Scheff, Thomas J. (1988). "Shame and Conformity: The Difference-Emotion System." *American Sociological Review* 53:395–406.

Tangney, June P.; Miller, Rowland S.; Flicker, Laura; and Barlow, Deborah Hill. (1996). "Are Shame, Guilt, and Embarrassment Distinct Emotions?" *Journal of Personality and Social Psychology* 70:1256–1269.

Tedeschi, James T., and Felson, Richard B. (1994). *A Theory of Coercive Actions: A Social Analysis of Aggression and Violence.* Washington, DC: American Psychological Association.

Zillmann, Dolf. (1983). "Arousal and Aggression." In *Aggression: Theoretical and Empirical Reviews*, ed. Russell G. Geen and Edward I. Donnerstein. New York: Academic Press.

James T. Tedeschi

ALTERED STATES OF CONSCIOUSNESS

All three of the primary forms of altered states of consciousness—shamanic, possession, and meditative— use ritual, physical activities, and psychosocial processes to alter relations among emotions, the self, and others. In particular, they alter the self and incorporate "others" into one's identity.

Shamanic altered states of consciousness occur in a dramatic ritual encounter within the spirit world, which is induced by drumming, chanting, dancing, and in some cases, drugs. Collapsing into apparent unconsciousness, the shamans experience their soul leaving the body and flying to other worlds with spirit allies. In contrast, possession altered states of consciousness involve a dramatic transformation in the individual's personality, manifested in the behavior, voice, expressions, and identity of a person who is believed to be under the influence or control of external spiritual agencies. The enactment of behavior, social roles, and emotions through imitative and verbal mediums has dramatic effects upon the possessed person and others, with the spirit's presence changing relationships and identity and producing a range of emotional reactions. The dramatic shamanic and possession forms are complemented by the sedate meditative altered states of consciousness. The inward focus of attention dismisses the importance of the external world and its emotional attachments in an effort to achieve emotional equanimity and non-attachment to desires. While these three forms differ in the specific emotional transformations they produce, they share commonalities in their effects upon the brain and the emotions.

Psychobiology of Altered States of Consciousness

Altered states of consciousness constitute conditions akin to a "waking dream." Their similar manifestations cross-culturally reflect the wide variety of procedures and conditions that induce a common set of psychophysiological changes that involve activation of the limbic brain system and induction of a slow wave synchronization of the frontal cortex. Altered states of consciousness reflect coherent integrative information processing across the neuraxis, linking the limbic brain and the lower brain with synchronous slow-wave brain wave patterns that intensely project into the frontal cortex. Arnold Mandell (1980) considers the underlying neurobiochemical pathway of altered states of consciousness to involve connections of the limbic system and its serotonergic pathways with the lower brain areas. The hippocampus is the focal point for the production of altered states of consciousness. The limbic brain, specifically the hippocampal-septal circuits and hypothalamus, regulate emotions, synthesize internal and external information, and influence the brain structures that are responsible for memory, emotions, self-representation, and social behavior. The hippocampus is the gateway from the limbic system to the neocortex, functioning as an association area in the formation and mediation of memory and emotions and their integration into behavior. The limbic system plays an important role in eliciting emotional information and transforming it into physiological effects when the organism is confronted with threatening situations.

The limbic system is located between the frontal cortex and the lower brain centers, representing evolutionary developments referred to as the "paleomammalian brain." Paul MacLean (1990) suggests that the primary functions of the limbic system involve modulating emotion to guide behavior and providing functions that are essential to personal identity. The paleomammalian brain mediates patterns of social signaling that promote a sense of community and provide for cooperation—physically, socially, and mentally—in ways that enhance human adaptation and survival. The paleomammalian brain produces facial expressions, vocalizations, actions, and gestures that provide information about the mind, motives, and internal states. These communicative interactions involve mimesis, an imitative behavioral language manifested in art, music, theater, dance, and facial expressions. These communicative behaviors evoke similar experiences in other individuals, providing information about the mind, the self, and personal relationships and creating a common or collective awareness that is the basis of consciousness. Altered states of consciousness use these same mechanisms to alter relations among emotions, the self, and others.

Shamanic Altered States of Consciousness

Shamanic altered states of consciousness manage emotional loss and loss of the self, restoring and transforming the self and reinvigorating community relations and social bonds. The terms *soul flight, soul journey, out-of-body experience,* and *astral projection* reflect a universal element of shamanism: an altered state of consciousness that involves traveling to and/or encountering entities in the spiritual or supernatural world. This is induced by chanting, drumming, singing, and dancing, followed by sleep or "unconsciousness" (but with intact memory of an experience interpreted to be the flight of one's soul or a similar visionary experience). Although the shaman appears unconscious, awareness persists as evidenced in the reports of the visionary experience. The wide cross-cultural distribution of these experiences reflects the origins of their structure in biological processes.

Manipulation of the sympathetic-parasympathetic balance of the autonomic nervous system underlies

typical procedures for inducing shamanic altered states of consciousness, with extensive activity leading to collapse. Harry Hunt (1995) suggests that the very deep rest provided by these states of profound muscular relaxation produce a deep sense of calm, detachment, and acceptance. Shamanic rituals evoke the body's production of its own opioids (i.e., endogenous opiates). These substances mediate attachment and affiliation, and they promote psychobiological synchrony between individuals. This coordination of daily cycles and bodily rhythms through rituals that integrate the group reinforces identification and internalization of social relations and enhances community well-being and social attachments. Shamanic healing evokes opioid release through physical procedures (e.g., pain, extensive activity), as well as cultural symbols that are associated with endocrine systems during early socialization. This linking of mythological beliefs with bodily processes underlies shamanic healing. The use of hallucinogens is also a prominent aspect of sha-

A Dayak shaman wears amulets as he performs a ceremonial dance near the Mahakam River in Borneo. (Corbis/Charles & Josette Lenars)

manic altered states of consciousness. Their effects enhance the production of coherent integrated brain wave patterns across the brain.

Central to shamanic altered states of consciousness is the capacity to create inner representations, images, or visions. This type of imagery affects the brain-mind interface and produces healing by integrating experience, feeling, intuition, and reason through myth, symbol, and ritual. The prototype for shamanic altered states of consciousness is derived from "taking the role of the other" in using visual imagery to represent one's own body as it would appear from others' perspectives. This referencing of the self with feedback from others provides a self-awareness or consciousness that is based on internalization of social attributions of others toward the self. This visual-spatial self-referential capacity enables one to direct awareness at one's own ongoing subjective experiences.

A principal therapeutic application of soul flight is to recover the patient's "lost soul." Shamanic soul recovery involves dramatic enactments during which the shaman battles and overcomes frightful spirits to rescue the patient's soul. Soul loss involves an injury to the person's essence or being, representing fundamental aspects of the self and the individual's attachments to the social group. Soul loss involves disharmony in terms of the meaning of life and the feeling of belonging and being connected with others. Roger Walsh (1990) discusses shamanic illness with reference to the American Psychiatric Association's *Diagnostic and Statistical Manual of Mental Disorders* category of the "spiritual emergency"—mystical experiences with psychotic features, spontaneous shamanic voyages, and a renewal process manifested in the death and rebirth experience. The shamanic phenomena of death and rebirth reflects processes of transformation of the self through manipulation of basic emotional dynamics that involve self-representation. This is manifested in the shaman's illness, which results in a "death" from torment by spirits and their consumption of the initiate. This death is followed by a "rebirth," which gives the initiate power and spirit allies. Threatening spirit images symbolize the shadow—aspects of the self that are disowned and repressed. These structures are forced into consciousness in distressing symbolic forms, resulting in a collapse of the ego. The shaman's dismemberment reflects fragmentation of psyche and ego, an overwhelming psychological transformation that results from intrusion of unassimilated neural structures. This collapse of internal structures is experienced as dismemberment, autosymbolic images representing one's breakdown. The underlying conflicts lead to a destructuring of egoic consciousness, with the organization of the psyche—identity, beliefs, habits, and conditioning—collapsing, resulting in an extreme internal focus of attention and reduction of behavior.

Shamanic counseling involves training the client to make his or her own shamanic journey to restore personal power. The active aspect of the visionary experience helps instill a sense of mastery and control. Shamanic counseling involves personal empowerment through which the individual comes to recognize his or her inherent ability to obtain spiritual wisdom directly without the assistance of others. These transformational experiences involve acquiring a spiritual power that is used in the transformation of one's self by altering relationships with one's social and physical world. The spiritual world of shamanic altered states of consciousness provides a conceptual domain for organizing experiences of mental structures dissociated from consciousness. Because of their relationships to ego, symbolic manipulation of spiritual constructs affect emotions and other psychodynamic processes. Ritual manipulation of these structures represented in the spirit world affects conscious ego, emotions, and the body while operating through processes outside of consciousness.

Possession Altered States of Consciousness

The concept of forces outside of one's consciousness acting upon one's body and self is a central aspect of possession (or mediumistic) altered states of consciousness, which involve dramatic experiences interpreted as seizure by spirits. Possession altered states of consciousness change emotion-self dynamics by engaging alternate selves and socially prohibited emotional expressions, providing sublimation and catharsis. Erika Bourguignon (1976) characterized possession as a spirit entity or power that takes over the body and mind, but other forms of possession are also recognized, including pathology, communication, and social action involving manipulation of emotions in constructing relations between the self and others.

Common patterns of possession altered states of consciousness involve a dramatic transformation in personal appearance, personality, behavior, voice, emotional expression, movement, and identity, as well as changes in physiological responses. Initial possession altered states of consciousness generally involve spontaneous seizures or rapid onset of illness; excessive, agitated, violent, or uncontrolled motor behavior; tremors or convulsions; and amnesia. Nearly identical cross-cultural cases involving seizures, convulsions, and amnesia suggest a physiological bases for possession altered states of consciousness that is distinct from that of shamanism. The occurrence of amnesia, spontaneous seizures, compulsive motor behavior, and tremors with possession altered states of consciousness (but not shamanic altered states of consciousness) suggests the differential involvement of limbic structures, specifically the amygdala.

Bourguignon's cross-cultural research shows that this specific phenomena of possession altered states of consciousness occurs in socially complex societies that have distinct social classes, jurisdictional hierarchy, and agriculture. Research by Michael Winkelman (1986, 1992) found that possession altered states of consciousness occur in societies that have political integration, high population density, and distinct social classes (with political integration being the most important predictor). Possession altered states of consciousness are produced by processes that are associated with political integration, but political integration alone does not fully explain variations across societies in the incidence of possession altered states of consciousness. It seems that possession altered states of consciousness are caused by both psychobiological factors and social conditions, with physiological factors predisposing the development of possession altered states of consciousness and societal conditions contributing to the display of seizure-like phenomena. Possession altered states of consciousness are frequently associated with women's cults in societies where women face oppressive conditions. They also occur in the lower classes of societies that have distinct social classes, indicating that people's deprived status and resultant consequences—dietary and nutritional deficiencies and metabolic imbalances such as hypocalcemia and hypoglycemia—could predispose them to seizures, which are then interpreted as possession. Political integration may foster a predisposition toward possession altered states of consciousness by eliminating the cultural traditions that provide early direct training in the alteration of consciousness. Shamanic altered states of consciousness generally are deliberately induced at earlier ages (childhood or puberty) than possession altered states of consciousness (early adulthood), apparently precluding seizures in the shamanic form that are associated with the possession form.

Felicitas Goodman (1988) examines other forms of possession altered states of consciousness, conceptualizing them as a person inviting a spirit being who is without a physical body to enter the person's body and use it. Possession may also embody forms of enlightenment, a collective perfect harmony among the self, nature, and the universe, where the person's domination of the gods and spirits begins with the act of choosing to find the proper harmony. Brazilian spiritists recognize "grades" of possession relationships that may be established with a deity. These relationships range from dialogue, irradiation, and obsession (where the client feels under varying degrees of control by an alien spirit but manages to retain a basic sense of the self and identity) to hysterical personality syndromes and dissociation to control of the individual by spirits who may inhabit the person's body. Possession altered states of consciousness involve many psychodynamics, psychosocial conditions, and varying degrees of influence. Even pathological possession subsumes a range of phenomena that are specific to cultural psychodynamics as exemplified in culture-bound syndromes.

Variable self-other relations are emphasized in Janice Boddy's (1994, p. 407) characterization of *possession* as "a broad term referring to an integration of spirit and matter, force or power and corporeal reality, in a cosmos where the boundaries between an individual and her environment are acknowledged to be permeable, flexibly drawn, or at least negotiable." Possession altered states of consciousness entail many different kinds of cognitive and psychodynamic processes. Chandra Shekar (1989) distinguishes dissociation (related to emotional transactions that involve pathology), communication (related to interpersonal relations), and expectation or sociocultural explanations (related to self- or social transformations).

Pathological perspectives have identified possession altered states of consciousness as being hysterical dissociation, finding evidence of neurotic disorder in episodes that occur in response to traumatic, disturbing personal afflictions or experiences and in the presence of glazed eyes, psychomotor activity, change in facial expression and voice quality, constricted attention, sleep disturbances, depressed mood, psychosomatic ailments, anxiety, and panic attacks. Behaviors of the possessed individual may involve dramatic enactments of conflictive situations, including the symbolic and literal expression of repressed desires or behaviors that are unacceptable to ego or social norms. Goodman (1988) links possession to multiple personality disorder. She details a range of similarities between the two and suggests that multiple personality disorder might be more effectively addressed with possession therapies.

Some communication perspectives characterize possession altered states of consciousness as involving assumption of the sick role, affecting action of socially significant others toward the possessed person, and providing personal, emotional, social, and material benefits. However, the pathological models of culture-specific neuroses fail to account for its use by those who do not suffer pathological distress and for the cultural interpretation and significance of possession altered states of consciousness in reference to broader cultural norms. The spirits' communicational intent, their roles in the person's world, their effects upon behavior, and their cultural meanings shift responsibility from the self to the other, objectifying emotions in terms and referents that transcend the other and place a locus of responsibility in the broader social order. Bourguignon (1976) emphasizes that possession altered states of consciousness play a role in managing problems of everyday life, changing relationships between wives and husbands, enabling women to make demands indirectly, and allowing individuals to achieve a catharsis of emotions. Possession altered states of consciousness can instigate identity changes, alter power relations and interpersonal hierarchies, and provide a means of managing stress and exerting social power.

The perspective that views possession altered states of consciousness with regard to societal norms holds that people emulate possession behavior because of socialization through repeated exposures across their development. Possession altered states of consciousness have a range of adaptive sociocultural, political, acculturative, theatrical, expressive, and therapeutic functions. Boddy (1994) characterizes possession altered states of consciousness as being continuously transformative, enabling the exploration of morality and the external influences on one's selfhood and personal identity. Boddy also asserts that possession altered states of consciousness (1) flexibly articulate relations between reference groups, rendering benefits of group membership, (2) establish ties of fictive kinship, facilitating negotiation of self-constitutive interactions and providing mechanisms for incorporation of various "others" in the development of the self, and (3) reformulate identity in providing mechanisms of self-expression and knowledge that are characterized by reciprocal and reversible relationships between knower and known. These interactions provide mechanisms for constructing identities in dramatic social performances and establish social forms for expressing anxieties, fears, and other emotions. Roles in identity and self-transformation enable possession altered states of consciousness to have therapeutic as well as social and political effects. The possessing spirit's representation of the "other" and systems of morality give possession many roles in managing emotions, self construction, and social relations.

Meditative Altered States of Consciousness

The dramatic alterations in the self that are associated with possession altered states of consciousness are contrasted in the sedate, isolated meditative altered states of consciousness that may deny the reality of the self altogether. Meditative altered states of consciousness involve an internal focus of attention that is often combined with sleep deprivation, auditory

driving (e.g., chanting), fasting, and sensory deprivation. Meditative altered states of consciousness change emotions through attention control that enhances the emotional experience, its integration into thought, and its suspension to achieve greater objectivity, detachment, and freedom from suffering. Meditative practices vary considerably, but they share a common core that includes enhancement of the control of attention and emotions, disinhibition, and changes in sense of the self. Meditative altered states of consciousness allow the individual to develop the detached observational attitude that is necessary for the suspension of socially engaged evaluative processes. This suspension of cognitive constructs enables the emergence of nonverbal physical and organic processes and emotions, which can then be integrated into a more complete sense of the self. Mediators' intentional control of attention increases awareness of mental processes (including emotions) and enhanced control of cognitive functions (including feelings and intuition).

The framework for affective development within meditative altered states of consciousness is provided by the observing self that is developed in meditation. This "witnessing consciousness" observes its own forms in terms of an all-inclusive felt significance that is created through synthesis of a diffuse sense of space patterns and one's own bodily presence. Feelings, which provide a basis for appreciating opposing reasons, play an important role in the development of meditative forms of consciousness. Feelings also mediate social influences, providing the basis for the personal attachments that define the social group, the sense of self, and morality. Vedic psychology views feelings as having a role in interconnecting the different levels of the mind. At more mature levels of consciousness, feelings provide information that links ego, inner-self, the intellect, and motivations to guide decision-making processes through the intuitive mode. Earlier stages of emotional development, which involve internalization of social group symbolic constructions of the self and knowledge, are transcended in meditative altered states of consciousness. During these meditative states, individuals exhibit exceptional control in the ability both to elicit and suspend emotional processes. This can result in feelings of rapture, bliss, and overwhelming love and compassion that are independent of the immediate stimuli that are generally necessary for such pleasurable experiences.

Richard Castillo (1991) has analyzed these developmental experiences in Hindu yogis, and he asserts that they involve control of attention to change consciousness of the self by creating and separating the two co-conscious selves: the observing or transpersonal self (*atman,* "true self" or witness) that is uninvolved in the world and the personal or participating self that is engaged in the world of attachment and the accompanying personal mind, memories, and emotions. The observing self's experience of being an uninvolved witness to the participating self and its world frees it from the pain and suffering that comes from the identifications of the personal self. People in meditative altered states of consciousness experience both of the conscious selves simultaneously through restraining participating consciousness. Castillo suggests this split in consciousness is recognized within Western psychiatry as depersonalization. This involves the experience of being detached from one's own body or mental processes, an uninvolved witness to one's own behavior; it may be combined with the feeling that one's personality is unreal and is not associated with one's identity, which is the experience of the observing self.

Meditation has effects upon emotions through numerous mechanisms: as a release for repressed memories, as a self-regulation strategy, as an ego regression prompting manifestation of unconscious material, as a relaxation response, and as counter-conditioning that leads to desensitization. Eugene Taylor and his colleagues (1997) suggest that meditation reduces stress, as indicated in lower levels of adrenal hormones and lactate. Meditation is also useful for the treatment of psychosomatic disorders, anxieties, fears, phobias, addictions, neuroses, obesity, tension, and headaches. Meditation provides a sense of inner-directedness and an increased sense of self-responsibility. Meditation provides desensitization of distressing thoughts by permitting their occurrence in conjunction with extreme relaxation. Practices such as insight meditation allow for a focus on arising perceptions, thoughts, memories, sensations, and emotions, all of which provide primary material for the psychodynamic processing of patterns of thought and behavior. Enhanced awareness of unconscious processes may lead to the dissolution of the ordinary self-identity and to the development of an observing self. This deconstruction of the ordinary self may also lead to psychological complications, including intrusion of unprocessed material, repressed memories, and psychological conflicts, as well as intense feelings of anger, tension, and anxiety.

See also: BIOCHEMISTRY OF EMOTIONS; CONSCIOUSNESS; NEUROBIOLOGY OF EMOTIONS; PSYCHOPHYSIOLOGY OF EMOTIONS

Bibliography

Achterberg, Jeanne. (1985). *Imagery in Healing, Shamanism in Modern Medicine.* Boston: New Science Library.

Alexander, Charles N., and Langer, Ellen J., eds. (1990). *Higher Stages of Human Development: Perspectives on Adult Growth.* New York: Oxford University Press.

Boddy, Janice. (1994). "Spirit Possession Revisited: Beyond Instrumentality." *Annual Review of Anthropology* 23:407–34.

Bourguignon, Erika. (1976). *Possession.* San Francisco: Chandler and Sharpe.

Castillo, Richard. (1991). "Divided Consciousness and Enlightenment in Hindu Yogis." *Anthropology of Consciousness* 2(3–4):1–6.

Frecska, Ede, and Kulcsar, Z. Suzsanna. (1989). "Social Bonding in the Modulation of the Physiology of Ritual Trance." *Ethos* 17(1):70–87.

Goodman, Felicitas. (1988). *How About Demons? Possession and Exorcism in the Modern World.* Bloomington: Indiana University Press.

Harner, Michael. (1990). *The Way of the Shaman.* San Francisco: Harper & Row.

Hunt, Harry. (1995). *On the Nature of Consciousness.* Yale University Press.

Krippner, Stanley. (1987). "Cross-Cultural Approaches to Multiple Personality Disorder: Practices in Brazilian Spiritism." *Ethos* 15(3):273–295.

Krippner, Stanley, and Welch, Patrick. (1992). *Spiritual Dimensions of Healing: From Native Shamanism to Contemporary Health Care.* New York: Irvington Publishers.

MacLean, Paul. (1990). *The Triune Brain in Evolution.* New York: Plenum.

Mandell, Arnold. (1980). "Toward a Psychobiology of Transcendence: God in the Brain." In *The Psychobiology of Consciousness,* ed. Julian Davidson and Richard Davidson. New York: Plenum.

Shapiro, Dean. (1980). *Meditation.* New York: Aldine.

Shekar, Chandra C. R. (1989). "Possession Syndrome in India." In *Altered States of Consciousness and Mental Health. A Cross-Cultural Perspective,* ed. Colleen A. Ward. Newbury Park, CA: Sage Publications.

Taylor, Eugene; Murphy, Michael; and Donovan, Steven. (1997). *The Physical and Psychological Effects of Meditation: A Review of Contemporary Research with a Comprehensive Bibliography: 1931–1996.* Sausalito, CA: Institute of Neotic Sciences.

Wade, Jenny. (1996). *Changes of Mind: A Holonomic Theory of the Evolution of Consciousness.* Albany: State University of New York Press.

Walsh, Roger. (1988). "Two Asian Psychologies and Their Implications for Western Psychotherapists." *American Journal of Psychotherapy* 42(4):543–560.

Walsh, Roger. (1990). *The Spirit of Shamanism.* Los Angeles: Tarcher.

Winkelman, Michael. (1986). "Trance States: A Theoretical Model and Cross-cultural Analysis." *Ethos* 14:76–105.

Winkelman, Michael. (1992). "Shamans, Priests, and Witches: A Cross-Cultural Biosocial Study of Magico-Religious Practitioners." *Anthropological Research Papers #44,* Arizona State University.

Winkelman, Michael. (1996). "Psychointegrator Plants: Their Roles in Human Culture and Health." In *Sacred Plants, Consciousness, and Healing Cross-Cultural and Interdisciplinary Perspectives Yearbook of Cross-Cultural Medicine and Psychotherapy, Vol. 6,* ed. Michael Winkelman and Walter Andritzky. Berlin: Springer-Verlag.

Winkelman, Michael. (1997). "Altered States of Consciousness and Religious Behavior." In *Anthropology of Religion: A Hand-*

book of Method and Theory, ed. Stephen Glazier. Westport, CT: Greenwood.

Michael Winkelman

AMBIVALENCE

When one thinks about emotion, the thoughts are typically about pure feelings such as happiness, anger, or sorrow. These basic emotions are easily recognized in others and oneself. Yet, many emotional experiences are not so one dimensional. Sometimes, even happy occasions have a bitter-sweetness about them. For example, graduation days are typically thought of as joyful occasions, yet even amid the joy there is some sadness that one is leaving an important, familiar setting. Sadness at a funeral may be tempered with a sense of relief that the deceased is no longer suffering. Often, people's emotional experiences are blends of more than one emotion. At times, these emotions even oppose each other.

The term *ambivalence* refers to the experience of feeling two opposing emotions at once—to love something but also hate it, to want something but also be repelled by it. Paul Meehl (1964, p. 10) defined intense ambivalence as "the existence of simultaneous or rapidly interchangeable positive and negative feelings toward the same object or activity, with the added proviso that both the positive and negative feelings be strong." Very intense ambivalence tends to be characterized by distress and an inability to make decisions.

Ambivalence is confusing because the person is feeling two opposite emotions at one time. This confusion can also interfere with taking action. Being very ambivalent means never really feeling that one is wholly positive or negative about anything, so it is fitting that ambivalence itself cannot be categorized as either a wholly positive or a wholly negative experience.

A prime example of ambivalence is provided by the character of Hamlet in William Shakespeare's classic tragedy. Throughout the play, Hamlet is caught in indecision and doubt. Should he kill his stepfather? Should he kill himself? Even as he berates himself for his lack of action, he personifies the ambivalent individual—unable to stop thinking, ruminating, and worrying and take action. At the end of the famous "To be, or not to be" soliloquy in Act III, Scene i, Hamlet has put aside the thought of suicide and concludes

> Thus conscience does make cowards of us all;
> And thus the native hue of resolution
> Is sicklied o'er with the pale cast of thought,
> And enterprises of great pith and moment
> With this regard their currents turn awry,
> And lose the name of action.

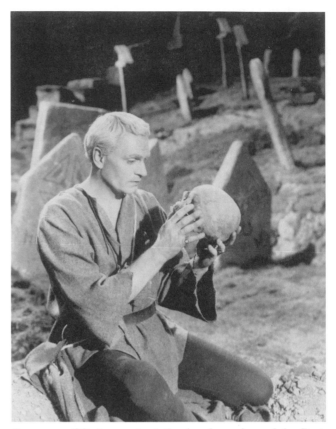

Laurence Olivier received the Academy Award for Best Actor in 1948 for his portrayal of Hamlet, the melancholy Dane tortured by his ambivalent feelings. (Corbis/Bettmann)

But Hamlet is not unique. This combination of emotions often causes people to "lose the name of action."

The Motivational Context of Ambivalence

Emotions have often been portrayed as feedback for people's goal pursuits—that is, they feel happy, relieved, joyful, sad, upset, or depressed because of how they are doing in achieving their important goals. In this context, it might be said that ambivalence is the emotional manifestation of a conflictful motivational situation in which an individual both wants and does not want the same goal. There are many reasons why a person might feel ambivalent. For example, the goal one is seeking may not be worth the effort, or it may involve sacrificing other important goals. Robert Wilensky (1983) has reviewed a taxonomy of goal relationships that might result in a feeling of ambivalence. He pointed out that goals may compete with each other for a variety of reasons—because of limited resources or because the accomplishment of one goal may be mutually exclusive with another.

Emotions may also be thought of as not just gauging individual progress in goal pursuit but motivating people to behave in different ways. For example, fear may include the action tendency to run away, or joy may include the act of embracing people nearby. What sort of action does ambivalence motivate? Not surprisingly, if an individual feels both fearful and happy, he or she experiences contradictory action tendencies and may simply do nothing. Thus, in talking about ambivalence one is often talking about an emotion that is not reflected in action but is experienced primarily inside the person. Robert Emmons and Laura King (1988) showed that goals that conflict with other goals are very likely to be thought about but very unlikely to be put into action, demonstrating the way ambivalence may be associated with thinking but not doing.

Clinical and Personality Approaches

Historically, ambivalence has been a matter of attention for clinical and personality psychologists. In 1911, Eugen Bleuler was the first to discuss ambivalence in a psychological context. He described three types of ambivalence. First, Bleuler described voluntary ambivalence: experiencing conscious conflict over whether to do or not to do something. This conflict is best exemplified by the previously discussed character of Hamlet, who spends much of the play trying to muster himself up to the task of murdering his stepfather. The second kind of ambivalence described by Bleuler was intellectual ambivalence: simultaneously interpreting an experience in both positive and negative ways. This ambivalence is akin to approach-avoidance conflict. For example, an individual may desire a slice of chocolate cake (approach) but realize at the same time that eating the cake will ruin his or her diet (avoidance). The third type of ambivalence discussed by Bleuler was emotional ambivalence: experiencing feelings of both love and hate toward the same object. This type of ambivalence was referred to by Sigmund Freud (1920, p. 532) as "direction toward the same person of contrary—affectionate and hostile—feelings." Freud felt that this sort of ambivalence characterized most human relationships and he asserted that the hostile bonds people feel toward others are just as binding as the affectionate ones. For individuals experiencing this kind of ambivalence there is a thin line between love and hate. Bleuler's emotional ambivalence is probably most similar to many subsequent views of ambivalence.

Ambivalence has never been portrayed as an optimal emotional experience. Hamlet is, after all, the "Melancholy Dane." Rarely would a person prefer to feel ambivalent. Theory and research has tended to examine the mental health correlates of ambivalence, focusing on its negative side. The problems associated with intense ambivalence have been the subject of much work in the area. Regardless of the type of ambivalence experienced, for example, Bleuler believed that people with severe mental illness were intensely ambivalent.

In his classic work "Mourning and Melancholia," Freud (1913) held that bereaved individuals who were ambivalent about their lost loved one were likely to experience depression as a result. This intuition by Freud has been supported by later empirical research. Individuals who had rocky relationships with loved ones who subsequently died do tend to have difficulty in the grieving process. Feelings of ambivalence about a lost loved one can interfere with attaining a sense of closure and resolution about the loss.

Research has also examined the relationship between ambivalence and psychological distress, apart from the grieving process. Michael Raulin (1984) used a self-report questionnaire to measure ambivalence. Some items from the Raulin Intense Ambivalence Scale include "Very often, even my favorite pastimes don't excite me" and "Many things that I enjoy have their painful side." Raulin reported that individuals who received very high scores on this scale were likely to be at risk for psychosis.

King and Emmons (1990) examined the ways that individuals' ambivalence over their emotional expressiveness might relate to their overall emotional style and their psychological well-being. A great deal of research has examined the relationship between emotional expression and psychological well-being. The purpose of the research by King and Emmons was to examine whether feeling conflict about one's emotional expressiveness would also relate to well-being. That is, some people are very expressive and wish they could hide their feelings better. Others are very inexpressive but wish they could be more expressive. A person could feel ambivalent about their emotional expressiveness regardless of how expressive they are.

Using a questionnaire to measure ambivalence, King and Emmons were interested in testing whether ambivalence, in fact, was related to poorer psychological functioning. The Ambivalence Over Emotional Expressiveness Questionnaire includes items such as "I want to express my emotions honestly but I am afraid that it may cause me embarrassment or hurt," "Often I'd like to show others how I feel, but something seems to be holding me back," "I try to show people that I love them, although at times I am afraid that it may make me appear weak or too sensitive," and "I try to keep my deepest fears and feelings hidden, but at times I'd like to open up to others." King and Emmons found that ambivalent individuals were more likely to be distressed, anxious, and depressed, regardless of the person's level of emotional expressiveness. In addition, ambivalence was negatively related to expressiveness—showing once again that, like Hamlet, ambivalent individuals are not likely to act on their ambivalent impulses. Subsequent research by King, Emmons, and their colleagues has shown that ambivalent individuals tend to be less satisfied in their marriages, to be less likely to benefit from social support, and to show confusion in reading the emotional messages conveyed in facial expressions. When presented with a very straightforward emotional facial expression, ambivalent individuals tend to see the expression as conveying not only the obvious emotion but also emotions of the opposite valence. Individuals who are ambivalent tend to experience a broad range of contradictory emotions. Apparently, they believe that others share their rather convoluted emotional life.

The Social Psychology of Ambivalence

Social psychologists have addressed the concept of ambivalence as it relates to attitudes. The term *attitude* refers to opinions about different things, including how people think about them, feel about them, and behave toward them. For example, a person who has a negative attitude about broccoli might think that broccoli tastes bad, might have negative feelings about broccoli, and finally, will probably avoid eating broccoli. Sometimes, as in this example, attitudes are quite simple and straightforward. But an individual who has a negative attitude about some aspects of broccoli might also believe that broccoli is a healthy food with a variety of benefits. Such a person might feel that the health benefits of eating broccoli are quite important, despite its flavor. The question remains: Would this person be more or less likely to eat the vegetable in question?

Initial attitude research did not measure ambivalence, so little was known about the consequences of having mixed feelings about an attitude object. Later research has looked at the antecedents of ambivalent attitudes as well as the consequences of these attitudes. Megan Thompson and Mark Zanna (1995) found that ambivalent attitudes were less likely to be found in individuals high in need for cognition (i.e., the tendency of individuals to enjoy thinking about all of the aspects of a situation). Individuals high in this need are more likely to have thought through their attitudes and are more likely to feel that they have reached a satisfactory conclusion in their attitude. Actively working toward one's attitude allows an individual to confront and resolve contradictory aspects of his or her feelings.

Another personality construct, personal fear of invalidity, has been shown to relate to heightened feelings of ambivalence. Personal fear of invalidity refers to the tendency to be very concerned that one is making the right decision. This fear is related to hesitance in decision making and to less confidence that one's decision is correct. According to Thompson and Zanna, individuals with the personal fear of invalidity tend to have difficulty prioritizing contradictory information and therefore tend to vacillate between opposing views. This kind of vacillation renders these individuals less able to make sense of the world.

These results demonstrate an important aspect of ambivalence. An ambivalent individual may have little difficulty seeing all sides of an issue. This ability is a strength in the sense that ambivalent individuals are likely to be keenly aware of all of the possible solutions to a problem. However, this ability may render these individuals unable to come to a resolution—making problem solving seem impossible. The ambivalent person sees an embarrassment of riches when it comes to all the possibilities to consider. Unfortunately, without a guiding principle for weighing the options, the ambivalent person may be paralyzed in thought.

Perhaps it is not surprising, then, that individuals are less likely to act upon ambivalent attitudes. A number of studies have shown that pre-existing ambivalence about an object tends to reduce the consistency between an individual's attitudes and his or her intention to act. This research agrees with that of King and Emmons, which shows that individuals who are ambivalent about their emotional expressiveness tend to be inexpressive. Returning to the broccoli example, these results would indicate that even though the person is aware of the health benefits associated with eating broccoli, he or she will not be likely to act on that ambivalent attitude.

Subsequent work has shown that, in looking at attitudes about unfamiliar objects, ambivalence may be related to more systematic thought about the attitude object. That is, if an individual is ambivalent about some new issue, he or she is likely to spend more time deliberately thinking about that issue. Thus, in attitude formation, ambivalence may serve as motivation for heightened intense thought about the issue. With regard to the broccoli example, if the person had never tried broccoli, his or her ambivalence would likely lead the person to explore the issue thoroughly, make a decision, and act on it.

Ambivalence, Conflict, and Personality Development

Although most of this entry has portrayed ambivalence as a negative state, the ability to recognize that one is ambivalent—to be aware of conflict—might actually be a sign of insight and wisdom. Certainly, ambivalence is a sophisticated emotion. It is unlikely that very young children could acknowledge ambivalence —indeed Julie Sincoff (1990) reported that children under ten years of age are unable to recognize ambivalence. The capacity to acknowledge contradictions in personal emotions is acquired developmentally. Even though individuals may not enjoy feeling ambivalent, it may be an inevitable part of growing up. Is it realistic to expect that people should never feel ambivalent when they live in a complicated world populated by a variety of different, complex individuals?

Although it might be easier to see the world in black and white, some theories of personality development suggest that being able to see all sides of an issue is a sign of maturity. Object relations theories, for example, portray the ability to experience ambivalence toward another person—to realize that even good people may have their darker sides—is a sign of healthy development. According to this approach, when people are born, they are unable to distinguish between themselves and the world. The process of development involves making more and more distinctions about themselves and the people around them. Harry Stack Sullivan (1953) suggested that individuals come to understand their social world by creating mental representations of their interactions with their caregivers. They make these representations in very simplistic ways—as a "good mother" and a "bad mother." The good mother is an internalized amalgamation of all positive interactions with the environment. The bad mother is an internalized amalgamation of all negative interactions with the environment. It should be noted that the good and bad mother may be products of interactions with the same person or group of persons. The infant is unable to view the social world in all of its complexity—complete with contradictory behaviors and emotions. Development requires that people ultimately come to view the world as characterized by inconsistent and sometimes contradictory individuals—to recognize that the good mother and bad mother are, in fact, one and the same. Similarly, Donald W. Winnicott (1986) theorized that the infant has an idealized view of the mother as perfect. Development requires that this perfect view be destroyed and the child accept the mother as an imperfect, fallible, but still lovable person in reality.

Another example of the value of ambivalence, from a different theoretical perspective, is provided by the theory of ego development as presented by Le Xuan Hy and Jane Loevinger (1996). This theory portrays the ego as the lens through which people view themselves and the world. This lens allows people to view themselves and the world in increasingly complex ways throughout development. According to this theory, people in the earliest stages of ego development tend to view the world in very simple ways—as if there is only one right answer to every question. As they mature psychologically, they come to see the world in more complex ways and recognize that every problem may have a variety of valid answers. In addition, as people become more mature they may come to recognize and acknowledge conflict in their world and in themselves. Ambivalence may be a sign of emerging wisdom—as people begin to realize that simple ways of viewing themselves and others may not adequately reflect the complexity of their world.

This perspective on ambivalence reflects back on the previous discussion in an important way. In thinking about ambivalence as a symptom of goal conflict, one might be tempted to state that the ambivalent person simply does not know what he or she really wants, implying that the person ought to be able to make up his or her mind by simply prioritizing. Within this consideration of psychological maturity one might look at the indecisive ambivalent person in another way. Perhaps ambivalence is not simply confusion about personal desires. Perhaps it is in fact a realistic appraisal of the many conflicting impulses and desires the individual experiences. It may be that the ambivalent individual's confusion is the most reasonable, open response to the complexities of his or her life.

Is adulthood, then, a time of complete ambivalence where nothing is certain? Is a lifetime of ambivalence the price of wisdom? One way to approach these questions is from the perspective of the theory of ego development. Individuals at the very lowest levels view issues in very clear-cut terms. They see that there is one right answer, and they are satisfied. As individuals develop, they become more aware of exceptions and distinctions—of contradiction and conflict. However, this awareness of conflict is not the end of development. A person at a high level of ego development need not be overwhelmed by the conflict that he or she sees. Rather, such an individual may find a way to resolve the conflict while acknowledging the many other ways that might exist for managing the same situation. With development comes an openness to experience and an ability to make the difficult decisions one must make. The developed person is not rendered inactive by ambivalence but rather is able to take responsibility for the well-informed and well-thought but potentially erroneous decisions that are required in life.

Is Ambivalence an Emotion?

Ambivalence is surely not a simple emotion, like joy or anger. No universal facial expression for ambivalence and no specific pattern of physiological responses associated with ambivalence have been identified. Unlike other emotions, ambivalent feelings are likely to be typically unexpressed. Ambivalence requires at least some cognitive activity on the part of the feeler—to be open to the conflicting emotions one is feeling and interpret them as truly ambivalent. Furthermore, it is not clear that a specific set of cognitive attributions or appraisals would lead one to feel ambivalent. While emotions are often considered to be instigators of action, ambivalence may have just the opposite effect. Yet, ambivalence may be a more and more common affective reaction to life's ups and downs as individuals mature and take their place in a complicated world. Indeed, though ambivalence may not be a basic or simple emotion, it is certainly a hallmark of the emotional life of adulthood.

See also: ATTITUDES; GRIEF; HOPELESSNESS; LONELINESS; MOTIVATION

Bibliography

Bleuler, Eugen. ([1911] 1950). *Dementia Praecox or the Group of Schizophrenia.* New York: International Universities Press.

Carver, Charles S., and Scheier, Michael F. (1990). "Origins and Functions of Positive and Negative Affect: A Control-Process View." *Psychological Bulletin* 97:19–35.

Emmons, Robert A., and King, Laura A. (1988). "Conflict among Personal Strivings: Immediate and Long-Term Implications for Psychological and Physical Well-Being." *Journal of Personality and Social Psychology* 48:1040–1048.

Freud, Sigmund. ([1913] 1958). "Mourning and Melancholia." In *The Standard Edition of the Complete Psychological Works of Sigmund Freud, Vol. 14,* ed. James Strachey. London: Hogarth Press.

Freud, Sigmund. ([1920] 1966). *Introductory Lectures on Psycho-Analysis.* New York: W. W. Norton.

Hy, Le Xuan, and Loevinger, Jane. (1996). *Measuring Ego Development,* 2nd ed. Mahwah, NJ: Lawrence Erlbaum.

King, Laura A. (1998). "Ambivalence over Emotional Expression and Reading Emotions in Situations and Faces." *Journal of Personality and Social Psychology* 74:753–762.

King, Laura A., and Emmons, Robert A. (1990). "Conflict over Emotional Expression: Psychological and Physical Correlates." *Journal of Personality and Social Psychology* 58:864–877.

Meehl, Paul E. (1964). *Manual for Use with Checklist for Schizotypic Signs.* Minneapolis: University of Minnesota Medical School, Psychiatric Research Unit.

Raulin, Michael L. (1984). "Development of a Scale to Measure Intense Ambivalence." *Journal of Consulting and Clinical Psychology* 52:63–72.

Sincoff, Julie B. (1990). "The Psychological Characteristics of Ambivalent People." *Clinical Psychology Review* 10:43–68.

Sullivan, Harry Stack. (1953). *The Interpersonal Theory of Psychiatry.* New York: W. W. Norton.

Thompson, Megan M., and Zanna, Mark P. (1995). "The Conflicted Individual: Personality-Based and Domain-Specific Antecedents of Ambivalent Social Attitudes." *Journal of Personality* 63:259–288.

Wilensky, Robert. (1983). *Planning and Understanding: A Computational Approach to Human Reasoning.* Reading, MA: Addison-Wesley.

Winnicott, Donald W. (1986). *Home Is Where We Start From: Essays By a Psychoanalyst.* New York: W. W. Norton.

Laura A. King
Christie K. Napa

ANGER

Anger as emotion is often discussed in terms of its experience (e.g., stress, frustration) and its behavioral outcomes (e.g., aggression, violence, rape). In the research literature, anger generally is discussed as an emotional reaction to negative, aversive states. Yet, anger is also a natural response that is necessary with regard to people's ability to cope with negative events in a social environment.

Very seldom in the literature is the emotion of anger clearly defined. One exception is James Russell and Beverly Fehr's (1994) explanation of anger as a set of scripts that people perform. In this manner, the experience and expression of anger would follow predictable lines. As Russell and Fehr explained, "to know the concept of anger is to know a script in which prototypical antecedents, feelings, expressions, behaviors, physiological changes, and consequences are laid out in a causal and temporal sequence" (p. 202). However, the script-based approach is only one of many. Perhaps a more inclusive approach would derive from an examination of where anger is said to arise and how it is manifested between people.

Origins of Anger

Scholars have speculated and tested the various *mechanisms* that produce anger or anger-like reactions. Some argue that anger arises out of an individual's motivation to explain behavior, while other researchers explain feelings of anger as an interaction between cognition and arousal. Still other scholars view anger as a reaction to behavior that blocks goal attainment. Finally, some researchers explain anger as the result of socialization processes. Each of these perspectives has merit in understanding anger as an emotional construct that involves physiological responses in addition to cognitive responses.

One way of studying the manner in which anger arises involves identifying the "sites" of anger, or the topics that give rise to both the experience and expression of anger. The nine basic sites of anger include identity management, aggression, frustration, lack of fairness, incompetence due to ignorance, incompetence due to egocentric motives, relationship threat, predispositions, and general learned response. As Table 1 indicates, issues that lead to anger vary from episodic, situation-specific items to more abstract, general factors. For example, an identity threat can occur within a single situation or across several episodes. On the other hand, other sites of anger appear to reflect more on the individual's personality (e.g., coping processes). Finally, some sites of anger imply that individuals control the manner in which anger is experienced in terms of coping responses and personal tendencies regarding aversive reactions.

It is possible that various forms of anger exist. One model that helps to demarcate reactions to different kinds of anger was proposed by Gerald L. Clore and his colleagues (1993), and it takes into consideration two factors: (1) whether or not the action is blameworthy and (2) whether or not the action personally causes a negative consequence. Table 2 summarizes the various outcomes that are expected to occur when one considers blameworthiness and the consequences. According to this model, one experiences "pure" anger when another person's reproachable behavior leads to negative consequences for the self. Imagine that a local restaurant does not accept reservations and serves customers only as they arrive on a first come, first serve basis. Also imagine that this restaurant serves good food, so it attracts many clients who wait in line. According to this model, if an individual has been waiting a long time in line and someone cuts in front of that individual (a blameworthy behavior) and causes the individual's wait to be much longer (a negative consequence), the individual might feel justified in being angry (i.e., "pure" anger). If, on the other hand, the individual is still given a table before the person who cut in line is given one, then the

Table 1 Sites and Subcategories of Anger

Site	Subcategories (with examples)
Identity Management	integrity threat 　　A teacher questions that one has read the assignment. condescension 　　A friend acts superior and talks down to one. insult 　　An in-law makes fun of an expensive new painting that one proudly displays in the living room. blame/reproach 　　Someone falsely accuses one of butting in line.
Aggression	physical threat/harm 　　One sees a man bully a much smaller woman. sexual aggression 　　One's coworker insists that one should get involved in a sexual relationship. verbal abuse 　　One's spouse often uses threats, swearing, and demeaning comments.
Frustration	goal interference 　　A driver cuts in front of one and then suddenly turns onto another street. expectation violation 　　An old friend visits from out of town but never spends any time with one. thwarted plans 　　One's airline cancelled a flight due to mechanical problems with the plane. impotence 　　One cannot convince the librarian that a book was returned on time and must pay a fine.
Lack of Fairness	inequity 　　One is expected to cook and clean even though a roommate never cooks or cleans. blameworthiness 　　One sees a classmate cheating on a final exam. hurt feelings 　　One's best friend was jilted by a boyfriend or girlfriend.

Table 1 (continued)

Site	Subcategories (with examples)
Incompetence Due to Ignorance	incompetent others One has been working with another person on a project, but that person has not produced anything of quality. thoughtless actions One's date arrives two hours late and acts as if nothing wrong has happened.
Incompetence Due to Egocentric Motives	self-centeredness An acquaintance acts as if he or she should be the center of attention at another person's birthday party. self-opinionatedness A roommate offers an opinion on each and every topic that is raised and consistently disagrees with one.
Relationship Threat	jealousy One's new love interest has an old flame that wants to go out one more time. unfaithfulness After weeks of denying it, one's partner finally admits being unfaithful during a summer trip.
Predispositions	predisposition due to experiences One's colleague is prejudiced, following a long family tradition. predisposition due to drug dependence One's friend acts edgy when he or she cannot get a drink and then gets aggressive when a drink is obtained.
General Learned Responses	coping processes One's acquaintance readily honks the car horn loudly at other drivers. response to aversion One becomes angry whenever he or she feels guilty.

Table 2 Anger As a Function of the Blameworthiness of the Other and the Outcomes for the Self and the Other

	The Other's Actions Are Blameworthy	The Other's Actions Are Not Blameworthy
Outcomes for the Self		
Negative	"pure" anger	frustration
Positive	relief	joy
Outcomes for the Other		
Negative	gloating	pity
Positive	resentment	pride

individual would feel relieved. If the manager sees this person cutting in line and asks him or her to go to the back of the line, then the individual might gloat. If the outcomes for the person who cut in line are positive, but the outcomes for the individual are no dif-ferent (e.g., both are given tables at the same time), then the individual might respond with resentment due to the lack of equity. If another person did not exhibit blameworthy behavior, but the individual is still somehow frustrated (e.g., the manager simply called the other person's name before calling the individual's name for some unknown reason), the individual would—hypothetically—feel frustration but no enmity toward that person.

Since it appears that many causes and types of anger exist, it is impossible to narrow the discussion of what is meant by anger to a single episode or type. Instead, it appears that the onset of anger arises from many plausible triggering events, potentially producing alternative responses.

Conceptual Models of Anger

There are a large number of social scientific theories that explain anger and predict how it might be expressed. Of these major theories of anger-arousal and expression, the following theories appear to be central to the discussion of anger: attribution theory, cognition-arousal hypothesis, neoassociational theory, frustration theory, social learning theory, and the communication deficit hypothesis.

Attribution Theory

Attribution theory, a group of related theories that are concerned with people's explanations for events, suggests that humans need to understand their own behavior and the behavior of others. In order to develop this understanding, people form attributions, or explanations, about why a particular behavior or set of behaviors has occurred. Within this framework, the causes for behavior can be explained as stable or unstable, controllable or uncontrollable, and internal or external.

Although research concerning attributions has focused mostly on explaining behavior, attributions also play a role in determining emotional responses to behavior. The attribution theory of motivation and emotion is based on the premise that individuals are motivated to think about and develop an explanation for behavior. Beginning with a search for the cause of behavior, this process leads to an attribution of causality, which, in turn, influences emotion. Lee Ross and Richard Nisbett (1991) explain a common assumption within this perspective—an individual's construal of an event determines how that individual will react both behaviorally and emotionally to that event. From this perspective, general arousal to a precipitating event does not provide sufficient information for determining particular emotions. The specific emotions that are felt depend on an individual's interpretation of his or her internal state.

Bernard Weiner (1986) suggests that emotions are determined in part by the attributions an individual makes during an interpersonal event. The explanation an individual provides for an event becomes a catalyst for the emotions that the individual feels. If the event elicits a negative causal attribution, then the resulting emotions will, in turn, be negative. As Weiner and his colleagues (1982) found, an individual will experience feelings of anger when he or she has attributed another's behavior to internal and controllable causes. Similarly, Hector Betancourt and Irene Blair (1992) explain that behaviors that are attributed to controllable and intentional causes elicit feelings of anger. For example, interpreting a friend's non-response to a wave across a crowded intersection as disinterest (an attribution of controllable and internal cause) will likely produce feelings of anger.

Examining anger from an attribution perspective provides a window through which one can see cognitive processes that are associated with feelings of anger. Alan Sillars (1980) found that roommates were more likely to engage in competitive and angry ways when they each attributed the cause of their conflicts to stable and internal properties of the other person. However, roommates were more likely to act in a cooperative manner when attributions for the problem were directed toward their individuals selves. Indeed, in their review of martial problems, Frank Fincham and his colleagues (1990) revealed that partners who attribute causes of relational problems to global, stable, internal, and selfish dimensions are more likely to use negative communicative behavior and are less likely to report positive relational outcomes.

Cognition-Arousal Hypothesis

As Betancourt and Blair (1992) note, anger is determined only in part by the cognitive processes that are associated with behavior. They suggest that such cognitions are themselves determined by an "instigating action." From this perspective, the experience of anger involves both cognitive and physiological processes.

Ellen Berscheid (1983) indicates that people feel emotions when their normal patterns of behavior are in some way disrupted. This disruption results in arousal that causes an individual to react either negatively or positively. The magnitude of this arousal is known to influence the intensity of experienced anger. The implication here, according to Dolf Zillmann (1994), is that a precipitating event will produce "significant elevations of the level of sympathetic excitation in the autonomic nervous system" (p. 47).

Zillmann's cognition-excitation hypothesis explains the link between thought, arousal, and anger. He highlights this relationship by explaining that excitation depends on the recognition of endangerment (cognition). This recognition, in turn, produces physiological arousal, which activates decision processes concerning the meaning of an event and how to manage it. Aroused by an unfavorable experience, an individual is likely to appraise the event as a direct, personal attack and feel angry.

One emotional enhancer of anger is stress. The experience of managing many tasks with critical dead-

---

Anger against those who have land and money drives the poor sharecropper, Abner Snopes, in William Faulkner's "Barn Burning" (1939) to take his own form of revenge by burning the barns of the plantation owners. Raging against having to work for them as a tenant farmer, Snopes retaliates by destroying the barn where the wealth of the land is stored.

line features can set the stage to trigger indifference to the needs of others, and it can lead to anger-like responses. James Makepeace (1983) has shown that, among undergraduate students, stress is associated with physical aggression toward one's partner.

From this perspective, anger is a product of the interplay between cognition and excitation. Thoughtful consideration of an event is not enough to produce feelings of anger. In fact, Zillmann (1990) claims that if cognitive appraisal is present without physiological arousal, an individual will most likely not experience anger because "cognitive scrutiny of circumstances fosters perceptions of diminished danger" (p. 202). When appraisal is accompanied by arousal and an individual does, indeed, perceive danger, anger is the likely emotional response.

Neoassociational Theory

According to Leonard Berkowitz's (1993) neoassociationistic theory, anger shares psychophysical responses with other aversive stimuli. Because the mind and body do not compartmentalize different processes for different negative events, the aversion that one experiences during anger is similar to the aversion that one feels during other negative events. Berkowitz noted that "any given emotional state is best regarded as an associative network in which specific types of feelings, physiological reactions, motor responses, and thoughts and memories are all interconnected" (p. 9). Theoretically, then, any negative arousal can bring about angry responses. For example, environmental problems can lead to anger, due to the idea that negative experiences are associated with the expression of anger. Such environmental problems include cigarette smoke and other foul orders, heat, and pollution.

People can experience anger in response to sadness or pain. Berkowitz summarized two experiments that tested women's anger-like reactions to pain. In these studies, women either experienced pain (by allowing their hands to be placed and kept in extremely cold water) or did not experience pain (by allowing their hands to be kept in lukewarm water). These participants then evaluated another person's ideas, and they were asked to reward or punish the other person. The women in the painful condition offered fewer rewards and more punishments, as opposed to the women in the non-painful condition. Apparently, no anger-provoking event occurred as one might expect—only pain. In a second experiment, women in pain recalled more conflict interactions with their boyfriends and mothers than did women in the painless condition.

It should be noted that anger is not the only outcome of painful, negative experiences. Of course, people also respond to negative experiences with *fear*. Ber-

kowitz, for example, argued that in light of aversive or threatening situations, people seek to escape or avoid the issue confronting them. Alternately, Joyce Hocker and William Wilmot (1995) asserted that people may respond to their fear in an angry manner, trying to regain control of the situation. They may rely on defensive behaviors that serve to evaluate or dominate the other person, control communication, or show indifference. Accordingly, people who are afraid and who choose not to use integrative behaviors may *act* as if they are angry.

Frustration Theory

Another body of research indicates that frustrations can incite individuals to anger. Frustration is discussed most often as a result of goal impediment. It is assumed that individuals hold expectations concerning the outcomes of events. When those expectations are thwarted, individuals will likely feel frustrated.

Paul Fraisse's (1964) theory of emotion and aggression explains the relationship between frustration and anger. Emotion is described as a response to a situation for which the individual is not prepared. When that situation produces unexpected frustration an individual will likely experience anger. Fraisse suggests that the intensity of anger will be greater in response to unanticipated events than in response to anticipated events.

Nancy Stein and Linda Levine (1989, p. 64) explain that anger is elicited when an individual has not been able to "avoid being put into an unpleasant state." Their model suggests that anger occurs when an individual believes that a goal that is obstructed by another person can still be attained. They suggest that in order to restore the conditions that allow for the attainment of a desired goal, an individual will attempt to understand why that goal has been obstructed. In essence, an individual recognizes an agonistic experience and refuses to accept its result. This refusal of a negative experience, Stein and Levine explain, produces feelings of anger.

It is important to note that Stein and Levine do not suggest, as attribution theorists do, that anger arises when an individual perceives intentional harm. It is simply the frustration of being blocked from achieving a goal that causes anger. For example, Berkowitz (1989) examined the effect of goal impediment on children's outward expression of emotion. In this study, children were exposed to an unintentionally frustrating event. They expected to see a highly entertaining movie but could not see the movie because of an inadvertent equipment malfunction. Frustrated by their inability to enjoy the pleasure that they had anticipated, these children exhibited anger and nasty behavior when the interacted with others.

Examining anger as a result of frustration highlights the other-oriented nature of this emotion. From this perspective, not only is anger directed outward, but the cause of that anger is from a source that is outside of the individual and that is blocking the individual's goal attainment. In addition, it is clear that anger may be a more general response than is indicated by the cognition-arousal hypothesis or the neo-associational theory.

Social Learning Theory

James Averill (1982) describes anger as a socially constituted syndrome that represents the way subjective experience, physiological arousal, and goal impediment are organized to reflect the rules and social norms that are related to anger. According to social learning theory, or the social cognitive theory of Albert Bandura (1986), modeling is the method by which most human behavior is learned. Individuals learn what to do and how to act by observing others. Bandura suggested that in order to learn an individual must be motivated to learn, must remember what he or she has observed, and must be able to perform the behavior he or she observed. In addition, the learned behavior must be positively reinforced if an individual is to continue to engage in it.

Carolyn Saarni (1993) explains that emotions are learned in much the same way as behaviors are learned. Individuals experience particular emotions as a result of their relationships over time with others. In other words, emotions are learned, or "socialized," during the course of a lifetime. Saarni suggests that the "emotional dynamics" of relationships affect how emotions are socialized. For example, a child whose parent reacts to a disappointment with anger and frustration will come to understand that reaction as appropriate and model it in similar situations.

Social learning theory would suggest that the arousal that is associated with a precipitating event could produce any number of emotional reactions depending on what responses were learned. However, based on norms of behavior, it is most likely that negative events will elicit negative consequences and, therefore, produce feelings of anger. It is also the case, according to K. Daniel O'Leary (1988), that negative arousal for which individuals have no explanation generally becomes labeled and felt as anger.

Communication Deficit Hypothesis

The final explanation reviewed here concerns how anger reflects one's inability to manage his or her social environment in a competent manner. Without the ability to control one's social world through message behavior, one experiences a variety of negative arousal cues and responds in an inappropriate manner. For example, Dominic Infante and his colleagues (1989, p. 169) speculated that violence emerges "if undissipated anger creates a latent hostile disposition in at least one partner and the individuals have an argumentative skill deficiency which increases the probability of verbal aggression." Similarly, Richard Gelles (1974, p. 163) emphasized that verbal deficiencies constitute a primary predictor of inappropriate anger expression: "When the husband and wife are engaged in a verbal fight . . . one partner simply runs out of ammunition . . . and begins to flail away at the other."

Examinations of abusive relationships indicate that a lack of communicative skills perpetuates psychological and physical abuse. Susan Clearhout and her colleagues (1982) examined the problem-solving skills of women from abusive and non-abusive relationships. The abused women, versus the non-abused women, created fewer and less-effective problem-solving alternatives. Gayla Margolin and her colleagues (1989) found that couples who used physical aggression exhibited more hostility toward each other during verbal conflicts. Margolin and her colleagues also found that husbands who were physically aggressive demonstrated a lack of involvement, defensiveness, and coldness in comparison to verbally abusive and withdrawn husbands. Marital partners in nondistressed (versus abusive) relationships used more problem-solving skills and signs of warmth during verbal conflicts.

People in general appear vulnerable to everyday angry exchanges. According to Aron Siegman (1994, p. 189), angry people typically "raise their voice, accelerate their speech rate, and interrupt their partner. However, the heightened levels of [blood pressure], [heart rate], and catecholmanines will further intensify the speaker's angry voice and feelings of anger."

Of course, most people do not have heated exchanges with only themselves. Instead, people will fight and bicker and escalate conflicts that ride the negative energy generated by the escalated anger. In other words, one person's negative behavior serves as a stimulus to the partner's behavior, and each new injection of negativity into the conversation raises the level of excitation and the lack of ability to cope in a calm manner with the partner.

An alternative response to the experience of anger is withdrawal. John Gottman's (1994) model of marital divorce indicates that men and women have alternative reactions to anger, with men experiencing higher levels of noxious emotions (called "diffuse physiological arousal"). Especially in unhappy involvements, partners feel "flooded" by diffuse negativity. According to Gottman, four messages appear to be especially corrosive and lead to "cascades" of isolation and withdrawal, as well as to rethinking the history and future of the marriage. Gottman labels these communicative

An argument between two men in Milan, Italy, escalates with the introduction of angry gestures. (Corbis/Ted Spiegel)

behaviors the "Four Horsemen of the Apocalypse," and they are said to occur in the following manner: *complaining/criticizing* some aspect or features of the partner leads to *contempt* (e.g., indications that one is sickened by one's partner), which then leads to *defensiveness* (i.e., countermeasures to protect self), which culminates in *stonewalling* (i.e., withdrawal from the partner and obstinate refusal to discuss the issue directly). Gottman claims that satisfied couples do not engage in such behaviors and satisfied couples avoid the reciprocation of negative comments and nonverbal messages.

The reciprocation of negative comments and nonverbal messages (e.g., those that criticize, show contempt, defend the self, and announce one's withdrawal) reflects the communicative skill deficit hypothesis in a clear way. Researchers have consistently found that all couples experience some negativity; however, satisfied couples find ways of shutting off the negativity, of breaking the tendency to reciprocate the negativity, and of searching for ways to mend the negativity. Gottman, for example, argued that satisfied couples pay attention to the redeemable, insightful content that might be conveyed during conflict, even in complaints (e.g., "Maybe I should be more considerate and call the next time I come home this late").

That partners provide the catalyst as well as the crucible for the creation of anger represents an irony of human behavior. The irony is that those one ostensibly loves are those who ignite one's anger and reciprocate one's own negative impulses to communicate in an anger-like manner.

It should be noted communicative skill deficits do not constitute the only interactional responses to anger. In fact, researchers and theorists have presented alternative, integrative ways to manage anger when it arises. For example, Averill (1993) offers the following clear advice regarding how people might respond more productively to anger:

1. People have the personal right to be angry in response to another person's intentional wrongdoing or unintended misdeeds if those misdeeds can be corrected (e.g., negligence).
2. People should direct their anger at events, people, or objects that are clearly responsible for the action(s).
3. People should not blame innocent third parties or blame someone for a behavior that is irrelevant to the instigation of one's anger.
4. One's conversational objective should be to remedy the situation and to restore fairness.
5. One's response to anger should be related to the degree of the blameworthy behavior or event (i.e., the response should fit the crime).
6. One's response to anger should closely follow the provoking event—it should not last longer than the time needed to repair the situation.
7. One's expression of anger should entail resolve and follow-through when necessary.

A comprehensive and less prescriptive taxonomy of anger responses was offered by Laura Guerrero (1994). Guerrero separated types of anger expressions along the dimensions of directness and threat. Distributive-aggression concerns direct and threatening messages, such as screaming, criticizing, and using threats. Integrative-assertion refers to behaviors that reflect a direct but nonthreatening orientation, such as listening, attempts to be fair, and sharing of feelings. Passive-aggression includes indirect and threatening actions, such as giving the partner the "silent treatment," leaving the scene, and giving dirty looks. Nonassertive-denial behaviors are those that are both indirect and nonthreatening (e.g., hiding from a partner, denying feelings). As one might expect, Guerrero's research found that integrative-assertiveness tactics were positively linked to perceptions that the person managed his or her anger in a competent manner.

Conclusion

Given the many causes and explanations for anger as a social phenomenon, one must be cautious in drawing conclusions from the diverse literature on the topic. Still, this mixture of information does indicate that the experience and the expression of anger reflect complex processes, that people do not (cannot) comprehend these processes as they occur, and that ultimately people must decide, however reflexively, how they will interact with their partner(s). Ultimately, people are responsible for their own behaviors. Although partners might provide sites for anger instigation, provoke negative arousal and excitation that works against rational thinking, and reciprocate negative affect to a self-defeating degree, they still possess the ability to cease, to stop, to count to ten, and to cool off.

People also have the capacity to discuss their problems in a more positive, cooperative manner—even when angry. People can be cooperative in a direct manner by exchanging information, seeking a partner's point of view, and facilitating agreement by owning responsibility for any problems they might have caused. In addition, people have the capacity to be positive in an indirect way about issues by using hints, posing questions that are related indirectly, and even teasing. Either direct or indirect cooperative behaviors are much less likely than direct or indirect negative behaviors to elicit and exacerbate anger. In addition, they are much more productive and relationally enhancing than negative behaviors that reflect deficits in communication skills.

See also: AGGRESSION; ANNOYANCE; ATTRIBUTION; COGNITIVE PERSPECTIVE; COMMUNICATION; CONFLICT; PSYCHOPHYSIOLOGY OF EMOTIONS; RELATIONSHIPS; STRESS

Bibliography

Ahmed, S. M. S. (1992). "Fraisse's Theory of Emotion and Aggression." *Journal of Social Psychology* 132(2):257–260.

Averill, James R. (1982). *Anger and Aggression: An Essay on Emotion.* New York: Springer-Verlag.

Averill, James R. (1993). "Illusions of Anger." In *Aggression and Violence: Social Interactionist Perspectives,* ed. Richard B. Felson and James T. Tedeschi. Washington, DC: American Psychological Association.

Bandura, Albert. (1969). *Principles of Behavior Modification.* New York: Holt, Rinehart, & Winston.

Bandura, Albert. (1973). *Aggression: A Social Psychological Analysis.* New York: McGraw-Hill.

Bandura, Albert. (1977). *Social Learning Theory.* Englewood Cliffs, NJ: Prentice-Hall.

Bandura, Albert. (1986). *Social Foundations of Thought and Action: A Social and Cognitive Theory.* Englewood Cliffs, NJ: Prentice-Hall.

Berkowitz, Leonard. (1974). "Some Determinants of Impulsive Aggression: Role of Mediated Associations with Reinforcement for Aggression." *Psychological Review* 81:165–176.

Berkowitz, Leonard. (1989). "Frustration-Aggression Hypothesis: Examination and Reformulation." *Psychological Bulletin* 106:59–73.

Berkowitz, Leonard. (1993). "Towards a General Theory of Anger and Emotional Aggression: Implications of the Cognitive-Neoassociationistic Perspective for the Analysis of Anger and Other Emotions." In *Perspectives on Anger and Emotion, Vol. 6: Advances in Social Cognition,* ed. Robert S. Wyer, Jr., and Thomas K. Srull. Hillsdale, NJ: Lawrence Erlbaum.

Berscheid, Ellen. (1983). "Emotion." In *Close Relationships,* ed. Harold H. Kelley, Ellen Berscheid, Andrew Christensen, John H. Harvey, Ted L. Huston, George Levinger, Evie McClintock, Letitia Anne Peplau, and Donald R. Peterson. Beverly Hills, CA: Sage Publications.

Betancourt, Hector, and Blair, Irene. (1992). "A Cognition (Attribution) Emotion Model of Violence in Conflict Situations." *Personality and Social Psychology Bulletin* 18:343–350.

Canary, Daniel J.; Cupach, William R.; and Messman, Susan J. (1995). *Relationship Conflict: Conflict in Parent-Child, Friendship, and Romantic Relationships.* Thousand Oaks, CA: Sage Publications.

Canary, Daniel J.; Spitzberg, B. H.; and Semic, Beth A. (1998). "The Experience and Expression of Anger in Interpersonal Settings." In *The Handbook of Communication and Emotion,* ed. Peter A. Andersen and Laura K. Guerrero. San Diego, CA: Sage Publications.

Clearhout, Susan; Elder, John; and Janes, Carolyn. (1982). "Problem-Solving Skills of Rural Battered Women." *American Journal of Community Psychology* 10:605–613.

Clore, Gerald L.; Ortony, Andrew; Dienes, B.; and Fujita, Frank. (1993). "Where Does Anger Dwell?" In *Perspectives on Anger and Emotion: Advances in Social Cognition, Vol. 6,* ed. Robert S. Wyer, Jr., and Thomas K. Srull. Hillsdale, NJ: Lawrence Erlbaum.

Fincham, Frank D.; Bradbury, Thomas N.; and Scott, C. K. (1990). "Cognition in Marriage." In *The Psychology of Marriage: Basic Issues and Applications,* ed. Frank D. Fincham and Thomas N. Bradbury. New York: Guilford.

Fraisse, Paul. (1964). "The Sources of Emotion." In *Readings in Psychology*, ed. John Cohen. London: Allen & Unwin.

Gelles, Richard J. (1974). *The Violent Home A Study of Physical Aggression between Husbands and Wives*. Beverly Hills, CA: Sage Publications.

Gottman, John M. (1994). *What Predicts Divorce? The Relationship between Marital Processes and Marital Outcomes*. Hillsdale, NJ: Lawrence Erlbaum.

Guerrero, Laura K. (1994). " 'I'm So Mad I Could Scream': The Effects of Anger Expression on Relational Satisfaction and Communication Competence." *Southern Communication Journal* 59:125–141.

Hocker, Joyce L., and Wilmot, William W. (1995). *Interpersonal Conflict*, 4th ed. Dubuque, IA: Wm. C. Brown.

Infante, Dominic A.; Chandler, Teresa A.; and Rudd, Jill E. (1989). "Test of an Argumentative Skill Deficiency Model of Interpersonal Violence." *Communication Monographs* 56:163–177.

Lemerise, Elizabeth A., and Dodge, Kenneth A. (1993). "The Development of Anger and Hostile Interactions." In *Handbook of Emotions*, ed. Michael Lewis and Jeannette M. Haviland. New York: Guilford.

Makepeace, James. (1983). "Life Events, Stress, and Courtship Violence." *Family Relations* 32:101–109.

Margolin, Gayla; Burman, Bonnie; and John, Richard S. (1989). "Home Observations of Married Couples Reenacting Naturalistic Conflicts." *Behavioral Assessment* 11:101–118.

Marshall, Linda L. (1994). "Physical and Psychological Abuse." In *The Dark Side of Interpersonal Communication*, ed. William R. Cupach and Brian H. Spitzberg. Hillsdale, NJ: Lawrence Erlbaum.

O'Leary, K. Daniel. (1988). "Physical Aggression between Spouses: A Social Learning Theory Perspective." In *Handbook of Family Violence*, ed. Vincent B. Van Hassett, Randall L. Morrison, Alan S. Bellack, and Michel Hersen. New York: Plenum.

Ross, Lee, and Nisbett, Richard E. (1991). *The Person and the Situation: Perspectives of Social Psychology*. New York: McGraw-Hill.

Russell, James A., and Fehr, Beverly. (1994). "Fuzzy Concepts in a Fuzzy Hierarchy: Varieties of Anger." *Journal of Personality and Social Psychology* 67:186–205.

Saarni, Carolyn. (1993). "Socialization of Emotion." In *Handbook of Emotions*, ed. Michael Lewis, and Jeannette M. Haviland. New York: Guilford.

Schachter, Stanley, and Singer, Jerome. (1962). "Cognitive, Social, and Physiological Determinants of Emotional State." *Psychological Review* 65:379–399.

Shaver, Phillip; Schwartz, Judith; Kirkson, Donald; and O'Connor, Cary. (1987). "Emotion Knowledge: Further Exploration of a Prototype Approach." *Journal of Personality and Social Psychology* 52:1061–1086.

Siegman, Aron W. (1994). "Cardiovascular Consequences of Expressing and Repressing Anger." In *Anger, Hostility, and the Heart*, ed. Aron W. Siegman and Timothy W. Smith. Hillsdale, NJ: Lawrence Erlbaum.

Sillars, Alan L. (1980). "Attributions and Communication in Roommate Conflicts." *Communication Monographs* 47:180–200.

Stein, Nancy L., and Levine, Linda J. (1989). "The Causal Organization of Emotional Knowledge: A Developmental Study." *Cognition and Emotion* 3:343–378.

Weiner, Bernard. (1986). *An Attributional Theory of Motivation and Emotion*. New York: Springer-Verlag.

Weiner, Bernard; Graham, S.; and Chandler, C. C. (1982). "Pity, Anger, and Guilt: An Attributional Analysis." *Personality and Social Psychology Bulletin* 8:226–232.

Weiner, Bernard, and Handel, S. (1985). "Anticipated Emotional Consequences of Causal Communications and Reported Communication Strategy." *Developmental Psychology* 18:278–286.

Zillmann, Dolf. (1988). "Cognition-Excitation Interdependence in Aggressive Behavior." *Aggressive Behavior* 14:51–64.

Zillmann, Dolf. (1990). "The Interplay of Cognition and Excitation in Aggravated Conflict." In *Intimates in Conflict: A Communication Perspective*, ed. Dudley D. Cahn. Hillsdale, NJ: Lawrence Erlbaum.

Zillmann, Dolf. (1994). "Cognition-Excitation Interdependencies in the Escalation of Anger and Angry Aggression." In *The Dynamics of Aggression: Biological and Social Processes in Dyads and Groups*, ed. Michael Potegal and John F. Knutson. Hillsdale, NJ: Lawrence Erlbaum.

Daniel J. Canary
Beth A. Semic

ANIMALS

See Attachment to Animals

ANNOYANCE

According to Robert Plutchik's psychoevolutionary model of emotions, as detailed in *The Psychology and Biology of Emotions* (1994), there are eight basic emotions, and annoyance is conceptualized as part of a category known as "rage/anger/annoyance." Plutchik distinguishes annoyance from other emotions by factors such as valence (positive to negative) and intensity (strong to weak) and by the nature of the trigger. For example, elation is perceived by people to be positive and strong, and it is felt when something good happens. In contrast, annoyance is perceived as negative and mild, and it occurs when something bad happens unexpectedly. Anger is more intense than annoyance, and rage is the most intense emotion in the category. Charles Spielberger (1988), who studies emotions using a psychometric model, also suggests that annoyance refers to a lower intensity level of anger, implying that there is one dimension that stretches from mild annoyance to extreme rage.

It is usually hypothesized that several elements exist in any emotional episode. These include the triggers, cognitive appraisals, physiological reactions, personal experience (awareness), action tendencies (desired actions), patterns of expression, and outcomes of the episode. For example, consider a student who earns an "A" as a final grade in a course. Seeing the grade

ANNOYANCE   51

of "A" (the trigger) may lead to a thought (the appraisal) such as "My hard work has been appropriately recognized," which then leads to a feeling of joy (the experience), which is shown by a big smile (the expression), and a telephone call to parents who indicate their pride in the student and suggest a celebration dinner (the outcome). Similarly, a person may want to buy a product by telephone. However, when he or she is put on "hold" by the telephone operator (the trigger), the individual may think "This service is totally unacceptable" (the appraisal), take a deep breath to calm an increased heart rate (the physiological reaction), which leads to a feeling of annoyance (the experience), and complain to a friend (the expression). The person may then hang up the telephone and call a different company to buy the product (the outcome).

Although all emotions can be broken down into such elements, none are themselves *necessary* or *sufficient* to produce a specific feeling. In fact, psychologists such as Leonard Berkowitz (1993) believe that aversive triggers lead simply to undifferentiated negative affect before specific experienced feelings, such as annoyance, develop. The specific feelings are determined by a combination of the elements, such as the specific social and cultural context and the unique personal learning history (i.e., personality) of the individual. For example, a trigger (e.g., being gently reprimanded by a parent) may lead to annoyance in an American adolescent, while the same trigger might not produce annoyance in a Japanese adolescent since that culture generally demonstrates more respect for elders. In the study of the Utku Eskimos, who were described by Jean Briggs (1970) as "never in anger," anthropologists and cross-cultural psychologists have investigated the display rules for negative affect. These "rules" are defined as the behaviors considered to be appropriate for a given situation. It is believed that specific elements in the evolution of a society allow for, or prohibit, annoyance and anger as well as rage and aggression. Interestingly enough, a 1997 review by Bruce Bonta provides a list of twenty-five peaceful societies wherein negative affect and behavior are rare to non-existent. He offers the importance of "cooperation" in these societies as the explanation for their nonviolence. Nevertheless, in spite of these cultural differences, discrete emotions such as annoyance can be described and understood by their elements.

For example, if one person sitting next to another person in a movie theater makes crunching noises while eating popcorn (the trigger), the second person may feel annoyed (the experience). The feeling is negative and of mild intensity. In addition, the second person may believe that the person eating the popcorn "should have better manners!" Would this annoyance

In Greek mythology, Io was the daughter of a river god. Zeus loved her and changed her into a white heifer to protect her from the jealousy of his wife, Hera. Hera, however, figured out that Io was Zeus's mistress, so she sent a gadfly to bite and sting and annoy Io. The tormented Io wandered in a state of misery until she went into the sea (the Ionian Sea, named for her), where the annoying gadfly could not bite her. The term gadfly still refers to some annoying, irritating pest.

generally be sufficient to make the second person say something to the offending individual? Probably not. Most people will simply wait and hope that the popcorn will soon be finished so that the noise will stop. In contrast, if the same person was talking during the show, making the same level of noise as produced by eating popcorn, most people might become annoyed and feel entitled to "shush" the talker. People are likely to take an action much earlier when others are talking in a theater than when they are eating popcorn. These action tendencies are determined by personal beliefs and the social rules established within cultures. In the United States, eating popcorn in a movie theater is appropriate but talking during the show is not. Therefore, if the talking continued, an individual's negative affect would likely escalate to anger and he or she might loudly ask the persons to keep quiet. However, if the popcorn eating persisted, people would be likely to continue to feel annoyed but still not act. Annoyance, in contrast to anger, is more often concealed than displayed. The emotion being felt is determined not only by the intensity or duration of the aversive stimulus but by the rules specified by the culture for the specific context or trigger that is associated with certain emotions.

Annoyance Versus Anger

Annoyance is typically viewed as a less intense form of anger that is caused by insignificant or petty events. When the annoying stimulus is discontinued (e.g., the person in the movie theater finishes the popcorn) the experience of annoyance stops. People usually do not ruminate or hold grudges about annoying events for very long. Thus, the duration of annoyance is shorter than that of anger. The cognitive appraisal or thought involved in the experience of annoyance involves perception of unpleasantness and may trigger thoughts such as "I wish this distracting stimulus (e.g., eating popcorn) was not present." In contrast, anger involves perceptions of a more important problem, such as being unfairly wronged by a close friend (e.g., a friend steals something from an individual), that trigger thoughts such as, "This should not have happened." Rage often involves perceptions of great social injustice (e.g., the televised beating of Rodney King in Los Angeles, which was perceived to be racially motivated). Anger and rage are intense and long-lasting experiences, which are more likely than annoyance to be associated with physiological arousal and strong action tendencies. After someone has been angered or brought to a state of rage, the person often wants to argue or retaliate and has to "cool off" for a period of time before the feeling disappears. But, after being annoyed, there is little desire for retaliation and little time is needed to regain one's composure.

Howard Kassinove and his colleagues (1997) studied annoyance and anger experiences in 747 American and Russian college students. More than 85 percent of the students reported that they knew the difference between those times when they felt annoyed and those when they felt angry, suggesting that these feelings are experienced differently. As expected, on a 1-to-100 scale, the average intensity of annoyance was rated 45, compared to 60 for anger. Regarding duration, annoyance was described as lasting for less than five minutes by 34 percent of the students and only 5 percent said it lasted more than a full day. In contrast, anger was described as lasting less than five minutes by only 17 percent of the students, while 16 percent indicated that it lasted more than a full day. Annoyance, thus, is shorter in duration. Regarding frequency, 28 percent of the students reported being annoyed once a day or more, while only 7 percent reported being angry once a day or more. Annoyance, thus, is a more frequent experience.

Earlier, James Averill (1983) examined the differences between anger and annoyance from a social-constructivist model. This model assumes that emotions are complex responses of the whole person that serve a social purpose and are governed by display rules generated within a culture. Averill had forty-eight American university students keep daily records of their anger and annoyance episodes over a one-week period. Of the total 1,536 recorded episodes, 73 percent were labeled as annoyance, 23 percent were labeled as anger, and only 4 percent were labeled as uncertain. Clearly, the students knew the difference between the two emotions and annoyance emerged as a much more frequent experience. In terms of intensity, as expected, Averill noted that anger was described as more intense. However, it was the "seriousness" of the situation that appeared to differentiate better between whether anger or annoyance were experienced. Averill concluded that the triggers of annoyance were subjectively less important to the partic-

ipants, whether or not there was a direct effect on them. "A person might get angry over the killing of baby seals, but only annoyed by someone loudly chewing gum" (p. 1151). Therefore, the subjective importance of the trigger seems to be partially responsible for the verbal labeling of the experience as annoyance or anger.

A further distinction involves the issue of moral judgment. As compared with annoyance, the essence of anger involves a perception of injustice and is, according to Averill, an attribution of blame more than anything else. To become angry, a person must know that something has been done wrong. Therefore, Averill concluded that anger has a moral connotation and that annoyance does not. As in the example given above, few people think it is morally wrong to make noise while eating popcorn in a movie theater. However, an accident caused by driving while intoxicated often yields anger and a moral judgment against the driver. Anger and annoyance are also distinguished by their action tendencies. Action tendencies refer to desired, as opposed to actual, behaviors. While annoyed people typically hide their feelings and try to leave the aversive situation, angry people want to do something to change the provoking situation. Of course, such tendencies are often not manifested. The final distinction proposed by Averill is more subtle and represents a notion about commitment to the emotion. Anger involves committing one's self, beliefs and principles to an emotion event, annoyance does not. To illustrate this point, Averill compared the difference between anger and annoyance to that between loving and liking. Similarly to loving, anger implies a commitment and a certain type of social relationship, while liking or annoyance do not.

Environmental Psychology: Noise, Odors, and People

Annoyance research has most often occurred in the context of environmental psychology. This is consistent with the observation that people become angry with unexpected and personally significant events but they become annoyed about relatively impersonal trivial events. Environmental noise, unpleasant odors, and inconsiderate neighbors are three examples of such events that cause many people to feel annoyed. Because they have been studied by environmental psychologists, some specific things are known about each of these sources of annoyance.

Noise can be viewed as a prototypical trigger of annoyance. Everyone can recall being annoyed with the loud humming of an air conditioner, honking of car horns, dripping water from a broken tap, and muffled voices that can be heard from behind a thin wall. By

Even music, when it is played in a crowded Paris subway train, can be a source of annoyance for individuals who are not in the mood to listen to the music and are unable to get away from it. (Corbis/David & Peter Turnley)

its definition as "unwanted sound," noise can be considered to be an aversive stimulus that often leads to annoyance. Susan Staples (1996) reviewed human responses to environmental noise, including psychological mediating factors and consequences of exposure to noise. Prolonged exposure to noise was found to be related to impaired scholastic performance, elevated blood pressure, lowered frustration tolerance, and increased levels of stress-related hormones. However, psychological factors were found to account for more variance in the response than the actual level of the noise. Annoyance is a central individual variable and it was found not to habituate or decrease as a function of exposure. However, a cause and effect relationship is unclear. While noise can definitely lead to annoyance, generalized hyperreactivity (a tendency to react strongly to all aversive stimuli) may underlie both specific noise annoyance and increased levels of distress.

Stephen Stansfeld (1992) reviewed the literature and found that two cognitive factors consistently emerged in investigations of the noise and annoyance: appraisal of the stimulus as being harmful and per-

ceived control of exposure to the stimulus. People who believe noise to be harmful and who believe that they cannot avoid exposure to it seem to experience higher levels of annoyance. Stansfeld, consistent with the belief of Staples, concluded that annoyance is the most common subjective response to noise. Five factors that influence the subjective experience of annoyance were found: the perceived meaning of the noise, the personality characteristic of neuroticism, the intrusiveness of noise into personal privacy, the interference of noise in everyday activities, and the context in which the noise is heard. Stansfeld concluded that general vulnerability to stress is a distinguishing feature of people who are easily annoyed in response to noise. The general tendency to experience annoyance (i.e., trait annoyance) was found by Gerhard Winneke and Manfred Neuf (1992) to generalize across environmental stressors and to explain 10 percent of the variance in reactions to specific aversive stimuli.

Environmental, particularly industrial, odors have also been studied as a source of annoyance. In 1993, Brigitte Steinheider and Winneke investigated annoyance with odors in the industrial districts of three German cities. A positive relationship was found between the degree of annoyance and the frequency of industrial odors in the neighborhood. Age and health satisfaction, however, correlated negatively with odor annoyance (i.e., older age and better health were linked to less odor annoyance), and women reported higher levels of odor annoyance than men. Two coping strategies were differentially related to annoyance—people oriented toward solving problems were more annoyed with odors than were people oriented toward avoiding problems. This finding can be linked to the previously discussed perceptions of harmfulness and coping strategies. Industrial odors, as studied in the German sample, are probably difficult to eliminate from the environment. Therefore, participants with an avoidant coping strategy might have paid less attention to these odors and perceived them as less harmful than those who were trying actively to do something about them. Steinheider and Winneke concluded that people oriented to avoiding problems experienced significantly less odor annoyance.

A group of Dutch researchers, P. M. Cavalini, L. G. Koeter-Kemmerling, and M. P. J. Pulles (1991), investigated the relationship between coping styles and annoyance with odors. In an epidemiological survey, almost 20 percent of the Dutch population was estimated to be annoyed by aversive odors. In their study of 558 residents who lived in neighborhoods where sugar and tobacco factories were present, it was found that more than 25 percent of variance in odor annoyance was explained by the concentration of odor. Next, they hypothesized that people who thought that the odor was harmful and had possible health effects would be annoyed and might engage in coping efforts. Their research found that, at the same levels of concentration, people who believed that the odors were harmful to their health *were* significantly more annoyed than people who did not hold this belief. Further, the relationship between the level of annoyance and two types of coping efforts—problem-oriented coping and emotion-oriented coping—were investigated. In dealing with environmental stressors, changing the actual situation (e.g., closing down the factory that is polluting the neighborhood air) is often less feasible than changing one's own emotional reactions to the stressor (thinking of the fumes as less health damaging). Emotion-oriented coping was hypothesized to be linked to lower levels of odor annoyance. This hypothesis was supported, as people higher in problem-oriented coping reported higher levels of odor annoyance than people higher in emotion-oriented coping. Comforting cognitions, such as "I assume that problems disappear by themselves," were found to moderate the effects of odor concentration and annoyance level.

Neighbors also have been studied as a common source of environmental annoyance. In their 1994 review of the literature on annoyance with neighbors, Gary Paquin and Eileen Gambrill concluded that "every annoyance [episode] seemed to indicate that the perpetrator was a person who would not respect others" (p. 23). In a telephone survey of 197 residents of urban California, they investigated the frequency, intensity, types, and outcomes of annoyance in response to neighbors. Ninety percent of the respondents reported being annoyed with their neighbors, with an average of 2.8 episodes in the past three years. The most frequent trigger for annoyance was a "neighbor's barking dog." There were, however, unique triggers that included the neighbor's ritualistic slaughter of a goat for religious purposes. Intensity of annoyance was related to the type of trigger. Barking dogs and noisy children were associated with lower intensities, while abusive neighbors and damage to property were associated with higher intensity. It is important to note with regard to the elimination of annoyance that the frequency of annoyance was negatively related to the amount of time spent thinking about it (i.e., the more frequent the event, the less it was thought about). Unfortunately, the picture is unclear as intensity of annoyance was positively related to the amount of time spent thinking about it (i.e., the more intense the event, the more it is thought about). As expected from the description provided above, most of the time annoyance was simply noticed but not dwelt upon. When asked about the amount of stress that annoyance with neighbors contributed to the overall stress of life, the average estimate was slightly more than 8 percent. Indeed, half of the respondents said that neighbors did not contribute to stress in their lives. At the same time, 12 percent of the respondents reported that they changed their residence due to problems with neighbors. Socio-demographic variables did not contribute significantly to the number of annoyance experiences. However, higher neighbor annoyance was reported by apartment dwellers than by people in single family houses. This suggests that physical proximity is a factor in neighbor annoyance.

A group of psychologists from Norway and Sweden, Oddvar Skjaeveland, Tommy Garling, and John Gunnar Maeland (1996), used factor analysis to study social life within neighborhoods. Four questions targeted how frequently one was annoyed with neighbors, how much noise was made by neighbors, how safe one felt in the neighborhood, and how much one desired to live elsewhere. These constituted an annoyance factor in the neighborhood questionnaire. The neighbor annoyance scale was further used to investigate characteristics that influence the amount of annoyance in a sample of fifteen hundred respondents of varying demographic characteristics. Dwelling time and respondent's age were negatively related to annoyance, number of children was positively related, and gender was unrelated to neighbor annoyance. In addition, neighbor annoyance was relatively independent from two other factors: supportive acts of neighbors and social ties. However, it was inversely related to attachment, the fourth dimension of neighboring. Apparently, feeling attached to one's residence and feeling at home in one's neighborhood were the factors negatively related to neighbor annoyance.

Another telephone survey of two hundred California residents investigated behavioral and cognitive coping with neighbor annoyances. The 1992 study conducted by Paquin was based on a three stage (naming, blaming, and complaining) model of conflict. In neighbor annoyance episodes, naming involves the perception of an event as damaging. The attribution of responsibility for the damage to a neighbor is referred to as blaming. Two additional cognitive processes were investigated: consideration of retaliative actions and perceived control over the situation. Three main behavioral strategies emerged in the study: passive forbearance (doing nothing), claiming (addressing the issue with a neighbor), and disputing (bringing the issue up with a third party). The results showed that in 60 percent of reported neighbor annoyance incidents people did nothing. The probability of active coping by ways of communicating with the annoying party or with a third party, which was reported in 40 percent of episodes, increased with increases in the level of annoyance. In other words, very annoying events had a higher likelihood of being acted upon. At the same time, this relationship might have been mediated by the thought processes (i.e., cognitions) involved in the appraisal of the annoying event. Intensity of annoyance varied with the category of the primary cognition involved in the appraisal. The lowest levels of annoyance were reported when there was a perception of damage, but it was evaluated as "not so bad" and when the "responsible party was known, but not to blame." This could be explained by either insignificance of damage or by the accidental nature of damage. On the other hand, these two types of cognitions can also be considered to be palliative coping strategies that are related to lower levels of annoyance. The highest annoyance was associated with cognitions of low control over the situation and not knowing who is responsible.

Conclusion

Annoyance is an emotion that is characterized, as compared to anger, by lower intensity, shorter duration, and higher frequency. In addition, annoyance is usually triggered by events of lower personal significance. Annoyance is associated with avoidance or escape action tendencies intended to discontinue exposure to the unpleasant situation. Compared to anger, annoyance does not have a moral connotation and usually does not involve interference with a person's core belief system. Culture and context also play a role, since people may label very similar experiences as either anger or annoyance.

Noise, aversive odors, and inconsiderate neighbors have been often investigated as sources of annoyance. General vulnerability to stress was found as one of the personality characteristics responsible for annoyance reactions. Cognitive appraisals of harmfulness, perceived control, and responsibility were also found related to intensity of environmental annoyance. Avoidance and emotion-oriented coping strategies were found more effective than problem-oriented strategies in alleviating annoyances, at least the ones caused by environmental stressors.

See also: ANGER

Bibliography

Averill, James R. (1983). "Studies on Anger and Aggression." *American Psychologist* 38:1145–1160.

Berkowitz, Leonard. (1993). *Aggression: Its Causes, Consequences, and Control.* New York: McGraw-Hill.

Bonta, Bruce D. (1997). "Cooperation and Competition in Peaceful Societies." *Psychological Bulletin* 121:299–320.

Briggs, Jean L. (1970). *Never in Anger: Portrait of an Eskimo Family.* Cambridge, MA: Harvard University Press.

Cavalini, P. M.; Koeter-Kemmerling, L. G.; and Pulles, M. P. J. (1991). "Coping with Odour Annoyance and Odour Concentrations: Three Field Studies." *Journal of Environmental Psychology* 11:123–142.

Kassinove, Howard; Sukhodolsky, Denis G.; Tsytsarev, Sergei V.; and Solovyova, Svetlana L. (1997). "Self-Reported Anger Episodes in Russia and America." *Journal of Social Behavior and Personality* 12:301–324.

Paquin, Gary W. (1992). "Coping and Disputing with Neighbors." *Journal of Applied Social Psychology* 22:1852–1870.

Paquin, Gary W., and Gambrill, Eileen. (1994). "The Problem with Neighbors." *Journal of Community Psychology,* 22:21–32.

Plutchik, Robert. (1994). *The Psychology and Biology of Emotion.* New York: HarperCollins.

Skjaeveland, Oddvar; Garling, Tommy; and Maeland, John Gunnar. (1996). "A Multidimensional Measure of Neighboring." *American Journal of Community Psychology* 24:413–435.

Spielberger, Charles D. (1988). *Manual for the State-Trait Anger Expression Inventory (STAXI).* Odessa, FL: Psychological Assessment Resources.

Stansfeld, Stephen A. (1992). "Noise, Noise Sensitivity, and Psychiatric Disorder." *Psychological Medicine* 22:1–44.

Staples, Susan. (1996). "Human Response to Environmental Noise." *American Psychologist* 51:143–150.

Steinheider, Brigitte, and Winneke, Gerhard. (1993). "Industrial Odours As Environmental Stressors: Exposure-Annoyance Associations and the Modification by Coping, Age and Perceived Health." *Journal of Environmental Psychology* 13:353–363.

Winneke, Gerhard, and Neuf, Manfred. (1992). "Psychological Response to Sensory Stimulation by Environmental Stressor:

Trait or State?" *Applied Psychology: An International Review,* 41:257–267.

Denis G. Sukhodolsky
Howard Kassinove

ANTHROPOLOGY OF EMOTIONS

Anthropological interest in emotion focuses on the question of whether emotions are universal in any sense, or whether emotion has cultural or social dimensions that shape emotions differently from culture to culture. This has led anthropologists to consider a number of issues: how cultures control emotional experience, whether emotion words label the same experience in all cultures, whether the subjective experience of emotion differs from the public expression of emotion (i.e., "sentiment"), how Western cultural assumptions and beliefs about emotion shape research on emotion, and what the cross-cultural study of emotions can reveal about the nature of this phenomenon.

Early Anthropological Approaches to Emotion

Anthropological attention to emotion goes back at least to the beginnings of the academic discipline in the late nineteenth century, though the nature of that interest as changed over time. Emile Durkheim (1912), the French sociologist whose cross-cultural perspective was a foundation of anthropological study, considered emotion to be a powerful factor in social life, one that could be manipulated (e.g., by ritual) in the harnessing of the emotions of individuals to the interests of the social group. Bronislaw Malinowski (1948), one of the founders of British social anthropology, treated emotional states as independent variables in explaining puzzling cultural practices—magic, for instance, could be considered a technique for reducing anxiety, whether the anxiety surrounded agricultural success or the uncertainty of romantic overtures. A. R. Radcliffe-Brown (1952), the other major figure in the establishment of social anthropology in the first half of the twentieth century, similarly appealed to a kind of commonsense concept of emotion to explain, for example, the special social bond between certain categories of relatives, relying on a psychological feeling to explain a social structural pattern. In the United States, Alfred Kroeber (1952) considered kinship terms to have emotional content embedded within their meaning—kin terms did not merely label nodes on a genealogical chart; they encoded the affective content of kin relations as well.

The rise of the "culture and personality" school of cultural anthropology in the late 1920s and 1930s ex-

tended interest in emotion, particularly in the ways in which child-rearing practices produced personality configurations that were adapted to those forms of social organization that in turn reproduced those child-rearing practices. Ruth Benedict's *Patterns of Culture* (1934) understood "personality" to be in large part a pattern of emotions, a pattern created in childhood and supported by cultural and social practices. Margaret Mead's (1928) classic research on adolescence similarly focused attention on the emotional upheavals of this stage of development and its social and cultural construction. Much of the early culture and personality research now seems naive (e.g., studies linked infant swaddling to both Russian authoritarian character and Kwakiutl Indian destruction of property in potlatches). But while many aspects of this early work have been criticized, culture and personality research was valuable for stressing the fact that "emotion" has an important social component, in the development of emotional experience, in its expression and subjective experience, and in the social contexts that elicit and reproduce emotion.

What is notable about the early appeals to emotion in anthropological explanations of unusual cultural and social practices is that they relied upon an uncritical acceptance of Western notions of emotion as universal and unproblematic. For Malinowski, "anxiety" was the same emotional experience among farmers in the Trobriand Islands as it was among English university students, and both used culturally appropriate forms of magic to reduce the emotion. What differed was the culturally and socially determined contexts in which such emotions were called forth, displayed, and responded to. Thus, Trobriand Islanders felt "shame" in the presence of their opposite-sex siblings, while English brothers and sisters could be emotionally close and affectionate.

Social Meanings of Emotion

Robert Levy's (1973) research on Polynesian personality and character produced one of the major advances in the anthropological study of emotion that emerged from culture and personality research. Levy did not suggest that members of different cultures experience different emotions, but he did propose that cultures may perferentially exaggerate the expression or experience of certain emotions (i.e., hypercognize) or suppress or dampen the expression of certain emotions (i.e., hypocognize). Subsequent anthropological research has identified numerous examples of such emotional hypercognizing and hypocognizing cultures. Among the Faroe Islanders, for example, anger is cultivated and quickly expressed; among the Inuit

(Eskimo), anger is so widely suppressed that Jean Briggs' classic ethnography of an Inuit community is titled *Never in Anger* (1970). Traditional Balinese sought to flatten affective highs and lows, while Mediterranean cultures encouraged the histrionic expression of affect. The anthropological insight in these studies is not merely the discovery of hypercognizant or hypocognizant states but an understanding of how social life and other cultural principles intersect with these configurations of emotion in relatively systematic ways.

Anthropology has extended the insight that different cultures may hypercognize or hypocognize specific emotions to explore the cultural meanings that surround emotions and their expression. Emotional expression, or sentiment, is also a form of communication, and the meanings that are communicated by emotions—and the meanings experienced by actors —vary from culture to culture. Thus, anthropologists caution against the simple translation even of "core" emotions that may be universally experienced by humans. Similarly, the issue of how emotion is expressed is also surrounded by cultural sanctions and prescriptions. Lila Abu-Lughod (1986), for example, has studied how Bedouin women use poetry and song to express sentiments in defiance of a rigid, gendered system of social hierarchy.

Perhaps the most detailed study of the cultural meaning and social production of emotions is Catherine Lutz's *Unnatural Emotions* (1988), a study of sentiments among the inhabitants of Ifaluk atoll in Micronesia. Lutz explores several key emotions such as *fago*, which she interprets as "compassion/love/sadness" and *song*, which she interprets as "justifiable anger." The subtle but significant differences between Ifaluk notions of *song*, for example, and Western notions of anger are, Lutz demonstrates, rooted clearly in Ifaluk conceptions of social order and personhood, where "moral anger" helps to maintain this culture's form of social hierarchy. Lutz also notes that the Ifaluk concept of *ker*, which she interprets as "happiness/excitement," offers an interesting contrast to the American concept of happiness; Ifaluk islanders consider *ker* amoral or even immoral, in part because it signals a lack of fear (and thus a failure to respond appropriately to "justifiable anger"), while Americans place such high positive value on happiness as to make its pursuit a basic human right.

Cultures also propose theories of emotion—where emotions come from or originate, how they are triggered, and their nature. Americans are taught from infancy that their emotional experiences are the embodied expressions of underlying "mental" states (e.g., crying is the expression of sadness, a smile is the expression of happiness). Among the Kulina Indians of western Brazil, emotion is regarded as primarily physical. For Kulina, persons are composed of bodies and spirits; emotion cannot be regarded as a mental state when persons are not believed to possess a "mental" component. Metaphors of emotion, such as the American "hydraulic" metaphor (in which emotion is fluidlike, as when it "builds up" and must be "released"), reveal implicit cultural assumptions about the nature of emotion. For Kulina, metaphors of emotion often draw upon such contrasts as soft/firm and flowing/ fixed, which are more appropriate to the bodily experience of emotional states.

Methodological Issues

Most anthropological research on emotion has assumed what Lutz and Geoffrey White (1986, p. 415) have called "commonsense naturalism," which they describe as "the view that emotions are primarily to be understood as feelings, and that those feelings are universal in their essential nature and distribution." Methodologically, commonsense naturalism allows anthropologists to study emotion through a kind of empathy, in which the researcher who enters into the life of a community can take on and directly experience those emotions. However, anthropologists appealing to commonsense naturalism about emotion increasingly qualify the assumption of simple, unmediated universality, and the assumption of simple, immediate empathy. At the very least, research shows that emotion concepts in any culture are so saturated with cultural meanings that any "core" emotional experience is unlikely to be more significant in social life than the often powerful connotations conveyed by sentiment.

Traditional anthropological fieldwork in the participant observation mode is well suited to the empathetic demands of commonsense naturalism, but anthropologists have also employed methodological strategies that reduce reliance on the researcher's own experience and incorporate a degree of reproducibility. William Lessa (1966), for example, modified a set of Thematic Apperception Test pictures for his early research in the South Pacific, a technique that has been used by a number of anthropologists since in settings as widely different as the New Guinea highlands and the west coast of Ireland. Anthropologists have also experimented with controlled elicitation in interviews to probe cultural dimensions of emotions. On the other hand, efforts to translate many psychological instruments for use in radically different cultural settings have often failed. For example, Robert Barrett (1997), an anthropologist and psychiatrist who has worked extensively with the Iban of Borneo, has noted that Western assumptions about the nature of mental illness have so shaped commonly used psychiatric examination protocols that the responses of his Iban informants to carefully translated questions could not be used to assess their mental state.

Anthropology of Western Emotion

Anthropological research points up the ethnocentrism implicit in a great deal of research on emotion, research that employs, often subtly or unknowingly, assumptions about emotion that are in fact uniquely Western. Among these assumptions is the separation of cognition from affect, or thinking from feeling, treating each term of the distinction as a distinct form of mental behavior. Moreover, Western (especially American) culture links cognition/thought to male gender, and affect/emotion to female gender; this cultural distinction is then used to justify gender-role associations and is even biologized by locating the supposed source of female emotionality in those unique physiological features that define biological female sex.

Western individualism is probably related to the additional cultural assumption that emotions are experiences that occur inside individuals and that even though they are often provoked by social events, an emotion itself is separable from the social context of its production. Anthropologists have noted that grief is regarded in the West as a response to social circumstances, such as death, but is experienced "inside" the grieving person. In such contexts, the grieving person typically believes that it is their grief—the emotion itself—that they must come to cope with and overcome. Donald Pollock (1993) reported that the Kulina Indians of Brazil, like members of many other cultures, offer the startling image of, apparently, a highly choreographed form of grief in which a death, for example, provokes a chorus of ritualized wailing and physical mutilation that, after a conventional period of time, suddenly ends. The Kulina expression of grief easily appears to Westerners as somehow false and purely theatrical, but the Kulina experience of grief focuses on the social circumstances of, in this case, a death and thus ends when those circumstances have been played out and finally resolved. Such examples suggest that the American experience of grief submerges the salience of the social circumstances and instead makes the experience an individual task— "grief work"—that is consistent with American values of individualism, productivity and work, and accomplishment through overcoming adversity. Anthropologists have begun to caution against the naive extension of Western conceptions of emotion, many of which have embedded within them cultural meanings that may not be apparent even to the Western researcher.

Anthropology of Disordered Emotions

Anthropological interest in emotion has also extended to the "pathologies" of emotion and their cultural shaping. At the forefront of this work is Arthur Kleinman (1986), an anthropologist and psychiatrist who has studied "neurasthenia" (a condition of weakness or exhaustion of the nervous system) extensively in China. Kleinman has noted that neurasthenia has all but disappeared in the United States and Europe since the late nineteenth century, while "depression" —the clinical disorder—has appeared to replace it; in China, depression is rare, while neurasthenia is common. The difference is not merely one of translation; neurasthenia is regarded as, and is experienced as, a physical ailment, while in the West, depression is regarded as and is experienced as a mental ailment, though it may have physical symptoms. Kleinman argues that the physicalization of neurasthenia in China has important political dimensions in a country where materialist ideology might render a "mental" illness politically suspect. Kleinman proposes that a "core depressive syndrome" is probably universal among human beings. Cultures interpret this syndrome along a continuum of physical to mental (and perhaps spiritual), so members of many cultures experience the syndrome as a physical ailment such as neurasthenia, while a small number of cultures construct the syndrome in such a way that their members experience it at least in part as a "mental" ailment. Some cases of chronic fatigue syndrome that resemble neurasthenia might be understood as a modern Western experience of this core depressive syndrome in physicalized terms, especially among people for whom a "mental" disorder would be highly stigmatizing.

While depression has been a convenient affective disorder to study anthropologically (in large part because its expression and subjective experience are highly sensitive to cultural shaping), anthropologists have studied a variety of other affective disorders in both Western and non-Western cultures. Anxiety disorders, for example, have proven equally sensitive to cultural influence and make up much of what are regarded as "culture-bound syndromes," disorders that are relatively unique to a few cultures. *Koro*, for instance, found in several Asian cultures, is expressed as a pathological fear among its male victims that the penis will retract into the body with a variety of harmful effects. Among Northern Algonkian Indians in Canada, Witigo, or "Windigo psychosis," is a pathological fear of being possessed by a Witigo cannibal spirit, which would produce an uncontrollable desire to kill and eat one's family members. Among many Hispanic cultures, mothers report that their infant children suffer "caida de mollera," or "fallen fontanel," which is typically an expression of the mother's anxiety about her maternal skills. In each case, the disorder reveals how cultural values shape the experience and understanding of emotions such as anxiety.

Conclusion

Anthropological interest in emotion is long-standing, but since the mid-1980s, it has undergone rapid expansion as anthropologists have increasingly turned their attention to cultural conceptions of personhood and as they have begun to explore new ways to think about individual development in its social and cultural context. This research has revealed a wide variety of ways in which other cultures understand emotion and attach meaning to it. It has also led Western scientists to be cautious about generalizing their own implicit assumptions about emotion when researching non-Western cultures.

See also: CROSS-CULTURAL PATTERNS; CULTURE-BOUND SYNDROMES; MOOD DISORDERS; UNIVERSALITY OF EMOTIONAL EXPRESSION

Bibliography

Abu-Lughod, Lila. (1986). *Veiled Sentiments: Honor and Poetry in a Bedouin Society.* Berkeley: University of California Press.

Barrett, Robert J. (1997). "Kurt Schneider in Borneo: Do First-Rank Symptoms of Schizophrenia Apply to the Iban?" Paper presented at the December meeting of the American Anthropological Association, Washington, DC.

Benedict, Ruth. (1934). *Patterns of Culture.* New York: Houghton Mifflin.

Briggs, Jean L. (1970). *Never in Anger: Portrait of an Eskimo Family.* Cambridge, MA: Harvard University Press.

D'Andrade, Roy, and Strauss, Claudia, eds. (1992). *Human Motives and Cultural Models.* Cambridge, Eng.: Cambridge University Press.

Durkheim, Emile. ([1912] 1995). *The Elementary Forms of Religious Life,* tr. Karen E. Fields. New York: Free Press.

Kleinman, Arthur. (1986). *The Social Origins of Distress and Disease.* New Haven, CT: Yale University Press.

Kleinman, Arthur, and Good, Byron. (1985). *Culture and Depression: Studies in the Anthropology and Cross-Cultural Psychiatry of Affect and Disorder.* Berkeley: University of California Press.

Kroeber, Alfred L. (1952). "Classificatory Systems of Relationships." In *The Nature of Culture,* ed. Alfred L. Kroeber. Chicago: University of Chicago Press.

Lessa, William. (1966). *Ulithi: A Micronesian Design for Living.* New York: Holt, Rhinehart, and Winston.

Levy, Robert. (1973). *Tahitians: Mind and Experience in the Society Islands.* Chicago: University of Chicago Press.

Levy, Robert, and Wellenkamp, Jane. (1987). "Methodology in the Anthropological Study of Emotion." In *The Measurement of Emotions,* ed. Robert Plutchik and Henry Kellerman. New York: Academic Press.

Lutz, Catherine. (1988). *Unnatural Emotions.* Chicago: University of Chicago Press.

Lutz, Catherine, and White, Geoffrey. (1986). "The Anthropology of Emotions." In *Annual Review of Anthropology, Vol. 15,* ed. Bernard Seigel. Palo Alto, CA: Annual Reviews.

Malinowski, Bronislaw. (1948). *Magic, Science, and Religion.* Glencoe, IL: Free Press.

Mead, Margaret. (1928). *Coming of Age in Samoa.* New York: Macmillan.

Nuckolls, Charles. (1996). *The Cultural Dialectics of Knowledge and Desire.* Madison: University of Wisconsin Press.

Pollock, Donald. (1993). "Death and the Afterdeath among the Kulina." *Latin American Anthropology Review* 5(2):61–64.

Radcliffe-Brown, A. R. (1952). *Structure and Function in Primitive Society.* Glencoe, IL: Free Press.

Rosenberg, Daniel. (1990). "Language in the Discourse of the Emotions." In *Language and the Politics of Emotion,* ed. Catherine Lutz and Lila Abu-Lughod. Cambridge, Eng.: Cambridge University Press.

Schwartz, Theodore; White, Geoffrey; and Lutz, Catherine, eds. (1991). *New Directions in Psychological Anthropology.* Cambridge, Eng.: Cambridge University Press.

Donald Pollock

ANXIETY

The twentieth century has been labeled "The Age of Anxiety." The threat of nuclear war, biological weapons, global warming, and AIDS, as well as other threats to public health and the environment, all create significant concerns for large numbers of people. Sarah Dunant and Roy Porter (1996, p. xi) note too that the "sense of helplessness is not limited to the environment or acts of random violence. For many people in the western world the unprecedented expansion of everything from technology through communication to shopping has brought with it not only increased demands of choice (in itself something of an anxiety) but also an expanding potential for feeling out of control."

Since 1950, a considerable amount of scholarly research has examined the nature, causes, and effects of anxiety. Psychologist Rollo May (1977, p. xiii) observed that "there has been an enormous amount of research and interest in anxiety. In contrast to the fact that only two books were written on anxiety before 1950, a score of volumes were published [between 1950 and 1977]. And in contrast to the half-dozen papers exploring the subject before 1950, it has been estimated that at least 6,000 studies and dissertations on anxiety and tangential subjects [appeared between 1950 and 1977]." Since May made that observation in 1977, scholarly interest in anxiety has dramatically increased. Today, there are professional journals, such as *Anxiety Disorders* and the *Journal of Anxiety Disorders,* that are devoted exclusively to the publication of theory and research on anxiety.

Anxiety is a common emotional response to many life experiences. The prospect of public speaking, a job interview, severe weather, and riding in an airplane are situations that arouse anxiety in many people. While the causes of anxiety may vary from individual to individual or culture to culture, everyone experiences anxiety from time to time. It is an emotional response that, in extreme cases, can have a profound and debilitating effect on the individual.

The Nature of Anxiety

Anxiety is a complex human emotion. This complexity is revealed in the lack of a consensus among researchers and philosophers regarding a definition for the emotion. Furthermore, as psychologist Richard Hallam (1992) notes, definitions do not always agree with the complexity and nuances of anxiety experienced by clinicians working with individuals who have anxiety disorders. According to Hallam, the term *anxiety* can refer to the behavioral and physiological responses directly caused by a situation, an appraisal of the responses and their effects, a person's intentions toward a situation, and a person's evaluation of the resources available for dealing with the situation.

The complexities of anxiety as an emotion stem, in part, from its association with other emotions, especially fear. Psychologist Carroll Izard (1977) contends that the term *anxiety* is rather imprecise, referring to a wide range of affect combinations that involve fear. According to Izard, anxiety involves a combination of fundamental emotions, including fear and two or more of the emotions of anger, shame/shyness, distress, guilt, and interest/excitement. Izard maintains that these six emotions are variable components of a complex pattern. The relative importance of these emotions in the anxiety pattern varies with the individual and his or her life situation. Izard further maintains that these individual variations in the pattern of emotions involved with anxiety are a function of both hereditary and experiential determinants.

Anxiety may be conceptualized as a transitory state (state anxiety) or as a personality trait (trait anxiety). The distinction between state anxiety and trait anxiety centers on time or duration of the emotion experience. State anxiety is a temporary condition that occurs in selected situations. For example, public speaking causes many people to experience state anxiety; it is only in this situation that they find themselves feeling anxious. Trait anxiety, on the other hand, refers to one's proneness to experience state anxiety. Trait anxiety is a personality characteristic that predisposes one to experience state anxiety in a wide range of situations. Psychologist Michael Eysenck (1992) contends that a person high in trait anxiety is one who has highly developed danger-detection processes that cause the individual to become hypervi-

gilant and grossly exaggerate the number and severity of threatening or dangerous events in the environment. The primary focus in this entry, however, is state anxiety.

Central to the understanding of anxiety is the concept of threat. Anxiety is aroused when some characteristic of a situation is perceived as being threatening. Psychologist Charles Spielberger (1976, p. 5) notes that "the appraisal of a particular situation as threatening will be determined by the objective stimulus characteristics of the situation, the individual's experience with similar situations, and the memories or thoughts that are reintegrated or evoked by the situation." Some threats are unique to an individual, while others may be shared by individuals within a group, an organization, a region, a culture, or a nation. For example, uncertainty about an upcoming exam or public speaking engagement may create anxiety for an individual. Work groups may experience anxiety regarding an impending project deadline. People who live in a certain city or region of a state may experience anxiety over some environmental concern, such as contamination of the ground water. At a global level, the changes in weather patterns, such as El Nino, or the testing of nuclear weapons may cause large groups of people to experience anxiety when their thoughts are directed to these uncertain situations.

Hallam (1992) suggests that threats may be physical, social, psychological, or material in nature. Physical threats center on one's health and welfare. That death or injury may result from severe weather, riding in an airplane, or swimming in a lake or pond creates anxiety for some people. Psychological threats center on one's emotional well-being. Situations where one, or one's loved one, may feel embarrassed or experience a loss of self-esteem may be very threatening to some people. The prospect of being rejected socially, a concern for public speakers, may be a threat that results in anxiety. Finally, anxiety may result when certain material possessions or earnings are threatened.

The term *stress* is used to refer to the objective properties of a situation that are characterized by some degree of psychological or physical danger, whereas threat refers to the "perception" of a situation as being more or less dangerous or personally threatening. Spielberger (1976, p. 5) offers this comparison of the concepts:

> Situations that are objectively stressful are likely to be perceived as threatening by most people, but whether or not a particular person will interpret a specific situation as threatening will depend upon that individual's subjective (idiosyncratic) appraisal of the situation. Thus, a stressful situation may not be perceived as threatening by an individual who either does not recognize the inherent dan-

An anxious woman holds up a picture of a relative who was displaced by the Turkish invasion of Cyprus in October 1974. (Corbis/David Rubinger)

ger, or has the necessary skills and experience to cope with it.

Complex cognitive processes are associated with anxiety. Eysenck (1992, p. 101) contends that worry is the cognitive component of anxiety and "occurs in response to the actual or potential non-achievement of goals associated with major sources of life satisfaction," including the domestic, social, and work areas of life. Chronic worry is seen by the American Psychiatric Association (1994) to be the central feature of generalized anxiety disorder (GAD), a condition in which one frequently or excessively contemplates various negative future events that most likely will not occur. Studies of GAD patients suggest that worry may serve a number of functions for the individual. Psychologists Graham Davey and Frank Tallis (1994) note that worriers believe that their worry will make a feared event less likely to occur, that worrying will generate strategies for avoiding some feared event, that worrying may serve to distract one from contemplating other more emotional issues, that worrying helps prepare one for the occurrence of an event, and that worrying serves to motivate one to perform certain tasks that must be addressed given that some event will occur. As with anxiety, worry may be experienced as a temporary state or as a pathological condition.

While anxiety may appear to be closely related to fear, there are important distinctions between the two concepts. Spielberger (1976, p. 6) distinguishes between fear and anxiety as follows:

Fear generally denotes an emotional reaction to the anticipation of injury or harm from some real, objective danger in the external environment. Another defining characteristic of fear is that the intensity of a fear reaction is proportional to the magnitude of the danger that evokes it. In contrast, anxiety is traditionally regarded as an "objectless" emotional reaction because either the stimulus conditions that evoke it are unknown or the intensity of the emotional reaction is disproportionately greater that the magnitude of the objective danger. Thus, the traditional distinction between fear and anxiety is based on the assumption that similar emotional reactions result from the operation of different mediating processes.

Causes of Anxiety

Are human emotions learned or are they innate? This question has been the source of considerable debate among researchers and philosophers for more than one hundred years. Some, such as Charles Darwin (1872), argue that biological forces are responsible for the presence of human emotions, while others, such as Ray Birdwhistell (1970), maintain that emotion expressions are learned much the same way that language is learned. Yet others, such as psychologist Paul Ekman (1978), maintain that human emotions involve both an innate and a learned component. Existing theory and research suggest that both nature and nurture are responsible for emotion experiences and responses. Nature programs individuals to experience certain emotions, while nurture or socialization

The playwright Tennessee Williams portrays anxiety-ridden characters in several of his plays. In A Streetcar Named Desire *(1947), anxiety about her promiscuous past, her loss of the family home, and her uncertain present finally pushes Blanche DuBois over the edge, and she is taken away to a mental institution, where she must depend upon the kindness of strangers.*

processes determine which emotion they will experience in any given situation and how they will express that emotion.

The argument that human emotions are biologically determined can be traced to Darwin's classic 1872 book *The Expression of the Emotions in Man and Animals*. In this work, Darwin argued that human emotions evolved or were shaped by a process of natural selection because they provided survival value for the species. He reasoned that fear, for example, evolved as an adaptive response to dangerous situations. Humans and other animals need to recognize dangerous situations and respond accordingly (e.g., fight or flight).

Hallam (1992) maintains that humans may be biologically predisposed to a number of physical and social threats. Physical conditions that present threats to humans include extreme cold and heat; very loud sounds; loss of support; pain; heights; bright, open spaces; darkness; confinement in small spaces; unknown or new objects, places, or sensations; sudden movements; and small animals and insects. The social conditions that humans, especially children, are predisposed to fear include interactions with strangers, touch from strangers, being alone, and being looked at by others. From an evolutionary perspective, then, humans appear to be programmed to experience anxiety in certain situations.

Some threats are learned through personal experiences and observations of others. James C. McCroskey (1984) maintains, for example, that reinforcement patterns in a person's environment, particularly during childhood, are responsible for the development of communication anxiety in many individuals. People learn to feel threatened or helpless when participating in a job interview, talking to superiors, and talking to strangers on the telephone, as well as in a variety of other situations.

Human emotions are manifested through patterns of overt behavior. Mark Knapp and Judith Hall (1992) note that the face is a rich source of information regarding the type and intensity of felt emotions. Paralinguistic cues (i.e., the non-content aspects of speech such as speech rate, intensity, and pitch) also provide meaningful signals of emotions. While there is consid-

erable evidence to show that overt expressions of emotion are consistent across cultures of the world, people learn display rules to manage their emotion expressions. Display rules are prescriptions regarding the extent to which individuals should mask (i.e., replace the expression of one emotion with another different emotion), neutralize (i.e., show no emotion), intensify (i.e., show more of the emotion than what was experienced) or de-intensify (i.e., show less of the emotion than what was experienced) their overt expressions of emotions. In some situations, an ability to mask or neutralize feelings of anxiety may be in one's best interest. In employment interviews, for example, a job candidate who appears overly anxious may cause the interviewer to perceive him or her as being immature and lacking confidence. With practice, one can learn to suppress or control various verbal and nonverbal behaviors that may signal anxiety. A study by Jinni Harrigan and Kristy Taing (1997) revealed that research participants who were high in state anxiety were able to mask their anxiety from judges—the judges were unable to distinguish between participants who were low in state anxiety and those who were high in state anxiety.

Three Components of Anxiety

Existing theory and research suggests that human emotions involve the interaction of three systems. When people experience an emotion, such as anxiety, a complex interaction of physiological activity, cognitive activity, and overt behavior takes place.

Researchers have long recognized that certain physiological changes occur during emotion experiences. In describing fear, Darwin (1872, p. 290) noted the following:

> The heart beats quickly and violently, so that it palpitates or knocks against the ribs; but it is very doubtful whether it then works more efficiently than usual, so as to send a greater supply of blood to all parts of the body; for the skin instantly becomes pale, as during incipient faintness. This paleness of the surface, however, is probably in large part, or exclusively, due to the vaso-motor center being affected in such a manner as to cause the contraction of the small arteries of the skin.

During periods of anxiety, an individual is in a heightened state of vigilance as the body prepares itself for a response. Hallam (1992, p. 12) writes,

> The event that threatens has not yet occurred and there is uncertainty as to when it will occur, how bad it will be, and whether it will be possible to deal adequately with it. The organism is attentive to all stimulus changes and responds by orientation to the source of change. There is an increased readiness to startle and orientation to stimulus change or signs of threat momentarily stops the or-

ganism in its tracks. The heart rate slows down and peripheral blood vessels constrict, resisting the flow of blood, thereby increasing blood pressure. These physiological changes function to prepare the organism for defensive action; blood flow is increased to the skeletal muscles and glucose and fatty acids are released from tissue as energy sources.

According to Mark Leary and Robin Kowalski (1995), a number of changes in the autonomic nervous system (which controls a number of involuntary responses, such as heart rate, respiration, blood pressure, digestion, and muscle tension) are associated with anxiety. During periods of increased anxiety, there is an increase in heart rate, respiration, and muscle tone. A tingling in the hands and feet, weakness of the limbs, a sinking feeling in the stomach, dryness in the throat and mouth, pale sweaty skin, dilated pupils, blurred vision, and feeling faint are also associated with anxiety.

Eysenck (1992) asserts that cognitive processes play an integral role in the anxiety experience. Anxiety results from one's appraisal of potentially threatening situations. The perceived inability to address or confront a threatening situation adequately or effectively results in anxiety. Hence, an individual's thoughts, beliefs, assumptions, interpretations, and expectations regarding life events play an important role in producing (and/or mediating) anxiety responses. Misinformation, lack of awareness, and irrational beliefs may be the source of some anxieties. For example, many people experience stage fright because they maintain a number of illogical or irrational beliefs about how an audience will perceive them (e.g., "If I make one mistake, I'll be ruined" or "I know I'm going to mess up"). Such thinking establishes a set of negative expectations and causes the speaker to perceive and interpret relatively minor errors as major shortcomings in a presentation. Cognitive processes play such an important role in mediating anxiety responses to situations that one major approach to treating or coping with anxiety requires one to develop new ways of thinking, interpreting or evaluating threatening situations.

Anxiety, like other emotions, may reveal itself through patterns of verbal and nonverbal behavior. Communication researchers Judee Burgoon, David Buller, and W. Gill Woodall (1996) note that a number of nonverbal behaviors are associated with anxiety. These behaviors include increases in random hand and foot movements, indirect body orientation, excessive self-touching, gaze avoidance, postural tension, indirect body orientation, and leaning away. In addition, anxiety may influence speech disruptions. Knapp and Hall (1992) point out that anxiety may cause one to stutter, to change sentences abruptly, to repeat words in a sentence, to omit words, to present incomplete sentences, and to introduce incoherent sounds within a sentence. The severity with which speech is disrupted will vary with the intensity of the felt anxiety —the more intense the anxiety experience, the more speech disruptions one would expect.

Consequences

Anxiety may have a number of negative consequences. The effects of anxiety will depend, however, upon a number of factors, such as the intensity of the anxiety response, the duration of the response, the nature of the threat precipitating the response, and methods or strategies available for coping with a threat.

Given that the perception of threat is central to the experience of anxiety, a common method of coping with anxiety involves avoidance behavior. To avoid threats, individuals avoid people, places, and things that present threats to them. John Madden, former National Football League coach and television announcer, is afraid to fly. Despite a rigorous work schedule and the obvious convenience that air travel would provide him, Madden prefers to travel across the United States by bus. Most colleges and universities offer a course in human communication that typically includes a unit on public speaking. Many of the students who withdraw from this course experience high levels of speech anxiety, a form of state anxiety that results from the prospect of real or imagined public speaking. Thus, unless one is able to develop mechanisms for coping with it, anxiety may cause one to avoid a variety of meaningful, rewarding, and enriching experiences.

Anxiety may negatively affect one's ability to perform various cognitive tasks. Eysenck (1992, p. 126) notes that "very high levels of state anxiety cause a general impairment in virtually all aspects of information processing." Irwin Sarason's (1988) interference theory maintains that worry, the cognitive aspect of anxiety, adversely affects one's ability to attend to a task. The research of Michael Humphreys and William Revelle (1984) suggests that anxiety adversely affects cognitive performance by disrupting short-term memory processes.

Robert Edelmann (1992) points out that chronic anxiety is associated with a number of physical ailments and diseases, such as asthma, gastrointestinal disease, and cardiovascular disease. Anxiety may be related to illness in two ways. First, the stress caused by chronic anxiety may make one susceptible to illness. Second, anxiety may occur as a result of illness or disease.

Anxiety experienced during social interactions may have a number of negative consequences for an individual. Social anxiety refers to feelings of apprehension, dread, and nervousness that arise in a wide range of social situations, from talking to one's superior, giving a speech at a parent-teacher association meeting, participating in job interviews, to conducting one-time conversations with strangers. Leary and Kowalski (1995, p. 6) maintain that social anxiety results from "the prospect or presence of interpersonal evaluation in real or imagined social settings." According to Leary and Kowalski, two conditions must both be present for an individual to experience social anxiety. First, one must be motivated to manage a particular impression, and second, the individual must feel that he or she will be unsuccessful in managing the desired impression. In an employment interview, for example, a job candidate typically wants the interviewer to perceive him or her to be, among other things, industrious, knowledgeable, and friendly. Social anxiety will result if the candidate does not believe that he or she will make the desired impression. If the candidate (a) does not care about the impression created or (b) feels confident that he or she will create the desired impression, social anxiety will not result.

Social anxiety is a significant problem for many people. A study by psychologist Phillip Zimbardo (1977) revealed that more than 90 percent of all Americans feel shy from time to time. Leary and Kowalski (1995) report that approximately one-third of the college students in the United States feel nervous when interacting with people of the opposite sex and that 20 percent of all adults report an excessively high level of concern or apprehension about public speaking. Approximately 2 percent of all adults are so chronically nervous in social situations that they may be classified as being social phobic. In a study of college students conducted by Dan Russell, Carolyn Cutrona, and Warren Jones (1986), 80 percent of the respondents reported that interactions with strangers and authority figures made them feel shy.

A considerable amount of research has examined the social-psychological consequences and correlates of social anxiety. The results of this research depict a rather bleak picture of the socially anxious individual. In their review of this literature, communication researchers John Daly and Laura Stafford (1984) report that social anxiety is consistently and negatively related to self-esteem and positively related to loneliness. Individuals who have high social anxiety (compared to those who have low social anxiety) are perceived by others to be less socially and interpersonally attractive, less credible, less friendly, less assertive, more detached, and less competent in communication. These individuals who have high social anxiety report having fewer friends and more difficulty establishing heterosexual relationships than do their counterparts who have low social anxiety.

Individual Differences

Given the biological basis of human emotions, all people should be expected to report similar experiential qualities for a given emotion. That is, the experience of anxiety in men should not differ from that in women. In addition, anxiety in the United States is experienced in the same way that anxiety is experienced in Australia. What does vary from person to person or from culture to culture, however, are (a) the stressors that may be perceived as threatening and (b) the rules for managing overt expressions of emotion.

The perception of threat is likely to vary significantly from individual to individual. A number of factors, such as age, sex, education, and ethnic background, may influence one's beliefs and expectations that may, in turn, influence one's perceptions of threat. Some people are threatened by insects, while others are not. What creates anxiety in Kenya may not arouse anxiety in Canada. Likewise, what children find threatening may not be cause for concern in adults. For example, many children are threatened by dark places and separation from significant others.

Individuals differ in their ability to manage the overt behaviors that are associated with anxiety. The ability to manage emotion expressions is a communication skill. In some social situations, such as an employment interview, one must mask or neutralize anxiety expressions to create and maintain a favorable impression. Research by Ross Buck, Robert Miller, and William Caul (1974) suggests that women may be more skilled than men at controlling facial expressions of emotion.

People also vary in trait anxiety, one's proneness to experience anxiety. While some research suggests that hereditary factors may play a role in shaping one's level of trait anxiety, environmental forces that shape one's cognitive processing are considered to play a major role in determining proneness to anxiety. Eysenck (1992) believes that the experience of an individual in a certain stressful situation affects the information concerning that event that is stored in long-term memory, which will in turn affect that person's susceptibility to anxiety when placed in a similar situation.

Ernest Hemingway, in "A Clean, Well-Lighted Place" (1933), describes the anxiety that an old man feels about facing nada *(nothingness) and the darkness that night brings. The old man wants to stay up all night drinking in a clean, well-lighted place so he will not have to face the emptiness and meaninglessness that is suggested by the night. His anxiety is shared by many people who are afraid of the dark, including the old waiter who tells the story.*

Coping with Anxiety

It should be noted that not all anxiety is negative or dysfunctional. In some situations, as in sports, a moderate amount of anxiety may be optimal. Spielberger (1989) notes that high levels of state anxiety typically interfere with performance, whereas low levels of state anxiety often create motivation problems in athletes. In other situations, however, anxiety may adversely affect one's ability to concentrate and solve problems. For these situations, the following three general types of strategies have been used to manage anxiety effectively: cognitive therapy, relaxation training, and skill training.

Given the fact that anxiety results from how individuals evaluate a situation, the way people think about threats plays a critical role in whether or not they experience anxiety. One way to reduce the anxiety experienced in some situations involves changing the way one thinks about perceived threats. The goal of cognitive therapy (including cognitive restructuring and rational-emotive therapy) is to identify negative, irrational, and unrealistic thoughts and expectations for a particular situation and replace them with more positive, rational, and logical thoughts that are also more productive.

A second approach to managing anxiety involves relaxation training. For some people, the assessment that a situation is threatening can lead to an extremely high level of physiological arousal. In severe cases, one may become incapacitated by the arousal. Therefore, one must learn to relax. In cue-controlled relaxation, one learns how to relax muscles and pair a specific word with being in a relaxed state. Through training, the cue word produces relaxation. Systematic desensitization, another technique that involves relaxation training, has been used to treat a wide range of anxiety disorders.

A third approach to managing anxiety involves learning new skills to eliminate the threat presented by certain situations. Leary and Kowalski (1995, p. 185) note that "people with poor interpersonal skills are more likely to experience social anxiety than socially skilled people." In the case of social anxiety, social skills training develops confidence that, in turn, leads one to perceive social interactions as being less threatening.

Generalized Anxiety Disorder

The major concern of this entry has been anxiety as an emotional state, a temporary affective response to some situation. The experience of state anxiety is a rather common and natural occurrence in everyday life. However, anxiety can become a long-term experience, lasting for more than a month, and be severely debilitating. In such cases, the anxiety may be considered a disorder. Psychologists Jerry Deffenbacher and Richard Suinn (1987, p. 332) offer the following assessment of one such condition:

> Individuals with a generalized anxiety disorder (GAD) experience a chronic, persistent anxiety. The anxiety tends to be moderate in intensity, although it may spike upward at times, and is usually pervasive across time and situations. Because it does not appear to be related to specific situations or external stressors, it has sometimes been labeled "general" or "free-floating." Individuals with GAD experience a kind of chronic cloud of arousal, doom, and apprehension that seems to follow them everywhere, ebbing somewhat from time-to-time, but never leaving for very long.

Individuals who experience GAD appear to engage in excessive or unrealistic worry for long periods of time. These concerns generally center on family issues, finances, and personal illness.

Estimates regarding the prevalence of GAD in the general population vary. Edelmann (1992) reports data suggesting a prevalence rate of 2.3 to 6.4 percent. Edelmann also notes that the prevalence rate of GAD appears to be higher for women than for men.

See also: ANXIETY DISORDERS; DEFENSE MECHANISMS; FEAR AND PHOBIAS; GUILT; HELPLESSNESS; SHYNESS; STRESS

Bibliography

American Psychiatric Association. (1994). *Diagnostic and Statistical Manual of Mental Disorders,* 4th ed. Washington, DC: American Psychiatric Association.

Birdwhistell, Ray. (1970). *Kinesics and Context: Essays on Body Motion Communication.* Philadelphia: University of Pennsylvania Press.

Booth-Butterfield, Melanie, ed. (1991). *Communication, Cognition, and Anxiety.* Newbury Park, CA: Sage Publications.

Buck, Ross; Miller, Robert E.; and Caul, William F. (1974). "Sex, Personality, and Physiological Variables in the Communication of Affect via Facial Expression." *Journal of Personality and Social Psychology* 30:587–596.

Burgoon, Judee K.; Buller, David B; and Woodall, W. Gill. (1996). *Nonverbal Communication: The Unspoken Dialogue,* 2nd ed. New York: McGraw-Hill.

Daly, John, and Stafford, Laura. (1984). "Correlates and Consequences of Social Anxiety." In *Avoiding Communication: Shyness, Reticence, and Communication Apprehension,* ed. John A. Daly and James C. McCroskey. Beverly Hills, CA: Sage Publications.

Darwin, Charles. ([1872] 1965). *The Expression of the Emotions in Man and Animals.* Chicago: University of Chicago Press.

Davey, Graham, and Tallis, Frank, eds. (1994). *Worrying: Perspectives on Theory, Assessment, and Treatment.* New York: Wiley.

Deffenbacher, Jerry L., and Suinn, Richard M. (1987). "Generalized Anxiety Syndrome." In *Anxiety and Stress Disorders: Cognitive-Behavioral Assessment and Treatment,* ed. Larry Michelson and L. Michael Ascher. New York: Guilford.

Dunant, Sarah, and Porter, Roy, eds. (1996). *The Age of Anxiety.* London: Virago.

Edelmann, Robert J. (1992). *Anxiety: Theory, Research, and Intervention in Clinical and Health Psychology.* New York: Wiley.

Ekman, Paul. (1978). "Facial Expressions." In *Nonverbal Behavior and Communication,* ed. Aaron W. Siegman and Stanley Feldstein. Hillsdale, NJ: Lawrence Erlbaum.

Eysenck, Michael W. (1992). *Anxiety: The Cognitive Perspective.* Hove, Eng.: Lawrence Erlbaum.

Friedrich, Gustav, and Goss, Blaine. (1984). "Systematic Desensitization." In *Avoiding Communication: Shyness, Reticence, and Communication Apprehension,* ed. John A. Daly and James C. McCroskey. Beverly Hills, CA: Sage Publications.

Goodwin, Donald G. (1986). *Anxiety.* New York: Oxford University Press.

Hallam, Richard. (1992). *Counseling for Anxiety Problems.* Newbury Park, CA: Sage Publications.

Harrigan, Jinni A., and Taing, Kristy T. (1997). "Fooled by a Smile: Detecting Anxiety in Others." *Journal of Nonverbal Behavior* 21:203–221.

Humphreys, Michael S., and Revelle, William. (1984). "Personality, Motivation, and Performance: A Theory of the Relationship between Individual Differences and Information Processing." *Psychological Review* 91:153–184.

Izard, Carroll E. (1977). *Human Emotions.* New York: Plenum.

Knapp, Mark L., and Hall, Judith A. (1992). *Nonverbal Communication in Human Interaction,* 3rd ed. New York: Harcourt Brace Jovanovich.

Lang, Peter J. (1985). "The Cognitive Psychophysiology of Emotion: Fear and Anxiety." In *Anxiety and Anxiety Disorders,* ed. A. Hussain Tuma and Jack D. Maser. Hillsdale, NJ: Lawrence Erlbaum.

Last, Cynthia G., ed. (1993). *Anxiety across the Lifespan: A Developmental Perspective.* New York: Springer.

Leary, Mark R., and Kowalski, Robin M. (1995). *Social Anxiety.* New York: Guilford.

MacLeod, Colin, and Donnellan, Avonia M. (1993). "Individual Differences in Anxiety and the Restriction of Working Memory Capacity." *Personality and Individual Differences* 15:163–173.

May, Rollo. (1977). *The Meaning of Anxiety.* New York: W. W. Norton.

McCroskey, James C. (1984). "The Communication Apprehension Perspective." In *Avoiding Communication: Shyness, Reticence, and Communication Apprehension,* ed. John A. Daly and James C. McCroskey. Beverly Hills, CA: Sage Publications.

Russell, Dan; Cutrona, Carolyn E.; and Jones, Warren H. (1986). "A Trait-Situational Analysis of Shyness." In *Shyness: Perspectives on Research and Treatment,* ed. Warren H. Jones, Jonathan M. Cheek, and Stephen R. Briggs. New York: Plenum.

Sanderson, William C., and Barlow, David H. (1990). "A Description of Patients With DSM-III-Revised Generalized Anxiety Disorder." *Journal of Nervous and Mental Disease* 178:588–591.

Sarason, Irwin G. (1988). "Anxiety, Self-Preoccupation, and Attention." *Anxiety Research* 1:3–7.

Silverstein, Shel. (1974). *Where the Sidewalk Ends.* New York: HarperCollins.

Spielberger, Charles D. (1976). "The Nature and Measurement of Anxiety." In *Cross-Cultural Anxiety,* ed. Charles D. Spielberger and Rogelio Diaz-Guerrero. Washington, DC: Hemisphere.

Spielberger, Charles D. (1989). "Stress and Anxiety in Sports." In *Anxiety in Sports: An International Perspective,* ed. Dieter Hackfort and Charles D. Spielberger. Washington, DC: Hemisphere.

Spielberger, Charles D., and Vagg, Peter R., eds. (1995). *Test*

Anxiety: Theory, Assessment, and Treatment. Washington, DC: Taylor & Francis.

Zimbardo, Phillip. (1977). *Shyness.* New York: Jove.

Mark E. Comadena

ANXIETY DISORDERS

The experiences of fear and anxiety are common, typically temporary, and have survival value in that they motivate "fight-flight" responses to danger. Normal anxiety and anxiety disorders vary along a continuum, with the degree of distress and interference with daily life distinguishing between what is normal and adaptive and what is dysfunctional. For some people, anxiety can become so problematic that they can be said to have an anxiety disorder. Disorders of this type are among the most common mental health problems, and a large proportion of health resources are spent on dealing with anxiety and its associated problems.

Diagnostic Features of Anxiety Disorders

The most common diagnostic systems in use are the *Diagnostic and Statistical Manual of Mental Disorders* (DSM-IV) of the American Psychiatric Association and the *International Classification of Diseases* (ICD) of the World Health Organization. In determining whether a problem warrants a formal diagnosis as an anxiety disorder, the clinician using these systems will consider the specific symptoms, the duration of the problem (which must have lasted a minimum length of time in order to avoid transient fears receiving a formal diagnosis), the interference caused by the problem, and whether the anxiety can be better explained by another problem such as drug abuse or a medical condition.

The DSM-IV discriminates between anxiety disorders that typically begin in childhood or adolescence and those usually diagnosed in adulthood. However, children can be diagnosed with any of the adult categories, and only one disorder is specific to children and adolescents: separation anxiety disorder. This disorder results from undue anxiety regarding separation from significant figures in the child's life. The child's reaction to such separations is beyond that expected for his or her developmental level (i.e., most children show transient separation fears in early childhood).

The anxiety disorders of adulthood include: agoraphobia, panic disorder, specific phobias, social phobias, and generalized anxiety disorder. Agoraphobia is a morbid fear and avoidance of public places such as shopping centers and public transport. Although the problem may be based on a previous experience of having suffered a panic attack in such places, panic is no longer a feature; a long standing pattern of avoidance is the primary manifestation. Panic disorder (with or without agoraphobia) is the repeated experience of uncontrollable panic attacks not associated with specific phobic stimuli (i.e., appear to come out of the blue) characterized by heart palpitations, sweating, breathing problems, nausea, and shaking, as well as thoughts of losing control, having a heart attack or stroke, and dying. Those individuals who exhibit panic disorder without agoraphobia show no secondary avoidance of particular places associated with the panic. Those individuals who also suffer from agoraphobia avoid certain places because they fear the onset of a panic attack, which they associate with those places. Sufferers develop a sensitivity to internal arousal that signals the possibility of a panic attack. Thus, any signs of bodily changes due to exertion, loss of breath, excitement, anger, and so on can come to elicit panic; often described as "fear of fear." Specific or simple phobias result from specific stimuli. These phobias tend to parallel the fears people normally have throughout the life span, except the phobias lead to a greater degree of fear and significant impairment. The most common stimuli for specific phobias include medical procedures, needles, blood, injury, heights, water, small spaces such as elevators, insects, and animals. Social phobia results from the morbid anxiety associated with being scrutinized by others. Sufferers show high levels of self consciousness and exaggerate other people's negative reactions to them on the basis of their own state of anxiety. Thus, sufferers find it difficult to attend social gatherings and perform tasks in front of people, which often makes them unable to lead normal social and work lives. Generalized anxiety disorder involves undue anxiety or worry about a range of areas that may include well-being of family members, self-consciousness, future or past events, performance, and competence. The worry is experienced as uncontrollable and is therefore ineffective as a problem-solving strategy. Theorists have argued that the worry is a narrowing of attentional focus that screens out all non-worry related events. Others argue that the worry may function to protect the worrier from other more distressing forms of cognitive activity, such as mental images of scenes that elicit unpleasant emotional states.

There are a number of other diagnoses that are usually grouped as anxiety disorders in the psychological and psychiatric literature, but more controversy exists about whether their categorization is correct. Three such disorders are obsessive-compulsive disorder, post-traumatic stress disorder, and hypochondriasis (i.e., health anxiety). An individual who suffers from obsessive-compulsive disorder feels compelled to perform rituals over and over to prevent tragedy from occurring. The most common forms of obsessive-compulsive disorder involve repeated checking to make

La malade imaginaire, *created by Honore Victorin Daumier, features a depressed hypochondriac who is visualizing various death scenes, including being bled, preparing a will, appearing as a cadaver, and being measured for a coffin.* (Corbis)

sure mistakes have not been made and repeated washing to avoid contamination. The rituals rarely bring any relief, so normal life is often sacrificed to a cycle of never-ending ritualization. Post-traumatic stress disorder involves a range of symptoms (including anxiety) that are directly attributable to the previous experience of a traumatic event (e.g., assault, rape, war experiences, car accidents). Hypochondriasis, or health anxiety, is a preoccupation with the belief or fear that one has a serious illness, even in the absence of organic pathology and despite medical reassurance. As in panic disorder, someone who suffers from hypochondriasis becomes sensitized to and fearful of bodily sensations that are incorrectly taken as evidence of serious illness. Such worries are also common in depression, so assessment must try to disentangle the primacy of the various symptoms. The validity of the above categories of anxiety disorders is still controversial. As new research and clinical practice evolves, so do the way scientists categorize disorders, and it is reasonable to predict that the diagnostic system may look markedly different in the future. The American Psychiatric Association has placed increasing emphasis on research, and resulting evidence is used in further developing the diagnostic system. For example, the childhood category of avoidant disorder was omitted from DSM-IV after research indicated that it did not differ sufficiently from social phobia.

Most sufferers of anxiety disorders have more than one type of anxiety disorder, and thus it is difficult to argue that the subtypes of anxiety disorder are really discrete entities. Further, anxiety disorders also tend to overlap with other emotional and behavioral problems, in particular depression and substance abuse. The latter may simply be due to people using drugs to cope with the anxiety. However, the co-occurrence of anxiety and depression is more complex, and the similarity of the two problems has led a number of researchers to argue they are one and the same. A consensual view holds that anxiety and depression are distinct yet overlapping events that share the common experience of negative affect but show distinctions in patterns of symptoms and response to treatment.

Prevalence and Developmental Course

Population surveys of the number of people suffering from one or more of the anxiety disorders typically average about 7 percent to 12 percent of the population, whether children, adolescents, or adults. In terms of stability, studies have produced rather discrepant results. Some studies have found that approximately half of the sample spontaneously improved regardless of treatment, whereas several other studies found that around 70 percent of the sufferers retained their diagnosis two years later. Where long-term anxiety problems are the case, the situation may be complicated by other problems such as dependency on others, poor problem-solving skills, or substance use.

Few longitudinal studies (which follow their subjects over a considerable span of time) have been conducted to review the continuities and discontinuities between childhood and adult anxiety disorders. Thus, scientists are mainly limited to the use of retrospective accounts given by anxious adults to study the pathways of anxiety through the life span. This evidence indicates that many adult anxiety disorders originally began in childhood or adolescence. Perhaps the most consistent connection is that many adult agoraphobic patients had separation anxiety and difficulty adjusting to school during childhood.

Models of Etiology

Sigmund Freud's (1909) description of a phobic disorder in a five-year-old boy was one of the first descriptions of an anxiety disorder. The child had phobias of horses and of leaving the family home, which Freud interpreted as stemming from Oedipal conflicts, specifically the anxiety caused by the boy's unconscious wishes to kill and replace his father. Thus, in the psychoanalytic approach, the feared stimuli are seen as being symbolic of unconscious conflicts. The usefulness of psychoanalytic treatments for anxious people have received little empirical support, and reanalyses of Freud's interpretations cast serious doubts about their validity in the opinion of some experts. Further, the need for reducing health costs through the development of brief effective treatments has seen the gradual decline in the psychoanalytic model.

Genetic transmission studies indicate a family pattern for anxiety disorders. However, it is not known whether the transmission results from genetic factors or from environmental factors, and it has not been established that it results in specific disorders. That is, anxious children often have parents with a range of psychiatric disturbances and anxiety problems in parents are associated with a similarly broad range of disturbances in their children.

Observational studies of families with anxious children indicate that parents with anxious children model threat and avoidance and are consistently more controlling and directive than are parents with non-anxious children. However, this does not indicate that the parents' behaviors are the cause of the children's anxiety, as the parents' behaviors are just as likely to be the result of the children's anxious behaviors. Instead, clinicians emphasize models of two-way influence in which parents and children become trapped in behavioral patterns that reinforce each other's strengths (in healthy systems) or vulnerabilities (in dysfunctional systems).

John Bowlby (1969) emphasized the infant's need for stable, nurturant, intimate attachments as prerequisites for psychological health, and numerous studies since that time have shown that different attachment processes characterize psychologically healthy adults and children versus distressed adults and children. It has been difficult to find, however, specific relationships between anxiety disorders and specific types of insecure attachment, and few treatments developed from an attachment perspective have been subjected to controlled outcome and process studies.

In all higher primates, certain individuals are more likely than others to respond to "challenge" situations with fear and behavioral inhibition (e.g., mutism, lack of eye contact, freeze responses), a characteristic more commonly shared by natural siblings than by adopted siblings. Jerome Kagan and his colleagues (1988) have shown that the trait of behavioral inhibition is one of the first visible risk factors for the development of anxiety disorders, especially in children who have highly stable behavioral inhibition and who have anxious parents.

Hans Eysenck's (1953) model of personality includes the traits of neuroticism and introversion as temperamental risk factors for anxiety problems. Jeffrey Gray (1988) has attempted to bridge behavioral and biological dimensions with regard to these personality traits. He argues that anxiety-prone people show ready activation of the behavioral inhibition system, which controls preparedness for inhibitory responses, sensitivity to punishment, and vulnerability to traumatic conditioning. Several abnormalities in neurotransmitter systems of anxious people have been identified that appear to be reversible through medication. These systems include norepinephrine, serotonin, dopamine, the gamma-aminobutyric acid benodiazepine receptor complex, and certain neuropeptides.

Important progress in understanding anxiety disorders has come from cognitive-behavioral models. These originated with Ivan Pavlov and his demonstration of conditioned associative learning and B. F. Skinner and his work on reinforcement theory. Classic learning explanations of anxiety disorders emphasize an interplay of these two forms of learning. Consider a person who has a morbid fear of elevators. Behaviorists would point to conditioning processes in which elevators, due to a previous traumatic experience, had come to signal an aversive consequence such as falling to one's death or being trapped in a small space. Once the fear has been established, avoidance of elevators keeps anxiety levels within the comfort zone, thus reinforcing avoidance behavior. Further, other people may inadvertently reinforce the fear by providing support and nurturance contingent upon fear displays. Cognitive-behavioral theory is a strongly empirical tradition, and its own research has pointed to limitations of the above conceptualization. In particular, it has been shown that not all people report an initial conditioning experience, fears are not randomly distributed (and it thus appears that different species have predispositions to learn fears of some things and not others), people show fears and anxieties that persist or even get worse in the absence of any trauma or avoidance, and many people are exposed to traumatic experiences without developing conditioned reactions. However, contemporary researchers have shown that updated "cognitive" models of learning are able to explain the above observations. For example, higher primates do not need to experience trauma to show conditioned learning; conditioning can occur by simply observing or hearing about a peer's experience of a traumatic event.

The incorporation of cognitive processes into learning theory has led to some innovative developments in anxiety disorders. For example, it has been shown that the tendency to allocate attention toward ambiguous stimuli and to interpret those stimuli as threatening is a reliable indicator of an adult with an anxiety. Similarly, the tendency to overinterpret a threat and respond with avoidance is characteristic of anxious children and their families. Thus, anxiety problems may be maintained in part by the perceptual and thinking style of the sufferer. Anxiety problems can be associated with acute and chronic stressors such as divorce, unemployment, school failure, sexual and physical abuse, physical illness, and the loss of a loved one. However, environmental stressors appear to precede the onset of nearly all psychiatric disorders and physical illnesses. Thus, stressors may increase one's vulnerability to anxiety but could not be considered to be a disorder-specific cause.

Psychosocial Treatments

When considering the success of any particular treatment, it is useful to discriminate between efficacy and effectiveness. The former refers to the outcomes associated with a treatment when it is delivered in its optimal form. The latter refers to the outcomes associated with the treatment in the real world, and thus includes consideration of many factors such as resources needed, skills of clinicians in the community, and acceptability of the treatment to consumers, as well as the efficacy of the treatment. While psychodynamic and family therapies have been used in the treatment of childhood anxiety disorders, the lack of controlled studies prohibits conclusions about their efficacy or effectiveness. In contrast, a wealth of evidence is available about the efficacy and, to a lesser extent, the effectiveness of cognitive-behavioral and pharmacological interventions.

Cognitive-behavioral treatments incorporate a range of treatment strategies, and most clinicians recommend combinations of procedures based on conditioning/exposure, reinforcement, physiology, and cognition. Common to all learning-based treatments is the premise that anxious patients can, through learning, minimize the threat value of the things they fear and learn to regulate their emotions and physiological reactions more comfortably as they explore life. Exposure techniques involve having the patient, under the support and guidance of a therapist, face the fear in order to learn that the feared stimulus is not in fact so threatening, thereby breaking the cycle of avoidance. Often, some exposure is undertaken in imagination (learning to imagine the feared events without getting anxious) prior to exposure in the real world. The underlying mechanisms that account for the success of exposure based procedures are still controversial. Originally Joseph Wolpe (1958) explained it as the inhibition of anxiety through relaxation learned as part of the exposure treatment. More recent views emphasize changes in thinking processes that occur during exposure. David Clark and his colleagues (1997) use exposure treatments that help the sufferer to "rethink" and devalue the threat associated with the things they fear as they face them.

Physiological strategies for dealing with anxiety include muscle relaxation skills and breathing techniques to help patients manage uncontrollable arousal, especially during exposure exercises. Most of these techniques were developed with anxious adults but can be used with children and adolescents. A number of other strategies have been developed more specifically for children. Modeling procedures often include the use of films, whereby the child learns to devalue the threat of the fear after watching other people confidently handle the feared situation. Modeling is an important procedure with children who may be manifesting a fear that is shared by other family members. The child is prompted to imitate the performance of the model (often a parent or peer) who is demonstrating nonfearful behaviors and is reinforced for coping behavior. The efficacy of modeling procedures in both the treatment of childhood phobias and in the preparation of children for stressful (e.g., medical and dental) events has been supported.

Treatments for anxious children often incorporate reward-based programs, especially in the treatment of school refusal, socially avoidant children, and specific phobias. In general, therapeutic success is enhanced when these programs are combined with other techniques such as exposure and cognitive reappraisal. Philip Kendall and his colleagues (1992) have demonstrated the efficacy of an integrated learning program. The treatment centers around having the child develop an individualized FEAR plan: F, for feeling good by learning to relax; E, for expecting bad versus good things to happen through positive self-talk; A, for approaching actions to take in the face of fear; and R, for rewarding oneself for efforts to overcome fear or worry. Research by Paula Barrett and her colleagues (1996) has shown that involving the family in such a learning program reliably improves outcomes for the children over and above the improvement rate of approximately 60 percent to 70 percent found by Kendall. Other studies have shown that similar success rates could be achieved by presenting the treatment in a group format, thereby significantly reducing costs of intervention.

Given the demonstrated efficacy and high cost of the above treatments, many authors are now arguing that a shift in emphasis (and funding priorities) should be made from clinical treatments to early intervention and prevention programs aimed at larger cohorts of people at risk for anxiety problems. Some evidence has emerged to indicate that the provision of learning programs (scheduled as part of the school curriculum) for anxious children can assist in preventing the development of anxiety disorders in a significant proportion of children.

Pharmacological Treatments

Medications are a common treatment for anxiety disorders in adults, and research supports their efficacy. Anxiolytic drugs have been shown to reverse specific abnormalities in the neurotransmitter systems of anxious people. Benzodiazepines (BZs) have been shown to be effective in treating adults with panic disorder, agoraphobia with panic, social phobia, and generalized anxiety disorder. Required dosage varies considerably across individuals and recommended practice is to start with a low dose and build up until a therapeutic effect is achieved, thus avoiding unnecessary toxicity and side effects. Physical dependence on BZs is a concern, and discontinuation of BZ treatment can be associated with a rebound in anxiety symptoms, so a gradual fading and augmentation of the medication with psychosocial treatments is recommended. Tricyclic antidepressants (TCAs, especially imipramine and clomipramine) and especially monoamine oxidase inhibitors (MAOIs) have been shown effective with panic disorder and social phobia. The advantages of these medications are that they can also produce an improvement in comorbid depressive symptoms. However, both of these antidepressants have significant side effects; the MOAIs require dietary restrictions and can cause hypertensive crisis. Thus, they are rarely a first choice for the treatment of primary anxiety. The selective serotonin reuptake inhibitors (SSRIs) are widely used as antidepressants and have been shown to have potential for the treatment of panic disorder, social phobia, obsessive-compulsive disorder, and post-traumatic stress disorder. However, little information is available about the long-term efficacy of these agents and the side effects, which can include agitation, insomnia, gastrointestinal problems, and sexual dysfunction.

A number of important clinical issues have been identified regarding medication treatments for anxiety disorders. The long-term outcomes and effects of medication are not clear, and the therapeutic benefits once medication has been discontinued remain dubious. Most clinicians, therefore, consider a combination of drug and cognitive-behavioral treatment to be optimal for handling anxiety disorders.

With regard to children, there is a lack of well-controlled and well-conducted research studies into psychopharmacological interventions, and there is little support for their use as sole treatments for anxiety disorders with younger people. BZs, which have received the most empirical support and are most commonly prescribed for children and adolescents with anxiety disorders, they are tolerated by most children with minimal side effects, although these can include unsteady gait, blurred/double vision, reduced mental acuity, sedation, slurred speech, tremor, drowsiness, and irritability. BZs are comparatively safe in overdose, but the risks associated with tolerance and dependence in children are unknown. Studies of the efficacy of TCAs with anxious children have focused on separation anxiety and school refusal and have produced conflicting results. Only one of four published studies has provided support for the efficacy of the TCAs in the treatment of separation anxiety (with or without school refusal). However, one of the three negative studies used an arguably sub-therapeutic medication dosage while the remaining two had small sample sizes. The most frequent side effects of TCAs include blurred vision, sedation, lightheadedness, dry mouth, urinary retention, and constipation. Overdosage can result in severe medical complications.

There is some evidence that buspirone may be effective in the treatment of generalized anxiety, and further controlled trials are merited, especially given its lack of major side effects, its limited potential for abuse, and its low probability of producing withdrawal symptoms following cessation. Fluoxetine (prozac) has shown promise in the treatment of childhood obsessive compulsive disorder and generalized anxiety in children. In one study, 81 percent of the children given fluoxetine showed moderate to marked improvement in their anxiety symptoms with few side effects.

See also: ANXIETY; BOWLBY, JOHN; CULTURE-BOUND SYNDROMES; EYSENCK, HANS JURGEN; FEAR AND PHOBIAS; FREUD, SIGMUND; HELPLESSNESS; MOOD DISORDERS; POST-TRAUMATIC STRESS DISORDER; STRESS

Bibliography

Allen, Albert John; Leonard, Henrietta; and Swedo, Susan E. (1995). "Current Knowledge of Medications for the Treatment of Childhood Anxiety Disorders." *Journal of the American Academy of Child and Adolescent Psychiatry* 34:976–986.

American Psychiatric Association. (1994). *Diagnostic and Statistical Manual of Mental Disorders,* 4th ed. Washington, DC: American Psychiatric Association.

Anderson, Jessie C.; Williams, Sheila; McGee, Rob; and Silva, Phil A. (1987). "DSM-III Disorders in Preadolescent Children: Prevalence in a Large Sample from the General Population." *Archives of General Psychiatry* 44:69–76.

Barrett, Paula M.; Dadds, Mark R.; and Rapee, Ronald M. (1996). "Family Treatment of Childhood Anxiety: A Controlled Trial." *Journal of Consulting and Clinical Psychology* 64:333–342.

Bowlby, John. (1969). *Attachment and Loss, Vol. 2: Separation, Anxiety, and Anger.* New York: Basic Books.

Clark, David M., and Fairburn, Christopher G. (1997). *Science and Practice of Cognitive Behaviour Therapy.* Oxford: Oxford University Press.

Dadds, Mark R. (1995). *Families, Children and the Development of Dysfunction.* Thousand Oaks, CA: Sage Publications.

Davey, Graham C. L. (1992). "Classical Conditioning and the Acquisition of Human Fears and Phobias: A Review and Synthesis of the Literature." *Advances in Behavior Research and Therapy* 14:29–66.

Eysenck, Hans J. (1953). *The Structure of Human Personality.* London: Methuen.

Freud, Sigmund. ([1909] 1955). "Analysis of a Phobia in a Five-Year-Old Boy." In *The Standard Edition of the Complete Psychological Works of Sigmund Freud, Vol. 10,* ed. James Strachey. London: Hogarth Press.

Gray, Jeffrey. (1988). "The Neuropsychological Basis of Anxiety." In *Handbook of Anxiety Disorders,* ed. Cynthia G. Last and Michel Hersen. New York: Pergamon Press.

Kagan, Jerome; Reznick, Steven; and Snidman, Nancy. (1988). "Biological Bases of Childhood Shyness." *Science* 240:167–171.

Kendall, Philip C.; Chansky, Tamar Elisas; Kane, Martha T.; Kim, Ray S.; Kortlander, Elizabeth; Ronan, Kevin R.; Sessa, F. M.; and Siqueland, Lynne. (1992). *Anxiety Disorders in Youth: Cognitive-Behavioral Interventions.* Boston: Allyn & Bacon.

Lydiard, R. Bruce; Brawman-Mintzer, Olga; and Ballenger, James C. (1996). "Recent Developments in the Psychopharmacology of Anxiety Disorders." *Journal of Consulting and Clinical Psychology* 64:660–668.

Suomi, Stephen J. (1986). "Anxiety-Like Disorders in Young Non-Human Primates." In *Anxiety Disorders of Childhood,* ed. Rachel Gittelman. New York: Guilford.

Wolpe, Joseph. (1958). *Psychotherapy by Reciprocal Inhibition.* Stanford: Stanford University Press.

World Health Organization. (1992). *The ICD-10 Classification of Mental and Behavioral Disorders: Clinical Descriptions and Diagnostic Guidelines.* Geneva: World Heath Organization.

Mark R. Dadds

ARISTOTLE

b. Stageria, Thrace, 384 B.C.E.; *d.* Chalcis, Euboea, 322 B.C.E.; *philosophy.*

Aristotle was a leading Greek philosopher and scientist. A student of the great philosopher Plato, he later broke with him over several philosophical matters after Plato's death. Aristotle is considered by many to be the greatest philosopher of the Western world, and his ideas had an enormous effect on the philosophers of the European Renaissance, which occurred between the thirteenth and the seventeenth centuries.

Aristotle was born in the Ionian colony of Stageria in Macedonia. His father, Nicomachus, was the physi-

An eighteenth-century etching depicts Aristotle and a companion contemplating the animals and other elements of nature. (Corbis)

cian of King Amyntas II of Macedonia, so as a boy Aristotle was exposed to science and medicine, in both of which he expressed an interest. At seventeen years of age, Aristotle went to Athens to study at Plato's Academy. He stayed there for twenty years, moving from being a student to being a scholar and teacher, but he left after Plato's death in 347 B.C.E. Aristotle moved to the town of Assos, joined a group of Platonists that was already active there, and then founded his own school. He also married Pythias, the niece and adopted daughter of Hermias, the ruler of the region in Asia Minor where Assos was located. Aristotle then spent two years at Mytilene on the island of Lesbos conducting scientific research on local plants and animals. In 343, he was asked by Philip of Macedon to tutor his son Alexander (the Great) and remained in that position until Alexander replaced his father in 336.

In 335, Aristotle returned to Athens and established his school at the Lyceum. The school did not follow the model of Plato's Academy but was more of a research institute where scholars analyzed and organized scientific collections, held discussions, and gave lectures. Because the scholars held discussions as they walked under a covered walkway, his followers were called Peripatetics. Aristotle enjoyed the protection of both Alexander and Antipater, the governor of Macedonia and Greece. Following Alexander's death in 323, the anti-Macedonian faction in Athens charged Aristotle with atheism, and he left the school and moved to Chalcis in Euboea, where he died the following year.

Aristotle's research, thought, and writings cover a wide range of topics, including ethics, logic, cosmology, politics, rhetoric, and psychology. Actually, the extent of his works is not fully known as some were lost and others attributed to him were probably written by students who were working under his supervision. His ideas about logic, which he viewed as being the basis of science are set forth in the six treatises that form the *Organon*. His ideas about existence and its meaning are set forth in works that were organized by later scholars as the *Metaphysica*, which covers a wide range of topics, including matter, form, time, and space. Other works reflect his life-long interest in science. Aristotle saw scientific study as being theoretical, practical, and purposive, and his works reflect these themes. *On the Heavens* covers his study of the solar system, *On Generation and Corruption* covers his study of evolutionary cycles, and *Meteorology* covers his study of the sky and the sea. Aristotle's work with regard to animal biology is presented in a series of four books that discuss the study of animals, the parts of animals, the reproduction of animals, and the movement of animals. In *Politics*, which reflects Aristotle's support of the city-state, he covers a wide range of topics, from the structure of society to civics to revolution to education, while his *Rhetoric* focuses on the art of persuasion and brings together ideas from logic, psychology, ethics, and techniques of argument.

Aristotle's interest in psychology reflects the importance that he placed on the role of humans and the individual in the universe. He described the structure of the human soul as a reflection of the structure of the universe and as consisting of three elements: nutrition, sensation, and thought. In addition, unlike many other philosophers, Aristotle considered emotion to be an entity in and of itself, and he provided a clear definition in his *Rhetoric:* "that which leads one's condition to become so transformed that his judgment is affected, and which is accompanied by pleasure and pain." Although he gave less attention to emotion than to other matters, Aristotle listed several emotions, including anger, fear, and pity, and discussed anger at some length in his *Rhetoric.* His analyses of anger reflected a deep understanding of emotion and included a consideration of the cognitive, social, behavioral, and biological components of emotional experience.

Aristotle's work was a major influence on later generations of philosophers, scholars, and others. His interest in science led to the emergence of scientific study as a legitimate intellectual activity alongside philosophy. His writings influenced other classical schools of philosophy (such as the Stoics), as well as early Christian theologians and leading theologians and philosophers of the Middle Ages and the Renaissance, including St. Thomas Aquinas and Francis Bacon. In fact, so many of Aristotle's ideas have been incorporated into accepted Western culture that they are now simply taken for granted with no concern abut where they first originated.

See also: ORATORY; PHILOSOPHY; PLATO

Bibliography

Adler, Mortimer J. (1997). *Aristotle for Everybody: Difficult Thought Made Easy.* New York: Scribner.

Barnes, Jonathan, ed. (1983–1984). *The Complete Works of Aristotle,* 2 vols., revised Oxford translation. Princeton, NJ: Princeton University Press.

Barnes, Jonathan, ed. (1995). *The Cambridge Companion to Aristotle.* Cambridge, Eng.: Cambridge University Press.

David Levinson

ARTS

See Dance; Drama and Theater; Literature; Music; Poetry; Visual Arts

ATTACHMENT

Love makes the world go around. Love is a source of pain and a cause for joy. Love feeds the highest highs and the lowest lows of human emotional experiences. But where does it come from? Why do people feel what they feel and do what they do in the name of love? Why must individuals love? Why are people attracted to only certain other persons? And why are some people seemingly capable of productive and rewarding relationships, while others appear destined only to experience pain and disappointment? These questions have been pondered by the greatest philosophers, poets, playwrights, and artists. And they are questions upon which consideration of attachment can shed some light.

The term *attachment* refers to a discriminating and specific affectionate relationship that is formed between one person and another. The behavioral marker of an attachment relationship is a striving to achieve and maintain physical closeness to the relationship partner. In more common terms, then, an attachment is a love relationship, and such relationships may occur between people of all ages. But from a scientific or psychological perspective, consideration of attachments began with an interest in the nature and potential importance of the very first such relationship each human forms—that between the infant and the primary caregiver. Traditionally and historically, the primary caregiver has been the mother, and most of the related research has dealt with mother-infant attachments (so, for simplicity, the term *mother* will be used in this entry to refer generally to the primary caregiver—even though this person does not have to be the biological mother). As this first relationship was studied and better understood, its importance for development beyond infancy became apparent, and with this came attention to a full variety of attachment relationships, including those between older children and their parents and between adults, as in marriage. What this work has revealed is that Sigmund Freud (1949) really did know what he was talking about when he suggested that the mother, as the first person the infant loves, is "unique, without parallel, established unalterably for a whole lifetime as the first and strongest love-object and as the prototype of all later love-relations" (p. 70). What the young child learns from his or her mother about the capacity for being loved and loving, the likelihood of having the most basic and most intense desires met, the value of expressing feelings and voicing needs—all of this and more—will be carried forward, affecting the close relationships formed after infancy.

Attachment Theory Overview

Two of the major issues addressed by attachment theorists concern *why* and *how* attachment relationships develop. Both are important to a full consideration of attachment.

Why Do Attachments Develop?

At a general level, attachment theory describes the development of the infant-mother relationship as a species-characteristic phenomenon that promotes the protection, survival, and felt-security of the infant who, though helpless in terms of assuring its own survival, is nevertheless endowed from birth with a repertoire of instinctive behaviors (e.g., sucking, clinging, gazing, crying) that are believed to contribute to the development of attachments. Reciprocally, adults are predisposed to respond to these attachment behaviors by initiating and/or maintaining closeness to the infant, providing necessary care, and thereby promoting the infant's safety and survival.

All of this is to say that infants develop relationships with a caregiver because they must. It is a matter of survival, a matter of connecting with another person —physically and emotionally—on the way to becoming the kind of social creature that defines the very basis of humanness. The inborn need for such a relationship is as strong as, or perhaps stronger than, the need for food and shelter. There is a long and tragic history of infants deprived of social and emotional contact with a caregiver suffering serious mental and physical retardation and even death, despite having their needs for food and shelter met. However, research shows that it is still possible for infants who are neglected and/or physically abused by their caregivers to become attached to the caregivers. The inborn drive to develop this intimate relationship is that strong. The human infant is ready, able, willing, eager, and even desperate to become attached to someone and given even the slightest opportunity of consistent contact with another, will do so. (This is to say nothing, of course, of the particular nature of the relationship that might result from any of the extreme scenarios suggested.) Attachments are not incidental occurrences. They are an absolutely essential ingredient of being human.

How Do Attachments Develop?

The theoretical position regarding the *process* by which attachments develop recognizes that the very young infant's attachment behaviors are independently and indiscriminately exhibited. That is, behaviors at the outset are not coordinated in any sophisticated way, and the infant does not "care" about who might be on the receiving end of his or her various signals. Over time, however, infant behaviors become organized in more complex ways, and the infants become more particular about the person or persons toward whom they prefer to direct these behaviors. In

fact, it is only when the infant's attachment behaviors are integrated into a coherent behavioral-motivational system and organized around particular figures who provide care, comfort, and safety that the term *attachment* is properly applied. A somewhat detailed accounting of this process has been provided by attachment theorists' delineation of four phases through which the development of attachments proceeds: initial preattachment, attachment in the making, phase of clear-cut attachment, and goal-corrected partnership.

During the preattachment phase (from birth to twelve weeks), the infant exhibits species-characteristic behaviors (e.g., visual orientation toward people, reaching, smiling) that are likely to evoke proximity to, and caretaking from, adults, but the infant does not effectively discriminate among these adults. The hallmark of the second phase, attachment in the making (from twelve weeks to six months), is the infant's ability to discriminate between familiar and unfamiliar figures. Also during this period, the infant typically demonstrates a preference for a particular figure, typically the mother, by being more likely to direct attachment behaviors (such as smiles) toward her and appearing more content when she is the person responding to those behaviors. Additionally, it is believed that during this second stage, the infant begins to develop a sense of those aspects of interaction with the attachment figure that are experienced consistently across interaction episodes. During phase three, the phase of clear-cut attachment (seven months to three years), the child becomes much more active in promoting and maintaining proximity to, and contact with, the preferred attachment figure, while becoming more active in exploring the environment. Perhaps most important in this stage, however, is that the behavior of the infant becomes organized on a goal-corrected basis, which is to say that the infant's behaviors toward the mother may now be viewed as directed by specific plans for the purpose of accomplishing particular attachment-oriented goals. For example, whereas the younger infant might cry when frightened and the mother might respond by picking up and comforting the infant, the infant in the third phase might respond to fear by crawling toward the mother and clambering up into her lap with the intention of seeking comfort. The onset of such goal-directed attachment behaviors (typically between six and nine months) may be viewed as an appropriate criterion for the onset of attachment. Finally, in the fourth phase, goal corrected partnership (older than three years of age), the attachment relationship takes on a more mature quality as the child becomes capable of viewing things from the caregiver's perspective. With this comes the ability to infer the feelings, motives, and plans that might influence the caregiver's behaviors, along with the capacity for a more complex, reciprocal partnership. It is during this phase, for example, that the child would be capable of adapting plans to accommodate the mother, causing the mother to accommodate her plans to the child or bringing about a compromise. Not surprisingly, these fairly sophisticated characteristics of attachment relationships are those that John Bowlby (1969) asserted are relevant to an understanding of attachments beyond childhood.

Three Central Propositions

Having provided a brief overview of some general notions of attachment theory, three specific theoretical propositions related to the development of attachment relationships provide a framework for further discussion of attachment.

Proposition One

On the basis of Mary Ainsworth's (1979) early empirical demonstrations of variation in attachment quality across mother-infant pairs, it became necessary for attachment theory to explain why attachment relationships differ from one dyad (i.e., pairing) to another. Accordingly, the first proposition holds that attachment relationships develop in the context of, and thus are directly influenced by, interactions between the mother and infant during the first year of life. Individual infant-mother pairs thus are expected to develop attachments that are distinctive given that these relationships grow out of the idiosyncratic patterns of behavioral exchange that have evolved within the dyad over time.

Identified as a most important element of interaction between the infant and the mother is sensitivity, the ability of the caregiver to attend to the infant's signals, interpret them accurately, and respond in a prompt, appropriate, and consistent manner. When a hungry infant cries and the mother immediately goes to the baby, picks him or her up, speaks in a soothing tone, and provides the required food, the mother has behaved sensitively. Sensitive caregiving behavior is also being exhibited when an infant vocalizes and the mother responds enthusiastically, as if the vocalization had a particular meaning. When this type of sensitivity characterizes interactions between a mother and an infant, it is likely that the infant will develop a "secure" relationship with the mother. Such a relationship is born of the infant's confidence in the mother's being available and having the ability to meet needs in a prompt and rewarding manner. The infant learns to trust that the mother will be there when needs dictate and that she can be counted on to do that which is most necessary and desired. In this process, the infant

A young father in San Antonio, Texas, provides his infant with food, an important sensitive caregiving behavior. (Corbis/Sandy Felsenthal)

also develops the confidence that is necessary to move away from the mother for the purpose of exploring the world, with full knowledge that safety is only as far away as the distance put between the two. (This is what Ainsworth referred to as the "secure base" phenomenon.)

Insensitive caregiving represents the opposite of sensitivity. While there are many ways in which insensitivity may be manifested, at root it may be viewed as the mother's tendency to ignore the infant's signals and/or respond to those signals in an inappropriate or untimely manner. Failing to respond to a crying infant, talking angrily at a crying infant, feeding an infant who is not hungry, or stimulating an infant who is already overstimulated (such as throwing a crying baby into the air) are all examples of insensitive caregiving. When insensitivity characterizes interactions between mother and infant, it is likely that an "insecure" relationship will develop. In essence, insecure relationships are characterized by the infant's lack of confidence in, and trust regarding, the mother's ability and willingness to successfully meet needs. The insecurely attached infant thus has a tendency to fear moving away from the mother for the sake of exploration.

Proposition Two

The second proposition central to attachment theory maintains that in the course of an infant's development over the first year and in the context of interactions with the mother, the infant eventually comes to represent the attachment relationship in the form of an internal working model. This representational model is made up of two components: a notion of the acceptability of self in the eyes of the attachment figure and a complementary notion of the accessibility and emotional supportiveness of that figure. In addition, it is expected that once the infant is capable of the representation necessary to form an internal model of the relationship, his or her choice of behaviors in interacting with the mother will be guided by this model (during the clear-cut attachment phase of development discussed above).

In effect, then, this proposition describes a mechanism by which the child symbolizes generalizations drawn from cumulative experiences in interaction with the mother over the first year of life. This generalized "record" of interactional history represents the child's attachment relationship with the mother, but it also serves to guide the infant's behaviors as he or she draws upon previous experience in making decisions about how to act in any given situation. Research has supported these claims. In circumstances believed to heighten one-year-old infants' attachment-relevant needs, securely attached infants have manifested their high levels of trust and confidence in their mothers in characteristic ways. These infants signal their needs in an efficient and age-appropriate manner. For example, a secure infant who is upset when the mother leaves briefly tends to cry to signal distress. Upon the mother's return, the infant moves and reaches toward the mother to signal the desire for contact. A secure infant also experiences comfort as a product of the mother's ministrations, calms quickly, and before long is comfortable leaving the mother's side in order to explore the surroundings. An insecure infant also behaves in characteristic ways that serve as exhibitions of low levels of trust and confidence in the mother. Such an infant often vigilantly monitors the mother's location and activity at the expense of exploration. He or she may signal distress at the mother's brief departure and even approach the mother upon her return, but an insecure infant often fails to be comforted by the mother despite her apparent attempts toward this end. An insecure infant may also become quite angry and hostile toward the mother. In addition, some insecure infants fail to exhibit their distress in an outwardly observable manner and/or exhibit a variety of disorganized behaviors with no logical motivation other than to avoid any greater discomfort than the given situation might arouse in them.

In essence, then, there is ample reason to believe, first, that an infant's experiences in interaction with his or her mother will influence the quality of the attachment relationship formed with her, and, second, that these experiences and the resulting relationship are represented within the infant in the form of an internal working (representational) model with components related to both the self and the caregiver. Once this model has formed, the infant's behavior will become organized in accordance with it, which highlights the central importance to the child's development of the attachment model.

Proposition Three

The third proposition from attachment theory, and perhaps the most important for considerations of attachment beyond infancy, holds that as the child grows older and moves into a broader social context, his or her model of the relationship with the mother will be transformed into a generalized model of self in relation to all others. Furthermore, this generalized (and modifiable) representational model is expected to influence subsequent development through its effect upon the individual's selection of, behaviors in, and interpretations of interactions with others. Here again, quite simply, the suggestion is that what is learned in the first and earliest intimate relationship between the infant and primary caregiver will serve as a template for all future relationships. What sets this proposition apart from Freud's much earlier, similar contention, however, is its consideration of a mechanism by which the past is played out in the present or future. An individual of any age must make decisions about when, where, with whom, and how to behave. These decisions will influence not only the individual's behavior but also, to some extent at least, the response of the environment to the individual. Finally, these responses and the entire interactional experience must be interpreted by the individual. Attachment theory suggests that all of this will be influenced by the representational model, thus again reinforcing the central role of the model in development, while at the same time providing some indication of the processes by which such models, to the extent they are reinforced by ongoing experiences, are likely to remain fairly stable over time. At the same time, attachment theory recognizes that representational models are open to revision, such that experiences counter to the expectations that define a particular model could lead to changes—either minor or dramatic—in that model.

It is with regard to this third proposition that the largest (and most diverse) body of research exists. While the data from this research are compelling, they are not perfect, which is to say that while the characterizations to be provided are convincingly supported by research, it also is apparent that exceptions to them exist. In addition, gender and ethnicity, in and of themselves, do not influence attachment in any known way. For example, neither boys nor girls are more nor less likely to develop secure or insecure attachments, and Hispanics are no more nor less likely to be secure, or insecure, than are Caucasians, Blacks, or any other ethnic group. To the extent, however, that either of these factors might combine with culture, socioeconomic status, attitudes, and so on (and in so doing influence parenting behavior), they may be related, if indirectly, to the individual's experience of attachment. Karin Grossmann and her colleagues (1985) found that for a particular sample of mothers and babies in Germany, insecure attachments were more common than in an American sample of similar socioeconomic status. These researchers linked insecurity to maternal behavior, as is common, and attributed the high rate of insecurity to the cultural tendency of German mothers to foster independence and self-reliance in their infants. Thus, these German infants were more likely to be insecure than their American counterparts, but not simply because they were German; rather, it was as a result of the interactions they experienced with their mothers, which were influenced by their nationality and culture.

Security, an outgrowth of sensitively responsive caregiving during infancy, has proven an optimal component of individual development. During toddlerhood (between two and three years of age), secure children, when compared to insecure children of the same age, are more autonomous, flexible, resourceful, cheerful, enthusiastic, capable of using their mothers to assist them without being overly dependent upon them, and cooperative despite their willingness to express and exert their independent will. As preschoolers, secure children, as compared to insecure counterparts, are more ego resilient and independent, have higher levels of self-esteem, more positive social skills, more friends, and more empathy toward their peers. Insecure preschoolers tend to be aggressive, victimized, unpredictable, disruptive, and unpopular in the eyes of their peers.

During middle childhood (between seven and twelve years of age), differences between secure and insecure children are apparent largely in the context of social relationships. Secure children are very adept at forming and maintaining close friendships charac-terized by mutual caring, respect, and, when necessary, effective conflict resolution. Insecure children have a difficult time forming such friendships, and the relationships they do form with their peers may be characterized by overdependence and jealousy. Also during this stage, insecure children, particularly boys, tend to be characterized by a variety of problem behaviors such as hostility, noncompliance, hyperactivity, nervous habits, or unhappiness.

During adolescence, secure teens are capable of speaking coherently and thoughtfully about their close relationships, particularly those with their parents. As compared to their insecure counterparts, secure adolescents are better able to handle conflicts with their parents, more adept at transitioning to college, and more capable of finding an optimal balance between numerous and varied age-appropriate demands (e.g., coping with stress, studying, and enjoying themselves). Insecure teens are much more limited in their abilities to access and express their thoughts and feelings associated with close relationships, and they tend to be more hostile, condescending, and anxious in interactions with their peers than are secure adolescents.

Many facets of adulthood also are affected by attachment, including marriage, parenting, and even the experience of pregnancy. Marriage represents an important attachment relationship, and the steadily growing divorce rate serves as a testament to the fact that not all marriages are successful. From an attachment perspective, a good marriage epitomizes all that is necessary and important in establishing healthy, mature relationships. For individuals who are secure in their sense of having been loved and are confident in their ability to both give and get love, there also is a confidence in seeking a partner who can and will fulfill their attachment needs. Indeed, there is some evidence that secure adults tend to seek out and marry secure partners. Additionally, such couples (secure-secure) are more satisfied with their marriages, and these relationships last longer than do marriages that involve an insecure individual.

Consideration of pregnancy and parenting serves to demonstrate the importance both of being capable

Lady Isabella Augusta Gregory's Workhouse Ward (1908) portrays two bedridden elderly men who spend their days arguing with each other. But when one of the men has a chance to leave the workhouse ward and go live with his sister, both men realize that their attachment to each other is too essential to break up.

of relying on someone and of having someone to rely on as factors that contribute to successful coping in the face of immense demands. Women who display secure characteristics of being able to seek support and assistance directly from appropriate persons are likely to fare well during pregnancy, experiencing fewer complications during pregnancy, labor, and delivery. These women also are likely to have a satisfying relationship with their husbands (as explained above), which itself serves as a primary source of support. Conversely, when women are not confident that support will be available to them, and thus have difficulty seeking such support or do so in a negative (e.g., aggressive, demanding) manner, emotional difficulties during pregnancy are more likely. It is not surprising, based on this information, that problems associated with insecurity would continue to show themselves beyond the birth of the child. Mothers who themselves are insecure, and thus are likely to be in a marital relationship that is not viewed by them as satisfying, are likely to behave toward their infants in an insensitive manner, thus fostering an insecure attachment. Secure mothers, on the other hand, would be likely to enjoy a satisfying and supportive marital relationship and to foster security with their infants via their willingness and ability to meet infants' needs in a sensitively responsive manner.

Conclusion

As the above discussion illustrates, the role of attachment is central in personal development across the entire life span. When a person experiences early secure attachment, there is fostered in that individual a strong sense of being loved, ultimate confidence in their ability to give love in return, and the capacity for seeking and accepting the care and support of others as circumstances dictate. This confidence and belief in a secure base (both of which characterize secure attachment) appear to serve as necessary and sufficient building blocks for a wide assortment of developmental accomplishments that from any perspective must be viewed as optimal. In the absence of security and the certainty of love (and the attending faith in its attainability), trust and confidence prove difficult. In their place lie uncertainty, self doubt, fear, anger, resentment, and, almost assuredly, disappointment.

Change in attachment style is possible, though positive experiences in the context of close relationships —and significant and repeated experiences at that— likely would be necessary to lead to lasting alterations in an individual's model of attachment. Models gain momentum, and the longer they are strengthened by experiences that validate their core assumptions, the more resistant to change they are likely to become. All

people begin life striving for attachment. Initially, it is a matter of survival, but ultimately, it is a matter of how they will approach all future relationships. Secure attachment is not the only thing that can lead to an optimal path through life. In fact, it is not even a guarantee of continued success. Nevertheless, as birthrights go, secure attachment is a strong asset to possess from the beginning.

See also: ABANDONMENT; ACCEPTANCE AND REJECTION; ATTACHMENT TO ANIMALS; BOWLBY, JOHN; HUMAN DEVELOPMENT; INTIMACY; JEALOUSY; LOVE; RELATIONSHIPS; SHYNESS; TRUST

Bibliography

Ainsworth, Mary D. Salter. (1979). "Attachment As Related to Mother-Infant Interaction." In *Advances in the Study of Behavior, Vol. 9,* ed. Jay S. Rosenblatt, Robert A. Hinde, Colin Beer, and Marie-Claire Busnel. New York: Academic Press.

Ainsworth, Mary D. Salter; Blehar, Mary C.; Waters, Everett; and Wall, Sally. (1978). *Patterns of Attachment.* Hillsdale, NJ: Lawrence Erlbaum.

Arend, Richard; Gove, Frederick L.; and Sroufe, L. Alan. (1979). "Continuity of Individual Adaptation from Infancy to Kindergarten: A Predictive Study of Ego Resiliency and Curiosity in Preschoolers. *Child Development* 50:950–959.

Belsky, Jay, and Isabella, Russell A. (1988). "Maternal, Infant, and Social-Contextual Determinants of Attachment Security." In *Clinical Implications of Attachment,* ed. Jay Belsky and Teresa Nezworski. Hillsdale, NJ: Lawrence Erlbaum.

Bowlby, John. (1969). *Attachment and Loss, Vol.1: Attachment.* New York: Basic Books.

Bretherton, Inge. (1985). "Attachment Theory: Retrospect and Prospect." In *Growing Points of Attachment Theory and Research,* ed. Inge Bretherton and Everett Waters. Chicago: University of Chicago Press.

Bretherton, Inge. (1987). "New Perspectives on Attachment Relations: Security, Communication, and Internal Working Models." In *Handbook of Infant Development,* ed. Joy D. Osofsky. New York: Wiley.

Cassidy, Jude. (1988). "The Self As Related to Child-Mother Attachment at Six." *Child Development* 59:121–134.

Fonagy, Peter; Steele, Howard; and Steele, Miriam. (1991). "Maternal Representations of Attachment during Pregnancy Predict the Organization of Infant-Mother Attachment at One Year of Age." *Child Development* 62:891–905.

Freud, Sigmund. ([1949] 1969). *An Outline of Psychoanalysis.* New York: W.W. Norton.

George, Carol, and Main, Mary. (1980). "Abused Children: Their Rejection of Peers and Caregivers." In *High-Risk Infants and Children: Adult and Peer Interaction,* Tiffany M. Field, Susan Goldberg, Daniel Stern, and Anita M. Sostek. New York: Academic Press.

Greenberg, Mark; Cicchetti, Dante; and Cummings, E. Mark, eds. (1990). *Attachment in the Preschool Years: Theory, Research, and Intervention.* Chicago: University of Chicago Press.

Grossmann, Karin; Grossmann, Klaus E.; Spangler, Gottfried; Suess, Gerhard; and Unzner, Lothar. (1985). "Maternal Sensitivity and Newborns' Orientation Responses As Related To Quality of Attachment in Northern Germany." In *Growing*

Points of Attachment Theory and Research, ed. Inge Bretherton and Everett Waters. Chicago: University of Chicago Press.

Hazan, Cindy, and Shaver, Phillip. (1987). "Romantic Love Conceptualized As an Attachment Process." *Journal of Personality and Social Psychology* 52:511–524.

Isabella, Russell A. (1993). "Origins of Attachment: Maternal Interactive Behavior across the First Year." *Child Development* 64:605–621.

Isabella, Russell A. (1995). "The Origins of Infant-Mother Attachment: Maternal Behavior and Infant Development." In *Annals of Child Development, Vol. 10,* ed. Ross Vasta. Bristol, PA: Jessica Kingsley.

Jacobson, Joseph L., and Wille, Diane E. (1986). "The Influence of Attachment Pattern on Development Changes in Peer Interaction from the Toddler to the Preschool Period." *Child Development* 57:338–347.

Karen, Robert. (1998). *Becoming Attached: First Relationships and How They Shape Our Capacity to Love.* New York: Oxford University Press.

Kobak, Roger R., and Sceery, Amy. (1988). "Attachment in Late Adolescence: Working Models, Affect Regulation, and Representations of Self and Others." *Child Development* 59:135–146.

Main, Mary; Kaplan, Nancy; and Cassidy, Jude. (1985). "Security in Infancy, Childhood, and Adulthood: A Move to the Level of Representation." In *Growing Points of Attachment Theory and Research,* ed. Inge Bretherton and Everett Waters. Chicago: University of Chicago Press.

Main, Mary, and Weston, Donna R. (1981). "The Quality of the Toddler's Relationship to Mother and to Father: Related to Conflict Behavior and the Readiness to Establish New Relationships." *Child Development* 52:932–940.

Pipp, Sandra. (1990). "Sensorimotor and Representational Internal Working Models of Self, Other, and Relationship: Mechanisms of Connection and Separation." In *The Self in Transition: Infancy to Childhood,* ed. Dante Cicchetti and Marjorie Beeghly. Chicago: University of Chicago Press.

Ricks, Margaret. (1985). "The Social Transmission of Parental Behavior: Attachment across Generations." In *Growing Points of Attachment Theory and Research,* ed. Inge Bretherton and Everett Waters. Chicago: University of Chicago Press.

Smith, Philip B., and Pederson, David R. (1988). "Maternal Sensitivity and Patterns of Infant-Mother Attachment." *Child Development* 59:1097–1101.

Sroufe, L. Alan. (1983). "Infant-Caregiver Attachment and Patterns of Adaptation in Preschool." In *Minnesota Symposia On Child Psychology,* ed. Marion Perlmutter. Hillsdale, NJ: Lawrence Erlbaum.

Sroufe, L. Alan; Egeland, Byron; and Kreutzer, Terrie. (1990). "The Fate of Early Experience Following Developmental Change: Longitudinal Approaches to Individual Adaptation in Childhood." *Child Development* 61:1363–1373.

Russell A. Isabella

ATTACHMENT TO ANIMALS

The early-twentieth-century entomologist William Morton Wheeler remarked that it would seem a very bizarre world if people were to take animals into their homes and feed them at the expense of their own children. He was seeking to describe a human equivalent of forms of social parasitism found in the insect world, whereby the host is fooled by some simple signals into responding to the parasite as if it were one of its own kind. Recent commentators have recognized that Wheeler's analogy describes a situation that is not too far from the way humans treat their pets. It is true that most people do not neglect their own children in favor of pets, but provisioning for animals may detract from providing for human children, simply because there will be less to go around.

According to this view, pets are seen as social parasites that actually provide no real benefits to their owners; human responses to like and care for pets are seen merely as accidental by-products of humans' tendency to care for any dependent being who behaves like a human child. A different view is advocated by James Serpell (1986), who sees pets as providing real benefits to humans; he emphasizes the hidden benefits to the owner's health and well-being conferred by the keeping of pets.

The Nature of the Bond

Whichever of these alternative views of ownership is correct, the immediate motivation for caring for pets is that the human owner has established an emotional bond or attachment to the animal. He or she has come to love the pet. Research on the type of relationship people have with their pets confirms the commonly held view that they are treated like children. Owners enjoy playing with them, they talk to them in baby-talk ("motherese"), they hold them and cuddle them as they would a baby or young child, and they might even explicitly refer to them as "baby."

Some pets assume more the role of an adult companion than a substitute child and provide a source of security when the owner feels anxious or upset. This probably applies more to the larger breeds of dog, as opposed to smaller dogs and cats, although there is no definitive research evidence on this point.

The emotions humans feel for their pets are therefore similar to those they feel for children and other family members. These are positive feelings involving playfulness or relaxed contentment in their company. The responses of the common pets, dogs and cats, reinforce these feelings. Dogs are very attentive to their owners and show signs of affection. Cats purr and seem to like being petted and stroked.

How Attachment to the Pet Begins

Positive feelings toward the animal underpin a continuing bond with it, but how does this bond begin to form? Humans choose as pets animals that fit in with their way of life and possess features that are pleasant and appealing. Pets must be safe in terms of not attacking their owners and not destroying their possessions; they should not urinate or defecate in the home; they should be active at around the same time as their owners; and they should be amenable to socialization and taming by humans. Of the animals that fit these criteria, the dog and cat have become the most popular pets in Western countries because of their initial proximity to humans.

There are also psychological reasons why humans are attracted to dogs and cats. People generally take young animals into their homes as pets. The young of all mammals possess features that humans find attractive. Large eyes, a high forehead, chubby cheeks, and short stubby limbs are viewed as cute whatever their setting, whether in a human infant, a teddy bear, a cartoon character such as Bambi, or a pet. The adults of some popular breeds of dog, such as the King Charles Spaniel, also possess these features.

Attractive "baby features" facilitate the initial decision to take the puppy or kitten into the home. The way the owner then interacts with the pet is helped by the emotions humans share with other mammals. People feel that they understand the moods and behavior

of other mammals, and to a degree they do. The pet also helps by behaving in a dependent and playful way. Many owners also feel that the dog or cat understands their speech, and the common use of baby talk to pets facilitates this feeling. Humans readily anthropomorphize—they attribute human characteristics to other animals. In the case of pets, this helps owners to treat them as if they were human companions and to view them as part of the human family.

Separation Reactions

One way of assessing the strength and type of any attachment to another individual is to examine what happens when that person is not there. Measures of the style of attachment shown by infants to their mothers and other caregivers are based on their reactions to brief separations. Longer separations typically evoke distress and, in older children and adults, continued thoughts of the person and efforts to be reunited with them.

Some people have paid ransoms for the return of a kidnapped pet, and others have engaged in expensive legal disputes over the custody of a pet. More commonly, owners search for a lost pet and offer rewards for its return. While there are no systematic studies of people's responses to separations from their pets, studies of situations where people mysteriously leave home or go missing indicate that the ones left behind experience a prolonged and painful period of searching and preoccupation with the missing person. A similar, if somewhat shortened version of this reaction can be expected in the case of a missing pet.

Reactions to a Pet's Death

The strength of grief following a pet's death reveals the strength of the attachment to it. Surveys of veterinarians and reports from counseling services for bereaved pet owners provide many examples of people showing grief reactions similar to those following the death of a loved human. The question raised by these accounts is how typical are such reactions.

Crying is one outward sign of emotional distress. A questionnaire study conducted in the United States by William Lombardo and his colleagues (1983) found that 23 percent of the men and 58 percent of the women said that they would be likely to cry over the death of a pet. The figures were higher (around 50 percent and 75 percent, respectively) in a comparable British study.

Studies of owner reactions to a pet's death usually examine a range of emotions, thought processes, motives, and ways of coping. North American studies conducted by Elaine Drake-Hurst (1991) and Marilyn

A child demonstrates the degree of attachment that he has formed with his spaniel puppy by allowing it to sleep in the same bed with him. (Corbis/Bettmann)

In Marjorie Kinnan Rawling's The Yearling (1938), Jody's beloved pet fawn, Flag, grows up to be a real threat to the survival of the boy's family because it eats the garden. Finally, in frustration, Jody's mother shoots the yearling deer, but her aim is poor, so Jody must shoot his pet to end its suffering.

Gerwolls and Susan Labott (1994) adapted a questionnaire used to study human grief and found levels comparable to those reported for death of a parent, child, or spouse. These surprisingly high levels of grief are not supported by other studies and may reflect the limitations of that particular questionnaire.

A British study by John Archer and Gillian Winchester (1994) used a questionnaire based on the reactions one would expect in the case of grief for another human. Although many of the reactions associated with human bereavement were reported by a large proportion of this sample, they did not generally show pronounced emotional upset following a pet's death. Around 20 to 30 percent reported items indicating that they felt particularly depressed or anxious or angry as a result of the loss. These are the main emotions that often accompany a human bereavement, and the findings suggest that it is only a minority who show these emotions when a pet has died. Consistent with this, Geraldine Gage and Ralph Holcomb (1991) found that the death of a pet was viewed as less stressful than that of a close friend or an immediate family member among a large sample of middle-aged couples in the United States.

It can therefore be concluded that although most people do not show the same strength of feeling that they would in the case of a human bereavement, the death of a pet still evokes a substantial degree of emotional upset among a minority of people. Several studies indicate that grief for the death of a pet tends to be more pronounced if the person lives alone or if the death is sudden. As would be expected, if the person's description of what the pet meant to him or her indicates a greater emotional bond, the grief will be more pronounced.

Conclusion

People's attachments to their pets are modeled on human relationships with family members, notably young children. The emotions felt for the pet are therefore similar in kind to those shown to children, albeit more limited in scope. People vary in the extent to which they are attached to pets, in some cases valuing them as strongly as humans. This variable level of attachment affects the reaction to a pet's death, a reaction that involves a range of emotions similar to those experienced when a human companion is absent or has died. For most people, however, the emotions are still not as intense as those experience with the loss of a human loved one.

See also: ATTACHMENT; GRIEF

Bibliography

Archer, John. (1997). "Why Do People Love Their Pets?" *Evolution and Human Behavior* 18:237–259.

Archer, John, and Winchester, Gillian. (1994). "Bereavement Following Death of a Pet." *British Journal of Psychology* 85:259–271.

Berryman, Julia C.; Howells, Kevin; and Lloyd-Evans, Meredith. (1985). "Pet Owner Attitudes to Pets and People: A Psychological Study." *Veterinary Record* 117:659–661.

Drake-Hurst, Elaine. (1991). "The Grieving Process and the Loss of a Beloved Pet: A Study of Clinical Relevance." *Dissertation Abstracts International* 51(10):5025.

Gage, M. Geraldine, and Holcomb, Ralph. (1991). "Couple's Perception of Stressfulness of Death of the Family Pet." *Family Relations* 40:103–105.

Gerwolls, Marilyn K., and Labott, Susan M. (1994). "Adjustment to the Death of a Companion Animal." *Anthrozoös* 7:172–187.

Hirsh-Pasek, Kathy, and Treiman, Rebecca. (1992). "Doggerel: Motherese in a New Context." *Journal of Child Language* 9:229–237.

Lombardo, William K.; Cretser, Gary A.; Lombardo, Barbara; and Mathis, Sharon L. (1983). "Fer Cryin' Out Loud— There Is a Sex Difference." *Sex Roles* 9:987–995.

Serpell, James. (1986). *In the Company of Animals.* Oxford, Eng.: Blackwell.

John Archer

ATTITUDES

Emotion plays a primary role in how people's attitudes are shaped and changed. Indeed, the feelings associated with a given attitude are often the most relevant, most easily interpretable, and most informative manifestations of an individual's attitudes. Research in a variety of disciplines have consistently found that emotion is a powerful tool for promoting attitude change. Yet to fully understand the process whereby emotion ultimately plays a role in the formation and changing of attitudes, it must first be understood what an attitude is and how it is structured.

The Structure of Attitudes

An attitude is generally defined as a "learned predisposition to respond in a consistently favorable or unfavorable manner with respect to a given object" (Fishbein and Ajzen, 1975, p. 6). Hence, an attitude is an enduring, generalized positive or negative feeling about some issue, person, or object. For example, "I'm afraid of the Internet," "I really like my teacher," and "I love the movie *Titanic*" would all be considered attitudes because each statement demonstrates a positive or negative feeling associated with each object. Furthermore, the feelings connected with these objects tend to be generally consistent; one does not lightly change one's mind about her or his fear of technology, respect for one's teacher, or choice of a favorite movie. The definition of an attitude as consisting of positive and negative feelings also underscores the importance that emotion plays in the construction of these attitudes.

Attitudes have traditionally been defined as consisting of three interrelated parts: the cognitive components, the affective components, and the behavioral components. The cognitive component represents the thoughts, beliefs, and judgments about an attitude object, whereas the affective component represents the feelings associated with the object. The behavioral component of an attitude consists of a predisposition toward action with regard to the attitude object. Hence, an attitude is not a single thought, nor a single feeling. Rather, an "attitude" is really a bunch of information and feelings all surrounding a single attitude object. For instance, consider a man's attitude about going to church. The cognitive components might consist of how involved he is (or is not) at church, how important attendance is to him, what his thoughts about organized religion are in general, how much effect faith has on his life, or any number of other beliefs he may have about going to church. The affective components might consist of relief, joy, frustration, anger, guilt, love, or a combination of several emotions he associates with going to church. The behavioral component of an attitude is how the man acts as a result of the attitude he holds about the attitude object; in this instance, he may decide to attend church, switch churches, not attend church at all, or attend church reluctantly. Hence, an attitude should not be conceived as a single isolated concept, but rather as a collection of related thoughts, ideas, beliefs, feelings, and behaviors that are all associated with a particular attitude object. The balance of these components change for different people; some attitudes may be primarily cognition-based in nature (i.e., logical attitudes), others may be predominantly emotion-based, and still other attitudes might be an equal blend of affect and cognition. In one sense, a given attitude might be depicted as a bunch of grapes; each grape represents one thought, feeling, or action that is associated with a specific attitude object, but it is the entire cluster of grapes that really defines the attitude itself.

With the realization that an attitude is defined by the thoughts, feelings, and behaviors associated with a given attitude, one might ask the question "Which component carries the most weight in shaping or changing an attitude?" Since the behavioral component is more or less a consequence of a given attitude, most research has focused on attempting to understand the link between emotion and cognition in attitude structures. That the two processes (emotion and cognition) can occur simultaneously is generally uncontested; as Robert Zajonc (1980, p. 154) notes, "In nearly all cases. . . , feeling is not free from thought, nor is thought free from feelings." However, the two do not always have to occur together; in fact, emotion may be experienced independently from cognitive thought. People can experience emotion on a primal, instinctual level that for all intents and purposes occurs without conscious thought. For example, when someone jumps out at an individual unexpectedly, that individual may experience a momentary stab of fear; the experience of that fear occurs as an instinctual response to a perceived danger, not as the result of a conscious assessment of the environment.

Indeed, emotional experience does not necessarily depend on cognition. Even when cognition and emotion are experienced together, emotion may often dominate cognition. Some researchers argue that inconsistencies between affective and cognitive components of an attitude are most readily resolved by changes in cognition rather than emotion. Suppose that a woman is completely against having a dog as a pet; her cognitions supporting this attitude might include that pets are an additional responsibility, feeding pets and cleaning up after them are hassles, and a dog can be hard on the home. However, one day she finds an abandoned puppy, and as much as she would like to rationalize ignoring the puppy or getting rid of it, the woman just falls in love with it. She now finds herself in something of a dilemma. Her attitude now has some inconsistencies between the cognitive components (i.e., she does not want a pet) and the emotional components (she adores the puppy!). Research in the area of attitude change suggests that the woman can more easily resolve the inconsistencies in her attitude by altering her cognitions (i.e., convincing herself that maybe pets do not require *that* much responsibility, feeding them and cleaning up after them is not all that time consuming, and the pet can live in the backyard) than she can by trying to change the emotional components (from loving the puppy to disliking it). This finding suggests not only that affect is at least as capable as cognitive thought in generating attitudinal change, but that affect may hold a position of primacy over cognition under certain conditions. Some research has found that predominantly emo-

The day after resigning from the presidency in August 1974, Richard Nixon manages to present a positive attitude during a farewell speech to his staff. Any negative emotions created by the situation seem to be dominated by a positive cognitive and behavioral manner. (Corbis/Wally McNamee)

tion-based attitudes exhibited greater change under emotional means of persuasion than under cognitive means of persuasion (such as logical argument), and that predominantly cognition-based attitudes exhibited equal amounts of change under both emotional and cognitive forms of persuasive appeals. Regardless of the ordering of these processes, it is clear that emotional experiences can, and do, significantly influence the means by which attitudes are formed and changed.

Attitude Formation and Change

Emotion can affect the formation and changing of attitudes in a number of ways. To gain a more comprehensive understanding of how emotions can affect this process, three different theories need to be examined with regard to their ability to explain the effect emotion has on the attitude formation and change process. These three models are the elaboration likelihood model, the heuristic-systematic model, and the motivational and cognitive capacity hypotheses. They have been selected for discussion because they each address the emotional components of attitude change in meaningful yet slightly different ways.

The elaboration likelihood model (ELM), proposed by Richard Petty and John Cacioppo (1986a), stipulates that certain variables can affect the amount

and direction of attitude change in one of three ways: by serving as a persuasive argument, by serving as a peripheral cue, and/or by affecting the extent or direction of issue and argument elaboration. The key hypothesis of this model is that argument elaboration—or the degree to which one focuses on and tests the quality of an argument—mediates the route to persuasion, whether it be by the central route (conscious processing of argument quality) or the peripheral route (where cues such as source attractiveness, emotion, social role, or impression management concerns are processed). The model predicts that as argument scrutiny and motivation to process arguments decrease, peripheral cues (such as emotion) become more important determinants of persuasion. From a general standpoint, the ELM suggests that emotional appeals act as a peripheral cue—meaning that emotional appeals are the most effective when the receiver's motivation or ability to process the message is low. Hence, if people attend a political rally where they are not really concerned with the issues being discussed (low motivation) or are unfamiliar with the concepts (low ability), they are much more likely to base changes in their attitude on such peripheral cues as how impassioned, articulate, or attractive a speaker may appear. Given that message cues are either processed centrally or peripherally—not both—emotional appeals appear only to operate as peripheral cues. Although the goal of attitude change may be realized through the use of the peripheral route, research suggests that such changes are more fleeting than changes brought about by central route processing. Hence, emotional appeals would appear to be most effective in situations where the receiver is unable or unwilling to process the cognitive aspects of the message and only attitude change in the short term is initially desired. However, there may be times when emotional appeals are processed centrally rather than peripherally. This holds the additional implication that emotional appeals may be used effectively to produce attitude change and in turn result in long-term rather than short-term effects. For instance, emotion may function as evidence in an argument. In many criminal cases, evidence is revealed in such a way as to shock and repulse the jury members; the purpose of this strategy is not only to introduce the evidence as support for an argument but to associate the strong, negative emotional reactions to the crime scene photos or video with the alleged criminal, thereby building animosity toward the individual purported to have committed the crime. In these cases, the function of emotional appeals is clearly to elaborate on the argument itself, either by acting as an integral part of the argument (i.e., the evidence) or by increasing the level of motivation to process the argument on the parts of the listeners.

The heuristic-systematic model (HSM), extends and improves upon noted inadequacies of the ELM with regards to the processing of messages. According to the model forwarded by Shelly Chaiken and her colleagues (1980), receivers of a message will reach some kind of attitude judgment about a message in one of two ways: via systematic processing, which relies on a content-oriented, critical examination of the message, or via heuristic processing, which occurs when the receiver develops judgments about the message based on cues external to the message itself, such as perceived source credibility, use of emotional appeals, or attractiveness of the source. Furthermore, Chaiken argues for a validity-centered assessment approach as a means of explaining the motivation to process messages. This approach stipulates that a person's primary goal is to hold accurate attitudes, with attitudinal accuracy defined as a measure of consistency with relevant facts.

Although similar in many respects to the ELM, the HSM differs from the former model in a number of ways. The primary difference that is most relevant to a discussion of the effect of emotion on attitude formation and change is that, from the perspective of HSM, messages may be processed simultaneously using both heuristic and systematic processes, whereas message processing as described by the ELM is limited to either central or peripheral processing at any given time. This activity is referred to as "concurrent processing." As the HSM proceeds from the assumption that systematic and heuristic processing can occur simultaneously, the effect of a functional approach of emotional appeals is less clear in the case of this model than in the case of the ELM. On the one hand, the functions of emotional appeals that promote argument scrutiny and systematic (or in the case of the ELM, central) processing remain similar for both models. When emotional appeals act as the evidence in a particular argument or attempt to increase the level of motivation on the parts of the receivers, emotional appeals will tend to be processed systematically. However, an important qualification here is that, according to the HSM, the multidimensional nature of the message means that these types of emotional appeals may be *primarily* processed systematically, although parts of the message may still be processed heuristically. The HSM approach does not mandate that messages must be processed in a purely dichotomous fashion, as is suggested by the ELM. Indeed, research into attitude formation and structure has suggested that attitudes are constructed of both affect-based and cognition-based components, which suggests that efforts to change such attitudes cannot be explained well by taking a purely cognition-versus-affect approach. Furthermore, as persuasive appeals are fundamentally multidimensional messages consisting of both logical and emotional components, it may be that the different dimensions of the persuasive appeal are being processed simultaneously via different cognitive paths. The effects of other functions of emotional appeals (such as the use of emotional appeals to heighten credibility or to provide an alternative to logic) are clearly heuristic in nature and are easily capable of affecting judgments about the heuristic cues. In essence, the functions of emotion provide individuals with sets of easily identifiable cues on which to make a judgment regarding either the accuracy or the validity of the persuasive argument without processing the argument systematically.

Both the ELM and the HSM attempt to explain the role of emotion and emotional appeals in producing attitude change. In each of these models, emotion is depicted as having a more or less direct effect on how attitudes might be changed and with what effect. Yet to look at emotion as being capable of only changing attitudes directly is to perceive only one part of the emotion-attitude puzzle. Another related body of research that bears interesting implications for gaining a better understanding of emotion's role in attitude change seeks to explore the relationship between mood and the effectiveness of attitude change attempts. Mood research is somewhat removed from the more specific study of emotional appeals, yet moods share much in common with the direct experience of emotion. Mood is often distinguished from emotion by defining mood as being more persistent, less intense, and generally more diffuse than the experience of emotion. But even the subtle influence of mood can have an effect on the process of attitude change. Mood is usually studied as a precursor to the processing of persuasive information and is assumed to be in existence prior to the reception of the persuasive message. One commonality that ties these two conceptual areas together lies in the fact that the use of emotional appeals may create a specific mood-state, which in turn affects the attitude change process. Thus, from this view, emotional appeals are an antecedent in creating mood rather than having a direct effect on persuasion itself. Yet another area of commonality is that both moods and emotions have as their basis some level of positive or negative feeling.

Norbert Schwarz and his colleagues (1991) posit five ways in which a recipient's mood state might influence the means by which attitudes are formed and changed. Each of these possibilities uses a slightly different set of assumptions regarding the means by which mood affects attitude change. A test of these competing frameworks found that two of these theories seem to be supported with the available research, while the others have failed to garner sufficient supporting evidence as to their accuracy. Discussion here will be limited to the two competing theories that have been found to be at least somewhat reflective of the effect of emotional states on information processing.

The first of these hypotheses, the motivational hypothesis, posits that recipients' affective states may influence their motivation to elaborate on the content of the message. In other words, depending on whether someone is in a good mood or a bad mood, that individual may be more or less predisposed to process the message consciously and actively (systematically) or rely upon peripheral cues (heuristically) to make judgments about the message. Moreover, if a person is in a bad mood, they are more likely to perceive the world as a threatening place and therefore would be more likely to process messages carefully in an attempt to avoid making costly mistakes in judgment about the state of the world. Good moods, on the other hand (or positive affective states), would be indicative of a relatively safe environment in which the need to process information critically is reduced. Furthermore, some research suggests that individuals experiencing positive affective states are less likely to elaborate on the messages in an effort to maintain the positive mood.

Given these explanations of positive and negative affective states, the motivational hypothesis predicts an interaction effect for affective state and argument quality. Specifically, when strong arguments are used, recipients of the argument should be more persuaded when they are in a bad mood rather than a good mood, as they should be concentrating on evaluating the strengths of the message. Conversely, recipients of weak arguments should be more apt to alter their existing attitudes when they are experiencing a positive affective state, as the weaknesses of the argument should not be apparent due to the failure to elaborate on the message.

The second hypothesis forwarded by Schwarz and his colleagues is the cognitive capacity hypothesis. This hypothesis is in some ways an extension of the motivational hypothesis, in that it too maintains that mood will affect the recipient's ability to elaborate on messages. However, the cognitive capacity hypothesis asserts that the presence of positive or negative affective states will interfere with the information-processing capacity of the individual, although it is unclear as to whether good moods or bad moods are more likely to cause this interference in the cognitive processing. On the one hand, previous research has suggested that positive moods increase the accessibility of positive material, which in turn leads to a predisposition to focus on related positive thoughts. Hence, as the individual becomes preoccupied with re-experiencing these positive thoughts, the positive mood state interferes with the processing of the message. On the other hand, negative events that result in negative mood states may be more likely to stimulate a search for a rationalization as to how the negative event came to pass in the first place. In this way, the search for explanations may inhibit the elaboration of the message, thus interfering with the cognitive processing.

In general, the cognitive capacity hypothesis predicts an interaction effect between argument quality and affective state, such that individuals whose cognitive capacity is reduced by their current affective state should be more persuaded by weak arguments rather than by strong arguments. This hypothesis is differentiated from the motivational hypothesis in that cognitive capacity limitations may be overridden by time factors, as well as by other factors that affect the capacity to process the information. Although the two are very similar in terms of outcomes, the explanatory framework of each hypothesis differs slightly. In the motivational hypothesis, effective attitude change depends on whether the recipient views the world as threatening or nonthreatening at the time, increasing or decreasing, respectively, the need for critical examination of the message. The cognitive capacity hypothesis maintains that it is not so much perceptions of danger in the world but rather the capacity of the individual to process the information while remaining free from distractions generated by his or her current affective state that determines the level of cognitive processing given to an incoming message.

As previously noted, there is empirical support for both of these hypotheses, but the findings are mixed. Some research has concluded that individuals in a positive affective state were able to process the content of the message if explicitly instructed to do so. However, this finding in itself does not go far enough to establish the primacy of one explanation over the other, due in large part to the difficulty of measuring cognitive capacity separate from motivational attributions.

See also: ACCEPTANCE AND REJECTION; ADVERTISING; AMBIVALENCE; ATTACHMENT; MOOD; MOTIVATION; PERSUASION; PROPAGANDA

Bibliography

Bless, Herbert; Bohner, Gerd; Schwarz, Norbert; and Strack, Fritz. (1990). "Mood and Persuasion: A Cognitive Response Analysis." *Personality and Social Psychology Bulletin* 16:331–345.

Bohner, Gerd, and Schwarz, Norbert. (1993). "Mood States Influence the Production of Persuasive Arguments." *Communication Research* 16:331–345.

Breckler, Steven J. (1993). "Emotion and Attitude Change." In *Handbook of Emotions*, ed. Michael Lewis and Jeanette M. Haviland. New York: Guilford.

Breckler, Steven J., and Wiggins, Elizabeth C. (1989). "Affect Versus Evaluation in the Structure of Attitudes." *Journal of Experimental Social Psychology* 25:253–271.

Chaiken, Shelly. (1980). "Heuristic Versus Systematic Information Processing and the Use of Source Versus Message Cues in Persuasion." *Journal of Personality and Social Psychology* 39:752–766.

Chaiken, Shelly. (1987). "The Heuristic Model of Persuasion." In *Social Influence*, ed. Mark P. Zanna, James M. Olson, and C. Peter Herman. Hillsdale, NJ: Lawrence Erlbaum.

Chaiken, Shelly; Liberman, Akiva; and Eagly, Alice H. (1989). "Heuristic and Systematic Information Processing Within and Beyond the Persuasion Context." In *Unintended Thought: Limits of Awareness, Intention, and Control*, ed. James S. Uleman and John A. Bargh. New York: Guilford.

Eagly, Alice H., and Chaiken, Shelly. (1993). *The Psychology of Attitudes*. New York: Harcourt Brace Jovanovich.

Edell, Julie A., and Burke, Marian Chapman. (1987). "The Power of Feelings in Understanding Advertising Effects." *Journal of Consumer Research* 14:421–433.

Edwards, Kari. (1990). "The Interplay of Affect and Cognition in Attitude Formation and Change." *Journal of Personality and Social Psychology* 59:202–216.

Fishbein, Martin, and Ajzen, Icek. (1975). *Belief, Attitude, Intention, and Behavior: An Introduction to Theory and Research.* Reading, MA: Addison-Wesley.

Frijda, Nico H. (1988). "The Laws of Emotion." *American Psychologist* 43:349–358.

Hass, R. Glen. (1981). "Effects of Source Characteristics on Cognitive Responses and Persuasion." In *Cognitive Responses in Persuasion*, ed. Richard E. Petty, Thomas M. Ostrom, and Timothy C. Brock. Hillsdale, NJ: Lawrence Erlbaum.

Holbrook, Morris B., and Batra, Rajeev. (1987). "Assessing the Role of Emotions as Mediators of Consumer Responses to Advertising." *Journal of Consumer Research* 14:404–420.

Isen, Alice M. (1984). "Toward Understanding the Role of Affect in Cognition." In *Handbook of Social Cognition*, ed. Robert S. Wyer, Jr., and Thomas K. Srull. Hillsdale, NJ: Lawrence Erlbaum.

Lewis, Michael; Sullivan, Margaret W.; and Michalson, Linda. (1984). "The Cognitive-Emotional Fugue." In *Emotions, Cognitions, and Behaviors*, ed. Carroll E. Izard, Jerome Kagan, and Robert B. Zajonc. Cambridge, Eng.: Cambridge University Press.

Morris, William N. (1989). *Mood: The Frame of Mind.* New York: Springer-Verlag.

Petty, Richard E., and Cacioppo, John T. (1981). *Attitudes and Persuasion: Classic and Contemporary Approaches.* Dubuque, IA: William C. Brown.

Petty, Richard E., and Cacioppo, John T. (1986a). *Communication and Persuasion: Central and Peripheral Routes to Attitude Change.* New York: Springer-Verlag.

Petty, Richard E., and Cacioppo, John T. (1986b). "The Elaboration Likelihood Model of Persuasion." In *Advances in Experimental Social Psychology*, Vol. 19, ed. Leonard Berkowitz. San Diego, CA: Academic Press.

Petty, Richard E.; Cacioppo, John T.; and Kasmer, Jeff A. (1988). "The Role of Affect in the Elaboration Likelihood Model of Persuasion." In *Communication, Social Cognition, and Affect*, ed. Lewis Donohew, Howard E. Sypher, and E. Tory Higgins. Hillsdale, NJ: Lawrence Erlbaum.

Petty, Richard E.; Wegener, Duane T.; Fabrigar, Leandre R.; Priester, Joseph R.; and Cacioppo, John T. (1993). "Conceptual and Methodological Issues in the Elaboration Likelihood Model of Persuasion: A Reply to the Michigan State Critics." *Communication Theory* 3:336–362.

Schwarz, Norbert; Bless, Herbert, and Bohner, Gerd. (1991). "Mood and Persuasion: Affective States Influence the Processing of Persuasive Communications." In *Advances in Experimental Social Psychology*, Vol. 24, ed. Mark P. Zanna. New York: Academic Press.

Sypher, Howard E., and Sypher, Beverly Davenport. (1988). "Affect and Message Generation." In *Communication, Social Cognition, and Affect*, ed. Lewis Donohew, Howard E. Sypher, and E. Tory Higgins. Hillsdale, NJ: Lawrence Erlbaum.

Zajonc, Robert B. (1980). "Feeling and Thinking: Preferences Need No Inferences." *American Psychologist* 35:151–175.

Zajonc, Robert B., and Markus, Hazel. (1982). "Affective and Cognitive Factors in Preferences." *Journal of Consumer Research* 9:123–131.

Peter F. Jorgensen

ATTRACTIVENESS

Interaction with others is central to being human. At a personal level, successful interaction allows individuals to form relationships with others who support their actions and confirm their views of the world. At a collective level, people develop shared meanings and understandings of the world and create networks that sustain social life by interacting with others.

Attraction is a basic ingredient of social interaction. The ability to draw others into interaction depends, in part, on an individual's attractiveness to them. Attractiveness is a valuable personal resource for accomplishing personal goals and satisfying needs for belonging, security, and self-esteem. It is also a valuable social resource for maintaining social life by bonding people to each other. However, it is a resource that benefits some at the expense of others.

Attraction refers to positive feelings toward another person. It is the impetus for affiliation with others. Social psychologists argue that, as social beings, humans need to associate with others. Belonging helps individuals feel safe, cared for, competent, needed, and worthwhile. Without affiliation with others, individuals become lonely, depressed, and anxious, have lower self-esteem, and withdraw from social life.

When an individual finds someone else attractive, his or her body gives signals, such as an increased heart rate, shortened breath, sweaty hands, or weak knees. Such physiological signals tell the individual to look for something in the situation that can help in making sense of the arousal by labeling it as an emotion. Of course, these bodily responses could be signs of fear rather than attraction. In fact, experimental research by Stanley Schachter and Jerome Singer (1962) and Stuart Valins (1966), has shown that participants who are aroused by drugs, fear, or exercise can interpret their body's signals as attraction to another person. When the reasons for arousal are unclear, the individual looks for situational cues to use in deciding how to interpret the body's signals. Standing on a swinging bridge over a mile-deep chasm, the individual might easily label the body's signals as fear. On the other hand, standing opposite a good-looking man or woman, the individual might label the body's signals as love.

Attraction can take several forms. When people like others, they feel affection, warmth, closeness and/or respect for those other people. Love is not just a more intense form of liking; it is qualitatively different. Both involve feelings of needing, caring, and trust. However, as Arthur and Elaine Aron (1986) point out, love places a premium on caring for and needing another, while trust is most important in friendships. Love also involves feelings of attachment. People in love want to know that they "belong to" each other. Threats to that attachment, such as fear that a loved one is attracted to someone else, evoke feelings of jealousy because self-esteem, identification with the other, and an important relationship are under attack. Although jealousy was once considered a normal part of a love relationship, it is now seen as a sign of personal insecurity that is damaging to relationships.

Social psychologists distinguish between different types of love—primarily, passionate and compassionate love. Passionate love is a compulsive attraction to another person that involves strong physiological responses and idealization of another. A pounding heart, the feeling of walking on clouds, and daydreaming are all associated with passionate love. This type of love is intense but relatively fleeting. Compassionate love, on the other hand, refers to a calmer but more stable form of affection that develops over time between those whose lives are deeply entwined.

Researchers such as Francesca Cancian (1987) have found that men are more prone to be romantic and impulsive, while women are more practical and cautious about love. This is a consequence of their different social and economic positions in society. Women have had to be more pragmatic about love, since their marriage partners have determined their standard of living. In keeping with these differences, women are more likely than men to regulate their emotions by analyzing and discussing their feelings of attraction rather than expressing them spontaneously.

In addition to the physiological responses that signal attraction to another, these feelings are reflected in body language. When an individual likes another, he or she has dilated pupils, looks into that person's eyes, leans forward, and moves closer, taking an open, relaxed stance. When an individual does not like someone with whom he or she is interacting, the pupils contract, the individual looks and leans away, keeps his or her distance, and takes a closed stance, perhaps folding the arms or crossing the legs.

Cultural expectations influence how men and women show attraction. In Western cultures, as Scott Coltrane (1998) notes, women are expected to flirt, smile, listen attentively while cocking their heads to the side, and find other ways of exuding the right combination of innocence, admiration, and sexiness to show their attraction to a man. Men, on the other hand, are expected to make the first move assertively, showing a combination of sensitivity and bravado. Expectations change across time and cultures, but because they are presented as ideals in the media, current Western norms spread rapidly to other cultures.

Elements of Attraction

The specific qualities that are liked in other people depend on both personal and social factors. Personal qualities and situational goals shape an individual's attraction to other people. One may find emotional sensitivity, earning ability, or good looks quite attractive when looking for a romantic partner, but honesty and problem-solving skills are usually more attractive in an automobile mechanic, particularly if the client knows nothing about cars. In addition, what an individual finds attractive is shaped by the values of the culture and social groups to which he or she belongs. While some cultures put a high value on honesty, other cultures find diplomacy to be more important. Such values shape what qualities people like in others. Likewise, what is considered attractive varies across history. Obesity was considered a standard for beauty in past Western cultures, whereas thinness, particularly for women, is the standard in the West today.

A look at what attracts two people to form a romantic relationship provides an example of how personal and social considerations come into play. Harold Kelley (1983) proposes that four types of factors influence a close relationship between two people: factors related to Person A, factors related to Person B, interactions between the two people, and environmental factors.

First, individuals are influenced by personal goals and circumstances. They are more likely to find another person attractive if they are not currently involved in a romantic relationship but desire intimacy, and if they are feeling lonely or temporarily lacking in self-confidence.

Second, the characteristics that are perceived to be possessed by an individual affect how attractive others find that person to be. Initial attraction is based on first impressions, so physical attributes, verbal skills, signs of success, and reputation are all important in attraction (or attractiveness) to others. Individuals are drawn to people who are warm—who maintain a positive attitude and who praise others. Individuals are also attracted to those they see as being competent, as long as they do not seem unattainable.

Physical attractiveness is especially important in forming first impressions, even though people often deny it. The amount of money spent on hair transplants and hair loss medication, liposuction, facelifts, and cosmetics each year testifies to the importance that is placed on physical appearance. Videodating and personal advertisements are additional examples of practices that emphasize the importance of physical looks in obtaining a mate.

Cultural standards of beauty vary across time, across cultures, and across social groups. As noted above, thinness has replaced obesity as a sign of beauty. However, this standard applies more to women than to men and does not hold among African Americans. While obesity is now considered unattractive in both women and men, muscular strength is considered more attractive in men than the excessive thinness that characterizes the ideal for women. Tallness is also a valued physical trait, especially for men. Finally, physical disabilities are generally considered to diminish attractiveness.

> Hans Christian Andersen's "The Ugly Duckling" (c. 1850) describes how the odd looking "duckling" is rejected by his siblings because he is different. They peck at him until he finally runs away and spends a miserable winter alone. When spring arrives and the bird sees his reflection in the water, he realizes that he is not an ugly duckling at all but a beautiful swan.

Gender differences attest to the importance of social factors in shaping ideas of attractiveness. While men are primarily drawn to partners they consider physically attractive, women place more importance on a partner's earning ability. Like differences in attitudes toward love, this reflects gender differences in position and access to power in Western society. As noted above, women's subordinate position in society has required them to place primary emphasis on a partner who can provide security and safety, while attracting beautiful women is considered a sign of men's social status and sexual prowess.

The interaction between two people makes up a third component of attraction. Extensive research has shown that individuals prefer those they see as similar to themselves in attitudes, interests, physical characteristics, sexual orientation, intelligence, age, education, class, race or ethnicity, and religion. There are several possible reasons for this. People use observable cues, especially in first meetings, to determine what to expect from others and how to interact with them. People expect similar others to confirm their view of the world and to accept them for who they are. People also find it easier to open up to those who are like them. Because expressing emotions heightens the sense of physiological and psychological well-being, people like those with whom they feel comfortable sharing emotions.

Another explanation for attraction to similar others comes from understanding interpersonal attraction as a kind of market exchange between individuals. In a process social psychologists have called status matching, individuals offer their own set of attributes and skills in trade for another's attributes and skills. Attraction to another is thus shaped by a consideration of another's personal attributes, an assessment of how personal attributes match those of the other person, and the availability of other potential partners. In short, individuals try to make the best match possible. The result is that they select a person who is roughly similar to themselves in attractiveness.

It is also true that "opposites attract." Bernard Murstein (1974) has demonstrated that rather than seeking others to complement one's personality, as is often thought, people usually seek those who can fill complementary role expectations and provide missing resources. This phenomenon can be seen in relationships between beautiful women and financially successful, but physically unattractive, men. Each gains in status by their association with the other. People seek to "trade up" in status when possible. Such trade-offs usually involve men dating "down" by choosing women who are beautiful but younger or in a lower class or status group, and women dating "up" by choosing older men who are more financially secure or ambitious.

People are also drawn to those who are familiar. Obviously, one must have some contact with a person before attraction can occur. Living or working closely increases chances for interaction and makes another person more familiar. Research by Barrie Morgan (1981) has shown that appreciation of others grows with repeated contact, as long as the initial interaction is positive. Even when the first interaction is negative, if an individual knows he or she will continue to see someone regularly (e.g., a coworker), that individual will focus on the person's good qualities and ignore the flaws in an effort to get along.

Finally, the interpersonal factors—similarity, familiarity, and proximity—that shape what one finds attractive in others are themselves shaped by environmental factors. Social arrangements, such as racial or class segregation in living, working, and schooling environments, limit whom one sees regularly, finds attractive, and chooses as friends and romantic partners. These processes help to maintain racial and class distinctions by further reinforcing patterns of segregation, because people become even more similar to those they like through sharing of emotions, ideas, and interests. However, individuals are more open to those they think of as different if they feel accepted by that group. For this reason, frequent interaction in daily activities with those who are perceived to be different is necessary for learning to appreciate those differences and build positive connections between conflicting groups.

Cultural ideals also influence the assessment of another's attractiveness. Every culture has rules that govern appropriate marriage partners. Individuals are expected to marry outside of their immediate family but within their own social group, proscriptions that quickly narrow the set of possible partners. In addition, reference groups shape whom individuals find attractive. One study cited by James Wiggins, Beverly Wiggins, and James Vanderzanden (1994) found that norms concerning love among adolescent girls limit attraction only to members of the opposite sex, only to those who are unattached, and only to one boy at a time, but prescribe being in love at all times.

Other people can also influence one's feelings toward a person. Individuals tend to mimic the expressions of others. Smiling in response to another's smile evokes pleasant feelings that can increase liking for that person and for the people they like. Usually, the more family and friends approve of an attraction, the greater the attraction becomes. However, Susan Sprecher and Kathleen McKinney (1993), point out that parental disapproval can sometimes heighten the attractiveness of a forbidden love. Individuals also compare others in terms of attractiveness. After seeing a very beautiful person, people tend to judge others as more attractive if they are friends with that beautiful person and less attractive if they are strangers. Along these same lines, people tend to judge friends of very unattractive people as less attractive themselves.

Attraction is also influenced by elements of the situation in which the first meeting occurs. In general, individuals like people more when they are associated with pleasant experiences. Unpleasant physical conditions, such as heat and crowding, reduce attraction to others, while certain kinds of music may increase it. Likewise, as noted earlier, people infer their emotions from a cognitive interpretation of physiological arousal. Because they can interpret situations that arouse them—due to fear, excitement, or physical exertion, for example—as attraction to another individual, people are more likely to experience attraction during exciting situations, such as football games, dances, health club workouts, or thunderstorms. Cultural views that see love as being something that "overwhelms one" or that one "falls into" further encourage interpreting physical arousal as attraction.

The Consequences

Attractiveness has ramifications for more than just romantic attachments. People judge others by how they look, sound, and act, especially if little else is known. In general, individuals assign other people status and expectations based on their degree of attractiveness. People assume that being attractive makes a person more desirable in other ways, such as being more sociable, sensitive, interesting, poised, warm, trustworthy, dependable, and moral. Individuals expect attractive people to be more successful and happier than others. As a result of these common expectations, attractive people are better received than others, are more persuasive, have an advantage in hiring and salary decisions, and receive lighter punishments.

Expectations are also shaped by stereotypes associated with certain groups. While attractive men are considered to be more capable than others, attractive women are considered to be less capable, reflecting the stereotype that beautiful women are dumb. Likewise, taller men are seen as being more mature, secure, confident, and outgoing, and they enjoy a higher status as a result. In fact, the taller candidate won every U.S. presidential election from 1900 to 1968. The negative stereotypes of people of color in the United States have fed into a standard of beauty that values lighter skin over darker skin, even within darker-skinned ethnic groups. On the other hand, because of negative stereotypes concerning vanity, physical attractiveness has its downside: Attractive people are seen as less faithful, more self-centered, and less sympathetic to others.

Every culture, in an attempt to divert attention from humans' animal nature, has rules governing eating, excretion, and copulation. Those individuals who violate these rules—intentionally or not—are considered unattractive. In addition, people assume that physical differences, such as disabilities or deviation from weight norms, are signs of personal flaws. Those considered unattractive are often assumed to be socially deviant as well. For example, Mary Dew (1985) found that women who do not meet conventional standards of beauty are often assumed to be homosexual.

People with physical disabilities are often seen as being sick, dependent, bitter, sinful, asexual, and incompetent. As a result they face strained relations with able-bodied people and discrimination in housing, employment, civil rights, and social activities. As Spencer Cahill and Robin Eggleston (1994) show, disabled people often must do "emotion work" to ease others' discomfort and gain their cooperation. This emotion work consists of efforts to bring one's own or other people's feelings into line with the social expectations for a particular situation. For example, by apologizing for or joking about his or her disability, a disabled person eases the discomfort others feel in his or her presence. By putting strangers at ease, the disabled person gains others' good will and help to maneuver in awkward public encounters, such as moving through doorways simultaneously.

Likewise people evaluate fatness negatively. Individuals who are obese are considered disgusting, mean, lazy, sexless, ugly, self-indulgent, dumb, and dirty. They are thought to be morally and socially unfit. The stigma associated with obesity is particularly strong because overweight people are considered personally responsible for their condition. As a result they often have lower education, salaries, and raises.

Enhancing Attractiveness

Most individuals are unhappy with some aspect of their looks. For example, Elaine Hatfield and Sprecher (1986) reported that one-half of all women

and one-third of all men are unhappy with their weight. The proliferation of diets and diet aids attests to this obsession with weight. Cultural standards shape self-image, and negative judgments of oneself with regard to those standards lowers self-esteem and can lead to social withdrawal, damaging relationships and personal health in the process.

If obese people and those with physical disabilities or other characteristics considered unattractive accept prevailing cultural standards, the stigma they endure is compounded by negative self-feelings. Because of this, people who are considered unattractive are often unhappy and live constricted lives. This is particularly true for women. Physical attractiveness is more important for a woman's self-esteem than a man's. However, unrealistic standards of attractiveness leave many women with a sense of perpetual deficiency, which increases incidences of dangerous eating disorders and unnecessary surgery and sustains a beauty industry that makes billions of dollars every year.

In contrast, those who are considered attractive gain in self-evaluation as well as social advantage from their attractiveness. Attractive people are indeed more independent, confident, self-accepting, outgoing, achievement-oriented, and resistant to peer pressure than are less attractive individuals. Attractive people see themselves as being more likable, have more friends, and have more social skills and influence.

Attractiveness influences much beyond selection of friends or romantic partners. The expectations held for attractive and unattractive people become self-fulfilling prophecies. Because others expect more and gain status from association with them, attractive people develop an aura of competence and charisma that provides them the self-confidence, the networks, and the resources to achieve more than those who are considered unattractive. Conversely, the stigma that unattractive people endure lowers their motivation and expectations of themselves and limits the support they can gain from others. The result is that beliefs about the association between competence and attractiveness are confirmed by personal behavior and response from others.

Because of the importance of attracting others, people try to manage the impressions they make on others to their own advantage. Erving Goffman (1959) argues that individuals present themselves positively to others by the way they dress and the things they say and do. They usually do this unconsciously in an effort to let others know who they are. However, because individuals have different expectations and goals in different situations, they present their most favorable side in a given situation, while holding back sides that may create an unfavorable impression. For example, what people consider appropriate to wear to a job in-

Both men and women alike participate in a step aerobics class at a Paris health club in order to improve their physical fitness and thereby increase their physical attractiveness. (Corbis/Peter Turnley)

terview is quite different from what they wear on vacation. Likewise, what people discuss with their bosses differs from what they talk about with friends.

The assessment of what is appropriate for different situations is based on cultural norms that define how different attributes are valued. When cultural norms define femininity in terms of innocence, dependence, and sexiness, women feel pressed to dress seductively and act demurely on a first date. Conversely, when cultural norms define masculinity in terms of strength, leadership, and sexual prowess, men feel pressed to make sexual advances on a first date but to withhold their emotional vulnerabilities.

Some individuals are particularly sensitive to how they are perceived and responded to by others. Monitoring self-presentations is especially important for stigmatized individuals who face negative expectations from others. According to Goffman (1963), stigmas are deeply discrediting to the self. Because physical characteristics, personal qualities, and membership in social groups are valued according to culturally-constructed hierarchies, those individuals with the more valued characteristics have the power to pressure

stigmatized individuals to conform to negative expectations about them.

To fight the negative self-evaluation and shame that can accompany stigmas like physical disabilities or obesity, stigmatized persons adopt different strategies of impression management. Some hide the offending characteristic as much as possible through dress, avoidance of situations that draw attention to their condition, and selective disclosure of their stigma to others. Some engage in self-deprecating humor or alternate strategies to ease others' discomfort during interaction. Some stigmatized individuals master areas or activities that are usually thought closed to them, taking pride in their accomplishments and challenging stereotypical thinking. Each of these strategies have different consequences with regard to self-evaluation.

In general, self-presentations are intended to increase attractiveness to others. In tailoring how they dress, speak, and act to conform to cultural definitions of attractiveness, individuals may enhance their feelings about themselves. If negative self-beliefs are banished and other people respond positively, these self-alterations may increase opportunities to form rewarding relationships and achieve personal goals. However, molding oneself to fit cultural expectations can also lead to feelings of inauthenticity. Arlie Hochschild's (1983) study of airline stewardesses and bill collectors whose jobs require them to express only those emotions that are in line with company expectations provides a classic example of how damaging this can be. In addition to distorting self-conceptions, constantly managing emotions to fit others' expectations can keep individuals from heeding the signals their emotions provide to guide their interactions and tell them who they are.

Tailoring self-presentations to fit cultural norms also reproduces cultural patterns that continue to give advantage to some individuals over others. As people draw on familiar symbolic representations to convey favorable impressions, they narrow the range of emotions, actions, and thoughts that they draw on to make themselves more attractive. Judith Howard and Jocelyn Hollander (1998) assert that over time these people conform to the stereotypes that shape their repeated performances and begin to think of the stereotypes as being who they "truly" are. In tailoring themselves to fit cultural standards of attractiveness, people reproduce those standards that constrain them. When people consciously present themselves in ways that challenge constraining ideas of who they can acceptably be, on the other hand, they create greater acceptance of differences among individuals and enhance individual emotional health.

See also: ATTACHMENT; ATTRIBUTION; JEALOUSY; LOVE; RELATIONSHIPS; SELF-ESTEEM

Bibliography

Aron, Arthur, and Aron, Elaine. (1986). *Love and the Expansion of Self: Understanding Attraction and Satisfaction.* Washington, DC: Hemisphere.

Cahill, Spencer E., and Eggleston, Robin. (1994). "Managing Emotions in Public: The Case of Wheelchair Users." *Social Psychology Quarterly* 57:300–312.

Cancian, Francesca. (1987). *Love in America.* New York: Cambridge University Press.

Clanton, Gordon, and Smith, Lynn G., eds. (1998). *Jealousy.* Lanham, MD: University Press of America.

Coltrane, Scott. (1998). *Gender and Families.* Thousand Oaks, CA: Pine Forge Press.

Crittenden, Kathleen S., and Wiley, Mary Glenn. (1985). "When Egotism Is Normative: Self-Presentational Norms Guiding Attributions." *Social Psychological Quarterly* 48:360–365.

Dew, Mary A. (1985). "The Effect of Attitudes on Inferences of Homosexuality and Perceived Physical Attractiveness in Women." *Sex Roles* 12:143–155.

Eagly, Alice H.; Ashmore, Richard D.; Makhijani, Mona G.; and Longo, Laura C. (1991). "What Is Beautiful Is Good, But . . . : A Meta-Analytic Review of Research on the Physical Attractiveness Stereotype." *Psychological Bulletin* 110:109–128.

Goffman, Erving. (1959). *The Presentation of Self in Everyday Life.* Garden City, NY: Doubleday.

Goffman, Erving. (1963). *Stigma: Notes on the Management of Spoiled Identity.* Englewood Cliffs, NJ: Prentice-Hall.

Harris, Mary B.; Walters, Laurie C.; and Waschull, Stefanie. (1991). "Gender and Ethnic Differences in Obesity-Related Behaviors and Attitudes in a College Sample." *Journal of Applied Social Psychology* 21:1545–1566.

Hatfield, Elaine, and Sprecher, Susan. (1986). *Mirror, Mirror: The Importance of Looks in Everyday Life.* Albany: State University of New York Press.

Heilman, Madeline E., and Stopeck, Melanie H. (1985). "Attractiveness and Corporate Success: Different Causal Attributions for Males and Females." *Journal of Applied Psychology* 70:379–388.

Hochschild, Arlie. (1983). *The Managed Heart.* Berkeley: University of California Press.

Howard, Judith A., and Hollander, Jocelyn. (1998). *Gendered Situations, Gendered Selves.* Thousand Oaks, CA: Sage Publications.

Kelley, Harold H. (1983). *Close Relationships.* New York: W. H. Freeman.

Kernis, Michael H., and Wheeler, Ladd. (1981). "Beautiful Friends and Ugly Strangers: Radiation and Contrast Effects in Perception of Same-Sex Pairs." *Personality and Social Psychology Bulletin* 7:617–620.

Morgan, Barrie S. (1981). "A Contribution to the Debate on Homogamy, Propinquity, and Segregation." *Journal of Marriage and the Family* 43:909–921.

Murstein, Bernard I. (1974). *Love, Sex, and Marriage Through the Ages.* New York: Springer.

Patzer, Gordon L. (1985). *The Physical Attractiveness Phenomena.* New York: Plenum.

Piliavin, Jane Allyn, and LePore, Paul C. (1995). "Biology and Social Psychology: Beyond Nature Versus Nurture." In *Sociological Perspectives on Social Psychology,* ed. Karen S. Cook, Gary A. Fine, and James S. House. Boston: Allyn & Bacon.

Schachter, Stanley, and Singer, Jerome E. (1962). "Cognitive, Social, and Physiological Determinants of Emotional State." *Psychological Review* 69:379–399.

Sprecher, Susan, and McKinney, Kathleen. (1993). *Sexuality.* Newbury Park, CA: Sage Publications.

Valins, Stuart. (1966). "Cognitive Effects of False Heart-Rate Feedback." *Journal of Personality and Social Psychology* 4:400–408.

Wiggins, James A.; Wiggins, Beverly B.; and Vanderzanden, James. (1994). *Social Psychology,* 5th ed. New York: McGraw-Hill.

Shealy Thompson

ATTRIBUTION

Attribution refers to the ways that people answer "why" questions—the reasons they give to explain events, specifically their own and others' behavior. Although the making of attributions was first studied as an intrapersonal (i.e., internal) cognitive process, research has pointed increasingly to the importance of interactions, communication, and social contexts in the formation of attributions. The attributions individuals make reflect their previous experiences, their conceptions of the world, their goals, and their interpretation of the situation at hand. In turn attributions affect the individuals' subsequent behavior and thinking and the social world in which they live.

Fritz Heider (1958) is credited with the original ideas about attribution. He proposes that, because people want to see the world as controllable, they seek explanations that help them form a coherent picture of the world. Making attributions helps them to predict how others will behave, so personal behaviors can be planned accordingly. Heider argues that individuals act as "naïve scientists," analyzing available information based on personal theories of human behavior gleaned from past experience. These explanations help people to understand and gain control over events in their lives.

Edward E. Jones and Keith E. Davis (1965) and Harold H. Kelley (1967, 1973) base their models of attribution on Heider's conception of the observer as "naïve scientist." These models, and many subsequent research efforts, assume that observers weigh two types of causes—internal and external—to explain the behaviors they see. Internal causes refer to characteristics of the acting individual, such as personal dispositions, moods, attitudes, preferences, health, and abilities. External causes refer to characteristics of the situation, such as pressure from others, the weather, chance, and social conditions. Kelley explores how people decide whether to attribute behavior to one or the other of these causes, while Jones and Davis look specifically at the circumstances that lead an observer to attribute behavior to an actor's internal characteristics.

These early models identify three dimensions of causality—locus, stability, and controllability—that guide people in making attributions. Locus refers to whether a cause is internal or external to an actor, as described above. Stability refers to the permanence or impermanence of a characteristic (whether of actors or situations). For example, over the long run, a pianist's performance depends on talent and skill (stable characteristics). However, performance may suffer temporarily if the pianist has influenza or must play a poorly tuned piano (unstable characteristics). Controllability refers to the extent to which an actor can manipulate a particular cause. For example, individuals may see effort as something they control but view the weather or the difficulty of a task as being beyond their control. Together, these three dimensions provide logical criteria for making attributions. In explaining success or failure, teachers' and students' attributions often refer to motivation (locus), ability (stability), and effort (controllability).

Two principles guide the process of attribution: the principle of covariation and the discounting principle. The principle of covariation states that people look for an association between cause and effect. If a cause is present when an effect occurs and absent when the effect is absent, the effect is attributed to that cause. If the above pianist is clumsy (effect) before concerts (cause) but not when practicing at home or when doing other things, an observer would attribute the clumsiness to nervousness about the upcoming concert rather than concluding that the pianist is generally a clumsy person. The discounting principle states that people give less weight to a particular cause if other plausible causes are available. In other words, an observer would be less confident about attributing the pianist's clumsy stumble on stage to nervousness if he or she knew that the stage floor had been recently waxed.

A number of studies show that the discounting principle is important in deciding between internal and external explanations. People usually attribute the behavior of others to personal disposition or stable characteristics, but when a situation is seen to constrain an actor's behavior—due to social expectations or coercion, for example—people turn to situational (external) factors to explain the behavior. Personal dispositions are discounted if external forces could also explain an actor's behavior. For example, if a parent cuddles and rocks a child at home, the behavior will likely be attributed to the parent being affectionate. However, if the parent behaves this way when the child cries at a concert, the behavior is more likely to be attributed to social expectations that require the audience to be quiet during performances.

In short, people usually make external attributions when they believe an actor's behavior is being influenced by external pressures, such as social norms or coercion. People are particularly confident in making those attributions when the actor's behavior is contrary to what is expected, based on knowledge of the actor's past behavior. If an observer knows that the above parent usually lets the child cry a while before providing consolation, he or she would feel certain that the social expectations of the concert setting explain the parent's cuddling behavior. On the other hand, when people act in ways that are contrary to what is expected in a given situation, an observer is more likely to attribute what they do to who they are. A parent who ignores a child's crying during a concert is likely to be seen simply as an insensitive person.

Kelley (1973) extends the principles of covariation and discounting by specifying the types of information that are used to make attributions. He argues that people compare an actor's current behavior to his or her behavior in previous similar situations (consistency), to his or her behavior in other situations (distinctiveness), and to the behavior of other people in similar situations (consensus). Kelley proposes that behavior is attributed to the actor's internal dispositions when consistency is high and distinctiveness and consensus are low. A student's failure to pass a test will be attributed to his or her being incapable or not trying (internal causes) if the student has failed the same test in the past (high consistency), if the student fails most tests (low distinctiveness), and if everyone else passed the test (low consensus). However, attribution of behavior will be attributed to external causes if all three types of information are high. In other words, the student's failure will be attributed to the test being too hard (an external cause) if the student has failed the same test in the past (high consistency), if the student usually passes other tests (high distinctiveness), and if other students also failed the test (high consensus).

Attributional Biases and Heuristics

While early research on attribution provided some support for "naïve scientist" models, it also pointed out biases in observers' cognitive processing of information. First, people tend to pay more attention to information that is perceptually salient (i.e., notable), such as objects that stand out by being brightly colored, loud, in motion, or different from viewer expectations in some way. Shelley Taylor and Susan Fiske (1975) assert that the more salient information takes precedence in attributions even when it is not the best explanation.

Second, research shows that people prefer to attribute behavior to the stable characteristics of actors rather than to changeable situational factors such as social roles, a bias referred to by Lee Ross (1977) as the "fundamental attribution error." Because attention is usually focused on the person's actions in the situation rather than the situation itself, the person's characteristics are the most salient element and therefore become the favored explanation.

However, people are more likely to explain their own actions by referring to the complexity of the situation at hand, a tendency referred to by Jones and Richard Nisbett (1972) as the "actor-observer bias." This bias can also be explained as a difference in salience. Actors and observers have different perspectives. In general, what is foreground to the outside observer (i.e., the characteristics of the actor) is background to the actor, and what is foreground to the actor (i.e., the situation at hand) is background to the outside observer. When the actor becomes the observer as well, his or her attributional foreground remains the situation at hand (rather than personal characteristics), which leads to the external attribu-

tion. Dennis Regan and Judith Totten (1975) have pointed out that when observers look at the situation from the perspective of the actor, they tend to make similar external attributions.

The final cognitive bias is a tendency to give more weight to personal experiences than to statistical information. People believe what they see for themselves and what they know firsthand more than what others tell them about general patterns of behavior. Furthermore, people assume their own behavior is typical—that everyone responds to situations in the same way—a tendency called the "false consensus bias."

In addition to these cognitive slants, attributions are biased in ways that reflect motivations. Self-serving biases refer to attributions that help individuals look good in comparison to others or provide protection in some way. For example, people enhance self-esteem and public self-presentation by using internal attributions to take credit for successes and using external attributions to exonerate themselves from blame for failures.

People also have a tendency to explain the world in ways that help them see it as controllable. They prefer attributions that confirm control, such as effort or mood, over those that point to vulnerability, such as chance or talent. One consequence of this is the tendency to believe in a "just world"—a world where good things happen to good people and bad things happen to bad people. Believing that people get what they deserve helps individuals feel that they control their own fate. However, it is also used to justify the continued oppression of disadvantaged people, as it exonerates others and social arrangements from responsibility for their plight.

Biases in attribution were originally viewed as "errors" made by observers searching for accurate explanations of events—mistakes made by "naïve scientists." Attempts to account for these errors led social psychologists to reexamine their assumptions about how and why people make attributions. Looking at observers as active participants in the situation, motivated by their own goals and guided by their personal conceptions of the world, helped to recast biases as heuristic devices—rules-of-thumb and shortcuts that aid observers in making attributions quickly and efficiently. According to this formulation, observers are "cognitive misers" who use attributions to guide their next actions. Observers—as actors themselves—look for clues about how to respond to other actors rather than about simply how to describe the behavior of others. According to this model, efficiency is more important than accuracy.

Cognitive research has identified other heuristics used to speed up attributions and reduce the amount of information processing needed. Among these are the use of stereotypes to make inferences; reliance on the most readily available plausible explanations; and a bias toward holding onto current beliefs, even in the face of disconfirming evidence. Finally, when people do not have easily available explanations, they construct possible scenarios, which they then use to make future attributions.

The debate about whether people make attributions in a deliberate, logical manner or on the run, using shortcuts and snap judgments, garnered support for both models in different situations. Research shows that when people make attributions casually, they follow familiar heuristics. However, when they expect to be held accountable for their explanations, valued social identities and relationships are at stake, so they analyze information more thoroughly, putting aside heuristic shortcuts in favor of logical criteria. In effect, people, as social knowers, can move flexibly among processes for making attributions, depending on their goals at the time.

Revised models of attribution acknowledge this flexibility by accounting for variations in social knowers' goals across situations and by conceiving of observers as "motivated tacticians" who have pragmatic goals and are active, engaged participants in the interaction. Fiske and Taylor (1991) argue that in the midst of interaction—when quick decisions and responses are needed—people rely on rules-of-thumb to provide explanations that are "good enough" for the moment. With time for reflection, people engage in a more careful, controlled processing of events. While situational goals may shift between efficiency and accuracy depending on the circumstances of the interaction, the overall goal is understanding.

Attribution and Emotion

While studies of attribution have focused primarily on cognitive processes, there has been increasing emphasis on the role of emotions in motivating, processing, and responding to attributions. Emotions affect whether or not people bother to make attributions because they motivate thinking about a particular situation. In general, people pay attention to situations and events that they care about. They pay particular attention to events that involve self-esteem, sense of competence, social standing, and relationships with others. Self-serving biases reflect emotional attachments to good self-conceptions. However, such biases may be overcome in favor of more careful information processing if valued identities or relationships depend on the accuracy of the attributions that are being made.

Emotions also influence how people make attributions. In addition to paying attention to situations that are important emotionally, people pay attention to particular information that is important emotionally. Because people think more about emotional information, it is more easily retrieved and used in attribution processes. Studies of mood and cognitive processing show that people remember information that confirms their current mood. In addition, Alice Isen (1987) has reported that good moods lead people to rate things more positively, to make judgments more quickly, to define categorizations more inclusively, and to be more receptive to persuasion.

Attributions influence emotions as well as being influenced by them. People identify their emotions by interpreting certain physical sensations—they know what they feel by attributing a cause to physiological arousal. People use the same situational and cognitive cues to figure out their own emotions as they do to explain the behavior of themselves and others. In addition, cognitive processes can generate emotions, since retrieval of emotion-charged thoughts from memory brings up not only the thoughts but the emotions associated with them.

Different attributions have different emotional consequences, a linkage that can be seen across the three dimensions of causality (locus, stability, and controllability). Internal and external attributions (locus) concerning success or failure generate strong emotions because of the implications for the self. When people take personal credit for success, they feel pride, greater self-esteem, and an enhanced sense of competence, whereas attributing success to others may spark gratitude or a sense of obligation. Failures that people blame on themselves can cause depression by lowering self-esteem and sense of competence, but those failures that are blamed on others can make people feel angry or frustrated.

This has important implications for future behavior. In general people who see their lives as being controllable tend to be less depressed, less lonely, and less shy. As this would suggest, mental health and motivation are related to attributions for success and failure. These connections also suggest that cognitive biases are attempts to elicit desired emotions and avoid undesired ones. Self-enhancing biases increase the credit people receive (and thus enhance pride) and deflect blame (and thus reduce guilt or shame). At times people also engage in self-defeating acts, such as choosing very difficult courses or getting drunk the night before a test. Such external, or at least unstable, causes excuse people if they fail and allow them to avoid the negative feelings that come with self-blame. Negative comparisons to others can further lower self-esteem, increase depression, and spark jealousy if the failure is attributed to internal causes.

While internalized failure leads to self-blame, the stability of those internal causes has different emo-

The amount of dejection that is felt by the members of a high school football team after a championship defeat will be determined to a certain degree by their attribution of the cause of the defeat. (Corbis/Paul A. Souders)

tional consequences. Attributing failure or problems to the "type of person I am" (a stable cause) can increase feelings of shame, hopelessness, depression, and loneliness. In contrast, attributing problems to behavior (an unstable, changeable cause) increases coping skills in times of crisis. A robbery victim who blames himself or herself for leaving the door unlocked may feel guilty, but will cope better than one who sees himself or herself as a generally careless person.

Perceptions of responsibility (controllability) also generate different emotions. In general, people who see their lives as controllable tend to be less depressed, less lonely, and less shy. People feel ashamed or guilty when they hold themselves responsible for their failures, but they feel angry when they believe others are to blame.

The emotions generated by perceptions of the controllability of causes have important implications for interactions with others. Theodore D. Kemper (1984) argues that because people feel strongly about their social positions, attacks on that social position evoke emotions that affect behavior. If people attribute a loss in status or power to controllable forces, their anger motivates them to regain their position. Status lost through uncontrollable forces, however, is seen as irredeemable, which causes depression and dampens motivation. The motivating effects of emotions help to explain whether disadvantaged groups accept or resist their oppression.

Research on altruism has also shown how perceptions of control affect emotions and behavior. People are less likely to help someone who is in trouble if they see the person as being responsible for his or her plight than if they see the person as a victim of uncontrollable circumstances. Sympathy and aid go more readily to people who are hit by drunken drivers than to individuals who injure themselves by drinking and driving. People's attitudes toward abortion also vary depending on whether a pregnancy is due to rape or poor planning. In a similar way, people can more easily justify retaliating aggressively if they think they are intentionally being hurt by another, but people will usually try harder to forgive hurts that are seen as being accidental. By extension, people evaluate stigmatized individuals more harshly if they perceive the cause of the stigma to be a matter of choice. The general public has been more sympathetic to AIDS victims who contract the disease from blood transfusions than to those who contract it from sharing heroin needles. Similarly, the debate over the biological basis of sexual orientation has important ramifications for attitudes toward homosexuality.

An interesting application of the research on controllability in attributions concerns the attributions that one spouse makes for the other spouse's negative and positive actions. Judging a partner's hurtful actions as being deliberate puts a strain on the marriage, whereas uncontrollable negative actions are more likely to be forgiven. In addition, when a couple is already experiencing marital problems, one partner is more likely to see the other partner's negative actions as being intentional and positive actions as unintentional, both of which heighten tensions further. Thus, without intervention, the emotional implications of perceptions of control can lead to a disastrous spiraling of marital problems.

Social Influences and Consequences

While attribution research has been able to isolate some general principles that guide explanations of behavior, it has also identified differences across groups that have not been as easily explained. Achievement research illustrates this problem.

Research in education, work, and sports psychology has looked at how attributions affect self-evaluations, motivation, and performance. The basic argument has been that the ways people explain their successes and failures generate emotions that influence subsequent performance. The pride generated by attributing successes to internal causes, such as effort, motivates people to work harder and increases confidence in personal abilities, both of which enhance future performance. Likewise, linking failures to external causes, such as the difficulty of the task, helps to protect self-esteem and reinforce motivation to continue. In contrast, feelings of shame or guilt that are associated with external attributions for success and internal attributions for failure affect future motivation and performance negatively.

Research in this area, while supporting this thinking, has found that men and women make different attributions about achievement—men more often making self-enhancing attributions and women more often making self-disparaging attributions. However, even when women make self-disparaging attributions, they maintain levels of achievement similar to men. Similar patterns in achievement attributions and performance exist across ethnic groups.

Attempts to explain gender differences have included the argument that attributions depend on whether the actor is performing a gender-consistent task or not. People may explain a woman's success at parenting by crediting her nurturing abilities but attribute her success at climbing the corporate ladder to luck or good professional contacts. However, Kay Deaux and Tim Emswiller (1974) point out that successful men are more likely to be perceived as being skillful and that successful women are more likely to be seen as being lucky, regardless of whether tasks are defined as masculine or feminine.

Amy J. Dabul and Nancy Felipe Russo (1996) argue that the meaning and standards of achievement vary across groups and cultures. For independent individuals and people from cultures that value individualism, internal attributions for achievement indicate success. However, in collectivist cultures and for individuals who value interdependence, internal attributions for achievement signify not success but lack of cooperation. As they argue, while independent people feel pride in their accomplishments, interdependent people feel gratitude. Thus, women may continue to succeed (even though they downplay their own role in their successes and emphasize the help of others) because they have learned to value cooperation over independent achievement.

This argument addresses attribution theory's asocial bias by paying attention to how social context influences attribution processes. However, it does not adequately explain the tendency to see men as being generally more skilled than women regardless of context. Social categorization theories suggest an explanation. One of the ways people reduce the amount of time and effort needed to process information is through the formation of categories, which allow them to assess and store information in an organized and easily retrievable format. Assigning people to social groups according to visible differences, such as gender, skin color, or age, helps to provide a quick reference about what to expect and how to interact on the basis of characteristics associated with those groups. Assigning characteristics to groups reduces the amount of information people have to retain, but it leads to stereotyping individuals because people assume similarities among all members of the group. Because people define gender in dichotomous terms, categorizations assign men and women contrasting personality traits, roles, skills, and physical characteristics. Men are thought of as being competitive and women are thought of as being cooperative, men are expected to be good at instrumental tasks and women are expected to be good at emotional tasks, and so on.

The tendency to attribute skill to successful men and luck to successful women, regardless of the gender-typing of the task, seems to go against this logic. However, as Judith Howard and Jocelyn Hollander (1997) and others argue, assigning contrasting characteristics to groups involves evaluation and ranking of groups on the basis of those characteristics. Western society places more value on characteristics associated with men, such as ambition and competitiveness, than on those associated with women. Because people's conceptions of men fit cultural models of what it takes to succeed, they attribute their success to internal causes, such as ambition and skill, regardless of the situation, while they attribute the success of women (who are assumed to be non-ambitious and non-competitive) to external causes, such as luck or help from others.

As this research suggests, the influence of social categorizations on attributions has important implications. Studies of stereotyping show that people's attributions for members of their own group tend to put them in a better light than members of other groups. If people have negative feelings toward another group, they make external attributions for the positive behaviors and internal attributions for the negative behaviors of members of that other group, while the reverse is true for attributions about members of their own group. In general, people tend to evaluate members of their own group more positively than members of other groups, and they see more variation and complexity in the behavior of members of their group than in that of members of other groups.

Group membership has important consequences for self-conceptions, so people shape group-level attributions to protect the image of valued groups to which they belong while denigrating other groups. Members of stigmatized groups may blame negative events on others' discrimination and prejudice to reduce negative evaluations of their groups. Dominant groups, on the other hand, attribute the same events to chance factors or to internal stable traits of members of the stigmatized group. Such differences in attributions have political implications, the former supporting liberal social programs and the latter supporting more conservative political agendas. Because the power of dominant groups is supported by stereotypes that reaffirm beliefs in their competence and moral superiority, their views usually carry more weight in political debates.

Research on how social arrangements influence attributions and how attributions affect social relations is important for addressing differences among groups in society. As research continues to explore these connections, the potential for a convergence of psychological and sociological interests and views is beginning to be realized. The marriage of insights from cognitive social psychology (which emphasizes intrapersonal and interpersonal processes) and from sociology (which emphasizes cultural beliefs and structural arrangements) can only enhance the understanding of attribution processes and their individual and social consequences.

See also: ATTRACTIVENESS; CONFLICT; EMBARRASSMENT; GUILT; RELATIONSHIPS; SELF-ESTEEM; SHAME

Bibliography

Anderson, Craig A.; Krull, Douglas S.; and Weiner, Bernard. (1996). "Explanations: Processes and Consequences." In *Social Psychology: Handbook of Principles*, ed. E. Tory Higgins and Arie W. Kruglanski. New York: Guilford.

Barone, David F.; Maddux, James E.; and Snyder, C. R. (1997). *Social Cognitive Psychology: History and Current Domains.* New York: Plenum.

Bradley, Gifford Weary. (1978). "Self-Serving Biases in the Attribution Process: A Reexamination of the Fact or Fiction Question." *Journal of Personality and Social Psychology* 36:56–71.

Dabul, Amy J., and Russo, Nancy Felipe. (1996). "Rethinking Psychological Theory to Encompass Issues of Gender and Ethnicity: Focus on Achievement." In *Women's Ethnicities: Journeys through Psychology,* ed. Karen Fraser Wyche and Faye J. Crosby. Boulder, CO: Westview Press.

Deaux, Kay, and Emswiller, Tim. (1974). "Explanations of Successful Performance on Sex-Linked Tasks: What Is Skill for the Male Is Luck for the Female." *Journal of Personality and Social Psychology* 18:80–85.

Fiske, Susan T., and Taylor, Shelley E. (1991). *Social Cognition,* 2nd ed. New York: McGraw-Hill.

Graham, Sandra, and Folkes, Valerie S., eds. (1990). *Attribution Theory: Applications to Achievement, Mental Health, and Interpersonal Conflict.* Hillsdale, NJ: Lawrence Erlbaum.

Harvey, John H.; Ickes, William J.; and Kidd, Robert F., eds. (1978). *New Directions in Attribution Research, Vol. 2.* Hillsdale, NJ: Lawrence Erlbaum.

Heider, Fritz. (1958). *The Psychology of Interpersonal Relations.* New York: Wiley.

Hewstone, Miles. (1990). *Causal Attribution: From Cognitive Processes to Collective Beliefs.* Cambridge, MA: Blackwell.

Higgins, E. Tory, and King, Gillian. (1981). "Accessibility of Social Constructs: Information Processing Consequences of Individual and Contextual Variability." In *Personality, Cognition, and Social Interaction,* ed. Nancy Cantor and John F. Kihlstrom. Hillsdale, NJ: Lawrence Erlbaum.

Howard, Judith, and Hollander, Jocelyn. (1997). *Gendered Situations, Gendered Selves.* Thousand Oaks, CA: Sage Publications.

Isen, Alice M. (1987)."Positive Affect, Cognitive Processes, and Social Behavior." In *Advances in Experimental Social Psychology, Vol. 20,* ed. Leonard Berkowitz. New York: Academic Press.

Jones, Edward E., and Davis, Keith E. (1965). "From Acts to Dispositions: The Attribution Process in Person Perception." In *Advances in Experimental Social Psychology, Vol. 2,* ed. Leonard Berkowitz. Orlando, FL: Academic Press.

Jones, Edward E., and Nisbett, Richard E. (1972). "The Actor and the Observer: Divergent Perceptions of the Causes of Behavior." In *Attribution: Perceiving the Causes of Behavior,* ed. Edward E. Jones, David E. Kanouse, Harold H. Kelley, Richard E. Nisbett, Stuart Valins, and Bernard Weiner. Morristown, NJ: General Learning Press.

Kahneman, Daniel; Slovic, Paul; and Tversky, Amos, eds. (1982). *Judgment under Uncertainty: Heuristics and Biases.* New York: Cambridge University Press.

Kelley, Harold H. (1967). "Attribution Theory in Social Psychology." In *Nebraska Symposium on Motivation, Vol. 15,* ed. David Levine. Lincoln: University of Nebraska Press.

Kelley, Harold H. (1973). "The Process of Causal Attribution." *American Psychologist* 28:107–128.

Kelley, Harold H., and Michela, John L. (1980). "Attribution Theory and Research." *Annual Review of Psychology* 31:457–501.

Kemper, Theodore D. (1984). "Power, Status, and Emotions: A Sociological Contribution to a Psychophysiological Domain." In *Approaches to Emotion,* ed. Klaus R. Scherer and Paul Ekman. Hillsdale, NJ: Lawrence Erlbaum.

Langer, Ellen J. (1975). "The Illusion of Control." *Journal of Personality and Social Psychology* 32:311–328.

McArthur, Leslie Z. (1972). "The How and What of Why: Some Determinants and Consequences of Causal Attribution." *Journal of Personality and Social Psychology* 22:172–193.

Menec, Verena H., and Perry, Raymond P. (1995). "Reactions to Stigmas: The Effects of Targets' Age and Controllability of Stigmas." *Journal of Aging and Health* 7:365–383.

Oakes, Penelope. (1987). "The Salience of Social Categories." In *Rediscovering the Social Group: A Self-Categorization Theory,* ed. John C. Turner. Oxford, Eng.: Blackwell.

Regan, Dennis T., and Totten, Judith. (1975). "Empathy and Attribution: Turning Observers into Actors." *Journal of Personality and Social Psychology* 32:850–856.

Ross, Lee. (1977). "The Intuitive Psychologist and His Shortcomings: Distortions in the Attribution Process." In *Advances in Experimental Social Psychology, Vol. 10.,* ed. Leonard Berkowitz. New York: Academic Press.

Schachter, Stanley, and Singer, Jerome E. (1962). "Cognitive, Social, and Physiological Determinants of Emotional State." *Psychological Review* 69:379–399.

Sears, David O., and McConahay, John B. (1973). *The Politics of Violence: The New Urban Blacks and the Watts Riot.* Boston: Houghton Mifflin.

Taylor, Donald M., and Jaggi, Vaishna. (1974). "Ethnocentrism and Causal Attribution in a South Indian Context." *Journal of Cross-Cultural Psychology* 5:162–171.

Taylor, Shelley E., and Fiske, Susan T. (1975). "Point of View and Perceptions of Causality." *Journal of Personality and Social Psychology* 32:439–445.

Tesser, Abraham; Pilkington, Constance J.; and McIntosh, William D. (1989). "Self-Evaluation Maintenance and the Mediational Role of Emotion: The Perception of Friends and Strangers." *Journal of Personality and Social Psychology* 57:442–456.

Weiner, Bernard. (1979). "A Theory of Motivation for Some Classroom Experiences." *Journal of Educational Psychology* 71:3–25.

Shealy Thompson

AUGUSTINE

b. Tagaste, North Africa, November 13, 354 C.E.; *d.* Hippo, North Africa, August 28, 430 C.E.; *philosophy, theology.*

Augustine (Aurelius Augustinus) was the most important Christian theologian of the ancient world and one of the most influential theologians in history. His opinions on the doctrines of Original Sin, Predestination, and the Fall were accepted by the Roman Catholic Church and by many Protestant denominations as well. Although, beginning in the thirteenth century, his ideas were revised and in some cases replaced by the ideas of other theologians, Augustine's two basic works, the *Confessions* (c. 397–400) and *The City of God* (c. 413–426), remain important Christian texts. Augustine was also an early psychologist in the sense that he stressed looking inward rather than outward for spiritual fulfillment and in that the *Confessions,* an open account of his personal journey to God, considers emotions such as sin, guilt, and happiness.

Tagaste, the birthplace of Augustine, was located in the region that is now known as Algeria. Augustine's mother, Monica, was a Christian, while his father, Patricius, was a pagan. Despite their different views about religion, both parents encouraged Augustine's education, and after attending schools in the neighboring village, he was sent to Carthage for a more proper education when he was nineteen years of age. In Carthage, Augustine worked as a teacher of rhetoric and entered into a relationship with a woman whom he did not marry but who bore him a son. During this period, Augustine also began to explore the teachings of ancient philosophers, to examine alternatives to Christianity, and to contemplate his own life. In 383, he moved first to Rome and then to Milan, where he met and came under the influence of Ambrose, the bishop of Milan, perhaps the best-known Christian in the Roman Empire. Augustine then converted to Christianity and was baptized by Ambrose in 387.

After his conversion, Augustine returned to North Africa, formed a monastic community, entered the priesthood in 391, and became the bishop of Hippo in 395 (a position he held until his death in 430). His time in Hippo coincided with a time of great turbulence in the Roman Empire, which was increasingly falling under the control of invaders from the north and east. In 410, Rome was sacked, and at the time of Augustine's death, Hippo was coming under siege from the invading Vandals. This period was also a time of considerable controversy within the Christian Church. Various schools of theology, including the Manichaeans (of which Augustine had once been a member), the Donatists, the Pelagians, and the Arianists, were competing for influence. However, Augustine attacked these schools in his writings, and his own views on many theological matters prevailed and were accepted by the Church in Rome.

Saints Augustine and Monica, as depicted by Ary Scheffer's 1854 painting. (Corbis/National Gallery Collection; by kind permission of the Trustees of the National Gallery, London.)

In addition to the *Confessions* and *The City of God,* Augustine produced a large body of sermons, treatises, biblical commentaries, letters, and reports. All of his works were catalogued in the *Retractationes,* which he compiled in 427 and 428. Augustine's works provide an important record of the development of Christian thought as well as a record of the fall of the Roman Empire. *Confessions* is part autobiographical, part commentary. In the first nine chapters, Augustine recounts his life from infancy through his thirty-fourth year and concludes with a confession to God. Augustine addresses the various emotional crisis of his early life and analyzes them in the context of Christian belief. The emotional issues that are covered in this publication include grief over his mother's death, the sin of his involvement with his mistress in Carthage, the turmoil of bad friendships, the struggles of his conversion experience, and the matter of human will. *The City of God* is a work of historical commentary in which Augustine attempts to refute the criticisms of Christianity that followed the fall of Rome. He argues that God *was* responsible for Rome's greatness and that Christianity *was not* responsible for its demise. In the remainder of the book, Augustine sets forth a number of theological ideas that cover evil, the millennium, death and resurrection, the two cities (of Heaven and Earth), prophecy, and judgment and punishment.

During his lifetime, Augustine's open discussion of his feelings and emotional turmoil as he sought to reconcile behavior and belief drew a readership from among the large number of people who espoused an emotional form of devotion to God. After his death, Augustine continued to have a great influence on theologians in the Middle Ages, including St. Thomas Aquinas in the thirteenth century, and on the Protestant reformers, including Martin Luther and John Calvin, in the early sixteenth century. As Christian theology became more sophisticated, Augustine's clear, emotional approach fell from general favor, but it continued to influence many theologians such as Francis de Sales, Pascal Reinhold Niebuhr, and Paul Tillich.

See also: PHILOSOPHY; SIN

Bibliography

Augustine. (1994). *The City of God,* tr. Marcus Dods. New York: Modern Library.

Augustine. (1998). *The Confessions,* ed. Susan B. Varenne. New York: Vintage Books.

Brown, Peter R. L. (1967). *Augustine of Hippo: A Biography.* Berkeley: University of California Press.

Chadwick, Henry. (1986). *Augustine.* New York: Oxford University Press.

Kirwan, Christopher. (1989). *Augustine.* London: Routledge.

David Levinson
Ben Manning

B

BIOCHEMISTRY OF EMOTIONS

Emotions serve as a primary method of communication and as a motivational state. They also have a functional role in humans' interactions with the environment. As important as they are, emotions are difficult to define, and the search for the causes or bases of emotion has been disappointing.

Early Research

The James-Lange Hypothesis represented one of the first attempts to describe the relationship between bodily sensations and the subjective experience of emotions. Independently formulated by William James and Carl Lange in the 1880s, this theory is based on the notion that emotions are secondary to the perception of physical sensations and that emotion could not exist without bodily experiences. This argument marked a major shift in focus from a concentration on the psychological causes of emotion to the inclusion of the physiological influences. This integration of the biological and psychological elements of emotion was also evident in the work of Walter Cannon (1929), who challenged the notion that unique physiological responses preceded and/or caused emotional experiences. Cannon argued that physical perceptions cannot account for the wide range of emotions that are exhibited by people. According to Cannon, the thalamus was chiefly responsible for the experience of emotion and bodily sensations, disputing the notion that one depended on the presence of the other. Through a series of experiments, Cannon demonstrated that epinephrine, a catecholamine (i.e., an amine that functions in the sympathetic nervous system as a hormone, neurotransmitter, or both), prepares the person for threatening situations by causing a wide range of emotional responses. These emotions, in turn, influence the person's flight-or-fight response. Although James Papez (1937) subsequently found that the thalamus was not the central control center for emotions, Cannon's work continues to influence researchers. In addition to linking the sympathetic nervous system with flight-or-fight situations, Cannon also argued that the sympathetic division of the autonomic nervous system served an adaptive function by supplying the person with the biological resources necessary to respond to threat (e.g., increased available glucose, increased cardiac output).

While Cannon focused primarily on catecholamines and activity of the sympathetic nervous system, the landmark contributions of Hans Selye guided the study of stress in a new direction. His work centered on the role of the adrenal gland and corticosteroids produced by the adrenal cortex. His research was based on the observation that people experience a consistent physical response as a result of any aversive threat or protracted insult, suggesting a nonspecific response to stress. Regardless of which stressor he applied, if it was maintained over time, Selye observed enlargement of adrenal glands, a shrinking thymus gland, and ulceration of the stomach. To account for these phenomena, Selye (1976) proposed the general adaptation syndrome, a model that depicts the processes that underlie the response to a stressor. According to this model, alarm, which is the initial phase of response, begins when the person experiences increased adrenal, cardiovascular, and respiratory activity as the stressor is detected. The massive release of corticosteroids associated with this alarm serves to prepare the person to deal with this threat. The second stage begins when the person's corticosteroid levels have reached heightened levels and coping is applied. This stage is marked by resistance, as the stressor is overcome or accommodated so that its effects are minimized. However, if resistance does not remove or resolve the stressful situation, the person may cycle back and forth between new alarm-like reactions and sustained periods of resistance. Selye defined the third stage as being the consequence of prolonged resistance or unabated cycling between alarm and resistance. Prolonged resistance to threat renders people increasingly vulnerable to physiological harm and possibly disease.

The nonspecific response quality that defined Selye's model has been strongly criticized, and most theories of the biochemical bases of emotional states require some degree of correspondence between emotion and biochemical substrates. One of the chief criticisms was that people do not respond to stressors in a nonspecific manner—different patterns of bodily activity are associated with different stressors. Many emotions involve activation such as that involved in stress, and some researchers have defined stress as being a strong and complex emotional state. However, research on emotions suggests that emotions extend beyond basic physiological activation and can reflect very different biological states.

This early research set the stage for more detailed analyses of the biochemical bases of emotion. To some extent, research and theory about these aspects of emotion are based on findings that suggest that hormones affect neurotransmitters and their metabolism. When a neuron is stimulated, it releases neurotransmitters into the space between it and another neuron. The neurotransmitter travels across this synaptic cleft and binds to the adjacent neuron, thereby stimulating it. At the same time, it is taken back up by the initiating neuron, and the remaining neurotransmitter is metabolized. This alters the amount of the neurotransmitter that is available, and the duration and concentration of the available neurotransmitter appears to affect mood. One of that the best places to look for evidence of biochemical mediation of emotions is in the synapse and postsynaptic ganglia. For example, greater availability of norepinephrine or serotonin in the synapse could be achieved by greater production of the neurotransmitter by presynaptic neurons or by slowed or reduced metabolism or reuptake of peptides released into the synaptic cleft. These changes may have implications for the study of mood and mood

disorders. Drugs that inhibit monoamine oxidase inhibitors have been used extensively as antidepressants. Their mechanism of action targets the enzyme monoamine oxidase, which is a key factor in the metabolism of monoamine compounds released by presynaptic neurons (e.g., norepinephrine, dopamine). Inhibition of monoamine oxidase leads to slower degradation and reuptake of the neurotransmitter and to greater availability of norepinephrine or dopamine. Antidepressant action is produced by the relatively greater levels of monoamine compounds, a phenomenon linked to improved mood.

Biological Theories of Emotion

James was one of the first theorists to draw attention to the complex issues that are related to emotion. For James, emotion represented the perception of the feelings that are associated with changes in bodily sensations. While this theory has evolved over the years, most researchers agree that multiple processes play a major role in the experience of emotion. On a psychological level, the subjective experience of emotion is based on appraisal (thoughts that incorporate past associations) and sources of external validation. On a physiological level, a number of biochemical compounds have been linked to specific corresponding emotions. While these associations are noteworthy, they do not necessarily imply causality. Instead, it remains unclear as to whether the subjective experience of emotion activates biological substrates or whether these biological underpinnings lead one to seek a label for perceived physical changes. Al Ax (1953) attempted to clarify this point by inducing feelings of anxiety or anger in subjects. Different patterns of physiological response emerged when subjects experienced anger and when they experienced anxiety or fear. These results, which supported Ax's contention that different biological changes reflect different emotions, also implied that the psychological and biological components of emotions are the same.

Malcolm Lader and Peter Tyrer (1972) argued that one's physical and social environment present stimuli that interact with individual variables. The processing of these stimuli is mediated by factors related to personal disposition, by past experiences with the stimuli, and by learned associations. Stimuli processed in this manner produce a nonspecific central nervous system arousal state, which in turn produces a particular emotion. According to the model, if the interaction between stimuli and individual factors occurs at the conscious level, the experience of a particular emotion will likely be expected. However, if the interaction occurs at an unconscious level, the emotion may be considered unexpected or irrational. This judgment may mediate the intensity of the emotion and the degree of emotional expression.

Another model that incorporates biological elements of activation into emotions was based on a provocative study by Stanley Schachter and Jerome Singer (1962). This two-factor theory represented a framework that linked the physiological experiences associated with emotion to the subjective experience of emotion. Arousal in emotional states was often undifferentiated, and it was the cognitive interpretation and labeling of these states that formed the core of emotional experiences. For example, the experience of physical arousal marked by an increase in heart palpitation and respiration rate must be explained, thereby initiating a search of the environment for a likely cause and explanation. Cognitive interpretation of arousal was the key variable in this system. That is, a true emotion, in addition to the psychological component, includes physiological and cognitive components. In addition, accurate identification of an emotion was facilitated by the presence of others who were experiencing the same emotion. Schachter and Singer tested this theory by injecting three groups of male subjects with epinephrine in a dose that would produce clear symptoms of sympathetic nervous system arousal. One group was forewarned of the effects of the compound, while the other groups were uninformed. Confederates used in this study were instructed to exhibit happiness or anger to the subjects after the injection in order to model a set emotion for the subject. The results of the study supported the two-factor model. Subjects who were informed of the effects of the drug before the injection was given did not seek an explanation for the symptoms they experienced after the injection—because they had already anticipated such experiences. Those subjects who were not informed in advance of the drug's effects sought an explanation by assessing and adopting elements of the confederate's mood. While subsequent investigations that have tried to replicate the results obtained by Schachter and Singer have produced mixed results, this landmark study underscored the role of social cues and the cognitive interpretation of physical sensations, thereby advancing researchers' understanding of emotions.

More recently, James Averill and his colleagues (1994) delineated four major sources of influence of emotion. These factors include environmental factors, inborn biological processes, traits and temperament, and characteristic variability. The interaction of these variables contributes to both the experience and intensity of emotion. The general framework of this model portrays the experience of emotion, the psychological and physiological components, as an output of information from varying sources.

Biochemical Correlates of Emotional States

Sympathetic nervous system activity is a major pathway through which one experiences stress and other emotions. A division of the autonomic nervous system, the sympathetic nervous system becomes highly activated during states of emotional arousal. Investigators have successfully stimulated the sympathetic nervous system to produce emotional responses in participants. Conversely, they have attempted to block the effects of the sympathetic nervous system as a way of preventing or minimizing the experience of emotions when a person is confronted by a stressor. This research has been fueled by the development of compounds that block adrenergic receptors.

The hypothalamic-pituitary-adrenal axis is another endocrine axis that is associated with stress and emotional arousal. Disturbance of this axis has been associated with different mood disorders, particularly with major depression. The hypothalamic-pituitary-adrenal axis can be characterized by a number of sequential steps that depend on the release of specific hormones. When a person is aroused, corticotropin releasing factor regulates the release of adrenocorticotropic hormone from the pituitary gland. This, in turn, causes the adrenal cortex to release glucocorticoids.

The systems involved in responding to stress generally play a role in what some would consider to be the complex emotions. High self-esteem, hardiness, and emotional stability have been associated with higher plasma cortisol levels and less psychological distress. Elevated levels of growth hormone in response to pyridostigmine suggests a cholinergic disturbance in depression. Endogenous opioids and corticosteroids have been associated with shyness, distress, and fear. Much of the research regarding these agents have been conducted in animal studies, where endogenous opioids appear to be a major factor in social behavior. Studies have found that stimulation of opioid receptors has resulted in play and dominant behavior, while blockade of opioid receptors has been linked to decreases in both play and dominance. These studies have not been replicated with humans; therefore, their applicability is limited.

Jerome Kagan and his colleagues (1987), who have conducted studies of shyness among humans, have suggested that inhibited children have greater stress-like reactivity. These inhibited children exhibit stable tendencies to react to changes in their environment with more inhibited, resistant, fearful affect. In addition, inhibited children generally exhibit higher urinary norepinephrine levels than less inhibited children. These findings suggest that shy individuals experience a greater level of stress than do less inhibited children and that this stress contributes to or results from inhibition of social behavior. Consistent with studies that have found associations between fear and cortisol levels, Kagan and his colleagues found that the resting levels of cortisol were elevated among these children as well, indicating a broad stress response among inhibited children and a heightened reactivity to acute stress.

Another source of data related to the endocrine bases of emotion are studies of treatment of emotional disorders. Schizophrenia, depression, and withdrawn affect have been treated experimentally with a variety of hormones and hormone extracts. Similarities between schizophrenia and hypothyroidism sparked initial attempts to treat schizophrenia with thyroid extract. These approaches were not useful in treating schizophrenia, but they were useful in the treatment of periodic catatonia. These approaches also proved ineffective in the treatment of depression, although thyroid hormones do appear to increase the effectiveness of some antidepressant drugs. This approach is useful if it provides information about thyroid deficiencies or other characteristics that might be causes or bases of emotional disturbances or mood. There is little or no evidence to suggest that a lack of thyroid hormones causes depression or that administration of thyroid hormones has much beneficial effect.

Elements of the hypothalamic-pituitary-adrenal axis have also been examined in relation to the treatment for mood disorders. In particular, adrenocorticotropic hormone and cortisol have been studied with mixed results. After many failed attempts to treat major psychoses with these steroids, scientists learned that people given doses of cortisone or adrenocorticotropic hormone can experience depressed mood, mania, or delirium. As would follow from this observation, they were not effective treatments for depression, and some evidence even indicated that they actually made symptoms worse. However, an altered pattern of cortisol release associated with depression has been observed, and several researchers have reported that some depression is related to excessive secretion of cortisol.

In a classic study of depressed patients and control subjects, Edward Sachar and his colleagues (1973) compared cortisol levels in circulating blood every twenty minutes for an entire day. The findings indicated that the normal pattern of cortisol release was altered in depressed people; relative to controls, depressed patients exhibited more frequent pulses of cortisol and the normal rhythms governing levels of cortisol at different times of day were blunted. As a result, cortisol was released more often and did not decrease as much as it did in controls at the end of the day. Similarly, studies in which the artificial steroid dexamethasone has been administered suggest important differences. In normal people, dexamethasone suppresses the production of cortisol by stimulating negative feedback to the brain. In depressed patients, dexamethasone has little effect on the production of cortisol, suggesting an insensitivity or defect in the negative feedback loop governing the hypothalamic-pituitary-adrenal axis.

Other hormones have also been used with varying success to treat emotional disorders, but this research has not yielded very much information about the endocrine bases of emotion. It is known that emotional states are associated with physiological and biochemical changes, but it is unclear whether these alterations are due to deficiencies or abnormalities in these compounds or whether these biological changes are due to disturbing situations or recognized distress. As noted, there is some evidence of changes in patterns of release of cortisol in depression (hypercortisolism) and anxiety disorders such as post-traumatic stress disorder. These changes in the release of cortisol may be due primarily to changes in biological rhythms in hormone production (which might reflect responses to distressing affect), or they may be produced as a function of particular coping activities.

The search for evidence of endocrine mediation of emotion is a complicated endeavor. Stress is associated with negative emotions, with increases in catecholamines (epinephrine and norepinephrine), cortisol, prolactin, and growth hormones, and with decreases in estrogen, testosterone, and insulin. To the extent that negative emotions such as anger, fear, and sadness are related to stress, the same changes in hormones are likely to occur when these emotions are experienced. This suggests that it is necessary for researchers to control for or remove the nonspecific effects of stress from those of the emotional state. As one might expect, this is a difficult task, one that is likely to produce mixed findings. However, differences between depressed and nondepressed people in how some hormones are secreted suggest that there is more involved than just stress.

Serotonin and other neurotransmitters have been implicated in a variety of emotional states. Serotonin appears to play an influential role in the regulation of mood, appetite, sleep, aggressive behavior, perception of pain, and circadian rhythms. In addition, serotonin affects the release of prolactin, cortisol, and growth hormone. Low levels of serotonin have been associated with major mood disorders; conversely, high levels of serotonin have been associated with states of mania or an extraordinary amount of euphoria. The drug action of serotonergic reuptake inhibitors, as implied by the name, prevents the reuptake of serotonin, thereby maintaining an increased level of the compound.

Conclusion

While available data are not extensive, they suggest that emotional states are associated with circulating levels of hormones, available neurotransmitters, and metabolism or reabsorption of these chemical messengers. Catecholamines (including dopamine, norepinephrine, and epinephrine), corticosteroids produced by the adrenal cortex, and endogenous opioids (such as beta-endorphin or met-enkephalin) have been considered to be important factors in stress, as well as in complex emotional states such as anger, shyness, and fear. Over time, examination of these biochemical compounds has become easier and less expensive, and techniques for collection of blood, urine, or saliva have been developed. Using measurements that are based on a few relatively simple biochemical principles, researchers have continued to search for causal relationships in the experience and expression of emotion that can be used to address a range of issues, including the diagnosis and treatment of emotional disturbances. In addition, the apparent role of the hypothalamic-pituitary-adrenal axis in the experience of emotion may suggest that health and emotion are related. Continuing advances in psychopharmacology will likely shed more light on the origin of emotions, as well as on other mechanisms that contribute to the experience of emotion.

See also: COGNITIVE PERSPECTIVE; JAMES, WILLIAM; MIND-BODY DICHOTOMY; MOOD; MOOD DISORDERS; NEUROBIOLOGY OF EMOTIONS; PSYCHOPHYSIOLOGY OF EMOTIONS; STRESS

Bibliography

Averill, James R.; Clore, Gerald L.; LeDoux, Joseph E.; Panksepp, Jaak; Watson, David; Clark, Lee A.; Ekman, Paul; and Davidson, Richard J. (1994). "What Influences the Subjective Experience of Emotion?" In *The Nature of Emotion: Fundamental Questions,* ed. Paul Ekman and Richard J. Davidson. New York: Oxford University Press.

Ax, Al R. (1953). "The Physiological Differentiation between Fear and Anger in Humans." *Psychosomatic Medicine* 15:433–442.

Baum, Andrew, and Grunberg, Neil E. (1995). "Measurement of Stress Hormones." In *Measuring Stress,* ed. Sheldon Cohen, Ronald C. Kessler, and Lynn Underwood Gordon. New York: Oxford University Press.

Cannon, Walter B. (1929). *Bodily Changes in Pain, Hunger, Fear, and Rage.* New York: Appleton.

Greenberg, Roger; Bornstein, Robert F.; Zborowski, Michael J.; Fisher, Seymour; and Greenberg, Michael D. (1994). "A Meta-Analysis of Fluoxetine Outcome in the Treatment of Depression." *Journal of Nervous Mental Disorders* 182:547–551.

Herbert, Tracy B., and Cohen, Sheldon. (1993). "Depression and Immunity: A Meta-Analytic Review." *Psychological Bulletin* 113:472–486.

Hollister, L. E.; Davis, K. L.; and Berger, P. A. (1980). "Subtypes of Depression Based on Secretion of MHPG and Response to Nortriptyline." *Archives of General Psychiatry* 37(10):1107–1110.

James, William. (1884). "What Is an Emotion?" *Mind* 9:188–205.

Kagan, Jerome; Reznick, Steven; and Snidman, Nancy. (1987). "The Physiology and Psychology of Behavioral Inhibition in Children." *Child Development* 58:1459–1473.

Kagan, Jerome; Reznick, Steven; and Snidman, Nancy. (1988). "Biological Bases of Childhood Shyness." *Science* 240:167–173.

Lader, Malcolm H., and Tyrer, Peter J. (1972). "Central and Peripheral Effects of Propranolol and Sotalol in Normal Human Subjects." *British Journal of Pharmacology* 45:557–560.

Lange, Carl. (1922). "The Emotions." In *The Emotions,* ed. Knight Dunlap. Baltimore, MD: Williams & Wilkins.

Mason, John W. (1975). "Emotion As Reflected in Patterns of Endocrine Integration." In *Emotions: Their Parameters and Measurements,* ed. Lennart Levi. New York: Raven Press.

O'Leary, Ann; Savard, Josee; and Miller, Suzanne M. (1996). "Psychoneuroimmunology: Elucidating the Process." *Current Opinion in Psychiatry* 9(6):427–432.

Panksepp, Jaak; Jalowiec, John; DeEskinazi, F. G.; and Bishop, Paul. (1985). "Opiates and Play Dominance in Juvenile Rats." *Behavioral Neuroscience* 99:441–453.

Papez, James W. (1937). "A Proposed Mechanism of Emotion." *Archives of Neurological Psychiatry* 38:725–743.

Prange, Arthur J.; Wilson, Ian C.; Knox, A.; McClane, T. K.; and Lipton, Morris A. (1970). "Enhancement of Imipramine by Thyroid Stimulating Hormone: Clinical and Theoretical Implications." *American Journal of Psychiatry* 127(2):191–199.

Ravindran, Arun V.; Griffiths, Jenna; Merali, Zul; and Anisman, Hymie. (1995). "Lymphocyte Subsets Associated with Major Depression and Dysthymia: Modification by Antidepressant Treatment." *Psychosomatic Medicine* 57:555–563.

Sachar, Edward J.; Frantz, A. G.; Altman, N.; and Sassin, J. (1973). "Growth Hormone and Prolactin in Unipolar and Bipolar Depressed Patients: Responses to Hypoglycemia and L-Dopa." *American Journal of Psychiatry* 130(12):1362–1367.

Schachter, Stanley, and Singer, Jerome E. (1962). "Cognitive, Social, and Physiological Determinants of Emotional State." *Psychological Review* 69:379–399.

Selye, Hans. (1976). *The Stress of Life.* New York: McGraw-Hill.

Suarez, Edward C.; Shiller, Andrew D.; Kuhn, Cynthia M.; Schanberg, Saul; Williams, Redford B.; Zimmermann, Eugene. (1997). "The Relationship between Hostility and Beta-Adrenergic." *Psychosomatic Medicine* 59(5):481–487.

Yehuda, Rachel; Giller, Earl L.; and Mason, John W. (1993). "Psychoneuroendocrine Assessment of Posttraumatic Stress Disorder: Current Progress and New Directions." *Progress in Neuro-Psychopharmacology and Biological Psychiatry* 17(4):541–550.

Zorrilla, Eric P.; DeRubeis, Robert J.; and Redei, Eva. (1995). "High Self-Esteem, Hardiness, and Affective Stability Are Associated with Higher Basal Pituitary-Adrenal Hormone Levels." *Psychoneuroendocrinology* 20(6):591–601.

Andrew Baum
John Paul Garofalo

BIOFEEDBACK

See Biochemistry of Emotions; Mind-Body Dichotomy; Neurobiology of Emotions; Psychophysiology of Emotions

BODY LANGUAGE

See Body Movement, Gesture, and Display; Emotion Experience and Expression; Emotion Suppression; Facial Expression; Universality of Emotional Expression

BODY MOVEMENT, GESTURE, AND DISPLAY

How people express emotions nonverbally through the body is a highly complex topic that has fascinated students of human behavior for centuries. From the early writings of the Greek philosophers, who identified the trio of pathos (emotions), logos (logic), and ethos (ethical appeals) as being elemental components in human discourse; through Charles Darwin's revolutionary thesis that emotional expressions are innate (inborn), with specific gestures and facial expressions corresponding directly to specific emotions; to contemporary treatments of the biological, psychological, social, and cultural bases of emotional expression, this topic has captivated scientists and humanists alike.

Even though the lion's share of attention has been directed to the face and facial expressions, there is clear evidence that people interpret the emotional states of others based on such nonverbal cues as gestures, postures, gait and other physical movement, touch, vocalizations, interpersonal distance, and so on. The focus of this entry will be these latter aspects of nonverbal communication. Four of the seven primary coding systems for nonverbal communication are kinesics (i.e., body movement), vocalics (i.e., use of the voice), haptics (i.e., touch), and proxemics (i.e., use of distancing and space). Other codes not discussed here, but which also have implications for emotional expression, are physical appearance (e.g., clothing, accessories, hair style, cosmetics, and grooming), environment and artifacts (e.g., colors in built environments, use of symbolic objects, personal possessions), and chronemics (i.e., use of time).

Conceptual Distinctions

The study of emotional meaning as conveyed by nonverbal behaviors has been approached from a number of different perspectives. As a result, several basic distinctions have been made, including experience versus expression, encoding versus decoding, and symbolic versus spontaneous emotional displays.

The literature on emotions can be divided into two rough categories, that which concerns emotional experiences or feelings and that which concerns the overt expression of those emotional states. Emotions themselves are chiefly considered to be internal physiological and cognitive experiences that can and do manifest themselves in outward expressions. However, since people exert some control over how they respond or behave in situations, and numerous influences in day-to-day encounters compel people to do just that, emotional experiences do not automatically translate into emotional expressions. This complicates matters for those individuals who are interested in studying emotional expression, both in terms of sending and in terms of receiving emotional signals, especially through nonverbal body communication.

Another important distinction is between encoding, what an individual (the encoder) is sending in the way of signals, and decoding, what another individual (the decoder) is receiving and interpreting in the way of signals. Because there is often a difference between what emotions people are experiencing (including how intensely those emotions are being experienced) and how, or even if, those emotions are being expressed, emotional expression should be considered from both the encoder's and the decoder's perspective for their respective contributions to the subject. A key reason for this is that while emotional expressions are sometimes reflex responses to various environmental challenges, they also function as a social signaling system. Often, the process of subjectively feeling an emotion will result in expressive behavioral displays that are indicative of that emotion, whether or not the person displaying the behaviors intends to signal anyone. When expressed in private, in other words when there is no audience present, such displays may be considered to be cathartic (rather than communicative), and they are likely to be authentic indicators of a person's internal experience. However, when expressed in the presence of others, emotional displays become part of the social signaling system, which is to say they are potentially communicative. Because such displays need not correspond perfectly with the internal state—senders may mask, neutralize, exaggerate, or fake different emotions—the study of emotional encoding concerns not only the characteristics of various emotional displays but also what might separate real displays from false displays. The study of emotional decoding concerns interpretations that recipients/observers assign to such displays, the specific cues responsible for those interpretations, and the ability to

The mastery of emotional display and masking can be critical in many social situations. One common example is the "poker face" that must be developed to hide all emotion during a poker game, such as the one depicted by Jay Hambidge in his 1895 The Draw on the Bowery. *(Corbis/Museum of the City of New York)*

identify accurately the emotions that the sender is experiencing or intends to convey.

Ross Buck (1994) has noted that one useful way to differentiate various bodily emotions is according to whether they are spontaneous or symbolic. Spontaneous displays are biologically programmed signs of internal states that are typically expressed automatically and perhaps involuntarily. Reflex acts, such as fleeing in a life-threatening situation or lunging, without forethought, toward an attacker, qualify as spontaneous communication. These forms of response are thought to be "hard-wired" into people. Symbolic displays, by contrast, are ones that are learned and employed with the intention of expressing a particular meaning. Such expressions typically rely on conventional or arbitrary means of expression. For example, communicating anger by shaking a fist or butting another's head would be considered symbolic displays. This distinction may seem to parallel the distinction made by Paul Ekman and Wallace Friesen (1969) between nonverbal behaviors that are indicative and those that are communicative. Indicative cues may reveal something about a person's internal states and feelings but are not intended to be communicative, whereas communicative cues are ones that are deliberately encoded to send a message, such as whether one is happy or sad. (A similar distinction was introduced at the beginning of the twentieth century between emotional communication—unintentional "bursting out" of emotion during speech—and emotive communication—strategic signaling of affective information, with no necessary correspondence to internal states). However, those individuals who subscribe to the spontaneous/symbolic classification of emotional expressions, as well as those who believe most emotional expressions come under some regulatory control, usually consider both classes of cues to be communication because they function as social signals—put another way, they have "meaning" for others.

Universality of Bodily Emotions

Perhaps no issue has loomed larger in the study of bodily communication than the extent to which such expressions are universal (which implies that they have a common genetic or neurological basis that reflects an evolutionary heritage that is shared by all humans) or relative (which implies that their form, use, and interpretation are tied to individual cultures and contexts). A blend of nature and nurture as joint influences on nonverbal emotional displays and their interpretation has attracted the most adherents, but with different scholars and disciplines emphasizing different degrees of influence from the biological to the social side of the equation.

Originating with Charles Darwin's treatise *The Expression of the Emotions in Man and Animals* (1872), the evolutionary perspective on nonverbal communication of emotion maintains that human emotional expressions (particularly facial ones) are innate. Darwin asserted that these signals functioned as adaptive physiological mechanisms that allowed humans to navigate and survive their environment. Over the course of time, these signals became specialized to serve only communicative functions. Ethologists and neurobiologists, among others, have carried this thesis forward with substantial scientific evidence of signals that are universally displayed and understood. Comparative analyses of interspecies and intraspecies displays, for example, find similarities between innate displays among other vertebrate animals and those displayed by humans. The way an animal sits, stands, or walks reflects and communicates its emotional state to others present. Animals of the same species, for example, assume the same posture when confronting prey or avoiding danger. They may communicate their lack of fear by sprawling in a relaxed posture and strutting about with their tails in the air. Fearful and subordinate animals crouch, head drawn into shoulders, and walk cautiously with their tails hanging down. Humans express arousal, approach-avoidance tendencies, and emotional states in similar manners. Fearful humans may adopt a contractive, stooped posture and hesitant gait. Depressed humans, like depressed animals, will droop and drag themselves along in slow motion. Other actions such as shaking a fist (rage, aggression), twisting hands together (anxiety), touching the face (shame), assuming expansive stances and gestures (antagonistic defense), showing the palm of a hand or lowering the head (submission, appeasement), yawning (boredom), producing high-pitched alarm cries (fear), offering soothing pats and hugs (love, attachment, comfort), and exhibiting a mock aggressive touch (playful affection) may be universal emotional displays. Physiological and neurobiological work on emotions similarly supports some degree of universality by virtue of reflexes, drives, arousal, and emotions being controlled anatomically by such structures as the ascending reticular activating system, R-complex, and limbic system (which includes, among other components, the hippocampus, hypothalamus, thalamus, and amygdala). Functionally, emotions are controlled by the transmission and reception of various neurochemicals such as dopamine, norepinephrine, endorphins, and hormones. Thus, all humans have the same brain circuitry that is responsible for emotional readouts, or what Buck (1988) calls "primes."

On the other side of the universality position is the extensive evidence of cultural differences in the form, function, and meaning of various emotional displays. This led Ekman and his colleagues (1969) to propose the neurocultural theory of emotional displays. According to this theory, all humans are endowed with the same genetic and physiological affective equipment, as well as many innate responses to environmental stimuli. But, the displays and their interpretations are also filtered through and modified by culture. Cultural display rules, as defined by Ekman and Friesen (1969), represent learned societal norms about what emotions may be displayed under what circumstances to whom and in what way. For example, cultures may differ in how grief is to be expressed in public—with prostrate wailing and gnashing of teeth, with restrained weeping and formal demeanors, with inscrutable impassivity, or with the raucous behavior of a wake. Because cultures have different views on whether touch conveys sexual interest, they will also vary in how frequently touch occurs as well as what meanings are ascribed to it—Western cultures may exhibit less touching between two males than is true in non-Western cultures. Relational display rules, situational display rules, and individual display rules may also be important factors. Employers may feel inhibited about expressing certain emotions in front of subordinates, formal settings may call for different standards of decorum than joyous celebrations, and people who rigidly control their emotions may avoid exhibiting extreme states of emotional agitation. Each of these situations is likely to be influenced in some way by the broader culture that encompasses it.

The position of contextual relativity is founded on the belief that the communication of emotion is necessarily adjoined to context. As Karen Barrett (1993, p. 152) says, "No aspect of emotion is invariant in form, nor invariably present when the emotion is in process." Context, whether it be environmental, societal, relational, or a combination of these, gives a meaning to behaviors that may otherwise have had different meanings or no recognized meaning at all. Therefore, to attempt to isolate emotional cues from context is counterproductive. The role of context in influencing and interpreting facial expressions has been well-established. From this, it can be surmised that the communication of emotion through nonverbal channels such as body movements, vocalics, and interpersonal distance may similarly require contextual information for there to be shared meaning for the people who are involved. William James (1932) pointed out that people may imagine a setting or context for the nonverbal cues they are seeing, using past experience or imagined situations to provide them with a framework that allows them to decipher those behaviors. The power of these influences is obvious, granting meanings that may differ widely based on the applied context. Seeing an individual shaking his fist, if taken as an emotional display, might reliably indicate anger, while taken simply in the context of movement, this exact same behavior may simply be the movement of someone's hand as they rattle dice. Context may similarly affect how emotions are displayed. Hugh Wagner and Jayne Smith (1991) found that women's emotional displays differed depending on whether they were with friends or with strangers.

It goes without saying that because emotional experiences differ from person to person, so should emotional expressions. One theory that addresses these individual differences is Buck's (1993) developmental-interactionist theory (also known as readout theory). According to this theory, humans acquire and hone their range of emotional behaviors from infancy forward through a process of emotional education. They learn from caregivers how they should respond to various stimuli and are given social feedback on the appropriateness of their emotional expressions. In this way, because each person has a unique developmental history, each person's manner of expressing emotions will also reflect unique, idiosyncratic properties. Other individual differences in personality, temperament, anatomy, and physiology will likewise influence how emotional expressions are displayed and interpreted. Evidence of individual variability, however, is not intended to dispute the thesis that emotional experience and expression have universal, biologically based and culturally shared features.

Emotional Meanings Conveyed by the Body

Several issues regarding emotional meanings conveyed by bodily expressions are particularly relevant. Such issues include the importance of viewing bodily expressions as a whole, the scope and precision of bodily cues, and what meanings are conveyed by the separate codes that contribute to bodily expressions.

Bodily Expressions As a Set of Cues

Nonverbal cues have long been held to be the primary site for emotional expression. Typically, however, emotions are not conveyed by a single indicator but rather by a set of cues, which can create considerable complexities for both senders and receivers. James (1932, p. 406) captures the essence of this complexity:

A single facial expression or bodily posture may be regarded as consisting of a number of variable factors such that a change in any one might be to expected to change the expression of the whole. There is, of course, a certain artificiality in assuming the independence of mimicry, gesture, and posture as modes of expression. The natural expression, we may suppose, is a total made up of a certain facial expression, certain gestures, and a bodily posture. There is, however, no guarantee that expression may not be based upon some single aspect of the total.

Michael Argyle (1988) reiterates this idea, contending that it is the combination of movements by the face, voice, arms, legs, and other body parts, as well as touching behaviors, that yields an overall display. Therefore, judgments of isolated body movements, postures, and gestures as signals of emotion should be accepted with a fair amount of caution and reservation.

Scope and Precision of Expressions

Many scholars regard emotional signals communicated by the body to be of a different nature than those signals communicated by the face. Emotions can be located roughly on a continuum ranging from gross affect, broadly judged as positive or negative, to more specific mood states (e.g., contentment, irritability) and emotions (e.g., anger, happiness, fear). Whereas people typically rely on the face or voice to detect specific emotional states, researchers including James (1932) and Ekman and Friesen (1967) have found that people are more apt to recognize gross affect and emotional intensity or emphasis rather than specific emotions from head and body movements.

A case in point is the ambiguity associated with posture. While some ritualized or conventional postures, such as bowing or prostrating oneself before royalty, have clear-cut meanings, postures may more often give rise to a range of possible interpretations and thus best function in a subsidiary role reinforcing or intensifying the specific affects signaled in other channels. For example, a wide range of hand and arm movements, and to a lesser extent head and trunk movements, communicate emphasis, presumably by coinciding with verbal or vocal punctuation. Yet other aspects of body movement, such as degree of postural relaxation and head movement or orientation, may signal a position along the emotional continuum (e.g., aroused to unaroused) or gross affect rather than particular emotions. Additionally, dynamic cues, such as kinesic movement and vocal variety, may be more helpful than static or slow signals in decoding the valence (i.e., positivity or negativity) and intensity of specific affects, and possibly even specific emotional categories. In short, in contrast to facial and vocal cues, other bodily movements tend to convey general rather than specific emotions.

Numerous researchers have attempted to capture the qualities of this more general information in the context of their studies and have found it productive to examine dimensions of judgments that underpin body movements and bodily expressions. These dimensions provide information that, while more basic, is nonetheless essential for its valuable adaptive cues. One study by Marco de Meijer (1989) found three dimensions of judgment underlying ratings of body movements: rejection-acceptance, withdrawal-approach, and preparation-defeatedness. Rejection is any behavior that communicates a person's readiness to react with force to remove a barrier or an unpleasant stimulus. Such behaviors include strong and bowed movements that may be fast and indirect. Acceptance, the opposite of rejection, is described as behavior that communicates a person's willingness to interact without violence. These behaviors are indicated by stretching, opening, lightness, and directness of movement(s). Bowing, closed movements, downward or backward movements of the body, often expressed strongly and/or directly, typify withdrawal. In this state, an individual indicates a shying away from a situation that might be associated with hiding, protecting, or fleeing. Approach, in contrast, involves moving toward an object or situation and is exhibited in stretching and opening movements. Preparation is communicated by opening, backward movements with the trunk of the body straight, particularly if these movements are direct but not forceful. These movements are typical of an individual's response to something that is unexpected. Conversely, defeatedness is conveyed by limp movements that would indicate a lack of motivation or energy to interact. These movements are generally slow and include bowing and downward-directed movements.

It is interesting to note that these factors compare closely with those outlined by James in 1932, even though the studies were conducted more than fifty years apart. The value of such information, particularly from an adaptive perspective, is often underestimated. In addition to signaling such basic responses as approach and avoidance, bodily displays may provide meaningful information for adaptive responses such as contextually appropriate interpersonal responses, affecting relational success as well as chances of survival.

Kinesic Cues

The term *kinesics* refers to those nonverbal behaviors that involve self-contained physical movements of the body, such as gestures, posture, and gait. They include what are typically thought of as body language. Highly developed systems exist for coding facial emotions. For example, John Gottman and Lowell Kro-

koff's (1989) Specific Affect Coding System (SPAFF) identifies various components of the face that are involved in different emotional expressions. Although systems have been developed to classify the building blocks of kinesic expressions and to catalogue normative patterns such as cultural variants in postures and gestures, no comparable systematic compilation exists for emotional expressions presented through body movements, gestures, and postures. What is known must be gleaned from a wide range of research investigations or inferred from coding systems that focus on other communication functions.

What these various investigations reveal is that some kinesic behaviors can be linked to particular emotions, especially when they occur together as collections of cues. Gross trunk movements, general unrest, and touching the hair may signify action tendencies such as approach or withdrawal that are closely linked with emotional states such as fear, anxiety, or aggression.

A variety of nonverbal cues indicates that this couple walking along the Danube in Budapest, Hungary, is enjoying a close personal relationship. (Corbis/Peter Turnley)

Interest may be communicated by forward lean, direct body orientation, and moderate postural erectness; its opposite, boredom, may be expressed via restless movements, stretching, turning the head away or lowering it, supporting the head on a hand, and leaning back. Open postures may convey emotional receptivity, and expansive, rhythmical, spontaneous, emphatic, self-assertive, fast, upward-directed movements with the arms raised may express joy and elation. Conversely, slow, hesitant, nonemphatic or downward movements, with arms closed in tight to the body, may convey grief. Gestures involving the hair, hiding the face, wringing and interlocking of hands, opening and closing of fists, plucking eyebrows, scratching the face, pulling hair, and aimless fidgeting may express anxiety. Dominance and threat may be communicated by standing with erect posture, moving expansively, swaggering, and using threat gestures, whereas submission may be expressed with head lowering or a head tilt, a crouching posture, or flight.

Emotions may also be conveyed implicitly through cut-off gestures that conceal emotions present in the face or crossed leg positions that attempt to hide anxiety. Other bodily movements are not intended to communicate. These have variously been called "autistic gestures" or "self-adaptors" on the theory that they were originally intended to satisfy some bodily need. Most gestures of this kind are body-focused, such as rubbing one's face or twisting one's hair.

On the decoding side, emotions can also be interpreted correctly from kinesic actions. Joann Montepare and her colleagues (1987) found that people identify, at better-than-chance levels, sadness, anger, happiness, and pride from walkers' gaits. Gaits are seen to be angry if they are heavyfooted, sad if they have less arm swing, proud if they have longer strides, and happy if they are faster paced.

Vocalic Cues

Vocalic cues make up one of the primary nonverbal codes and include all communicative features of the voice other than words themselves. As with other species, vocalizations are a major source of affective information. The wide range of cues, including fundamental frequency (pitch), tempo, pitch range, tempo range, loudness, inflection, resonance, and fluency, that are available for signaling emotional states, coupled with the human capacity to make fine discriminations among these complex and dynamic stimuli, makes possible highly nuanced emotional expressions.

Although the complexities of vocal emotions might make accurate recognition a challenge, research has shown conclusively that humans are quite accurate in detecting vocal emotions. After correcting for the number of accurate guesses expected by chance alone, Jeffrey Pittam and Klaus Scherer (1993) found that the accuracy rate for emotion recognition by listeners is quite often 50 percent or higher (with regard to fear, joy, sadness, and anger). Only the accuracy rate for identifying disgust fell below 50 percent. One reason for this degree of accuracy is that vocal emotions are expressed not as single cues but as patterns of cues. Anger, for example, is conveyed by an increase in all of the following: pitch, intensity, high-frequency energy, and articulation rate. The vocal characteristics that are associated with happiness involve such cues as extreme pitch variation, moderate loudness variation, and a fast tempo. Sadness is conveyed by a decrease in all of the following: pitch, intensity, high-frequency energy, and articulation rate.

With the high rates of vocal emotional recognition and the evidence of individual acoustical properties for different emotions, there can be little doubt that the voice is a remarkably useful channel for expressing emotions—outside of the words as well as through them.

Haptic and Proxemic Cues

Two fundamental elements that indicate how people are feeling toward someone or something are how close they are willing to get to that person or thing and whether they engage in any kind of contact. Although cultural and individual differences wield a not inconsiderable influence, people commonly assess relational messages such as intimacy, dominance, familiarity, and connectedness between others by observing how closely they interact with one another and what kind of touching behaviors (if any) they engage in with one another. People also encode particular messages regarding their affect or emotion by using certain touch and interpersonal distance behaviors. The term *haptics* refers to touching cues that are used to communicate messages, and the term *proxemics* refers to distancing or spacing cues that are used to communicate messages.

In the course of investigating the communicative properties of touch, a number of researchers have developed categories of touch. These various lists of touching behaviors describe such things as types of touch as well as situations and likelihood of occurrence, special categories of touching behaviors, compilations of touching norms, touches commonly used by particular cultures, and the functions of touching behaviors. The communication of emotion or affect through touching is self-evident in these categorical treatments of touch. For example, the categories of touch developed by Stanley Jones and Elaine Yarbrough in their 1985 study include the following: positive affect touches, an example of which might be a touch that is appreciative or sexual in nature; playful touches, which might include playful aggression or playful affection; control touches, which might involve a touch designed to exert influence; ritualistic touches, such as greeting or departure touches; hybrid touches, whereby touch functions to bridge two purposes such as a greeting and a sign of affection; and task-related touches, which involve touch as a by-product of a task, such as the hairdresser's touch as he or she cuts hair.

Emotion factors into proxemic behaviors in terms of people's choice of interpersonal distance maintained between themselves and others. Closer proxemic distances are often associated with affiliative interactions (such as would be expected between friends), while more distant proxemic behaviors tend to be associated with negative affect, with the exception of retaliative behaviors (whereby someone might counter hostility by reducing interpersonal distance in an effort to be intimidating). D. Russell Crane and his colleagues (1987) have found that people employ bigger conversational distances when talking to strangers and to spouses with whom they are dissatisfied than to friends and to spouses with whom they are satisfied. These behaviors may be understood within the broader framework of general affect toward another rather than specific emotional displays. It has been found that men and women differ in their use of conversational distance or interpersonal space. John Aiello (1987) has found that men customarily converse with each other across greater conversational distances than do women; women interact with each other across the smallest distances, while mixed-sex couples will adopt intermediate conversational distances or small conversational distances, depending upon the intimacy of the couple.

See also: DARWIN, CHARLES ROBERT; DEFENSE MECHANISMS; EMOTION EXPERIENCE AND EXPRESSION; EMOTION SUPPRESSION; EMPATHIC ACCURACY; FACIAL EXPRESSION; NEUROBIOLOGY OF EMOTIONS; UNIVERSALITY OF EMOTIONAL EXPRESSION

Bibliography

Aiello, John R. (1987). "Human Spatial Behavior." In *Handbook of Environmental Psychology*, ed. Daniel Stokols and Irwin Altman. New York: Wiley.

Argyle, Michael. (1988). *Bodily Communication*, 2nd ed. New York: Methuen.

Barrett, Karen Caplovitz. (1993). "The Development of Nonverbal Communication of Emotion: A Functionalist Perspective." *Journal of Nonverbal Behavior* 17:145–169.

Buck, Ross. (1988). *Human Motivation and Emotion*. New York: Guilford.

Buck, Ross. (1993). "Emotional Communication, Emotional Competence, and Physical Illness: A Developmental Interactionist View." In *Emotion, Inhibition, and Health*, ed. James W. Pennebaker and Harald C. Traue. Seattle, WA: Hogrefe & Huber.

Buck, Ross. (1994). "The Neuropsychology of Communication: Spontaneous and Symbolic Aspects." *Journal of Pragmatics* 22:265–278.

Bull, Peter E. (1987). *Posture and Gesture: International Series in Experimental Social Psychology, Vol. 16*. Elmsford, NY: Pergamon.

Burgoon, Judee K.; Buller, David B.; and Woodall, W. Gill. (1996). *Nonverbal Communication: The Unspoken Dialogue*, 2nd ed. New York: McGraw-Hill.

Crane, D. Russell; Dollahite, David C.; Griffin, William; and Taylor, Vincent L. (1987). "Diagnosing Relationships with Spatial Distance: An Empirical Test of a Clinical Principle." *Journal of Marital and Family Therapy* 13:307–310.

Darwin, Charles. (1872). *The Expression of the Emotions in Man and Animals*. John Murray: London.

de Meijer, Marco. (1989). "The Contribution of General Features of Body Movement to the Attribution of Emotions." *Journal of Nonverbal Behavior* 13:247–268.

Ekman, Paul, and Friesen, Wallace V. (1967). "Head and Body Cues in the Judgment of Emotion: A Reformulation." *Perceptual and Motor Skills* 24:711–724.

Ekman, Paul, and Friesen, Wallace V. (1969). "Nonverbal Leakage and Clues to Deception." *Psychiatry* 32:88–105.

Ekman, Paul; Sorenson, E. Richard; and Friesen, Wallace V. (1969). "Pan-Cultural Elements in Facial Displays of Emotion." *Science* 164:86–88.

Goleman, Daniel. (1995). *Emotional Intelligence*. New York: Bantam.

Gottman, John M., and Krokoff, Lowell J. (1989). "Marital Interaction and Marital Satisfaction: A Longitudinal View." *Journal of Consulting and Clinical Psychology* 57:47–52.

Hall, Edward T. (1966). *The Hidden Dimension*. Garden City, NY: Doubleday.

Heslin, Richard, and Alper, Tari. (1983). "Touch: A Bonding Gesture." In *Nonverbal Interaction*, ed. John M. Wiemann and Randall P. Harrison. Beverly Hills, CA: Sage Publication.

Izard, Carroll E. (1994). "Innate and Universal Facial Expressions: Evidence from Developmental and Cross-Cultural Research." *Psychological Bulletin* 115:288–299.

James, William T. (1932). "A Study of the Expression of Bodily Posture." *Journal of General Psychology* 7:405–437.

Jones, Stanley E., and Yarbrough, A. Elaine. (1985). "A Naturalistic Study of the Meanings of Touch." *Communication Monographs* 52:19–56.

Montepare, Joann M.; Goldstein, Sabra B.; and Clausen, Annmarie. (1987). "The Identification of Emotions from Gait Information." *Journal of Nonverbal Behavior* 11:33–42.

Pittam, Jeffery, and Scherer, Klaus R. (1993). "Vocal Expression and Communication of Emotions." In *Handbook of Emotions*, ed. Michael Lewis and Jeannette M. Haviland. New York: Guilford.

Scherer, Klaus R. (1979). "Nonlinguistic Vocal Indicators of Emotion and Psychopathology." In *Emotions in Personality and Psychopathology*, ed. Carroll E. Izard. New York: Plenum.

Wagner, Hugh L., and Smith, Jayne. (1991). "Facial Expression in the Presence of Friends and Strangers." *Journal of Nonverbal Behavior* 15:201–214.

Lisa E. Allspach
Judee K. Burgoon

BOREDOM

The perceptive heroine of Jane Austen's novel *Emma* (1816) offers a succinct and evocative description of boredom: "[t]his sensation of listlessness, weariness, stupidity, this disinclination to sit down and employ myself, this feeling of everything being dull and insipid about the house." More formally, boredom can be defined as a state of relatively low arousal and dissatisfaction that is attributable to an inadequately stimulating situation. This definition highlights several key characteristics of the emotion. Attributes of low arousal and dissatisfaction position boredom between sadness and depression (emotions characterized by displeasure) and sleepiness (a state of low arousal) in the range of emotions. Unlike sadness and depression, however, which are typically associated with a sense of loss, boredom usually occurs in response to inadequate stimulation and does not have a negative effect on the self-esteem of the sufferer. Although both depression and boredom can lead to a sense of hopelessness, in the case of boredom this feeling is more diffused and related to a generalized existential sense of pessimism. While loneliness can cause boredom, socially isolated individuals who maintain various external interests or who possess a rich inner life may never experience low levels of arousal or feelings of dissatisfaction.

The fact that boredom is a state and not a trait highlights its fleeting nature. This distinguishes boredom from ennui, a feeling that is typically more pervasive, less fluctuating, and less responsive to the immediacy of one's environment. In everyday language, the often synonymous use of the term *boredom* with the term *ennui* is a potential source of confusion. Whereas boredom is typically experienced as a negative and aversive state that produces a strong desire to escape, the same is not true of ennui. Many adolescents and members of countercultural groups take considerable pride, if not joy, in responding with ennui to the perceived hypocrisy and lack of meaning of the dominant culture. Ennui as a means of social criticism was depicted by Federico Fellini in such films as *La Dolce Vita* (1960) and *8½* (1963).

The fact that the experience of boredom is a result of an attribution made about the level of stimulation present in one's immediate surroundings highlights the connection between boredom and the individuals internal and external reality. Boredom is experienced typically in response to monotonous, highly repetitive tasks that require concentration and that constrain and preclude avoidance. Work on an assembly line or listening to a lecture that is incomprehensible and delivered in an impassive manner are two examples of situations that can elicit boredom. Since feelings of boredom are in part the result of an attribution, this means, of course, that not all individuals feel bored in response to the same environment. From a cognitive perspective, boredom has been associated with the tendency to construct events in an undifferentiated and homogeneous way and with a rigid, dogmatic way of thinking. In terms of a more global personality style, the inclination to experience boredom has been variously associated with extraversion (particularly when the extrovert's tendency to seek out stimulation is constrained or blocked), narcissism, and neuroticism.

Mixed findings have been reported concerning the relation between boredom and psychophysical arousal. Laboratory studies indicate that boredom is usually associated with low physical activation, including low levels of adrenaline, a slowing of heart rate, and a decrease in oxygen consumption. Cognitively, boredom is associated with decreased attentiveness and slower thought processes. This slowing down of the body and of thought processes constitutes a potential threat to safety among individuals performing routine and monotonous jobs (e.g., airline pilots, truck drivers, and assembly workers). However, a lowered state of arousal can easily change to agitation once the bored individual experiences constraint and feels deprived of a means of escape.

Theories of Boredom

According to Mihaly Csikszentmihalyi (1988), feelings of boredom are produced when personal skills surpass environmental challenges. In other words, individuals become deprived of the exhilaration of flow and experience boredom whenever they are confronted with a situation that lacks an adequate level of complexity, difficulty, or novelty. Because feelings of flow are pleasurable and boredom is aversive, Csikszentmihalyi's model points to the motivating power of boredom avoidance. A similar view was expressed by Friedrich Nietzsche in *The Gay Science* (1974, p. 108): "For thinkers and all sensitive spirits, boredom is that disagreeable 'windless calm' of the soul that precedes a happy voyage and cheerful winds."

The basic premise of the model of human functioning provided by Marvin Zuckerman (1994) is the existence of an optimal level of arousal (OLA). Persons with very high OLAs (i.e., sensation-seekers) are susceptible to boredom. In turn, a low threshold for boredom leads to risk seeking behaviors such as pathological gambling, drug use, and promiscuity. Alternatively, a low threshold for boredom can result in overeating.

As indicated, boredom is a feeling of dissatisfaction that results from experiencing a low level of stimulation. But why should a lack of stimulation lead to boredom rather than feelings of pleasure or contentment? There are two theories that try to resolve this apparent paradox. First, in experiments on the effect of sensory deprivation, Woodburn Heron (1957) demonstrated that a changing and stimulating sensory environment is essential for the normal functioning of human beings. The human brain depends for normal functioning on a continuing arousal reaction, which in turn depends on constant sensory bombardment. Boredom, therefore, may be aversive because it is a sign of suboptimal arousal level. Second, the psychoanalyst Otto Fenichel (1953) argued that the unpleasurable experience of lack of impulse that is associated with boredom is the result of repression. In other words, the central problem of boredom, according to Fenichel, lies in the inhibition of aggressive or sexual impulses, which results in a paralysis of will accompanied by a sense of displeasure. Psychoanalytic object-relations theorists, however, conceive of boredom as a

The classic play that defines boredom is Samuel Beckett's Waiting for Godot *(1953), which features two tramps who try to entertain themselves while they wait for someone they are not sure will even appear (he never does). The tramps get terribly bored because nobody comes and nothing happens, but they think that they must keep waiting in case Godot does show up. While they wait, the tramps make up songs and stories, interrupt each other, lose their train of thought, forget why they are there, and then remember that they are waiting (forever).*

Performing repetitive tasks, such as sorting biscuits in this factory in Perugia, Italy, can lead to an increased level of boredom. (Corbis/Vittoriano Rastelli)

by-product of a false self or narcissistic personality structure. According to Heinz Kohut (1971), for example, one of the key features of narcissism is a mismatch or misalignment between one's inner ambitions (true self) and one's external pursuits or current goals (false self). This in turn leads to feelings of boredom and dissatisfaction and a sense of lack of fulfillment. Both Kohut and Csikszentmihalyi explain the presence of boredom in terms of a lack of tension between intrapsychic and external factors.

The fact that the word *boredom* was introduced into the English language only toward the end of the eighteenth century has led cultural and literary critics to suggest that the current concern over lack of self-stimulation is a product of modern times. As argued by Patricia Spacks in *Boredom: The Literary History of a State of Mind* (1995), boredom was born in the same era as (a) the emergence of leisure as a condition, (b) the rise of individualism and a concomitant increase in personal sense of entitlement (to respond with displeasure to a lack of stimulation one has to feel the right to be entertained), and (c) the rise of capitalism and a corresponding decline of orthodox religion leading to progressive disenchantment with the world. In particular, the rapid growth of interest in boredom in the twentieth century has been linked to increased consumerism, rationalization, and information technology, which some observers allege have resulted in sterility and homogenization of culture and an overload of the senses with irrelevant, meaningless, banal—and hence boring—messages on television, radio, and the internet. The relation between boredom and such existential themes as meaninglessness and inauthenticity are explored in the writing of Albert Camus. When asked whether he regrets a senseless murder, Meursault—the protagonist of Camus's novel *The Stranger* (1956)—responds: "What I felt was less regret than a vague boredom."

If feelings of boredom are indeed socially constructed and are an artifact of a cultural shift in the industrialized world, this undermines the thesis that all human emotions have an evolutionary basis. Clearly, more research needs to be done to substantiate this claim. In particular, little is known about the experience of boredom in different cultures. It is also not known whether there is a common (universal) facial expression associated with being bored.

Social Differences in Boredom

It is typical for members of an ingroup to attribute boredom to outsiders. For example, members of the upper class tend to perceive the life of the working class as monotonous, lacking in stimulation, and boring. Conversely, members of the lower class tend to disparage the lack of challenges and authentic experiences that come with affluence. Although boredom was more frequently attributed to women than men in the past, recent empirical evidence suggests that men score higher than women on measures of sensation seeking, boredom, and risk taking. Both cross-sectional and longitudinal data indicate that older adults experience less boredom than younger adults, though there is some indication that boredom increases after the age of sixty-five. A small body of cross-cultural research suggests that boredom is positively related to the perception of social constraints and absence of opportunities. For example, Asian women tend to score higher on measures of boredom than Euro-American women and Black Americans score higher than White Americans.

Conclusion

Boredom is a much understudied emotion that has come into prominence only since the 1970s. It could be argued that boredom is a feeling of modern times and that it points to the existential and cultural dilemmas confronting the Western world.

See also: HELPLESSNESS; HOPELESSNESS; LONELINESS; NIETZSCHE, FRIEDRICH WILHELM; SENSATION SEEKING AND RISK TAKING

Bibliography

Csikszentmihalyi, Mihaly. (1988). *Beyond Boredom and Anxiety.* San Francisco: Jossey-Bass.

Farmer, Richard, and Sundberg, Norman D. (1986). "Boredom Proneness: The Development and Correlates of a New Scale." *Journal of Personality Assessment* 50:4–17.

Fenichel, Otto. (1953). "The Psychology of Boredom." In *Collected Papers of Otto Fenichel, First Series,* ed. Hanna Fenichel and David Rapaport. New York: W. W. Norton.

Fisher, Cynthia D. (1993). "Boredom at Work: A Neglected Concept." *Human Relations* 46:395–417.

Heron, Woodburn. (1957). "The Pathology of Boredom." *Scientific American* 196:52–56.

Klapp, Orin E. (1986). *Overload and Boredom.* Westport, CT: Greenwood Press.

Kohut, Heinz. (1971). *The Analysis of the Self.* New York: International Universities Press.

Mikulas, William L., and Vodanovich, Stephen J. (1993). "The Essence of Boredom." *The Psychological Record* 43:3–12.

Nietzsche, Friedrich. (1974). *The Gay Science.* New York: Vintage.

Spacks, Patricia M. (1995). *Boredom: The Literary History of a State of Mind.* Chicago: University of Chicago Press.

Wink, Paul, and Donahue, Karen. (1997). "The Relation between Two Types of Narcissism and Boredom." *Journal of Research in Personality* 31:136–140.

Zuckerman, Marvin. (1994). *Behavioral Expressions and Biosocial Bases of Sensation Seeking.* New York: Cambridge University Press.

Paul Wink

BOWLBY, JOHN

b. London, England, February 26, 1907; *d.* London, England, September 2, 1990; *attachment theory, human development, psychoanalytic theory.*

John Bowlby was a British psychiatrist and psychoanalyst whose research and writing about child development substantially revised the dominant psychoanalytic perspective of the mid-twentieth century and influenced subsequent treatment approaches for children and adults with emotional problems. Bowlby was educated at Cambridge University and spent 1933, the year following his graduation, working at a school for emotionally disturbed children, an experience that led him to choose the behavioral sciences as a career with the goal of helping children with emotional problems. He was especially interested in the effect of the family situation on personality development, an interest that was to define his career. Bowlby later returned to Cambridge and earned a medical degree in 1939, received psychoanalytic training, and began his career in psychiatry at the Tavistock Clinic in London.

Bowlby's research with young criminals and then five years of service in the military during World War II (as a psychology officer evaluating officer candidates) convinced him that there was a close link between experiences in infancy and childhood and emotional health as an adult. He was particularly interested in the role of separation from a primary caregiver—usually the mother—in infancy and early childhood on emotional development and behavior. Bowlby's research convinced him that such separation had harmful consequences—children often reacted by being angry and unhappy, creating emotional distance between themselves and others, and later experiencing separation anxiety. He also found that infants and young children seem naturally to bond with people (especially their mothers) who take care of them and that they turn to these people for support, protection, and comfort.

From this research and his clinical psychiatric work, Bowlby developed a theory of attachment or emotional bonding that sought to explain these patterns of emotional attachment and the harmful consequences that often resulted when such attachments failed to form or were broken. Bowlby did not find the existing psychoanalytic interpretations of such behavior useful and instead looked to research on young animals for a model that better explained attachment and its consequences. In doing so, he developed the basic framework for what is now known as attachment theory, a model of human development that was later elaborated by psychologist Mary Ainsworth and other colleagues in America. Attachment theory and the issue of social and family ties has, since the 1960s, remained influential in the treatment and prevention of emotional problems, including severe anxiety, depression, and the inability to form close emotional relationships (both in the childhood and adulthood).

In accord with his use of ethology (the study of animal behavior), Bowlby suggested that attachment is a biological trait that all infants are born with and that motivates infants to seek to establish close emotional bonds with people who take care of them. When these bonds are established, infants feel safe and secure; when the bonds fail to form or are broken, infants feel anxious and scared. The underlying cause of this biological need for attachment, in Bowlby's view, is physical dependency in adult caregivers. Bowlby further suggested that attachment developed in stages over the first year of life, that one person (usually the mother) was more important than others as an object of attachment, and that attachment occurs in adults as well as infants and children. Many of these basic ideas were subsequently revised, expanded, and tested by other researchers, producing a somewhat deeper view of attachment than was originally set forth by Bowlby. Nonetheless, his original observations and theory set the groundwork, and the nature of early family relationships are now routinely considered in programs that are designed to both prevent and treat emotional problems in children and adults.

For his work on attachment, Bowlby received numerous honors, including an honorary doctorate from Cambridge and awards from the American Academy of Arts of Sciences, the New York Academy of Medicine, and the American Orthopsychiatric Association. As these awards suggest, although he worked mainly in England, his ideas became popular among psychologists in the United States as well and have remained so.

See also: ATTACHMENT; HUMAN DEVELOPMENT; PERSONALITY; PSYCHOANALYTIC PERSPECTIVE

Bibliography

Ainsworth, Mary D. Salter; Blehar, Mary C.; Waters, Everett; and Wall, Sally. (1978). *Patterns of Attachment.* Hillside, NJ: Lawrence Erlbaum.

Bowlby, John. (1969–1980). *Attachment and Loss,* 3 vols. New York: Basic Books.

Bowlby, John. (1988). *A Secure Base: Parent-Child Attachment and Healthy Human Development.* New York: Basic Books.

Holmes, Jeremy. (1993). *John Bowlby and Attachment Theory.* London: Routledge.

Van Dijken, Suzan. (1998). *John Bowlby: His Early Life: A Biographical Journey into the Roots of Attachment Theory.* London: Free Association Books.

David Levinson

C

CATHARSIS

See Happiness; Hope; Pleasure; Satisfaction

CATTELL, RAYMOND BERNARD

b. Staffordshire, England, March 20, 1905; *d.* Honolulu, Hawaii, February 2, 1998; *personality, psychology.*

Raymond Bernard Cattell was one of the leading academic psychologists of the mid-twentieth century. His major contributions were in the areas of personality and the use of statistical techniques in psychological research. His studies on the combined and cumulative influences of the social environment and culture on intelligence, emotions, and personality development influenced several generations of psychologists and pointed to the complex nature of human psychological development and functioning.

Cattell was educated at the University of London, receiving a B.S. in chemistry in 1924 and a Ph.D. in 1929. After a five-year teaching stint at the University of Exeter, he moved into clinical work as the director of the Leicester Child Guidance Center. He held this position until 1937, when he returned to research at the urging of the eminent psychologist Edward Thorndike. From then on, Cattell's career was devoted primarily to research and writing. After brief assignments at Clark University (1939–1941) in Worcester, Massachusetts, and Harvard University (1941–1943), he settled as a research professor at the University of Illinois,

Urbana-Champaign, retiring as an emeritus professor in 1973. Cattell's contribution to psychology did not end with his formal retirement; he continued into the 1990s to study and write about personality, ability, motivation, and other matters that had been the focus of his life's work.

Cattell's interests focused on research methods, statistical analysis, and the study of personality. He was one of the first psychologists to recognize the complexity of human behavior, and much of his work was devoted to the careful study of the dynamics of human personality. He emphasized a multimethod, multivariate approach to research in which clinical observations were combined with the results of various personality tests, questionnaires, and rating scales to assess the interaction of different components of and influences on personality. In this regard, he was among the leaders of the new, more scientific psychology that has dominated research in psychology throughout the twentieth century. Cattell was instrumental in developing the use of the statistical method of factor analysis in order to identity the key features of personality and the major environmental and genetic influences on personality development.

Unfortunately, many of Cattell's findings were highly technical in nature and were published only in scientific journals, so they often did not influence psychologists involved in the treatment of emotional problems or the general public. Nonetheless, many people have become familiar—if only in a general way—with Cattell's best-known work, his so-called trait theory of personality, in which he distinguished between ability (skill and intelligence), temperament (emotions), and dynamic (motivation) traits and developed various rating scales to measure these personality traits. One such scale is the sixteen personality factor questionnaire, which measures both general emotional personality configurations, such as outgoing or reserved and warm or cold, as well as specific emotions, such as tension and guilt. These and other scales created by Cattell have been widely used in the study of personality and his research has influenced later researchers who have further refined trait theories of personality.

See also: PERSONALITY

Bibliography

Cattell, Raymond B. (1965). *The Scientific Analysis of Personality.* Baltimore, MD: Penguin.

Cattell, Raymond B. (1979–1980). *Personality and Learning Theories,* 2 vols. New York: Springer-Verlag.

Cattell, Raymond B. (1987). *Intelligence: Its Structure, Growth, and Action.* New York: North-Holland.

Schultz, Duane P., and Schultz, Sydney Ellen. (1994). *Theories of Personality,* 5th ed. Pacific Grove, CA: Brooks/Cole.

David Levinson

CHILDREN AND EMOTIONS

See Emotional Abuse: Children; Human Development: Childhood

COGNITIVE PERSPECTIVE

Until the mid-twentieth century, the dominant school of thought regarding emotions was derived from Plato, who argued that emotions are wild and uncontrollable forces of the soul that are non-rational and that serve no psychological purpose. His theory was subsequently elaborated and disseminated by eminent philosophers such as René Descartes, John Locke, and David Hume. Indeed this view still pervades everyday thinking, where emotions are often thought to cloud judgment rather than facilitate it. For example, people are frequently warned of the danger of making rash decisions in the "heat of the moment" or of thinking with their hearts and not their heads.

The ideas of Aristotle regarding emotions stand in contrast to those of Plato. Aristotle suggests that emotions involve rationality rather than act in opposition to it. A good example to illustrate the difference between the Platonic and Aristotelian stances is that of anger. Plato would argue that anger is an intense force, challenging rationality and reason—it is a hindrance rather than a help. In contrast, Aristotle would argue that anger serves a distinct psychological

purpose—it represents a psychological state that facilitates vengeance of the wrong that has occurred and is thereby a rational response to wrongdoing.

For a long time, the Aristotelian theory remained on the periphery of received thinking about emotions. However, as a result of the work of philosophers such as Benedict (Baruch) Spinoza and St. Thomas Aquinas who disputed the Platonic view, and due to psychological research investigating emotions, it is Aristotle's approach that now forms the mainstay of so-called cognitive theories of emotions.

The Cognitive Approach to Emotions and Functionalism

The essence of the cognitive approach to emotions is that emotions are meaningful "takes" on the world and the current human position within it. That is, they provide a legitimate and rational account of a situation that may or may not be in accord with the conclusions derived from a cold, logical examination of the facts. Sometimes the head and the heart communicate different things, but both messages are valid.

Allied to this focus on the meaning behind emotions is the idea of functionality (i.e., the purpose served by emotions). Within the functionalist tradition, emotions are seen as having the important job of reallocating limited mental resources in order to deal with urgent problems at hand. They are not just by-the-way experiences, they actually play an essential psychological role in negotiating the ups and downs of day-to-day life. So, a cognitive functionalist perspective on positive emotions would hold that they are responsible for informing people that all is well and that personal goals are being achieved. In contrast, negative emotions would effectively be viewed as the emergency services of the mind—a set of psychological responses that signify that all is not well.

In a cognitive analysis of mind, every person has hundreds of goals and plans concerning themselves, others, and the world. These goals and plans run concurrently in the context of a world that is characterized by a great deal of uncertainty. Assuming the capacity for cognition is finite, there needs to be some means of prioritizing some goals over others in the light of rapidly changing circumstances. Emotions, it can be argued, facilitate this prioritization. For example, an individual is lying in bed trying to get a good night's sleep before a job interview when he or she hears the bedroom window being smashed. Two (probably subconscious) goals that are running in parallel at that moment would be the aim to sleep and the goal of personal survival. In this situation, it is likely that the emotion of fear will prioritize the goal of personal survival and inhibit the goal of sleep. This involves a rapid reconfiguration of the cognitive system, and leads the individual to decide whether to roll over and tell the burglar to be quiet because he or she needs to sleep or to leap out of bed and leave the room as fast as possible.

What are these cognitive changes that occur as emotions reconfigure the mental system in order to service newly prioritized goals? Psychological research suggests that most basic cognitive processes such as perception, attention, and memory are affected by emotional states. Andrew Mathews and Colin MacLeod (1985) found that anxious individuals seem more attentive to danger and threatening stimuli than non-anxious individuals. Therefore, fear seems to prioritize cognitive mechanisms for detecting immediate threat. In the case of sadness or depression, David Clark and John Teasdale (1982) suggest that people in this state seem to selectively remember negative material from the past. Mick Power and Tim Dalgleish (1997) have argued that this may reflect a reconfiguration of the cognitive system such that information concerning loss is easily accessible, thus enabling the reallocation of resources to cope with the change in circumstances.

Cognitive Theories of Emotion

The theories attempting to explain emotion from a cognitive perspective seem to fall into three broad camps: automatic (network) theories, appraisal theories, and theories that integrate the strengths of the other two approaches.

Network Theories of Emotion

The initial aim of network theories was to provide a model of memory, but they were subsequently developed to incorporate emotion as well. The basic tenet of the network approach is that concepts (e.g., death), events (e.g., spouse's funeral), and emotions (e.g., sadness) are represented as nodes in a memory network that are all linked together—rather like stations on a subway map. Activation in one of the nodes spreads to other nodes via their associative connections. For example, activation of the "vacation" node may spread to activate the "happiness" and "beach in Spain" nodes. Activation depends on the proximity of nodes, strength of initial activation, and time elapsed. The network theory of emotion is regarded as a cognitive theory in that whether or not an emotion is activated in a given situation depends on the pattern of associations (a type of meaning) linked to that emotion node in memory.

Network models have suffered from considerable criticism. First, within the network approach all emotions are treated as equal—they are all just nodes in the system. However, research data indicate that this is not the case. For example, the cognitive processes associated with the emotions of fear and sadness are very different. Second, there is the "hot" and "cold" problem. Network models predict that if someone talks about an event that is linked to an emotion node, activation will spread to that emotion node and evoke the corresponding emotion. However, this does not always hold. People often talk about emotional topics in a cold unemotional way, so the cognitive model of emotions that is used needs to reflect this.

Appraisal Theories of Emotion

An alternative cognitive approach to understanding emotions hinges on the concept of appraisal. The underlying premise is that individuals evaluate or appraise events in the world, usually subconsciously, in terms of the events' significance to themselves and their ongoing goals and plans. Richard S. Lazarus (1991) posits that the initial appraisal of an event occurs with respect to three goal-related dimensions: whether there is goal relevance, whether there is goal congruence or incongruence, and the degree of ego involvement in the event. For example, negative emotions occur when an event is moving a person away from a desired goal instead of towards it (goal relevance and goal incongruence) and has implications for the self (ego involvement).

Other authors, including Phoebe Ellsworth and Craig Smith (1988), have expanded on Lazarus's position and suggested that appraisals or evaluations are made according to a number of features, such as pleasantness, situational control, importance, predictability, and effort required. The emotion depends upon the combination of these appraisal features. For example, happiness would be linked to events that are appraised as pleasant, low in effort, and high in certainty.

An influential appraisal theory of emotions was proposed by Keith Oatley and Philip Johnson-Laird (1987), who suggested that there are five basic emotions that underlie human emotional life: sadness, happiness, anger, fear, and disgust. They relate these emotions to appraisals at key junctures in a person's goals and plans. So, sadness occurs when loss or failure (actual or possible) of a valued goal is appraised; happiness occurs when a successful move toward or completion of a valued goal is appraised; anger occurs when a goal is blocked or frustrated; fear occurs when there is a physical or social threat to the self or a valued goal; and, disgust occurs when an idea is appraised as repulsive to the self or a valued goal.

As with network approaches, appraisal theories also attract their critics. They too meet with the "hot" and "cold" problem described above. Sometimes people may act calmly at a juncture of a plan, whereas at other times on a similar occasion they may become very distressed. Similarly, sometimes people can appraise situations in a cold, calculating way, whereas at other times strong emotions are invoked. Another problem with appraisal theories is that there are times when emotions appear to be generated automatically, even when the individual seems to appraise the situation as non-emotional. So, for instance, the person who is arachnophobic will readily admit that spiders are not really threatening or dangerous—they are appraised as benign—but he or she will still experience an intense fear reaction in the presence of a spider.

Integrated Cognitive Models of Emotion

Because both network and appraisal theories seem to fall short of being completely convincing explanations of emotional phenomena, more complex models have been developed that integrate the strengths of both approaches in an attempt to overcome some of the shortfalls. The core argument is that in any given situation there is the potential for emotion to be generated by appraisal of the implications of that situation for the individual's goals and plans—an appraisal component. However, aspects of any situation that the individual has learned to associate with particular patterns of appraisal will, on later occasions, automatically lead to the relevant emotions, without the initial appraisal having to take place again. In this way, the emotional response can be, and often is, a mixture of the old and the new. Up-to-date appraisal of a situation combines with learned emotional responses to aspects of the situation that have been commonly encountered in the past.

In addition to these two emotion-related ways of analyzing what situations might mean, integrated models also allow a non-emotional or propositional route to assess situations—a way of thinking with the head as well as with the heart. The combination of this idea of more than one route to emotion and the means to generate a non-emotional analysis of a given situation allows for the understanding of how emotional conflict and emotional confusion can arise and provides a good framework for looking at both normal emotions and emotional disorder. However, one problem with the new generation of integrated models is that they are very general and thus sometimes difficult to disprove—a problem for any scientific theory.

Integrated cognitive models of emotion offer a good account of phobic states by indicating how automatically generated emotional reactions and appraisals of a situation such as encountering a spider can be in conflict. Integrated models of emotion can also provide plausible accounts of more complex disorders such as depression. For example, the argument would be that, for depressed individuals, events are systematically appraised in a way consistent with the generation of negative emotions. Depression, then, can be thought of in terms of a vicious circle of cognitive processing in which biased appraisals of this kind lead the individual to feel more depressed. The depression then biases the appraisals even further in a negative direction.

Comparison of Cognitive Approaches with Other Theories

Although, within the psychology of emotion, the cognitive approach to emotions is probably the dominant theory, there are a number of other approaches that attract a considerable intellectual following.

Psychoanalytic ideas about emotion have been highly influential in clinical psychology in the twentieth century, and indeed, their influence has spread to the far flung corners of Western culture. There is nothing inherently incompatible between the cognitive approach to emotions and the ideas in psychoanalysis. If the term *cognitive* refers to the idea that emotions are a function of what events mean, then psychoanalytic ideas are cognitive in their conception. The crucial differences lie in how the psychoanalytic approach, in comparison to the cognitive theories discussed above, represent this processing of meaning. In psychoanalytic writings, emotions relate to largely unconscious meaning structures, whereas in more mainstream cognitive theories, although much of the semantic processing associated with emotion generation is viewed as subconscious, it is assumed that the semantic content involved is available to awareness.

The differences between the cognitive approach and so-called behaviorist approaches to emotion are more profound. The essence of the behaviorist manifesto is that emotions are no more than the sum of emotional behaviors. In sadness, for example, it is crying and a glum expression that are key rather than any internal processing of meaning associated with loss. The traditional argument against the behaviorist theory is that behaviors do not reliably map onto the causal events in this way. Sometimes, following a supposedly sad event, a person will cry, but at another time, following the same event, he or she may do something else—even laugh in a defensive manner. Similarly, people can pretend to be sad by deliberately looking glum, and it is unclear in the behavioral analysis how this can be distinguished from genuine sadness.

The final alternative theory of emotions that merits some discussion here is the so-called feeling theory. This approach is derived from the work of Descartes and William James. The suggestion is that emotions are no more than the experience of physiological reactions cued by certain events in the world. As with behaviorist approaches, feeling theory does not address the issue of how reliably physiological reactions map onto certain events. Also, for both the feeling theory approach and the behaviorist analysis, it is unclear how the system "knows" what behavior or physiological reaction to generate in a given situation without some analysis of the meaning of that situation.

See also: ANGER; ANTHROPOLOGY OF EMOTIONS; ARISTOTLE; DESCARTES, RENÉ; DISGUST; FEAR AND PHOBIAS; HAPPINESS; HUME, DAVID; JAMES, WILLIAM; PHILOSOPHY; PLATO; PSYCHOANALYTIC PERSPECTIVE; PSYCHOLOGY OF EMOTIONS; SADNESS; SOCIOLOGY OF EMOTIONS; SPINOZA, BARUCH

Bibliography

Aristotle. (1991). *The Art of Rhetoric.* London: Penguin.

Clark, David M., and Teasdale, John D. (1982). "Diurnal Variation in Clinical Depression and Accessibility of Memories of Positive and Negative Experiences." *Journal of Abnormal Psychology* 91:87–95.

Ellsworth, Phoebe C., and Smith, Craig A. (1988). "From Appraisal to Emotion: Differences among Unpleasant Feelings." *Motivation and Emotion* 12:271–302.

James, William. (1884). "What Is an Emotion?" *Mind* 9:188–205.

Lazarus, Richard S. (1982). "Thoughts on the Relationship between Emotion and Cognition." *American Psychologist* 37:1019–1024.

Mathews, Andrew, and MacLeod, Colin. (1995). "Selective Processing of Threat Cues in Anxiety States." *Behaviour Research and Therapy* 23:563–569.

Oatley, Keith, and Johnson-Laird, Philip N. (1987). "Towards a Cognitive Theory of Emotions." *Cognition and Emotion* 1:29–50.

Plato. (1977). "The Republic." In *The Classics of Western Philosophy,* 3rd ed., ed. Steven M. Cahn. Indianapolis, IN: Hackett.

Power, Mick J., and Dalgleish, Tim. (1997). *Cognition and Emotion: From Order to Disorder.* Hove, Eng.: Psychology Press.

Skinner, B. F. (1974). *About Behaviourism.* New York: Knopf.

Tim Dalgleish
Jessica Bramham

COLOR

Do colors affect people emotionally? Surely most individuals would react negatively if they were served blue meat. The color would conflict with their sense of the natural appearance of edible food. Also, people prefer particular colors for clothes, the preference changing with the change of fashion. But aside from liking things to have particular colors, can colors in and of themselves make people feel happy, sad, angry, and so on? Is there a connection between colors and the experience of emotions?

A few individuals do indeed see vivid colors when they experience emotions or hear music. Others experience colors when looking at people, words, or letters of the alphabet. Thus, they may see a purple aura behind the person at whom they are angry or experience colored shapes when listening to music. Such crossing of the senses is inborn and involuntary. The color associations, which are stable over time for a particular individual but vary from person to person, are generally reported to be pleasant, life-enriching experiences. This phenomenon is known as synesthesia and is authoritatively discussed by Richard Cytowic in *Synesthesia: A Union of the Senses* (1988).

Synesthesia is experienced by only a minority of individuals. For them, it is apparently a neurological event. But for the rest of the population, there is no evidence that colors spontaneously accompany emotions or induce emotions. There is no known case of anyone ever becoming enraged solely for sitting in a room painted entirely in, for example, red. Yet what then causes the majority of people to make synesthesia-like cross-sensory associations as in the assertions of Americans, Germans, Mexicans, Poles, and Russians that red and black are the colors of anger? What is it about colors that makes it so easy to attach emotion labels to them? Do colors really arouse emotions, or are the claims due to features of language, such as the metaphorical expressions "He got red with anger" or "I was beginning to see red"?

The usual procedure for assessing the effect of color on emotions is to require volunteers to rate small patches of color on scales listing words of emotions. This approach studies visual-verbal associations. For example, looking at a patch of red, the volunteers rate how much they associate it with concepts of emotions, such as anger, happiness, sadness, pleasure, arousal, and so on. Less common are studies on verbal-verbal associations, which use similar rating scales but involve reading the names of colors. Both formats cause people to make color-emotion associations, but the reason for the associations differs for each procedure.

Visual-Verbal Associations

Much research has been done on the relationship between color and emotions. Unfortunately, most of it is uninformative because researchers failed to recognize that color stimuli are characterized by the psychological dimensions of hue (i.e., wavelength; the attribute that permits the label of red, blue, etc.), brightness (light to dark), and saturation (i.e., purity). Various combinations of these three characteristics elicit different emotion associations; therefore, they must be carefully controlled in experiments, something most researchers failed to do. For example, red has been reported to be arousing. However, the red chips used in experiments are typically high in saturation. It is the high saturation and brightness, not the hue, that accounts for the association of red with arousal.

Roy D'Andrade and Michael Egan (1974) were the first social scientists to observe that hue, or the light wavelength, is not the main cause of the associations between emotions and colors—it is the degree of saturation and brightness of the hue. The researchers had respondents select the color chip that best corresponded to a particular emotion term from a set of chips varying in hue, saturation, and brightness. They found that chips of the highest saturation and brightness, regardless of color, were described as "happy" and "good." Chips of unsaturated color, on the other hand, were associated with "sadness" and described as the "worst" chips. Darker unsaturated chips were cast as "worried," whereas lighter unsaturated color chips were cast as "fright" and "weak." But dark saturated chips, again irrespective of the hue, were perceived as strong. The findings in the initial study were found to be similar for Americans and native Mexican Indians, two historically distinct cultures, and the results have since been corroborated in additional cultures. This would suggest that the focus on saturation and brightness in color stimuli and the particular emotional associations they elicit might well be innate responses, human universals so to speak. Not enough is known about the neural correlates of emotions and color vision to attempt an explanation of the D'Andrade and Egan findings based on human neuroanatomy, but perhaps an explanation lies in evolutionary psychology.

For most of human history, the principal unending task was the daily search for food. Lacking an acute sense of smell, the search depended on vision, possibly setting the stage over time for the evolution of innate color-emotion associations. Visually, ripe fruit and vegetables generally come in bright, highly saturated hues. Emotionally, the satisfaction of hunger when eating them is gratifying and joyful; therefore, vivid colors may have come to be associated with pleasurable experiences. Conversely, when in decay, food often takes on a dark saturated hue. The inability to prevent the decay of the precious commodity was probably the source of much frustration, possibly giving rise to the attribution of power to dark colors. New growth, particularly unripe fruit, lacks saturation and brightness. Since new growth was not able to satisfy hunger, it may have led to the association of washed-out colors with weakness, disappointment, and sadness.

Of course, there is the possibility that the findings with the D'Andrade and Egan research format apply only to the context of the experiment. Perhaps, as they have found, any hue, as long as it is highly saturated

and bright, will indeed be described as "happy" and "good" when presented on a small chip, possibly even when seen in a painting or as the color of a shirt. But how many individuals would want the interior of their homes to be painted with this "happy" and "good" color?

Verbal-Verbal Associations

Because the verbal-verbal research format examines the association of emotion terms with the names for colors, the issue of hue, saturation, and brightness is not raised. Ralph Hupka (1997) and his collaborators in Germany, Mexico, Poland, and Russia found black and red to be associated in all nations with anger. Black was also connected with fear. The latter finding conflicts with the D'Andrade and Egan observation (in the visual-verbal format) that lighter unsaturated

The cultural differences in the emotional meaning and significance of specific colors are illustrated by a bride in Rajasthan, India, who is dressed in a traditional red sari embroidered with gold even though Western observers would typically expect a bride to be wearing white. (Corbis/Craig Lovell)

hues are associated with fear, not the dark saturated attributes of black.

Charles Osgood, George Suci, and Percy Tannenbaum (1957) speculated that such associations between color names and emotions originate in learned associations of common features of the environment to which all human beings are exposed. For example, the black of night, a period of sleep and hence vulnerability to danger, might universally be associated with fear. Blood rushes to the face during intense anger, possibly explaining the connection with red. This may explain why Hupka found similar color-emotion associations in several nations. It may also explain the origin of some metaphors, such as "She was scarlet with rage" or "I was beginning to see red." The facial flushing dissipates when the anger subsides. Perhaps this is the reason that the word for feeling peaceful or reconciled in Selepet, a language of New Guinea, is rendered literally by "the anger becomes white."

A second type of learned association may be due to the arbitrary conjunctions of colors and emotions in the myths and literature of cultures. Yellow is the color of envy in German literature ("He turned yellow with envy"). In English plays and novels of the seventeenth and eighteenth centuries, the face of jealousy was described as yellow. On the one hand, black tends to symbolize, for some people, deceit, fear, and hatred, but on the other hand, black is worn by priests and judges and is the expected attire at funerals. While red can symbolize anger, blood, danger, and vengeance, it can also represent lust and carnal passion.

The variety of meanings associated with colors suggests that the connections between colors and their meanings are most likely learned, not innate. But because such associations do exist, they can be a source of dismay to international corporations when choosing the color of the wrapping for a new product. Consider purple as an example. Americans associate purple with virility: powerful, strong, masterful, and vigorous. The Japanese, on the other hand, connect it with sin and fear. Therefore, what suggests virility in one country suggests sin in the other, making purple an unwise choice for the packaging of particular products, such as prophylactics.

The willingness to make cross-sensory associations, as with colors and emotions, occurs in other sensory domains as well. Lawrence Marks (1982) found that individuals readily set the brightness of a light and the loudness of a tone to match the levels suggested by auditory-visual metaphorical expressions (e.g., "the bright sound of battle"). In another study, individuals easily rated words of colors on pencil and paper scales of brightness and pitch. Such findings tempted Marks to propose that they are due to some fundamental property of the makeup of sensory experience, perhaps something akin to what causes synesthesia. Alter-

natively, they may simply be due to the willingness of people to apply glibly or poetically the linguistic categories established for describing one particular sensory domain, say audition, to another unrelated sensory domain, say vision. This gives rise to poetic metaphors that appeal to the ear (e.g., "the dawn comes up like thunder") but lack the descriptive precision required in scientific experiments.

Conclusion

People have strong opinions about what colors they like for their home decor, the clothes they wear, the cars they drive, and the food they eat. People also readily make associations between colors and emotions. However, researchers have been unable to provide evidence to prove that colors directly increase or decrease emotions. Perhaps all one can say is that color makes life more pleasurable and engaging. But even that conclusion may be incorrect. There is no evidence that color-blind individuals find life less interesting than individuals with normal color vision.

See also: CROSS-CULTURAL PATTERNS; PSYCHOLOGY OF EMOTIONS; SOCIOLOGY OF EMOTIONS

Bibliography

Adams, Francis M., and Osgood, Charles E. (1973). "A Cross-Cultural Study of the Affective Meanings of Color." *Journal of Cross-Cultural Psychology* 4:135–156.

Cytowic, Richard E. (1988). *Synesthesia: A Union of the Senses.* New York: Springer-Verlag.

D'Andrade, Roy, and Egan, Michael. (1974). "The Colors of Emotion." *American Ethnologist* 1:49–63.

Hupka, Ralph B.; Zaleski, Zbigniew; Otto, Jürgen; Reidl, Lucy; and Tarabrina, Nadia V. (1997). "The Colors of Anger, Envy, Fear, and Jealousy: A Cross-Cultural Study." *Journal of Cross-Cultural Psychology* 28:156–171.

Johnson, Allen; Johnson, Orna; and Baksh, Michael. (1986). "The Colors of Emotions in Machiguenga." *American Anthropologist* 88:674–681.

Marks, Lawrence E. (1982). "Bright Sneezes and Dark Coughs, Loud Sunlight and Soft Moonlight." *Journal of Experimental Psychology: Human Perception and Performance* 8:177–193.

Osgood, Charles E.; Suci, George J.; and Tannenbaum, Percy H. (1957). *The Measurement of Meaning.* Urbana: University of Illinois Press.

Valdez, Patricia, and Mehrabian, Albert. (1994). "Effects of Color on Emotions." *Journal of Experimental Psychology: General* 123:394–409.

Ralph B. Hupka

COMMITMENT

Commitment is an integral component of the most important social relationships. It binds people together in friendships, partnerships, and romances and forms the foundation on which these relationships can grow. It is the force that enables relationships to withstand adversity and overcome obstacles. It fosters a sense of security and connection between partners that often lasts a lifetime. In short, commitment is the glue that keeps a relationship intact and provides a sense of continuity and stability for the individuals who are involved.

Although such descriptions generally are consistent with most people's conception of what interpersonal commitment is, they ultimately fail to convey the truly complex nature of the bonds that exist between people. Indeed, commitment may be referred to metaphorically as the glue that keeps relationships intact, but questions still remain regarding the composition of the glue and how it is applied. Moreover, one might ask if the glue is of only one type or several, or whether its adhesive properties are uniform across different types of relationships. All of these points illustrate that there is a great deal more to interpersonal commitment than initially meets the eye.

Definition and Conceptualization

Despite its familiarity and prevalence in everyday discourse, commitment has proven to be a rather difficult concept for researchers to describe. The main reason for this seems to be that commitment can take on several shades of meaning depending on the context and manner in which the word is used. For example, in describing their commitment to one another a newlywed couple might say they are "devoted," "dedicated," "faithful," and "in it for the long haul." From such a description, one could deduce that commitment involves pursuing one's marriage enthusiastically, with the expectation that it will last forever. A different couple, however, might indicate that they have committed themselves to their marriage and cannot back out of it, even if they wanted to, because they would lose too much or incur too many costs if they did. In this situation, one still could infer that the couple expects their marriage to last into the future, but rather than reflecting an enthusiastic pursuit of the marriage, this couple's commitment seems to be characterized by begrudging endurance or feelings of entrapment. Yet another couple might remain committed to their marriage because it is "God's law" or the morally responsible thing to do. For this couple, commitment has taken the form of a virtuous act or a moral imperative to remain in one's marriage regardless of what happens. Commitment, then, has many faces, rendering the task of defining it an especially challenging one.

Attempts to understand interpersonal commitment are further complicated by the fact that people often confuse the meaning of commitment with its behavioral manifestations. For example, as mentioned above, commitment is linked with the duration of the marriage. While it certainly is the case that the relationships of committed individuals are much more likely to persist over time than are the relationships of relatively uncommitted individuals, one must take care not to equate commitment with relationship longevity. Equating the two would create a circular argument in which commitment is deduced from the very occurrence of the act that it is supposed to explain— a fundamentally unsound inference. Similarly, one must refrain from equating relationship status (e.g., strangers, friends, spouses) with commitment. Here again, although it might be reasonable to assume that as people's relationships become more intimate their commitment becomes stronger, this also is an inappropriate way to characterize interpersonal commitment. Indeed, it is possible for less intimate relationships to demonstrate a considerable degree of commitment and for highly intimate relationships to end because commitment has dissolved. In other words, the extent to which two people are committed to one another is not necessarily dependent upon the type of relationship they are in.

It is not surprising that the aforementioned descriptive difficulties have led to the accumulation of an assortment of formal definitions in the scientific literature. For example, marital commitment has been defined as the voluntary binding together of two people, both legally and emotionally; the strength of an individual's desire and determination to continue a particular marital relationship; a global, internal, subjective summarization of the factors that underlie stay-leave decisions; a desire to maintain one's relationship; and a decision to build and maintain a marriage relationship with a particular person and acting in accordance with that decision over time. Other definitions reflect slightly different themes, including the feeling that marriage is an institution based on a lifelong commitment and should be preserved even if it becomes unfulfilling; an obligation to put forth effort in a relationship and meet the needs of one's partner; a tendency toward relational stability/instability; and the consequences of the initial pursuit of a relationship that constrain the actor to continue that relationship. Clearly, commitment is a highly complex human experience that defies simple explication.

By even the most optimistic standards, it would appear that contemporary understanding of the fundamental structure of interpersonal commitment is murky at best. Fortunately, several investigations have begun to cast light on this issue by examining the entire body of definitions and attempting to identify the key features of interpersonal commitment that are common to most of these definitions. Through such efforts, a clearer picture of this important construct has begun to emerge.

Beneath the surface of a seemingly confused and confusing literature lie several common threads that appear to capture the most basic features of interpersonal commitment. For example, most researchers agree that commitment is a psychological state that reflects an individual's intention to maintain or persist in a particular relationship. That is, the decision to become committed to a person or relationship and the effort expended to sustain that commitment over time are willful acts—people choose to make and break their commitments to others. This is an important characteristic because it helps to differentiate commitment from more passive sources of behavioral consistency such as social norms. Moreover, and perhaps more obviously, virtually all scholarship on interpersonal commitment indicates that commitment is a causal factor in the long-term stability of relationships. People who are committed to a particular relationship, regardless of the reason for the commitment, ultimately intend to maintain that relationship into the foreseeable future. Accordingly, committed relationships remain intact even when stress, tribulation, and adversity threaten them. Thus, at the most basic level, interpersonal commitment involves an act of will and leads to the continuance of close relationships.

At a somewhat deeper level, a growing number of scholars are beginning to acknowledge the fact that, despite superficial differences, most definitions of interpersonal commitment seem to reflect a relatively small number of underlying dimensions. One dimension (referred to variously as commitment to spouse, personal commitment, and attraction force) reflects an individual's personal desire to see a relationship continue. Because a person who is committed in this way *wants* the relationship to last, he or she acts in ways that are supportive of the relationship and is willing to make sacrifices, if necessary, to ensure its continuation. For example, personally committed individuals are deeply devoted to their spouses and work diligently toward resolving conflict, accommodating negative partner behavior, and otherwise improving the relationship. In short, this dimension of commitment is strongly associated with the degree to which an individual feels attracted and attached to a relationship and thereby bound to it through force of desire.

A second dimension reflects the constraining or entrapping features of commitment, wherein a particular relationship is maintained not necessarily because the partners want to see it continue but because they feel that they *have* to maintain it. Like the first dimension, the second dimension of interpersonal commitment has received different labels in the literature,

In "A Worn Path" (1941) by Eudora Welty, the ancient African-American grandmother, Phoenix, makes her several-mile journey on foot through woods and farms in order to get medicine for her grandson. Her commitment to his care gives her the strength and courage to climb through barbed wire fences, ford streams, and stand up to a patronizing hunter. The worn path and the recognition by the nurses at the health center indicate that Phoenix has made the trip many times.

including feelings of entrapment, structural commitment, constraint commitment, and barrier forces. In each case, though, the labels refer to the feeling of resignation that accompanies the recognition that even though one's relationship is no longer personally satisfying one must stay in it or face severe emotional, social, and/or financial penalties.

A third dimension, called (by various authors) commitment to marriage, moral commitment, institutional commitment, and marital commitment to permanence, represents an individual's intention to maintain a relationship because it is the right thing to do. Individuals who are committed in this way tend to hold strong values regarding the importance of consistent behavior, the stability of particular kinds of relationships (e.g., casual acquaintanceships versus marriages), and the value of keeping one's promises. This morally or normatively based dimension also may have religious undercurrents whereby marriages should be maintained for biblical or spiritual reasons.

Although not all researchers interested in interpersonal commitment have settled on this three-dimension conceptualization, there is compelling evidence that the three dimensions described above adequately represent interpersonal commitment. First, Jeffrey Adams and Warren Jones (1997) and Michael Johnson (1999) have found that the results of statistical analyses designed to identify underlying patterns in empirical data suggest that people's responses to commitment questionnaires tend to coalesce into three general categories corresponding to the attraction, moral/normative, and constraining dimensions. Second, most existing theoretical models of interpersonal commitment refer, in some way, to the three dimensions. This is not to say that all models clearly specify a three-component conceptualization; indeed, different models present numerous structural variants of interpersonal commitment. However, careful examination of these models reveals that they share a number of similarities and, as a set, are reflective of the attraction, moral/normative, and constraining dimensions.

Finally, Adams and Jones have found that the three dimensions are evident in the free responses of married couples to questions about their relationships, suggesting that all three dimensions are meaningful from the perspective of actual relationship participants. Thus, the three-dimension model of interpersonal commitment appears to have considerable theoretical, empirical, and phenomenological support.

One final undercurrent of the commitment literature deserves mention. Although commitment often is considered to be strictly or primarily a cognitive variable, it is important to recognize the fact that commitment is closely tied to emotional experience. For example, the attraction dimension is commonly associated with positive feelings of satisfaction and love. In contrast, the constraining dimension tends to be accompanied by negative emotional states such as frustration, anger, and resentment. The moral/normative dimension may be accompanied by either positive or negative emotional states, depending on whether the moral obligation to maintain a relationship is perceived to be a constraint or a virtue. Thus, although it is not completely accurate to say that commitment *is* an emotion, it certainly is the case that the different ways in which people may be committed to a relationship are associated with different affective states.

Interpersonal commitment, then, is a multidimensional, cognitive-affective process that reflects an individual's intention to maintain a relationship with another person. This definition not only encompasses the various manifestations of interpersonal commitment found in the literature but also distinguishes commitment from other variables of interpersonal relevance. For example, by defining commitment as being a state of intentionality, it is possible to separate commitment conceptually from such relationship qualities as satisfaction and intimacy, which are perhaps better regarded as outcomes of couple interaction than intentions per se. Furthermore, the emphasis on relationship maintenance helps distinguish commitment from love, as it is possible to love someone to whom one is not committed and, conversely, to be committed to someone whom one does not love. Perhaps most important, though, the aforementioned definition captures the extent to which interpersonal commitment is integrated with numerous cognitive, emotional, and social processes, a fact that places commitment in a truly unique position among interpersonal variables.

Theories of Interpersonal Commitment

Having laid the groundwork for a more complete understanding of interpersonal commitment by describing its central features, it is now possible to examine some of the theoretical models that have been developed to explain how people become and remain committed to one another. As will be seen, most formal theories of commitment processes are rooted firmly in social or social-cognitive principles. However, interpersonal commitment can be explained from several other perspectives as well. Although these alternative explanations have not yet received much scientific support and, in fact, represent minority viewpoints in the literature, they nevertheless offer some intriguing interpretations of commitment and thus are worthy of consideration.

Social-Cognitive Approaches

In virtually all contemporary theories of interpersonal commitment, social-cognitive processes play the largest role in explaining how and why interpersonal ties are made, maintained, and broken. Central to this approach is the supposition that commitment is largely a function of how a person thinks about his or her relationships. Thus, most existing models of interpersonal commitment reflect, to varying degrees, a decision-making model wherein an individual will become committed to another person or relationship if, in that individual's estimation, a certain number of preconditions have been met.

To illustrate the social-cognitive approach, three theoretical models—George Levinger's (1965, 1976) cohesiveness model, Johnson's (1973, 1991) commitment framework, and Caryl Rusbult's (1980, 1983) investment theory—will be briefly examined. These are not the only social-cognitive models, but they are the three that have been especially influential in shaping contemporary thinking about commitment in close relationships.

According to Levinger's cohesiveness model, interpersonal commitment is a function of attraction, repulsion, and barrier forces acting on an individual and affecting his or her decision to remain in or leave a particular relationship. Attraction forces, in this context, refer to feelings of love, satisfaction, respect, and security, as well as material resources acquired during the course of the relationship. Such forces are attractive for obvious reasons and serve to draw relationship partners together. However, repulsion forces also may exist in a relationship, serving to drive partners away from one another. Also referred to as costs, repulsion forces include disagreements and arguments that might arise, negative feelings (i.e., irritation or frustration) that partners might experience with each other, and the expenditure of time, energy, and financial resources necessary to maintain a relationship. Finally, most intimate relationships (especially formal, voluntary relationships such as marriage) are embedded in a network of barrier forces that prevent partners from terminating the relationship. Examples of barrier forces include the legal bonds of marriage, pressure from friends and family members, internal feelings of obligation, the threat of social stigmatization, financial costs associated with divorce, and the loss of irretrievable investments (e.g., time, effort, money). Commitment, then, represents a person's net attractions to the relationship (attraction forces minus repulsion forces) plus perceived barriers or restraints against relationship termination—the more rewarding the relationship is and the more costly its dissolution, the more committed an individual will be to the relationship. While the attraction and barrier forces surrounding a given relationship are relevant determinants of a person's commitment to that relationship, it is important to recognize the fact that relationships are not isolated entities—they are embedded in broader social networks. According to the cohesiveness model, these broader social networks also play a significant role in couple commitment by making available to the partners certain alternatives that have their own set of attraction and barrier forces. To the extent that the attraction forces surrounding an alternative relationship exceed those surrounding one's primary relationship, commitment to the primary relationship should be reduced. However, if the barrier forces surrounding the primary relationship are strong enough, then commitment to the primary relationship should remain high, even though the alternative relationship is more attractive. Thus, from the perspective of the cohesiveness model, when considering the causes of interpersonal commitment, one must take into account not only the internal forces of the relationship itself but also the external forces produced by alternative relationships.

According to Johnson's commitment framework model, commitment takes three forms: personal, moral, and structural commitment. Personal commitment, which reflects an individual's desire to continue a relationship, has three components. The first two components are attitudinal in nature and involve the degree to which an individual is satisfied with the relationship and with the partner, respectively. Although it might seem that these components refer to the same thing, the distinction between them is important (as evidenced by the fact that someone can have a favorable attitude toward a partner even if the relationship is a bad one). The third component is relational identity, or the degree to which an individual internalizes or identifies with membership in a given relationship. A personally committed individual considers the relationship role (i.e., husband or wife) to be a central element of his or her self-concept. The second type of commitment, moral commitment, also has three major sources. The first of these is a belief in the value of

The commitment that Michael and Catherine Brady have shared was acknowledged officially on February 4, 1999, when the Guinness Book of Records *authenticated them as Great Britain's longest-married living pair. At the time, the couple (Michael was 98 and Catherine was 104) had been married for 78 years and 190 days.* (Corbis/AFP)

behavioral and attitudinal consistency. An individual who is morally committed to his or her partner tends to subscribe to the notion that it is important to be predictable and to finish what one begins. Second, morally committed individuals hold values about the importance of maintaining certain types of relationships (i.e., marriages should be preserved because they are important institutions). Finally, moral commitment derives from a person-specific sense of obligation in which an individual maintains a relationship because he or she feels that it would be wrong to break the promise of life-long commitment. In general, then, moral commitment results from an internalized moral code regarding the stability of behavior, the importance of particular relationships, and the value of keeping one's promises. The final type of commitment, structural commitment, reflects a person's intention to maintain a relationship because of concern over the penalties associated with relationship dissolution. In particular, there are four areas of concern that lead to the experience of structural commitment. The first of these is the loss of irretrievable investments. People may feel entrapped in an unhappy relationship because they feel that they would lose important investments of time, energy, and money if they ended the relationship. Second, structural commitment is engendered by concern over possible social reactions to the dissolution of one's relationship. For example, one might remain in an unsatisfying relationship if he or she fears being chastised or rejected by friends and/or family members. Third, an individual may feel entrapped in a relationship if he or she perceives the costs of terminating the relationship (e.g., the expense of divorce proceedings, emotional costs) to be too great. Finally, structural commitment is affected by one's perception of the availability of acceptable alternatives to one's relationship. A person may remain in an unattractive relationship because there are no other options (i.e., acceptable alternative partners or living arrangements).

Perhaps the most thoroughly social psychological description of commitment processes in close relationships is Rusbult's investment model. According to this model, commitment is affected by three factors. First, an individual's commitment to a relationship is closely related to his or her satisfaction with that relationship. Satisfied couples are those who perceive that they are receiving more interpersonal rewards than costs in their relationship and that the ratio of rewards to costs is equivalent to or higher than that which the couple has come to expect from relationships in general. Second, commitment is affected by the quality of alternatives to which a person has access. Certainly one would expect a satisfied individual to remain committed to the relationship. However, if satisfaction falls below some acceptable level, the quality of the individual's alternatives to the relationship will become a more potent predictor of commitment. Specifically, the less attractive one's alternatives, the greater one's commitment to the relationship will be. Finally, commitment is affected by the degree to which an individual has invested resources in the relationship. Examples of such investments include time, self-disclosure, money, and mutual friends. All other things being equal, the more one has invested in the relationship, the greater the commitment will be.

Of course, not all people perceive and think about their relationships in the same way. Differences in relationship history, for example, undoubtedly contribute to variations in people's interpersonal commitments. In this regard, an individual whose past relationships were characterized by deception and betrayal might be more vigilant in evaluations of a current relationship in an attempt to detect signs of potential betrayal. While such vigilance might be warranted and may indeed be a successful method of self-protection, it might also hinder someone from making a solid commitment to another person; it is difficult to commit oneself to someone whom one does not trust. In contrast, one would not expect an individual with a positive relationship history to be so diligent in searching for relationship pitfalls. Accordingly, such a person would be likely to have little difficulty forming and maintaining interpersonal ties. Following this line of reasoning, it is easy to see how variations in the commitment experience could be linked to differences in religious orientation, sensitivity to social reactions, perceptual set, or virtually any other social-cognitive process.

Alternative Explanations

While the social-cognitive models represent the major thrust of inquiry into the inner workings of interpersonal commitment, it is important to recognize that other explanations are possible. Two of the many possible alternative approaches to the study of interpersonal commitment are a dispositional perspective that emphasizes the role of attachment history and personality and a learning perspective that highlights the importance of modeling.

For all of their strengths, social-cognitive models of interpersonal commitment tend to ignore the potential role of dispositional factors in forming and maintaining commitments with other people. While it certainly is the case that social forces have a strong effect on how people think about and behave in their relationships, it also is true that people bring to their social interactions enduring personality traits and behavioral tendencies that may be equally as powerful in affecting interpersonal dynamics. Consider, for example, the effect of attachment style on relationship stability. According to attachment theory, as presented by John Bowlby (1958, 1969, 1973), adult attitudes, feelings, and behaviors in close relationships are governed, in large part, by interaction patterns established early in life. To be more specific, different patterns of upbringing are translated by children into enduring templates of relationships that shape the expectations that adults have about their relationships and the ways they behave in them. Thus, individuals who, as infants, enjoyed secure, warm, and responsive relationships with their primary caregivers tend to trust, enjoy, and feel safe in their adult relationships. Conversely, individuals who, as infants, had relationships with their primary caregivers that were marked by inconsistency, rejection, and anxiety tend to feel less secure and more anxious about the stability of their adult relationships. On the basis of these differences in attachment history one might predict that securely attached individuals would be more committed to their romantic relationships than insecurely attached individuals. Indeed, this is precisely what researchers have found, supporting the idea that certain aspects of personality are linked to tendencies to commit (or not commit) to close relationships.

Whereas the social-cognitive perspective emphasizes the role of social evaluations in the formulation of interpersonal commitment, the personality perspective highlights the importance of predisposing personal characteristics that make certain types of commitment experiences more or less likely. Although the exact mechanisms by which personality might influence commitment is unclear at this point, several possibilities exist. For example, as mentioned above, differences in attachment style represent dispositionally-based variations in relationship orientation. An individual who, for example, had an insecure attachment to his or her primary caregiver is likely to develop negative expectations about the availability of significant others that might affect his or her inclination to commit to close relationships. If important social figures are unavailable or unreliable, why should one commit to them? Alternatively, personality may influence commitment through specific dominant traits. For example, an individual who is conscientious, self-efficacious, and has an internal locus of control (i.e., believes that the outcomes in life are determined by personal effort) probably is more likely to weather the interpersonal storms that could erode commitment than is an individual who is not conscientious, has a low sense of self-efficacy, and has an external locus of control (i.e., believes that the outcomes in life are determined by fate or external circumstances). In either case, according to the personality perspective, variations in interpersonal commitment are rooted in broader individual differences.

While the foregoing discussion supports a personality-based interpretation of relationship dynamics, it also is possible to view the development of commitment to close relationships from the social learning theory perspective. In this situation, differences in the experience of commitment are judged to result from exposure to models who exhibit varying degrees of commitment to their partners. Indeed, this explanation often is invoked to explain the phenomenon of intergenerational transmission of divorce, in which the children of divorce experience firsthand how their parents resolve conflict and learn that when things get bad enough it is acceptable simply to walk away. The same argument may be applied to the acquisition of specific orientations toward interpersonal commitment. For example, it is reasonable to expect that individuals whose social models were personally committed to their relationships and demonstrated devotion and dedication toward their spouses would adopt a similar approach to their own relationships. Similarly, individuals who were raised in strict religious environments (for example) would be likely to follow the example of their parents or other significant models and honor their marital commitments on moral grounds. In the case of the constraining dimension of commitment, one can readily imagine an individual remaining in an unsatisfying (or even abusive) relationship because he or she learned through observation that resignation is the only realistic response to distressing circumstances.

As these brief descriptions suggest, interpersonal commitment can be explained in several different ways. Depending upon one's theoretical orientation, it is possible to view commitment as a decision process guided by relationship-specific evaluations, a behavioral tendency influenced by dispositional characteristics, or a learned response based on observations of others. While it is tempting to ask which of these perspectives is the correct one, it is important to keep in mind the fact that no human experience is adequately explained by a single viewpoint. Interpersonal commitment, like other variables relevant to close relationships, undoubtedly has several causes.

Personal and Interpersonal Effects of Commitment

The implications of interpersonal commitment are far reaching, touching not only individual functioning and interpersonal dynamics but social issues as well. At the individual level, the three dimensions of interpersonal commitment are related to personal dispositions and behavioral tendencies that are connected to health, happiness, and well-being. For example, the attraction dimension has been compared to the psychological state that Mihaly Csikszentmihalyi (1990) has termed *flow*, which is an aspect of optimal experience characterized by complete absorption in a particular task or endeavor. Someone who is personally committed to a relationship typically derives great pleasure from interacting with his or her partner, experiences the ongoing dynamics of the relationship as being an effortless process, and looks forward to a lifetime of shared experiences with that partner. In addition, personally committed individuals may be more likely than less personally committed individuals to withstand hardships and the effects of stress. In contrast, individuals who feel constrained to remain in unsatisfying relationships often feel resentful, defeated, and unhappy and may be more likely to experience some forms of psychological disturbance. Thus, the manner in which an individual is committed to another person can have profound effects on his or her overall emotional (and even physical) health.

It is not surprising that the greatest effects of interpersonal commitment are related to the relationship itself. All three dimensions of commitment have an effect on the stability of relationships. However, each dimension is related to unique aspects of couple interaction that directly affect the quality of the relationship. For example, the attraction dimension is related to a broad range of positive relationship states and processes, including relationship satisfaction, intimacy, love, closeness, and congruence. Moreover, personally committed partners tend to engage in behaviors that are relationship enhancing, including devaluing attractive alternatives, accommodating one another's potentially disruptive or destructive behaviors, and resolving conflict in a constructive manner. The moral/normative dimension also has positive effects on relationships, but these effects have more to do with the endurance properties of relationships than with relationship dynamics per se. For example, married couples who are committed to their relationship on moral or religious grounds often hold the institution of marriage in high esteem, a fact that enables the relationship to endure even through times of adversity. By weathering negative periods in their relationship, morally committed individuals have the opportunity to experience the upturns in relationship quality that often follow the downturns, an experience that may not be available to their less morally committed counterparts. Finally, feelings of entrapment in relationships often are related to withdrawing from interactions and allowing the relationship to decay, resulting in an "empty shell" marriage.

Finally, the interpersonal commitments people form affect society as a whole. Perhaps the clearest illustration of this lies in the effects of divorce on social institutions. When most marriages end, for whatever reason, it can safely be assumed that the commitment the partners once had has dissolved (although this is not always the case). Indirectly, this dissolution of commitment may lead to the involvement of marriage counselors, divorce lawyers, financial officers, and, if the couple has children, daycare or child welfare agencies. To be sure, each of these institutions would be severely affected if divorces never occurred. In a more positive vein, Robert Hogan (1983) maintains that the capacity to form and maintain interpersonal commitments simply may be a mark of good citizenship. Indeed, from a sociobiological point of view, it seems unlikely that the human species would have survived

had its ancestors been unable to form stable social relationships. Interpersonal commitment, then, is a versatile construct that can be applied to a wide range of intra- and interpersonal phenomena.

Conclusion

For most of its history, research on close relationships has tended to focus on the variables that are relevant to interpersonal quality. However, there is now growing interest in the factors that influence the stability of relationships regardless of their quality. Foremost among these is commitment. As the preceding discussion has shown, commitment is a complex construct that is fundamentally implicated in a broad range of interpersonal processes. Accordingly, scholars in close relationships would do well to focus increased attention to this variable in subsequent research. In a time when the stability of marriage has become a critical social issue, it may be that increased efforts to understand commitment will affect not only the course of scholarship on close relationships but also the growing number of social structures that are affected by the breakdown of the family.

See also: ATTACHMENT; BOWLBY, JOHN; FRIENDSHIP; HEALTH AND ILLNESS; INTIMACY; JEALOUSY; LOVE; PERSONALITY; RELATIONSHIPS; SATISFACTION; TRUST

Bibliography

Adams, Jeffrey M. (1999). "Future Directions for Commitment Research." In *Handbook of Interpersonal Commitment and Relationship Stability*, ed. Jeffrey M. Adams and Warren H. Jones. New York: Plenum.

Adams, Jeffrey M., and Jones, Warren H. (1997). "The Conceptualization of Marital Commitment: An Integrative Analysis." *Journal of Personality and Social Psychology* 72:1177–1196.

Adams, Jeffrey M., and Jones, Warren H. (1999). "Interpersonal Commitment in Historical Perspective." In *Handbook of Interpersonal Commitment and Relationship Stability*, ed. Jeffrey M. Adams and Warren H. Jones. New York: Plenum.

Becker, Howard S. (1960). "Notes on the Concept of Commitment." *American Journal of Sociology* 66:32–40.

Bowlby, John. (1958). "The Nature of the Child's Tie to His Mother." *International Journal of Psycho-Analysis* 39:350–373.

Bowlby, John. (1969). *Attachment and Loss, Vol. 1: Attachment.* London: Hogarth Press.

Bowlby, John. (1973). *Attachment and Loss, Vol. 2: Anxiety and Anger.* London: Hogarth Press.

Csikszentmihalyi, Mihaly. (1990). *Flow: The Psychology of Optimal Experience.* New York: Harper & Row.

Hogan, Robert. (1983). "A Socioanalytic Theory of Personality." In *Nebraska Symposium on Motivation, 1982*, ed. M. M. Page. Lincoln: University of Nebraska Press.

Johnson, Michael P. (1973). "Commitment." *Sociological Quarterly* 14:395–406.

Johnson, Michael P. (1991). "Commitment to Personal Relationships." In *Advances in Personal Relationships: A Research Annual,*

Scott McPherson's Marvin's Room *(1992) features a daughter who has committed her life to care for her bedridden father, who is helpless after having suffered several strokes. The daughter does not begrudge the time and effort that is required for the care of her father; she feels she is living a full, rich life that is committed to caregiving.*

Vol. 3, ed. Warren H. Jones and Daniel Perlman. London: Jessica Kingsley.

Johnson, Michael P. (1999). "Personal, Moral, and Structural Commitment to Relationships: Experiences of Choice and Constraint." In *Handbook of Interpersonal Commitment and Relationship Stability,* ed. Jeffrey M. Adams and Warren H. Jones. New York: Plenum.

Kelley, Harold H. (1983). "Love and Commitment." In *Close Relationships,* ed. Harold H. Kelley, Ellen Berscheid, Andrew Christensen, John H. Harvey, Ted L. Huston, George Levinger, Evie McLintock, Letitia Anne Peplau, and Donald R. Peterson. New York: W. H. Freeman.

Leik, Robert K., and Leik, Sheila A. (1977). "Transition to Interpersonal Commitment." In *Behavioral Theory in Sociology,* ed. Robert L. Hamblin and John H. Kunkel. New Brunswick, NJ: Transaction.

Levinger, George. (1965). "Marital Cohesiveness and Dissolution: An Integrative Review." *Journal of Marriage and the Family* 27:19–28.

Levinger, George. (1976). "A Social Psychological Perspective on Marital Dissolution." *Journal of Social Issues* 32:21–47.

Lydon, John E. (1996). "Toward a Theory of Commitment." In *The Psychology of Values,* ed. Clive Seligman, James M. Olson, and Mark P. Zanna. Hillsdale, NJ: Lawrence Erlbaum.

Rusbult, Caryl E. (1980). "Commitment and Satisfaction in Romantic Associations: A Test of the Investment Model." *Journal of Experimental Social Psychology* 16:172–186.

Rusbult, Caryl E. (1983). "A Longitudinal Test of the Investment Model: The Development (and Deterioration) of Satisfaction and Commitment in Heterosexual Involvements." *Journal of Personality and Social Psychology* 45:101–117.

Rusbult, Caryl E., and Van Lange, Paul A. M. (1996). "Interdependence Processes." In *Social Psychology: Handbook of Basic Principles,* ed. E. Tory Higgins and Arie W. Kruglanski. New York: Guilford.

Rusbult, Caryl E., and Verette, Julie. (1991). "An Interdependence Analysis of Accommodation Processes in Close Relationships." *Representative Research in Social Psychology* 19.9–33.

Stanley, Scott M., and Markman, Howard J. (1992). "Assessing Commitment in Personal Relationships." *Journal of Marriage and the Family* 54:595–608.

Thibaut, John W., and Kelley, Harold H. (1959). *The Social Psychology of Groups.* New York: Wiley.

Jeffrey M. Adams

COMMUNICATION

Everyone experiences emotions. Anger, happiness, fear, and many other emotions are felt frequently by virtually every person. At one time emotions were thought of as entirely private experiences. Individuals certainly perceive emotions as internal feelings to which only they themselves have direct access. But emotions are more than private experiences; usually emotions are communicated to other people.

Emotions are internal control mechanisms, but they are more than that: Emotions are universal communication systems that evolved to signal personal feelings to others. Emotional communication enables other people to observe a person's emotional display and adjust their own actions accordingly. Avoiding an angry, enraged individual, comforting a sad member of one's family, mating with an individual expressing love, or reading a person's fear as a sign of impending danger had survival value for humans. The universality and power of human emotional displays suggests that emotionally unexpressive people may not have survived to pass their genes along to contemporary humans.

Communication of Basic Emotions

Throughout human history emotions have been communicated primarily through nonverbal communication. Humans experienced and expressed emotions long before verbal language developed. The high degree of universality of emotions in every culture suggests they are old, evolutionary adaptations that served important functions for the human species. Similarly, people are able to express emotions nonverbally long before they can express them verbally. In fact, prior to socialization, infants show little control over their emotional expression. Infants are biologically programmed to express their emotions so adults can react to their emotions and provide the appropriate caregiving response. Even in adults most emotions evoke spontaneous, nonverbal expressions that are communicated through one's voice, body, arms, and particularly the face. Each emotion has a unique nonverbal display that is recognizable to most other humans and particularly to members of one's own group or culture. Likewise each emotion results in a different kind of verbal behavior.

Anger, one of the most basic and powerful of human emotions, is an intense feeling of displeasure resulting from injury, harm, or mistreatment by another person. Usually angry people feel another person has illegitimately harmed them. Although anger does occur outside of interpersonal communication, it is usually the result of a troubling social event involving interpersonal communication. The most common causes of anger are physical or verbal attacks or injuries, thoughtlessness, rudeness, frustration of a person's goals by another person, threats to a person's identity or reputation, and relational threats such as infidelity or disloyalty. Anger is quickly and unmistakably communicated both nonverbally and verbally. Anger displays are an important form of communication that warns other people of the dangerous state of the angry person and the possibility of an attack. Without such a warning, anger could result in death or injury to one of the interactants. Angry communication, on the other hand, results in flight, avoidance, symbolic aggression, apologies, explanations, and reparations. Verbal expressions of anger are common and are generally directed at the supposed cause of one's anger. Sharing one's angry feelings with friends, family, therapists, or loved ones is frequently used to try to cope with angry feelings or gain sympathy for the alleged wrongdoing. Anger is most clearly manifested in the face. The anger expression consists of knit and lowered eyebrows, a direct, menacing stare, and a tense jaw with teeth often exposed. Like other basic facial expressions, anger is universally and cross-culturally recognized, suggesting its innate origins. Anger is also communicated through vocal behavior, including sounds and utterances that are louder, lower pitched, and harsher than the vocalization of other emotions. Verbal behaviors may include swearing, berating the other person, threats, or making the other person feel guilty for the alleged harm. Anger may result in changes in spatial behavior, such as invading a person's space, shaking a fist at the other person, or walking out on the presumed perpetrator of the harm. Anger is expressed physically through stomping feet, slamming doors, breaking things, throwing tantrums, making threatening gestures, becoming withdrawn, or terminating the relationship. Research has consistently shown that anger displays are far more common during social interaction than when an individual is alone.

Disgust was one of Charles Darwin's fundamental emotions and has been included on the list of basic facial expressions by modern researchers. Humans originally experienced disgust when they encountered the foul taste or smell of rotten food or dead, decaying animals. The expression that resulted is well known to even preschool children: a downturned mouth, sometimes accompanied by a protruding and downturned tongue, a wrinkled nose, and the eyes nearly shut. It appears that the original function of this expression was to close sensory channels and expel the disgusting stimulus. Disgust often is accompanied by vocal utterances such as "yuck," "ick," or "agghh" but only occasionally by verbal utterances such as "gross" or "disgusting." Today, the creative minds of human being have applied the disgust expression to unpleasant people, relationships, situations, groups, and interactions. The basic facial expression has remained the same, arguably a prewired response to disgusting stimuli.

Embarrassment is an inherently social emotion stemming from a failure of self-presentation, loss of face, or reduced esteem in one's own display of the self to others. Just as embarrassment occurs as the result of interpersonal interaction, communication is also the tool for repairing embarrassment. Verbal explanations, accounts, and excuses, as well as nonverbal apologies such as shrugs, sheepish looks, and feeble smiles designed to appease onlookers, are commonly associated with embarrassment. Other nonverbal reactions include hiding the face, reduced eye contact, blushing, lowering the head, turning away from others, and leaving the scene.

It is both common and important for human beings to experience fear. Feelings of fear warn of impending danger and make people react in ways designed to protect themselves. Fear is usually a transient but very negative emotion that humans seek to avoid in one of two ways. Usually fear promotes danger avoidance, a functional response in which people flee, fight, or take other actions to minimize the threat posed by the impending danger. However, people may also engage in fear avoidance, such as not thinking about fear, or rationalizing and minimizing the danger, which are probably dysfunctional ways to avoid experiencing fear. Unrealistic or imaginary fears, called phobias or paranoia, produce much the same reactions as do fears with more realistic external causes. Fearful feelings often are accompanied by increases in heart rate, muscular tension, and increased skin conductance. Likewise, other physical symptoms occur that may be perceived by other communicators as danger signals, including excessive perspiration, cold extremities,

A man displays the classic fear expression in this detail from Fortunato Onelli's Religious Zeal. *(Corbis/Araldo de Luca)*

shaking, trembling, and muscular rigidity or agitation. Fear produces a classic facial expression, vocal exclamations, and rapid changes in body positions. The fear expression involves raised eyebrows and a narrowing of the eyes, creating eyes that appear to be triangular in shape. The upper eyelid is raised and the lower eyelid is tightened. The lips are stretched horizontally to reveal the lower teeth. Defensive avoidance behavior such as covering the face, hiding, cowering, or outright flight are also common nonverbal reactions to fear. Vocal fear behaviors include shouts, screams, and cries. Fear appeals are commonly used by advertisers, health agencies, politicians, teachers, and parents to get people to eat less fat, wear seat belts, practice safe sex, brush their teeth, and change their behavior in variety of other ways.

Guilt is a social emotion that is closely linked to communication in personal relationships. Guilt is an emotion that happens in the context of human interaction, not just inside people. Guilt arises out of a perceived transgression by one person against another, usually in the context of a close relationship. Guilt is considered a basic, primary emotion because it can occur without other emotions. However, frequently, guilt is accompanied by regret, shame, and embarrassment. Research conducted by Klaus Scherer and Harald Wallbott (1994) in thirty-seven countries revealed that guilt is a common emotion in virtually all cultures. Guilt is communicated nonverbally through hiding, isolation, or other behaviors designed to compensate for one's transgressions. Although there is not a specific facial expression associated with guilt, a sad or worried facial expression, a lump in the throat, and a remorseful or sorry expression during apologies are common communicative reactions to guilt. Guilty nonverbal behaviors include fewer smiles, a less pleasant tone of voice, and a less pleasant facial expression. Similarly, avoidance and silence are behavioral responses to guilt across a variety of cultures. Guilt functions to exert social control over one person's actions in a group. Indeed, Rowland Miller and Mark Leary (1992) suggest that social emotions such as guilt are important because they show remorse to the injured party rather than disregard for others, which is crucial when those who act with consistent disregard for others may be ostracized, banished, or even killed. Guilt may also prevent individuals from engaging in behavior that deviates too greatly from group social standards. The "guilt trip" is a specific example of guilt used as a strategic behavior in an attempt to change the behavior of another person.

One of the most basic emotions is happiness, which is expressed and recognized around the world. Happiness is a concept that virtually every person includes when asked to compile a list of emotions. Happy people touch more, hug their friends more, and are more likely to refrain from violent behavior. Happiness is related to increased vocal pitch, a more melodious tone of voice, closer interpersonal distances, and an increased level of laughing and smiling. Happy expressions are most likely to occur during social occasions when they can be shared with other people and much less likely to be displayed when a person is not in social contact with others. Because people rarely are dangerous when they are displaying positive expressions, smiling and other happy expressions may have survival advantages for humans and other primates. Among all primates, including humans, smiles are a central part of appeasement and submission displays, designed to calm other individuals and build positive relationships.

Jealousy is experienced when a person perceives that a third party rival is a threat to a primary relationship. Jealousy has a genetic basis—the protection of one's mate or friends from defection into other relationships—but it is encouraged or discouraged in different cultures and subcultures in a variety of ways. While jealousy is a unique emotion, it is often accompanied by other emotions, including sadness, anger, fear, hate, and hurt. A jealous individual communicates (both verbally and nonverbally) negative affect toward his or her partner and the rival. In such situations, constructive problem solving about the feelings is the strategy that generally works best in alleviating the jealousy. Individuals experiencing jealousy may also engage in avoidance behaviors, denial, threats, violence, increased affection, flirtation with potential new partners, improvement of their appearance or image, and stalking or other surveillance behaviors.

Love, regarded as one of the most basic emotions (as well as one of the strongest), is universally experienced in various forms throughout the world. Love occurs in the context of interpersonal communication and is almost always directed at people with whom one has shared a long and rich relationship. Love may have evolved in humans to serve the purpose of creating lasting bonds that helped ensure the survival of pairs or groups of people in a dangerous world. Love can be experienced in many ways: passionate, sexual, fun, intimate, committed, pathetic, or sacred. Love is also communicated in many ways. Saying "I love you" is an overt expression of the emotion. However, more subtle nonverbal expressions are often more powerful communicators of love. Prolonged eye contact, various forms of intimate touching (including hugging, kissing, and sexual activity), increased smiling, and more time spent together are commonly associated with love. It is the manifestation of love through these nonverbal actions that make the expression of love believed and reciprocated by one's partner.

Despite its inclusion as one of the "seven deadly sins," pride has generated less research than many other emotions. Pride is viewed as both a positive and a negative emotion. Excessive pride communicates boastfulness, conceit, and arrogance, and immoderately proud people are warned that "pride cometh before a fall." Pride can also be a barrier to people who need support, assistance, or comfort. Conversely, pride is part of self-esteem and is the natural emotional reaction to compliments and success. As such, pride may actually be part of the delight emotion. Pride is an inherently interpersonal or social emotion that depends upon a social audience. In the rare instance of private pride, an imaginary audience is often pictured. While less research has been done on the expression of pride than most other emotions, several nonverbal behaviors have been associated with pride. Proud individuals stand and sit straighter and taller, make themselves larger, exhibit signs of strength, display their bodies to others, smile broadly, and produce celebratory behaviors such as hugs, "high fives," and handshakes. Occasionally, pride is manifested verbally through either appropriate disclosures or inappropriate boasting.

Sadness and other melancholic emotions, such as depression and grief, are considered to be basic emotions, both in experience and expression. Social interaction has been shown to be the primary cause of sadness. Even infants are likely to show sadness and distress in response to the distress of their parent or caregiver. Depression, like sadness, is both a cause of and a result of disturbed or troubled relationships. Some of the ways in which sadness is communicated are well known even to preschoolers: a downturned mouth, crying, and fussing. People also communicate sadness verbally to potential comforters in order to gain relief from an unpleasant state. They are likely to speak in a monotone voice, use shorter utterances, and employ longer pauses when speaking. Sad people also avoid social interaction, become immobilized, and engage in a number of other nonverbal behaviors, including sad facial expressions, slouching, moping, reduced smiling and eye contact, and less open body positions.

Sexual desire or lust is often characterized as an emotion, although some researchers think it is simply a human drive or motivational state. Sexual desire includes a unique set of subjective feelings, physiological arousal, sexual thoughts, and an object of one's sexual desire, all characteristics typically associated with an emotional state. Sexual desire is mixed with many other emotions, including love, happiness, loneliness, jealousy, fear, and guilt. Sexual desire is communicated in many ways, including telling the object of one's desires about one's feelings, sexual propositions, requests for dates, increased eye contact, touch behaviors, erections, flushed skin, and even sexual harassment and coercion. Likewise, a group of flirtation behaviors have been discovered including increased grooming behaviors, hair flips, flirtation, self-touching, open palm presentations, pelvic rolls, breast thrusts, standing straighter, chest expansions, pulling in one's stomach, and revealing more of one's body.

Shame is a social emotion that both originates and is displayed in interpersonal interaction. It is the product of one's perceived transgressions against others and their negative reactions. Shame is an intense, negative feeling of inferiority and loss of respect resulting from failing to live up to other's and one's own expectations. Shamed individuals feel that they are unworthy of the respect and love of others. Researchers disagree about whether shame is a basic emotion or a blend of other emotions (including sadness, dejection, depression, anger, and helplessness). The primary communicative response to feelings of shame are behaviors manifesting a desire to disappear, including hiding, sulking, avoiding interaction with others, shrinking of the body, slouching, lowering of the head, increased facial touching, hiding the face, and weak, forced smiles. Verbally shamed individuals may proclaim their worthlessness or helplessness, apologize, and promise to improve.

Nonverbal researchers since Darwin have considered surprise to be one of the most basic of all emotions. Surprise is somewhat unique among emotions because it is a neutral emotion that often blends quickly into another emotion consistent with the sources of the surprise (e.g., fear from danger or happiness from seeing someone you like). Surprise is the most fleeting of facial expressions, usually lasting only milliseconds before blending into another emotion such as fear, anger, or happiness. Surprise has its own facial expression consisting of wide-open eyes (such that the whites of the eyes become more visible), raised eyebrows, and an open mouth with parted teeth. Vocal behaviors, such as shrieks or screams, occasionally accompany surprise, but little verbal behavior results from surprise, probably due to the transient nature of surprise compared to other emotions.

Warmth and intimacy is not always thought of as an emotion. However, a considerable body of research suggests that the feeling of interpersonal warmth constitutes a unique emotion. Warmth is most likely to occur in close relationships characterized by comfort, intimacy, contentment, bondedness, and attraction. Warmth is communicated through touch, close distances, spending time together, and a host of other behaviors collectively called immediacy behaviors.

Cultural Display Rules

In every culture, rules and norms governing when, how, and where emotions should be expressed regulate the communication of emotion. As individuals mature, they learn display rules through the process of socialization. Parents, teachers, and peers socialize children to show the proper emotions through the learning of five types of display rules: simulation, inhibition, intensification, miniaturization, and masking.

In many situations, it is important to show or simulate an emotion even if it is not the one being felt. In certain situations, people may smile when they do not feel happy, express guilt when they have no remorse, and act somber when they feel no sadness. Showing happiness at a coworker's wedding announcement or sadness at a distant cousin's funeral even in the absence of these feelings are important aspects of communication competence. Children begin learning simulated expressions in infancy but do not perfect them until early adulthood. An adult who cannot display the appropriate emotion for the situation is often thought of as immature or incompetent.

Inhibition is the reverse of simulation in that it involves not showing an emotion when you have one. Appearing fearless in the face of danger, keeping a straight face when something is really funny, and hiding attraction to a third party when one's spouse is present are all important skills involving emotional inhibition. Perhaps the main developmental trend as children develop and improve their communication skills is the inhibition of inappropriate emotions. Gender roles are often the function of inhibition; for example, girls are taught to inhibit anger displays and boys are taught to inhibit sadness displays. Failure to inhibit emotional displays can have very negative consequences on relationships with family members, friends, or colleagues.

Sometimes called maximization, intensification involves showing stronger emotions than one is experiencing. Unlike simulation one may actually feel the emotion but exaggerate it to make sure it is communicated. Showing more sadness at a coworker's failure to be promoted than one is really experiencing or laughing heartily at a friend's mildly funny joke are examples of intensification. Children learn this early. They may scream when only slightly injured to gain attention or they may show affection and love for a parent when they want something.

The opposite of intensification is miniaturization, sometimes called deintensification or minimization. This involves showing an emotion with less intensity than one is really experiencing. Showing just liking for a date with whom one is totally infatuated, showing mild anger when one is completely furious, or being blasé and merely smiling instead of laughing at a hilarious joke are examples of miniaturization. This display rule is used strategically to avoid complete emotional disclosure or to conform to rules of social appropriateness.

Masking, or substitution, is the process of communicating an emotion when one actually feels a completely different emotion. Masking is the last skill that children and adolescents acquire because it is the most difficult of the display rules to master. Indeed, masking requires a knowledge of emotional communication and considerable acting skill to create a believable display. A gambler showing disappointment in a poker game over his or her straight flush rather than glee or parents showing joy rather than disappointment over their child's bad athletic performance are examples of competent emotional masking.

Conclusion

Emotional communication is the result of both biology and learning. Certainly, emotional communication evolved to help the individual, the group, and the human species survive. However, culture and individual decisions always play a role in emotional expression. The communication of emotion will always be a complex mix of inherited, spontaneous emotional expressions along with the enculturated displays under the strategic control of individuals. Researchers now recognize that emotions are more than private experiences; they are interpersonal messages that are designed to be a central part of the process of human communication.

See also: ANGER; BODY MOVEMENT, GESTURE, AND DISPLAY; CROSS-CULTURAL PATTERNS; DARWIN, CHARLES ROBERT; DESIRE; DISGUST; EMBARRASSMENT; EMOTION EXPERIENCE AND EXPRESSION; EMOTION SUPPRESSION; FACIAL EXPRESSION; FEAR AND PHOBIAS; GRIEF; GUILT; HAPPINESS; INTIMACY; JEALOUSY; LOVE; SADNESS; SHAME; SURPRISE

Bibliography

Andersen, Peter Alex. (1999). *Nonverbal Communication: Forms and Functions.* Mountain View, CA: Mayfield.

Andersen, Peter Alex, and Guerrero, Laura Knarr. (1998a). "The Bright Side of Relational Communication." In *Handbook of Communication and Emotion: Research, Theory, Applications, and Contexts,* ed. Peter Alex Andersen and Laura Knarr Guerrero. San Diego, CA: Academic Press.

Andersen, Peter Alex, and Guerrero, Laura Knarr. (1998b). "Principles of Communication and Emotion in Social Interaction." In *Handbook of Communication and Emotion: Research, Theory, Applications, and Contexts,* ed. Peter Alex Andersen and Laura Knarr Guerrero. San Diego, CA: Academic Press.

Barrett, Karen Caplovitz. (1995). "A Functionalist Approach to Shame and Guilt." In *Self-Conscious Emotions: The Psychology of*

Shame, Guilt, Embarrassment, and Pride, ed. June Price Tangney and Kurt W. Fischer. New York: Guilford.

Burgoon, Judee K.; Buller, David B.; and Woodall, W. Gill. (1996). *Nonverbal Communication: The Unspoken Dialogue,* 2nd ed. New York: McGraw-Hill.

Canary, Daniel J.; Spitzberg, Brian H.; and Semic, Beth A. (1998). "The Experience and Expression of Anger in Interpersonal Settings." In *Handbook of Communication and Emotion: Research, Theory, Applications, and Contexts,* ed. Peter Alex Andersen and Laura Knarr Guerrero. San Diego, CA: Academic Press.

Cupach, William R., and Metts, Sandra. (1994). *Facework.* Thousand Oaks, CA: Sage Publications.

Ekman, Paul. (1972). "Universal and Cultural Differences in Facial Expression of Emotion." In *Nebraska Symposium on Motivation,* ed. James K. Cole. Lincoln: University of Nebraska Press.

Ekman, Paul. (1982). *Emotion in the Human Face.* Cambridge, Eng.: Cambridge University Press.

Ekman, Paul. (1993). "Facial Expression and Emotion." *American Psychologist* 38:384–392.

Ekman, Paul, and Friesen, Wallace V. (1975). *Unmasking the Face: A Field Guide to Recognizing Emotions from Facial Clues.* Englewood Cliffs, NJ: Prentice-Hall.

Guerrero, Laura Knarr, and Andersen, Peter Alex. (1998). "Jealousy Experience and Expression in Romantic Relationships." In *Handbook of Communication and Emotion: Research, Theory, Applications, and Contexts,* ed. Peter Alex Andersen and Laura Knarr Guerrero. San Diego, CA: Academic Press.

Izard, Carroll E. (1977). *Human Emotions.* New York: Plenum.

Kraut, Robert E., and Johnson, Robert E. (1979). "Social and Emotional Messages of Smiling: An Ethological Approach." *Journal of Personality and Social Psychology* 37:1539–1553.

Metts, Sandra; Sprecher, Susan; and Regan, Pamela C. (1998). "Communication and Sexual Desire." In *Handbook of Communication and Emotion: Research, Theory, Applications, and Contexts,* ed. Peter Alex Andersen and Laura Knarr Guerrero. San Diego, CA: Academic Press.

Miller, Rowland S., and Leary, Mark R. (1992). "Social Sources and Interactive Functions of Emotion: The Case of Embarrassment." In *Review of Personality and Social Psychology, Vol. 14,* ed. Margarett S. Clark. Newbury Park, CA: Sage Publications.

Scherer, Klaus R., and Wallbott, Harald. (1994). "Evidence for Universality and Cultural Variation of Differential Emotional Response Patterning." *Journal of Personality and Social Psychology* 66:310–328.

Shaver, Phillip; Schwartz, Judith; Kirson, Donald; and O'Connor, Cary. (1987). "Emotional Knowledge: Further Explorations of a Prototype Approach." *Journal of Personality and Social Psychology* 52:1061–1086.

Taraban, Carolyn B.; Hendrick, Susan S.; and Hendrick, Clyde. (1998). "Loving and Liking." In *Handbook of Communication and Emotion: Research, Theory, Applications, and Contexts,* ed. Peter Alex Andersen and Laura Knarr Guerrero. San Diego, CA: Academic Press.

Van Hoofe, J. A. R. A. M. (1972). "A Comparative Approach to the Phylogeny of Laughter and Smiling." In *Non-Verbal Communication,* ed. Robert A. Hinde. Cambridge, Eng.: Cambridge University Press.

Witte, Kim. (1998). "Fear as Motivator, Fear as Inhibitor: Using the Extended Parallel Process Model to Explain Fear Appeal Successes and Failures." In *Handbook of Communication and Emotion: Research, Theory, Applications, and Contexts,* ed. Peter Alex Andersen and Laura Knarr Guerrero. San Diego, CA: Academic Press.

Peter Alex Andersen

CONFLICT

Conflict that escalates to violence is fast becoming the societal norm. By 1985, physical spousal abuse occurred in one in six households, and during the 1990s, news reports broadcast stories about motorists being killed on the road (road rage). Also, by the mid 1990s, murder was the primary cause of death in the workplace. Is it any wonder, then, that when one thinks of conflict, the image that comes to mind is a vision of two people yelling loudly at each other and trying to physically hurt each other? These behaviors, however, represent only one of three possible overall response strategies. When individuals engage in conflict, they may choose to use an avoidance strategy (e.g., do not bring up the topic, leave when the topic is discussed, withdraw from the conversation when the topic arises), an integrative strategy (e.g., provide information about goals, ask the other person's opinions, support the other person's opinions, be willing to concede interests), or a distributive strategy (e.g., threaten the other person, attack the other person's self concept, devalue or reject the other person). The spousal abuse, road rage, and murder in the workplace discussed above are examples of a distributive strategy. As one might guess, this strategy has been found to leave conflicting parties with negative emotions, while the use of integrative strategies often result in positive emotions.

Criteria for Conflict

According to William Wilmot and Joyce Hocker (1998), at least one member of the party must have a goal if conflict is going to occur. This goal can be anything, such as wanting to get better hours at work or wanting an "A" on an examination. The person with the goal must also perceive that the other person is acting as a barrier to that goal. This barrier can result because the other person has the same goal (e.g., a person wanting the same work schedule) or a competing goal (e.g., someone who wants a friend to go out on the night that person needs to study).

The next criteria needed for conflict to occur is interdependence between the parties. John Thibaut and Harold Kelley (1959) define this interdependence as the ability for one person to affect the cost and rewards of another. Because a friend can give rewards (e.g., sharing time) and exact costs (e.g., not

Public anger over an Israeli girl having gone out on a date with an Arab boy has lead to a public confrontation outside of the Damascus Gate in Jerusalem. (Corbis/Ted Spiegel)

sharing time), an individual cannot just say that he or she wants to study instead of going out without some consequence (e.g., the cost of feeling guilty). It is the inclusion of interdependence between two parties that distinguishes conflict from interactions that do not involve emotion, such as a debate. Researchers have found that interdependence leads to states of heightened emotion, and the heightened emotion usually prompts individuals to express their dissatisfaction with the other party, the final criteria necessary for conflict to occur. Once someone tells a friend that he or she is upset with that friend, the two individuals are engaged in conflict.

Emotions Associated with Conflict

Typically, people view conflict as a negative event that often yields angerlike responses. This is illustrated in the Garth Brooks song "She's Every Woman," in which he sings, "And when she gets mad, you best leave her alone, 'cause she'll rage just like a river." While there are a number of emotions that are associated with conflict—contempt, guilt, sadness, loneliness, anxiety, fear, jealousy, and uncertainty—anger is by far the most common. Wilmot and Hocker (1998) argue that anger is most often connected to conflict because adults are not encouraged to acknowledge feelings of fear, loss, abandonment, or loneliness. Moreover they claim that anger may be a secondary emotion, most often coming from the feeling of fear. One reason the emotion felt may be labeled anger rather than fear is that, according to Stanley Schachter and Jerome Singer (1962), people often interpret their own emotions using the behavior of the other person, and the other party may appear angry, not frightened. So while anger is the emotion most commonly referred to, fear may be the emotion most commonly experienced during conflict.

Emotion As an Antecedent to Conflict

Emotion occurs prior to, during, and after the conflict and is related to several of the criteria necessary for the conflict to occur. For example, when an individual first perceives that the other person is acting as a barrier to a goal or that rewards will be affected, the individual's body experiences tension. In his theory of psychodynamics, Sigmund Freud (1923) states that when a need is threatened, the id creates energy. The id wants the body to release the energy as quickly as possible. This is often referred to as an emotional outburst or temper tantrum. The superego and ego, however, try to control the release of this energy so that it is let out in a socially acceptable fashion. When individuals first perceive that a goal is being blocked or their rewards are being threatened, they feel a surge of energy and a strong desire to release that energy. Usually, but not always, the superego and ego will intercede and force the body to wait to dispel the energy until a more appropriate time or target is found. The emotion experienced may affect this process. According to Nancy Stein and Linda Levine (1987), individuals who are angry continue trying to meet their goals, while those who feel sad when their goals are blocked often abandon their goals or seek substitute goals. This new goal may be to release the energy through exercise, in which case there is no expression of disagreement, so there is no conflict. Exercising to release energy is actually one of the recommendations psychoanalysts make for dealing with potential for conflict. Another recommendation would be to channel the energy to a more vulnerable or acceptable target. This explains the behavior of abusive partners. Often the abusive spouse experiences conflict with someone of higher power (e.g., a boss) and releases the energy on his or her partner later in the day since the partner is considered a more vulnerable or acceptable target.

Experiencing emotion, then, leads one to express dissatisfaction and engage in conflict, though not necessarily with the party blocking the goal. While it may appear as though emotion leads to negative conflict management strategies (e.g., violence), John Gottman, in his book *What Predicts Divorce? The Relationship between Marital Processes and Marital Outcomes* (1994), argues that if an individual does not feel emotion, he or she is not interested in maintaining the relationship. He refers to this lack of emotion as withdrawal or stonewalling. Gottman argues that emotions are important; most marriages typically end with a whimper because the couple no longer cares enough to engage in conflict.

Gottman and many other conflict researchers argue that conflict and emotional feelings about topics of conflict indicate the importance of an issue and the relationship with the other party. Engaging in conflict, then, is a sign that one cares about the other's thoughts and actions. However, engaging in conflict in a destructive manner can be just as problematic as not engaging in conflict at all.

Emotion during Conflict

Emotions may actually affect how people choose to engage in conflict. Susan Crockenberg and Deborah Forgays (1996) report that children who feel sad are more likely to use internal behaviors (e.g., depression, withdrawal), while those who are angry react with physical behaviors. Both responses, however, are considered negative reactions, and it is important to engage in conflict in a positive manner. But how does one do that? First, researchers would argue that individuals will need to acquire communication skills that allow them to defuse the conflict. Amy Holtzworth-Munroe and Kimberly Anglin (1991) found that conflicts characterized by violence tend to escalate because violent couples do not know how to break the cycle. Wilmot and Hocker (1998) label this cycle a "spiral," explaining that individuals tend to engage in constructive spirals (one partner uses an integrative strategy and the other responds with an integrative strategy) or a destructive spiral (one partner uses a distributive strategy and the other reciprocates). What spirals illustrate is the human tendency to reciprocate another person's behavior. If someone yells at a person, that person feels a strong urge to yell back. This concept is demonstrated in a scene between the characters David and Dee in the movie *Indecent Proposal* (1993). David suspects that Dee has been seeing the

"other man." David walks in and shows Dee the business card he found with the other man's name on it. Dee tries calmly to explain that she has never seen the card but David starts yelling at her. David accuses Dee of seeing this man behind his back. Dee then yells and attacks David's character. While Dee initially resists the temptation to reciprocate David's strategy, she eventually matches his volume and begins to cast insults and accusations of her own. The moment Dee starts using the distributive strategy and raising her voice, she and David begin a destructive spiral. Destructive spirals, characterized by negative emotions, can be defused in several different ways. One way is to choose not to reciprocate the tone or emotion of the other person. If Dee had continued to keep her voice down, David may have begun to reciprocate her use of the integrative strategy. This is illustrated in an example given by Roxane Lulofs in her book *Conflict: From Action to Theory* (1994, p. 118):

> I was at a friend's house when her husband came downstairs to look for an extension cord. . . . [H]e had a hard time. . . . He was really angry and yelled at [my friend] about the drawer [he tried to look in], the house in general, and how he could never find anything. She just asked him what he was looking for, found it, handed it to him. . . . She never raised her voice. I asked her how she could do that, and she said, "He's not mad at me. He's just mad at the world. If I yell back, I'll just make it worse."

The husband in this example got what he wanted and, because his wife did not yell back, the couple did not engage in a destructive conflict spiral.

A second way to diffuse emotion, according to David Mace (1982), is for the parties to describe how they feel without acting on that emotion. While some scholars argue that suppression of emotion can lead to stress, depression, and illness and that expression leads to a reduction in the amount of rage felt, Carol Tavris, in her book *Anger: The Misunderstood Emotion* (1982), claims the benefits of expressing anger, as well as the connection between suppressed anger and illness, have been overstated. Several researchers have in fact found that the expression of anger, one of the emotions linked to conflict, does not reduce the tension. Tavris concluded that expressing anger in an unrestrained way simply makes people angrier; it does not reduce the feeling. One reason for this may be that talking reinforces the anger and makes individuals feel it even more deeply. Another reason expression of anger may not help dispel the emotion is that acting directly on anger as well as other negative emotions (such as self-righteousness) detracts from the more primary issue—why one feels the emotion. As a result, scholars recommend defusing emotions in conflict by discussing the emotion, not venting it. Researchers have provided scripts to help individuals recognize the emotion, clearly state it, and discuss it with their partners in a calm, rational fashion. For example, Gottman and his colleagues put forth an XYZ model in their book *A Couple's Guide to Communication* (1976). They recommend that an individual who is angry say "when you do X, in situation Y, I feel Z." So Dee, the character in the movie *Indecent Proposal* could have said, "When you accuse me of cheating on you, knowing you were the one who suggested I spend the night with him, I feel hurt."

In addition to the XYZ formula, there is the DIE formula proposed by John Wendt (1984): describe what one sees without adding any meaning to it; interpret what one thinks or believes about what is observed; and evaluate what is observed using should-ought language. Both formulas are very similar in that they start with what is observed and move to the feelings a person experiences in response to those observations. These approaches drastically depart from Freud's theory of psychodynamics in which he states individuals need to vent the tension (emotion) that builds up.

While many therapists agree that the XYZ and DIE formulas help their clients in a conflict situation, Gordon Bower (1981) argues that if the clients learn these behaviors while they are in a calm state, they will not use them when they are emotionally charged. According to Bower and his theory of state-dependent learning, information acquired in a particular emotional state is more readily remembered when the person is in the state in which learning took place. Because a person will be angry during a conflict, the therapist must make that individual angry before teaching him or her how to respond in a competent way.

Results of Conflict

Therapists and researchers argue that when emotion is addressed through description, rather than enactment, both parties experience more positive emotions. Leslie Greenberg and Susan Johnson (1986) argue that couples in martial therapy who learn to identify their primary emotion and describe that information to their spouse (using either the XYZ or the DIE formula) become more emotionally accessible. These couples also report that they are more satisfied, secure, and intimate. Other positive emotional outcomes from conflict resolution include feelings of relief and excitement.

However, negative emotions may also be experienced during conflict resolution. After a disagreement, one may feel hurt, anxious, angry, frustrated, sad, and/or guilty. According to William Cupach and Daniel Canary, in their book *Competence in Interpersonal*

All of William Shakespeare's plays deal with conflict in one form or another. In the tragedies, such as Hamlet *(1601) and* King Lear *(1605), the conflicts tend to end with death, destruction, and the breakup of the community. In the comedies, such as* All's Well that Ends Well *(1602) and* The Taming of the Shrew *(1593), the conflicts tend to be resolved and the couples are together at the end. In his histories, such as* Julius Caesar *(1600) and* Macbeth *(1606), conflicts over who has power and how it should be used lead to the overthrow of political leaders and to civil strife.*

Conflict (1997), the intensity and importance of the conflict and the overall climate of the relationship between the two parties affect whether the emotions experienced after a conflict are positive or negative, the magnitude of the emotion, and the duration of the emotional experience. They argue that if negative feelings persist, they will probably emerge in subsequent conflicts.

Conclusion

Emotional conflict has the potential to lead to negative emotional displays or positive emotional displays. Because the difference in the outcomes depends on how the emotion is handled, conflict researchers and therapists hope to stop conflict that escalates to violence by training individuals to discuss, not display, their emotions. Most researchers and therapists argue that discussing the emotion and why it exists will lead to more positive outcomes than will enacting the emotion. These positive outcomes that result from the correct handling of conflict include solving the problem, energizing the relationship, and increasing marital satisfaction. Hopefully, in the future, conflict that escalates to violence will no longer be the norm.

See also: ANGER; ANXIETY; EMOTIONAL ABUSE; GUILT; JEALOUSY; SADNESS

Bibliography

Bower, Gordon H. (1981). "Mood and Memory." *American Psychologist* 36:129–148.

Crockenberg, Susan, and Forgays, Deborah K. (1996). "The Role of Emotion in Children's Understanding and Emotional Reactions to Martial Conflict." *Merrill-Palmer Quarterly* 42:22–47.

Cupach, William R., and Canary, Daniel J. (1997). *Competence in Interpersonal Conflict.* New York: McGraw-Hill.

Deutsch, Morton. (1973). "Conflicts: Productive and Destructive," In *Conflict Resolution Through Communication,* ed. Fred E. Jandt. New York: Harper & Row.

Freud, Sigmund. ([1923] 1961). "The Ego and the Id." In *The*

Standard Edition of the Complete Psychological Works of Sigmund Freud, Vol. 19, tr. James Strachey. London: Hogarth Press.

Gottman, John M. (1994). *What Predicts Divorce? The Relationship between Marital Processes and Marital Outcomes.* Hillsdale, NJ: Lawrence Erlbaum.

Gottman, John M.; Notarius, Clifford; Gonso, Jonni; and Markman, Howard. (1976). *A Couple's Guide to Communication.* Champaign, IL: Research Press.

Greenberg, Leslie S., and Johnson, Susan M. (1986). "Affect in Martial Therapy." *Journal of Marital and Family Therapy* 12: 1–10.

Holtzworth-Munroe, Amy, and Anglin, Kimberly. (1991). "The Competency of Responses Given by Maritally Violent Versus Nonviolent Men to Problematic Marital Situations." *Violence and Victims* 6:257–269.

Infante, Dominic A.; Sabourin, Theresa C.; Rudd, Jill E.; and Shannon, Elizabeth A. (1990). "Verbal Aggressiveness: Messages and Reasons." *Communication Quarterly* 38:361–371.

Lloyd, Sally A. (1990). "Conflict Types and Strategies in Violent Marriages." *Journal of Family Violence* 5:269–284.

Lulofs, Roxane S. (1994). *Conflict: From Theory to Action.* Scottsdale, AZ: Gorsuch Scarsbrick.

Mace, David R. (1982). *Close Companions: The Marriage Enrichment Handbook.* New York: Continuum.

Schacter, Stanley, and Singer, Jerome E. (1962). "Cognitive, Social, and Psychological Determinants of Emotional State." *Psychological Review* 69:379–399.

Stein, Nancy L., and Levine, Linda. (1987). "Thinking about Feelings: The Development and Organization of Emotional Knowledge." In *Aptitude, Learning, and Instruction, Vol. 3: Conative and Affective Process Analysis,* ed. Richard E. Snow and Marshall J. Farr. Hillsdale, NJ: Lawrence Erlbaum.

Tavris, Carol. (1982). *Anger: The Misunderstood Emotion.* New York: Simon & Schuster.

Thibaut, John W., and Kelley, Harold H. (1959). *The Social Psychology of Groups.* New York: Wiley.

Wendt, John R. (1984). "DIE: A Way to Improve Communication." *Communication Education* 33:397–401.

Wilmot, William W., and Hocker, Joyce L. (1998). *Interpersonal Conflict,* 5th ed. Boston: McGraw-Hill.

Yvonne Kellar-Guenther

CONSCIOUSNESS

During the 1990s, there has been an increasing recognition of the importance of emotion research and theory for any comprehensive approach to the study of human consciousness. Similarly, emotion researchers have become increasingly concerned with understanding the role of conscious experience in emotion. Most researchers would agree that emotion is a nearly constant aspect of the human phenomenal experience. It has been suggested that emotions play a necessary role in reasoning processes, creativity, and any adequate neural network model of consciousness. In addition, developments in basic and clinical neuroscience have resulted in rapid progress toward understanding the neural bases of emotion.

Distinguishing Conscious from Nonconscious Aspects of Emotion

Addressing questions concerning the conscious experience of emotion from a scientific perspective requires that one be able to contrast conscious emotional experience with nonconscious emotional responses. For both the general public and many scientists, emotion is identified with feeling and, thus, is inextricably linked to consciousness. Some theorists, such as Gerald Clore (1994) and Richard Lazarus (1982), assert that conscious experience or feeling is a necessary component of emotion, with cognitive appraisal (of the personal significance of information) seen as preceding other emotional reactions. For such individuals, the notion of "nonconscious emotion" would be a contradiction of terms. However, it has become increasingly clear that the conscious experience of emotion is not invariably correlated with other emotion components, nor is it a necessary contributor to all emotional behavior. Although there are disagreements concerning the necessary and sufficient conditions for identifying an emotion, most analyses typically describe four components: physiological (central nervous system and autonomic) arousal, cognitive appraisal, subjective experience, and action tendency (including facial expression). In humans, the autonomic physiological and action tendency components of emotion can occur in response to an emotional stimulus that is not consciously recognized or is outside of the subject's attentional focus. Although some cognitive appraisal (in terms of positive or negative valuation in relation to personal goals, need states, or self-preservation) may be a necessary condition for emotional arousal, such appraisals need not necessarily be conscious.

Other evidence that is consistent with the interpretation that important functions of emotion can occur nonconsciously comes from nonhuman animal research. As Joseph LeDoux's (1996) studies of fear (in rodents) have shown, the amygdala structure in the brain appears to be key in both the stimulus evaluation of threatening events and the production of defensive responses. These defensive responses appear to be evolutionarily selected, involuntary, automatic consequences of the initial rapid evaluation of stimulus significance, and they appear not to require cortical mediation. Thus, LeDoux emphasizes subcortical (e.g., thalamic-amygdala circuitry) emotion systems being involved in fast, evolutionarily-selected, and probably nonconscious aspects of emotion. In contrast, he suggests that cortical inputs (through multiple pathways) are necessary for the conscious experience of emotion. Functional brain imaging studies have provided evidence that is consistent with Le-

Doux's view that the amygdala can perform its role in the processing of emotional stimuli nonconsciously. Employing functional magnetic resonance imaging, Paul Whalen and his colleagues (1998) have demonstrated amygdala activation in response to emotional stimuli (e.g., facial expressions) even when conscious awareness of the stimuli are prevented by backward masking (which involves the presentation of a second stimulus immediately after a first stimulus in order to prevent conscious perception of the first stimulus).

Searching for the Neural Correlates of Conscious Emotion

If one accepts the distinction between the conscious and nonconscious aspects of emotion, then what kinds of contrastive observations or experiments might be possible in searching for the neural correlates of conscious emotion? One approach would be to examine patients for whom there appears to be a dissociation (i.e., there is impairment in the conscious experience of emotion, but the nonconscious emotional behavior is intact). *Alexithymia,* a term originally proposed to describe people who seem to lack an adequate language for their emotional experience, has been shown by Richard Lane and his colleagues (1996) to be more properly conceptualized as a general problem in the conscious experience and discrimination of emotion. In 1997, Lane, Geoff Ahern, Gary Schwartz, and Alfred Kaszniak argued that alexithymia might be considered to be an emotional equivalent of blindsight (i.e., the state where a person's primary visual cortex is damaged but the capacities for visual localization, discrimination, and acuity are demonstrably preserved despite phenomenal blindness—an absence of conscious visual experience). If this is a reasonable characterization of alexithymia, then it should be possible to compare the brain structure and physiology of alexithymic individuals to those of nonalexithymic individuals as a way of exploring the neural correlates of conscious emotion. This approach would be analogous to that in which studies of blindsight patients have been used to explore the neural correlates of visual consciousness. Such studies, with patients who meet the clinical criteria for the diagnosis of alexithymia, are not yet available. However, Lane, Eric Reiman, Beatrice Axelrod, and their colleagues (1998) have examined the neural correlates of varying degrees of "emotional awareness" among normal volunteers, employing positron emission tomography. Differences between these volunteers in emotional awareness were measured with the Levels of Emotional Awareness Scale (LEAS), which had been shown to correlate with the ability to recognize verbal and nonverbal emotion stimuli accurately.

Higher scores on the LEAS were found to be associated with greater blood flow in a supra-callosal region of the anterior cingulate cortex, for both film-elicited and recall-elicited emotion conditions.

The search for the neural correlates of conscious emotional experience might also be pursued by contrasting conscious and nonconscious aspects of emotion experimentally. In positron emission tomography studies, Lane, Gereon Fink, and their colleagues (1997) found that during attention to subjective emotional experience that was elicited by visual scenes (as contrasted with attention to the spatial context of the scene), activity was elicited in rostral anterior cingulate cortex and medial prefrontal cortex. Based upon the differences in regions of the anterior cingulate that were activated in this, versus other positron emission tomography studies, Lane, Reiman, Schwartz, and their colleagues (1998) speculate that the primary or phenomenal conscious experience of emotion may be more dependent upon the rostral anterior cingulate, while secondary or reflective emotional consciousness (involving the evaluation, representation, and reflection upon primary emotional experience) may depend more upon the supra-callosal region of the anterior cingulate.

Similar conclusions concerning the important role of the anterior cingulate gyrus in conscious emotional experience come from studies of people who have damage to this area. Damage to the anterior cingulate (e.g., in the case of surgical destruction of brain tissue for the treatment of intractable pain) has been associated with alterations in emotional experience. Approximately 50 percent of cingulotomy patients experience emotional blunting after surgery. Further, in a series of studies by Antonio Damasio and his colleagues (as reviewed by Ralph Adolphs and his colleagues, 1996), it has been shown that patients with ventromedial frontal damage (typically including the anterior cingulate) do not show the normally expected differentiation of skin conductance response (SCR) magnitude in response to neutral versus emotionally significant visual scenes. Damasio (1994) has hypothesized that frontally damaged patients who do not have an SCR to emotionally salient stimuli will not have the "conscious body state characteristic of an emotion" (p. 209). In support of this hypothesis, Damasio has provided anecdotal examples of frontally damaged patients who do not show SCRs when they are exposed to strongly negative (e.g., mutilation) pictures and who volunteer that they do not feel the expected emotion. In an attempt to further test Damasio's hypothesis, Kaszniak and his colleagues (1999) found that patients who have ventromedial frontal lobe damage (including the anterior cingulate) show a lack of SCR differentiation in response to neutral versus negatively or positively arousing visual stimuli. These same patients also showed a corresponding lack of differentiation in consciously experienced emotional arousal. Despite their abnormal SCR differentiation and subjective arousal ratings, these patients indicated a normal appreciation of the general meaning of emotionally salient stimuli, as reflected in valence ratings of the stimuli, which were similar to those of normal controls. Thus, patients with ventromedial frontal damage provide evidence that is consistent with the interpretation that the anterior cingulate (and possibly the related frontal structures) plays an important role in both the conscious experience of emotional arousal and the differentiation of autonomic physiologic response to emotional stimuli.

What Is the Functional Role of Conscious Emotional Experience?

If various aspects of emotional response (e.g., amygdala activation, facial muscle activity, autonomic physiologic response) can occur without the conscious awareness of an eliciting stimulus, then it might appear to make sense to ask what functional role conscious (as distinguished from nonconscious) emotion might play. It should be noted, however, that in some studies, such as those of Whalen and his colleagues (1998), backward masking prevents conscious awareness of the emotionally salient stimulus itself but does not necessarily prevent the person from being aware of at least some aspects of emotional experience in response to the nonconsciously processed stimulus.

Such conscious experience of emotion, despite unawareness of the eliciting stimulus, might occur through an awareness of bodily signals. Thus, within backward masking or similar experimental models, the participant may have a conscious emotional experience even though he or she cannot consciously identify the eliciting stimulus. It may be the case that there are components of emotional experience that are dependent upon the conscious perception of the eliciting stimulus and others that are independent of a conscious perception. Research, by Kaszniak and his colleagues (1999), on people who have ventromedial frontal lobe damage has shown that emotional valence and arousal experience are dissociable (i.e., they can be differentially impaired by brain damage) and has suggested the possibility that the former (valence) may be more dependent upon conscious perception of the eliciting stimulus while the latter (arousal) may be dependent upon feedback from the somatic periphery (or brainstem somatic effectors).

Specific testing of this possibility would require further experiments with frontally damaged individuals, during which the eliciting stimuli would be prevented (e.g., through backward masking) from being consciously perceived. Such studies, in which experimental manipulations disrupt conscious experience of one aspect (the eliciting stimulus) while an "experiment of nature" (i.e., ventromedial frontal damage) disrupts conscious experience of another (conscious emotional arousal), may be able to scientifically address the question of what functional role is played by these apparently distinguishable aspects of conscious emotion.

How Should the Conscious Experience of Emotion be Measured?

Some research aimed at exploring the neural correlates of conscious emotion has employed the Self-Assessment Manikin (SAM) to assess conscious emotional experience. The SAM is designed to minimize the effects that language may have in reporting experience in response to emotionally arousing stimuli. Both valence and arousal dimensions of emotional experience are ordinally scaled with five cartoon-like figures, and the option is given to make ratings at the midpoint between any two figures, thus providing a scale ranging from 1 to 9 for each emotion experience dimension. The justification for obtaining separate self-reports on these two dimensions (valence and arousal) of emotional experience comes from studies of affective language and from psychophysiological experiments.

Several studies of the covariation between different emotional adjectives have consistently found that valence and arousal are reliable factorial dimensions that account for most of the variance in affective judgments. Further, self-reported experiences of emotional valence and arousal (using the SAM procedure) have been found to relate differentially to various physiologic measures. Peter Lang and his colleagues (1993) have found that facial muscle electromyography, heart rate, and magnitude of the eye-blink startle reflex co-vary with self-reported valence, while SCR, electrocortical activity, and functional brain imaging measures of regional activation co-vary with self-reported arousal. The conceptualization of emotion as having a fundamental valence dimension is supported by both electroencephalographic and brain functional magnetic resonance imaging evidence that shows there is differential cerebral hemispheric involvement in approach emotion versus withdrawal-related emotion.

The primacy of a valence dimension in emotional experience is also supported by human developmental research. Positive or negative reactions to gustatory and olfactory stimuli can be observed in newborns, although identifications of distinct patterns of sadness, anger, and fear cannot be coded reliably until the end of the first year. The limitation of the SAM emotional experience rating procedure is that it may oversimplify the complexity and richness of human emotional experience. The advantage of this simplification is, however, the known relationship of valence and arousal experience dimensions to biologic measures and the probability that these dimensions do represent fundamental and differentiable components of conscious emotion.

An alternative to such laboratory stimuli might involve efforts to obtain self-reports through emotional experience sampling at various times throughout an individual's daily life. This would have the advantage of possibly capturing a wider range of evoking stimuli (and a presumably wider range of emotional experience). The difficulties with such an approach include reduced experimental control over the eliciting stimuli and problems in securing other kinds of correlative data (e.g., many physiologic signals are difficult to measure in moving individuals).

Similarly, a more naturalistic approach to obtaining self-report data on emotional experience may be necessary. If individuals are given the opportunity to provide natural language descriptions of their emotional experiences in daily life, what commonalities might emerge in such descriptions across individuals? Such an approach might have the potential for capturing more of the variety, richness, and nuance that may be missed by other more structured self-report protocols (e.g., the SAM). However, more open-ended self-report formats are notoriously difficult to code for research purposes. Further, depending upon the method by which such self-reports are sampled, one must be concerned with various threats to the reliability and validity of introspective self-report data (e.g., forgetting, particularly when the interval between elicitation and report lengthens; selective reporting/editing). The risks may be outweighed by the benefits, if indeed such open-ended self-report formats capture dimensions of the conscious emotional experience that are potentially lost within more structured self-report formats.

See also: FACIAL EXPRESSION; NEUROBIOLOGY OF EMOTIONS; PSYCHOLOGICAL ASSESSMENT; PSYCHOPHYSIOLOGY OF EMOTIONS

Bibliography

Adolphs, Ralph; Tranel, Daniel; Bechara, Antoine; Damasio, Hanna; and Damasio, Antonio R. (1996). "Neuropsychological Approaches to Reasoning and Decision-Making." In *Neurobiology of Decision-Making*, ed. Antonio R. Damasio, Hanna Damasio, and Yvonne Christen. Berlin: Springer-Verlag.

Canli, Turhan; Desmond, John E.; Zhao, Zuo; Glover, Gary; and Gabrieli, John D. E. (1998). "Hemispheric Asymmetry for Emotional Stimuli Detected with fMRI." *NeuroReport* 9:3233–3239.

Clore, Gerald L. (1994). "Why Emotions Are Never Unconscious." In *The Nature of Emotion: Fundamental Questions*, ed. Paul Ekman and Richard J. Davidson. New York: Oxford University Press.

Clore, Gerald L.; Schwarz, Norbert; and Conway, Michael. (1994). "Affective Causes and Consequences of Social Information Processing." In *Handbook of Social Cognition*, 2nd ed., ed. Robert S. Wyer and Thomas K. Srull. Hillsdale, NJ: Lawrence Erlbaum.

Davidson, Richard J. (1992). "Anterior Cerebral Asymmetry and the Nature of Emotion." *Brain and Cognition* 20:125–151.

Damasio, Antonio R. (1994). *Descartes' Error: Emotion, Reason and the Human Brain.* New York: G. P. Putnam.

DeLancey, Craig. (1996). "Emotion and the Function of Consciousness." *Journal of Consciousness Studies* 3:492–499.

Griffiths, Paul E. (1997). *What Emotions Really Are: The Problem of Psychological Categories.* Chicago: University of Chicago Press.

Kaszniak, Alfred W.; Reminger, Sheryl L.; Rapcsak, Stephen Z.; and Glisky, Elizabeth L. (1999). "Conscious Experience and Autonomic Response to Emotional Stimuli following Frontal Lobe Damage." In *Toward a Science of Consciousness, III: The 1998 Tucson Discussions and Debates*, ed. Stuart R. Hameroff, Alfred W. Kaszniak, and David Chalmers. Cambridge, MA: Massachusetts Institute of Technology Press.

Lane, Richard D.; Ahern, Geoff E.; Schwartz, Gary E.; and Kaszniak, Alfred W. (1997). "Is Alexithymia the Emotional Equivalent of Blindsight?" *Biological Psychiatry* 42:834–844.

Lane, Richard D.; Fink, Gereon; Chau, Phyllis M.-L.; and Dolan, Ray J. (1997). "Neural Activation during Selective Attention to Subjective Emotional Responses." *NeuroReport* 8:3969–3972.

Lane, Richard D.; Nadel, Lynn; Allen, John B.; and Kaszniak, Alfred W. (1999). "The Study of Emotion from the Perspective of Cognitive Neuroscience." In *The Cognitive Neuroscience of Emotion*, ed. Richard D. Lane, Lynn Nadel, Geoff E. Ahern, John B. Allen, Alfred W. Kaszniak, Stephen Rapcsak, and Gary E. Schwartz. New York: Oxford University Press.

Lane, Richard D.; Reiman, Eric M.; Axelrod, Beatrice; Yun, Lang-Sheng; Holmes, Andrew; and Schwartz, Gary E. (1998). "Neural Correlates of Levels of Emotional Awareness: Evidence of an Interaction between Emotion and Attention in the Anterior Cingulate Cortex." *Journal of Cognitive Neuroscience* 10:525–535.

Lane, Richard D.; Reiman, Eric M.; Schwartz, Gary E.; Fink, Gereon; Chua, Phyllis M.-I.; and Dolan, Ray J. (1998). "Subregions within the Anterior Cingulate Cortex May Differentially Participate in Phenomenal and Reflective Conscious Awareness of Emotion." Plenary Paper presented at the "Toward a Science of Consciousness III" April conference. Tucson, AZ.

Lane, Richard D.; Sechrest, Lee; Riedel, Robert; Weldon, Victoria; Kaszniak, Alfred W.; and Schwartz, Gary E. (1996). "Impaired Verbal and Nonverbal Emotion Recognition in Alexithymia." *Psychosomatic Medicine* 58:203–210.

Lang, Peter J.; Greenwald, Mark K.; Bradley, Margaret M.; and Hamm, Alfons O. (1993). "Looking at Pictures: Affective, Facial, Visceral, and Behavioral Reactions." *Psychophysiology* 30:261–273.

Lazarus, Richard S. (1982). "Thoughts on the Relations between Emotion and Cognition." *American Psychologist* 37:1019–1024.

LeDoux, Joseph. (1996). *The Emotional Brain: The Mysterious Underpinnings of Emotional Life.* New York: Simon & Schuster.

Öhman, Arne. (1999). "Distinguishing Unconscious from Conscious Emotional Processes." In *Handbook of Cognition and Emotion,* ed. Tim Dalgleish and Mick Power. Chichester, Eng.: Wiley.

Whalen, Paul J.; Rauch, Scott L.; Etcoff, Nancy L.; McInerny, Sean; Lee, Michael B.; and Jenike, Michael A. (1998). "Masked Presentations of Emotional Facial Expressions Modulate Amygdala Activity without Explicit Knowledge." *Journal of Neuroscience* 18:411–418.

Alfred W. Kaszniak

CREATIVITY

The concept of creativity is often associated with a degree of mystique and elitism. Initially, creativity was perceived as an aspect of intelligence that was an inherited skill possessed by only a few individuals. The investigation of creativity as a major construct in the domain of intelligence has a rich history, yet it was only in the 1980s that the bridge between creativity and emotion began to gain the increased interest of researchers and theorists. Studies indicate that creativity depends, in complementary fashion, not only on intelligence but also on a range of feelings, emotions and affective states. In this entry, creativity is discussed not as a rare or unique skill attributed to a few but as an ability that all people possess to some extent and can develop.

Nature of Creativity

Some people limit their view of creativity to an artistic outcome-based product, but creativity is both a process and a way of thinking. Because creative thinking and creative products typically involve originality and adaptiveness, identification of problems and problem-solving strategies are important cognitive components of the creative process. Two additional aspects of creativity are divergent thinking and transformation abilities. Creative problem solving involves concepts of insight and synthesizing skills, and creative individuals use knowledge in unique and different ways to find relationships between unrelated elements, another central cognitive concept of creativity.

While many intelligence theorists emphasize the limitations of the traditional unidimensional cognitive view of intelligence and creativity as an outcome-based product, Robert Sternberg (1985) and Howard Gardner (1983) have developed multidimensional theories of intelligence and creativity. Sternberg's theory involves three types of intelligence: componential, contextual, and experiential. Componential intelligence, which is analytic and abstract thinking, most closely resembles the traditional view of intelligence. Contextual intelligence is related to the practical skills and abilities that are necessary to adapt to a specific environment. Experiential intelligence involves insightful and creative thinking used in problem-solving strategies. Sternberg acknowledges that intelligence is a necessary component of creativity, but he maintains that high levels of intellectual function are not in themselves sufficient for creativity. Gardner, who agrees with Sternberg's view that creativity is more than a phenomenon of intelligence, suggests that there are seven distinct intellectual competencies: linguistic, logical-mathematical, spatial, body-kinesthetic, interpersonal, intrapersonal, and musical intelligences. According to Gardner, being creative in any of these intellectual competencies is the highest level of functioning. These perspectives on creativity and intelligence have led to the reexamination of the construct of creativity as not only multidimensional but as an area of study that also deserves multidisciplinary inquiry, including the social-emotional dimensions.

Creative Personality

There is a wealth of research on the creative personality, which has allowed creativity researchers to identify a personality profile for the creative individual. These traits include tolerance of ambiguity, openness to experience, possession of unconventional values, independence of judgment, curiosity, preference for challenge and complexity, self-confidence, propensity for risk taking, and intrinsic motivation. Additionally, the creative individual is one who perseveres, is self-disciplined, and can delay gratification.

A number of these identified personality characteristics have associated emotional components. For example, it can be argued that creativity is an attitude derived from emotional experiences in which the individual is receptive to uncertainty and open to surprise. Individuals open to these experiences are sensitive to their feelings and impulses and are more tolerant of ambiguity, thus enabling thoughts and feelings to be simultaneously processed. Additionally, other creative characteristics such as curiosity, preference for challenge, and risk taking all have underlying emotional aspects. They can involve excitement, as well as positive and negative tension, and these emotional components can be highly motivating for creative behavior.

Emotion and Creativity

Attitudes and personality may predispose a person to creative functioning, but it is the motivational and emotional states that serve as the catalyst for creative behavior. Israel Scheffler (1982) has presented two emotions associated with creativity: the joy of verification and the feeling of surprise. Joy of verification comes when an individual's approach to resolving a problem is proven correct. The feeling of surprise occurs when a creation does not turn out as expected. Scheffler emphasizes that the feeling of surprise and the cognitive conflict that arises when unexpected results occur is a central and intrinsic part of the creative process. Likewise, Sandra Russ (1993) has identified several affective processes that are important to creativity. She emphasizes the affective states of pleasure in challenge, which is related to the excitement of problem identification, and the emotional pleasure in problem solving, which is associated with the passion and drive to create solutions. Furthermore, Russ notes that control over the affective process is critical to the creative process. Adaptive creative functioning involves the integration of both cognitive and emotional balance.

Several researchers have offered explanations of how emotion influences creativity. Positive feelings can facilitate creative thinking by enhancing problem-solving efforts, and they can increase cognitive flexibility and the retrieval of memory, thus influencing creativity. The fluctuations of mood states are also important to the creative process. One area of creativity research in relation to mood that has received attention is in the domain of psychopathology. In a review of research on the connection between creativity and psychopathology, Robert Prentky (1989) postulated that there may be an association between a certain genetic predisposition for mental illness and a cognitive style that promotes creativity. Another researcher, Colin Martindale (1989) has concurred that there is data supporting the notion that mood disorders are more prevalent in creative individuals, but he does not think this is determined by the same genetic code site. In another review of creativity and mental health, Ruth Richards (1990) concluded that mild emotional problems may be associated with creativity but that intermediate levels of affect, such as moderate anxiety, stimulate creative processes. Richards also emphasized in her review that positive affect was important to creative endeavors.

Emotional variability has been hypothesized as advantageous to creativity. For example, imagination, enthusiasm, and openness are associated with individuals with more variable moods unlike less moody people who tend to be more rigid and cautious. There may be many psychological origins of creative behavior, and this can include mental disorders as well as healthy emotional development. The primary ingredient that each of these destinies may share is openness to affective thoughts, states, and experiences.

Teresa Amabile (1996) has conducted one of the major research efforts focusing on the personal-social variables related to creativity. She suggests that passion is the primary factor necessary to motivate the most creative individuals. Underlying the creative phenomenon is a passion in a specific area of interest to the individual. This strong positive affect associated with creating can be a powerful internal motivation.

Related to the motivational state of passion are the "flow" experiences described by Mihaly Csikszentmihalyi (1997). These experiences are flashes of intense living that provide immediate feedback in a setting where a person's skills are fully involved in overcoming a challenge that is manageable. Csikszentmihalyi proposes that these optimal experiences usually involve a contextual balance between one's ability to act (skills) and the availability opportunities for action (challenges).

Amabile and Csikszentmihalyi both believe that the powerful motivator behind creative passion and flow experiences is intrinsic motivation. Amabile suggests three methods that serve as a catalyst for this intrinsic motivation. First, the individual needs a knowledge base, technical skills, or talent to be motivated to create. Second, the environment needs to be void of extrinsic constraints that are unnecessary and inhibit the creative process. And third, early in an individual's life there needs to be a general sense or set of experiences that enhance intrinsic motivation. For young children, these earliest intrinsically motivating experiences often center on play.

Play and Creativity

Children's play is important to examine because it involves the same affective processes that are thought to be important in creativity. Play provides opportunities to express positive and negative feelings in a nonthreatening situation through role-playing, experimentation, and discovery. These unstructured experiences, which are typically nonevaluative and free from failure, can promote cognitive and behavior processes that can enhance creative potential. For example, Lev Vygotsky (1962) believed that children's play was the origin of creative imagination. Additionally, Dorothy and Jerome Singer (1990) have shown that a number of cognitive skills are enhanced through play, including increased vocabulary, development of divergent thinking, and problem solving.

Bryan Sutton-Smith (1971) emphasized the role of play in the development of problem-solving skills. Children can engage in conflict resolution by playing out a problematic situation. He found that play could facilitate divergent thinking in young children by providing opportunities for children to explore new ideas

Three young girls in a New York City classroom engage in creative play that also serves to strengthen their problem-solving skills. (Corbis/Jacques M. Chenet)

and develop new associations with ordinary objects. Given the importance of creativity in cognitive and emotional development, it is important to explore strategies in which parents and teachers can facilitate the creative process.

Emotion, Creativity, and Environment

Creativity is a critical component in children's intellectual and emotional development. Schools and homes play important roles in enhancing the emotional aspects of creativity. Unfortunately, there are many aspects of these environments that may instead inhibit creative functioning. There tends to be a pedagogical bias in many schools and homes where traditional academic and intellectual skills are emphasized over creative and emotional abilities. This is evident in schools where an emphasis on standardized tests ignores the creative and emotional dimensions of intelligence. Frequently, there is an overcommitment to traditional forms of learning (e.g., tasks that involve rote memorization, competition, and grading), which can undermine creative potential and diminish healthy emotional development. Ironically, parents often support the greater emphasis schools place on academic skills and ignore the relationship between creativity, intelligence, and emotion. However, based on the previously discussed research, there are a number of ways that parents and teachers can facilitate creativity and emotional development. Four specific areas are (1) providing opportunities for children to express their feelings, (2) enhancing the play environment,

(3) cultivating curiosity and interest, and (4) providing creative role models.

Creative children are allowed freedom to express positive and negative emotions. This freedom of expression allows conflicts to be brought into the open, so children do not repress negative feelings. Children need to deal with a wide range of emotions, including anger, frustration, fear, love, and jealousy. This type of openness in communication facilitates the development of flexibility of thought, curiosity, and fantasy. Children who are not given this opportunity are less likely to develop new ideas and associations and are less likely to develop their creative potential.

Environments that encourage creativity value play and playful behaviors that are important for emotional expression. Children attempt to deal with emotions through play and role-playing situations where they can express feelings in a safe, acceptable way. Creative play environments also allow children to be free to explore and make discoveries. This type of environment would include a wide variety of materials that reflect a range of interests and hobbies. The home and school can include reading materials, musical instruments, art supplies, and so on. Adults in these environments can place an emphasis on the importance of ideas and varied interest that will encourage children to experiment. These experiences will facilitate the development of the emotional aspects of creativity, such as excitement in discovery, that motivate children to further their creative development.

Adults in the home and school can encourage curiosity and exploration. It is important for teachers and parents to demonstrate that they value curiosity, exploration, and original ideas. Children should be made to feel that their ideas and the products they create are valued and respected. This will build the children's self-esteem and self-confidence. And when children have an intense interest in an area, adults should encourage this passion and help the children become absorbed in tasks in that area. In addition, children must have the feeling that attempting new experiences is more important than success or failure. Although failure can be associated with negative emotions such as frustration and anger, it is perseverance that is characteristic of creative individuals. Indeed, it is often the failure experiences that result in individuals growing and developing in different ways.

Finally, and most importantly, children need models of creative behavior in their homes and schools. One of the most important characteristics of teachers and parents is their positive attitudes toward creativity. The presence of such models can provide children with exposure to new skills and creative behaviors in a variety of areas. Adults in children's lives should share the positive feelings they get from being creative such as the excitement of discovery and the joy of problem solving.

Conclusion

Creativity, which is inextricably intertwined with emotion, constitutes a unique and integral aspect of human experience that can bring multiple rewards to individuals in particular and society in general. For this reason, creativity is an important aspect of children's intellectual, social, and emotional growth, and it is essential for healthy development. Therefore, the development of creative abilities is an important parenting and educational goal.

See also: ADVERTISING; COGNITIVE PERSPECTIVE; DANCE; DRAMA AND THEATER; HUMAN DEVELOPMENT; LITERATURE; MUSIC; POETRY; TEMPERAMENT; VISUAL ARTS

Bibliography

Amabile, Teresa. (1996). *Creativity in Context.* Boulder, CO: Westview Press.

Barron, Frank, and Harrington, David. (1981). "Creativity, Intelligence, and Personality." *Annual Review of Psychology* 32:439–476.

Costa, Paul, and McCrae, Robert. (1984). "Personality as a Lifelong Determinant of Well-Being." In *Emotion in Adult Development,* ed. Carol Malatesta and Caroll Izard. Beverly Hills, CA: Sage Publications.

Csikszentmihalyi, Mihaly. (1996). *Creativity: Flow and the Psychology of Discovery and Invention.* New York: HarperCollins.

Csikszentmihalyi, Mihaly. (1997). *Finding Flow: The Psychology of Engagement in Everyday Life.* New York: Basic Books.

Gardner, Howard. (1983). *Frames of Mind: The Theory of Multiple Intelligences.* New York: Basic Books.

Getzels, Jacob, and Csikszentmihalyi, Mihaly. (1976). *The Creative Vision.* New York: Wiley.

Guilford, Joy Paul. (1950). "Creativity." *American Psychologist* 5: 444–454.

Isen, Alice, and Daubman, Kimberly. (1984). "The Influence of Affect on Categorization." *Journal of Personality and Social Psychology* 47:1206–1217.

Mackie, Diane, and Worth, Leila. (1989). "Processing Deficits and the Mediation of Positive Affect in Persuasion." *Journal of Personality and Social Psychology* 57:27–40.

Martindale, Colin. (1989). "Creativity, Consciousness, and Cortical Arousal." *Journal of Altered States Of Consciousness* 3:69–87.

McCrae, Robert, and Costa, Paul. (1997). "Conceptions and Correlates of Openness to Experience." In *Handbook of Personality Psychology,* ed. Robert Hogan, John Johnson, and Stephan Briggs. New York: Academic Press.

Prentky, Robert. (1989). "Creativity and Psychopathology." In *Handbook of Creativity,* ed. John Glover, Royce Ronning, and Cecil Reynolds. New York: Plenum.

Richards, Ruth. (1990). "Everyday Creativity, Eminent Creativity and Health." *Creativity Research Journal* 3:300–326.

Runco, Mark, and Charles, Robyn. (1993). "Judgements of Originality and Appropriateness as Predictors of Creativity." *Personality and Individual Differences* 15:537–546.

Russ, Sandra. (1993). *Affect and Creativity: The Role of Affect and Play in the Creative Process.* Hillsdale, NJ: Lawrence Erlbaum.

Scheffler, Israel. (1982). "In Praise of the Cognitive Emotions." In *Science and Subjectivity,* ed. Israel Scheffler, Indianapolis: Hackett Publishing.

Singer, Dorothy, and Singer, Jerome. (1990). *The House of Make-Believe.* Cambridge, MA: Harvard University Press.

Sternberg, Robert. (1985). *Beyond I.Q.: A Triadic Theory of Intelligence.* Cambridge, MA: Harvard University Press.

Sullivan, Michael, and Conway, Michael. (1989). "Negative Affect Leads to Low-Effort Cognition: Attributional Processing for Observed Social Behavior." *Social Cognition* 7:315–337.

Sutton-Smith, Bryan. (1971). *Children's Play.* New York: Wiley.

Terman, Lewis. (1925). "Mental and Physical Traits of a Thousand Gifted Children." In *Genetic Studies of Genius, Vol. 1,* ed. Lewis M. Terman. Stanford, CA: Stanford University Press.

Vygotsky, Lev. (1962). *Thought and Language,* tr. Eugenia Hanfmann and Gertrude Vakar. Cambridge, MA: MIT Press.

Cheryl A. Wright

CRIME

See Hate Crimes

CROSS-CULTURAL PATTERNS

A technical definition of many, if not all, emotion episodes might read as follows: A multicomponent reaction pattern (involving changes in neurophysiological parameters, motor expression, motivational tendencies, and subjective experience) in response to a particular evaluation of the significance of an antecedent event. From the vantage point of comparing emotional reactions in different cultures, the task is to determine to what extent cultures differ with respect to (1) the nature of antecedent events giving rise to emotions, (2) the way such events are evaluated, (3) the multicomponent reactions generated by a particular appraisal pattern, and (4) the communication and regulation of the respective emotional process.

Before reviewing the evidence available with respect to these points, one must understand the important distinction between potential or competence on the one hand and practice or performance on the other. Potential is built into the human organism or acquired early in childhood development. In consequence, it is determined by both prewired psychobiological structures and learning and socialization patterns that establish stable cognitive representations and behavior models. Thus, with respect to emotion, potential refers to antecedent evaluations and reaction patterns that are available to individuals in all cultures but that may not necessarily occur very frequently due to lack of opportunity or suppression as part of normative regulation. Practice, on the other hand, refers to the actual occurrence of particular emotional reactions as they are observed in a particular cultural setting. Practices are determined by a large number of cultural factors such as values, norms, habits, or environmental constraints that may call forth certain types of evaluations of events and subsequent emotional reactions. Most likely, the potential for reactions inherent in the emotion mechanisms is more extensive than the repertoire that is consistently used in the day-to-day reality of a specific cultural context.

One would expect psychobiological potential to be universally shared and emotional practice, in contrast, to vary across cultures. Much of the cross-cultural emotion research in psychology has been exclusively concerned with the potential for certain emotion mechanisms (e.g., the potential for members of one culture to recognize the facial expressions produced by members of another culture). It is assumed that this ability constitutes evidence for a universally available meaning system for specific expressions. Issues concerning the usefulness of such skills in a particular social context, the frequency of observed expressions, or the importance assigned to such signals in particular cultural groups are consequently considered to be of lesser importance. In contrast, anthropologists and ethnologists have concentrated almost exclusively on the cultural practices of emotion in the people they studied, focusing on the meaning and importance given to specific emotional reactions in a given cultural context and the way people communicate about emotional episodes. Examples of emotional behaviors that are noticeably connected to a groups culture include the low incidence of apparent anger among the Utku Inuit reported by Jean L. Briggs (1970) and the high incidence of a particular variant of shame (i.e., *hasham*, following threats to honor or autonomy) among the 'Awlad Ali Bedouins reported by Lila Abu-Lughod (1986). Robert I. Levy (1984) has suggested that these differences result from under- or over-emphasizing the cognitions that are related to certain antecedent events and the resulting emotions.

The study of the variations of emotional experience across cultures is rendered extremely difficult by the fact that there are very strong *individual* differences in emotional experience and expression, even within a given culture. Often, this important point is neglected. For example, when anthropologists or ethnologists report on the role of emotion in cultures that are relatively isolated from Western influence, they tend to compare their findings implicitly to standard urban cultures in the Western world. In most cases, their objects of study are small tribal societies that live on islands, in deserts, in mountainous areas, or in other remote regions and survive on fishing or agriculture. The researchers tend to disregard the fact that one might find similar—although probably weaker differences—between isolated rural villages and major urban centers in most Western countries. Unfortunately, little evidence about such group and individual differences within any one culture is available. Such evidence, however, is essential for determining to what extent differences in emotional experience between two or more countries are due to cultural differences (e.g., linguistic, geopolitical, or historical) rather than to differences in sociodemographic or psychological variables (e.g., urban-rural habitat, social class, education, temperament, personality, or other dispositional factors).

A further difficulty in analyzing cultural variations in emotional experience and expression is that virtually all evidence on cross-cultural differences is based on emotion talk rather than on objective assessments of reaction or feeling differences. Both anthropologists, who interview their informants about the role of emotion in the societies studied, and comparative psychologists, who use standardized and carefully translated questionnaires to obtain cross-cultural data, forcibly rely on verbal reports of reactions and feelings. In consequence, one major determinant of the results is the way in which the respective language encodes emotion-related information (i.e., what kinds of words or expressions are available in the respective language to describe emotional reactions). Languages differ in the way in which they cut up the emotional meaning space by verbal concepts. However, these differences cannot necessarily be taken as evidence that underlying thought or behavior processes are different or that certain emotional meanings cannot be communicated. In consequence, one has to guard against interpreting differences in emotion words across languages to be evidence for underlying differences in reactions or feelings. However, there is much disagreement in this field about how useful the analysis of "emotion talk" really is.

Antecedent Events

Most emotion theorists consider the elicitation and differentiation of an emotional reaction to depend on the subjective evaluation or appraisal of an event. The results of this process can strongly vary between individuals and culture. However, it remains true that the nature of the emotion-antecedent event has a strong effect on the range of emotions that are likely to be evoked. Thus, while it is unlikely that the ensuing emotion can be completely predicted based on the event alone, the available alternatives will be restricted. For example, while an attack by a knife-wielding individual in a dark street will produce somewhat different emotions depending on the potential victim's perceived coping potential, such an event is unlikely to produce many positive emotions. Thus, if knife-wielding individuals—or similar events—are frequent in one culture and rare in another culture, this may influence the relative frequency with which certain emotions are likely to occur in the two cultures. In order to determine to what extent cultural differences could be due to different antecedents, it is important to examine whether there are differences in the frequency with which particular types of antecedent events occur in particular cultures.

A number of cross-cultural studies have shown similarities and differences of emotion-eliciting situations across cultures. In a large-scale questionnaire study on recalled emotional experiences, the psychologists Klaus Scherer and his colleagues (1986) found a high degree of similarity across eight European countries with respect to the general nature of the eliciting events. The most important event categories were good and bad news, continuation of or problems with relationships (e.g., contact with friends, being socially rejected, quarrels), temporary meetings (e.g., meeting one's friend for dinner), separation (e.g., journey), permanent separation, birth and death, enjoyment (e.g., sex, music), interaction with strangers, and success and failure in achievement situations. However, differences were found with respect to the strength of underlying needs or goals such as personal welfare versus social order and the nature of the causal attribution. In an extension of this cross-cultural study to respondents in the United States and Japan, Scherer and his colleagues (1988) found that Japanese

respondents reported less body-related joy, fewer death- and separation-induced sadness episodes, less stranger-induced fear but much more stranger-induced anger, and fewer anger episodes produced by perceived injustice. The researchers suggest that specific living conditions, cultural values, norms, interactional practices, demographic and socioeconomic factors, and the frequency of certain types of events (e.g., crime) are all possible reasons for such cultural differences.

It is important to note that what is seen as differences or similarities in antecedent conditions depends partly on the degree of concreteness or abstractness used in describing the situations. For example, is having one's car stolen similar to or different from having one's horse stolen, assuming that these commodities play a similar role in the lives of the people concerned? Clearly, many concrete aspects of a situation that may differ greatly between cultures are structurally equivalent with respect to the emotional meaning of the situation and may elicit the same emotion.

Apart from the possibility that the actual frequency of certain types of events differs from country to country, even situations that are objectively determined to be highly similar can be interpreted differently across cultures and thus elicit different emotions. For example, one can demonstrate interesting differences in interpreting the condition of "being alone." Whereas Utku Inuits, Tahitians, and the Pintupi aborigines of Australia, for example, dread finding themselves alone (which is interpreted as social isolation), many people in Western cultures would view the same condition much more positively, seeing it as an opportunity for privacy and time to concentrate on oneself. Another example is the rather universal situation of a child becoming seriously ill. Whereas in many cultures this is seen as a sad but inevitable bit of bad luck, members of cultures with strong beliefs in sorcery or witchcraft may interpret the situation as being the work of evil spirits and react with fear and/or anger. Clearly, in such cases, the eliciting event is objectively the same—what makes it psychologically different is the interpretation of the causes and the consequences of the event. There can be little doubt that what is the determining factor for the emotion evoked is the subjective interpretation of the event. Emotion psychologists use the term *appraisal* to refer to this subjective interpretation.

Appraisal Processes

Several appraisal theories of emotion based on the pioneering work of Magda Arnold (1960) and Richard Lazarus (1966) have been developed since the early 1980s. The fundamental principle of all of these theories is that people will interpret, evaluate, or appraise

While death is a common emotion-eliciting event around the world, the display of the grief and the ceremonies that are involved can vary from culture to culture. These Hindu pallbearers serve in a funeral procession that is part of a traditional worship, celebration, and cremation along the riverside at Varanasi, India. (Corbis/Chris Rainier)

an event with respect to a number of criteria or dimensions related to the significance of the event to them and their ability to cope with its consequences. The major dimensions suggested are attention to changing conditions (novelty/familiarity), a sense of unpleasantness or pleasantness, a sense of uncertainty or certainty, the perception of reaching a goal or encountering an obstacle, the attribution of agency or responsibility, a sense of relative ability to cope with an event (control and/or power), a sense of compatibility with one's self-image or social norms and values. Theorists in this tradition predict, in a highly convergent manner, different profiles of appraisal outcomes as necessary conditions for the occurrence of specific emotions. For example, this tradition asserts (in a simplified version) that anger will be elicited when an individual believes that an obstacle to his or her plans can be removed by aggression, whereas fear will result if an individual considers his or her power to be insufficient to avoid the negative consequences of another person's actions. The major value of these theories (whose predictions mostly sound rather plausible) is that they systematized the appraisal patterns presumed to underlie the major emotions and they have stimulated investigations that generally support the theoretical assumptions.

While the results of studies conducted in different Western cultures by appraisal theorists from different countries (e.g., the United States, Germany, the Netherlands, and Switzerland) show much agreement, there have been few systematic cross-cultural comparisons. Studies on the appraisal profiles associated with particular emotion words have found a relatively high degree of cross-cultural similarity. Generally, the appraisal dimensions accounting for the differentiation between emotion words seem to be similar for all languages studied.

Another way to study appraisal cross-culturally is to ask respondents to remember powerful emotional experiences and to describe the appraisal processes that accompanied the emotion. Similarities and differences in the appraisal patterns for comparable emotions across cultures can be determined in this way. One of the most comprehensive data sets comes from a long-term study performed by Scherer and his colleagues (1994, 1997). The approximately three thousand respondents from thirty-seven countries were asked to recall episodes for each of seven major emotions. They then described details of their appraisal processes and their emotional reactions with the help of a specially developed questionnaire. The results show strong similarities for emotion-specific appraisal profiles across geopolitical regions. This suggests that the appraisal process—as a potential—may indeed be universal. Furthermore, the profiles found empirically by this study correspond in large measure to the theoretical predictions made by appraisal theorists. As Phoebe Ellsworth (1994) has pointed out, however, it is possible that appraisal dimensions that are particularly important in certain non-Western cultures have not yet been identified by Western appraisal theorists.

Still, the study by Scherer and his colleagues did find sizable differences between geopolitical regions with respect to practice (e.g., in the way in which certain appraisal dimensions are used). In particular, respondents in African countries tended to appraise events as being more immoral, more unfair or unjust, and more externally caused. Respondents in Latin American countries tended to appraise emotion-antecedent events as immoral less than did those respondents in other regions. To explain these differences, the researchers evaluated a number of key culture variables related to climate, cultural values, and socioeconomic and demographic variables. Scherer (1997) tentatively explained the differences based on the prevalence of sorcery and witchcraft beliefs in the African countries studied (which, as anthropologists have shown, tend to produce external causal attribution together with moral disqualification of witchcraft) and the high degree of urbanization in the Latin American countries studied (which may lower moral concerns or increase normative tolerance due to habituation to a relatively higher degree of deviance).

Other studies have confirmed that appraisal processes in general show a high degree of similarity except for socially significant appraisal dimensions such as agency, morality, or justice—where considerable cultural differences are found. Robert Mauro and his colleagues (1992), in a comparative study of students in the United States, Japan, the People's Republic of China, and Hong Kong, found few differences between cultures for the more "primitive" dimensions such as pleasantness, attentional activity, certainty, coping ability, and goal/need conduciveness, but the found pronounced differences for more complex appraisal dimensions such as responsibility. Jonathan Haidt and his colleagues (1993) found that, with regard to social transgressions and unconventional food and sex practices, Brazilians more readily than Americans appraised them as being immoral, while highly educated respondents in both countries were less likely than the less educated respondents to appraise in terms of morality. These findings demonstrate that morality is a complex appraisal dimension that may be used in very different ways in different cultures.

It is possible to explain these cultural differences in appraisal—at least partly—as differences in practice

(i.e., the propensity to use certain appraisal dimensions). David Matsumoto and his colleagues (1988) found that Japanese subjects were less willing than American subjects to attribute the responsibility for joy, fear, anger, disgust, shame, and guilt antecedent events to either themselves or other people. Similarly, Scherer and his colleagues (1988) found that, compared to American and European groups, Japanese subjects reported relatively fewer instances of injustice as anger antecedents. These findings were confirmed by Mauro and his colleagues (1992), who found that students from the United States made more use of the responsibility dimension than did students from Japan. Another example for culture-specific appraisal propensities was suggested by Robert Solomon (1978), who explained the low incidence of anger among the Utku Inuit as a reluctance to blame another person for a negative event.

Reaction Patterns

The literature concerning cross-cultural similarities and differences can be analyzed in terms of a number of response forms, including neurophysiological changes, motor expression, motivational tendencies, and subjective experience.

Neurophysiological Changes

Theories of discrete or differential emotions, as presented by Paul Ekman (1992) and Carroll Izard (1992), postulate specific, unique patterns of responses for each of the presumably pancultural fundamental emotions. This specificity of patterning is particularly expected to hold for the motor expression response modalities, although some discrete emotion theorists also expect specific neurophysiological signatures for basic emotions. Of the psychophysiologists studying emotion, Robert Levenson (1992) strongly advocates this position, hypothesizing that there is a large extent of universality for the typical physiological response patterns in the peripheral or autonomous nervous system—in other words, that the nervous systems of people across the world respond in a similar fashion to emotion-inducing events. A clear validation of this hypothesis requires extensive physiological response measurement for cross-culturally comparable emotional states. Due to the difficulties in experimentally inducing strong emotions and of obtaining reliable physiological measurements outside of specialized laboratories, only one such study exists. This study, which was conducted by Levenson and his colleagues (1992), dealt with young Minangkabau men in West Sumatra. While the results did not completely replicate earlier findings with American college students, there is sufficient overlap to allow the researchers to claim support for the existence of pancultural physiological differentiation between the basic emotions. However, the results of this unique study of potential cross-cultural stability in physiological response patterns need to be evaluated on the basis of a lively debate concerning the evidence (or the lack thereof) for stable, specific response patterns for certain basic emotions.

Batja Mesquita and her colleagues (1997) point out that even if physiological response patterning is cross-culturally similar, cultures may differ in its practice (e.g., in the degree to which certain responses are suppressed or amplified in accordance with cultural norms). For example, among the Bedouins in the Egyptian desert crying is considered to be a sign of weakness, whereas—under certain circumstances—it is perfectly acceptable in Western cultures. However, one must keep the possibility in mind that different reactions to comparable events are due to different patterns of situation evaluation or appraisal and may thus constitute different emotions.

In another approach to the study of cross-cultural similarity in physiological patterns, respondents are asked to report verbally the physiological symptoms that accompanied a remembered emotional experience. The available evidence suggests a high degree of similarity across cultures in emotion-specific physiological symptom reports. For example, in the thirty-seven-country study conducted by Scherer and his colleagues (1994, 1997), joy was characterized on average by a warm feeling and an accelerated heart rate, and sadness was characterized by tense muscles, a lump in the throat, and crying/sobbing. While a considerably larger part of the variation in reported physiological responses was explained by the type of emotion, the variation due to country differences is not negligible. Again, some of the country differences found in such verbal reports might be due to practice rather than potential. For example, in an earlier study of eight European countries, Bernard Rimé and his colleagues (1986) found that the reputedly "hot-blooded" southerners reported significantly more blood pressure changes (in feeling joy, sadness, and anger) than did the "cold" northerners, whereas the northerners reported significantly more stomach sensations (in feeling joy and fear) and muscle symptoms (in feeling anger) than did the southerners. One possible explanation for these findings is that specific symptoms elicit more attention, and therefore more comments, in some countries than in others. Similarly, the finding that Japanese students generally reported fewer symptoms than did Europeans or Americans can possibly be related to the respective cultural norms that regulate the reporting of such bodily symptoms.

The emotion-specificity and intercultural stability found in these verbal reports contrasts with the weak and inconsistent findings reported in studies, such as the on conducted by Gerhard Stemmler (1989), that actually measure physiological parameters for laboratory-induced emotions. Based on the generally low correlations between objective measurement and subjective reporting, the stable reporting of specific symptoms for particular emotions has been credited to stereotyped expectations concerning the changes that should occur with certain emotions. However, this interpretation neglects the fact that studies involving objective measurement have used relatively weak emotion induction procedures whereas the studies involving subjective verbal report have asked respondents to recall the strongest emotional experiences they could remember. Still, verbal report of physiological symptoms is obviously an unreliable method of investigation, and cross-cultural studies using objective measurements of intense emotional episodes are urgently needed.

Motor Expression

The expression component of emotion has been by far the most frequently studied with respect to cross-cultural similarities and differences. One reason for this is that Charles Darwin (1872) proposed a very explicit hypothesis concerning the universality of expression (across cultures as well as across species) in his pioneering monograph on emotional expression. Furthermore, while all other emotion components are very difficult to observe, facial and vocal expression is readily observed and can be analyzed objectively. One can also obtain an indirect assessment of the universality assumption by studying whether people in different cultures can recognize expressions produced by members of other cultures (as presented in photographs of facial expressions or sound recordings of vocal expressions). The vast majority of cross-cultural research on expression since the 1960s has indeed been concerned with the pancultural recognition of emotion. The results of this massive research effort are unequivocal: While there are differences in the degree of accuracy with which members of Western and non-Western (particularly illiterate) cultures recognize emotional experiences, the general level of accuracy across cultures vastly exceeds the one that would be expected if the responses were based on chance (i.e., guessing). This strongly suggests the existence of a universal potential for emotion communication.

Obviously, the existence of such a *potential* does not mean that the *practice* of expression is similarly universal. While there are plausible arguments for why this might be the case and while informal observations during travel to foreign countries seem to support this assumption, there is no conclusive formal evidence. One of the few sets of data of this kind has been obtained by the human ethologist Irenäus Eibl-Eibesfeldt (1989), who has filmed, often in an unobtrusive fashion, sequences of emotional expressions in a number of non-Western societies. This, admittedly unsystematic, selection from a wide variety of cultures shows many similarities in the expressions of different emotions. However, Eibl-Eibesfeldt has also documented various culture-specific bodily expressions. A prime example for a culture-specific expression pattern is the tongue protrusion as a sign of shame in the Indian Orissa culture reported by Usha Menon and Richard Shweder (1994).

Thus, the available evidence points to the existence of a universal core of emotional expressions in face, voice, and body that may be based on a combination of the appraisal of emotion-eliciting situations, psychophysiological adaptations, action tendencies or behavioral intentions, and the communicative signaling of the latter. However, there is an extraordinary flexibility in this expressive system allowing for a large number of individual, contextual, and cultural variations in expressive behavior. Part of this variability is due to the fact that expressions are influenced by both the "push effects" that are the adaptive psychophysiological changes occurring in a situation and the "pull effects" that are the social and cultural rules guiding personal behavior in a specific context. The need to adapt the expressions of emotion to cultural norms and expectations have been frequently commented on. The psychologist Wilhelm Wundt (1874) provided one of the first systematic treatments of the issue, and the sociologist Norbert Elias (1977) proposed the intriguing thesis that civilization is a product of affect control (including the development of social rules concerning emotion expression).

Motivational Tendencies

One of the major components of emotion is motivational change, the emergence of a particular action tendency or action readiness (e.g., approach, withdrawal and avoidance, rejection, help-seeking, hostility, breaking contact, dominance, and submission). Different emotions tend to produce different kinds of action readiness that are often only felt as impulses and do not necessarily result in the production of the respective behavior. There are exceedingly few cross-cultural studies on action readiness patterns. In the extensive cross-national study conducted by Scherer and his colleagues (1994, 1997), subjects were asked whether their emotional experience had led them to move toward, move away from, or move against (aggress against) the object of emotion. Considerable cross-cultural similarity was found in the action readiness patterns for the emotions studied. As would have been expected, joy caused more approach behaviors than the other emotions studied, anger elicited more aggression, and withdrawal was most common in sadness, disgust, shame, and guilt. The differences in action readiness responses were mostly due to differences in emotion and only partly due to culture or to a combination of emotion and culture.

In a study of lexically equivalent words in Japanese, Indonesian, and Dutch, Nico Frijda and his colleagues (1995) found a remarkable degree of similarity for the action tendencies perceived to be associated with these words. Five major factors (that might be considered universal dimensions of action readiness modes) were found: moving away, moving towards, moving against, helplessness, and submission. In addition to the overall similarities, some intercultural differences were found. The Japanese subjects reported more frequently than others groups a wish to depend on someone else, as well as apathy, feelings of helplessness, and urges to protect themselves. Hazel Markus and Shinobu Kitayama (1994) proposed that these findings reflect the value placed on depending on intimate others and acceptance by others in Japan.

Subjective Experience

The definition of subjective emotional experience poses serious problems for the study of emotion. While some theorists believe that the lack of an external reference for such feelings prevents them from being conveniently analyzed or studied in depth, most emotion researchers are more pragmatic. One of the suggestions for a definition of subjective emotional experience is to see it as a reflection (which the individual may or may not be conscious of or able to put into words) of the changes in all of the other emotion components (i.e., appraisal of the situation, physiological changes, motor expression, and action tendencies). As long as techniques for neuropsychological recording or imaging of such reflections are lacking, researchers must continue to rely on verbal report of that part of the reflection that the subject is conscious of and capable of putting into words.

Using verbal report, one can attempt to assess some of the major aspects or dimensions of subjective experience and to determine to what extent these are similar or different across cultures. Among the most readily available aspects are the perceived duration and intensity of different types of emotions. The intercultural studies conducted by Scherer and his colleagues (1994, 1997) provide rather reliable information on these aspects. While most of the differences in intensity or duration are due to the differences between emotion, a sizable amount of the variation is accounted for by country differences. One of the strongest effects found is that a longer duration of all emotional experiences is reported in poorer countries (particularly those located close to the equator). One possible explanation is that because of a slower pace of life and fewer external diversions, emotion processes are less likely to be interrupted or superseded by mood changes due to new events.

Other dimensions that were proposed, on the basis of introspective analysis, by Wundt (1874) are experienced valence or hedonic tone (pleasure versus pain), activity or arousal, and degree of tension. The first two of these dimensions have been reliably found across cultures in people's responses to emotion words, similarities of facial expressions, and emotional experiences. This provides evidence that subjective experience can be mapped onto two or three comparable dimensions across different cultures. However, these dimensions are very general and do not represent the richness and detail of subjective emotional experience.

This richness in experience is reflected in the specific emotion terms, labels, or multi-word expressions that abound in many languages. To compare details of emotional experience, one can investigate the verbal description of emotional experience in different cultures. Unfortunately, as mentioned above, such comparisons are complicated by language-specific semantic representations of the emotion domain. While such differences in emotion semantics may reveal cultural differences in the attention paid to certain emotion facets or their evaluation in a culture-specific meaning system, this is not necessarily the case. Subjective experience or feeling is nonlinguistic much of the time—often people start trying to find the word for a feelings only when they are required to talk about it. In consequence, differences in emotion semantics over languages may not provide information about similar differences in nonlinguistic feeling states.

One can imagine large-scale cross-cultural differences in feeling state without resorting to justifications based on linguistic differences. Subjective feeling reflects all of the other components of emotion, in particular, the underlying appraisal process. Thus, all of the culture-specific elements of those components mentioned above can produce cultural differences in feeling states. If one takes an event that is highly comparable across cultures—the death of a spouse, for example—it is likely that the subjective feeling states in different cultures are quite different because the emotion process as a whole, starting with appraisal and its effect on all other components, is different. Appraisal may depend on social structure (e.g., monogamy versus polygamy, relation between sexes, role of the couple in the extended family), values such as romantic love, and the attitude toward death, as well as a large number of other factors. However, as noted earlier, such factors may also explain differences in emotional reactions between individuals within any one culture.

Regulation and Communication

Inasmuch as emotion words are used for the communication of emotion in social interaction, differences in denotation (i.e., specific meaning) and connotation (i.e., associated meaning) may well be of importance and may indeed play a role in the social construction of emotion experiences. This may be of particular interest with respect to emotion regulation, which concerns both the culturally prescribed control of emotion and its components (as in the case of display rules) and the amplification or even induction of desirable emotional states (as in the case of feeling rules). Again, this concerns practice rather than potential. The emotion mechanism can be made to work within a system of cultural rules and expectations, partly because of the extreme flexibility of the appraisal mechanism that drives the changes in the other emotion components and partly because of sensitivity to emotional experiences and their effect on social environment. Ever since Darwin, the importance of emotional expression to signal reactions and intentions related to specific events has been emphasized. The reason is that emotion, through expression, is one of the major mediators of social interaction. It allows for smooth interpersonal adaptation through the communication of reactions and behavioral intentions. This communication occurs through negotiable nonverbal expressions rather than binding verbal utterances. For example, while people can explain away an angry facial expression if they notice that they have overreacted or that negative consequences are to be expected, this is not possible for a verbally uttered threat. To the extent that cultural factors affect interactional episodes, emotion regulation and communication will be affected equally.

Conclusion

There are many reasons to assume that the emotion mechanism consists of psychobiological building blocks that constitute a universally shared potential to react in specific ways to important life events. In practice, these building blocks are assembled according to rules and practices that can be highly culture specific, particularly with respect to how the subjective experiences are verbally communicated to others. Although the research shows that all components of emotion can show strong cross-cultural variations, researchers have only started to understand what cultural factors determine these variations. Socioeconomic variables, history, demographic factors, social structure, norms, values, expectations, socialization, personality, and interpersonal interaction patterns are all potential determinants of cultural differences in emotion practice. Only a more systematic exploration of the role that these factors play in emotion will allow researchers to understand the sources of cross-cultural variations in emotional processes.

See also: ANTHROPOLOGY OF EMOTIONS; BODY MOVEMENT, GESTURE, AND DISPLAY; COMMUNICATION; CULTURE; CULTURE-BOUND SYNDROMES; DARWIN, CHARLES ROBERT; EMOTION EXPERIENCE AND EXPRESSION; EMPATHIC ACCURACY; FACIAL EXPRESSION; NEUROBIOLOGY OF EMOTIONS; PSYCHOPHYSIOLOGY OF EMOTIONS; UNIVERSALITY OF EMOTIONAL EXPRESSION

Bibliography

Arnold, Magda. (1960). *Emotion and Personality.* New York: Columbia University Press.

Abu-Lughod, Lila. (1985). "Honor and the Sentiments of Loss in a Bedouin Society." *American Ethnologist* 12(2):245–261.

Brakel, Jaap van. (1994). "Emotions: A Cross-Cultural Perspective on Forms of Life." In *Social Perspectives on Emotion, Vol. 2,* ed. William M. Wentworth and John Ryan. Greenwich, CT: JAI Press.

Briggs, Jean L. (1970). *Never in Anger: Portrait of an Eskimo Family.* Cambridge, MA: Harvard University Press.

Darwin, Charles. ([1872] 1998). *The Expression of the Emotions in Man and Animals.* London: HarperCollins.

Davitz, Joel R. (1969). *The Language of Emotion.* New York: Academic Press.

Eibl-Eibesfeldt, Irenäus. (1989). *Human Ethology.* Hawthorne, NY: Aldine de Gruyter.

Ekman, Paul. (1973). "Darwin and Cross-Cultural Studies of Facial Expression." In *Darwin and Facial Expression,* ed. Paul Ekman. New York: Academic Press.

Ekman, Paul. (1992). "An Argument for Basic Emotions." *Cognition and Emotion* 6(3–4):169–200.

Elias, Norbert. (1977). *The Civilizing Process.* New York: Urizen.

Ellsworth, Phoebe C. (1994). "Sense, Culture, and Sensibility." In *Emotion and Culture: Empirical Studies of Mutual Influence,* ed. Shinobu Kitayama and Hazel R. Markus. Washington, DC: American Psychological Association.

Frijda, Nico H.; Markam, Suprapti; Sato, Kaori; and Wiers, Reinoud. (1995). "Emotions and Emotion Words." In *Everyday Conceptions of Emotion: An Introduction to the Psychology, Anthropology, and Linguistics of Emotion,* ed. James A. Russell, José-Miguel Fernandez-Dols, Anthony S. R. Manstead, and Jan C. Wellenkamp. Dordrecht, The Netherlands: Kluwer Academic.

Haidt, Jonathan; Koller, Silvia H.; and Dias, Maria G. (1993). "Affect, Culture, and Morality, or Is It Wrong to Eat Your Dog?" *Journal of Personality and Social Psychology* 65(4):613–628.

Heider, Karl G. (1991). *Landscapes of Emotion: Mapping Three Cultures of Emotion in Indonesia.* Cambridge, Eng.: Cambridge University Press.

Izard, Carroll E. (1992). "Basic Emotions, Relations among Emotions, and Emotion-Cognition Relations." *Psychological Review* 99(3):561–565.

Lazarus, Richard S. (1966). *Psychological Stress and the Coping Process.* New York: McGraw-Hill.

Levenson, Robert W. (1992). "Autonomic Nervous System Differences among Emotions." *Psychological Science* 3(1):23–27.

Levenson, Robert W.; Ekman, Paul; Heider, Karl; and Friesen, Wallace V. (1992). "Emotion and Autonomic Nervous System Activity in the Minangkabau of West Sumatra." *Journal of Personality and Social Psychology* 62(6):972–988.

Levy, Robert I. (1984). "The Emotions in Comparative Perspective." In *Approaches to Emotion,* ed. Klaus R. Scherer and Paul Ekman. Hillsdale, NJ: Lawrence Erlbaum.

Lutz, Catherine. (1987). "Goals, Events, and Understanding in Ifaluk Emotion Theory." In *Cultural Models in Language and Thought,* ed. Dorothy Holland and Naomi Quinn. Cambridge, Eng.: Cambridge University Press.

Markus, Hazel R., and Kitayama, Shinobu. (1994). "The Cultural Construction of Self and Emotion: Implications for Social Behavior." In *Emotion and Culture: Empirical Studies of Mutual Influence,* ed. Shinobu Kitayama and Hazel R. Markus. Washington, DC: American Psychological Association.

Matsumoto, David; Kudoh, Tsutomu; Scherer, Klaus R.; and Wallbott, Harald G. (1988). "Antecedents of and Reactions to Emotions in the United States and Japan." *Journal of Cross-Cultural Psychology* 19(3):267–286.

Mauro, Robert; Sato, Kaori; and Tucker, John. (1992). "The Role of Appraisal in Human Emotions: A Cross-Cultural Study." *Journal of Personality and Social Psychology* 62:301–317.

Menon, Usha, and Shweder, Richard A. (1994). "Kali's Tongue: Cultural Psychology and the Power of Shame in Orissa, India." In *Emotion and Culture: Empirical Studies of Mutual Influence,* ed. Shinobu Kitayama and Hazel R. Markus. Washington, DC: American Psychological Association.

Mesquita, Batja; Frijda, Nico H.; and Scherer, Klaus R. (1997). "Culture and Emotion." In *Handbook of Cross-Cultural Psychology, Vol. 2: Basic Processes and Human Development,* 2nd ed., ed. John W. Berry, Pierre R. Dasen, and T. S. Saraswathi. Boston: Allyn & Bacon.

Oatley, Keith. (1993). "Social Construction in Emotions." In *Handbook of Emotions,* ed. Michael Lewis and Jeannette M. Haviland. New York: Guilford.

Osgood, Charles E.; May, William H.; and Miron, Murray S. (1975). *Cross-Cultural Universals of Affective Meaning.* Urbana: University of Illinois Press.

Rimé, Bernard, and Giovannini, Dino. (1986). "The Physiological Patterns of Reported Emotional States." In *Experiencing Emotion: A Cross-Cultural Study,* ed. Klaus R. Scherer, Harald G. Wallbott, and Angela Summerfield. Cambridge, Eng.: Cambridge University Press.

Russell, James A., and Fernandez-Dols, José-Miguel, eds. (1997). *The Psychology of Facial Expression.* Cambridge, Eng.: Cambridge University Press.

Russell, James A.; Lewicka, Maria; and Niit, Toomis. (1989). "A Cross-Cultural Study of a Circumplex Model of Affect." *Journal of Personality and Social Psychology* 57(5):848–856.

Scherer, Klaus R. (1997). "The Role of Culture in Emotion-Antecedent Appraisal." *Journal of Personality and Social Psychology* 73:902–922.

Scherer, Klaus R.; Matsumoto, David; Wallbott, Harald G.; and Kudoh, Tsutomu. (1988). "Emotional Experience in Cultural Context: A Comparison between Europe, Japan, and the United States." In *Facets of Emotion: Recent Research,* ed. Klaus R. Scherer. Hillsdale, NJ: Lawrence Erlbaum.

Scherer, Klaus R., and Wallbott, Harald G. (1994). "Evidence for Universality and Cultural Variation of Differential Emotion Response Patterning." *Journal of Personality and Social Psychology* 66(2):310–328.

Scherer, Klaus R.; Wallbott, Harald G.; and Summerfield, Angela B., eds. (1986). *Experiencing Emotion: A Cross-Cultural Study.* Cambridge, Eng.: Cambridge University Press.

Solomon, Robert C. (1988). "On Emotions As Judgements." *American Philosophical Quarterly* 25:183–191.

Stemmler, Gerhard. (1989). "The Autonomic Differentiation of Emotions Revisited: Convergent and Discriminant Validation." *Psychophysiology* 26(6):617–632.

Wallbott, Harald G., and Scherer, Klaus R. (1988). "Emotion and Economic Development: Data and Speculations Concerning the Relationship between Economic Factors and Emotional Experience." *European Journal of Social Psychology* 18(3):267–273.

Wundt, Wilhelm. ([1874] 1905). *Fundamentals of Physiological Psychology*, 5th ed. Leipzig, Germany: Engelmann.

Klaus R. Scherer

CRYING

Crying is a complex collection of behaviors that are associated with the expression of several emotions. These behaviors include characteristic vocalizations and respiratory patterns (in infants), facial expressions, and the secretion of tears from the lacrimal glands in the absence of physical irritation of the eyes. Crying is associated with a number of situations and physical and emotional states, and it may be elicited by a number of appraisals. Researchers who study crying in infants focus primarily on crying as a form of distress vocalization and draw parallels between the crying of human infants and the distress calls of other animals. Researchers who study adult crying focus exclusively on crying as the shedding of tears in an emotional context. (Some researchers have advocated the use of the term *weeping* to differentiate the shedding of tears in an emotional context from crying as a form of distress vocalization.) While there are many similarities between nonhuman distress calls and human distress vocalizations, the secretion of tears associated with emotion appears to be unique to humans. Because of this, the focus of this entry is on crying defined as the shedding of emotional tears (manifested as the appearance of tears in the eyes, as tears flowing down the face, or as sobbing, all with or without accompanying vocalizations), and most of what is said, except where otherwise noted, pertains to adults only.

Crying behavior, as opposed to the simple secretion of tears, is associated with a complex pattern of both sympathetic and parasympathetic nervous system arousal. (The sympathetic nervous system is involved in emergency responses to perceived environmental threats and prepares the body for vigorous activity. The parasympathetic nervous system is involved in the conservation of energy and counteracts, to some extent, the activity of the sympathetic system.) Tears contain lysozyme, an antibacterial agent, adrenocorticotropic hormone (ACTH), leucine-enkephalin, and several proteins. Because tears and the lacrimal glands also contain relatively high concentrations of the hormone prolactin, it has been hypothesized that prolactin may act to lower the threshold of crying. It has also been hypothesized that irritant and emotional tears should differ in ACTH levels, the reasoning being that the secretion of tears is the body's way of ridding itself of the toxic by-products of stress. Irritant and emotional tears, however, have been found to differ primarily in terms of the protein albumin, with emotional tears having higher levels.

Why Do People Cry?

When people are asked to describe the kinds of situations in which they cry, the most frequently cited situations are those that involve the death of loved ones or friends, the dissolution of romantic relationships, and watching sad films or television programs. Positive events such as weddings and reunions with loved ones or friends are also frequently mentioned. In addition, people report crying when they see others who are crying or in distress, during sporting events when their team wins or loses, and when they hear their national anthem played. When people are asked to describe the most recent occasion during which they cried, a somewhat different question, interpersonal conflicts such as arguments, being rejected by others, and simply feeling lonely or inadequate are the kinds of situations that are most often reported. The situations in which people report crying, although diverse, may share a resemblance in that all of them are situations in which bonds of attachment have been broken, are in danger of being broken, or are being reestablished. This resemblance may be one of the ways in which adult crying is similar to the crying of infants. As John Bowlby pointed out (1969), crying is one of the primary means by which infants establish and maintain an attachment relationship with their caregivers.

As might be expected, given its association with situations that involve loss and interpersonal conflict, crying has been found to be most often accompanied by feelings of sadness, grief, disappointment, anger, frustration, self-pity, and, in women in particular, powerlessness. Crying is also associated with feelings of sympathy, pity, relief, great joy, elation, and aesthetic and religious rapture. People often report feeling several emotions during an episode of crying, with powerlessness or helplessness blending with other emotions such as sadness or anger.

It is unclear precisely what patterns of appraisal elicit crying, as few studies have explicitly examined the issue. However, the strong association of crying with feelings of helplessness and powerlessness and individuals' reports of crying when they feel that they have no other resources left suggest that the predominant theme in the appraisals that lead to crying may be the recognition that one is powerless to change the situation. Indeed, the philosopher Helmuth Plessner (1970) argues that crying is an admission that nothing more can be done in the situation, and others have pointed to the recurring motifs of "giving in" or surrendering in reports of the experience of crying. The association of crying with the realization that one is powerless or helpless may suggest another way in which the crying of adults is similar to that of the crying of infants, because some infant researchers regard at least some episodes of infant crying to be an indication that the infant's ability to respond to a situation

A young girl was overcome by feelings of helplessness and began to cry when she was confronted by a photographer who was visiting Taipei, Taiwan (then known as Formosa), shortly after the city became the seat of the Chinese Nationalist government in 1949. (Corbis/Bettmann)

is disorganized and that it is overwhelmed with stimulation.

As befits such a complex collection of responses, a variety of functions have been attributed to crying. In *The Expression of the Emotions in Man and Animals* (1872), Charles Darwin argued that the production of emotional tears originally served simply to protect the eyes from the violent contraction of the facial muscles that accompanies screaming in infancy. The association of tears with sadness and other emotions was merely accidental. This argument is in line with the hypothesis that emotional tears may help maintain the body's equilibrium by draining off toxic chemicals.

Crying is thought by many to serve as the primary means by which infants communicate their needs to their caregivers and as part of the infant's arousal regulation system. It is likely that the crying of adults, although vastly different in form, serves similar purposes. Just as the crying of infants serves to elicit from others behaviors that establish and maintain bonds of attachment, the crying of adults serves to elicit sympathy and support from others. It is no accident that crying occurs in situations where emotional attachments are broken or are in jeopardy and that it is a powerful elicitor of sympathy. Whatever else it might do, crying is a means of social communication in both infants and adults.

Crying, in adults, as in infants, may also serve to help regulate arousal in two ways. There may be direct effects of crying on arousal, as when a "good cry" leads to a reduction in negative affect or arousal, although the evidence for this is inconclusive. There may also be indirect effects of crying on arousal, as when the sympathy and concern of others, elicited by crying, help to calm the crying individual.

The Effects of Crying

In folk psychology and in the psychological literature associated with psychodynamic psychotherapy, crying is often described as being followed by increases in positive affect and a release from emotional tension. Indeed, when people are asked to describe how they generally feel after crying or how they felt after a specific episode of crying, respondents commonly describe themselves as feeling "relieved" and more relaxed after they have cried. People also show significant increases in self-rated positive affect and decreases in depression scores after crying. Such positive changes are typically not found, however, when the effects of crying are assessed in more controlled laboratory settings.

In the most commonly used laboratory model for studying crying and its effects, self-report and physiological measures of affect are taken before, during, and after participants are exposed to a sad film. In such studies, it has been found that crying leads to significant increases in sadness, depression, other negative affects, muscle tension, and heart rate and decreases in happiness and immunity (as indicated by decreases in secretory immunoglobulin A).

Differences between the outcomes of self-report and laboratory studies of the effects of crying may be due to specific features of the laboratory situations in which crying is elicited and assessed. Perhaps people do not feel better after crying because their crying is in response to something about which they can do nothing and nothing in the situation has changed as a result of their crying. It may also be the case that it takes longer for the beneficial effects of crying to appear than is usually allowed in laboratory studies. Memory biases may also affect the results of these studies. It is possible that people tend to recall only episodes of crying in which they felt better afterward or they allow their recall to be influenced by the generally recognized notion that one should feel better after crying.

Variability in Crying

Men and women appear to differ considerably in the frequency and intensity with which they cry. Although there are marked cultural differences in the frequency of crying, in both European and non-European cultures, women report crying more frequently and more intensely than do men. Men in the United States who endorse less traditional gender roles, however, report crying more frequently than do men who endorse more traditional gender roles. Studies that have correlated global self-reports of crying frequency with actual crying in a laboratory setting or crying frequency as assessed by daily diaries suggest that these gender differences are not the result of self-report bias. Gender differences in crying in infants and young children appear to be slight, but by the time children reach puberty, the gender differences already resemble those of adults.

In addition to differences in the frequency and intensity with which they cry, men and women appear to differ somewhat in the kinds of things that elicit tears from them, although the differences are not very pronounced. There appears to be no difference in the tendency of men and women to cry in response to highly emotional events, such as the death of a loved one. Women, however, appear to cry more frequently than men in situations that involve interpersonal conflict and when they feel angry or frustrated. Women are more likely to report crying for purely physical reasons (e.g., during certain phases of the menstrual cycle). Men are less likely to cry in the presence of another man.

The subjective experience of crying appears to be quite similar for men and women. Women who have cried in their place of work, however, report feeling helpless, embarrassed, and out of control, which appears to be a function of the context of their crying and the reactions, real and imagined, of others to it.

Crying, like all emotional expressions, takes place within the context of social and cultural norms that define when and how it is appropriate to express particular emotions. While crying is almost certainly a universal form of human emotional expression, cultures undoubtedly differ in the extent to which they value crying, especially in public. Hence, one would expect there to be cultural and historical variation in the expression and experience of crying. There is some evidence that the acceptance of public displays of crying, especially for men, has increased considerably in the United States between the 1950s and the 1990s. Unfortunately, aside from variations in the frequency of crying, cultural differences in crying have not been well documented.

Self-reported monthly crying frequency is highest for women in Turkey, Chile, and the United States, and for men in Italy, the United States, and Austria. Monthly crying frequency is lowest among women in Nigeria and men in Spain. It is not clear what the countries with the highest or lowest frequencies of crying have in common. A study of self-reported annual crying frequency among English and Israeli university students and faculty found that estimates of crying frequency were much lower among the Israeli sample. Israelis were less likely to cry in the presence of a person that they knew well, in the presence of a close female friend, and when alone. However, there was no difference between the English and Israeli samples with regard to whether they felt they could stop themselves from crying once they had begun.

The tendency to cry has been found to correlate with a number of personality characteristics. In particular, crying is associated with higher levels of femininity, empathy, extroversion (in women only), and self-monitoring. Crying has also been found to be associated with lower levels of alexithymia, the tendency to be out of touch with one's emotions, a "distancing" coping style, higher levels of neuroticism, and, paradoxically, ego-strength. The common threads that unite these associations, except for that of crying and ego-strength, appear to be emotional flexibility and expressiveness. Crying may be associated with ego-strength because those who are more secure in their sense of self may not regard crying as a sign of weakness.

Reactions to Crying

Crying, whether the distress vocalizations of infants or the tears of adults, is a compelling emotional expression, and reactions to the crying of others are usually positive. People take notice of another person who is crying and almost always respond in some manner, sometimes, depending upon the context, by crying themselves. Reactions to crying do differ, however, as a function of the gender of both the person who is crying and the person who is witnessing the crying. Self-report questionnaire studies indicate that people generally respond to crying with sympathy and acceptance. Men, however, are more likely to report feeling awkward, confused and irritated, or manipulated in the presence of another person who is crying. Men are also more likely than women to consider the crying of men to be inappropriate and a sign of weakness. Perhaps for this reason, men are less likely to cry in the presence of another man.

In laboratory studies in which people are exposed to the crying of another person who is actually a confederate of the experimenter (and has been trained to appear as if he or she were crying), confederates of both genders who cry in response to a sad film are seen to be more emotional and depressed and elicit more sympathy than those who do not cry. Male confederates who cry, however, are considered to be the most likable by both women and men, while female confederates who cry are considered to be the least likable.

Differences in the outcomes of the two types of studies may be due to the different methodologies that were employed, changes in attitudes toward men's crying, the commonly observed disjunction between what people say they do and what they actually do, or a combination of all three. It could also be that, because crying by men in public is such a rare event, when people observe a man crying they feel that something of great emotional significance must have occurred and therefore do not negatively evaluate him.

There is evidence that the reactions of others may have important effects on the expression and experience of crying. Data from both questionnaire and laboratory studies indicate that peoples' reports of feeling better after a bout of crying are associated with positive changes in the situation in which they cried and in the relationship they shared with whomever was present when they cried.

See also: DARWIN, CHARLES ROBERT; GENDER AND EMOTIONS; GRIEF; HELPLESSNESS; HOPELESSNESS; SADNESS; SMILING

Bibliography

Botelho, Stella Y. (1964). "Tears and the Lacrimal Gland." *Scientific American* 221:78–86.

Bowlby, John. (1969). *Attachment and Loss, Vol. 1: Attachment.* New York: Basic Books.

Cornelius, Randolph R. (1997). "Toward a New Understanding of Weeping and Catharsis?" In *The (Non)Expression of Emotions in Health and Disease,* ed. Ad J. J. M. Vingerhoets, Frans van Bussel, and Jan Boelhouwer. Tilburg, The Netherlands: Tilburg University Press.

Darwin, Charles. ([1872] 1965). *The Expression of the Emotions in Man and Animals.* Chicago: University of Chicago Press.

Efran, Jay S., and Spangler, Timothy J. (1979). "Why Grown-Ups Cry: A Two-Factor Theory and Evidence from the Miracle Worker." *Motivation and Emotion* 3:63–72.

Frey, William H.; Desota-Johnson, Denise; and Hoffman, Carrie. (1981). "Effect of Stimulus on the Chemical Composition of Tears." *American Journal of Ophthalmology* 92:559–567.

Gross, James J.; Fredrickson, Barbara L.; and Levenson, Robert W. (1994). "The Psychophysiology of Crying." *Psychophysiology* 31:460–468.

Kraemer, Deborah, and Hastrup, Janice L. (1986). "Crying in Natural Settings." *Behaviour Research and Therapy* 24:371–373.

Labott, Susan M.; Martin, Randall B.; Eason, Patricia S.; and Berkey, Elayne Y. (1991). "Social Reactions to the Expression of Emotion." *Cognition and Emotion* 5:397–417.

Lester, Barry M., and Boukydis, C. F. Zachariah, eds. (1985). *Infant Crying: Theoretical and Research Perspectives.* New York: Plenum.

Plessner, Helmuth. (1970). *Laughing and Crying: A Study of the Limits of Human Behavior.* Evanston, IL: Northwestern University Press.

Vingerhoets, Ad J. J. M.; Assies, Johanna; and Poppelaars, Karin. (1992). "Weeping and Prolactin." *International Journal of Psychosomatics* 39:81–82.

Vingerhoets, Ad J. J. M.; Geleuken, Aly J. M. L. van; Tilburg, Miranda A. L. van; and Heck, Guus L. van. (1997). "The Psychological Context of Crying Episodes: Toward a Model of Adult Crying." In *The (Non)Expression of Emotions in Health and Disease,* ed. Ad J. J. M. Vingerhoets, Frans van Bussel, and Jan Boelhouwer. Tilburg, The Netherlands: Tilburg University Press.

Randolph R. Cornelius

CULTURE

Since the 1960s, scholars have been interested in the relations between culture and various emotional phenomena because of what these relations might reveal about human nature and cultural processes. Most cross-cultural studies of emotional phenomena have focused on the recognition of emotional facial expressions, the incidence of emotional experiences, and the events that elicit emotional reactions. Relatively little attention has been paid to cultural influences on emotional reactivity (i.e., the changes in physiology, subjective emotional experience, and expressive behavior that occur at the moment individuals feel angry, happy, or sad). Furthermore, the focus of most past investigations has been either to demonstrate the universality of emotion (by documenting cultural similarity) or the culture-specific nature of emotion (by documenting cultural difference). Evidence suggests, however, that these perspectives cannot adequately capture the complex relations between culture and emotional reactivity. Consequently, research is moving beyond mere descriptions of cultural similarities and differences, examining instead the specific ways in which culture influences emotional reactivity.

Ethnographic notions and clinical accounts by people such as Karl Heider (1991), Catherine Lutz (1988), and Sulamith Potter (1988) suggest that cultural contexts and heritages influence individuals' emotional responses. Most cultural comparisons have been made between members of Asian and Western cultures. Members of Asian cultures have been described by James Russell and Michelle Yik (1996) as moderating and controlling their emotions more than members of Western cultures due to Confucian and Buddhist beliefs that view emotional moderation and control as a means of maintaining individual health and harmonious interpersonal relations. In clinical settings, Arthur Kleinman (1986) reported that Asian patients were inhibiting and somatizing (i.e., expressing in bodily terms) their affective symptoms more than their European American counterparts. Few studies, however, have examined how these cultural differences relate to emotional reactivity.

The few cross-cultural studies of emotional reactivity that do exist primarily compare the emotional reactions of members of Asian and Western cultures. Most of these studies do not find differences in overall levels of emotional reactivity between members of Asian and Western cultures. Instead, culture appears to influence emotional reactivity in very specific ways. The first cross-cultural studies of emotional reactivity, however, were primarily interested in whether Asians were less emotionally reactive than their Western counterparts, as suggested by ethnographic and clinical descriptions, and whether these differences could be attributed to genetic factors.

Research on Infants

In the 1970s, Daniel Freedman (1974) and his wife Nina hypothesized that the relative differences between Asian and Western emotional reactivity depicted in the ethnographic literature resulted from genetic factors. Based on this hypothesis, they predicted that differences in emotional reactivity could be observed in Asian and Western newborns who had little prior contact with their cultural environments. To test this prediction, they conducted some of the first and still most widely cited studies comparing the responses of U.S. Caucasian and Asian (Chinese, Japanese) newborns on the Cambridge Neonatal Scales developed by T. Berry Brazelton. These scales included a variety of behavioral indices of temperament, sensory development, autonomic and central nervous system maturity, motor development, and social interest and response. For example, in order to measure "defensive movements," these investigators placed a cloth over the infant's face, removed it, and then recorded the infant's responses.

In support of their hypothesis, Freedman and Freedman found temperamental differences between Caucasian and Asian newborns. Asian newborns were less emotionally changeable, less irritable, took longer to reach peak excitement, grew accustomed to novel stimuli sooner, and were better able to stop crying by themselves than were Caucasian newborns. There was only one contradiction to this general pattern: Asian infants were more "tremulous" (i.e., demonstrated more body and facial tremors) than Caucasian infants.

Consistent with Freedman and Freedman's findings, Linda Camras and her colleagues (1992, 1998) found that five-month-old American children more rapidly show negative facial expressions than five-month-old Japanese children during an arm restraint procedure used to elicit anger and frustration. Unlike Freedman and Freedman, who made subjective ratings of behavior, Camras and her colleagues used an objective behavioral coding system (Harriet Oster's Baby Facial Action Coding System) to compare the minute facial movements of Japanese and American infants.

A set of findings by Jerome Kagan and his colleagues (1994) corroborates this general pattern of results. Their study compared the behavior of four-month-old Chinese, Irish, and American (Caucasian) infants in response to a variety of stimuli to their senses of smell, sight, and touch. Again, Chinese infants were less reactive than the Western infants. American infants cried the most and were the most active and fretful, followed by Irish and then Chinese infants. American and Irish infants also vocalized more than the Chinese infants did. The groups, however, did not differ in how much they smiled.

The Freedmans and Jerome Kagan interpreted their findings to mean that differences in reactivity were due to genetic factors. However, it is possible that these differences were due to cultural differences in prenatal and postnatal environments. For example, Joan Kuchner (1989), using spot observations in the home, compared the parenting styles of Chinese-American and European-American mothers when their infants were three weeks, one month, two months, and three months old. She found that European-American mothers consistently introduced change and novel stimuli into their infants' environment more than Chinese-American mothers. Chinese-American mothers also used calming as a method of soothing their distressed babies more than European-American mothers did. Sara Harkness and Charles Super (1983) have found that the constant presentation of stimuli is related to increases in sleep difficulties and higher levels of physiological arousal in childhood. Thus, differences in overall levels of arousal between European-American infants and Chinese-American infants may be very much mediated by cultural differences in parenting styles.

Other evidence that group differences in infant reactivity are cultural rather than genetic exists. When culturally different, but genetically similar Asian groups are included in the same study, differences in emotional reactivity emerge. For example, Freedman and Freedman found differences in reactivity between Chinese-American and Japanese-American newborns. Although Japanese-American infants were better able to stop crying than their Caucasian-American counterparts, they were less able to do so than their Chinese-American counterparts. In addition, Japanese-American newborns were more tremulous and demonstrated more spontaneous startle responses than Chinese-American newborns.

Camras and her colleagues (1998) have also compared eleven-month-old American, Chinese, and Japanese infants' responses to emotion-eliciting stimuli and found significant differences between Chinese and Japanese groups. During the arm restraint procedure and the presentation of a growling gorilla head, Chinese infants moved their faces less and demonstrated less variable facial expressions than did both American *and* Japanese infants, who did not differ from each other. Camras and her colleagues also found differences between Asian groups in specific facial movements. For example, American and Japanese infants demonstrated before the arm restraint procedure more Duchenne smiles (i.e., smiles of felt happiness) than did Chinese infants. Thus, Japanese infants were more behaviorally reactive than Chinese infants.

These differences between Chinese and Japanese groups imply that cultural variables rather than genetic factors may influence emotional reactivity in infants. For example, Chinese people have been described as placing lesser emphasis on relationships between groups and greater emphasis on relationships between individuals, as having less rigid social boundaries, and as encouraging individual accomplishments more than Japanese. Thus, emotional moderation and control may be more the responsibility of the individual in Chinese culture and the responsibility of the group in Japanese culture. Nonverbal transmission of these norms may cause Chinese infants to be less emotionally reactive than Japanese infants.

Research on Adults

Evidence from the adult literature even more strongly supports notions that group differences in emotional reactivity are cultural and that culture influences emotional reactivity in specific ways. Harry Triandis and his colleagues (1986) have argued that group differences can only be attributed to cultural variables if they are measured and found to be directly related to emotional reactivity. Although few studies have actually measured cultural variables (e.g., orientation to a particular culture and beliefs about emotional expression), those that have addressed this issue suggest that such a relationship exists. For example, Jeanne Tsai and Robert Levenson (1997a) found that the more "American" both Chinese Americans and European Americans reported being, the more variable their reports of affect were. These findings support ethnographic notions that American culture emphasizes open expression of emotion more than Chinese culture. Tsai and Levenson (1996) also found that the more Chinese Americans believed that emotional responses should be controlled, the more likely they were to control their negative emotion during conflict with a dating partner.

Fewer studies have found a relationship between cultural variables and physiological responses; however, there is some evidence that culture influences this component of emotional reactivity. Kathryn Lee and Levenson (1992) found that in response to a loud noise, the ear pulse transmission times of more Americanized Chinese Americans' matched those of European Americans more closely than did less Americanized Chinese Americans. These findings are consistent with studies of the relations between levels of cultural contact and physiological arousal. One such study by Koji Takenaka and Leonard Zaichowsky (1990) examined the autonomic responses of female Japanese immigrants during stressful tasks. They found that immigrants who had been in the United States for more than one year demonstrated less physiological arousal (i.e., reduced heart rates and increases in skin temperature) than did the immigrants who had been in the United States less than one year. The latter group of immigrants demonstrated slight increases in heart rate and no change in skin conductance levels. Similarly, Daniel Brown (1982) found that cultural contact affected the levels of cortisol (a hormone that is secreted during stress) present in Filipino Americans residing in Hawaii. Thus, these findings suggest that as individuals have more contact with their dominant culture, their physiological responses change.

Specific Modes of Cultural Influence

As mentioned above, studies of cultural influences on emotional reactivity demonstrate both that culture has an effect on emotional reactivity and that culture influences emotional reactivity in very specific ways. These cultural influences may depend on the *component* of emotional reactivity and on the *context* in which those emotional reactions occur.

Component of Emotional Reactivity

One of the functions of culture is to regulate social relations. Therefore, cultural influences may have a greater effect on those components of emotional reactivity that have greater social consequences. Thus, cultural differences may emerge more in self-reported emotion and expressive behavior than in physiology reactions since the latter is generally less socially visible than the former. For example, people observing an individual who becomes angry would be more likely to notice a change in facial expressions than a change in heart rate. Although cultural differences have been found in all components of emotional reactivity, fewer cultural differences have, in fact, been found in physiology than in self-reports of emotion or expressive behavior. Levenson and his colleagues (1992) compared the emotional responses of the Minangkabau of West Sumatra and those of European Americans. Participants were instructed to move specific muscles of their faces in configurations that signaled specific emotional states. The two groups did not differ in autonomic activity induced by the facial posing. However, cultural differences did emerge in reports of subjective emotional experience: Minangkabau reported experiencing less emotion than did the European American participants. The authors attributed this difference to the Minangkabau's greater emphasis on emotion in the context of interpersonal relationships. Tsai and Levenson (1996, 1997a, 1997b) have found more cultural differences in self-reports of emotional experience than in physiology across three studies of Chinese-American and European-American couples engaging in emotional conversations.

When cultural differences in physiology do emerge, they both confirm and disconfirm hypotheses that Asians are less emotionally reactive than Westerners. Kagan and his colleagues (1978, 1994) found evidence in both behavior and physiology that supported hypotheses that Chinese would be less reactive than their Caucasian counterparts. Behaviorally, Chinese-American infants demonstrated more stable vocalization (behavior) and were also more inhibited (i.e., stayed close to their mothers, were more irritable, and vocalized and played less) when introduced to unfamiliar peers than were Caucasian infants. Physiologi-

In Indonesia, a Minangkabau bridegroom, who wears a songket cloth skullcap, appears to be somewhat more open in his display of emotion than is his bride, who wears an elaborate gold headdress. (Corbis/Lindsay Hebberd)

cally, Chinese-American infants also demonstrated less variable heart rates than Caucasian infants. Tsai and Levenson (1997a) found evidence in their study of Chinese-American and European-American dating couples that supported notions of greater reactivity in Western than in Asian groups. In addition to Chinese Americans reporting less variable affect and less positive affect during conflict, they also demonstrated less variable heart rates.

Other findings, however, do not support the notion that members of Asian cultures react less than members of Western cultures. Tsai and Levenson (1997a) found that Chinese Americans demonstrated more variable skin conductance responses than European Americans. Michael Lewis, Douglas Ramsay, and Kiyobumi Kawakami (1993) compared the affective behavior and cortisol responses of four-month-old Caucasian and Japanese infants during a pediatric inoculation. Caucasian infants demonstrated more affective behavior and took longer to quiet than did Japanese infants. However, contrary to expectation, Japanese infants demonstrated *greater* cortisol responses than did Caucasian infants. Thus, although Japanese infants were less behaviorally reactive than Caucasian infants, they were more physiologically reactive. These findings are consistent with those of James Gross and Levenson (1993), who have found that the voluntary suppression of emotional expression increases autonomic activity.

The findings described above suggest that cultural influences on emotional reactivity vary by component of emotional reactivity. Those components that may have greater social consequences (e.g., self-reported emotion and expressive behavior) may be more influenced by culture than those components that have lesser social consequences (e.g., physiology). Understanding the mechanisms by which different components of emotion are shaped by culture is an important challenge for future researchers.

Context of Emotional Reaction

Cultural influences on emotional reactivity have been studied using a variety of stimuli and across a variety of contexts. Findings from existing studies suggest that the immediate social context may be an important mediator of cultural influences on emotional reactivity. In the mid-1960s, Richard Lazarus and his colleagues (1966) conducted one of the first studies of culture and emotional reactivity. In discussing their results, they identified the social context as a mediator of cultural influence. They compared the reports of distress and skin conductance responses of Japanese and American adults first to a "benign" film (about rice farming for Japanese samples and corn farming for American samples) and then to a distressing film (about the "mutilation of male adolescent genitals in a puberty ceremony"). There were *no* cultural differences in self-reports of distress during each film or in mean levels of physiological responding during the stressful film. However, Japanese samples demonstrated higher levels of skin conductance responding during the benign film. Lazarus and his colleagues suggested that these differences were due to cultural differences in the appraisal of the social context. That is, they proposed that the Japanese samples were more sensitive to the experimental context and therefore reacted with "marked general apprehension" during the experiment.

Paul Ekman (1972) and Wallace Friesen (1973) conducted a seminal study to examine the effect of the social context on emotional expression. As in the study performed by Lazarus and his colleagues,

Japanese and European-American men were shown distressing films. However, half of the subjects watched these films in a room alone (private context), while the other half watched the films in the presence of the experimenter (public context). Only in the public context did cultural differences emerge in negative and positive emotional expression. In the public context, Japanese men demonstrated more positive and less negative expressive behavior than Japanese men in the private context, whereas American men's emotional expressive behavior did not differ between the public and private contexts. Ekman and Friesen attributed the observed cultural differences during the public context to cultural differences in display rules (i.e., cultural rules about the expression of emotion).

Until the 1990s, no studies had pursued the suggestion by Ekman and Friesen that the social context may be a powerful mediator of cultural influence. It was with this in mind that Tsai and Levenson (1997a) conducted their studies to examine what effect the social context had on Chinese-American and European-American emotional responses during conflict. They were interested in whether the social context mediates cultural influences on reports of subjective emotional experience and physiological responding in these groups. In order to elicit strong negative emotion, they instructed Chinese-American dating couples and European-American dating couples to discuss the area of greatest conflict in their relationships. During these discussions, Tsai and Levenson measured their couples' physiological responses. After the discussions, the couples were shown videotaped recordings of their conversations and asked to rate how much positive and negative emotion they felt during the conversation. Half of the participants had their conversations in a room by themselves, constituting a private context, and the other half had their conversations in the presence of an authority figure, constituting a public context. Consistent with the findings of Ekman and Friesen, Chinese Americans moderated and controlled their reports of negative emotion, but only in the presence of the authority figure. The social context did not influence European Americans' reports of negative emotion. Physiological responses were not altered by the social context for either group.

The Tsai and Levenson studies also demonstrated that cultural influences on emotion depend on the specific demands of the situation (in addition to the presence of an authority figure). Members of Asian cultures, for example, have been shown to be more sensitive to contextual demands than members of Western culture. Therefore, in a given situation, members of Asian cultures may behave in ways that are more consistent with contextual demands than with specific cultural values. In the study where Tsai and Levenson compared the physiological and subjective responses of Chinese Americans and European Americans during conflict (a context in which there were strong demands for participants to experience negative affect), they found that Chinese Americans and European Americans did not differ in reports of negative affect (the "contextually appropriate" emotion) but did differ in reports of positive affect (the "contextually inappropriate" emotion). Specifically, Chinese Americans reported less *positive* affect than did their European-American counterparts. To further examine the effect of contextual demands on reported affect, Tsai and Levenson (1997b) had Chinese-American and European-American couples discuss enjoyable topics in their relationships, a context in which there were strong demands for participants to experience positive affect. Again, no cultural differences emerged in reports of positive affect (the "contextually appropriate" emotion). However, cultural differences emerged in reports of negative affect (the "contextually inappropriate" emotion)—but for men only. Chinese-American men reported less *negative* affect than did European-American men.

Future Directions for Research on Culture and Emotional Reactivity

What future research is needed to advance understanding of culture and emotional reactivity? Clearly, researchers must continue to move beyond merely describing cultural differences in emotion toward understanding other specific ways in which culture influences emotional reactivity. This may be best achieved by examining other cultural groups and by assuming a developmental perspective.

As demonstrated above, the current knowledge of cultural influences on emotional reactivity stems largely from a literature comparing Asian and Western cultural groups. Other cultural groups, such as Navajo, African Americans, Australian aborigines, and Mexican Americans, have been included in studies of emotional responding, but to a much lesser degree. More studies of this type are needed before the findings related to Asian and Western cultural groups can be generalized to other cultures. These studies are also necessary for the identification of other ways in which culture may influence emotional reactivity, ways that may be specific to non-Asian and non-Western cultural groups.

Because both culture and emotion develop over the life span, longitudinal studies may be the best way to examine the specific ways in which culture influences emotional reactivity. Longitudinal studies will allow for the examination of the effects of parenting, language, and other cultural variables on emotional reactivity

over time. However, few studies have taken a developmental perspective beyond examining the first few years of life, and there are almost no studies that have examined culture and emotional reactivity in old age. Because older individuals have experienced a lifetime of cultural influence, studying older samples can greatly inform researchers' understanding of the specific ways in which culture influences emotional reactivity. Findings by Tsai, Levenson, and Laura Carstensen (1992) suggest that although physiological differences between Chinese Americans and European Americans may for the most part disappear during adulthood, they may re-emerge in old age. In this study, Chinese-American and European-American men and women, equally divided between two age groups (younger: 20–35 years of age, older: 70–85 years of age), watched sad and amusing film clips. There were no cultural differences in physiological responding, reports of subjective emotional experience, or expressive behavior during the amusing film clip. However, during the sad film clip, older Chinese Americans demonstrated less intense cardiovascular responses (perhaps indicating less intense emotional arousal) than younger Chinese Americans. These age differences were not found among the European Americans. Thus, it is possible that these physiological differences reflect cultural influences whose effects are only observable in old age. Studying cultural influences across the life span opens the door to other sources of cultural influence. One potential source of cultural influence is language, which as Anna Wierzbicka (1992) has pointed out, varies in the elaboration of emotion terms. For example, although there is no semantic equivalent in Hmong for the general term *emotion*, there are more terms to describe the emotion *shame* in Hmong than in English. Do Hmong speakers experience emotion differently (especially shame) than English speakers? How do such language differences affect emotional experience? Although some studies have examined how language alters the affective experience of bilinguals, none have examined how the acquisition of specific languages influences emotional reactivity.

Research on culture and emotional reactivity has several potential implications for counseling and other multicultural settings. Given demographic trends toward a more multicultural world, it is guaranteed that in multiple arenas (i.e., at work, at home, at school), individuals will come into increasing contact with people from other cultural backgrounds. Therefore, an accurate understanding of how cultural context influences how people feel, think, and behave is critical. Thus far, the empirical findings convey one main message—that cultural influences on emotional reactivity are complex and dynamic. Cultural influences on emotional reactivity vary by specific component of emotion and context in which emotion occurs. Thus, in counseling and other multicultural settings, one must relinquish simplistic notions that cultural groups differ in overall levels of emotional reactivity. For example, as a growing number of Asians (and other ethnic minority individuals) in the United States seek mental health care services, it becomes increasingly clear that certain diagnostic and treatment methods of Western psychiatric practices are not applicable to individuals of Asian cultural descent. According to Kleinman (1986), affective disorders are more difficult to diagnose in Asian patients than in European-American patients because Asian patients tend to describe their affective states more in physical terms. Moreover, Asian patients are described as possessing more controlled emotional styles, which may be misdiagnosed as depressed or flat affect. By and large, clinicians have attributed differences in symptom presentation to cultural differences in emotional expression and conceptions of emotion. However, as demonstrated in the studies reviewed above, it is not at all clear that cultural differences in values regarding emotional expression translate into overall cultural differences in emotional reactivity. In fact, research suggests that Asian patients may or may not be moderating and controlling their emotions, depending on their specific social context. Thus, prior to diagnosis and treatment, clinicians are encouraged to ask family members (and others with whom the patient may demonstrate different emotional responses) about the patient's symptoms of emotional distress.

Given the tremendous variety of cultures that make up the world, it would be impossible to describe the details of emotional response for every culture. A more fruitful approach to understanding how cultural context can shape emotional response is to focus on the specific ways in which culture influences emotional reactivity. By assuming this approach, researchers might be able to achieve a more accurate understanding of culture and human behavior, an understanding that grows in significance as cultural contexts become increasingly enmeshed in everyday life activities.

See also: CROSS-CULTURAL PATTERNS; CULTURE-BOUND SYNDROMES; UNIVERSALITY OF EMOTIONAL EXPRESSION

Bibliography

Brown, Daniel E. (1982). "Physiological Stress and Cultural Change in a Group of Filipino-Americans: A Preliminary Investigation." *Annals of Human Biology* 9(6):553–563.

Camras, Linda; Oster, Harriet; Campos, Joseph; Campos, Rosemary; Ujiie, Tatsuo; Miyake, Kazuo; Wang, Lei; and Meng, Zazuo. (1998). "Production of Emotional Facial Expressions in American, Japanese, and Chinese Infants." *Developmental Psychology* 34(4):616–628.

Camras, Linda; Oster, Harriet; Campos, Joseph; Miyake, Kazuo; and Bradshaw, Donna. (1992). "Japanese and American Infants' Responses to Arm Restraint." *Developmental Psychology* 28(4):578–583.

Ekman, Paul. (1972). "Universals and Cultural Differences in Facial Expressions of Emotion." *Nebraska Symposium on Motivation, Vol. 19*, ed. James K. Cole. Lincoln: University of Nebraska Press.

Ekman, Paul, and Friesen, Wallace V. (1971). "Constants across Cultures in the Face and Emotion." *Journal of Personality and Social Psychology* 17:124–129.

Freedman, Daniel G. (1974). *Human Infancy: An Evolutionary Perspective*. Hillsdale, NJ: Lawrence Erlbaum.

Friesen, Wallace V. (1973). "Cultural Difference in Facial Expressions in a Social Situation: An Experimental Test on the Concept of Display Rules." *Dissertation Abstracts International* 33(n8-B):3976–3977.

Gross, James, and Levenson, Robert W. (1993). "Emotional Suppression: Physiology, Self-Report, and Expressive Behavior." *Journal of Personality and Social Psychology* 64(6):970–986.

Harkness, Sara, and Super, Charles. (1983). "The Cultural Construction of Child Development: A Framework for the Socialization of Affect." *Ethos* 11(4):221–231.

Heider, Karl G. (1991). *Landscapes of Emotion: Mapping Three Cultures of Emotion in Indonesia*. Cambridge, New York: Cambridge University Press.

Kagan, Jerome; Arcus, Doreen; Snidman, Nancy; Wang, Yu Feng; Hendler, John; and Greene, Sheila. (1994). "Reactivity in Infants: A Cross-National Comparison." *Developmental Psychology* 30(3):342–345.

Kagan, Jerome; Kearsley, Richard; and Zelazo, Philip. (1978). *Infancy : Its Place in Human Development*. Cambridge, MA: Harvard University Press.

Kleinman, Arthur. (1986). *Social Origins of Distress and Disease: Depression, Neurasthenia, and Pain in Modern China*. New Haven, CT: Yale University Press.

Kuchner, Joan F. (1989). "Chinese American and European American Mothers and Infants: Cultural Influences in the First Three Months of Life." Presented at the Biennial Meeting of the Society for Research in Child Development, Kansas City, MO, April 27–30.

Lazarus, Richard; Opton, Edward; Tomita, Masatoshi; and Kodama, Masahisa. (1966). "A Cross-Cultural Study of Stress-Reaction Patterns in Japan." *Journal of Personality and Social Psychology* 4(6):622–633.

Lee, Kathryn J., and Levenson, Robert W. (1992). "Ethnic Similarities in Emotional Reactivity to an Unanticipated Startle." Presented at the meeting of the Society for Psychophysiological Research, San Diego, CA.

Levenson, Robert W.; Ekman, Paul; Heider, Karl; and Friesen, Wallace V. (1992). "Emotion and Autonomic Nervous System Activity in the Minangkabau of West Sumatra." *Journal of Personality and Social Psychology* 62:972–988.

Lewis, Michael. (1989). "Culture and Biology: The Role of Temperament." In *Challenges to Developmental Paradigms: Implications for Theory, Assessment, and Treatment*, ed. Philip R. Zelazo and Ronald G. Barr. Hillsdale, NJ: Lawrence Erlbaum.

Lewis, Michael; Ramsay, Douglas; and Kawakami, Kiyobumi. (1993). "Differences between Japanese Infants and Caucasian American Infants in Behavioral and Cortisol Response to Inoculation." *Child Development* 64:1722–1731.

Lutz, Catherine. (1988). *Unnatural Emotions: Everyday Sentiments on a Micronesian Atoll and Their Challenge to Western Theory*. Chicago: University of Chicago Press.

Potter, Sulamith. (1988). "The Cultural Construction of Emotion in Rural Chinese Social Life." *Ethos* 16(2):181–208.

Russell, James, and Yik, Michelle. (1996). "Emotion among the Chinese." In *The Handbook of Chinese Psychology*. Hong Kong: Oxford University Press.

Takenaka, Koji, and Zaichkowsky, Leonard. (1990). "Physiological Reactivity in Acculturation: A Study of Female Japanese Students." *Perceptual and Motor Skills* 70:503–513.

Tsai, Jeanne L., and Levenson, Robert W. (1996). "Beyond Ethnographic Notions: Cultural Influences on Emotional Responding." Presented as part of the Culture and Psychological Processes symposium conducted at the June meeting of the American Psychological Society, San Francisco, CA.

Tsai, Jeanne L., and Levenson, Robert W. (1997a). "Cultural Influences on Emotional Responding: Chinese American and European American Dating Couples during Interpersonal Conflict." *Journal of Cross-Cultural Psychology* 28:600–625.

Tsai, Jeanne L., and Levenson, Robert W. (1997b). "Culture, Physiology, and Reported Affect: Couples during Enjoyable Conversations." Presented at the October meeting of the Society of Psychophysiological Research, Cape Cod, MA.

Tsai, Jeanne L.; Levenson, Robert W.; and Carstensen, Laura L. (1992). "Physiological and Subjective Responses of Chinese Americans and European Americans to Emotional Films." Presented at the October meeting of the Society of Psychophysiological Research, San Diego, CA.

Triandis, Harry C.; Kashima, Yoshihisa; Shimada, Emiko; and Villareal, Marcelo. (1986). "Acculturation Indices As a Means of Confirming Cultural Differences." *International Journal of Psychology* 21(1):43–70.

Wierzbicka, Anna. (1992). *Semantics, Culture, and Cognition: Human Concepts in Culture-Specific Configurations*. New York: Oxford University Press.

Jeanne L. Tsai

CULTURE-BOUND SYNDROMES

The term *culture-bound syndrome* refers to a category of distinct behavioral patterns that are commonly assumed to be abnormal and unproductive, with a learned rather than physical cause. By definition, culture-bound syndromes are understood to be restricted in their occurrence; that is, they are assumed to be linked with specific cultures or cultural areas. Some culture-bound syndromes, such as *latah, amok,* and *koro,* are dramatic and have a long history of Western description and interpretation, allowing them to be viewed as classic examples. Others, such as anorexia nervosa, while long noted, have been only recently added to the category as the basic definition has been extended to cover the culture-based illnesses of Western societies in addition to non-Western ones. Most culture-bound syndromes are gender-specific or gender-related; that is, they occur exclusively or predominantly among either males or females. Formerly (and sometimes still) referred to by terms such as *ethnic psychosis* or *folk illness,* culture-bound syndromes fall outside of the usual diagnostic categories of Western psychiatry. However, they are of particular interest in the fields of transcultural psychiatry, psychological anthropology, and medical anthropology.

History of the Concept and the Classic Forms

The awareness of the classic culture-based mental illnesses and behavioral abnormalities resulted from the encounter between European colonists and non-European peoples, especially in Southeast Asia. The term *culture-bound syndrome* was formulated by P. M. Yap (1966), a Malaysian Chinese who was trained in psychiatry in England and who, by virtue of his own background, was attuned to matters of cultural and medical difference. Yap initially used the phrase *culture-bound reactive psychosis* but subsequently dropped both *reactive* and *psychosis* from the phrase and added *syndrome.* He thought, as did his predecessors, that the culture-bound syndromes could be classified as variants of mental abnormalities defined in Western psychiatric terms.

Yap's concept was directed at a fairly small number of non-Western patterns that form the classic cases. The three most famous of the classic culture-bound syndromes are *amok, latah,* and *koro,* all of which were first encountered by European observers among Malay, Javanese, or other Indonesian peoples. As a result, scholars commonly refer to all three of these syndromes by using the original Malayan terms, even in instances where the syndromes occur in other regions of the world (e.g., Chinese koro). Amok was noted by Westerners as early as the sixteenth century, and the term was long ago incorporated into the English language to mean any sort of crazed assault. Malayan amok is specifically a homicidal rampage that is conducted by males and is directed at both innocent bystanders as well as (or instead of) any persons believed to have provoked the incident. True Malayan amok involves a state of trance, as a result of which the aggressor experiences temporary amnesia and is thus unaware of his actions. The practice of amok probably originated in warfare, with which it has continued to be associated.

Latah, a hyper-startle pattern, is the most extensively described and analyzed of the classic culture-bound syndromes, and also the most controversial. It was first observed among Malays and Javanese around the middle of the nineteenth century, although reports of similar or identical patterns soon followed in several other areas of the world. Hyper-startle patterns consist of exaggerated reactions to sudden noises, movements, or touch and involve various verbal and physical responses that typically include jumping and exclaiming obscene words. In Malayan latah and a few other similar instances (most of which occur in northern Asia among various Siberian peoples and the Ainu of northern Japan), the pattern is much more developed and may involve a loss of consciousness, the compulsive imitation of the words and actions of others, and the involuntary following of orders—all of which, however, may also be performed for amusement or attention. Latah involves mainly females among Malayan peoples and similar North Asian groups. In other areas, including North Africa, the southern Arabian peninsula (where a few instances have been reported), and North America (where instances have been noted among French Canadians in Canada and Maine), culturally recognized hyper-startle patterns involve mainly males.

Koro is the shrinking or disappearing penis syndrome. The koro sufferer believes that his penis is retracting into his abdomen, which will lead to death. From the Malay word for turtle, the koro syndrome was reported early in the twentieth century by Dutch colonial doctors in present-day Indonesia. Similar patterns have been extensively reported elsewhere as well, especially in China, where the occurrences frequently take on epidemic proportions.

Further Developments and Controversies

By the 1980s, the list of culture-bound syndromes had been greatly expanded through the reporting of new types or instances. A glossary published in the book *Culture-Bound Syndromes* (1985), which was edited by Ronald Simons and Charles Hughs, lists 185 culture-bound syndromes, although there is no claim made that the list is exhaustive or without duplication. By 1985, however, both the general concept of culture-bound syndromes and some specific forms were being sharply disputed. For example, one researcher, Lou Marano (1985), found that *windigo* (the cannibal compulsion syndrome reported among Algonkian Native American groups) existed only in myth and folklore. In other instances, the behavioral reality of the pattern was not denied but its interpretation was disputed. In regard to the concept of culture-bound syndromes in general, four related issues emerged concerning both the culture-bound and the syndrome parts of the phrase.

The first of these issues concerns whether similar culture-bound syndromes found among distant, culturally diverse and unrelated peoples actually constitute the same syndrome. Here opinion has been polarized between generalists (who argue for cross-cultural similarity or sameness) and relativists (who argue for the importance of cultural specificity). This issue has been argued most clearly (and vehemently) regarding latah, with Michael Kenny (1985) taking the extreme relativist position that this pattern can only be understood in relation to Malayan culture and that other putative non-Malayan instances in Siberia and elsewhere are only superficially similar. The generalist position, as formulated especially by Ronald Simons (1985), is not that latah or the other culture-bound syndromes are entirely the same wherever they occur —for such a position would amount to a categorical denial of the value of the concept. Instead, the generalist position claims that such patterns have both cultural and innately universal dimensions that are developed in some cultures but not in others. This position, however, turns out to be rather hypothetical. In attempting to refute relativism, generalists have tended to stress biological or psychological universals and show less interest in cultural distinctiveness and an explanation about why a culture-bound syndrome develops among one cultural group and not others.

The second issue concerns the adequacy or utility of the term itself. While not denying the reality of the culture-bound syndromes as a type, the generalist position creates a problem regarding the concept. If the same syndrome does occur cross-culturally, especially in many places (as has wrongly been argued regarding latah), how can it be called culture-bound? At least, it would appear necessary to change the phrase to something much weaker such as culture-influenced or culture-related syndromes. There is also a relativist objection to the redundancy of these terms: If all syndromes, especially those based on mental state, vary from one culture to another, then there is really nothing unique about those that have been called culture-bound. For these reasons, some scholars have advocated the abandonment of the term. Its problematic nature notwithstanding, however, most scholars seem inclined to retain it, if only because it has become so widely known and because no one has proposed an attractive alternative.

A third issue concerns the syndrome part of the concept. Syndromes are abnormal or harmful patterns of behavior that people suffer from, even if the behavior provides some positive benefits (such as sympathy). Here again there is a relativist position (that cultures define what is abnormal or harmful) and a generalist one (that deviant behavior is cross-culturally similar or identical). The anthropology-oriented transcultural psychiatrists Roland Littlewood and Maurice Lipsedge (1985) suggest an interesting but exaggerated contrast between syndromes and useful rituals. They argue that some of the same patterns of behavior may be defined as rituals or syndromes depending on the training and status of the observer; that is, a medical practitioner may see as a syndrome what an anthropologist sees as an adaptive ritual. Therefore, whether a given pattern of behavior from some far-off place has entered Western scholarly awareness as a culture-bound syndrome or as an exotic ritual is a matter of what type of observer described it first. Spirit possession (the belief that a person's body and mind are occupied by an alien spirit, either hostile or friendly) is a particularly apt example of something that, depending on the specific cultural context, can be either a socially useful ritual or a malady (or in some instances both). Latah is also ambiguous and contingent upon cultural context. Most of the other culture-bound syndromes, however, have been interpreted by members of the culture in question, as well as by anthropologists and medical practitioners, as maladies.

The fourth and final issue has been the nosological (classificatory) status of the culture-bound syndromes within modern Western psychiatry. This issue arose especially with the 1987 publication of the third revised version of the *Diagnostic and Statistical Manual of Mental Disorders* (DSM-III-R), the official diagnostic handbook of the American Psychiatric Association. The DSM-III-R included neither the general category of culture-bound syndromes nor any of the specific instances. The issue here was whether the various culture-bound syndromes could be made to fit with the DSM-III-R classification, and therefore whether the latter had universal applicability. Here again, generalists argued for the careful applicability of general categories to culture-specific instances while the relativists took the position that the DSM-III-R was itself culture-bound and not useful in understanding many non-Western patterns. The fourth edition of the *Diagnostic and Statistical Manual of Mental Disorders* (DSM-IV), which was published in 1994, has incorporated the culture-bound syndromes at several points, more or less along the lines of the generalist position. Most of the classic syndromes, including latah and amok, are placed in the category of "dissociative trance disorders" in the main body of the work. In addition, the manual explicitly addresses the culture-bound syndromes in an appendix that makes reference to the role of culture in mental illness and provides a glossary of twenty-five instances.

Western and Other Postindustrial Culture-Bound Syndromes

Despite continuing definitional problems and disputes, the concept of culture-bound syndromes has, if anything, continued to grow in importance as it has been reconsidered and applied to a wider range of instances. The glossary of twenty-five culture-bound syndromes in Appendix 1 of DSM-IV includes traditional instances. With the partial exception of "spell" and "rootwork" (both said to occur among African

Americans and European Americans in the southern United States) and "falling out" or "blacking out" (said to occur primarily in the southern United States and among Caribbean groups), all of the DSM-IV examples involve non-Western populations. Such a list is subject to the criticism that it gives the impression that Westerners have regular syndromes while non-Westerners (and occupants of the southern United States) have culture-bound syndromes.

Perhaps the most important aspect of reconsideration of the culture-bound syndromes has been the effort to apply the concept to various maladies in Western and other postindustrial societies. Anorexia nervosa, bulimia, noneconomic shoplifting, and obesity, as well as various modern Japanese phobias, have all been analyzed as culture-bound syndromes, as have (though more dubiously) general life conditions such as Western adolescence and menopause. The initial efforts along this line may have been partly motivated by the relativist desire to show the ethnocentric bias of a concept applied only to non-Western societies. The results, however, have been a very productive analysis of the cultural bases of much taken-for-granted social and individual pathology.

Although none of these new Western culture-bound syndromes fit into the set of classification designations developed in 1985 by Simons and Hughs, they have been the focus of some of the same sorts of arguments as the older, non-Western ones, though in reverse. Anorexia nervosa was, for example, initially thought to be a uniquely Western culture-bound syndrome. It has since been widely reported in non-European places, including China, resulting in the question of whether it can still be regarded as culture-bound in the context of the global spread of Western ideals, images, and neuroses regarding body size and shape. While anorexia may have initially been a pathological expression of the uniquely Western preoccupation with thinness (extending back, it has been argued, to ancient Christian practices and values), the Western thinness syndrome has diffused readily throughout the world, including the upper classes of societies where hunger and malnutrition remain or recur among the poorer populations.

The growing interest in the 1980s and 1990s in the concept of culture-related illnesses and conditions and its applicability to various modern Western maladies has several bases beyond intellectual and medical relativism. The expansion of the culture-bound syndrome category to include what were once thought to be inevitable conditions of life (adolescence, menopause, menstruation) is related to medicalization—the biomedical co-opting of the body resulting in the medical (and hence social) redefinition of deviance. Female conditions have been particularly subject to medicalization. Premenstrual syndrome, for example, was created as a diagnostic category in 1953 although the symptoms described were the same as those associated with premenstrual tension, which was identified in 1931. While the symptoms of premenstrual syndrome have yet to be consistently qualified using scientific measures, some of them, particularly those relating to emotional inconsistencies, have their roots in ancient Western ideas of women, animality, and hysteria.

New Immigrants and Culture-Bound Syndromes

In dealing with the late-twentieth-century influx of non-Western immigrants, Western medical practitioners have been faced with many unfamiliar maladies and modes of curing maladies. For example, along with *nervous* or nerves (found among inhabitants of the Spanish-speaking Caribbean and among immigrants from that region), Latin Americans frequently suffer from *susto,* which involves various physical symptoms that are culturally attributed to soul loss, usually due to fright. Again, the widespread occurrence of susto throughout Latin America and the occurrence of similar syndromes elsewhere make its status as a true culture-bound syndrome a matter of doubt. But whether or not it is a culture-bound syndrome, susto is a culturally defined malady that would make little sense to Anglo-American medical practitioners who are not already familiar with it or aware of the category of culture-bound syndromes.

In the case of Asian immigrants and refugees, all have brought (or developed) their own culturally defined maladies. However, those from Southeast Asia have been especially vulnerable to serious culture-bound syndromes, in part because the forced (for many) emigration from their homeland was so traumatic and because their adaptation to life in the United States was particularly stressful. Cambodian women, for example, have been reported to have developed psychosomatic blindness as a result of the horrors they witnessed in their homeland. Another culture-bound syndrome, called sudden unexpected nocturnal death syndrome, has occurred among several ethnic groups in the United States, including Cambodians, Vietnamese, Mien, and Filipinos, with Hmong males having suffered the greatest number of fatalities. Although several possible physiological causes for this syndrome, which occurs while the victim is asleep, have been proposed, none have been confirmed. Based on survivors' reports of being tormented by a spirit during the attack, Shelley R. Adler (1995) argues that the events immediately preceding death are a culture-specific expression of the cross-cultural experience of having a nightmare.

As immigration continues and as Western and other postindustrial societies continue to discover or develop and medicalize new maladies, the concept of culture-bound syndromes will continue to be needed, although its definition will continue to evolve.

See also: ANXIETY DISORDERS; CULTURE; FEAR AND PHOBIAS; MOOD DISORDERS; POST-TRAUMATIC STRESS DISORDER

Bibliography

American Psychiatric Association. (1987). *Diagnostic and Statistical Manual of Mental Disorders,* 3rd ed., rev. (DSM-III-R). Washington, DC: American Psychiatric Association.

American Psychiatric Association. (1994). *Diagnostic and Statistical Manual of Mental Disorders,* 4th ed. (DSM-IV). Washington, DC: American Psychiatric Association.

Adler, Shelley R. (1995). "Refugee Stress and Folk Belief: Hmong Sudden Deaths." *Social Science and Medicine* 40(12):1623–1629.

Bliatout, Bruce Thowpaou. (1982). *Hmong Sudden Unexpected Nocturnal Death Syndrome: A Cultural Study.* Portland, OR: Sparkle Publishing.

Hahn, Robert A. (1995). *Sickness and Healing: An Anthropological Perspective.* New Haven, CT: Yale University Press.

Karp, Ivan. (1985). "Deconstructing Culture-Bound Syndromes." *Social Science and Medicine* 21(2):221–228.

Kenny, Michael G. (1985). "Paradox Lost: The Latah Problem Revisited." In *The Culture-Bound Syndromes: Folk Illnesses of Psychiatric and Anthropological Interest,* ed. Ronald C. Simons and Charles C. Hughes. Dordrecht, The Netherlands: D. Reidel Publishing.

Lebra, William P. (1976). *Culture-Bound Syndromes, Ethnopsychiatry, and Alternate Therapies.* Honolulu: The University Press of Hawaii.

Lee, Sing. (1996). "Reconsidering the Status of Anorexia Nervosa as a Western Culture-Bound Syndrome." *Social Science and Medicine* 42(1):21–34.

Littlewood, Roland, and Lipsedge, Maurice. (1985). "Culture-Bound Syndromes." In *Recent Advances in Clinical Psychiatry, Vol. 5,* ed. Kenneth Granville-Grossman. Edinburgh: Churchill-Livingstone.

Lock, Margaret. (1987). "DSM-III as a Culture-Bound Construct: Commentary on Culture-Bound Syndromes and International Disease Classifications." *Culture, Medicine, and Psychiatry* 11:35–42.

Low, Setha M. (1985). "Culturally Interpreted Symptoms or Culture-Bound Syndromes: A Cross-Cultural Review of Nerves." *Social Science and Medicine* 21(2):187–196.

Marano, Lou. (1985). "Windigo Psychosis: The Anatomy of an Etic-Emic Confusion." In *The Culture-Bound Syndromes: Folk Illnesses of Psychiatric and Anthropological Interest,* ed. Ronald C. Simons and Charles C. Hughes. Dordrecht, The Netherlands: D. Reidel Publishing.

Rodin, Mari. (1992). "The Social Construction of Premenstrual Syndrome." *Social Science and Medicine* 35(1):49–56.

Rozee, Patricia D., and Van Boemel, Gretchen B. (1989). "The Psychological Effects of War Trauma and Abuse on Older Cambodian Refugee Women." *Women and Therapy* 8:23–50.

Rubel, Arthur J.; O'Nell, Carl W.; and Collado-Ardón, Rolando. (1984). *Susto: A Folk Illness.* Berkeley: University of California Press.

Simons, Ronald C., (1985). "The Resolution of the Latah Paradox." In *The Culture-Bound Syndromes: Folk Illnesses of Psychiatric and Anthropological Interest,* ed. Ronald C. Simons and Charles C. Hughes. Dordrecht, The Netherlands: D. Reidel Publishing.

Simons, Ronald C., and Hughs, Charles C., eds. (1985). *The Culture-Bound Syndromes: Folk Illnesses of Psychiatric and Anthropological Interest.* Dordrecht, The Netherlands: D. Reidel Publishing.

Tseng Wen-Sing; Mo Kan-Ming; Li Li-Shuen; Chen Guo-Qian; Ou Li-Wah; and Zheng Hong-Bo. (1992). "Koro Epidemics in Guangdong, China: A Questionnaire Survey." *Journal of Nervous and Mental Disease* 180(2):117–123.

Winzeler, Robert L. (1995). *Latah in Southeast Asia: The History and Ethnography of a Culture-Bound Syndrome.* Cambridge, Eng.: Cambridge University Press.

Yap, P. M. (1966). "The Culture-Bound Reactive Syndromes." In *Mental Health Research in Asia and the Pacific,* ed. William Caudill and Tsung-Yi Lin. Honolulu: East-West Center Press.

Robert L. Winzeler

D

DANCE

Dance may communicate ideas, values, and emotions. Dance is a medium for expressing one's own emotion, a subjectively experienced state of feeling, as well as the emotion of a character one may portray. For some dancers, dance is primarily a vehicle for communicating emotion to viewers and eliciting the viewers' own emotion. The expression of all of these various emotions may inspire and sustain a dancer's creativity in choreography and performance.

Variation

Dance can relate to all emotions. An emotion can play one or more roles in the creation, performance, and viewer perception of dance. These roles vary among and within different forms of dance. The dancer's intention, culture, aesthetics, and symbolism create variation. Personal and cultural experiences influence a viewer's perception of emotion in dance—regardless of the choreographer's or performer's intention.

In secular and ritual settings, dance often accompanies important emotion-laden events and concepts in human life, from the joyous celebrations of birth and marriage to the painful loss at death. Serving as a venue to express emotion that is inappropriate in other settings, dance may criticize or embarrass people. Dance staged apart from emotion-laden events can arouse emotion about current events and change, as well as about the basic values a society wants to perpetuate. Because knowledge is retained longer if it is learned through several senses and emotion, dance may also be a useful communication tool.

The emotion of dancing may serve peak experiences, transcendent moments, spirituality, and "magic." People may lose themselves in dance to escape negative emotions. Religious belief systems throughout the world respect the dancing body as a medium for the emotions of reverence, propitiation, and atonement toward the divine. Dance may entertain the supernatural, appease divinities, or exorcise demons or malevolence caused by the supernatural. In therapy and in education, dance is often a way for people to express and deal with emotions that are related to conflict and stress.

Complexity

Dance is more than the expression of different emotions, each with its own continuum of intensity and complexity. Created from the dancer's perspective (which is typically shared by audience members who belong to the same culture), dance is purposeful; individual choice and social learning play a role. Dance is intentionally a rhythmical event made up of culturally influenced sequences of nonverbal body movements, which are mostly different from those movements performed in ordinary motor activities. The motion, with its elements of time, space, and effort, has an inherent aesthetic value (the notion of appropriateness and competency held by the dancer's culture) and symbolic potential.

Sensory stimulation contributes to the communication of emotion through dance: the sight of dancers moving in time and space; the sound of physical movement; the smell of the dancers; the tactile sense of body parts touching the ground, other body parts, people or props, and the air around the dancers; the sense of distance between dancers and audience; and the kinesthetic experience (i.e., the feeling of bodily movement and tension). Audience members may empathize with the dancers' multisensory engagement and convey multisensory emotional feedback to the dancers (e.g., through clapping, joining the dance, or booing). While dancers and viewers can sense the performing body, the intellect (also referred to as mind, cognition, and ego) influences how the choreographer and dancer express emotion in dance and how they and the viewers perceive it. Ideas are communicated through both verbal language and dance, which is language-like with many "languages" and "dialects." The cognitive, physical, and emotional elements of the choreographer, dancer, and audience intertwine in a dance performance.

A dancer may choose to conceptualize through dance or to play with the movement itself, emotion having no (or low) salience. A dancer's concentration on dance structures, abstraction, and rhythms may preclude the intentional communication of emotion.

Because emotions and their dance expression communicate meanings that influence special and everyday activities, the audience must look for clues to meaning. These clues are contextual, mostly culturally and historically specific.

Dance can draw upon multiple devices and spheres to convey the meaning of emotion. Dancers may use the devices of portraying the outward aspect of something, its symbol (a metaphor or metonym), or a stylization. In Western ballet, extending one's arms toward a beloved; partners' touching, embracing, or extending their arms toward each other; mutual gazing; and pointing to one's heart all show love. By simply appearing as a deity or monarch whom viewers treat as real (the actualization device), a dancer may communicate awe.

The emotional meaning of dance may involve several spheres. A specific emotion-laden event is one such sphere of meaning. Clues to emotional meaning in dance may lie in the spheres of the total human body or the sequence of unfolding movement, including who does what to whom and how. Emotions about gender relations evolve in this way. Specific movements and how they are performed (e.g., slow or fast, narrow or wide, high or low, stylized or unstylized) may communicate emotion. For example, tension and frowning commonly express anger. Slow, repetitive dances—depending on the context—may evoke the emotions of tranquility, detachment, or boredom.

The sphere of a dancer's presence or charisma frequently conjures excitement. Skillfully executed technical feats in Western ballet and other dance media inspire wonderment. But "electric" performances involving emotion beyond the ordinary, such as those given by the technically accomplished Rudolf Nureyev and Natalia Makarova, arouse strong emotion, a visceral engagement, in the spectator. The interconnections between dance and other modes of communication, such as speech, song, music, or costume, may carry clues to the significance of dance and emotion.

A group's dances may display neutral facial expression but rely on the color of body decoration or type of costume to convey emotion. An example of combining movement and costume to convey pain is the American modern dance pioneer Martha Graham's "Lamentation," in which the dancer, covered in stretch fabric and mostly maintaining a seated position, moves her body diagonally. (At the turn of the twentieth century, modern dance began challenging the 400-year-old ballet tradition of systematized movements, technique, and style.) Complex emotions such as jealousy, envy, greed, and suspicion that cannot be read by facial or bodily expression alone need other culturally-based clues such as the context of the theme being danced.

Codified Expression

Some forms of dance have codified expressions for different emotions. The basic principles of Indian classical dance, gesture, and mime are set out in the ancient treatise on dance, the *Natyasastra.* There are nine basic emotions (*rasa*) in the classical dance: eroticism-love, anger-fierceness, laughter, disgust, sorrow-pathos-compassion, fear-terror, amazement-wonder, heroism-valor-chivalry, and peace-tranquility. The *bhava* are the situations and acts that evoke the sentiments the dancer expresses; the dancer attempts to evoke the corresponding rasa in the spectator.

Classical Indian dance themes come from the mythological epics, the *Ramayana* and *Mahabharata,* and the legends about the lives and loves of the gods (who are conveyed in human images with all the human moods and passions). Stylized poses and movements of separate parts of the body and face convey the meaning of emotion in the context of the episode or idea being danced. *Mudras,* or gestures, convey a poetic language. Each mudra may combine two or more of the twenty-four basic *hastas,* or hand poses. Poses emphasize balance or perfect stillness. Distinct postures express heroic and furious moods. A level pose of the head conveys serenity and usually begins a dance. Raising the head indicates dignity or divinity. Vigorously nodding the head expresses anger, threat,

A Kathak dancer who wears bells on her ankles and steps with precise movements to the rhythm of the tabla drum performs at the Khajuraho Dance Festival in India. (Corbis/Lindsay Hebberd)

or boasting. Moving the eyeballs in circles means valor, passion, and fury. Up and down movements of the eyeballs express wonder; horizontal shifts suggest heroism, fear, direction, and mystery. Diagonal movements denote grief. Eyelid fluttering conveys excitement and terror. Sidelong glances refer to dalliance, whereas a projected wide-eyed look signifies anger and challenge. The chest movement "drawn in" denotes fear and modesty; "heaved up" denotes pride, courage, and anger. Folding in the waist expresses female shyness and seductiveness. Rhythmic and spatial patterns help to convey specific emotions.

In the classical Kathakali dance-drama from Kerala, India, the facial colorings correspond to the moods of the characters. For example, the erotic mood is allied with light green, and the furious mood is associated with red. Eye twitches, vibrating hands, and trembling hands with one arm extended stiffly and the other bent express anger mixed with a feeling of retribution.

The process of dance creation is considered complete when the ideal viewer responds by reaching an ultimate state of bliss. In an interweaving of art and religion, both dancer and spectator seek to expand the unique self toward the universal divine self.

Fervor

Fervor appears in different forms of dance. In the Heyalo dance of the preliterate Kaluli in Papua New Guinea, guests dance for their hosts. As many as twenty dancers enter a torchlight illuminated loghouse. Their dances are accompanied by nostalgic songs about different landmarks in their hosts' land that remind them of the past, particularly of beloved friends and relatives now absent or dead. In a successful dance, the hosts burst into sorrowful tears from the strong sentiment aroused by the dancers. Following the tearful outburst, the hosts jump up angrily and burn the dancers on the shoulders with the torches used to light the ceremony. The dancers show no visible signs of pain as they continue performing. However, after the night-long vigil of dancing, singing, weeping, and burning, the dancers (who frequently have second- or third-degree burns on their arms and shoulders) pay compensation to the host individuals they saddened. This compensation is a gesture of reconciliation and friendship. Some dancers wail in sympathy with grief-stricken relatives who may be among the hosts.

Pain and daring are experienced by dancers and seen by viewers during performances of the American Elizabeth Streb Ringside Dance Company. Streb choreographs extremely demanding daredevil acrobatic stunts. Her dancers even punish their bodies by throwing themselves against wall surfaces.

The Old Testament refers to rejoicing with a person's entire being. Jews dance to praise their God in sublime adoration and to express thanks for his beneficence.

Ecstatic dance is performed as an outcome of strong religious emotion in order to bring about union with deities or achieve enlightenment. During church services of some Christian denominations, the attendees' dancing manifests "feeling the spirit." Pentecostal Churches of the Holy Christ treat dance as a divine occurrence, a revelation of God to those upon whom he has bestowed the Holy Ghost.

Muslim religious orders of dervishes ("at the door to enlightenment") practice Sufi mysticism and seek to become one with God. The repetition of short invocations to Allah with movements made to vocal or instrumental accompaniment help to free physical effort from consciousness, to eliminate desires from the heart, and to replace the desires with the love of God.

Known as the whirling dervishes, the Mevlevi order from Konya, Turkey, practices a stately ecstasy toward self-transcendence. These dervishes begin their dance with a slow turning movement that increases in speed. Dancers, with arms crossed on their breasts, heads bent, and feet close together, start turning very slowly, resting on each heel as they circle the hall. The whirling represents the celestial motions of Earth turning on its axis as it revolves around the Sun. As the speed of the spinning increases, the dancers' long white skirts flare outward, their heads lift, and their arms stretch outward. At times the right hand rises, palm up, and the left lowers, palm down, to symbolize the belief that the influence of Heaven is handed down to the world.

In Brazil, Trinidad and Tobago, Grenada, New Orleans, and places with a large West Indian immigrant population (e.g., Toronto, Canada, and Brooklyn, New York), Carnival is a time of exciting dancing. Some participants spend the entire year preparing for the event.

The social and theatrical flamenco dance of Spain expresses personal emotions of longing, human separateness, liberation of instinct, suffering, joy, love, passion, and pride. The concept of *duende* refers to a spirit or energy taking a dancer into a kind of ecstatic state. Passion manifests itself in body tension and sensual release, facial concentration, hard-hitting foot stamping and staccato striking of heels on the floor, curvaceous fast movement, and knife-sharp pivots, in addition to the accompanying music and song. The dancer uses upper torso arching, hands delineating the horns of a bull, and side stepping with skirt or cape like a bullfighter in action. The history of the "passionate" nature of the dance contributes to its being understood as erotic. Although flamenco has its roots in private gatherings among the Gypsies and has come to be associated with Spanish nationalism, the dance has (at various times) been associated with other ethnic groups as well, including Moors, Jews, and other marginalized groups.

Similarly, the tango of Argentina evokes personal feelings, the sense of national identity, and nostalgia for one's homeland among Argentineans living abroad. Originating at the end of the nineteenth century, the tango was performed by marginalized, displaced people in slums and brothels. Passion, aggression, betrayal, and desire shape the tango. In its early history, respectable people rejected the tango as being scandalous and immoral. The public display of a couple in a passionate embrace performing suggestive intricate footwork can have the effect of arousing sentiments of sexuality and power, as well as feelings about gender, class, and religion. For outsiders, the tango often evokes emotions of mystery, exoticism, or desire.

Prior to the twentieth century, some African ethnic groups' warrior dances emotionally readied men to fight in a coming raid. Successful battles warranted warrior dances in celebration. Today warrior dances are performed for many kinds of celebration (e.g., national independence, patriotism, earned postgraduate degrees in Western higher education). Warrior dances include mock attacks, angry leaping and charging, weapon brandishing, and unflagging vigorous movements performed to an exhilarating throbbing sonic accompaniment. Among Kenya's Samburu warriors, shaking expresses anger when they are frustrated by life situations.

Health and Healing

Dance in various settings (e.g., homes, courtyards, community gathering places, dance studios, theaters) may induce the feeling of well-being to promote health and healing. For example, communal dancing often creates a sense of support, infectious joy, and identification with the community, which all prevent or reduce feelings of alienation and loneliness. Physical fitness from dance and mastery of a dance technique contribute to feelings of self-control and well-being. Of course, a dancer's experiences, instructors, and the difficulty of dance may elicit both positive and negative emotions.

A person may escape or divert painful emotion by achieving an altered state of consciousness through dance, feeling the physical discomfort of dance excess, or engaging in fantasy. A dancer can be royalty, an animal, a lover, or a fighter.

Confronting painful emotions by projecting them in dance allows individuals to work through ways of handling these emotions. Because dance representations of ideas are pretend and without the effect of real life, dance participants can play with them at a distance and, consequently, make them less threatening. Holding up problems for scrutiny through dance may allow the dancers and spectators to evaluate and reflect on possible resolution. Children at play often create their own dances about matters that disturb them—death, drugs, and discrimination. Catharsis (i.e., the recollection and release of past repressed distressful emotions such as anger and fear) is also possible through dance.

When a person has gone to a healer (or shaman) and is possessed by a deity or spirit who dances using the possessed person's body (an event found in some parts of Africa, the Caribbean, the Middle East, Brazil, and Asia), the dance often conveys emotions that assist in the diagnosis and contribute to healing. Sometimes the healer is the possessed spiritual medium who dances. At times possession leads to trance states.

A devil dancer on the south coast of Sri Lanka wears an exorcist mask covered with pythons. (Corbis/ Charles & Josette Lenars)

Sri Lanka's Buddhist healing rituals that are performed throughout the night include elaborate dances to sever the relationship between a patient and evil demons or ghosts. During the exorcist's dance, the demonic deity enters his body, permitting him to control and expel the demon. The dance builds up emotional tension and energetic power that controls the demon realm and flows across to embrace the patient. Both the exorcist and patient may enter a trance state. In their effort to amuse a deity and encourage his assistance in the cure, some dancers provoke laughter among the patient and onlookers. Lampooning the demons allows the audience to laugh away its fear and terror.

In the Korean *kut* healing rituals performed by female shamans and housewives, trance dancing provides euphoria, enjoyment, and relief. A woman finds pleasure in entertaining her own personal god by dancing in the god's costume in order to bring good fortune. The deity ascends, possesses her, and dances. Ecstatic jumping creates frenzy.

Western dance therapy began to develop in the mid-twentieth century. Psychotherapists who are also trained in dance can facilitate a client's receptivity to confronting conflicts (regardless of whether they are in or out of the person's awareness) and to expressing the emotions that are aroused through dance or other movement in a censor-free setting. Dance therapists believe dance movements reveal a person's emotions, thoughts, and range of adaptive behaviors.

Since the 1960s, Western culture has included dance in education from preschool through college. One of the goals of dance in education has been to facilitate students' sense of well-being, which can contribute to academic success.

Theory and Practice

The West has had a disproportionate influence on dance throughout the world, first as a result of colonial contact and then as a result of cultural exchanges. Television, film, and the internet have led to further globalization.

Western thought from Biblical and early Greek times divided mind and body, the emotionally expressive body supposedly undermining the integrity and purity of the mind. Plato and Lucian feared that common dancing could arouse passions and undermine civil society. Some religions feared dancing would subvert morality. Advances in cognitive science in the latter part of the twentieth century led to the integration of the mind-body split.

François Delsarte, in the first part of the nineteenth century, and Rudolph Laban, in the first part of the twentieth century, theorized how body gestures and other movements reveal inner feelings. Delsarte, a French singer, influenced American modern dancers who interpreted his study of expression as saying that emotion produces bodily movement that expresses emotion, and motion creates emotion. Challenging the stylization of emotion in acting in nineteenth-century France, Delsarte developed techniques of emotional expression based on relaxation and naturalness in the body.

Laban explored the temporal and dynamic qualities of expression in movement. He thought movement originates from emotion. The particular emphases on, or selections from, a combination of space, time, weight, and flow render emotional states in dance. Laban and his followers provided descriptors of movement qualities. These are systematized in effort-shape analysis. Laban disciple and modern dance pioneer Mary Wigman believed that without ecstasy there was no dance. She wanted spectators to empathize with the dancer's ecstatic emotional experience.

In contrast with the view that dance reveals the dancer's immediate inner feelings, Susanne Langer argued that dance conveys symbolic emotion. Recalling an experienced emotion, and possibly then feeling it, the dancer conveys this emotion in dance.

The controversy about whether dancers conveyed real or symbolic feelings led to Judith Lynne Hanna's (1983) study of dancer-audience encounters. Unidimensional views of emotion in dance were incorrect. Choreographers and performers reported that there was more than one way of expressing emotion through dancing (no one way being more important than any other) and that it was possible for more than one way to occur during a single performance:

1. Feeling a particular emotion, the performer may immediately physicalize it through dance.
2. A dancer may recall an emotion from earlier personal experience and use the memory as a stimulus to express the emotion in dance.
3. The dancer may recall an emotion and express it symbolically, creating an illusion of the emotion rather than feeling its actual presence.
4. Dancing may induce emotion through energetic physical activity or interaction between or among dancers during a performance. High speed, sensory rhythmic stimulation, and overexertion may increase the dancer's susceptibility to an altered state of consciousness. In addition, dancers may experience emotion in reaction to the drama onstage.
5. Audience reaction to an ongoing performance may evolve the performer's emotions, which may or may not be expressed in dance.
6. However the dancer expresses emotion, through immediate or recollected feeling, the dancer usually attempts to evoke emotion (although not necessarily a specific one) in the audience.

Emotions expressed in dance are not universally understood, even within the same culture. The audience reaction to a postmodern performance makes the point. (Developed in the late 1960s, postmodern dance dismissed the emotional expression of modern dance.) After viewing a couple dance, nearly half of the audience reported that they saw no feeling and considered the movement to be mechanical, stilted, robot-like, and computerized. The other half of the audience reported that they perceived a wide range of emotions and observed eroticism in the intertwining and rolling of the couple on the floor and the dancers lying as if spent.

Variation in recognizing emotions and clues to them as presented in dance correlates with ethnic group, gender, occupation, and knowledge about dance. At the Indian Hindu Kathakali and Kuchipudi performances, Indians overwhelmingly identified anger (seeing it in the face, eyes, and hands), whereas less than one-third of the American spectators did the same. The Indians were better informed about the Indian dance tradition of emotional expression of the face and eyes, both in gesture and makeup, and of the hands in articulated signs and symbols. Moreover, the Indians were more familiar with the context of the dances—the mythological stories and personalities of the characters.

Salience of Emotion

Innovation has been a key principle of Western theater dance in the twentieth century. This has led to different emphases on the salience (or importance) of conveying emotion.

Emotional expressiveness has been part of the ballet and modern dance traditions. A dancer may develop emotional expressiveness through becoming familiar with the story, characters, or moods in the repertory of dramatic dance; having personality and imagination; and observing or being taught how to portray a character or mood. Dancers learn emotional expressiveness from other dancers, teachers, and coaches. Modern dance choreographer Maida Withers speaks of the sensitivity and consciousness of a dancer releasing or projecting in performance general feelings of self, including the dancer's internal world and body image. The mood of the music and characteristics of the dance role may support the dancer's ability to project emotion.

Postmodern dance tended to shun the salience of emotion in favor of everyday movement or abstraction. Dance movements in themselves, stripped of choreographic intentional content, became important. These innovations stimulated the creation of inexpressive, abstract ballets and modern dances.

The salience of emotion in Western theatrical dance reemerged in the 1990s. Many dances express deep-seated emotions about ways of defining existence and issues of individual or group identity (e.g., gender, sexual orientation, ethnicity, race, nationality, persons with physical disability, and older persons). As in dance therapy and dance education, dancers onstage once again portray comfort, pride, self-loathing, dislike by others, shame, disgust, pain, sorrow, and resignation. Dancers use stories and movements onstage to illustrate offstage emotional issues. Dancer/choreographer Bill T. Jones, for example, has expressed strong emotions in dance related to his identity as a black, gay, HIV-positive man. He communicates the sorrow, acceptance, and mourning involved in losing his partner and lover, Arnie Zane, as well as other people, to AIDS.

The emotional effect of all kinds of dance reaches beyond the performances themselves and can reflect as well as emotionally influence social interactions. Western language and literature are filled with dance metaphors that comment on personalities, science, religion, and politics and thereby move people emotionally.

See also: BODY MOVEMENT, GESTURE, AND DISPLAY; CREATIVITY; DRAMA AND THEATER; MIND-BODY DICHOTOMY; MUSIC

Bibliography

Chodorow, Joan. (1995). "Body, Psyche, and the Emotions." *American Journal of Dance Therapy* 17(2):97–114.

Dell, Cecily. (1970). *A Primer for Movement Description Using Effort-Shape and Supplementary Concepts.* New York: Center for Movement Research and Analysis, Dance Notation Bureau.

Deren, Maya. (1970). *Divine Horsemen: The Voodoo Gods of Haiti.* New York: Dell.

Ghosh, Manomohan, tr. (1951–1961). *The Natyasastra: A Treatise on Ancient Indian Dramaturgy and Histrionics,* 2 vols., ascribed to Bharata-Muni. Calcutta: Asiatic Society.

Hanna, Judith Lynne. (1983). *The Performer-Audience Connection.* Austin: University of Texas Press.

Hanna, Judith Lynne. (1987). *To Dance Is Human: A Theory of Nonverbal Communication,* rev. ed. Chicago: University of Chicago Press.

Hanna, Judith Lynne. (1988a). *Dance and Stress: Resistance, Reduction, and Euphoria.* New York: AMS Press.

Hanna, Judith Lynne. (1988b). "Theories and Realities of Emotion in Performance." *Polish Art Studies* 9:44–66.

Hanna, Judith Lynne. (1995). "The Power of Dance: Health and Healing." *Journal of Alternative and Complementary Medicine* 1(4):323–327.

Hanna, Judith Lynne. (1999). *Partnering Dance and Education: Intelligent Moves for Changing Times.* Champaign, IL: Human Kinetics.

Jones, Bill T. (1995). *Last Night on Earth.* New York: Pantheon Books.

Kapferer, Bruce. (1983). *A Celebration of Demons: Exorcism and the Aesthetics of Healing in Sri Lanka.* Bloomington: Indiana University Press.

Kendall, Laurel. (1985). *Shamans, Housewives, and Other Restless Spirits: Women in Korean Ritual Life.* Honolulu: University of Hawaii Press.

Laban, Rudolf von. (1960). *The Mastery of Movement,* 2d ed., revised and edited by Lisa Ullmann. London: MacDonald & Evans.

Langer, Susanne K. (1953). *Feeling and Form: A Theory of Art Developed from Philosophy in a New Key.* New York: Scribners.

Langer, Susanne K. (1957). *Philosophy in a New Key: A Study of the Symbolism of Reason, Rite and Art.* 3rd ed. Cambridge, MA: Harvard University Press.

Savigliano, Marta. (1995). *Tango and the Political Economy of Passion.* Boulder, CO: Westview Press.

Schieffelin, Edward L. (1976). *The Sorrow of the Lonely and the Burning of the Dancers.* New York: St. Martin's Press.

Schieffelin, Edward L. (1979). "Mediators as Metaphors: Moving a Man to Tears in Papua New Guinea." In *The Imagination of Reality,* ed. A. L. Becker and Aram A. Yengoyam. Norwood, NJ: ABLEX Publishing.

Shawn, Ted. (1954). *Every Little Movement: A Book about François Delsarte.* New York: Dance Horizons.

Vatsyayan, Kapilla. (1968). *Classical Indian Dance in Literature and the Arts.* New Delhi: Sangeet Natak Akademi.

Vatsyayan, Kapilla. (1996). *Bharata, the Natyasastra.* New Delhi: Sahitya Akademi.

Washabaugh, William. (1996). *Flamenco: Passion, Politics and Popular Culture.* Oxford, Eng.: Berg.

Woodall, James. (1992). *In Search of the Firedance.* London: Sinclair-Stevenson.

Judith Lynne Hanna

DARWIN, CHARLES ROBERT

b. Shrewsbury, England, February 12, 1809; *d.* Downe, England, April 19, 1882; *evolutionary theory, expression of emotion.*

Charles Darwin was born the son of Robert Waring Darwin, a successful physician, and Susannah Wedgwood, the daughter of porcelainware manufacturer Josiah Wedgwood. Darwin studied medicine for two years in Edinburgh before dropping out because he could not endure surgery—there being no anesthesia in use at that time. Darwin then entered Cambridge University, preparing to become a clergyman, and graduated in 1831. A devoted amateur naturalist, Darwin obtained the position of ship's naturalist for the five-year voyage of the H.M.S. *Beagle.* It was on this journey around the world that Darwin developed his theory of human origins.

Although Darwin is probably best known as a famous evolutionary theorist, he also wrote a major work on emotion, *The Expression of the Emotions in Man and Animals,* which was published in 1872, ten years before his death. This book on expression was originally intended to be a chapter in *Descent of Man* (1871), but when that book became quite long, Darwin chose to publish his treatment of expression—itself quite long—separately. Darwin, who founded the modern study of facial expression of emotion, was the first to use what is now a common method in this field of research—showing photographs of different expressions to people and asking them what emotion they saw. He was among the first to use photography to study the face, and his book on expression was the first scientific book in English to use photographs as illustrations. He did not use photographs, however, in his cross-cultural studies. Instead he wrote to individuals traveling or living in different parts of the world and asked them to answer a number of questions about how emotions appeared in facial expression. He

Charles Darwin. (Corbis/Bettmann)

asked, for example, "Is astonishment expressed by the eyes and mouth being opened wide, and by the eyebrows being raised? When a man is indignant or defiant does he frown, hold his body and head erect, square his shoulders and clench his fists?" A large part of his book on expression is devoted to providing his analysis of the replies, which strongly supported the idea that human expressions of emotion are universal. This finding, he asserted, proved that all humans had descended from a common progenitor.

Darwin was directly challenging the racists of his time who had claimed the opposite—that Europeans had descended from a more advanced progenitor than the Africans. Darwin's claim that emotional expressions are universal was generally disregarded during most of the next century, when behaviorism dominated psychology and relativism dominated anthropology. However, data gathered independently by Paul Ekman (1973, 1982) and his colleagues and Carroll Izard (1971) and his colleagues in many Western and non-Western cultures (including two preliterate cultures) strongly supports Darwin's claim about universals in expression.

The second issue Darwin addressed was one that few researchers had asked before (or indeed have asked since). He did not ask when or how an expression occurred but why a particular expression occurred for a particular emotion. Darwin proposed three principles to answer this question. The first principle was what he called the principle of serviceable habits, by which he meant that actions that were at one time of service to the organism during a particular emotional state came to be signs of that emotional state. For example, puffing out the chest in anger makes the angry person seem bigger. Modern ethologists have preserved this idea under the concept of intention movements. Darwin's second principle was antithesis, the idea that some movements were selected as signals because they were the opposite of movements that might have been serviceable. The movements involved in the shrug, said Darwin, are of little use, but this expression of helplessness is the antithesis of what people do with their chest, arms, and hands when they are angry. Darwin's third principle was that some expressions result directly from nervous system activity.

Darwin used his three principles to explain the expressions not just of humans but of all animals. In this way, he meant to support his claim for the continuity of the species. Differences in mental state, in particular of emotion, were matters of degree, not of kind. Emotions, Darwin said, are not limited just to humans, nor just to the primates. Among scientists today who study signaling in non-human primates, there is still disagreement about whether these animals are actually showing emotions. And few scientists grant what Darwin and pet lovers believe—that dogs, cats, and horses experience emotion.

In addition to his theoretical explanations for the expression of emotions, Darwin provided theoretical explanations for the nature of emotion itself. He took for granted that emotions are best understood as discrete, categorical phenomena, such as anger, fear, disgust, and so forth. In doing so, Darwin became the founder of one approach to emotion—discrete emotion theory. This approach is in contrast to the one supported by scientists who believe that emotions can be best understood in terms of a few dimensions such as pleasantness or activity, with one emotion shading off into another rather than being discrete.

Darwin's extensive discussion of blushing provided both theory and observations relevant to modern interest in embarrassment. He noted that children blush more than adults, that women blush more than men, and that there are *families* who blush a great deal. It is attention to the self—to appearance—that Darwin claimed to be at the core of this phenomenon.

Perhaps Darwin's most important contribution to the study of emotion was his view that emotions are the product of evolution—that both the biological and the social (nature and nurture) must be considered in order to understand emotions.

See also: BODY MOVEMENT, GESTURE, AND DISPLAY; EMBARRASSMENT; FACIAL EXPRESSION; HISTORICAL STUDY OF EMOTIONS; UNIVERSALITY OF EMOTIONAL EXPRESSION

Bibliography

Darwin, Charles R. ([1872] 1998). *The Expression of the Emotions in Man and Animals*, 3rd ed. London: HarperCollins.

Ekman, Paul, ed. (1973). *Darwin and Facial Expression: A Century of Research in Review.* New York: Academic Press.

Ekman, Paul, ed. (1982). *Emotion in the Human Face,* 2nd ed. New York: Cambridge University Press.

Izard, Carroll E. (1971). *The Face of Emotion.* New York: Appleton-Century-Crofts.

Paul Ekman

DEFENSE MECHANISMS

At the end of the nineteenth century, when Sigmund Freud began his clinical work with patients suffering from various psychiatric disorders, he discovered that very often the symptoms they displayed resulted from an unconscious memory of some past traumatic event. The symptom prevented the memory from becoming conscious and protected the patient from experiencing overwhelming anxiety. This idea—that there were unknown contents of the mind—was then expanded to include wishes, thoughts, and feelings that exist within the mind but of which the person is ordinarily unaware. These thoughts are kept out of awareness because the conscious mind of the person would find them unacceptable; if they were to become conscious, the person would experience great anxiety.

Basic Defenses

At first, Freud recognized only one mental mechanism used by people to keep thoughts and feelings out of awareness, which he termed *repression*. Subsequently, however, a variety of different defense mechanisms were discovered. Today, there is no firm agreement among clinicians as to how many different defense mechanisms exist, but most would include the following in addition to repression: denial, displacement, projection, turning against the self, reaction formation, isolation, rationalization, intellectualization, and sublimation.

Repression involves the motivated forgetting of a thought or feeling that, if recognized, would cause excessive anxiety. The banished material, however, continues to exist in the unconscious mind and may affect the person's conscious behavior. Thus, a person may feel that there is something he or she could or should remember but cannot quite recall. Or, one may experience a strong emotion, such as sadness or fear, but not have any idea what the source of that emotion is. This split between the repressed idea and the felt emotion may also result in the person engaging in behavior without realizing the implications of the behavior, as when a girl is very flirtatious with a boy but does not realize she is inviting his sexual interest in her. Repression may also lead to "slips of the tongue," in which the repressed idea is inadvertently expressed through the choice of an apparently erroneous word —as when, in one of Freud's (1901) examples, a man says of his competitor, "He's a great *idiot,*" and then adds with embarrassment, "Of course I meant to say, a great *patriot.*" In a sense, repression is at the base of all other defense mechanisms, since all are involved in keeping certain thoughts and feelings out of awareness. When used excessively, this defense contributes to the neurotic disorder of hysteria and to anxiety disorders.

Denial is one of the less complex defenses. A person using denial fails to perceive troublesome aspects of external reality or disturbing aspects of inner, psychic life. In both cases, the function of the defense is to protect the person from excessive anxiety. By "warding off" these disturbing perceptions, the person maintains psychological equilibrium. In popular lore, the defense of denial is personified in the three monkeys who "see no evil, hear no evil, and speak no evil." In contrast to repression, in which the idea is banished from consciousness but the attendant emotion may be felt, with denial, neither the cognition nor the emotion is recognized. Because this defense is relatively easy for adults to see through (e.g., the child who has just lost his beloved dog says, "I don't care") the use of denial is only effective and to be expected with young children. When denial—especially perceptual denial (not seeing something that is actually present)—is used by adults, it may be indicative of psychotic psychopathology. Excessive use of cognitive denial—thinking of something as more pleasant than it actually is—is characteristic of the histrionic personality disorder, which involves pervasive and excessive emotionality and attention-seeking behavior.

Displacement is a somewhat more complicated defense in which a person displaces his or her feelings about one person onto another. The feelings are not denied or repressed, but the true object of the feelings is not consciously recognized. For example, a man who is angry at his boss may take out this anger on one of his coworkers or on a family member. Often, the emotion is displaced onto a weaker or less important person, where the consequences of expressing the feeling are less.

> One way in which people defend themselves against emotions that they cannot express to the source (such as to a supervisor who infuriates them) is to displace that emotion onto some innocent person who has nothing to do with the situation. James Joyce's "Counterparts" (1916) describes how a father has a bad day at the office and loses an arm wrestling match at a pub on the way home from work. He takes his fury and frustration out on his son by beating him with a stick, even though the little boy has done nothing to provoke the attack.

Projection is a defense somewhat similar to displacement, but more complex. In projection, the person's own unacceptable thoughts, feelings, or wishes are not consciously recognized. Rather, they are falsely attributed to another person. For example, rather than recognizing that he or she is angry with a teacher, a student may feel that the teacher does not like *the student.* (Of course, if in fact the teacher *does* dislike the student, it would not be an example of projection.) People who are prone to the use of projection are often suspicious or wary of others; they are on the lookout for instances of both hostility and unwanted attention from others. The inclination to attribute malevolence to others, when carried out in the extreme, can produce delusions of persecution and the psychopathology known as paranoia.

Turning against the self is a defense that functions in the opposite direction from projection. Rather than expelling unwanted feelings to the outside, as happens in projection, the angry or aggressive feelings about others are turned back on the person's own self. Rather than attacking or criticizing someone else, the person attacks or criticizes him- or herself. Using this defense may result in the person feeling guilty or worthless, as though he or she somehow deserved to be attacked in this way. The defense may result in persons being "accident prone" or doing other things that inadvertently harm themselves. Clinicians often find that this defense mechanism contributes to psychopathological depression. The defense is found more often in women than men, which is probably due to social and cultural expectations that women not be overtly aggressive.

Reaction formation is a defense in which unacceptable thoughts, feelings, or impulses are kept out of awareness by means of the person expressing the opposite thought, feeling, or impulse. For example, someone who feels extremely competitive and jealous of another may, in terms of behavior, be extremely helpful and praising of that person, thereby keeping

less noble feelings out of awareness. Whether or not a person's behavior is a true indication of good will or whether it exemplifies the defense of reaction formation can sometimes be determined by the response of others to the behavior; when the good will behavior is experienced as being "too nice" or "too perfect," the behavior may be a result of reaction formation.

Isolation is a defense in which the emotional and cognitive parts of an experience are kept separate, so that the person does not experience them at the same time. More often, the thought is available to consciousness but the feelings associated with the idea are not. Sometimes, the emotion may be felt, while the associated idea is not available to awareness; this case corresponds to the defense of repression. Persons who use isolation excessively appear to be cold, removed, and excessively "objective" in their everyday life.

Rationalization is a defense mechanism that functions by providing self-serving or self-reassuring but incorrect explanations for behavior that would otherwise be considered unacceptable. Although these explanations may keep the person from feeling anxious about his or her behavior or the behavior of others, an outside observer may recognize the defensive quality of the explanation. Thus, the teenager who eats all of a younger sibling's Halloween candy with the rationalization, "It wouldn't be good for him to eat all that sugar" thereby avoids the recognition of personal feelings of greediness. However, a parent may not be taken in by this explanation. The "sour grapes" phenomenon—in which the person says, "If I can't have it, I don't want it"—is another example of rationalization.

Intellectualization is related to rationalization in that they both use thinking as a way to avoid disturbing feelings. However, whereas rationalization creates reasons to explain behavior that would otherwise be unacceptable, intellectualization avoids negative feelings by excessively engaging in abstract thinking about the situation. In this process of excessive thinking about a problem, the related feelings are kept at bay and are not experienced. Persons who rely on intellectualization may focus on abstract or inanimate problems, avoiding interpersonal closeness; they may focus excessively on external reality, to the exclusion of considerations about inner life; or they may focus so exclusively on details that they lose a sense of the larger picture ("seeing the trees, but not the forest"). Long, abstract conversations about the nature of love, morality versus immorality, or the ethics of death may allow persons to air personally important issues without having to experience the potentially disruptive emotions associated with these issues.

Sublimation is a unique defense mechanism in that it allows the disturbing underlying thought, feeling, or impulse to be expressed but in a way that is socially acceptable. This is accomplished by changing the goal of the impulse from an object or activity that is socially unacceptable to one that is acceptable. Freud believed that sublimation was associated with the creation of great works of art. The contributions of many humanitarians may also be understood to involve the sublimation of personal egoistic drives into channels that benefit society.

Development of Defenses

Although psychologists have been concerned with both how and why defense mechanisms develop, the question of *why* they develop is the more easily answered of the two. As suggested above, defense mechanisms protect a person from experiencing overwhelming anxiety. By preventing any unacceptable thoughts or feelings from entering the person's conscious thought and by "warding off" ideas or emotions that people do not want to know exist within themselves, defense mechanisms function to maintain some degree of psychological equilibrium in the individual. In addition to protecting against excessive anxiety, defenses may shield the individual from feeling guilt about having violated some prohibition of their conscience. In other cases, defenses may function to preserve the person's self-esteem when something has happened to threaten their positive self-regard. In more extreme cases, defenses may help preserve the individual's self-cohesion and prevent feelings of being abandoned by those on whom the individual is dependent.

The question of *how* defense mechanisms develop is more complicated. One model that is useful here takes a developmental approach, tracing the origins of each defense back to the earliest days of life and the behaviors available to the infant to ensure survival. Shortly after birth, the infant has a number of reflex behaviors available; many of these serve protective functions. For example, the young infant, when exposed to too much stimulation, may simply fall asleep. By withdrawing in this way, the baby protects itself from becoming overstimulated; the infant no longer sees or hears what is there in reality. This withdrawal of attention from perceptual stimuli can be understood as the beginning of the defense of denial. As the child develops, this automatic physiological response of withdrawal changes into a voluntary behavior that the baby can use to avoid experiencing painful emotions. Research shows that a young child will avoid looking at, or "not see," a person or picture of a face that has been associated with unpleasant experiences. As the child develops further, denial may be carried out through the use of language. The child may see

or feel something upsetting but can protect him- or herself from emotional upset by saying, "It *wasn't* scary; I am *not* afraid." The verbal negation—the word *no*—provides the child with a new way to prevent anxiety. Language provides other opportunities for defense; the child who feels small and confused may proclaim, "I'm the biggest and smartest in my class," which is really a restatement of "I am *not* small, and I am *not* confused." Thus, with development, words may increasingly be used to deny the unpleasant or unacceptable aspects of a situation or of oneself and mentally to turn it into something more desirable. Eventually, this process may take place entirely in the mind of the individual. When this occurs automatically, without the awareness of the person, the process has become a mental mechanism of defense.

The origin of another defense, projection, is also found in an early reflex behavior. When the infant experiences something inside the mouth that feels or tastes bad, he or she will spit it out. This reflex of spitting out something unacceptable can be seen as the beginning of projection. Subsequently the child may voluntarily displace unpleasant internal stimuli onto the outside world; eventually, even unpleasant emotions may be placed outside of the self and attached to objects or people in the external world. Rather than feeling angry at another person, a child may experience the anger as coming from that person. Now the mechanism for shifting what is inside to the outside has moved from being a reflex to being a mental operation.

Defenses and Human Development

Although defense mechanisms were originally discovered in the context of psychopathology, it is now generally understood that defenses occur as part of normal development, as in the examples above. It has further been suggested that different defenses become prominent at different chronological periods of development, and empirical research has supported this idea. Of the defenses discussed above, denial is frequently used by very young children, but by the age of six, most children begin to give up this defense as its function becomes apparent to them. The use of projection is common in later childhood and early adolescence. Reaction formation and turning against the self (in men) have been found to decrease from adolescence to adulthood. Repression, displacement, rationalization, and intellectualization are all considered to be more mature defenses, developing more fully in adolescence and continuing into adulthood. Sublimation is considered to be the most mature of the defense mechanisms and would most likely be found in a psychologically mature adult.

Research studies have shown that children do use different defenses at different ages. This is found both when children of different ages are compared and when the same children are followed over time from early to later childhood. It has also been found that children use more defenses when they are under stress, and that this use prevents them from becoming too upset. College students also increase their use of defense mechanisms when their self-esteem or sense of identity is threatened. As people grow older, their well-being, happiness, and even socioeconomic status has been found to be related to the kind of defenses they use; those who use more mature defenses are better off than those who use immature defenses. It has also been found that seriously disturbed psychiatric patients are likely to use immature defenses. However, after treatment and with improved mental health, these patients use fewer immature defenses.

It should be kept in mind that one problem researchers and clinicians face in conducting these studies is how to measure defenses. Many different methods have been tried. These approaches can be divided into two large groups—those that ask a person to self-report in a questionnaire on their own use of defenses and those that rely on an independent observer to assess a person's use of defenses through an interview or other observational procedure. Both approaches have associated difficulties. Self-report measures are seen by some to be theoretically contradictory; how can a person report on a process of which they are supposed to be unaware? However, relying on the report of an observer runs the risk that the observer will be unreliable or otherwise biased in what is reported. This problem can be reduced by having more than one observer and then pooling the results.

See also: EMOTION SUPPRESSION; FREUD, SIGMUND; HUMAN DEVELOPMENT

Bibliography

Ablon, Steven L.; Carlson, Gabrielle A.; and Goodwin, Frederick K. (1974). "Ego Defense Patterns in Manic-Depressive Illness." *American Journal of Psychiatry* 131:803–807.

Cramer, Phebe. (1987). "The Development of Defense Mechanisms." *Journal of Personality* 55:597–614.

Cramer, Phebe. (1991a). *The Development of Defense Mechanisms: Theory, Research, and Assessment.* New York: Springer-Verlag.

Cramer, Phebe. (1991b). "Anger and the Use of Defense Mechanisms in College Students." *Journal of Personality* 59:39–55.

Cramer, Phebe. (1997). "Evidence for Change in Children's Use of Defense Mechanisms." *Journal of Personality* 65:233–247.

Cramer, Phebe. (1998). "Threat to Gender Representation: Identity and Identification." *Journal of Personality* 66:335–357.

Cramer, Phebe, and Blatt, Sidney J. (1990). "Use of the TAT to Measure Change in Defense Mechanisms Following Inten-

sive Psychotherapy." *Journal of Personality Assessment* 54:236–251.

Cramer, Phebe; Blatt, Sidney J.; and Ford, Richard Q. (1988). "Defense Mechanisms in the Anaclitic and Introjective Personality Configuration." *Journal of Consulting and Clinical Psychology* 56:610–616.

Cramer, Phebe, and Davidson, Karina. (1998). "Defense Mechanisms in Contemporary Personality Research." *Journal of Personality* 66:879–1157.

Cramer, Phebe, and Gaul, Robin. (1988). "The Effects of Success and Failure on Children's Use of Defense Mechanisms." *Journal of Personality* 56:729–742.

Dollinger, Stephen, and Cramer, Phebe. (1990). "Children's Defensive Responses and Emotional Upset Following a Disaster: A Projective Assessment." *Journal of Personality Assessment* 54:116–127.

Fenichel, Otto. (1945). *The Psychoanalytic Theory of Neurosis.* New York: W. W. Norton.

Freud, Anna. (1936). *The Ego and the Mechanisms of Defense.* New York: International Universities Press.

Freud, Sigmund. ([1894] 1962). "The Neuro-Psychoses of Defense." In *The Standard Edition of the Complete Psychological Works of Sigmund Freud, Vol. 3,* ed. James Strachey. London: Hogarth Press.

Freud, Sigmund. ([1901] 1960). "The Psychopathology of Everyday Life." In *The Standard Edition of the Complete Psychological Works of Sigmund Freud, Vol. 6,* ed. James Strachey. London: Hogarth Press.

Freud, Sigmund. ([1905] 1953). "Fragment of an Analysis of a Case of Hysteria." In *The Standard Edition of the Complete Psychological Works of Sigmund Freud, Vol. 7,* ed. James Strachey. London: Hogarth Press.

Freud, Sigmund. ([1910] 1957). "Leonardo da Vinci and a Memory of His Childhood." In *The Standard Edition of the Complete Psychological Works of Sigmund Freud, Vol. 11,* ed. James Strachey. London: Hogarth Press.

Freud, Sigmund. ([1926] 1959). "Inhibition, Symptoms and Anxiety." In *The Standard Edition of the Complete Psychological Works of Sigmund Freud, Vol. 20,* ed. James Strachey. London: Hogarth Press.

Freud, Sigmund. ([1939] 1964). "Moses and Monotheism." In *The Standard Edition of the Complete Psychological Works of Sigmund Freud, Vol. 23,* ed. James Strachey. London: Hogarth Press.

Haan, Norma. (1977). *Coping and Defending.* New York: Academic Press.

Perry, J. Christopher, and Cooper, Stephen. (1989). "An Empirical Study of Defense Mechanisms." *Archives of General Psychiatry* 46:444–452.

Semrad, Elvin V; Grinspoon, Lester; and Fienberg, Stephen E. (1973). "Development of an Ego Profile Scale." *Archives of General Psychiatry* 28:70–77.

Smith, Gudmund J. W., and Daniellson, Anna. (1977). *Anxiety and Defense Strategies in Childhood and Adolescence.* New York: International Universities Press.

Smith, Wendy P., and Rossman, B. Robbie. (1986). "Developmental Changes in Trait and Situational Denial Under Stress During Childhood." *Journal of Child Psychology and Psychiatry and Allied Disciplines* 27:227–235.

Vaillant, George E. (1974). "Natural History of Male Psychological Health, II: Some Antecedents of Healthy Adult Adjustment." *Archives of General Psychiatry* 31:15–22.

Vaillant, George E. (1976). "Natural History of Male Psychological Health, V: The Relation of Choice of Ego Mechanisms of Defense to Adult Adjustment." *Archives of General Psychiatry* 33:535–545.

Vaillant, George E. (1977). *Adaptation to Life.* Boston: Little, Brown.

Vaillant, George E. (1986). *Empirical Studies of Ego Mechanisms of Defense.* Washington, DC: American Psychiatric Press.

Vaillant, George E. (1993). *The Wisdom of the Ego.* Cambridge, MA: Harvard University Press.

Vaillant, George E. (1994). "Ego Mechanisms of Defense and Personality Psychopathology." *Journal of Abnormal Psychology* 103:44–50.

Phebe Cramer

DEPRESSION

See Anxiety; Hopelessness; Mood; Mood Disorders; Sadness; Seasonal Affective Disorder

DESCARTES, RENÉ

b. Touraine, France, March 31, 1596; *d.* Stockholm, Sweden, February 11, 1650; *philosophy.*

René Descartes was a leading French philosopher and mathematician of the late medieval period. As the founder of modern scientific philosophy, he remains a seminal figure in philosophy. Decartes's approach to philosophy, known as Cartesianism, remains a model that is routinely followed in philosophical inquiry and scientific research. To the general public, he is best known for his statement "I think; therefore, I am," although this simple formulation does not adequately represent the depth and breadth of his influence, nor the mathematical approach that he brought to knowledge and philosophy.

Descartes was born the second son of Joachim Des Cartes, a low-level noble who, after a military career, had become an advisor and assistant to the Parliament of Brittany. Descartes's mother died within a year of his birth, and at age ten Descartes began his formal education at the Jesuit College of La Fleche. Unlike many of his contemporaries, Descartes was an eager and dedicated student and spent eight years studying the full curriculum at the college and demonstrating a particular interest in and ability at mathematics. Descartes was a sickly child and his education was abetted by a lenient school policy that allowed him to remain in bed when he felt ill or too weak to study. It was also made more pleasurable by his close friendship with Abbe Mersenne, a scholarly monk who introduced Descartes to the practice of meditation, an activity Descartes engaged in regularly for the rest of his life and one that produced many of his intellectual insights.

Feeling that he had learned all that the college had to offer, Descartes left school at eighteen, moved to Paris, and joined the Dutch army. As it was a time of peace, Descartes had much free time to mingle with the mathematicians who served with him in the engineer corps and developed a greater appreciation for mathematics as a tool for understanding the world. In 1619, he joined the army of the Duke of Bavaria, who was then engaged in the Thirty Years War. During this period of service, Descartes, while in one of his meditation sessions, discovered that mathematics held the key to understanding the world. As a result of this, he vowed, in accord with his strong Catholic belief, to make a pilgrimage to the shrine of Our Lady of Loreto to devote his life to using this discovery to help explain the world. Descartes left military service in 1621, and since he had received a sizable inheritance from his father, he was able to begin a rather comfortable life in the pursuit of knowledge. He traveled through Europe for several years, made his pilgrimage to Loreto in 1625, and then settled in the Netherlands, where he spent most of the rest of his life and wrote his philosophical treatises.

Descartes was a private man, so relatively little is known about his personal affairs—other than that he

René Descartes. (Corbis/Bettmann)

remained a devout Catholic throughout his life and that in 1635 he had a daughter with a young servant. The daughter, named Francine, died five years later, an event that devastated Descartes and from which he perhaps never fully recovered. As a leading intellectual of his time, Descartes was able to move among nobles and royals, and in 1642, he became friendly with Princess Elizabeth of Palatine, who was living in the Netherlands and to whom he dedicated his *Principles of Philosophy* (1644). In 1646, Descartes became friendly with Queen Christina of Sweden, corresponded with her, and dedicated his psychological treatise *The Passions of the Soul* (1649) to her. He moved to Stockholm to serve as her personal tutor, a move that perhaps led to his death at the age of fifty-four in 1650. Descartes was used to a relaxed, leisurely life and had great difficulty adjusting to the cold climate and the early hours kept by Queen Christina. He took ill with pneumonia and died soon thereafter. In 1667, his body was returned to France, where he was buried at Sainte-Genevieve-du-Mont.

Descartes was an original and creative thinker who broke with the philosophical methods and approaches of Medieval Europe and began moving philosophy toward the modern era. He is viewed by modern philosophers as the father of modern philosophy because he was the first philosopher to set forth many of the basic concerns of modern philosophy, such as the relationship between mind and matter and the use of mathematical concepts to account for reality. Descartes predated the scientific revolution in Europe and was not a scientist himself, although his ideas about intuition, deduction, and related matters became the basis of scientific inquiry and he did revise some basic principles of geometry. Descartes was also a gifted writer and many of his works, such as *Discourse on the Method* (1637), are considered to be masterpieces—because of their style as well as their content.

Like his contemporaries and many philosophers who followed him, Descartes was far less interested in the emotions than in thought, reason, and ethics. His major work on the emotions, *The Passions of the Soul*, was perhaps motivated by his feelings for Queen Christina, but it has been dismissed by experts as his least important work. Descartes classified the emotions as one form of the passions, with the primary passions being wonder, love, hatred, desire, joy, and sadness. These passions were all distinct from thought and often had a confusing and negative effect on thought, which Descartes clearly believed was more valuable and human than the passions, which he believed were more primitive and animal. According to Descartes, emotions were a product of interaction between the mind and the body, which took place in a small gland (the pineal gland) at the base of the brain. However, Descartes also held a somewhat more modern view of the emotions because he also saw that emotions could be set off by external events, such as fear of a situation, and that they could also cause physical reactions. Since Descartes died shortly after writing *The Passions of the Soul*, these ideas went undeveloped and had little effect on later scientific study of emotion.

Despite his philosophical innovations, Descartes was actually quite conservative in most other matters, including loyalty to the state and to the Catholic Church. Descartes believed strongly in God, and he clearly believed that human thought and creativity were bestowed by God. As a devout Catholic, Descartes feared the power of the Church. For example, when he learned in 1633 that Galileo had been condemned by the Church, he halted the publication of *The World* because he set forth in it ideas that were in agreement with Galileo. Similarly, when his *Discourse* was criticized by the Church, even though it was lauded by other scholars, he dedicated his next work, *Meditations on the First Philosophy* (1641), to the faculty of theology in Paris.

See also: PHILOSOPHY

Bibliography

Cottingham, John. (1992). *The Cambridge Companion to Descartes.* Cambridge, Eng.: Cambridge University Press.

Cottingham, John; Stoothoff, Robert; and Murdoch, Dugald. (1985). *The Philosophical Writings of Descartes,* 2 vols. Cambridge, Eng.: Cambridge University Press.

Cottingham, John; Stoothoff, Robert; Murdoch, Dugald; and Kenny, Anthony. (1991). *The Philosophical Writings of Descartes, Vol. 3: The Correspondence.* Cambridge, Eng.: Cambridge University Press.

Descartes, René. ([1649] 1989). *The Passions of the Soul,* tr. Stephen Voss. Indianapolis, IN: Hackett.

David Levinson
Ben Manning

DESIRE

Desire is generally viewed as a conscious motivational state that is often described as "wishing," "wanting," "longing," "yearning," or "coveting," in addition to "desiring." Moreover, although the term *desire* frequently is used synonymously with these and other terms, the associations between them often have been little studied. For example, researchers studying addictions have often assumed that the term *craving* refers to a strong desire and have frequently used it in questionnaires concerning substance use. However, an investigation by Lynn Kozlowski and his colleagues (1989) of the ways in which smokers and alcoholics distinguished the terms *desire* and *craving* found, contrary to expectations, that their behavior did not indicate that they considered craving to be synonymous with strong desire. The term *drive,* which is sometimes used to refer to many of the same phenomena as desire, usually connotes innate biological needs and urges of which the individual may or may not be consciously aware.

As a motivational state, desire is linked to action and purposeful striving toward attainment of the object of desire. Usually the goal of desire is possession of an object (including psychological possession of and proximity to another person), but it also sometimes is associated with an event or activity (e.g., a desire to engage in a specific activity). Although many emotion theorists, such as Ellen Berscheid (1983) and George Mandler (1975), would not classify desire as an emotion in itself, the motivational state of desire often sets the conditions for the experience of a variety of emotions associated with the pursuit of the goal of desire, with its attainment, or with failure to achieve the desired object. For example, joy has been viewed as the unexpected attainment of a desired end and despair is often the result of frustrated desire.

Desire is sometimes also differentiated from the concept of need; that is, people do not always desire what they know they need (e.g., medicine) and often do not need what they desire if the term need is used to refer to objects and events that will simply maintain the individual's customary level of well-being. The difference between desire and need is perhaps most apparent in cases of chemical addiction, where ingestion of the addictive substance allows the individual to maintain his or her usual state of comfort but failure to ingest it leads to discomfort. *Need* often connotes more urgency to attain the object than desire does.

Such discrepancies between actual use and dictionary definitions indicates the care that must be taken when interpreting findings.

Desire and Pleasure

The most extensive psychological analysis of desire was conducted by Fritz Heider (1958), a social psychologist, who examined the manner in which people use the term *desire* in their everyday language and discourse. From his examination of the role the concept plays in the "common-sense" psychology people use to understand the behavior of others, Heider concludes that desire plays a fundamental role in people's causal theories about the behavior of others.

Central to the concept of desire in common-sense psychology is the link between desire and pleasure, which, Heider argues, is inviolable. If the individual is disappointed upon obtaining the object of desire, people tend to conclude that the individual did not truly desire the object, that he or she did desire the object but the object obtained was different, or that the individual was mistaken in his or her initial displeasure

upon attaining the object. Thus, people believe that if the desire for the object does exist and if the individual actually obtains the desired object, pleasure necessarily must result. Anticipated pleasure, Heider concludes, is an essential component of desire.

Desire and Psychological Distance

Heider (1958) also observes that states of desire are always characterized by a separation between the person and the desired object. As the American psychologist William James (1890, p. 486) put it, "We desire to feel, to have, to do, all sorts of things which at the moment are not felt, had, or done." The motivational state of desire, then, reflects the awareness that one wishes to be doing or feeling or having something that one is not now doing, feeling, or having and the belief that fulfillment of this wish would create pleasure.

Both the current and the expected degree of "distance" between the person and the desired object have implications for the emotions that the individual is likely to experience. Hope, for example, is often felt when an individual believes that the desired object can be attained, and sadness may be experienced if it becomes apparent that capture of the desired object is impossible. In the latter circumstance, Heider hypothesizes that the desire eventually will die. He hypothesizes, too, that as the individual's expectation that the desired object can be obtained increases, desire for the object will increase as well.

Perceived psychological distance from the desired object also has consequences for the experience of emotion when actions taken in pursuit of the object are blocked. John Dollard and his colleagues (1939), who derived their research from the classic "frustration-aggression" hypothesis, found that the closer the individual is to capturing the desired object, the greater his or her frustration if progress toward attainment is blocked. Frustration is associated with a variety of strong negative emotions (e.g., anger toward the individual perceived to be impeding progress). People sometimes manipulate an individual's distance from the object of desire in order to intensify the individual's desire—or "whet the appetite"—for the object; teasing, or moving the object of desire closer to the individual and then withdrawing it, appears to increase both desire and frustration and often energizes the individual to move even more vigorously toward capture of the object.

Desire and Action

Considered as a motivational state, desire evidences a strong action component—specifically, action that will remove the distance between the individual and the desired object. Nevertheless, desire is not always manifested in action. For example, the individual may perceive that although the object is desirable, the means to attain it are neither available in the present nor are they likely to be available in the future. The research of Kurt Lewin and his colleagues (1944) indicates that people will not take action to attain even highly desirable goals if they believe their actions will be unsuccessful. For this reason, and despite the fact that people often infer the existence of desire from observance of an individual's behavior, the absence of action is a poor indicator of whether or not the individual desires the object. Moreover, even if desire does result in action, there is no direct link between desire and a particular action pattern because it is usually the case that a number of different actions may serve to achieve the same end-goal of achieving the object.

Objects of Desire

Heider (1958) observes that some objects are seen as desirable by almost everyone whereas the desirability of other objects resides in the eyes of a single beholder whose unique properties interact with his or her situation to make a particular object desirable to that individual at that time. Thus, almost any object or event has the potential to become desirable to someone at some time—even fleas, as in the case reported by Carole Carlson (1983) of a Nazi concentration camp prisoner who regarded the fleas that infested her cell as being very desirable because the guards refused to enter the cell to take her to the gas ovens and death.

Studies have tended to separate the kinds of objects and events that people appear to desire (apart from chemical substances to which they are addicted) into four overlapping categories: (a) objects that increase control of the individual's fate and can be used to enhance well-being, such as a desire for information,

money, or a job; (b) abstract states that often reflect the individual's principles and values, such as a desire for privacy, freedom, and independence; (c) interpersonal objects and the variety of events and states associated with them, such as a spouse, children, love, marriage, support, and companionship; (d) and, finally, sex. Of these objects of desire, psychologists have most frequently discussed and investigated sexual desire, often referred to as *lust*.

Sexual Desire

Many contemporary theorists view sexual desire as a psychological state that is subjectively experienced by the individual as an awareness that he or she wishes to attain a sexual goal. Historically, however, and regrettably, many researchers have used such terms as *sexual desire, subjectively perceived sexual arousal,* and *sexual activity* interchangeably, despite the fact that they are distinct experiences. For example, physiological-genital sexual arousal may occur without conscious awareness (i.e., without subjective sexual arousal); for example, some women are not able to report their current level of physiological-genital sexual arousal. Even subjective sexual arousal, or awareness that one is currently experiencing the physiological-genital indicants of sexual arousal (e.g., an erection, vaginal lubrication), is a different state from an awareness that one is interested in sexual activities or wishes sexual contact with another. In a study conducted by J. Gayle Beck and his colleagues (1991), a majority of both men and women reported that they had engaged in sexual activity in the absence of sexual desire, and in a study by Pamela Regan (1997), more than half of the women and nearly a quarter of the men said that had engaged in noncoercive but undesired sexual activities. Unfortunately, subjective sexual arousal has often been used as an index of sexual desire even though subjective arousal and sexual activity do not necessarily imply a desire for such activity. Not only is sexual activity an unreliable indicant of sexual desire, sexual desire also is a poor predictor of sexual activity for a variety of reasons (e.g., unavailability of partner, moral norms). In sum, physiological-genital sexual arousal, subjective sexual arousal, and sexual desire are distinct experiences, although they frequently occur at the same time or in various pairings.

Regan and Berscheid (1999) observe that sexual desire may vary along at least two dimensions. First, it may vary quantitatively (in frequency and intensity). Stephen Levine (1987), for example, views an individual's fluctuations in intensity and frequency as one of the essential characteristics of sexual desire; in addition, people undoubtedly differ in the frequency and the intensity of sexual desire they typically experience.

> *Eugene O'Neill's* Desire Under the Elms *(1924) pits the desire of the son, Eben, to inherit his father's farm against the desire of his stepmother, Abbie, to have a home of her own. Abbie persuades Eben that if he cuckolded his father, he could get revenge on his father for his brutal treatment of Eben's mother. Abbie becomes pregnant by Eben but makes her husband believe the child is his. In a shocking ending, those who have manipulated each other come to realize that they really desire and love each other, but by that time Abbie has killed her baby, the incestuous lovers are under arrest, and the old father is left alone on the farm that everyone was fighting to own.*

Second, sexual desire may vary qualitatively (in the specificity of the desired sexual activity as well as in the specificity of the object or person involved).

In the traditional and still most common theoretical framework within which sexual desire has been discussed by psychologists, sexual desire is viewed as an innate motivational force (e.g., instinct or drive) that compels the individual to seek out sexual objects or engage in sexual activities. For example, the German physician and sexual pathologist Richard von Krafft-Ebing (1886) viewed sexual desire as a potent "physiological law" that arises jointly from cerebral activity and pleasurable physical sensations.

Sigmund Freud (1905), who coined the term *libido* to refer to sexual desire, also viewed it as an innate and instinctive motivational force that is analogous to hunger. In Freud's psychoanalytic theory of neurosis, humans are said to be propelled through successive developmental stages by the necessity to resolve their desires, the strongest of which are those that emanate from libido: "Certain as it is that the libidinal tendencies are reinforced later by regression and reaction-formation . . . I still think that we must not overlook the fact that those first impulses have an intensity of their own which is greater than anything that comes later and may indeed be said to be incommensurable with any other force" (1932, p. 296). Freud believed that the libido attaches to various objects as a person develops, beginning, for example, in the "oral stage," where the mother's breast is the primary object of desire. The majority of neuroses, Freud (1968, pp. 306–307) believed, are caused by conflict between libidinal desires and "ego-instincts."

Although Freud's psychoanalytic theory highlighted the role sexual desire may play in human development and in neurosis, his theory failed to generate empirical research relevant to his theses and to sexual desire. Subsequent sexuality research also neglected sexual desire, focusing more on the description of sexual practices and on the physiology of the human sexual response cycle. It is ironic that theoretical and empirical interest in sexual desire since the late 1970s has been prompted more by problems occasioned by the absence of sexual desire than by its presence—people more frequently seek help from clinicians and sex therapists because of too little interest in sexual activity than because of too much interest.

Helen Singer Kaplan, in her seminal book, *Disorders of Sexual Desire and Other New Concepts and Techniques in Sex Therapy* (1979), added sexual desire to the human sexual response cycle, proposing a three-phase model of human sexuality: desire, excitement, and orgasm. In accordance with the general concept of desire, Kaplan regards sexual desire as a subjective state "experienced as specific sensations which lead the individual to seek out, or become receptive to, sexual experiences" (p. 10). Like Freud, Kaplan and many other contemporary sexologists view sexual desire as a motivational drive that is internally generated in an as yet unspecified manner, perhaps from biochemical sources in the brain.

In contrast to traditional theoretical views, some contemporary theorists of sexual desire have developed social relational theoretical frameworks in which sexual desire is viewed as an externally generated phenomenon; desire is seen as originating from an external source of stimulation (e.g., an attractive person) rather than from a need within the desiring individual. Johan Verhulst and Julia Heiman (1979, p. 30) state that "desire is located in the partner rather than in oneself, since it is a feeling of being drawn to the other." Yet other theorists are advocating models that integrate both internal and external causes of sexual desire. Levine (1987) believes that sexual desire is best viewed as an interaction among three components: (a) the neuroendocrine system, reflecting a biologically-based sexual drive, (b) cognitive processes that generate the wish to behave sexually, and (c) psychologically-based motivational processes that result in a willingness to behave sexually. Levine theorizes that changes in any one of these components will affect both the likelihood that an individual will feel sexual desire and the intensity of the experience. For example, anger or other negative affects and emotions stemming from interpersonal conflict between partners appear to suppress sexual desire, and several studies now document that sexual desire disorders frequently signal other problems in a couple's relationship.

Although some motivation theorists, such as Peter Bertocci (1988) (whose theory of motivation regards "lust-sex" as a primary emotion), view sexual desire as an emotion in itself, the emotion most frequently associated with sexual desire is romantic love. Many early sexologists, such as Havelock Ellis (1933), believed sexual desire to be an important component of romantic love. Freud, Ellis's contemporary, theorized that romantic love stems from a primitive, sexual urge and is produced when the sexual instinct is suppressed or sublimated. Although Freud originally viewed sexual attraction to be the same as romantic love, he later modified his original view, concluding that tender and affectionate feelings combine with sensual feelings to produce the sentiment of love.

Sexual desire has played an important role in most clinical psychologists' discussions of romantic love, but social psychologists, who have conducted most of the empirical research on the phenomenon, initially neglected the role of sexual desire. That omission was subsequently corrected. Most contemporary theories of romantic love now include sexual desire as an important component, and empirical research findings strongly justify that inclusion. Sarah Meyers and Berscheid (1997) found that when individuals were asked to name those with whom they were in love and those to whom they were sexually attracted, virtually all of the romantically loved persons were among those to whom the individual was sexually attracted, but the reverse was not true. Thus, it appears that people do not fall in love with all those for whom they feel sexual desire, but if they do not feel sexual desire for the other, they are unlikely to describe their feelings as romantic love even if they like and care about the other. Given the strong association between sexual desire and romantic love, many researchers have concluded that to advance the understanding of these phenomena, it will be necessary for sexologists and social psychologists to collaborate in their efforts rather than continue to work in relative isolation from each other.

See also: FREUD, SIGMUND; HOPE; JAMES, WILLIAM; LOVE; LUST; MOTIVATION; PSYCHOANALYTIC PERSPECTIVE

Bibliography

Beck, J. Gayle; Bozman, Alan W.; and Qualtrough, Tina. (1991). "The Experience of Sexual Desire: Psychological Correlates in a College Sample." *Journal of Sex Research* 28:443–456.

Berscheid, Ellen. (1983). "Emotion." In *Close Relationships,* ed. Harold H. Kelley, Ellen Berscheid, Andrew Christensen, John H. Harvey, Ted L. Huston, George Levinger, Evie McClintock, Letitia Anne Peplau, and Donald R. Peterson. New York: W. H. Freeman.

Berscheid, Ellen, and Walster [Hatfield], Elaine. (1974). "A Little Bit About Love." In *Foundations of Interpersonal Attraction,* ed. Ted L. Huston. New York: Academic Press.

Bertocci, Peter A. (1988). *The Person and Primary Emotions.* New York: Springer-Verlag.

Carlson, Carole C. (1983). *Corrie Ten Boom: Her Life, Her Faith.* Old Tappen, NJ: F. H. Revell.

Carr, Harvey A. (1929). *Psychology: A Study of Mental Activity.* New York: Longmans, Green.

Dollard, John; Doob, Leonard W.; Miller, Neal E.; Mowrer, O. H.; and Sears, Robert R. (1939). *Frustration and Aggression.* New Haven, CT: Yale University Press.

Ellis, Havelock. ([1933] 1963). *Psychology of Sex.* New York: New American Library of World Literature.

Freud, Sigmund. ([1905] 1938). "Three Contributions to the Theory of Sex." In *The Basic Writings of Sigmund Freud,* ed. and tr. A. A. Brill. New York: Random House.

Freud, Sigmund. (1932). "Female Sexuality." *International Journal of Psycho-Analysis* 13:281–299.

Freud, Sigmund. (1968). *A General Introduction to Psychoanalysis.* New York: Liveright Publishing.

Hatfield, Elaine. (1988). "Passionate and Companionate Love." In *The Psychology of Love,* ed. Robert J. Sternberg and Michael L. Barnes. New Haven, CT: Yale University Press.

Heider, Fritz. (1958). *The Psychology of Interpersonal Relations.* New York: Wiley.

Heiman, Julia R. (1975). "Responses to Erotica: An Exploration of Physiological and Psychological Correlates of Human Sexual Response." *Dissertation Abstracts International* 36(5-B): 2472.

Hendrick, Susan S., and Hendrick, Clyde. (1992). *Romantic Love.* Newbury Park, CA: Sage Publications.

James, William. ([1890] 1950). *The Principles of Psychology, Vol. 1.* New York: Dover.

Kaplan, Helen Singer. (1979). *Disorders of Sexual Desire and Other New Concepts and Techniques in Sex Therapy.* New York: Simon & Schuster.

Kinsey, Alfred C.; Pomeroy, Wardell B.; and Martin, Clyde E. (1948). *Sexual Behavior in the Human Male.* Philadelphia: W. B. Saunders.

Kozlowski, Lynn T.; Mann, Robert E.; Wilkinson, D. A.; and Poulos, Constantine X. (1989). "'Cravings' Are Ambiguous: Ask About Urges or Desires." *Addictive Behaviors* 14:443–445.

Krafft-Ebing, Richard von. ([1886] 1945). *Psychopathia Sexualis,* 12th ed. New York: Pioneer Publications.

Levine, Stephen B. (1987). "More on the Nature of Sexual Desire." *Journal of Sex and Marital Therapy* 10:83–96.

Lewin, Kurt; Dembo, Tamara; Festinger, Leon; and Sears, Pauline S. (1944). "Level of Aspiration." In *Personality and the Behavior Disorders: A Handbook Based on Experimental and Clinical Research,* ed. Joseph McVicker Hunt. New York: Ronald Press.

Mandler, George. (1975). *Mind and Emotion.* New York: Wiley.

Masters, William H., and Johnson, Virginia E. (1966). *Human Sexual Response.* Boston: Little, Brown.

Meyers, Sarah A., and Berscheid, Ellen. (1997). "The Language of Love: The Difference a Preposition Makes." *Personality and Social Psychology Bulletin* 23:347–362.

Regan, Pamela C. (1997). "The Impact of Male Sexual Request Style on Perceptions of Sexual Interactions: The Mediational Role of Beliefs About Female Sexual Desire." *Basic and Applied Social Psychology* 19:519–532.

Regan, Pamela C., and Berscheid, Ellen. (1999). *Lust: What We Know About Human Sexual Desire.* Newbury Park, CA: Sage Publications.

Sternberg, Robert J. (1988). "Triangulating Love." In *The Psychology of Love,* ed. Robert J. Sternberg and Michael L. Barnes. New Haven, CT: Yale University Press.

Verhulst, Johan, and Heiman, Julia R. (1979). "An Interactional Approach to Sexual Dysfunctions." *American Journal of Family Therapy* 7:19–36.

Ellen Berscheid
Matthew Heller

DESPAIR

See Hopelessness

DISGUST

The topic of disgust appears in virtually every discussion of the basic or fundamental emotions. Charles Darwin, in *The Expression of the Emotions in Man and Animals* (1872), defined the term *disgust* as referring to "something revolting, primarily in relation to the sense of taste, as actually perceived or vividly imagined; and secondarily to anything which causes a similar feeling, through the sense of smell, touch and even of eyesight" (p. 253). In the classic psychoanalytic treatment of disgust, Andras Angyal (1941) claimed that "disgust is a specific reaction towards the waste products of the human and animal body" (p. 395). Angyal related the strength of disgust to the degree of intimacy of contact, with the mouth as the most sensitive focus. Silvan Tomkins (1963) has offered the more general contention that disgust is "recruited to defend the self against psychic incorporation or any increase in intimacy with a repellent object" (p. 233).

All of these scholars, as well as most others, suggest that a special relation exists between disgust and the mouth, as well as between disgust and food rejection. The relation has to do both with the central importance of food in the emotion of disgust and the idea that food rejection is the origin of disgust. William Miller (1997) has rejected both of these claims, arguing instead that the central elicitor of disgust is animal life, that touch and smell are the senses most related to disgust, and that taste became associated with disgust only in the modern era. In spite of Miller's assertions, the arguments for a food origin of disgust are very strong. The English term *disgust* means "bad taste," and the facial expression of disgust functions to reject unwanted foods and odors. Nausea, the distinctive physiological sign of disgust, is a food-related sensation that inhibits ingestion. The definition proposed by Paul Rozin and April Fallon (1987) of what is taken to be the original form of disgust, or core disgust, builds on the definition of Angyal, and has a clear food focus: "Revulsion at the prospect of (oral) incorporation of an offensive object. The offensive objects are contaminants; that is, if they even briefly contact an acceptable food, they tend to render that food unacceptable" (p. 23). The idea of contamination links disgust to the anthropological concept of pollution, particularly as expounded by Mary Douglas in *Purity and Danger* (1966).

Disgust is unique among the basic emotions in that it is specifically related to a particular motivational system (hunger) and to a particular part of the body (the mouth). It also serves as a primary means for socialization—an object or event made disgusting is prohibited with a power that goes beyond reason.

The Response Side of Disgust

Emotions are frequently analyzed or described in terms of a set of eliciting conditions and appraisals (input conditions) that trigger a set of responses (outputs), including subjective experience, facial and/or

bodily expressions, physiological changes, and motivated behaviors.

Behaviorally, disgust triggers the motivation or "action tendency" of moving away from some object, event, or situation; it can be characterized as avoidance or rejection. Physiologically, disgust is perhaps the only emotion associated with a specific physiological state, nausea. In terms of the type of autonomic features generally used to diagnose emotions, disgust is associated with either minimal or a predominantly parasympathetic (de-arousing) response. Autonomically, disgust is therefore more like sadness and less like fear and anger, with their sympathetic arousal.

The expressive component of disgust has been studied almost entirely with reference to photographs of the face. There are dynamic facial and bodily movements associated with disgust, but these have rarely been elaborated, with the exception of the ancient Hindu text of the *Natyasastra*. Although there are minor disagreements among researchers about the characteristics of the "disgust face," there is general agree-

A two-year-old boy curls his lip in disgust at broccoli that he refuses to eat. (Corbis/Laura Dwight)

ment that the disgust expression centers on the mouth and nose and involves wrinkling of the nose, raising of the upper lip, and a gape. There is some evidence that the facial expression of disgust differs somewhat as a function of different elicitors. There is also some evidence that there is an increase in the fundamental frequency of speech associated with disgust and that there are some basic characteristic modes of verbal expression (e.g., "yuck" in English).

Qualia, the mental or feeling component of emotion, may be at once the most central component of disgust and the most difficult to study. The qualia of disgust is often described as revulsion. In comparison to other basic emotions, the experience of disgust appears to be rather short in duration.

Elicitors and Meanings of Disgust

Disgust elicitors cover an enormous range. For Americans and Japanese, the items that cause disgust can be ordered into nine basic categories: foods, body products, animals, sexual behaviors, contact with death or corpses, violations of the exterior envelope of the body (including gore and deformity), poor hygiene, interpersonal contamination (direct or indirect contact with unsavory human beings), and certain socio-moral offenses. Disgust is clearly about offensiveness and is a negative (withdrawal) emotion. But there are many kinds of negative events, such as pain, loss, and frustration, that are not disgusting. The challenge, therefore, is to understand the full range of disgust elicitors—their meaning, their development, their cultural evolution and cultural variation.

Disgust may have originated in animals as a response to distasteful food; the gape response and nausea protected mammals from ingesting potentially dangerous foods. In cultural evolution, the output side of disgust (expression, physiology, behavior) remained relatively constant, but the range of elicitors expanded dramatically, coming under cultural control. In this expansion, the original elicitor of the disgust program (i.e., distaste) ceased to function as an elicitor of disgust, or at least failed to share some of the offensiveness and contamination features of the newer elicitors of disgust. By the process of preadaptation in cultural evolution (the use of a mechanism evolved in one system for a novel use in another system), the elicitor category gradually expanded as the offense/disgust system was harnessed to a wider and wider range of entities that a given culture considered negative and to be avoided. The guardian of the mouth became a guardian of the soul.

Core Disgust

Disgust has been described as one of four categories of food rejection, the others being distaste (motivated by negative sensory properties), danger (motivated by fear of harm to body), and inappropriateness (motivated by cultural classifications that label an item as not edible). Disgust is differentiated from distaste and danger in that the basis for disgust rejection is ideational (i.e., based on knowledge of the nature or origin of the elicitor), as opposed to the sensory basis for distaste and the fear basis for danger. Disgust differs from the category of inappropriateness (which involves items such as paper, marigolds, and sand) in that while both are ideational rejections, potential foods classified as disgusting are thought to be offensive and contaminating.

Core disgust has three components: a sense of oral incorporation (and hence a link with food or eating), a sense of offensiveness, and contamination potency. The mouth is the principal route of entry into the body for material things, and hence it can be thought of as the gateway to the body. Since putting external things into the body can be thought of as a highly personal and risky act, the special emotion associated with ingestion is understandable. The threat of oral incorporation is framed by a widespread belief that one takes on the properties of the food one eats ("You are what you eat"); there is evidence for an implicit belief of this sort even among educated Westerners.

Body products are quintessential elicitors of core disgust. There is widespread historical and cultural evidence for aversion to virtually all body products, including feces, vomit, urine, and blood (especially menstrual blood). More generally, almost all elicitors of core disgust have to do with animals, their body parts as well as their body products. In most cultures, only a few of the whole range of potential animal foods are not considered to be disgusting.

The contamination response (e.g., the rejection of a potential food if it even briefly comes in contact with a disgusting entity) appears to be powerful and universal among adults—it as a defining feature of disgust. This is an instance of the sympathetic magical law of contagion, which essentially holds that "once in contact, always in contact."

Animal Nature Disgust

The prototypical odor of disgust is the odor of decay, which is, of course, the odor of death. This centrality of death in disgust suggests a more general construal of disgust within a modified psychoanalytic framework. Where Sigmund Freud (1905) saw disgust as a defense against culturally unacceptable sexual urges, it is perhaps better understood as a defense against a universal fear of death. Ernest Becker (1973) has argued that the most important threat to the psyche is neither sexuality nor aggression—it is the certainty of death. Humans are the only organisms that know they are destined to die, so only humans need to repress this threat. In this framework, disgust helps to suppress thoughts or experiences that suggest human mortality.

These speculations about death lead naturally to an overarching description of disgust elicitors: Anything that reminds people that they are animals elicits disgust. Humans must eat, excrete, and have sex, just like other animals. However, each culture prescribes the proper way to perform these actions—by, for example, placing most animals off limits as potential foods and by placing all animals and most people off limits as potential sexual partners. People who ignore these prescriptions are reviled as being disgusting and animal-like. Furthermore, humans are like other animals in that they have fragile body envelopes that when breached reveal blood and soft viscera. These envelope violations (along with death) are disgusting because they are uncomfortable reminders of humans' animal vulnerability. Hygienic rules govern the proper use and maintenance of the human body, and the failure to meet these cultural standards places a person below the level of humans.

Interpersonal and Moral Disgust

Direct or indirect contact with other people can elicit disgust. There is a widespread reluctance to make contact with possessions, clothing, cars, and rooms used by strangers or undesirable people. Such items carry with them a sense of contamination. This form of disgust clearly discourages contact with other humans who are not intimates and can serve the purpose of maintaining social distinctiveness and social hierarchies. In Hindu India, interpersonal contagion, mediated in part by contacts with food, is a major feature of society and a major basis for the maintenance of the caste system.

In many languages, the word for disgust is often applied to a variety of immoral acts that do not involve the body and its products or physical defects. Disgusting moral violations show not just the property of offensiveness but also the property of contamination. Indirect contact with people who have committed moral offenses (such as murders) is highly aversive. What could possibly unite all morally disgusting actions into a single disgust domain is that they reveal a lack of normal human social motivation. People who betray friends or family or who kill in cold blood are seen as inhuman and revolting; criminal acts with "normal" human motivations, such as robbing banks, are seen as immoral but not disgusting. This sociomoral disgust may represent a more abstract set of concerns about being human, focusing not so much on the human body but on the soul. The most terrifying monsters in many Hollywood horror films look human on the outside yet lack a human soul within.

Like anger and contempt, disgust can be a moral reaction to other people, implying that their actions or character have violated certain norms. These three emotions compose a triad of related emotions that express moral condemnation toward others (in contrast to the three self-directed moral emotions: shame, embarrassment, and guilt). Richard Shweder and his colleagues (1997)) identify three types of moral codes that occur in cultures around the world: the ethics of community, the ethics of autonomy, and the ethics of divinity. The ethics of community focuses on issues of duty, hierarchy, and the proper fulfillment of one's social roles. Violation of this code seems to map on to the emotion of contempt. The ethics of autonomy encompass issues of rights and justice. This is the most fully elaborated code in Western societies; violations of this code are associated with anger. The ethics of divinity focus on the self as a spiritual entity and seek to protect that entity from acts of degradation or pollution. Violation of this code can result in disgust, making it the emotion that guards the sanctity of the soul as well as the purity of the body. Miller (1997) has provided an excellent general perspective on social and moral aspects of disgust, within a Western historical framework.

Development of Disgust

Distaste is the only one of the four basic food rejection mechanisms that is present in newborns. In parallel with the results from rats and other animals, human newborns show an innate rejection of bitter substances, accompanied by a gape. In North American children, disgust becomes distinct from distaste at some later point, perhaps between four and eight years of age. There seems to be no sense of offensiveness or rejection outside of the sensory realm in either infants or nonhumans, and there appear to be no gape elicitors other than bad tastes. Disgust seems to require cultural transmission—a supposition confirmed by the absence of disgust in feral (i.e., "uncivilized") humans.

Ursula Le Guin, in her utopian story "The Ones Who Walk Away From Omelas" (1973), creates a beautiful world with healthy, caring citizens who are at peace. However, the perfect nature of the world depends on a filthy child sitting in its own feces. Young people who are taken to see the child feel disgust, anger, and outrage that this child must suffer misery in order for everyone else to be happy. Those who cannot overcome their disgust are the ones who walk away from the utopia.

There does not seem to be an innate rejection of feces or other body products in nonhuman animals or human infants even though feces and the odor of decay are strong elicitors of disgust for adults. In fact, children do not seem to have an aversion to feces until they have gone through the toilet training process. It appears that toilet training, with all of the attendant negative affect from significant others toward feces, plays an important role in the development of disgust. Following toilet training and the rejection of feces, there is a spread of rejection responses, but little is known about the mechanisms and events that account for this spread.

The idea of contamination is quite sophisticated because it requires a separation of appearance and reality—there need be no sensory residue in a contaminated entity; it is the history of contact that is critical. This separation of appearance and reality is a cognitive achievement that may be a major barrier to a full childhood acquisition of disgust. Contamination responses to disgusting entities do not appear in children until they are four to seven years of age.

Presumably, parental reactions to disgusting things play a central role in the development of disgust. Since individuals vary markedly in their disgust sensitivity, one might expect that parental disgust sensitivity would be transmitted to their children. In fact, significant positive correlations have been found between the disgust sensitivity of parents and the disgust sensitivity of their college-age children.

Individual Differences in Disgust Sensitivity

A thirty-two-item Disgust Scale has been constructed to measure individual differences in disgust sensitivity for the seven domains of core and animal nature disgust. Research with this scale, in the United States and Japan, has found that disgust sensitivity seems to be higher for people of lower socioeconomic status, for females, and for people who are low in sensation seeking.

Disgust is involved in some types of animal phobias, and presumably in obsessive compulsive disorder. Cleaning obsessions and compulsions, the most common symptoms, have an obvious relation to contamination. However, checking, the second most common symptom, has no obvious relation to disgust. Research indicates that people with obsessive-compulsive disorder (primarily checkers) show a severe deficit in the recognition of disgust faces.

Disgust and Cultural Variation

Although most research on disgust has focused on the English-speaking minority of the world, it appears that cultural differences, rather than being related to the output side of disgust, are related primarily to elicitor/meaning elements (the input) of the disgust system. In other words, cultures vary less in how they express or experience disgust and more in what elicits disgust. For example, most cultures value a special sort of decayed/fermented food (e.g., cheese for Europeans, meat for Inuit, fish in fermented fish sauce for Southeast Asians). However, each of these "desirable" exceptions would be viewed as "disgusting" by other cultures. The act of kissing, which involves an intimate exchange of body fluid, varies from being disgusting in all cases in some cultures to being highly desirable with certain intimates in other cultures. Similarly, cultures differ about whether dogs are best friends or dirty scavengers and about whether or not a corpse should be touched during mourning. In spite of these differences in elicitors, it appears that core and animal nature disgust are expressed in a similar manner across cultures.

It is primarily in the last two steps of the expansion of disgust—interpersonal and moral disgust—that cultural differences seem to become more important. Liberal Westerners, particularly those of higher socioeconomic status, often try to de-moralize the emotion of disgust, preferring instead to base their moral evaluations on judgments of rights and justice. Among most other Westerners, however, actions that are considered to be disgusting (e.g., violations of sexual norms) are likely to be seen as moral violations. In Hindu India, with its elaborate moral ethic of divinity, purity and pollution issues play a central role in morality. Hence, interpersonal and moral disgust, especially in relation to contact with lower castes, are more salient in India than in the West.

Disgust in Relation to Other Emotions

Fear and disgust share a behavioral component: withdrawal based on a threat. Anger and socio-moral disgust share the appraisal of moral condemnation and the common facial gesture of raised upper lip. Contempt and disgust share the appraisal that someone (or something) is base and inferior. Shame has been described as disgust turned inward, a judgment that the self is disgusting. Students of emotion have often puzzled over identifying an emotion that is opposite to disgust, a quest encouraged by attempts to draw emotion "circles" to represent graphically these kinds of overlap. Based on the analysis that disgust is about rejecting things that are negatively contaminating, love would appear to be the opposite of disgust. Love involves acceptance, the elimination of boundaries and barriers, and (sometimes) positive contamination.

See also: ANGER; CULTURE; DARWIN, CHARLES ROBERT; EMBARRASSMENT; FEAR AND PHOBIAS; FOOD AND EATING; FREUD, SIGMUND; GUILT; HORROR; SHAME; UNIVERSALITY OF EMOTIONAL EXPRESSION

Bibliography

Angyal, Andras. (1941). "Disgust and Related Aversions." *Journal of Abnormal and Social Psychology* 36:393–412.

Becker, Ernest. (1973). *The Denial of Death.* New York: Free Press.

Darwin, Charles R. ([1872] 1965). *The Expression of the Emotions in Man and Animals.* Chicago: University of Chicago Press.

Douglas, Mary. (1966). *Purity and Danger.* London: Routledge & Kegan Paul.

Ekman, Paul. (1992). "An Argument for Basic Emotions." *Cognition and Emotion* 6:169–200.

Ekman, Paul., and Friesen, Wallace V. (1975). *Unmasking the Face.* Englewood Cliffs, NJ: Prentice-Hall.

Freud, Sigmund. ([1905] 1953). "Three Essays on the Theory of Sexuality." In *The Standard Edition of the Complete Psychological Works of Sigmund Freud, Vol. 7,* ed James Strachey. London: Hogarth Press.

Haidt, Jonathan; Koller, Silvia H.; and Dias, Maria G. (1993). "Affect, Culture, and Morality." *Journal of Personality and Social Psychology* 65:613–628.

Haidt, Jonathan; McCauley, Clark R.; and Rozin, Paul. (1994). "A Scale to Measure Disgust Sensitivity." *Personality and Individual Differences* 16:701–713.

Haidt, Jonathan; Rozin, Paul; McCauley, Clark R.; and Imada, Sumio. (1997). "Body, Psyche and Culture." *Psychology and Developing Societies* 1:107–131.

Izard, Carroll F.. (1971). *The Face of Emotion.* New York: Appleton-Century-Crofts.

Izard, Carroll E. (1977). *Human Emotions.* New York: Plenum.

Miller, William I. (1997). *The Anatomy of Disgust.* Cambridge, MA: Harvard University Press.

Rozin, Paul, and Fallon, April E. (1987). "A Perspective on Disgust." *Psychological Review* 94(1):23–41.

Rozin, Paul; Haidt, Jonathan; and McCauley, Clark R. (1993). "Disgust." In *Handbook of Emotions,* ed. Michael Lewis and Jeannette Haviland. New York: Guilford.

Rozin, Paul, and Nemeroff, Carol J. (1990). "The Laws of Sympathetic Magic: A Psychological Analysis of Similarity and Contagion." In *Cultural Psychology: Essays on Comparative Human Development,* ed. James Stigler, Gilbert Herdt, and Richard A. Shweder. Cambridge, Eng.: Cambridge University Press.

Scherer, Klaus R., and Wallbott, Harald G. (1994). "Evidence for Universality and Cultural Variation of Differential Emotion Response Patterning." *Journal of Personality and Social Psychology* 66:310–328.

Shweder, Richard A.; Much, Nancy C.; Mahapatra, Manamohan, and Park, Lawrence. (1997). "The 'Big Three' of Morality (Autonomy, Community, Divinity), and the 'Big Three' Explanations of Suffering." In *Morality and Health,* ed. Allan M. Brandt and Paul Rozin. New York: Routledge.

Tomkins, Silvan S. (1963). *Affect, Imagery, Consciousness, Vol. 2: The Negative Affects.* New York: Springer.

Paul Rozin
Jonathan Haidt
Clark R. McCauley

DISORDERS

See Anxiety Disorders; Culture-Bound Syndromes; Fear and Phobias; Mood Disorders; Post-Traumatic Stress Disorder; Seasonal Affective Disorder

DISPLAY

See Body Movement, Gesture, and Display; Emotion Experience and Expression; Facial Expression; Universality of Emotional Expression

DRAMA AND THEATER

There are several modes of dramatic experience: improvisation, theater, ritual, drama therapy, educational drama, and theater for children. Drama, in all of its forms, is capable of evoking a deep response from its participants, both actors and audience. It allows people to experience emotions while being removed and distanced from them. In the process, people are helped to better understand themselves and their dramatic experiences. Ken Robinson (1980) states that teachers, students, directors, and actors use the same medium of drama, allowing the term *theater* to refer to the occasion of presenting a performance to an audience. Theater, with its rehearsals, costumes, and history, allows people to transform their emotional responses, from the simple to the heroic, into a form of artistic expression. Drama, on the other hand, is a medium in which people participate as players around an event, entering the activity as though it were real, yet fully engaged in the "here and now."

Drama is a vehicle for the creation, re-creation, or representation of states of emotion. During a theater experience, members of the audience may be familiar with the emotion portrayed; at other times, the performance may constitute their first recognized experience with that emotion. While emotions in a drama are not "firsthand" experiences but emotions growing from drama, their representation can teach people how emotions are reflected in behaviors, in relationships with others, and in dealings with the world at large. However, emotion represents only one aspect of the activity that takes place among players and audience members; in practice and theory, it should be incorporated within an overall understanding of the dramatic act.

As a general rule, the satisfaction both performers and audience members experience during and after a performance relates directly to how the dramatic action matches each individual's emotional needs and experiences. Richard Courtney (1989, p. 125) maintains that emotion serves many purposes in dramatic action:

- to let off steam (catharsis)
- to work as the unconscious subtext of waking life
- to activate a response through actions or expression
- to adjust inner conflicts through dramatization (to "act out" emotional difficulties)
- to improve mental health and emotional balance
- to transform perceptions of the world so that people can work with them
- to bring about an affective-cognitive synthesis
- to unify imagination, knowledge, and feeling into a new species of knowledge through dramatic expression
- to work for hemispherical balance through drama activities
- to promote and control externalized associations
- to "try out" possible futures through drama
- to allow "a sufficient level" of emotion in a particular context for adequate motivation
- to promote adjustments to contexts, including adaptation to the dramatic situation
- to change how people look at things.

For a member of an audience watching a theatrical performance, emotions can be triggered in powerful ways because strong performances from the theater stay with the viewer as powerful life icons. For players in improvisation, feelings can be activated to much the same degree since they experience the tensions in the dramatic moment. Any performance exists on two levels. On the aesthetic level, the performer takes what is known and imagined and re-plays it inside the performance, and in this sense, cognition is re-synthesized. On the theater level, the actors gain reflective knowledge as they both perform and witness their own performances, which equips the actors with another kind of knowledge, a secondary emotion created through the act form of theater. Drama transcends barriers of time, because people can experience emotions in real (the actor) and imagined (the role) events simultaneously. Theatrical art, viewed as an aesthetic object, oscillates between the subjectivities of the creator and the perceivers. The stage can endow even the most mundane event with a power it otherwise lacks. Theater provides a range of meanings that are full of feeling, and its knowledge is as culture bound as language.

Drama can cause a range of emotions: trust in fellow actors or in the actors who are viewed; empathy for others in a range of situations, only some of which may be familiar; trust in the situation since the performance, in a sense, allows the audience members to experience emotions at the same time that it shelters them from the emotions; fulfillment in creating and viewing drama; and the confidence that comes from creating a drama experience.

Richard Schechner and Mary Schuman (1976) examine the relationship between ritual and theater:

- in ritual, all are performers; in theater, some are audience
- ritual is a form of drama that is related to the aesthetic
- the efficacy of performance to changes in life relates to the appreciation of performance for entertainment and critical ends
- the transformation of performers into a different state (as with initiation rites) relates to the transformation of performers into the fictional world of theater.

Gavin Bolton (1984) feels that the arts are deliberately created second-order experiences that are removed from the "rawness of living," where the substance of the playing is an abstraction. Lev Vygotsky (1933, p. 549) characterizes the emotional quality of the drama as having a dual affect: "the child weeps in play as a patient, but revels as a player." Vygotsky states that the crying is not on the same level as that of a child weeping in real life; however, the child— the player—can feel the emotion as intensely or even more intensely because the child knows that this is a "second-order" experience and can therefore feel it on both levels, secure in the knowledge that it is a game. This is not to say that the pain of the drama is not real, but that emotion allows people to create a new reality. The balance between drama and reality is a delicate one, as Johan Huizinga (1955, p. 30) points out: "[As] soon as the rules are transgressed the whole play-world collapses. The game is over. The umpire's whistle breaks the spell and sets real life going again." Conversely, when players have difficulty differentiating between reality and fiction, they run the risk of experiencing the emotion "first-hand."

Emotions occur in response to actual events, but they can also occur when people imagine events. These imagined events, then, become, to some degree, real, through the emotional responses that are generated because of them. Dramatic actions can trap people into believing that they are in actual events. Drama and make-believe play, unlike other second-order experiences, can look like real events because of the concreteness of the medium. Geoff Gillham

(1979) raises the question of why young children are not generally confused by the two. He feels that the child freely enters the make-believe world secure in the signals received from the real world that it continues to exist. According to Gillham, then, people can only believe in drama when they are secure in their belief of what constitutes the real world.

Bolton states that the logical relationship between "emotion occurring" and "emotion described" has been of central interest to both aestheticians and drama theorists. For example, Susanne Langer (1975, p. 90), in writing on aesthetics, asserts that emotion expressed through art is derived from, but is not the same as, that felt in real life: "[What] the creative form expresses is the nature of feelings conceived, imaginatively realized, and rendered by a labor of formulation and abstractive vision."

No emotional experience—dramatic or direct—can be ranked higher or lower than another, but the behavior that is experienced in each form differs. In the dramatic experience, people consider the emotion to be an object, since it has been created for or by them. This concept allows people to experience the emotion while they are, in a sense, cut off from it, simultaneously experiencing and reflecting on the dramatic action.

The Emotional State of the Actor

After William Shakespeare's time, as societies prospered, the performance of the actors reflected their audience's experiences and expectations. This eventually led to the almost total lack of individuality and emotional truth expressed by actors in the nineteenth century, where artistic expression was frowned upon. Instead, roles were clearly defined, and actors were expected to conform precisely to those roles. A particular style of acting made famous by the eighteenth-century English actor David Garrick focused on an accomplished technique by which "natural expressions of real life became distilled on stage by artifice," not by emotion. Denis Diderot (1773) admired Garrick's work and considered that the key to acting lay in its repeatability and that it was the actor's art to find the conventional signs of theater. As Richard Sennett (1974, p. 112) said, "A feeling can be conveyed more than once when a person, having ceased to suffer it, and now at a distance studying it, comes to define its essential form." A lack of imprint on the role on the part of the actor was not only expected, it was praised. Courtney (1995) cites the case of the American actor Mark Smith, who was praised in 1869 for his "most unexceptional Brabantio." Contrary to what one may think, these attitudes tended to hold sway for decades, and one need only look at the proliferation and rigid-

ity of actors' manuals that were produced through the mid-twentieth century for proof. Mainstream theater did little to change this for the actor; fare for large venue theaters centered on safe dramas that appealed to a wide range of audiences and did not examine emotional events. Rather, the focus was placed on the drama's spectacle appeal—music, dancing, and other visual effects. The return of theater that reached its actors and audience on an emotional level was due in large part to the Russian director Konstantin Stanislavsky. Born in 1863, Stanislavsky adopted a psychological approach to acting that centered on actors bringing personal experiences to their roles and drawing on past life to help define those roles. His approach to acting was introduced to America in 1925 when, after a visit to New York, two members of the Moscow Art Theatre decided to stay in the United States to teach Stanislavsky's system, a system completely opposed to what had been celebrated only years before. Stanislavsky believed in the importance of natural expression and saw the actor's feelings as being the cornerstones of performance. His philosophy eventually led to the "method" acting espoused by Lee Stras-

Konstantin Stanislavsky was the director and general stage manager of the Moscow Art Theatre players when they toured the United States in the 1920s. (Corbis/Bettmann)

berg's New York Actor's Studio. Today, many actors train in this same studio, using much of Stanislavsky's original philosophy.

The reasons why Stanislavsky's method took such a firm hold on America may be due in part to a pendulum effect that can occur in reaction to an extreme stance—the unnatural performances required of actors—and the limited range of theatrical experiences. In addition, the introduction of his techniques coincided with a time in history when people began to accept the new science of psychology. With the advent of Sigmund Freud, the unconscious took on a new meaning; no longer could one accept that observation of actions was all one needed to determine a person's motivation. Now, an understanding of thoughts and feelings—conscious or unconscious—was needed in order to truly know the reasons for one's actions.

Such a way of looking at the world fit perfectly with Stanislavsky's way of working. Actors now found themselves at "the center of the stage." They needed to draw on personal thoughts, understandings, and emotions in order to discover what the part required. The actor's stamp on a role was once again acceptable. In fact, an actor's effectiveness in Stanislavsky's model relied on personal understanding of the character in relation to the drama and the character's motivations and personality given a particular time and place, as well as the actor's ability to draw on life's emotional experiences that related to the portrayal of the character. The flavor of the experience and the emotions it evoked in the actor's past had to be similar to that of the character. Courtney (1995) states that the theory behind emotional memory (a disputed element of Stanislavsky's system) is that any actor (or any human, for that matter) has a reservoir of innumerable experiences, emotional moods, and psychological states at his or her disposal, which can be drawn on to increase the actor's perfection of a role.

In this scenario, the director also assumed a new role. Under Stanislavsky's approach, the responsibility of the director was to ensure that the actor was exploring areas that reflected his or her portrayal of the role. The director, in this model, was not there to direct, necessarily, but to shape aspects of the actor's explorations, subtly helping the actor to tap into related emotional experiences. If the actor found this to be an impossible task, the director could then help the actor to imagine a set of experiences that would arouse the same emotions as that required in the role.

In this way, Stanislavsky brought to the fore a technique—improvisation—that had been largely lost since the time of commedia dell'arte, allowing the actors to tap into a range of emotions, some having been experienced in the "real world" and some simply imagined. Improvisation is now practiced by almost all drama practitioners, from those in educational settings through professional drama coaches. The technique is effective in helping to explore all aspects of a drama, from its chronology of events through characters' relationships.

Stanislavsky and his system allowed actors to explore their emotions in order to portray the characters from a grounded, emotional base. This marked a radical departure from past expectations of fulfilling a role according to rigid expectations where actors had little input into the shaping of their performance. Stanislavsky had actors and directors focus on real life and on the feelings, events, and interrelationships that shape human existence, and hence, affect the portrayals of characters in a drama. Stanislavsky, in a sense, freed actors and directors to engage in self-exploration that eventually filtered through the actor's performance. The one cautionary note is that method acting, with its focus on an individual's experiences, can easily be modified to include exploration that has no place within a drama. Actors and directors alike need to keep in mind that the emotional exploration an actor engages in must focus on the character and relate directly to what the actor will portray on stage. Stanislavsky was aware of the dangers of actors focusing on personal emotions as opposed to that of the character and thus stated that their concentration should be centered on the "mainspring of action" in the character's behavior, not on personal feelings. That said, it can be difficult for actors to work in this method since the exploration of their own feelings and emotional memories are what allows them to bring a fullness to a character on stage

Forms of Behavior

Alan Tormey (1971) says that there is a double valence to behavior. Expressive behavior suggests a state of emotional arousal, while representational behavior "detaches the surface of emotional [behavior]" and does not involve arousal. Expressive behavior, according to Tormey, points toward some state of emotional arousal in the person at the same time that it points toward an intentional object, something outside the person to which the state of arousal is related. This object can be thought of as the "content" of the emotional arousal since it is the person's relationship with an object or context that shapes emotions and gives them a particular definition. Any emotion—anger, sadness, joy—does not exist on its own; rather, it exists in relation to an object or context. Tormey's definition of expressive behavior does not differentiate between types of behavior (voluntary, involuntary) since in all behaviors there is an element of the behavior that remains elusive—only the person experiencing the emotion truly knows or feels the emotion in its entirety.

Conversely, all emotions are clear in representational behavior. As an example of representational behavior, Tormey uses an actor who rages on stage as King Lear but who could not possibly be expressing his own rage or he would never complete the performance. Diderot (1773, p. 14) writes, "If the actor were full, really full, of feeling, how could he play the same part twice running with the same spirit and success! Full of fire at the first performance, he would be worn out and as cold as marble at the third."

According to Tormey, actors communicate to the audience the emotions of the character and not the actor's personal emotions. The behavior of the actor, then, cannot be considered expressive since the audience is viewing only the character's emotions. Tormey does not confine this assumption to drama, instead stating that all art forms, whether they be visual or auditory or both, are not expressive. The meaning of each art form is realized through the finished product. The skills of the artists are rated by their ability to represent feelings, emotions, and events. If the artist were to express feelings through art, some emotions would need to be hidden from the viewer and thereby lessen the effect of the endeavor.

Charles Marowitz (1978), a director who works in the Stanislavskian tradition, refers to acting as "An Act of Being." According to Marowitz, an actor can become emotionally engaged during a performance. Since it is a performance, however, the actor will only be able to approximate the character's emotions. The actor is one who, by definition, remembers:

> On the simplest level, someone who remembers his lines, his cues, his moves, his notes, to do up his flybuttons, to tie his shoe-laces, to carry his props, to enter, to exit. Simple things, complex things. An actor is someone who remembers.
>
> On another level, an actor is someone who remembers what it felt like to be spurned, to be proud, to be angry, to be tender—all the manifestations of emotion he experienced as a child, as an adolescent, in early manhood and maturity. An actor remembers the "feel" of all the feelings he ever felt or ever sensed in others. He remembers what happened to other people through all periods of recorded time—through what he has read and been taught. In tracing the lineaments of his own sensibility, he has the key to understanding everyone else.
>
> On a deeper level, an actor is someone who remembers the primitive primordial impulses that inhabited his body before he was "civilized and educated." He remembers what it feels like to experience intense hunger and profound thirst, irrational loathing and sublime contentment. He recalls the earliest sensations of light and heat, the invasion of infernal forces and the coming of celestial light. He remembers the anguish of disapproval and the comforting security of guardians. He remembers vividly (not necessarily articulately) what it feels like to be isolated, to be partnered, to be set adrift, to be reclaimed.

He remembers that miasmic stretch of time before becoming aware of the details of his own identity. He remembers the world before it became his world and himself before he became his self. To be without memory and to be an actor is inconceivable. An actor is someone who remembers [pp. 26–27].

Stanislavsky's theory, however, demands much of actors. The "Art of the Actor" entails that they must translate subjective meanings in a form that is understood by the audience at a deep level of feeling, thereby holding nothing back from their performance. It is in this way that it can be said that Stanislavsky viewed theater as representational art. Michael Goldman (1975) suggests that what is in vogue in acting relates, in some degree, to what is deemed proper regarding an actor sharing private feelings with an audience.

Role relationships that are explored in drama differ from those that are experienced in reality, since the latter are spontaneous while the former are planned experiences designed to evoke their real-life counterparts; they are what Stanislavsky referred to as "imaginative and artistic fiction." The emotions actors portray in a drama are presented as though they are real, but they are created. Both the performers and the audience recognize this, but they believe in what they are creating and what they are watching because what is presented on stage represents a form of truth. Everyone, actor and audience alike, must believe in the drama on stage for it to be effective.

Educational Drama

Participants in educational drama must balance the need for personal expression with the need for finding a way to communicate with others who are taking part in the drama. The more complex the mode of communication, the closer the participant is to reaching the performance mode within drama. The most extreme form of educational drama would be self-centered dramatic play.

Students who are improvising exist in a constant state of tension as they represent an experience while they take part in the experience and are affected by the other members involved in the drama. Bolton (1984) says that teachers need to be very sensitive to the emotional demands that they make on students. Encouraging emotional responses requires a careful grading of structures so that self-esteem, personal dignity, personal defenses, and group security are never compromised. "Some subjects are painful, sensational, controversial, or just a bit too exciting. To open up the central issue that arouses the pain, sensationalism, or the controversy is not necessarily the best way of protecting children into emotion. Indeed, with some topics if the teacher does not handle them indirectly, the class will hastily protect themselves by opting out" (p. 125).

A response at this depth of feeling is not, of course, the prerogative of drama; all of the arts are capable of touching people deeply. But drama happens to be one of the arts in which the response is shared by members of a group, as it is in dancing and music-making. When the actors set out to "represent" to an audience, they are using dramatic art in its theater form; when the participants have no audience and no sense of rehearsing for an audience, they are sharing their creation with each other. Both can be art of the highest kind because drama is both a performance and a communal art.

Theater for Children

In a performance that is designed for children—their needs, their experiences, their expectations—the emotions that the experience gives rise to can be deeply felt by them. When a child is entranced with a performance, the emotional experience may have several motivations. Often, when one member of an audience becomes involved in a drama, others will follow suit. When all children experience the same emotion, the tendency is for the group to experience the emotion at a heightened level. On other occasions, all children will become involved because they identify with one or more characters. For children whose concept of self is not as defined as that of adults, the ability to identify and connect with a character is of great importance in a drama.

It can be extremely difficult to gauge a child's emotions as related to a drama performance. Many children will describe the circumstances in which they felt the emotion rather than the emotion itself. The performance, however, can affect their emotional life. Children will see the emotions arising from a drama as being both real and fictitious, and the degree to which they see this will, naturally, vary from child to child.

For children, a performance must balance the "work" required of the spectator with his or her needs. In the case of children's theater, it should include situations in which there are no serious consequences for the audience—the tensions should cause some small anxiety over which each child has control. As a guide, the tensions should be consistent with what

A 1996 theater performance for children in Lafayette, Louisiana, features the characters from Maurice Sendak's popular children's book Where the Wild Things Are. *(Corbis/Philip Gould)*

children experience in games, where they can frighten themselves and then laugh about their fears.

A child's reaction to drama is tempered by experience, needs, and emotions. When children do not know how to react to a drama, they may "overreact." What the child needs, but which may be unavailable at the time, is an emotional means of responding. Reasons for "overreacting" may vary. The situation the drama presents to the child may be new, unusual, or sudden. The younger the children, the more they feel emotions because many situations are new. As such situations are repeated, the emotions become less sharp. Unusual or sudden situations, such as a loud noise or sudden darkness, can also threaten children because there is no response that they can call on to assist in dealing with the incident. Maturation can lessen these fears, but it can also create others since the child is increasingly able to anticipate risks and situations. When a performance does not meet a child's needs, she or he can become frustrated. As in other instances of frustration, the child may make comments to a character, withdraw from the situation, or become interested in something else, such as other children in the audience.

Another cause of excessive emotion may occur when children perform drama. Often, what a child can do privately or spontaneously can become stilted and difficult when performed in front of others. For this reason, public performance followed by critical judgment, should be handled sensitively.

Drama and Therapy

Drama therapy can be effective when someone has lost control of the emotional self, such as when an adolescent "acts out," raging against authority figures, friends, and self. Efforts to have the participant talk about feelings are often counterproductive. It is for this reason that drama can serve as a vehicle of communication. When the participants are encouraged to express themselves in their own language in a safe environment with a trained drama therapist, they can experience a wide range of emotions while being secure in the knowledge that they are "acting out" their emotions. Drama, then, becomes their therapy, and the participant has the opportunity to come to grips with his or her feelings.

Drama therapy centers on the interplay and balance between expression and containment. As participants become practiced and engaged in drama therapy, they increase control of their feelings, often to the point where they can relinquish them. As a facilitator, one must constantly be on guard for the point when one or more of the participants will move beyond what he or she can safely handle. The dynamics of the group, and the material its members explore, should never exceed this point. When it does, the facilitator needs to help the individual and/or the group practice distancing and containment. Without intervention, the participants can become overwhelmed by the emotion, resulting in acting out, disassociation, or a delayed reaction. The nature of the intervention can vary. In extreme cases, it can take the form of disbanding the performance. In others, the facilitator can ask the participant to view a situation from his or her current age (effective when an adolescent explores an incident that occurred at an earlier age), ask the participant to leave the stage to role play phoning a friend to talk about the incident, switch roles with a group member, or identify his or her feelings and then have others in the group role play these feelings.

While drama therapy can help participants control and manage their emotions, it can also serve as a creative outlet. When adolescents shape the output of their emotions, they begin to see themselves as actors as well as reactors, as able individuals who have the valuable insights necessary to make sound decisions regarding the editing, refining, and production stages of their work. Such self-knowledge does not disappear when the creative work is finished. Instead, the participants may learn that they call on these abilities when necessary. In addition, the opportunity to make their experiences concrete can help the participants to understand and assimilate the experience in their lives, and others can visibly see and appreciate their experiences.

Jacob Moreno (1964) can be considered to be the founder of psychodrama. His belief centers on the concept that every person—every self—is a composition of roles played. Perhaps at adolescence, more so than at any other point, people need to experiment with roles in order to develop a sense of self, integrating past roles with roles they may wish to adopt in the future. For some adolescents, however, role experimentation can be frightening, perhaps because of a lack of parental support or other causes of inner turmoil. In these cases, many adolescents want an identity that will help them to deal with the instability in their lives. There are two potentially dangerous pathways these adolescents can follow: extremism and over constriction. In the first instance, the adolescent forms an attachment to a group or identity that will serve as a total break from his or her past. In the latter, the adolescent assumes the role of an adult.

Drama therapy can be a valuable experience for adolescents, allowing them to try on roles without risk. In fact, they are encouraged to experiment with roles—to discard them, to alter them, to adopt them for a time. As they improvise, participants come to see that they do not have to fully adopt the role or make a permanent change in how they act—the point is to experiment and manipulate roles that interest them, that haunt them, that impress them. They will not become "stuck" in roles, and the facilitator is there to ensure that they are able to move forward when necessary.

Most drama therapy sessions begin with adolescents exploring fictional, social roles that have some resonance for them. The fact that the roles are fictional provides the participants with the distance they need, at least initially. The fact that they are familiar allows the participants to recognize themselves and others in the action. As their confidence grows, participants can role play figures of importance before finally playing family members and themselves in situations. In this way, their role playing will deepen, allowing them to resolve earlier issues in their life and to assume roles at a level that allows them to experience what it would be like in real life. A final benefit of drama therapy is that it can allow participants to merge how they see themselves with how others see them.

Conclusion

Drama transcends any attempts to reduce it to a single definable emotional meaning. It can have meaning on many levels for individual audience members or for participants in the drama experience. Each individual has a different experience, on both the emotional and intellectual planes. Communication takes place, but in the end, the participant should emerge having had an emotional, poetic, and intellectual experience of an intensity and significance that is as great, perhaps even greater, than one of the pivotal, decisive experiences of "real life." That is what Antonin Artaud (1938) meant when he dreamed of a theater that would shake its audience to the very core of their personality. Drama can enhance people's existence and play a valuable part in enriching their world, extending the scope of their experience and their understanding of the human condition.

Such is, of course, the ultimate achievement of all art—the point at which an aesthetic experience can approach the intensity of a religious experience. But drama, especially those forms of it that are witnessed by an audience or where an individual experience is enhanced by sharing it with others, is particularly able to produce experiences of overwhelming intensity and profundity for its actors and audience members. It is for this reason that drama and ritual are related—why drama experiences are a part of ritual and ritual is a part of a drama.

See also: DANCE; LITERATURE; MUSIC; ORATORY

Bibliography

Alter, Jean. (1990). *A Socio-Semiotic Theory of Theater.* Philadelphia, PA: University of Philadelphia Press.

Artaud, Antonin. ([1938] 1981). *The Theater and Its Double,* tr. Victor Corti. London: Calder.

Bennett, Susan. (1990). *Theater Audiences: A Theory of Production and Reception.* London: Routledge.

Bolton, Gavin. (1979). *Towards a Theory of Drama in Education.* London: Longman.

Bolton, Gavin. (1984). *Drama as Education: An Argument for Placing Drama at the Centre of the Curriculum.* Essex, Eng.: Longman.

Bolton, Gavin. (1992). *New Perspectives on Classroom Drama.* Herts, Eng.: Simon & Schuster.

Booth, David, and Martin-Smith, Alistair, eds. (1988). *Re-Cognizing Richard Courtney: Selected Writings on Drama and Education.* Markham, Canada: Pembroke.

Burgess, Roma, and Gaudry, Pamela. (1985). *Time for Drama: A Handbook for Secondary Teachers.* Melbourne: Longman.

Cohen, Robert, and Harrop, John. (1974). *Creative Play Direction.* Englewood Cliffs, NJ: Prentice-Hall.

Courtney, Richard. (1980). *The Dramatic Curriculum.* New York: Drama Book Specialists.

Courtney, Richard. (1989). *Play, Drama, and Thought: The Intellectual Background to Dramatic Education,* 3rd ed. Toronto: Simon and Pierre.

Courtney, Richard. (1995). *Drama and Feeling: An Aesthetic Theory.* Montreal: McGill-Queen's University Press.

Davis, Desmond. (1981). *Theater for Young People.* Don Mills, Canada: Musson.

Davis, Ken. (1988). *Rehearsing the Audience: Ways to Develop Student Perceptions of Theater.* Urbana, IL: ERIC Clearinghouse on Reading and Communication Skills.

Diderot, Denis. ([1773] 1957). *The Paradox of Acting.* New York: Hill and Wang.

Esslin, Martin. (1978). *An Anatomy of Drama.* London: Abacus.

Esslin, Martin. (1987). *The Field of Drama: How the Signs of Drama Create Meaning on Stage and Screen.* London: Methuen.

Fleming, Michael. (1995). *Starting Drama Teaching.* London: David Fulton.

Gillham, Geoff. (1979). "What's Happening when Children Are Doing Drama in Depth?" *Schooling and Culture,* Issue 4, Spring, pp. 32–39.

Goldman, Michael. (1975). *The Actor's Freedom: Toward a Theory of Drama.* New York: Viking Press.

Heilpern, John. (1977). *Conference of the Birds: The Story of Peter Brook in Africa.* Harmondsworth, Eng.: Penguin.

Hornbrook, David. (1991). *Education in Drama: Casting the Dramatic Curriculum.* London: Falmer.

Huizinga, Johan. (1955). *Homo Ludens.* Boston: Beacon Press.

Jennings, Sue, ed. (1995). *Dramatherapy with Children and Adolescents.* London: Routledge.

Langer, Susanne. (1975). *Mind: An Essay on Human Feeling, Vol. 1.* Baltimore, MD: Johns Hopkins Paperback.

Marowitz, Charles. (1978). *The Act of Being.* London: Secker & Warburg.

Moreno, Jacob. (1964). *Psychodrama.* New York: Beacon House.

O'Toole, John. (1992). *The Process of Drama: Negotiating Art and Meaning.* London: Routledge.

Robinson, Ken. (1980). *Exploring Theater and Education.* London: Heinemann.

Schechner, Richard, and Schuman, Mary. (1976). *Ritual, Play, and Performance: Readings in the Social Sciences/Theater.* New York: Seabury Press.

Schmitt, Natalie Crohn. (1990). *Actors and Onlookers: Theater and Twentieth-Century Scientific Views of Nature.* Evanston, IL: Northwestern University Press.

Sennett, Richard. (1977). *The Fall of Public Man.* New York: Knopf.

Stanislavsky, Konstantin. (1936). *An Actor Prepares.* New York: Theatre Arts Books.

Tormey, Alan. (1971). *The Concept of Expression.* Princeton, NJ: Princeton University Press.

Vygotsky, Lev. ([1933] 1976). "Play and Its Role in the Mental Development of the Child." In *Play: Its Role in Development and Evolution,* ed. Jerome S. Bruner, Alison Jolly, and Kathy Sylva. London: Penguin.

Way, Brian. (1967). *Development through Drama.* Atlantic Highlands, NJ: Humanities Press.

David Booth

E

EATING

See Food and Eating

ECSTASY

See Happiness; Hope; Pleasure; Satisfaction

EDUCATION AND TEACHING

Anyone who has ever been a student can testify to the array of emotions associated with schooling. Everyone, regardless of their overall academic capability, can remember feelings of elation connected with completing a difficult assignment or scoring well on an important test. On the other hand, almost no one escapes, even occasionally, feelings of apprehension on approaching a difficult test or bewilderment when listening to an incomprehensible lecture. During childhood and adolescence, the changing array of emotional experiences that provide the color and texture of human experience are largely played out in classrooms and on school campuses. This is so, in part, because during the school years students spend many of their waking hours at school, where classmates and teachers may be seen as much as or more than parents and siblings. School is simply a central component of child and adolescent life. Equally important, it is during these years that students develop broad feelings of self-worth and personal competencies, as well as narrower ideas about their ability to perform certain

tasks, such as mathematics or spelling. Biological maturation and personality development also converge so that students confront important social and developmental tasks—initial separation from parents, establishment of relationship with peers, development of attachment to non-family adults (teachers)—and each of these is apt to produce many varied human emotions.

Schools and Stress

Each child's school-related emotional experiences depend on the social environment and school culture where he or she is taught. How schools operate and what they emphasize depends on the even wider-reaching concerns of society. During the 1980s and 1990s, the United States underwent a series of educational reforms designed to improve its students' academic skills. These reforms arose because of concern that students were failing to acquire the necessary thinking and academic skills that are necessary for life in a highly complex, information-rich world. Various researchers have suggested that these reforms promote academic competence at the expense of students' emotional well-being. A particularly negative consequence may be competition among students for grades. In competitive academic environments, all but the most able students are apt to experience much failure and, consequently, negative emotions. Ultimately, so much frustration and discouragement may build up that students chose no longer to compete. Indeed, there has been an increase in the high school drop out rate in the United States during the last few years after declines during most of the century. Further, as today's students may already experience elevated levels of stress related to poverty, violence, drugs, sexuality, and compromised family functioning, further pressure to outperform classmates may represent an additional, sometimes overwhelming, stressor. Susan Forman and Patricia O'Malley (1984) have reported that as many as 30 percent of school-age children experience stress-related reactions. These reactions may be characterized by feelings of guilt, frequent or excessive crying, sleep problems, depression, anxiety, anger, bodily complaints (e.g., headaches or lack of stamina), concentration problems, social isolation, blunted emotions, suicidal thinking or planning, and a tendency to overreact emotionally. There is debate about whether schools should be involved in emotional and life satisfactions concerns or whether they should confine themselves to more traditional academic and cognitive domains. However, alternative societal values and competing notions about schools' roles in fulfilling them will prevent an immediate, conclusive resolution to the debate.

Thoughts about Performance Influence Emotions

To better understand emotional expression and student motivation, many researchers have become interested in students' thinking styles, particularly thoughts associated with routine school successes and failures. When success or failure occurs, attribution researchers are interested in locating factors to which students attribute these events. This area of investigation shows that interactions with parents and teachers can influence students' thinking about their own chances of success and failure and the emotions expressed when they encounter events. It also provides teachers with a rich framework for encouraging effective thinking styles.

As they explain their own behavior and that of those around them, students and teachers rely on differing reconstructions. Attribution theory researchers have found that some learners consistently believe that they control events, whereas other learners consistently interpret events in the world as being beyond their immediate control. When students fail or succeed at school, these beliefs may determine which emotions they experience. For example, one student who has just excelled on a math test may attribute the success to factors that are internal and under direct control ("I studied hard and have good math aptitude"). This student would likely feel pride in the accomplishment because it demonstrates the possession of good qualities and shows that events can be influenced if the student chooses to exert effort. The student is likely

to retain high levels of motivation for future work in math. In contrast, another student's success may be ascribed to external factors that are beyond control ("I was lucky that the teacher gave an easy test"). This student would feel little positive emotion and would presumably be less self-satisfied and pleased than the student who attributed the success to internal factors and believes in the personal ability to control events. Both students experienced the same objective event, but they differ on their attributions about it, their subjective emotional experiences, and their motivation for subsequent learning.

Differing attributions may also follow failure. One student may ascribe failure to lack of ability ("I'm dumb"), which reflects a belief in internal characteristics that cannot be controlled by the student. Such attributions in the face of failure are likely to lead to negative emotions, including shame and discouragement. A student who explains personal behavior in this manner is also likely to be unmotivated, as the prospects of future success is viewed as being dim. Another student, however, may attribute exactly the same school failure to lack of preparation ("I should have worked harder on the term paper"). Attributing failure to controllable factors may save this student from severe feelings of discouragement. Moreover, it may promote future motivation to study harder.

A focus on attributions is particularly important because a certain amount of success and failure at school is inevitable. To maintain positive emotions and motivation, students need to learn to make salutary attributions. Carol Dweck, Ying-yi Hong, and Chi-yue Chiu (1993) have found that generally it appears most beneficial to emphasize to students that they can control their own success by hard work while discouraging them from blaming external factors or inherent lack of ability for failures. To do so consistently may produce students who take pride in their work, feel positive emotions, and seek additional learning opportunities when they are successful while suffering only moderate discouragement that can be overcome with hard work when they fail.

Knowledge of how attribution styles influence emotions and motivation may help guide teachers, although at times attribution theory may suggest actions that seem counterintuitive or even emotionally cold. Consider two courses of teacher action when a student fails a test. One course is to respond sympathetically by indicating to the student that the material was too difficult ("I think I gave you work that was too hard"). Although this may mitigate against the student's experience of negative emotions in the short term, it may encourage counterproductive student attributions in the long term. Such statements may be interpreted by the student to reflect the teacher's underlying belief in the student's lack of ability. As mentioned before, attributions about limited ability are particularly destructive to emotional well-being and motivation to learn. An alternative course of action is for the teacher to withhold expressions of sympathy and to express disappointment in the student's substandard performance, even if the student then feels embarrassment, frustration, or shame over not working hard enough. Teacher disappointment may carry the implicit message that the student is capable of better performance (i.e., personal ability) but that failure was due to lack of effort (i.e., a controllable factor). At times, teachers may chose to provide explicit statements of disappointment. Students' feelings of embarrassment and frustration, though subjectively unpleasant, may increase their motivation to succeed.

Family and cultural factors, not just teachers, seem to influence the attributions that students make. For example, minority students as a group have been shown to believe that external factors, such as luck, influence success; this may contribute to lower overall levels of performance. However, James Coleman and his colleagues (1966) have shown that when members of minority groups believe events are under their control, their overall levels of performance match or exceed those of non-minority students. It is important for teachers to avoid stereotypes about students that assume lack of ability and instead seek to encourage students of all groups to control events in their own lives.

Self-Efficacy As a Goal of Education

Research by Albert Bandura has shown that students who have high perceived "self-efficacy" (i.e., students who make high appraisals of their own skills, expect that they will succeed academically, and look forward to challenges) do well in a variety of educational situations and tend to maintain a positive emotional outlook even in the face of difficult tasks. Freed of self-doubt and troubling anxiety that may hamper others, these students can seek the kinds of difficult and inherently interesting educational experiences that carry the greatest potential for producing feelings of self-satisfaction. Because these learners also tend to be comfortable in interpersonal situations, they may work effectively with other students and openly seek information and support from teachers. Barry Zimmerman (1989) points out that their degree of confidence in their own skills enables them to take risks, to withstand failure and frustration, and to state what they need from other people without fear of being criticized or rebuked.

It is believed that several factors contribute to feelings of self-efficacy. First, prior experiences with success often contribute. Students who have done well in the past expect to do well in the future. Therefore, many teacher training programs advocate providing all students with experiences where they may be perceived as being successful. This may mean that some students complete some tasks whereas other students complete alternative ones, that different scoring standards are used, or that teachers develop ways to highlight unique learner skills. David Johnson and Roger Johnson (1985) have suggested diminishing competitive grading practices and using techniques that let each student demonstrate his or her own unique competency. Lev Vygotsky (1978) has found that satisfaction associated with task completion seems to be especially powerful if students accomplish tasks that are neither too difficult nor too easy—tasks that are just beyond their range of comfort. Thus, teachers must also be prepared to select tasks carefully according to each student's current performance level. Second, confidence expressed by others seems to matter. Teachers who express pleasure in past accomplishments and are optimistic about the prospects for future accomplishments seem to aid feelings of self-efficacy. School experiences that foster close, unconditionally supportive, nurturing student-teacher relationships would seem to contribute to these outcomes. In addition, Teresa Jacobsen and Volker Hofmann (1997) have found that students who have close attachments to parents and are confident in those attachments are more attentive in the classroom and achieve higher grades. Third, it may be beneficial to provide students with opportunities to observe successful peers, especially those perceived to be similar to themselves. Students who have positive role models (models with common ethnic, cultural, gender, and age characteristics) may develop personal feelings of confidence. They may also attempt to attain levels of achievement that might otherwise be avoided. Each of these considerations implies that schools must be vigilant concerning the emotional needs of students and be prepared to invest resources and personnel sufficient to foster positive learning experiences.

Emotional Traits May Help Guide Teachers

Not all students need or benefit from the same type of school experiences. Even as preschoolers, individual students possess different ways of responding to the world around them. Parents are able to report reliably that some preschoolers, for example, are outgoing, happy, and emotionally placid, while others report that their children are withdrawn, irritable, and emotionally intense. These long-standing characteristics or predispositions may be part of the child's biological make-up, a result of child-rearing practices, or

A teacher at the Kennedy Institute in Baltimore, Maryland, works with a student in a one-on-one situation to help him increase his academic performance and foster greater feelings of self-efficacy. (Corbis/Richard T. Nowitz)

a combination of both factors. Regardless of their origins, individual differences in temperament or underlying personality traits are evident early in life, are more or less stable, and generally become more obvious as individuals mature. Without attempting to alter the child's underlying basic emotional character, educators may, by recognizing these individual differences, select learning activities that maximize educational progress.

Consider students who differ on the trait of anxiety. Researchers are able to distinguish between students with high levels of anxiety and those with low levels by using questionnaires that inquire about tendencies to worry, to be upset by minor events, or to feel subjectively nervous. N. L. Gage and David Berliner (1992) have reported that when these two groups are compared, the high anxiety group, as a whole, does worse on tasks that are timed, described as difficult, or filled with challenge. It is widely recognized that mood states may affect the degree to which information can be processed efficiently. When pressure is removed, on the other hand, such as by eliminating time requirements, the high anxiety group tends to perform as well or better than their low anxiety classmates. In very challenging situations, the demanding nature of tasks appears to jeopardize seriously the students who have high levels of anxiety. The grade point averages of high anxiety students, for example, are generally substantially below the grade point averages of low anxiety

students who have comparable scholastic aptitude. It is presumed that the intense demands and pressure to compete produce these differences in grades and that if adjustments and accommodations to individuals' differences occurred that the two groups would produce more similar results. Steps such as adding structure, reducing the pace at which lecture material is introduced, and allowing tests that are not timed have been advocated as ways of diminishing differences and allowing students with high levels of anxiety to succeed.

Children with depressive characteristics are common in school. Carroll Izard and Gail Schwartz (1986) report that such children tend to make negative self-evaluations, have a low tolerance for frustration, give up easily, hold pessimistic views of events, and express little enjoyment during normally pleasant activities. These students may report subjective feelings of sadness and may isolate themselves socially or behave in ways that alienate themselves from others. As a group, children with depressive characteristics also perform more poorly academically than control groups of non-depressed children and adolescents.

Teacher actions may benefit students with these types of depressive characteristics. Such children are likely to attribute success and failure to external factors that are beyond their control. Even worse, they may be particularly apt to assign these explanations only when they are successful ("I got a good score on my history test—I must have guessed well"), while assigning more stable and internal explanations for failure ("I failed my English test because I'm stupid"). Furthermore, such students are likely to be particularly aware of failure and retain strong impressions of those events but overlook or quickly forget success experiences. Cumulatively, this manner of thinking produces feelings of discouragement, diminished self-worth, pessimism, and what has been described by Lyn Abramson, Gerald Metalsky, and Lauren Alloy (1989) as a "hopeless and helpless" attitude. Effort for school work is often hard to muster as students in this situation tend to believe that what they do has little bearing on their prospect of success. Teachers may view these students as being lazy or intellectually dull. These teacher attributions are, of course, not helpful because they explain student failure using internal, stable factors that do not lend themselves to helping the student.

Teachers who recognize individual emotional differences seem to be prepared to aid students with depressive tendencies. Encouraging attributions that identify effort and study skills (events that are controllable by the student) in evaluating both success and failure may be used. To disrupt the failure-negative expectation cycle, some teachers reduce assignment difficulty to a level where student success is guaranteed. After a period of success (which permits unaccustomed positive feedback to the student), the difficulty of assignments can be slowly increased. Furthermore, to counteract inadequate intrinsic motivation that often accompanies depressive feelings, teachers may use temporary systems of extrinsic reward to permit prompt and obvious positive feedback and to motivate work completion. They may also structure school days to discourage inactivity and isolation, as solitude may provide a chance for unhappy and discouraged students from reflecting obsessively on their negative feelings. Finally, teaching social interaction skills (e.g., how to start and maintain a conversation) may help diminish the social isolation experienced by many children and adolescents who have depressive feelings. Enhanced social contact may ultimately contribute to improved mood.

Alternative Services

Controversy exists regarding how to treat students with extreme emotional problems that preclude educational success. Many educators and psychologists contend that all children's emotional needs should be addressed in the general education curriculum through regular classroom settings. Proponents of the general education approach cite concerns about labeling and stigmatizing children with emotion problems. They suggest that to remove students with severe problems from their "normal" classmates deprives them of essential opportunities to observe peers who model acceptable behavior. They also note that there is little justification for identifying learners with severe emotional problems—research has yet to demonstrate conclusively that specialized education placement, as compared to continuation in a general education environment, helps such students.

Others disagree with the general education approach and insist that it is most productive and humane to identify students with severe emotional problems and treat them with specialized services. It is argued that formal diagnosis of students with severe emotional disorders permits educators to understand the cause of student behavior better (rather than inaccurately attributing behavior to a unhelpful cause such as "laziness" or "defiance"); allows educators and other involved professionals, such as physicians and psychologists, to formulate a plan based on scientific knowledge of mental disorders; enables teachers with specialized training and reduced students loads to aid the students; and provides otherwise unavailable legal guarantees and protections of students' rights.

The last two points argued by the opponents of general education are directly related to special education laws that exist in the United States. Since 1975, mandatory special education services have existed for all school children. The laws, which encompass, in one form or another, those from birth to twenty-one years of age, spell out explicitly the types of handicaps that warrant special educational services, the rules for identification, and a set of rights and protections for affected students. Among the categories of "disabilities" that are outlined is "serious emotional disturbance"; other disabilities include learning disability, mental retardation, and visual impairment. Public school districts throughout the United States are obligated to identify students who suffer from serious emotional disturbance. According to the Individuals with Disabilities Education Act (1991), the term *serious emotional disturbance* refers to a condition exhibiting one or more of the following characteristics over a long period of time and to a marked degree that adversely affects a child's educational performance:

1. an inability to learn which cannot be explained by intellectual, sensory, or health factors,
2. an inability to build or maintain satisfactory interpersonal relationships with peers and teachers,
3. inappropriate types of behavior or feelings under normal circumstances,
4. a general pervasive mood of unhappiness or depression,

5. a tendency to develop physical symptoms or fears associated with personal or school problems.

The term includes schizophrenia, but it does not apply to children who are socially maladjusted (unless it is determined that they have a serious emotional disturbance).

The phrase "socially maladjusted" in this definition has been widely debated. At one time, it was argued to mean that children with conduct and delinquent behaviors were ineligible for special education services, but more recent interpretations have reasoned that this provision neither includes nor excludes students with these types of acting out behaviors. The five itemized characteristics (i.e., the descriptors) have been criticized as being imprecise, and there is great debate among school psychologists, who are often involved in diagnosis, about what exactly is being outlined by each of the descriptors. Some diagnosticians believe that descriptor 4 is an attempt to portray symptoms of depression, whereas descriptor 5 is an attempt to portray symptoms of anxiety. Since these disorders (i.e., depression and anxiety) have been comprehensively defined in the American Psychiatric Association's *Diagnostic and Statistical Manual of Mental Disorders* (1994), some diagnosticians use that source rather than the federal definition's limited descriptors to diagnose children who are eligible for serious emotional disturbance services. In addition to the problems over the imprecise characteristics, confusion exists about how to establish whether the disorder is extreme and if it has had a sufficiently lengthy history. Educators and psychologists also encounter uncertainty about how to establish whether the student has sustained adverse educational effect because of the emotional problems. Taken together, these factors impede an easy and assured diagnosis of serious emotional disturbance. This may be one reason why relatively few students have received these services. Although Beth Doll (1996) reports that 18 percent to 22 percent of all students may at one point in their educational career suffer from a diagnosable emotional disorder, the U.S. Office of Education (1995) reports that during a given school year only 1 percent of all students receive services related to serious emotional disturbance.

For students with serious emotional problems, a formal diagnosis may have certain benefits. Students who are deemed eligible must first go through a detailed evaluation that may illuminate the nature and degree of their emotional problem and outline their needs to address it—a list of rights and entitlements follows. These students are to be afforded a "free, appropriate public education," the provisions of which are outlined in a document called an "individualized education program." The precise elements of the individualized education program depend on each student's needs, but examples include individual tutoring, participation in a separate specialized classroom or school, and revised methods of instruction or testing designed to match emotional needs. Some eligible students may receive individual or group counseling at school as part of their related services. The intensity of services can be modified according to student needs as each school's obligation is to meet needs rather than to channel students into preexisting programs. Furthermore, the law guarantees that clearly stated annual goals must be established and progress toward them must be monitored. Parents are also afforded rights with regard to planning, period progress reviews, and confidentiality of records. Debate about benefits and disadvantages of identifying students with serious emotional disturbance is likely to continue.

See also: ANXIETY; ATTRIBUTION; CREATIVITY; HUMAN DEVELOPMENT; MOTIVATION

Bibliography

Abramson, Lyn Y.; Metalsky, Gerald I.; and Alloy, Lauren B. (1989). "Hopelessness Depression: A Theory-Based Subtype of Depression." *Psychological Review* 96:358–372.

American Psychiatric Association. (1994). *Diagnostic and Statistical Manual of Mental Disorder,* 4th ed. Washington, DC: American Psychiatric Association.

Bandura, Albert. (1974). "Behavior Theory and Models of Man." *American Psychologist* 29:859–869.

Bandura, Albert. (1986). *Social Foundations of Thought and Action: A Social Cognitive Theory.* Englewood Cliffs, NJ: Prentice-Hall.

Coleman, James S.; Campbell, Ernest Q.; Hobson, Carol J.; McPartland, James; Mood, Alexander M.; Weinfeld, Frederic D.; and York, Robert L. (1966). *Equality of Educational Opportunity.* Washington, DC: Government Printing Office.

Doll, Beth. (1996). "Prevalence of Psychiatric Disorders in Children and Youth: An Agenda for Advocacy by School Psychology." *School Psychology Quarterly* 11:20–47.

Dweck, Carol S.; Hong, Ying-yi; and Chiu, Chi-yue. (1993). "Implicit Theories: Individual Differences in Likelihood and Meaning of Dispositional Inferences." *Personality and Social Psychology Bulletin* 19:644–656.

Forman, Susan G., and O'Malley, Patricia. (1984). "School Stress and Anxiety Interventions." *School Psychology Review* 13:162–170.

Gage, N. L., and Berliner, David C. (1992). *Educational Psychology,* 5th ed. Boston: Houghton Mifflin.

Izard, Carroll, and Schwartz, Gail M. (1986). "Patterns of Emotion in Depression: Developmental and Clinical Perspectives." In *Depression in Young Children,* ed. Michael Rutter, Carroll E. Izard, and Peter B. Read. New York: Guilford.

Jacobsen, Teresa, and Hofmann, Volker. (1997). "Children's Attachment Representations: Longitudinal Relations to School Behavior and Academic Competency in Middle Childhood and Adolescence." *Developmental Psychology* 33:703–710.

Johnson, David W., and Johnson, Roger. (1985). "Classroom Conflict: Controversy over Debate in Learning Groups." *American Journal of Educational Research* 22:237–256.

Spielberger, Charles D. (1966). "The Effects of Anxiety on Complex Learning and Academic Achievement." In *Anxiety and Behavior*, ed. Charles D. Spielberger. New York: Academic Press.

United States Office of Education. (1995). *Seventeenth Annual Report to Congress on the Implementation of the Individuals with Disabilities Education Act.* Washington, DC: United States Office of Education.

Vygotsky, Lev S. (1978). *Mind in Society: The Development of Higher Psychological Processes.* Cambridge: Massachusetts Institute of Technology Press.

Zimmerman, Barry J. (1989). "Models of Self-Regulated Learning and Academic Achievement." In *Self-Regulated Learning and Academic Achievement*, ed. Barry J. Zimmerman and Dales H. Schunk. New York: Springer-Verlag.

David L. Wodrich
Glenn D. Reeder

EMBARRASSMENT

"I was at my senior prom and had too much to drink. As I was dancing, I got a little out of control and tripped, catching my slip on my heel. My slip came flying off, and I broke my heel. I ran into the bathroom crying—I was so embarrassed. Then I discovered I was in the men's room!" This description by a participant in research on embarrassment illustrates one of life's unpleasant experiences. The "dis-ease" of embarrassment is an undesirable emotion not bound by culture or ethnicity, age, or social status.

Embarrassment is a self-conscious emotion that may be understood as "a form of social anxiety." Most people would agree that feeling the anxiety of embarrassment typically occurs in the presence of another person (or thought of a person), when people are aware of being the center of attention, and when they feel judged or discredited. People like to feel in control, but when they lose the capacity to manage how others see them, embarrassment is one possible outcome. In a sense, people are motivated to appraise themselves as they communicate with others. Individuals feel embarrassed if they see themselves having a shortcoming, if they make some kind of social mistake, or if someone points out a problem. For example, when an acquaintance makes an unflattering comment about the suit a coworker is wearing, the attention and judgment by a colleague embarrasses this person. The comment compromises the way the coworker thinks he or she looks and attracts negative from colleagues. Hence, the coworker feels the emotion of embarrassment because he or she is being judged in a public arena, and is made the center of attention.

The most immediate response exhibited by people who are embarrassed is physiological. Based on research results, Rowland Miller (1995) advises that embarrassment may stimulate a unique set of physiological reactions. Physiologically, embarrassment is, according to Robert Edelmann (1987, p. 68), "characterized by blushing, rising in temperature, increased heart rate, muscle tension, grinning, smiling, or laughing, avoidance of eye contact and self-touching."

Physiological reactions to embarrassment appear to differ from related emotions such as shame and fear. For embarrassment, smiling is a nonverbal response, whereas smiling does not seem to be part of the repertoire for shame and fear. With embarrassment there tends to be more nervous touching of the body, including clothing, face, and hair. However, feelings of shame and fear do not result in as many gestures toward the self. In a sense, these physical reactions work as a communicative signal to alert others that something has gone wrong in the interaction. Some of these physiological differences, particularly between embarrassment and shame, may be explained by considering conceptual differences between these emotions. As opposed to embarrassment, shame may be considered a much more devastating experience that has the potential to impose a greater threat to the individual's sense of self. Embarrassment appears to depend more on an audience than does shame. Hence, shame results from not meeting some internal, private standard about the self, whereas embarrassment results from a public judgment based on social approval or appraisal in comparison to others.

Certain conditions may influence the extent to which a person feels embarrassment. In addition, some people are more or less susceptible to embarrassment. It is likely that things such as the need for social approval from others, fear of negative evaluation, being more self-conscious, or being introverted might influence levels of embarrassability. Besides these psychological tendencies, certain circumstances may prompt individuals to feel the emotional upheaval of embarrassment. For example, how intensely individuals feel embarrassed may depend on the number of people involved in the event, their status, and their relationship with others witnessing the event.

Sherwood Anderson, in "I Want to Know Why" (1921), describes an innocent fifteen-year-year-old boy who has a crush on a wonderful racehorse and on the horse's trainer. When the boy follows the trainer to a brothel, he is embarrassed and chagrined to discover that the man could look at a prostitute in the same way that he could look at the splendid, "pure" racehorse.

There is relatively little information on how people suffer embarrassment across cultures. However, Todd Imahori and William Cupach (1991) found that Japanese respondents typically report feelings of embarrassment when they make mistakes as compared to North Americans who typically report feelings of embarrassment when an accident occurs.

Although cultural issues are not yet fully understood, it is known that experiencing the emotion of embarrassment starts at a relatively young age. However, the very young (four years of age and younger) are less understanding of and susceptible to embarrassment. Embarrassment is somewhat more complex than other emotions such as happiness or sadness. As the definition of embarrassment shows, it requires an understanding of the part an audience plays in evaluating oneself. Feeling the emotion also depends on grasping when a person has failed to meet some standard (of one's own or another's), and there needs to be some type of emotional reaction. Children younger than eight years of age tend to have difficulty meeting these criteria. Between seven and eight years of age, children begin to comprehend this more elaborate set of factors necessary to experience the emotion of embarrassment. As children advance to adolescence, the occurrence of embarrassment steadily increases, with elevated activity during adolescent years. When individuals reach adulthood, embarrassment remains an emotion they periodically encounter.

Types of Embarrassment

There are two kinds of embarrassment: unintentional and strategic. Unintentional embarrassment takes place when there is an accident or mistake that results in negative self-appraisal in a social situation. Strategic embarrassment results from events provoked by other people.

When embarrassment is unintentional, the event inadvertently happens to a person and is outside his or her control. There are many cases of unintentional embarrassment. Predicaments such as spilling food during a meal, saying the wrong thing at the wrong time, having a stranger witness an extremely private moment, calling someone by the wrong name, and exhibiting general forgetfulness are but a few examples of the endless, commonly encountered examples.

Experiencing embarrassment when it is unintentional is definitely unpleasant. However, as Lisa Bradford and Sandra Petronio (1998) point out, strategic embarrassment, the emotion invoked by a situation that another person has purposefully created, may be more difficult to handle because developing strategies to make a person deliberately feel embarrassed may have positive as well as negative goals.

The fact that it was an unintentional event did not limit the public embarrassment that it caused President Gerald Ford when he slipped and fell as he was deplaning Air Force One *on June 1, 1975.* (Corbis/Wally McNamee)

The negative goals of strategic embarrassment may be more obvious. These are cases where individuals wish to jeopardize, discredit, compromise, or tarnish a person's image. The basis for public humiliation is in the desire to achieve a negative goal through embarrassment. Exposing failures, revealing secrets, and openly ridiculing embarrasses a person thereby achieving a negative outcome. Aggressively embarrassing someone else may be motivated by a desire for personal gain, or it may be motivated by a larger social objective. When people want to cause emotional discomfort for personal reasons, they may embarrass an individual so that they themselves look good by comparison. On a societal level, strategic embarrassment may be used for social control in a negative way. For example, if there is hope of political gain, one group may "leak" embarrassing information about the behavior of another group. The expectation is that the information revealed will result in controlling the other group's behavior. Sometimes the goals may not be all that clear until after the strategic embarrassment takes place. For example, relational partners may deliberately embarrass each other to reveal some hidden problem. Using a public forum, such as when friends are around, might make it easier to talk about personal problems within the relationship. Individuals might believe that friends would provide needed support. However, when the embarrassment involves breaching relational privacy and is used often, the relationship suffers. For example, one partner frequently revealing information about the couple's sexual life in front of friends or relatives causes embarrassment for the other partner, undercutting the stability and quality of the relationship.

Although there are many examples of strategically embarrassing someone for negative reasons, strategic embarrassment is also used to obtain positive goals. In many situations, embarrassment is used to show affection, to place people in the "limelight" for their achievements, or to help socialize others. These are motivated by admirable intentions even though the route is somewhat discomforting. For example, when friends give bridal or baby showers, one of the main features of these rituals is an element of embarrassment. Silly games such as making a hat for the bride out of a paper plate decorated with all of the ribbons from gifts are designed to embarrass the bride or mother-to-be. The bride is expected to sit through the shower with this embarrassing hat on her head. With the increasing occurrence of co-ed showers, men who have not traditionally been invited to these showers now become the focus of embarrassment as they attend. Initiations into clubs, celebrations of birthdays, recognition of achievements, and remembrance of special events all represent ways that the motivation for strategic embarrassment is positive. Parents often use strategic embarrassment to teach their children more appropriate ways of coping with the social world. By gently embarrassing children about their hairstyles, clothing, or manners, parents try to shape the children's behavior to fit the way parents believe they should act in a social arena. In elementary and secondary schools, children embarrass each other to become noticed, to influence their peers, to show their affection, or to communicate their expectations. Through strategic embarrassment, both the parents and peers help socialize children to perform appropriate or acceptable behaviors. Increasingly, strategic embarrassment is also being used as a means of social control in a larger societal setting. The groups initiating embarrassment may be motivated to achieve a positive outcome. Yet, sometimes the target groups may not initially see this goal as positive. Bradford and Petronio (1998) argue that when those people who are orchestrating the embarrassment help targets overcome their discomfort, a signal is sent alerting the embarrassed person that the intent is meant to be positive. Overall, strategic embarrassment appears to be a powerful tool to curb unwanted societal behavior. The move by judges and citizens across the United States to use public humiliation to force individuals to comply with social and legal expectations is evidence of strategic embarrassment. The goal is probably considered by the larger society to be positive, but the target of the embarrassment may not think it is positive. For example, as a condition of probation related to a charge of assault, a sixty-two-year-old farmer had a sign posted in his driveway by a judge stating, "Warning, A violent felon lives here. Travel at your own risk" (Hoffman, 1997). Deadbeat fathers find their names or their faces posted on billboards. "Johns" who are convicted of using prostitutes may find themselves on cable television. In California, the state attorney general's office set up booths with computer terminals listing the sixty-four thousand registered sex offenders.

Coping with Embarrassment

Whether the embarrassment is unintentional or strategically used by others, the person experiencing the emotional reaction is forced to cope with unpleasant feelings. In general, individuals either try to avoid embarrassment (where possible) or rectify the predicament by using face-saving strategies. The use of avoidance might be more likely if people are aware that a person is trying to embarrass them. When the embarrassment is unintentional, however, the individual may be less able to anticipate the precipitating event, which means that he or she will need to use face-saving strategies.

There are a number of face-saving strategies used in response to embarrassing predicaments. Apologies help save face for the embarrassed person by accepting responsibility for an inappropriate action. For example, an embarrassed person my say, "I am sorry for coming to your party so late." Accounts, typically either excuses or justifications may also redeem the embarrassed person. Excuses tend to deny responsibility for actions (e.g., "I fell asleep, I was so tired"). Justifications take responsibility for the action that lead to embarrassment but deny the disparaging outcome of the event (e.g., "I guess I deserved that"). In addition, humor may serve as a repair strategy, although it is not always appropriate. At best, humor may reduce the tension of the event or shifting the attention onto some other focal point. Sometimes humor can backfire. Rather than shift attention away from the embarrassed person, attempts at humor may exacerbate the situation. For example, joking about someone else's incompetence to relieve embarrassment may result in exposing hidden feelings about a coworker, thereby exaggerating feelings of embarrassment. Remediation, correcting the cause of the embarrassment (e.g., cleaning up the spilled coffee, picking oneself up quickly after a fall on the ice), is also a way to reduce emotional discomfort.

Of all the possible ways to relieve embarrassment, accounts tend to be used the least. The level of discomfort that the emotions of embarrassment evoke may make it difficult for people to reduce this arousal enough so that they can construct reliable accounts. When a people's ears are buzzing and they wish the whole situation would simple disappear, it is difficult to give a rational excuse for the event. For accounts to work, they demand control over emotions and physiology. Alternatively, avoidance is sometimes reported to be used with more frequency than accounts. In some research, avoidance is also defined as withdrawal or escape, which may explain why this is a valid choice for embarrassed people. Perhaps too, people may anticipate embarrassment more often and alleviate the effects by ignoring the event or retreating from the situation. Sometimes people use a simple description to overcome embarrassment (e.g., "Is today your birthday? I forgot"). At other times, however, they may become aggressive and verbally attack those witnessing the embarrassing event. Alone, these repair strategies lessen some of the embarrassment. However, William Cupach and Sandra Metts (1989) argue that most people use remedial strings that tie together several of these strategies to overcome embarrassment. For example, when people use an apology, they most frequently string several other repair strategies onto the initial face-saving attempt. Thus, Metts and Cupach found that apologies were at times followed by remediation or by description. In some situations, both description and remediation accompanied apologies. At other times, remediation, and escape followed apologies. In fact, 35 percent of all respondents reported combinations of two, three, or four strategies.

In an early gender study on strategies to reduce embarrassment, Petronio (1984) found that men and women differ in the way they reduce their emotional discomfort. For example, the men in the study tended to use more justifications to ease their feelings of embarrassment. When the men took control of the situation, they apologized to others present but verbally blamed something else for the event (e.g., "the stupid sidewalk"). However, the men also expected others to come to their aid. They wanted those involved to act as though nothing had happened; they even hoped that the others would change the topic of conversation. The men also saw withdrawal from the situation as a viable way to overcome these emotional situations. The women in the study tended to use more excuses than justifications. In other words, alleviating embarrassment meant shifting the responsibility to others.

> In "Everything That Rises Must Converge" (1971), Flannery O'Connor creates Julian, who is continually embarrassed by his mother's appearance and by the conventionally prejudiced behavior that she demonstrates toward African Americans. When Julian's mother realizes that a black woman is wearing the same hat that she is, Julian experiences such a vindictive pleasure at her discomfort that it takes him a while to realize that his mother is having a stroke.

For example, they thought that blaming the incident on others present helped them overcome feeling embarrassed (e.g., "Why did you make me do this?"). In addition, these women wanted others to make themselves the center of attention (e.g., "Well, you spilled your coffee too"). These findings only represent one study, and since other studies have not completely replicated the outcomes of this research, more information is needed to determine if men and women definitely differ in the basic way they experience embarrassment and relieve the emotional feelings.

When embarrassment occurs, those who witness the event often come to the aid of the embarrassed person. Thus, observers may attempt to save face for the embarrassed person using some of the same repair strategies as the person would use him- or herself. For example, humor is used with some frequency, as are accounts. Sometimes the actions of the observers increase the feelings of embarrassment a person feels, but at other times, observers provide support and empathy to help the embarrassed person overcome his or her humiliation. When individuals engage in "empathic embarrassment," they endure the emotional discomfort of embarrassment by imagining themselves in the same situation as the person who is embarrassed. Even if a person does not show signs of blushing or any other physical indicators, someone could recognize that the person is in an embarrassing predicament and respond with a certain degree of discomfort for the person. The empathic person feels these emotions for the other. Thus, if a teacher makes a disparaging remark about a student's performance in front of the class and the student does not exhibit signs of emotional discomfort, the empathic person may become embarrassed for the student. Empathic embarrassment also happens when the target of embarrassment does show emotional uneasiness. In these cases, the embarrassment becomes contagious, illustrating further the sense of dis-ease endured by all participants in an embarrassing situation.

However, giving support (empathic or otherwise) to someone may require overcoming one's own feelings of concern for potentially embarrassing situations. Not all people want assistance, and sometimes it is difficult to comprehend when help is desired. Consequently, individuals may feel embarrassed themselves to offer aid to others in an embarrassing situation. On the other hand, people often avoid asking for help because seeking help may make people feel compromised or indebted to others, which can be embarrassing in itself.

Conclusion

Although embarrassment is an uncomfortable emotion, it is important to understand how people experience it and cope with the aftermath. There are too many situations where embarrassment has the potential to do harm for people not to try to understand the way individuals cope in such situations. For example, embarrassment may interfere with important activities such as requesting the use of condoms prior to sexual activities, disclosing one's health status to partners, revealing secrets that have relational consequences, and talking frankly to physicians about medical concerns. Therefore, learning how to relieve the dis-ease of embarrassment may have long-term positive consequences in many facets of people's lives.

See also: ANXIETY; EMPATHY; GUILT; SELF-ESTEEM; SHAME; SHYNESS

Bibliography

Babcock, Mary, and Sabini, John. (1990). "On Differentiating Embarrassment from Shame." *European Journal of Social Psychology* 20:151–169.

Bradford, Lisa. (1993). "A Cross-Cultural Study of Strategic Embarrassment in Adolescent Socialization." Unpublished doctoral dissertation, Arizona State University, Tempe.

Bradford, Lisa, and Petronio, Sandra. (1998). "Strategic Embarrassment: The Culprit of Emotions." In *Handbook of Communication and Emotion: Research, Theory, Application, and Contexts,* ed. Peter A. Andersen and Laura K. Guerrero. San Diego, CA: Academic Press.

Braithwaite, Dawn O. (1995). "Ritualized Embarrassment at 'Co-Ed' Wedding and Baby Showers." *Communication Reports* 8:145–157.

Cupach, William, and Metts, Sandra. (1990). "Remedial Processes in Embarrassing Predicaments." In *Communication Yearbook, Vol. 13,* ed. James Anderson. Newbury Park, CA: Sage Publications.

Cupach, William, and Metts, Sandra. (1994). *Facework.* Thousand Oaks, CA: Sage Publications.

Edelmann, Robert J. (1987). *The Psychology of Embarrassment.* Chichester, Eng.: Wiley.

Fink, Edward L., and Walker, Barbara A. (1975). "Humorous Responses to Embarrassment." *Psychological Reports* 40:475–485.

Goffman, Erving. (1956). "Embarrassment and the Social Organization." *American Journal of Sociology* 70:1–15.

Gorov, Lynda. (1997). "LA Fair Has New Attraction: Information on Molesters." *Arizona Republic,* September 13, p. A6.

Greenberg, Martin S. (1980). "A Theory of Indebtedness." In *Social Exchange: Advances in Theory and Research,* ed. Kenneth Gergen, Martin S. Greenberg, and Richard H. Willis. New York: Wiley.

Griffin, Sharon. (1995). "A Cognitive-Developmental Analysis of Pride, Shame, and Embarrassment in Middle Childhood." In *Self-Conscious Emotions: The Psychology of Shame, Guilt, Embarrassment, and Pride,* ed. June Price Tangney and Kurt W. Fischer. New York: Guilford.

Gross, Edward. (1984). "Embarrassment in Public Life." *Society* 21:48–53.

Gross, Edward, and Stone, Gregory, P. (1964). "Embarrassment and the Analysis of Role Requirements." *American Journal of Sociology* 70:1–15.

Hoffman, Jan. (1997). "Public Humiliation is Punishment for '90s." *Arizona Republic,* January 19, p. A22.

Imahori, Todd, and Cupach, William R. (1991). "A Cross-Cultural Comparison of the Interpretation and Management of Face: American and Japanese Responses to Embarrassing Predicaments." Paper presented at the Conference on Communication in Japan and the United States. California State University, Fullerton.

Latane, Bibb, and Darley, John. (1970). *The Unresponsive Bystander: Why Doesn't He Help?* New York: Appleton-Century-Crofts.

Metts, Sandra, and Cupach, William. (1989). "Situational Influences on the Use of Remedial Strategies in Embarrassing Situations." *Communication Monographs* 56:151–162.

Miller, Rowland. (1987). "Empathic Embarrassment: Situational and Personal Determinants of Reactions to the Embarrassment of Another." *Journal of Personality and Social Psychology Bulletin* 18:190–198.

Miller, Rowland. (1995). "Embarrassment and Social Behavior." In *Self-Conscious Emotions: The Psychology of Shame, Guilt, Embarrassment, and Pride,* ed. June Price Tangney and Kurt W. Fischer. New York: Guilford.

Modigliani, Andre. (1968). "Embarrassment and Embarrassability." *Sociometry* 31:313–326.

Petronio, Sandra. (1984). "Communication Strategies to Reduce Embarrassment Differences between Men and Women." *Western Journal of Speech Communication* 48:28–38.

Petronio, Sandra. (1990). "The Use of a Communication Boundary Perspective to Contextualize Embarrassment Research." In *Communication Yearbook, Vol. 13,* ed. James Anderson. Newbury Park, CA: Sage Publications.

Petronio, Sandra; Olson, Clark; and Dollar, Natalie. (1989). "Privacy Issues in Relational Embarrassment: Impact on Relational Quality and Communication Satisfaction." *Communication Research Reports* 6:21–27.

Sattler, Jerome M. (1965). "A Theoretical, Developmental, and Clinical Investigation of Embarrassment." *Genetic Psychology Monographs* 71:19–59.

Schlenker, Barry R. (1980). *Impression Management: The Self-Concept, Social Identity, and Interpersonal Relations.* Monterey, CA: Brooks/Cole.

Scott, Marvin B., and Lyman, Stanford M. (1968). "Accounts." *American Sociological Review* 33:46–62.

Sharkey, William, and Stafford, Laura. (1990). "Responses to Embarrassment." *Human Communication Research* 17:315–342.

Tedeschi, James T. (1990). "Self-Presentation and Social Influence: An Interactionist Perspective." In *The Psychology of Tactical Communication,* ed. Michael J. Cody and Margaret L. McLaughlin. Clevedon, Eng.: Multilingual Matters.

Weinberg, Marvin S. (1968). "Embarrassment: Its Variable and Invariable Aspects." *Social Forces* 46:382–388.

Sandra Petronio

EMERSON, RALPH WALDO

b. Boston, Massachusetts, May 25, 1803; *d.* Concord, Massachusetts, April 27, 1882; *philosophy, theology, poetry.*

Ralph Waldo Emerson, or Waldo Emerson as he preferred to be called, was a major American philosopher, essayist, and poet of the nineteenth century. He could perhaps be considered to be the first "American" philosopher, a classification that rests on his rejection of the rational, rigid, scientific, tradition-bound approach that was characteristic of much of European philosophy and theology and his embrace of a more fluid, undefined form of thinking that was closer to poetry than to philosophy. His approach, which has been referred to as New England Transcendentalism, was developed by Emerson and his associates in Concord and Boston and stressed open inquiry, spirituality, nature, life experiences, and forces beyond complete human understanding. Emerson's approach to philosophy and New England Transcendentalism are viewed by some scholars to be uniquely American philosophical expressions since they reflect the core values of the expanding early nineteenth-century America, values that include individuality, liberty, opportunity, and reverence for nature. Emerson's ideas were set forth in numerous lectures, essays, and poems that were widely read during his life and remain a major contribution to the American literary tradition.

Emerson was one of six sons born to the Unitarian minister William Emerson and the former Ruth Haskins. Following his father's death in 1811, Emerson was raised by his aunt Mary Moody Emerson and studied at the Boston Public Latin School. He entered Harvard College in 1817 and began writing his journals, in which he set forth many of the ideas that were expanded upon in his later lectures and essays. After graduating in 1821, he taught at a girl's finishing school for four years while preparing for part-time study at the Harvard Divinity School. Due to illness and residence in the South to recuperate, his ordination to the Unitarian ministry at the Second Church in Boston (where his father had been minister) was delayed until 1829, when he began delivering Sunday sermons. An eloquent speaker and a kind person, he was well-liked by the parishioners. The same year, he married Ellen Louisa Tucker, whose death from tuberculosis eighteen months later caused Emerson such grief that he began to question his religious beliefs and the nature of Christian worship. In 1832, he ended the traditional practice of regularly administering the Eucharist and, despite his popularity, was forced to resign by the congregation. Still grieving the death of his wife, in poor health, and without employment, Emerson traveled to Italy and then England, where he meet and shared his ideas with several leading literary figures of the time, including William Wordsworth, Thomas Carlyle, and Samuel Coleridge. Emerson returned to America, evidently now at peace with himself and his ideas, and settled in Concord, Massachusetts, where he could enjoy the rural life— only a few hours by stage from Boston, the center of intellectual life in America. In 1835, he married Lydia Jackson and they had two sons and two daughters. In Concord, Emerson thrived. He farmed, took an active role in town affairs, assisted in the library, and socialized with other prominent citizens, such as Henry David Thoreau, William Ellery Channing, and Nathaniel Hawthorne. From this base in Concord, Emerson embarked on his successful career as a philosopher, essayist, lecturer, and poet.

Emerson published anonymously a ninety-five-page book entitled *Nature* in 1836, set forth a new model for American philosophy in a lecture at Harvard in 1837, criticized the rigid expression of religion in a lecture at Harvard Divinity School in 1838, and published his first collection of lectures as *Essays* in 1841. These lectures and writings became the basis for his future work and initiated New England Transcendentalism. By the end of the 1840s, Emerson had formed a Transcendentalist group that met regularly in his home. New England Transcendentalism was a reaction to and an attempt to correct the rational, scientific, reason-based philosophies of Europe. Emerson believed that humans are part of nature and that both shared a spiritual essence that is beyond full human understanding. Thus, he also believed that what could be truly known was knowable through the senses. His ideas about emotion focused mainly on religious expression. Having rejected what he saw as the rigid, cold, distant Unitarian Protestantism of Boston, he argued instead that believers must look into themselves to find God and, through having the courage to trust their own "inner feeling," to obtain the guidance that the God offers. Such a view of religious experience is commonly labeled spirituality, although its personal, experimental nature makes the concept difficult to define and describe. Although Emerson's ideas drew large audiences on the lecture circuit in the United States and in Europe in 1847, it was only later in life that he was accepted back into the Harvard-based in-

In an 1882 woodcut, Ralph Waldo Emerson addresses a large audience in Concord, Massachusetts, during a meeting of the Summer School of Philosophy. The school was set up by Emerson, Bronson Alcott, Henry David Thoreau, and other members of the Transcendentalist movement. (Corbis/Bettmann)

tellectual life of Boston. His early philosophical and religious crimes had not been forgiven, but they had been forgotten as American culture had changed and spirituality and emotional expression were more widely accepted. Although Emerson's views were shared by other Transcendental philosophers, it was his clear expression—in his lectures, essays, and poems—and breadth of vision that made him the leader of the movement and a lasting influence in American culture. In 1872, tragedy struck again—his home in Concord was partially consumed by fire. Although he and his wife escaped, Emerson never fully recovered from the trauma, and his intellectual work diminished. Emerson was a well-known public figure whose ideas lived on long after he died. In fact, his work was an important influence for many later intellectual leaders, including the psychologist William James, the educator John Dewey, and the social critic Louis Mumford.

See also: JAMES, WILLIAM; PHILOSOPHY

Bibliography

Atkinson, Brooks, ed. (1968). *The Selected Writings of Ralph Waldo Emerson.* New York: Random House.

Boller, Paul F., Jr. (1974). *American Transcendentalism, 1830–1860: An Intellectual Inquiry.* New York: Putnam.

Ben Manning

EMOTIONAL ABUSE

This entry consists of the following four subentries: Women; Children; Siblings; Men.

WOMEN

Emotional abuse of women generally is defined as (1) the use of verbal and nonverbal acts that symbolically hurt a woman or (2) the use of threats about causing physical harm. Verbal acts of emotional abuse include criticizing, making belittling remarks, screaming, and badgering. Nonverbal acts of emotional abuse include destroying personal belongings; emotionally or physically hurting a woman's family, friends, or pets; limiting access to resources such as money; and isolating a woman socially.

Although there is some agreement among experts that particular behaviors constitute emotional abuse, researchers and mental health professionals are not able to agree on a complete, specific, or exclusive definition of emotional abuse. Some proposed definitions focus on the forms of behaviors that constitute emotional abuse, such as humiliation and threats. Other definitions focus on the psychological effect of the behaviors, such as fear or anxiety. Still others focus on the function of the behaviors, such as control and coercion of the victim. Definitions of emotional abuse that focus on the emotional effect or the function of the abusive behaviors are especially limited because, by definition, the extent to which a behavior is abusive is determined by the recipient or victim. While defining emotional abuse of women is quite controversial among researchers, there are five major themes that characterize the behaviors that are included in the numerous definitions of emotional abuse: humiliation and degradation, threatened or actual emotional or physical control and terrorization, threatened or actual emotional or physical rejection/neglect, social isolation, and exploitation.

Regardless of the definition that is used, emotional abuse occurs in private and is not readily observable by outsiders such as researchers or clinicians. Further, what is perceived as abuse varies from person to person. For example, one woman being threatened by a husband or boyfriend may view the situation as a coercive act and label it as emotional abuse, while another woman in the same situation may be unaffected with regard to her feelings, thoughts, or behaviors and therefore not label it as emotional abuse.

Although differences in definitions and the subjective and private nature of the behaviors may prevent the experts from agreeing on what exactly constitutes emotional abuse, people in abusive situations do not appear to have difficulties in identifying it. Research suggests that partners in a relationship agree just as much in their reports of the rate of occurrence of emotional abuse as they do in their reports of other events in the relationship.

Prevalence of Emotional Abuse

Emotional abuse is quite frequent among married, cohabiting, and dating couples of all ages. Researchers estimate that approximately 50 to 80 percent of women report being emotionally abused by an intimate partner. Emotional abuse frequently co-occurs with physical abuse among teenage and adult women—95 to 97 percent of the women who are physically assaulted by an intimate partner are also emotionally abused. While approximately two-thirds of the men studied report being emotionally abusive to a partner but not physically aggressive, less than 1 percent of the men report physical abuse of a partner but

Celie, the main character in Alice Walker's The Color Purple (1982), suffers both physical and emotional abuse from her stepfather, her husband, and the culture around her. With no chance at an education, she is expected to cook and clean and care for children and wait on the men; Celie has no self-respect. After Shug teaches her how to stand up for herself and be independent, Celie goes into business for herself, making pants.

no emotional aggression. Thus, it seems that not only does emotional abuse accompany physical abuse, it is usually a precursor to it as well. Men often move from not abusing a partner, to emotionally abusing her, and then to physically abusing her as well. This progression from emotional abuse to physical abuse is more likely to occur among men who grow up in homes where their fathers physically abused their mothers. Accordingly, experts now see physical abuse as a developmental process in which emotional abuse necessarily occurs first.

Causes of Emotional Abuse

Although both men and women in intimate relationships are victims of their partners' emotional abuse, research on the consequences of abuse has been limited mainly to female victims because women appear to suffer more severe physical and psychological consequences. Further, women's greater social and economic dependence is believed to prevent them from escaping abusive relationships, thereby exposing them to more and more severe abuse over time. Attempts to uncover the causes of emotional abuse have focused on the sociocultural, intrapersonal, and interpersonal variables of the male perpetrators. First, emotional abusers are young, as rates of emotional abuse appear to be higher among young dating or cohabiting couples relative to older and married couples. Second, childhood exposure to family emotional and physical abuse, either as a victim or a witness, increases the probability that a man will emotionally abuse an intimate partner. Third, emotionally abusive individuals often face stressful events, have low levels of self-esteem and self-efficacy, and are unassertive with their partners. Fourth, abusive individuals have higher rates of alcohol and drug use and abuse. Fifth, emotionally abusive men are jealous, blame their partners for their own problems, are self-centered, need control, and anger easily.

Power and its distribution between intimate partners is often cited as a cause of emotional abuse. Relationship power refers to the ability to influence the behavior of one's partner and to persuade him or her to do what one wants. Two prominent theories of power as a cause of emotional abuse of women have emerged: feminist theory and resource theory. Feminist theorists focus on the social and political climate in which the abuse of women by men occurs. Specifically, feminist perspectives highlight Western society's patriarchal values and view men's abuse of women as attempts to enforce and maintain their social advantage over women. On the other hand, resource theorists suggest that relationship power is derived from the relative amount of available resources such as money, education, and communication skills. When the male lacks these or other resources, abuse is used to maintain and restore a sense of power in the relationship. But what seems to matter most is one's *perception* of power. The most significant predictor of abuse of women is men's dissatisfaction with the amount of power and control they have in relationships rather than the actual amount of control and power they possess. Accordingly, a man with very little power in the relationship will not abuse his partner if he is satisfied with what power he has. On the other hand, a man who has almost absolute power is at risk for abusing his partner if he desires even more control than he already has.

Consequences of Emotional Abuse

Researchers have given little attention to the effect of emotional abuse on women's physical and mental health. This lack of interest may be a function of the need to respond to the severe consequences of physical abuse and the expectation that emotional abuse will cause less severe and less permanent damage than will physical abuse. However, emotional abuse does cause serious damage to women's emotional and physical well-being. It seems that emotional abuse makes the victim fearful and dependent on her abuser, and it diminishes her sense of self-esteem. In turn, this damage can lead to health problems, poor work performance, and problems in other relation-

"The Yellow Wallpaper" (1892), by Charlotte Perkins Gilman, portrays a woman who is probably suffering from a depression after the birth of her child. Her physician-husband, instead of supporting her, insists that she rest and remain inactive, not even reading or writing. For all practical purposes, he has imprisoned the woman and forced her into an unbearable boredom and loneliness that finally drives her insane.

ships. Emotional abuse can cause women to be less satisfied with their relationships, to attempt to leave the partners, to have lower levels of perceived power and control, to exhibit lower self-esteem, to feel anxious and depressed, and to engage in abusive drinking. In terms of physical functioning and health, emotionally abused women have more serious or chronic illness, more often use psychotherapeutic services and psychotropic medication, more often visit a physician, and more often use over-the-counter and prescription medications for fatigue, backache, headache, gynecological dysfunctions, gastrointestinal problems, and insomnia.

A significant consequence of emotional abuse is post-traumatic stress disorder (PTSD), a set of characteristic emotional, behavioral, and cognitive symptoms that follows exposure to life-threatening events. PTSD occurs frequently among physically abused women, with estimates of the prevalence of the disorder ranging from approximately 30 to 80 percent. PTSD has been shown to be more likely to develop among women who engage in dissociative coping strategies, such as distraction, during the trauma and afterward. Perceptions of control over stressful events and the use of problem-focused coping strategies (e.g., developing a plan of action) instead of emotion-focused coping strategies (e.g., fantasizing about good outcomes) have been shown to be effective in reducing distress. In the case of physical battering, women who remained with their abusers were more likely to employ emotion-focused strategies to cope with their abuse than were women who terminated the abusive relationships. A similar pattern of findings characterizes emotionally abused women. Emotionally abused women are at increased risk for developing PTSD, and the use of emotion-focused rather than problem-focused coping strategies increases the probability that PTSD will develop. Further, PTSD interferes with emotionally abused women's intentions to leave their abusive partners—women who develop PTSD do not respond to their emotional abuse by distancing themselves from their abusive partners. In general, only women who are not hampered by PTSD are able to leave and remain away from their abusive partners.

The research evidence underscores the importance of assessing and addressing emotional abuse among physically battered and nonbattered women. Emotional abuse of women appears to be a strong and significant predictor of psychological adjustment and physical health. More important, the effects of emotional abuse appear to be significant even after controlling for the effects of physical abuse. Frequently, the effects of emotional abuse appear to be greater than those of physical abuse; approximately three-fourths of women who are both emotionally and physically abused experience emotional abuse as being the more damaging. The ability of emotional abuse to predict significantly and independently both psychological adjustment and intentions to terminate the relationship may reflect that, relative to physical abuse, emotional abuse exerts considerable influence on these variables. There are several reasons that may account for the relatively more robust effect of emotional abuse. First, it is possible that women experience emotional abuse more frequently than physical abuse. More frequent exposure to emotional abuse may allow it to have a greater effect on women's functioning than the relatively less frequent physical abuse. Second, relative to discreet episodes of physical violence, episodes of emotional abuse may be of longer duration functionally if women internalize emotional abuse, especially emotional abuse that assaults self-esteem and self-concept, such as humiliation. That is, a physically violent episode has a beginning and an end. Emotional abuse, on the other hand, may be prolonged if events such as name-calling (e.g., "You're crazy/stupid.") are incorporated into the self-concept (e.g., "I'm crazy/stupid."). Third, psychological assaults and trauma simply may have a greater effect on psychological well-being than physical assault. By definition, emotional abuse is psychological in nature. Its targets are emotions and cognitions of the victim.

Because emotional abuse of women by their intimate partners has a negative effect on women's psychological adjustment, their parenting skills and abilities are compromised, placing the children at risk for behavioral problems. Victims are likely to neglect and maltreat their children, who (both sons and daughters) are then likely to become depressed, lose self-esteem, and fight with other children.

Intervention and Treatment

Few treatments have been designed specifically for emotionally abused women. Consequences of emotional abuse, such as depression and PTSD, typically are treated with cognitive-behavioral techniques that have been developed to treat these problems in general. Accordingly, there is very little information regarding the effectiveness of interventions among emotionally abused women. Although no specific treatments exist, research on the consequences of emotional abuse has been used to generate guidelines or suggestions for intervention.

How much and how severely a woman is abused do not alone predict whether or not a woman will leave the abusive partner. Only women who are relatively unscathed psychologically strongly intend to leave their abusive partners. It may be that when abuse produces significant psychological damage, women are

In the mid-1970s, these victims of domestic violence lived in crowded conditions at a women's refuge in Chiswick, England, because only a handful of such places existed around the world. But by the 1990s, there were more than one thousand such shelters in the United States alone. (Corbis/Hulton-Deutsch Collection)

less ready or able to leave the relationship and live alone. Further complications, such as alcohol problems, also inhibit the desire and ability to leave. Thus, interventions with emotionally abused women may need to take the women's psychological well-being into account before expecting them to choose to leave the relationship. While women should not be dissuaded from attempting to leave their abusers, it appears crucial to assess the extent to which psychological well-being has an effect on women's evaluations of their ability to carry out plans to terminate the relationship and their appraisals of being able to be self-sufficient. Countering psychological distress or its effects by increasing social support, for example, appears to be an important action.

Encouraging women to engage in problem-focused or active coping (e.g., creating a plan of action) rather than emotion-focused or avoidance strategies (e.g., distraction or thinking about the good things in life) may be productive. In addition to increasing or maintaining psychological distress in the context of abuse, emotion-focused coping may decrease women's ability to stay out of the abusive relationship even if they intend to leave an abusive partner permanently and do carry out plans in that direction. Continued use of emotion-focused coping may increase the risk of the development of psychological distress in response to the difficulties that may be experienced after leaving the abusive partner, such as financial, employment, and housing difficulties. High levels of psychological distress, in turn, may increase the probability of returning to the abusive partner. Results suggesting that coping and distress have a negative effect on women's ability to terminate their abusive relationships underscore the need for shelter stays that extend beyond the common thirty-day limit. Focusing on the development of transitional housing and designing interventions that can be implemented over a longer period of time seem to be critical. Protective and supportive environments of longer duration would allow women to improve self-esteem, decrease psychological distress, and stabilize their improved affective and cognitive reactions enough to be able to focus on the complex task of independent living. Further, such interventions may increase the probability of maintaining constructive changes and independent living.

Because children of emotionally abused women also are at risk for emotional and behavioral problems, interventions may need to address directly the potential consequences of exposure to interparental emotional abuse. Children who observe interparental emotional abuse frequently observe interparental physical abuse as well. Further, children who observe interparental emotional or physical abuse are often emotionally and physically abused by a parent themselves. Children who observe interparental abuse and are abused themselves show the highest levels of emotional and behavioral problems. However, the destructive effect of emotional abuse, even after controlling for the effects of exposure to interparental physical abuse and child physical abuse, has been documented. Researchers have shown that women's physical victimization and their psychological adjustment appears to be nonexistent when the effect of emotional abuse is statistically controlled. Likewise, it would be interesting and important to assess the extent to which children's exposure to interparental emotional abuse accounts for the effect of their exposure to interparental physical abuse.

Effective prevention of physical and psychological abuse in general is difficult. Efforts to prevent the emotional abuse of women is in its infancy, and little is known of the effectiveness of the related programs and strategies. Prevention efforts typically consist of school-based educational programs that are designed to limit hostile and negative attitudes toward women, reduce the acceptability of and tolerance for emotional and physical assaults on women of all ages, reduce the need to control women, and provide problem-solving skills for addressing conflicts in relationships. Programs have been designed and implemented in middle and high schools, and programs for elementary schools have been proposed. Preliminary results indicate that school-based programs are successful in changing both boys' and girls' attitudes toward women and toward abuse. However, it is not clear to what extent attitudes cause abuse, and it remains to be seen if school-based prevention programs are successful in decreasing the emotional abuse of girls and women.

See also: DEFENSE MECHANISMS; POST-TRAUMATIC STRESS DISORDER; RELATIONSHIPS; SELF-ESTEEM

Bibliography

Arias, Ileana. (1998). "Women's Responses to Physical and Psychological Abuse." In *Violence in Intimate Relationships,* ed. Ximena Arriaga and Stuart Oskamp. Newbury Park, CA: Sage Publications.

Arias, Ileana; and Pape, Karen T. (1999). "Psychological Abuse: Implications for Adjustment and Commitment to Leave Violent Partners." *Violence and Victims* 14:1–13.

Follingstad, Diane R.; Rutledge, Larry L.; Berg, Barbara J.; Hause, Elizabeth S.; and Polek, Darlene S. (1990). "The Role of Emotional Abuse in Physically Abusive Relationships." *Journal of Family Violence* 5:107–120.

Jezl, David R.; Molidor, Christian E.; and Wright, Tracy L. (1996). "Physical, Sexual, and Psychological Abuse in High School Dating Relationships: Prevalence Rates and Self-Esteem Issues." *Child and Adolescent Social Work Journal* 13: 69–87.

Marshall, Linda L. (1996). "Psychological Abuse of Women: Six Distinct Clusters." *Journal of Family Violence* 11:379–409.

Molidor, Christian E. (1995). "Gender Differences of Psychological Abuse in High School Dating Relationships." *Child and Adolescent Social Work Journal* 12:119–134.

Murphy, Christopher M., and Cascardi, Michelle A. (1993). "Psychological Aggression and Abuse in Marriage." In *Family Violence: Prevention and Treatment,* ed. Robert L. Hampton, Thomas P. Gullotta, Gerald R. Adams, E. H. Potter, III, and Roger P. Weissberg. Newbury Park, CA: Sage Publications.

Murphy, Christopher M., and O'Leary, K. Daniel. (1989). "Psychological Aggression Predicts Physical Aggression in Early Marriage." *Journal of Consulting and Clinical Psychology* 57:579–582.

Ronfeldt, Heidi M.; Kimerling, Rachel; and Arias, Ileana.

Toni Morrison, in Beloved *(1987), describes the lives of slaves as they are physically and emotionally abused by whites who treat them as property and sell the children of the slave women. The novel also explores the continuing effects of abuse after the slaves have reached the precarious freedom of Ohio. Sethe kills one child and tries to kill them all rather than have them taken back into slavery.*

(1998). "Satisfaction with Relationship Power and the Perpetration of Dating Violence." *Journal of Marriage and the Family* 60:70–78.

Tolman, Richard M. (1989). "The Development of a Measure of Psychological Maltreatment of Women by Their Male Partners." *Violence and Victims* 4:159–177.

Ileana Arias

CHILDREN

Emotional abuse involves two categories of people: (1) those who suffer the abuse and (2) those who inflict the abuse. The term *emotional abuse* is commonly used to refer to child victims, but people of all ages may suffer emotional abuse, and people of all ages are capable of inflicting emotional abuse.

Emotional Life

Understanding emotional abuse necessitates basic knowledge of emotional life and emotional development. The emotional life simply means one's experience (through feeling) of emotions and the way one expresses those emotions. The emotional life actually begins before a person is born. The fetus has been observed experiencing a number of emotions, and it can be stimulated to experience more. Charles Darwin, as reported in *The Expression of the Emotions in Man and Animals* (1872), discovered that humans are born capable of feeling and expressing basic emotions that are necessary for survival. There is no truly accurate figure saying precisely how many emotions an average healthy human is capable of feeling and expressing, but the approximations of between sixty to eighty nevertheless indicate the richness and diversity of the emotional life. All emotions fall into two basic categories, positive and negative. Negative emotions (e.g., hatred, despair, distress, anger, mockery, frustration, contempt, humiliation, malice, repugnance, dejection, shame, and grief) outnumber positive emotions (e.g., joy, pity, pride, compassion, happiness, elation, and gratification) by approximately three to one. This is an important point to remember in understanding the consequences of emotional abuse. To say that emotions are negative emotions does not imply that they are necessarily harmful; it merely suggests that they are not "feel good" emotions. Nor are they necessarily dysfunctional; there are situations and experiences that will naturally stimulate many such emotions without causing harm. But negative emotions would be harmful if they were all pervasive, that is, if one endured such emotions over long periods of time and never had cause to feel and express positive emotions. Emotionally abused children experience negative, feel-bad emotions during and after the perpetration of emotional abuse, and they seldom experience feel-good emotions at any time.

The health of one's emotional life is partly dependent upon the number and variety of emotions one is capable of feeling and expressing; but far more important, it is dependant upon one's ability to feel and to express emotion appropriately. Emotional abuse adversely affects the emotional life of children. It diminishes their emotional repertoire, ensures that they experience and express many more negative emotions than positive, and limits their ability to establish healthy emotional and social relationships.

Emotional Development

The quality of one's emotional life is determined to a large extent by the quality of one's emotional development. The younger children are, the more dependent they are upon emotions. Newborn children are entirely dependant upon their emotions to communicate and to relate to the world. The healthy emotional development of a child depends upon adequate and appropriate emotional responses from caregivers. If the newborn baby cries, the mother comforts and feeds it; if the six-month-old baby is frightened, the caregiver reassures it; if the one-year-old child laughs heartily, the parents are likely to join in. Through this constant healthy emotional interaction, the child's emotional repertoire expands rapidly. It expands generally in terms of the number of emotions the child can feel and express, and it expands specifically in enabling the child to experience and express more positive emotions. There are a number of milestones in a child's emotional development: (1) the child learns to dissociate emotion and the accompanying expression of emotion; that is, the child learns that it is sometimes inappropriate or ineffective to be demonstrating the way he or she feels and acquires the means of controlling his or her expression of emotion, (2) the child acquires the ability to empathize, that is, to understand and to feel the emotional experiences of others,

---

Gabriel Garcia Marquez, in "The Tale of Innocent Erendira and Her Heartless Grandmother" (1978), tells the story of a twelve-year-old girl who accidentally sets fire to the house where she lives with her grandmother. The grandmother, deciding that Erendira must pay her back for the loss, sells the girl into prostitution in order to make money. The story takes on the characteristics of a bizarre fairy tale, with the evil grandmother forcing her Cinderella-like granddaughter to sell her body.

(3) the child is able to observe and interpret the emotional expression of others, (4) the child acquires the ability to mask their emotions, that is, being able to feel a particular emotion yet produce a facial expression or behavior that is indicative of another emotion. Researchers often debate (and argue) when precisely children achieve these emotional milestones and how children's understanding of their own emotions and the emotions of others develop. This is well illustrated in Paul Harris's *Children and Emotion* (1989) and in regular claim and counterclaim in child development journals. There is some evidence to suggest that children from differing cultures may reach these milestones at different times, but child-care experts are unanimous that the milestones, whatever age they are achieved, are crucial in children's development overall. These milestones are universally perceived to be necessary for ensuring normal social development and social relationships in adolescence and adult life.

A Definition of Emotional Abuse

The child who is being emotionally abused from an early age is unlikely to reach any of the important milestones of emotional development. The emotional interactions between the child and the abuser are characterized not by reciprocity or feel-good emotions but by a wholly inappropriate emotional negativity. Consider the following example:

> Four-year-old Tom meets a child of the same age from a family that has moved in next door. They get along well. Tom gets excited at the prospect of bringing his friend home to meet his mother. He feels a mixture of pride, excitement, enthusiasm, anticipation, happiness, and gratification. He anticipates that his mother will feel much the same way. But she does not. When Tom and his friend enter, she expresses an unmistakable anger; she is then irritable and snappy; then she is indifferent to them. Tom's enthusiasm for the venture quickly dissipates. He feels humiliated and helpless. Neither of the children can relax or enjoy themselves; Tom accompanies his friend back home next door.

The principal feature in this scenario is the entirely inappropriate emotional responses of the caregiver. Tom's dominant emotion at the outset is pride; his mother's first response is anger. Imagine that a very young child's pride is consistently met by a parent's anger, followed by irritability. What is the likely outcome? The obvious first consequence is that the child will quickly sense that being proud is much too costly; the predictable anger of his mother is too much for him to bear. Pride is an important emotion in the development of children. It spurs them on intellectually, educationally, and socially. Like all other emotions,

however, pride needs cultivation, role modeling, and practice. Children need to observe pride and the causes of pride in others (particularly their caregivers, who normally demonstrate a pervasive pride in the child's existence, looks, ability, and development). Children need to be encouraged to be proud in their achievements. Tom needed to know and to understand that when he felt and expressed pride, his mother would reciprocate that pride, would share in his excitement and anticipation in bringing his friend home, and would fulfill all of his expectations for her warmth, enthusiasm, and joy in welcoming his new friend. It is this appropriateness and inappropriateness of emotional responses that are crucial in understanding the following definition of emotional abuse: the sustained, repetitive, inappropriate emotional responses to (a) the child's experience of emotion and (b) how the child expresses the emotion.

The core feature of emotional abuse is that the emotions the child is feeling and expressing stimulate or provoke opposing and wholly inappropriate emotional responses on the part of the caregiver. Anger and aggression are entirely inappropriate emotional responses when a three-year-old child feels and expresses curiosity; indifference or resentment are entirely inappropriate responses when a ten-year-old child feels proud and expresses that pride. The crucially important words in the above definition are *sustained* and *repetitive*. Emotional abuse does not consist of one, single inappropriate emotional response. Emotional abuse is sustained, repetitive emotional responses over a long period of time. In the case of Tom and his friend, his mother's behavior caused a great deal of emotional hurt, but it did not necessarily constitute emotional abuse. It may have been a one-time situation. She may have had a fight with her husband; her elderly mother may be dying; she may be facing unemployment or a complicated pregnancy. More important, she may later have realized how poorly she treated her son and his friend and wanted to apologize and make amends. All parents are capable of single incidents of inappropriate emotional responses toward their children. Such incidents do not constitute emotional abuse. If, however, the emotional interactions between Tom and his mother were typical of the way they interacted each time they came into contact, that certainly would constitute emotional abuse. Emotionally abused children experience countless numbers of such inappropriate (emotionally painful) responses throughout their daily lives.

In addition to frequency and duration, emotional expressiveness is another important component in the above definition of emotional abuse. Often the caregiver will be more provoked by the expressive behavior accompanying the emotion that the child is feeling rather than the emotion itself. For example, the child's emotion of excitement may just be tolerable to the caregiver, but if the child is expressing that excitement by substantial noise and movement, it may become intolerable. The emotion of distress similarly may be tolerable, but sustained crying and kicking by a baby experiencing distress may provoke a whole range of negative emotions (and violence) on the part of the caregiver. Even the expressive smile or laughter in a child who is happy (rather than the happiness itself) may be the trigger that provokes a wholly inappropriate and damaging emotional response.

The term *emotional abuse* is often used synonymously with the term *psychological abuse*. Psychological abuse impedes psychological development and impairs mental (i.e., psychological) faculties, such as intelligence, reasoning, perception, memory, recognition, and imagination. The confusion arises because behavior that is emotionally abusive is likely to be psychologically abusive too, and vice versa. Marital violence for example, inflicts both kinds of abuses upon the child. Child abuse generally is multiple in its effects. That means that when a perpetrator inflicts one kind of abuse upon a child, the child will suffer other kinds of abuse (but that does not justify using abuse terms synonymously). Sexual abuse is nearly always psychologically and emotionally abusive. Physical abuse is always emotionally and psychologically abusive. Neglect of children (i.e., leaving them alone for long periods and inadequately feeding and clothing them) is also both emotionally and psychologically abusive.

Cross-Cultural Perspectives

There is much diversity of opinion on child abuse in general within separate cultures. For example, many parents in Great Britain smack their children, contrary to government advice and child-care laws; they believe that they are doing no wrong and that the occasional physical chastisement is necessary. Many others believe that physical chastisement of any kind is harmful and should be eradicated. The experts are as divided as the parents on this subject. Similar observations can be made in many other countries. Such differences of opinion are magnified in a cross-cultural perspective, as indicated in the work of Jill Korbin (1981) and Helen Noh Ahn (1994). This has led to some difficulty for professionals in child-care work. Cultural relativism is a concept that emerged in the 1980s to explain why some child-protection workers in Great Britain tolerated differing levels of child abuse within families from differing cultures. They believed that certain child-rearing practices regarded as child abuse within their own agency were generally

Marital violence, as this 1840 engraving of children attempting to restrain their drunken father as he lunges for his wife shows, is not a new phenomena. However, the emotional abuse sustained by the children in situations of domestic violence did not become a serious area of study until the early 1960s. (Corbis/Christel Gerstenberg)

acceptable within certain cultures and that intervening to stop it would constitute oppressive practice. This attitude was exposed as being detrimental to the welfare of the child in many reports.

As yet there are no studies that explore perceptions of emotional abuse cross-culturally. Anthropological studies, such as those of Signe Howell (1981) and Michelle Zimbalish Rozaldo (1980), suggest that emotions and the emotional life are perceived differently within differing cultures, but there is no evidence to suggest that behavior that constitutes emotional abuse as defined and explained in this entry is any more acceptable in one culture than in another. A number of studies, including those by Kieran O'Hagan (1993) and Daniel Reschly and Susan Graham-Clay (1987), have explored emotional abuse as a consequence of racism and cultural bias. The term *emotional abuse* may cause some difficulty within differing cultures, but it is reasonable to assume that the majority of the population in most countries would acknowledge that children's feelings and their expression of emotion requires appropriate emotional responses from their caregivers (particularly for younger children) and that there are certain emotional responses and behaviors that are definitely not appropriate. The sustained repetitive inappropriate emotional responses to children of any race or culture constitutes emotional abuse and will have a profoundly damaging effect on the children's emotional development.

Consequences of Emotional Abuse

There are many adverse consequences of emotional abuse. Emotionally abusive interactions can be extremely hurtful and disorientating. The child is likely to experience any combination of unpleasant emotions, including fear, humiliation, dejection, distress, despair, shame, resentment, or anger.

Emotional abuse inhibits the child from experiencing spontaneous, appropriate, positive, emotional feeling and emotional expression. Within the emotionally abusive situation, the child, as with Tom in the above example, quickly learns that it is too costly to feel good, happy, joyful, and so on. They also learn that it is and even more costly to express any of these emotions.

Consequently, many emotionally abused children appear to withdraw from the world around them. They are then perceived to be "unemotional" or "emotionally unresponsive." This is misleading. There is no such thing as "the unemotional child." Children, far more than adults, function through emotions. They relate and communicate through emotion. Emotionally abused children who *appear* to be unemotional or emotionally unresponsive are, in fact, feeling and ex-

pressing an abnormal intensity of emotion. But the emotions they are experiencing (as a consequence of the abuse) are most likely to be silent, inexpressive emotions such as apathy, despair, and hopelessness. As negative and damaging as these emotions can be, they are probably less risky for the child—they are less likely to attract anyone's attention, particularly the attention of the abuser.

Emotional abuse impairs emotional development. If the child is repetitively discouraged from feeling and expressing positive emotions, then it will become difficult for the child to be able to feel and to express such emotions. The child's emotional repertoire, therefore, is contracting rather than, as it should in normal development, expanding.

Emotional abuse deprives a child of the opportunity to learn about the appropriateness and inappropriateness of emotions and how to regulate and modulate emotional expression. This becomes crucial in the child's social and educational development.

The emotionally abused child's perception and understanding of emotion become distorted. This distortion applies to their own emotional experiences and the emotional expression of others. For example, the child who is emotionally abused by and within a situation of pervasive marital violence may perceive the emotions of anger and hatred as being normal and functional.

The emotionally abused child learns nothing about the subtleties of emotional life, and these subtleties are fundamental in understanding not just their own relationship with others but in understanding the relationships portrayed in literature, drama, poetry, music, and art.

Risk Factors and Identifiable Groups

Given the definition of emotional abuse, it is possible to recognize environments and relationships in which the risk of such abuse is high. Inappropriate emotional responses can easily be observed in the home and in a variety of other locations, but single incidents of inappropriate emotional responses reveal little about the quality of the emotional relationships

---

In Roddy Doyle's Paddy Clarke Ha Ha Ha *(1993), young Patrick is so distressed over his parents' fighting with each other that he stays up all night trying to prevent their quarrels. Like many children whose parents break up, Patrick thinks he is somehow responsible, but he does not understand what is going wrong or why.*

between children and their caregivers. The inappropriate emotional responses and all of the consequential emotional pain endured by the child has to be repetitive and sustained, and some of the consequences listed above need to be substantiated before one can confidently claim that the child is living in an emotionally abusive situation. There are, however, many such situations. The most obvious arises when the parents of children were themselves subjected to emotional abuse over many years during their own childhood. Their emotional repertoires are extremely limited. Their emotional lives are dominated by negative painful emotions, such as anger, despair, resentment, apathy, or indifference. They are often unable to respond in emotionally appropriate ways to their children's emotions and expressions of emotion.

Marital violence is another high-risk emotionally abusive situation. Every incident of violent conflict in a marital relationship consists of many inappropriate emotional responses on the part of the parents. The responses are not directed to the children, but often they are more acutely felt by the children. Research by Peter Jaffe, David Wolfe, and Susan Wilson (1990) clearly indicates the serious damage that marital violence inflicts upon children. The younger they are, the greater that damage. Many young children who observe marital violence will endure the emotions of fear, horror, and panic as they watch the mother being systematically pummeled by the father. Yet the only emotional responses the children get in return are hatred, anger, and aggression (usually from father) and terror, fear, and anguish (usually from the mother). As many child-care professionals will testify, this is emotional abuse of the most damaging kind.

Mentally ill parents are seldom able to respond in an emotionally appropriate way to their children. Their lives may often be characterized by sustained periods of depression and despair, guilt and shame, fear and unpredictability. During such periods, it may simply be impossible for them to feel enthusiastic, curious, joyful, or happy about anything. Very young children in particular find this distressing. To watch as the principal caregiver repeatedly breaks down can be a terrifying experience. They cannot cope with the enormity of the transformation from sanity to insanity. They do not understand what is happening, but they have an acute sense of foreboding that cautions them about any spontaneous expression of emotion and its consequences. It is vitally important that young children be rescued from the most extreme manifestations of a parent's mental breakdown. The other parent, or a significant other person in the family, can be crucial in enabling children to cope in such situations.

Poor, isolated, unsupported single parents, subject to grinding poverty and harassment by officials and debt collectors, are another group that poses a risk to the emotional life and development of their children. The cold, unfriendly, and threatening world in which they live is oppressive to their own emotional well-being and makes it difficult for them to respond to their children in an emotionally appropriate way. The origins of the problem are deep-rooted; many of these parents have been emotionally abused themselves by the same grinding poverty and relentless pressures that bore down upon their own parents. Little progress can be made by professionals in such situations without tackling these root causes of poverty and isolation. This is one of the reasons why some governments concentrate upon alleviating poverty (and its consequential hopelessness and despair) through work schemes and the provision of child-minding facilities, in addition to enhancing the quality of emotional interactions between child and parent in the home situation.

Treatment and Prevention

Much progress has been made by child-protection workers in treating and preventing emotional abuse. It is no longer perceived as something abstract or mysterious, to be avoided or ignored in the search for more tangible forms of abuse. The identification of high-risk factors is often the first stage of the process. The most significance advance has been the realization that many parents are well capable of understanding emotional abuse and that they can recognize the situations and circumstances that are conducive to the occurrence of such abuse.

Treatment and prevention are preceded by ongoing assessment and re-creation of the emotionally abusive interactions between parents and their children. This re-creation may be facilitated by video recordings made over many weeks, in the family home, in a daycare center, or in an alternative temporary accommodation. Parents have the opportunity to observe how they have been responding emotionally to their children, to comment, analyze, and to suggest alternatives. If there are obstacles to alternative emotionally healthier ways of interacting, these have to be exposed and acknowledged by both professionals and parents, and strategies for overcoming them need to be formulated. Sometimes the obstacles can be easily identified and overcome. On other occasions, the problem may be deep-rooted and complex, requiring a substantial investment of time and effort. The involvement and full participation of the parents is crucial, and the whole process of assessment, treatment, and prevention must be conducted entirely without blame and condemnatory overtones.

Conclusion

In 1962, C. Henry Kempe and his colleagues convened a symposium on child abuse at the annual national meeting of the American Academy of Pediatrics. They coined the term *battered child syndrome* and wrote numerous papers that influenced legislation and led to the establishment of mandated child abuse reporting laws in all fifty states of the United States. Kempe suggested then that it would be some considerable time before emotional abuse could be understood and given the recognition it deserved. For some thirty years after, emotional abuse was largely ignored in child-protection work, despite the fact that many child-protection workers not only believed it was occurring but that it was the most common form of abuse children were enduring.

The main reasons for the neglect of emotional abuse were (1) a lack of definition and (2) a lack of confidence among child-protection workers to articulate on emotional abuse. Thankfully, substantial literature and research has since been published, and no assessment of a child referred to a child-protection agency today is complete without a comprehensive exploration of the child's emotional life, establishing whether or not the child's emotional development is being impeded or impaired in any way. One of the most challenging and sobering discoveries made during this research is the fact that emotional abuse is so easily perpetrated without the perpetrator realizing it. Even loving, devoted parents and child-protection workers themselves are capable of engaging in damaging emotional interactions with their children. It is the emotional intensity of these regrettable moments that blinds one to the more objective realization of precisely what is happening, which is why the words of three well-known researchers on emotional abuse, Stuart Hart, Robert Germain, and Marla Brassard (1987, p. 7), are so important to remember: "It is doubtful that any of us escape being victims or perpetrators."

See also: ACCEPTANCE AND REJECTION; ATTACHMENT; BOWLBY, JOHN; DARWIN, CHARLES ROBERT; HUMAN DEVELOPMENT

Bibliography

Ahn, Helen N. (1994). "Cultural Diversity and the Definition of Child Abuse." In *Child Welfare Research Review, Vol. 1,* ed. Richard Barth and Jill D. Berrick. New York, Columbia University Press.

Aldgate, Jane. (1991). "Attachment Theory and its Application to Child Care Social Work." In *Handbook of Theory for Practice Teachers in Social Work,* ed. Joyce Lishman. London: Jessica Kingsley.

Bowlby, John. (1953). *Child Care and the Growth of Love.* Hammondsworth, Eng.: Penguin.

Brassard, Marla R.; Hart, Stuart N.; and Hardy, Daniel B. (1991). "Psychological and Emotional Abuse of Children." In *Case Studies in Family Violence,* ed. Robert T. Ammerman and Michel Hersen. New York: Plenum.

Channer, Yvonne, and Parton, Nigel. (1991). "Racism, Cultural Relativism, and Child Protection." In *Taking Child Abuse Seriously,* ed. The Violence Against Children Study Group. London: Unwin Hyman.

Darwin, Charles. (1872). *The Expression of the Emotions in Man and Animals.* London: Murray.

Evans, Ruth S. (1997). *Emotional Milestones from Birth to Adulthood: A Psychodynamic Approach.* London: Jessica Kingsley Publishers.

Goleman, Daniel. (1996). *Emotional Intelligence.* London: Bloomsbury.

Harris, Paul L. (1989). *Children and Emotion: The Development of Psychological Understanding.* Oxford, Eng.: Basil Blackwell.

Hart, Stuart N.; Germain, Robert W.; and Brassard, Marla R. (1987). "The Challenge: To Better Understand and Combat Psychological Maltreatment of Children and Youth." In *Psychological Maltreatment of Children and Youth,* ed. Marla A Brassard, Robert W. Germain, and Stuart N. Hart. New York: Pergamon.

Howell, Signe. (1981). "Rules Not Words." In *Indigenous Psychologies,* ed. Paul Heelas and Andrew Lock. London: Academic Press.

Iwaniec, Dorota. (1996). *The Emotionally Abused and Neglected Child: Identification, Assessment and Intervention.* London: Wiley.

Jaffe, Peter G.; Wolfe, David A.; and Wilson, Susan K. (1990). *Children of Battered Women.* Newbury Park, CA: Sage Publications.

Kempe, C. Henry. (1972). "Paediatric Implications of the Battered Baby Syndrome." *Archives of Disease in Childhood* 46 (245):28–37.

Kempe, C. Henry; Silverman, Frederick; Steele, Brandt; Droegemueller, William; and Silver, Henry. (1962). "The Battered Child Syndrome." *Journal of the American Medical Association* 181:17–24.

Korbin, Jill E. (1981). *Child Abuse and Neglect: Cross-Cultural Perspectives.* Berkeley: University of California Press.

O'Hagan, Kieran P. (1995). "Emotional and Psychological Abuse: Problems of Definition." *Child Abuse and Neglect: The International Journal* 19(4):449–461.

O'Hagan, Kieran P. (1993). *Emotional and Psychological Abuse of Children.* Buckingham, Eng.: Open University Publications.

Ortony, Andrew; Clore, Gerald L.; and Collins, Allan. (1988). *The Cognitive Structure of Emotions.* Cambridge, Eng.: Cambridge University Press.

Reschly, Daniel J., and Graham-Clay, Susan. (1987). "Psychological Abuse from Prejudice and Cultural Bias." In *Psychological Maltreatment of Children and Youth,* ed. Marla A Brassard, Robert W. Germain, and Stuart N. Hart. New York: Pergamon.

Rozaldo, Michelle Zimbalish. (1980). *Knowledge and Passion: Ilongot Notions of Self and Social Life.* Cambridge, Eng.: Cambridge University Press.

Kieran O'Hagan

SIBLINGS

"Sticks and stones may break my bones, but words will never hurt me." This popular children's saying suggests that physical assaults may hurt but that verbal attacks do not. Those people who have been victims of repeated verbal assaults from a sibling would not agree with this statement. For some, the abuse has had a serious effect on their lives, even prompting many to seek psychotherapy. Unfortunately, society in general does not regard emotional abuse in the form of verbal attacks by a sibling to be a serious problem. Instead, these attacks are viewed as sibling rivalry, which is considered to be part of the normal process of growing up.

The Nature of the Problem

Sibling emotional abuse or psychological maltreatment may be defined as verbal attacks of one sibling toward another, including name-calling, ridiculing, insulting, degrading, or threatening the victim. Also included in the definition are the exacerbation of a fear that a sibling may have and the destruction of a sibling's personal property, such as deliberately destroying a prized possession or pet.

When a child engages in name-calling, ridiculing, insulting, and degrading a sibling, the abuse is often focused on a personality or physical characteristic of the victim that distinguishes the child from other siblings or peers. For example, the abuse may focus on a sibling being shy or withdrawn, the inability to pronounce certain syllables or words, or the sibling's height, weight, or lack of physical agility. Frequently a sibling's fear, such as a fear of the dark or a fear of becoming lost, becomes the target of an attack. The destruction of personal property, a prized possession or pet may be viewed as emotionally abusive because of the loss of the object and the emotional investment the victim had in the object.

Three basic theoretical perspectives aid in understanding emotional sibling abuse. First, the abuse may indicate an attempt on the part of one sibling to exert power and control over another. The victim may be perceived as a threat to the sibling perpetrator because the perpetrator may not be as successful in school as the victim. Or the perpetrator may perceive

the victim to be in higher favor with the parents. The use of power and control may be exacerbated in instances of brothers abusing sisters if the males have been socialized in an atmosphere of gender inequality. Second, a perpetrator may be modeling verbally abusive behavior seen among peers at school, on television, or in behaviors that are engaged in by the parents toward each other. Third, parents may simply ignore the behavior, based on their own childhood experiences or on their belief that emotionally abusive behavior is a part of sibling rivalry, which is a part of normal child development.

The Extent of the Problem

Little statistical data exist on the extent to which sibling emotional abuse occurs; however, this is not to deny the existence of the problem. Incidents of emotional abuse between adults and children rarely appear in court because of the lack of physical evidence in substantiating such abuse. Even more rare are cases of sibling emotional abuse because of the reluctance of parents to bring charges against one of their children who may be perpetrating such abuse.

Murray Straus, Richard Gelles, and Suzanne Steinmetz (1980), in one of the initial studies on violence in American families, reported that violent acts between siblings occurred far more frequently than violence between spouses and violence between parents and children. Although the researchers were referring to acts of physical violence, subsequent research indicates that emotional abuse generally underlies physical abuse. In a study of 150 adults who were seeking treatment from a mental health resource, Vernon Wiehe (1997) found that 7 percent of the respondents indicated that they had only been emotionally abused by a sibling as they were growing up, but 78 percent indicated they had been physically, emotionally, and sexually abused, thus supporting earlier data that indicated that emotional abuse underlies other forms of family violence.

Effects of Emotional Abuse on the Victims

Victims of sibling emotional abuse report that most often the abuse affects their self-esteem. Victims often internalize the emotionally abusive comments as statements of truth (e.g., that they are ugly, stupid, or incompetent). These comments then become self-fulfilling prophecies that create problems-in-living for the individuals that extend even into adulthood

Problems in self-esteem appear to underlie or spill over into other problems-in-living that are reported by victims of sibling emotional abuse, including problems in relationships with the opposite sex, difficulty in in-

Sam Shepard's True West *(1980) portrays two brothers who confront and challenge each other in an escalating conflict. Each makes the other feel inadequate, and each trespasses on the other's "turf." Their actions trigger jealousy and angry retaliations that lead to the trashing of their mother's house, which is where they have been trying to live together. The play closes with the two brothers in a fight to the death.*

terpersonal relationships in general, being overly sensitive to criticism, self-blame for the abuse, and the attempt to cope with these problems through the abuse of drugs, alcohol, and food. The repetition of the victim role in interpersonal relationships can frequently be seen in victims who have internalized the emotionally abusive behavior to which they have been subjected. They have been left with feelings of worthlessness that they enact in their poor choice of friends and mates or in their fear of attempting to succeed in the tasks they undertake.

Preventing Sibling Emotional Abuse

A significant issue in the prevention of sibling emotional abuse is the parents' recognition of this social problem, its potential destructive effects, and appropriate intervention. Sibling rivalry is normal behavior engaged in by many siblings; sibling abuse is not. Sibling abuse occurs when one sibling repeatedly is the victim of another sibling. A victim of emotional abuse is someone who needs help, just as the victims in an automobile accident may be trapped in the wreckage and need help to extricate themselves.

When parents ignore sibling emotional abuse or tell the victims that this will toughen them up for life or that they must have done something to deserve the abuse, the victims are further victimized. Since emotionally abusive behavior often prompts similar behavior in self-defense from the victim, parents must engage in a problem-solving approach that helps both the perpetrator and the victim to understand the destructive nature of the behavior and to learn new, more effective ways of communicating with each other. Logical consequences may need to be enforced when a perpetrating sibling persists in the use of emotionally abusive behavior toward another sibling.

See also: CONFLICT; HUMAN DEVELOPMENT; SELF-ESTEEM

Bibliography

Ayalon, Ofra, and Van Tassel, Elizabeth. (1987). "Living in Dangerous Environments." In *Psychological Maltreatment of Children and Youth,* ed. Marla A. Brassard, Robert W. Germain, and Stuart N. Hart. New York: Pergamon.

Brassard, Marla, and Gelardo, Mark. (1987). "Psychological Maltreatment." *School Psychology Review* 16:127–136.

Briere, John; Berliner, Lucy; Bulkley, Josephine A.; Jenny, Carole; and Reid, Theresa, eds. (1996). *The APSAC Handbook on Child Maltreatment.* Thousand Oaks, CA: Sage Publications.

Claussen, Angelika, and Crittenden, Patricia. (1991). "Physical and Psychological Maltreatment: Relations among Types of Maltreatment." *Child Abuse & Neglect* 15:5–18.

Straus, Murray A.; Gelles, Richard J.; and Steinmetz, Suzanne K. (1980). *Behind Closed Doors: Violence in the American Family.* Garden City, NY: Doubleday/Anchor.

Telzrow, Cathy. (1987). "Influence by Negative and Limiting Models." In *Psychological Maltreatment of Children and Youth,* ed. Marla A. Brassard, Robert W. Germain, and Stuart N. Hart. New York: Pergamon.

Varia, Rachma; Abidin, Richard; and Dass, Patsy. (1996). "Perceptions of Abuse." *Child Abuse & Neglect* 20:511–526.

Wiehe, Vernon R. (1997). *Sibling Abuse.* Thousand Oaks, CA: Sage Publications.

Vernon R. Wiehe

MEN

While there has been some attention in the study of intimate and family violence paid to the emotional abuse of children and women, there has been little attention paid to the emotional abuse of men. Some advocates in the field of domestic violence argue that men's privileged position in society and the family make it logically impossible for men to be victims of any form of psychological or emotional abuse. Advocacy positions notwithstanding, men are yelled at, belittled, scolded, ignored, torn down, and otherwise victimized by behavior that would fit within a definition of emotional abuse. Wives, ex-wives, girlfriends, male homosexual partners, and children victimize them.

For the purposes of this entry, the term *emotional abuse* refers to acts that have the intent or perceived intention of emotionally injuring the partner. These can include overt acts, such as yelling, screaming, or belittling, or lack of action, such as shunning or ignoring the other person.

Prevalence

There have been few attempts to quantify the extent of emotional abuse in intimate relationships and even fewer efforts to assess the experiences of men. The Second National Family Violence Survey, conducted in 1985 by Richard Gelles and Murray Straus (1988), assessed acts of psychological aggression along with measuring physical violence and abuse. This survey asked men and women whether they had insulted or swore at their partners; sulked or refused to talk about an issue; stomped out of the house or yard; did something to spite partners; threatened to hit partners; or threw, or smashed, or kicked something.

Overall, 75 percent of the women surveyed reported using at least one of these behaviors, at least once in the previous twelve months. The results of this survey suggest that, at least in terms of the occurrence of the behavior, emotional abuse of men (and women—who reported the same level of experiencing emotional abuse) is widespread.

Emotional abuse in intimate and family relationships is generally a two-way street. In half of the relationships where emotional abuse occurs, both part-

In Edward Albee's play Who's Afraid of Virginia Woolf?, *Martha (played by Diana Rigg) is devastated when George (played by David Suchet, right) decides to take the ultimate revenge for all of the emotional abuse that he has received and tells Martha that their (fictional) child is dead.* (Corbis/Robbie Jack)

ners use it; in one quarter of the relationships, only the man is emotionally abusive; and in one-quarter of relationships, only the female partner is abusive.

Causes of Abuse

There has been a great deal of speculation about the causes of emotional abuse. A number of students of domestic violence suggest that men are physically and emotionally abusive in order to maintain coercive control over their partners. Women, on the other hand, are viewed as using emotional and physical violence only as a means of self-defense. Research on physical and emotional violence suggests that women use emotional violence for the same reason men do—to control their partners.

The nature of family and intimate relationships helps explain why men are more likely to experience emotional abuse in intimate relations than in most other social, group, or institutional settings—the family is a private social institution. Family relations are shielded from public view and from both formal and informal sanction by the physical privacy of the home or residence and by the cultural privacy that constrains outsiders from becoming involved in what are considered to be "private" matters. Outsiders only respond to the most outrageous or dangerous behaviors. Thus,

emotional and psychological attacks tend not to elicit either formal or informal sanctions. This absence of social controls enhances the likelihood of emotional violence occurring.

The family is also an intimate setting where there is no backstage. There is no place to hide or flee to escape conflict. Thus, intimate conflicts can escalate from mild to major, from minor rebukes to outright abusive hostility.

The various structural components of the family, such as mixed sex, mixed age, emotional investment and attachment, and zero sum activities (many family and intimate relationship decisions result in a winner and loser), not only enhance the likelihood of conflicts but create the expectation that intimate relationships will have screaming, yelling, and insulting. Intimate partners who bicker and fight have long been a staple of media representations of family life, including cartoon strips (e.g., *Andy Capp*), radio programs (e.g., *The Bickersons*), and television series (e.g., *The Honeymooners, All in the Family,* and *Love and Marriage*). Such expectations accept as "normal" a certain level of family conflict and emotional abuse. Moreover, media depictions typically cast the wife as the "shrew" and the husband as either the hapless victim or one who is deserving of the wife's sarcasm and cutting remarks. The end result is a cultural expectation that men and

Angels in America, Parts I and II (1991, 1992), explores many of the major issues of late twentieth-century America. One is self-serving manipulation of others, characteristic of Roy Cohn, who likes throwing his weight around and does not care who gets hurt. Cohn borrows money from clients, bribes judges, and threatens, bullies, and cheats to get his way. In almost all of his relationships, Cohn emotionally abuses the men who almost always have less power than he does.

Bibliography

Gelles, Richard J., and Straus, Murray A. (1988). *Intimate Violence*. New York: Simon & Schuster.

Murphy, Christopher, and O'Leary, K. Daniel. (1989). "Psychological Aggression Predicts Physical Aggression in Early Marriage." *Journal of Consulting and Clinical Psychology* 57:579–582.

Straus, Murray A. (1974). "Leveling, Civility, and Violence in the Family." *Journal of Marriage and the Family* 36:13–29.

Straus, Murray A., and Sweet, Stephen. (1992). "Verbal/Symbolic Aggression in Couples: Incidence Rates and Relationships to Personal Characteristics." *Journal of Marriage and the Family* 54:346–357.

Richard J. Gelles

women will bicker, argue, and yell, that women can be the protagonists and men the objects of abuse, and that the behavior is private and does not require informal or formal social controls.

The probability of frequent emotional abuse declines with age and the number of children in the family and increases with occurrences of alcohol abuse and use of other drugs. Race, income, education, and occupation are not related to emotional abuse of men.

One explanation for the widespread occurrence of intimate physical and emotional violence and abuse is that it occurs because *it can*. As mentioned above, the privacy of the family, the lack of internal and external social controls, and the expectation that some physical and emotional aggression will occur all allow for and even encourage a certain level of emotional abuse of men. A key tenet of prevention and treatment efforts is to make it so that emotional abuse of either partner *cannot happen*.

Intervention

Counseling interventions, either for individuals or couples, need to focus on anger management. Research demonstrates that couples who use rational discussion to deal with conflict and disagreement are less likely to use emotional aggression and/or physical violence.

One ineffective intervention is the notion that if people release their pent-up aggression and frustration, by yelling, screaming, or hitting objects, it will reduce the likelihood that such pent-up frustration and aggression will lead to dangerous emotional and physical aggression, violence, and abuse. Not only is there no evidence to support the assumption that "letting it all hang out" reduces the likelihood of harmful aggression, research indicates that yelling and screaming and "letting it all hang out" enhances the escalation of conflict to harmful emotional and physical abuse.

See also: CONFLICT; RELATIONSHIPS

EMOTIONAL DISORDERS

See Anxiety Disorders; Culture-Bound Syndromes; Fear and Phobias; Mood Disorders; Post-Traumatic Stress Disorder; Seasonal Affective Disorder

EMOTIONAL INTELLIGENCE

The term *emotional intelligence* was first used in a 1990 article by Peter Salovey and John D. Mayer that appeared in the journal *Imagination, Cognition, and Personality*. Salovey and Mayer described emotional intelligence as a form of social intelligence that involves the ability to monitor the feelings and emotions of oneself and of other people, to discriminate among the various feelings and emotions, and to use this information to guide one's thinking and action. Salovey and Mayer coined the term as a challenge to intelligence theorists to contemplate an expanded role for the emotional system in conceptual schemes of human abilities and to investigators of emotion who had historically considered the arousal of feelings to be a hindrance to rational mental activity. In the spirit of Charles Darwin, who in *The Expression of the Emotions in Man and Animals* (1872) viewed the emotional system as necessary for survival and as providing an important signaling system within and across species, Salovey and Mayer emphasized the functionality of feelings and described a set of competencies that might underlie the adaptive use of affectively charged information.

Associated Concepts and Formal Definition

The idea of an emotional intelligence was anticipated, at least implicitly, by various theorists who argued that traditional notions of analytic intelligence were too narrow. Emotional intelligence adds an affective (feeling) dimension to Robert Sternberg's work on practical intelligence, is consistent with theorizing by Nancy Cantor and John Kihlstrom about social intelligence, and is directly related to research by Carolyn Saarni and others on children's emotional competencies. Emotional intelligence is most similar to one of the multiple intelligences characterized by Howard Gardner in *Frames of Mind* (1983). Of the kinds of intelligence described by Gardner, intrapersonal intelligence is most similar to emotional intelligence. Gardner delineated intrapersonal intelligence (one of the personal intelligences) as access to one's own feeling life and the capacity to effect discriminations among these feelings, label them, enmesh them in symbolic codes, and draw upon them as a way of understanding and guiding one's behavior.

In a chapter titled "What is Emotional Intelligence?," Mayer and Salovey (1997) described emotional intelligence more formally by outlining the specific competencies it encompasses. They organized these competencies along four branches including (a) the ability to perceive, appraise, and express emotion accurately; (b) the ability to access and generate feelings when they facilitate cognition; (c) the ability to understand affect-laden information and make use of emotional knowledge; and (d) the ability to regulate emotions to promote growth and well-being. Individuals can be more or less skilled at attending to, appraising, and expressing their own emotional states. These emotional states can be harnessed adaptively and directed toward a range of cognitive tasks including problem solving, creativity, and decision making. Emotional intelligence also includes essential knowledge about the emotional system; the most fundamental competencies at this level concern the ability to label emotions with words and to recognize the relationships among elements of the affective lexicon. Finally, emotional intelligence includes the ability to regulate feelings in oneself and in other people. Individuals who are unable to manage their emotions are more likely to experience negative affect and remain in poor spirits.

Measuring Emotional Intelligence

When the book *Emotional Intelligence* (1995) by *New York Times* science writer Daniel Goleman became a worldwide bestseller, the concept of emotional intelligence gained enormous popular appeal and attracted considerable media attention. Attempts to operationalize and directly measure emotional intelligence were inevitable. Guided by their original framework, Salovey and Mayer initially examined the meta-experience of mood. Two self-report scales to assess meta-mood cognition (i.e., reflection on the experience of mood) have been employed: a trait scale

and a state scale. The former, for example, is the thirty-item Trait Meta-Mood Scale (TMMS), which taps into people's beliefs about their propensity to attend with clarity to their own mood states and to engage in mood-repair. The items of this measure are straightforward; for example, "I pay a lot of attention to how I feel" (attention), "I can never tell how I feel" (clarity, reverse scored), and "I try to think good thoughts no matter how badly I feel" (repair). The reliability (consistency of measurement) of the TMMS is quite good, and some empirical findings have been generated from the use of it. The TMMS, however, like other self-report measures of aspects of emotional intelligence such as the Emotional Quotient Inventory (EQ-i) developed by Reuven Bar-On (1997), essentially asks individuals whether or not they have various competencies and experiences consistent with being emotionally intelligent; it does not require individuals to demonstrate their emotional competencies. A more valid measure of core emotional intelligence is likely to require a test that relies on tasks and exercises rather than on self-assessment. Such a performance-based instrument has not yet been published, although David Caruso, Mayer, and Salovey have begun to circulate the Multifactor Emotional Intelligence Scales (MEIS), a measure of emotional intelligence relying on performance-based (ability) tests rather than self-report.

Although the construct of emotional intelligence has generated considerable interest, measures of it have emerged rather slowly, and data to substantiate the validity of the measures are especially scarce. There is a converging sense among researchers of what emotional intelligence is—a set of competencies concerning the appraisal and expression of feelings, the use of emotions to facilitate cognitive activities, knowledge about emotions, and the regulation of emotion—yet there is considerably less consensus on how best to measure it. Although the advantages of task-based and behavioral assessment are mentioned above, various self-assessments have also appeared that may measure important aspects of individuals' perceptions of their competencies in this domain. Such self-assessments may or may not correlate with actual skills and abilities. Other self-tests that have been repackaged as tests of emotional intelligence appear to have little to do with the basic construct itself.

Some relevant findings have begun to appear in the literature. For example, Bar-On (1997) reported that the EQ-i differentiates U.S. Naval Academy students who feel personally successful from those who do not and distinguishes Latina immigrants who score high versus low on an acculturation scale. The TMMS also appears to correlate with real-world outcomes. Salovey and his colleagues (1995) found that those individuals who are less likely to ruminate or report illnesses during stressful experiences score highly on the TMMS clarity and repair subscales, respectively. Despite what has been learned about the measurement of emotional intelligence during the 1990s, research on the psychometric (measurement) properties, generally, and the validity, in particular, of most emotional intelligence tests is still quite preliminary.

Emotional Intelligence in the Schools

During the 1980s and 1990s, the idea that the social problems of young people—school dropout, illicit drug use, teenage pregnancy—could be addressed through school-based prevention programs became popular among educational reformers. Early programs focused primarily on social problem-solving skills or conflict-resolving strategies, but more recent programs have dealt with the emotions explicitly. For younger children, these programs focus on building a feelings vocabulary and recognizing facial expressions of emotion. Middle school students learn how to control their impulses and regulate feelings such as sorrow and anger. Those programs focused on high school students address the role of emotions in resisting peer pressure to engage in risky sexual behavior and drug or alcohol use. It is likely that these programs are helpful to students, and the evaluation research that has been conducted generally reveals that they are liked by participating students and teachers and that they can have an effect on social behavior, especially at school.

Challenges for the Future

Despite the popularization of the construct in the mid-1990s, empirical research on emotional intelligence is still in its infancy. The problematic issues in this area of work are not surprising, given the relative immaturity of this research domain. For one, the term *emotional intelligence* is used to represent various aspects of the human condition. Salovey and Mayer (1990) and other investigators prefer to focus narrowly on specific abilities and competencies concerned with appraising, understanding, and regulating emotions and using them to facilitate cognitive (mental) activities. However, journalists writing for the general public, such as Goleman (1995), have defined emotional intelligence in terms of motivation (persistence, zeal), cognitive strategies (delay of gratification), and, even, character (being a good person). Emotional intelligence may contribute to motivation, cognitive strategies, and character, but they are not the same thing. The con-artist may be especially skilled at reading and regulating the emotions of other people but may have little of what is commonly thought to be good character.

This area of research will not prove to be productive unless the abilities that make up emotional intelligence can be measured reliably and unless these abilities are related to important, real-world outcomes. It is likely that research using ability (performance-based) measures will reveal that emotional intelligence is better characterized by a pattern of underlying strengths and weaknesses across various skills than by a monolithic emotional quotient (EQ). Future research is likely to address the independence of emotional intelligence from analytical (traditional) intelligence, cultural differences in the definition of emotionally intelligent competencies, and the ability of measures of emotional intelligence to predict important outcomes in school, work, and social life over and above the variance accounted for by the traditional intelligence quotient (IQ).

See also: EMPATHIC ACCURACY; SELF-ESTEEM

Bibliography

Bar-On, Reuven. (1997). *EQ-i: Bar-On Emotional Quotient Inventory.* Toronto: Multi-Health Systems.

Cantor, Nancy, and Kihlstrom, John F. (1987). *Personality and Social Intelligence.* Englewood Cliffs, NJ: Prentice-Hall.

Darwin, Charles. ([1872] 1965). *The Expression of the Emotions in Man and Animals.* Chicago: University of Chicago Press.

Gardner, Howard. (1983). *Frames of Mind: The Theory of Multiple Intelligences.* New York: Basic Books.

Goldman, Susan L.; Kraemer, Deborah T.; and Salovey, Peter. (1996). "Beliefs about Mood Moderate the Relationship of Stress to Illness and Symptom Reporting." *Journal of Psychosomatic Research* 41:115–128.

Goleman, Daniel. (1995). *Emotional Intelligence.* New York: Bantam.

Mayer, John D., and Salovey, Peter. (1993). "The Intelligence of Emotional Intelligence." *Intelligence* 17:433–442.

Mayer, John D., and Salovey, Peter. (1997). "What is Emotional Intelligence?" In *Emotional Development and Emotional Intelligence,* ed. Peter Salovey and David Sluyter. New York: Basic Books.

Saarni, Carolyn. (1990). "Emotional Competence: How Emotions and Relationships Become Integrated." In *Nebraska Symposium on Motivation, Vol. 36,* ed. Ross A. Thompson. Lincoln: University of Nebraska Press.

Salovey, Peter, and Mayer, John D. (1990). "Emotional Intelligence." *Imagination, Cognition, and Personality* 9:185–211.

Salovey, Peter; Mayer, John D.; Goldman, Susan L.; Turvey, Carolyn; and Palfai, Tibor P. (1995). "Emotional Attention, Clarity, and Repair: Exploring Emotional Intelligence Using the Trait Meta-Mood Scale." In *Emotion, Disclosure, and Health,* ed. James Pennebaker. Washington, DC: American Psychological Association.

Sternberg, Robert J. (1985). *Beyond IQ: A Triarchic Theory of Human Intelligence.* New York: Cambridge University Press.

Peter Salovey

EMOTION EXPERIENCE AND EXPRESSION

Emotions are fundamental features of daily life. The essence of humanness is the experience and expression of feelings, emotions, and moods. The initiation, escalation, and maintenance of relationships are largely based on the inner feelings and outward display of positive and even negative emotions. Likewise, the downside of relationships—deterioration and dissolution—is also a function of the degree and intensity of the experience and expression of negative emotion. In short, the inner feeling and the outward expression of emotions can both make and break relationships.

Like much of human behavior, rules and norms greatly influence the experience and expression of emotions. For example, full disclosure of emotions is potentially costly, often in terms of the discloser's vulnerability and the recipient's hurt feelings. It is not surprising that people typically feel emotions to a greater degree than they express them. For example, one may feel irritated with an instructor or boss when given a difficult assignment to complete on short notice. Yet one would most likely minimize the expression of irritation to maintain a favorable impression in such situations that involve people who are in a higher position of power. On the other hand, under-expression of emotions can also be problematic. Situations are quite common where one is obligated to express more gratitude or happiness than is felt. For example, when given a gift that is not particularly liked or needed, one may over-express happiness or joy in order to avoid offending the person who gave the gift. Failure to express emotions to the extent others expect may lead to awkward interactions and unfavorable impressions.

Rules governing the experience and expression of emotions are referred to respectively as feeling rules and display rules. Arlie Hochschild (1979) points out that children learn about the nature and appropriateness of particular feelings and expressions from their parents and others through socialization. Children learn early that some feelings are considered inappropriate to express in certain situations and that they are expected to engage in emotion work rather than express the emotion. Emotion work or emotion management involves the attempt to change the inner experience or outward display of the emotion. Display rules, according to Paul Ekman and Wallace Friesen (1975), may require people to minimize the emotion expression (i.e., show less than is felt), replace the emotion (i.e., display a different emotion than the one felt), or enhance the expression (i.e., show more of the emotion than is felt).

The socialization process does not end with childhood. Rather, the process continues throughout adult life, particularly in the context of adult romantic relationships. In the initial stages of relationship development, social and cultural rules influence the behavior of each partner and the trajectory of the relationship. As relationships become more personal, rules unique to each relationship are developed. Partners learn more about each other, developing a larger knowledge base that helps them predict how they will respond to each other's behavior. In addition, as relationships develop, partners are more willing to give each other feedback. The increases in feedback along with the expanding knowledge base lead to the development of feeling and display rules that are more specific to the relationship. Ross Buck (1989) describes this as a social biofeedback process in which unique rules—rules that are idiosyncratic to the relationship—are developed that govern each partner's emotions in the relationship.

As mentioned above, ethnic and cultural background also plays a role in the socialization and management of emotions. The development of feeling and display rules in relationships must always be examined within the context of this cultural backdrop. Consequently, the focus of this entry will be on the influences of relationship development and culture on emotion experience and expression.

Emotions across Relationship Stages

Theories of relationship development suggest that partners typically begin their relationships by exchanging positive disclosures in which partners take turns revealing positive information about themselves. Initially, potential partners will engage in an even exchange of relatively safe, innocuous public information. In essence, partners audition one another for potential friendships or romantic relationships, showing their most positive qualities at first. Emotions during the beginning of a relationship are often a blend of mostly positive feelings. Negative emotions are likely to be minimized in order to maintain a positive impression.

As the partners get to know one another, they begin to reveal their vulnerabilities by exchanging more personal information. Both negative and positive emotions are generally revealed more freely as confidence in the growing strength of the relationship bond increases. However the unique rule system that will eventually govern the feelings and expressions of the relational partners is just beginning to be developed; social and cultural guidelines still provide the basis for the relevant display rules. On the other hand, because there is still a great deal of uncertainty about where the relationship will ultimately lead, partners may experience and display emotions at a higher level of intensity.

After the more turbulent middle stages of relationship development, during which most of the negotiation of emotion feeling and display rules takes place, couples who "survive" may experience and express less intense emotions because uncertainty about the partner and the relationship has been reduced and there are fewer surprises of both the positive and negative variety. The relationship becomes more predictable. During this stage in the relationship, the partners' lives are more intertwined than ever before, and this creates a greater potential for conflict and emotional upheaval. However, the partners also have a better idea about which situations should get more attention, which situations must be dealt with delicately, and when to be more careful in the choice of emotion displays. In short, partners in long-term, satisfying relationships may manage their emotions in order to keep the relationship running smoothly.

A number of studies have investigated emotion management across stages of relationship development. Krystyna S. Aune, R. Kelly Aune, and David Buller (1994) tested the hypothesis that partners early and late in relationship development would feel and display emotions to a lesser degree than couples in middle stages of relationship development. On the other hand, the researchers believed that ratings of appropriateness of emotions would increase across stages. They argued that even though couples in more developed relationships may choose not to express some emotions, they would find it more appropriate to express emotions in more developed relationships than in less developed relationships. The responses from research participants were partially consistent with expectations. Couples in the middle stage of relationship development felt and displayed negative emotions more than couples in the early and late stages. However, the experience and expression of positive emotions did not vary across relationship stages in the expected manner. Perceptions of the appropriateness of both negative and positive emotions also did not vary across stages.

Aune, Buller, and Aune conducted another study in 1996, and this time they did find that perceptions of appropriateness of emotions varied across relationship stages. Early daters (relationships between one and three months in duration) were compared with cohabiting partners and married couples. Both groups reported that positive emotions were more appropriate to express than negative emotions. The expression of negative emotions was perceived as being least appropriate for the early daters. Another indication of display rules, the degree to which people claim to

manage or control their emotions, was also explored in this study. Women in early dating relationships reported that they minimized the display of negative emotions more than did women in married or cohabiting relationships. They also reported managing negative emotions more than positive emotions. Men in early dating relationships, however, reported that they managed their positive emotions to a greater extent than did men in married or cohabiting relationships. These results suggest that married women feel more free to express their negative feelings (e.g., anger and frustration) and married men feel more free to express their positive feelings (e.g., love and joy).

In a follow-up study that examined romantic partners in three stages of relationship development, the tendency to minimize negative emotions was most pronounced among those in the least and most developed relationships and least obvious among couples in the middle stage. Positive emotions were managed the least, regardless of the stage of relationship development. In addition, women reported more emotion management than did men. Perceived appropriateness of emotion expression was found to increase across the three relationship stages. It is interesting to note that the emotion expressions of women in early dating relationships were considered least appropriate. Appropriateness ratings of the experience of emotions did not vary across relationship stages. This latter

This couple's relationship has developed to a stage where both partners are comfortable with a public expression of their positive emotions for each other. (Corbis/Danny Lehman)

finding suggests that inner feelings, which are less obvious or accessible to others, are less rule governed than is the expression of such feelings.

It is important to note that perceptions of the quality and appropriateness of one's own and one's partner's emotions are subjective judgments based on the limited information gathered from interactions with partners. It is also noteworthy that these same limited perceptions provide the foundation for the development of a couple's display rule system. It stands to reason that partners will not always agree on their perceptions of events and that these differences in perceptions may change across levels of intimacy. Evidence of this can be found in a study by Krystyna S. Aune (1997) that compared perceptions of the appropriateness of emotions across relationship stages. Couples in the earliest stages of relationship development showed the biggest difference in ratings of emotion expression appropriateness, while participants in the later stages of relationship development tended to have more similar ratings—further indicating the development of a unique rule system.

Relationship Influences on Emotion Management

Ruth Ann Clark and Jesse Delia (1979) identified three general communication objectives or goals: instrumental, interpersonal, and identity. Instrumental goals involve accomplishing tasks such as obtaining resources from another. Interpersonal goals involve beginning or maintaining a relationship with another. Identity goals relate to self-presentation concerns. Aune and Aune (1997a, 1997b) have argued that emotion management can be understood within Clark and Delia's framework.

As relationships develop, romantic partners experience an increasing sense of unity or cohesion. Partners in more developed relationships should feel more comfortable and communicate more openly with one another over time. They should be more comfortable revealing things about themselves to their partners. Consequently, Aune and Aune (1997a) expected that identity management concerns would provide less motivation for engaging in emotion management as relationships develop. Research results indicated that was the case. As relationships developed, participants reported that they were less concerned with managing their emotion expressions to protect their sense of self or their image with their partner. In addition, participants in more developed relationships reported less inclination to manage their emotions to protect their partner's image. It appears that relationship development allows partners to feel more free to express their emotions spontaneously, without as much concern for maintaining their own or their partner's image.

Aune and Aune (1997a) expected that interpersonal motives would increase across relationship stages as the relationship itself took on an increasing value in the lives of relational partners. People should be more motivated to manage their emotions if it would be good for the relationship. This, too, was consistent with the findings of the study. As relationships developed, participants reported that uncertainty regarding a partner's response to emotion displays became less of a motivation for emotion management.

Instrumental objectives for managing emotions apparently did not vary as relationships developed. Specifically, the researchers examined the use of emotion management as a way of getting or holding on to power in a relationship. Participants in general did not endorse this objective as a motivation for managing motivations.

This research provides an indication of how people experience and express emotions in one of life's most emotionally arousing contexts, romantic relationships. However, emotion experiences are not limited to the world of romance. Emotion experience permeates people's lives and is influenced in large part by another aspect of life that is equally pervasive: culture.

Culture and Emotion

There is some evidence that a small number of emotion displays (i.e., enjoyment, sadness, anger, disgust, surprise, and fear) are interpreted in a very consistent manner across cultures. This lends support to the argument that human emotions are rooted in biological processes and that the experience and the expression of these emotions are rather universal.

However one would be seriously mistaken to assume that the results of these studies indicate that there is no variance in the manner in which people display emotions across cultures. Even if one agrees that some basic emotion experiences and expressions are constrained by biological processes, a growing body of research testifies to the effect that culture has on the manner in which emotions are displayed.

Culture has been described as the belief systems, value systems, customs, and traditions that are passed down from generation to generation. Social norms and patterns of behavior, rituals, and even ways of thinking are all, in part, influenced by the culture in which one is raised. In addition, culture is central in shaping emotion experience and expression.

Cultures are often conceptualized as being more individualistic (e.g., United States) or more collectivistic (e.g., Japan). Individualistic cultures encourage choice, openness, and maintenance of one's personal self-image. One is more likely to be guided by individualized beliefs and goals rather than those of the group. An individual's unique and self-motivated behaviors are more tolerated and accepted in individualistic cultures, and the expression of conflict and dissatisfaction is more acceptable. Collectivistic cultures, on the other hand, value interdependence—the connections among group members—and group harmony. Members of collectivistic cultures tend to be concerned with positive face needs, the concern that others think well of them. The goals, needs, beliefs, and social norms of the group provide the primary influence on an individual's behavior. Open disagreement in such cultures would be perceived to be inappropriate or impolite. In collectivistic cultures, silence may be more indicative of disagreement than in individualistic cultures.

The communication style of collectivistic cultures has been described as a high-context style, wherein the message conveyed by an individual is largely implicit or unspoken and based on internalized information or context cues. In a high-context culture, message receivers are expected to infer more meaning from a source's message than a surface analysis of the message offers. In short, members of a high-context culture are expected to be mind readers to some extent. In contrast, the communication style of individualistic cultures is typically more a low-context style, and the intended message is expressed more directly and explicitly. A message source is encouraged to "say what you mean" and not "beat around the bush." Thus, less meaning must be inferred by the receiver based on the context of the conversation.

Given such basic differences in beliefs and communication styles, it is reasonable to expect that emotion displays would also differ between more collectivistic and more individualistic cultures. In collectivistic cultures, emotions that facilitate group harmony and cohesion would be encouraged. On the other hand, in individualistic cultures, members are typically more free to be unique. As such, people in individualistic cultures may be free to express more fully the entire range of their emotion experiences.

A study by Aune and Aune (1996) illustrated some of these differences. The researchers collected data from Japanese Americans, Euro-Americans, and Filipino Americans, three groups known to differ in the collectivistic/individualistic and high/low context tendencies. Participants reported the intensity and perceived appropriateness of emotions they had recently experienced. The results did not produce the global differences across the cultures that the researchers had expected. Rather, the experience, expression, and perceived appropriateness of positive emotions—but

not negative emotions—varied across cultures. The researchers speculated that rules constraining negative emotions are probably similar across cultures because the detrimental influence of the experience and expression of negative emotions on individuals and groups is similar across cultures. On the other hand, the experience and expression of positive emotions may be used as a tool for creating and enhancing cohesion. This may lead to the cultural variation found in positive emotions.

Filipino Americans reported the highest degree of positive emotion experience, expression, and perceived appropriateness. In addition, Euro-Americans reported lower positive emotion expression than did Japanese Americans. These findings may reflect the relative importance of group harmony among collectivistic cultures such as the Filipino and Japanese Americans. Positive emotions typically facilitate group harmony; consequently, such emotions may be more important to express among Filipino and Japanese Americans relative to the Euro-Americans.

Krystyna S. Aune and Min-Sun Kim (1995) conducted a follow-up study in which Japanese-American and Euro-American couples were videotaped while engaging in a discussion about a problem or issue that was affecting their relationship. Again, the degree of emotion experience, expression, and perceived appropriateness were examined. After completing their discussions, each relational partner independently reviewed the videotape and recorded his or her emotion experiences, expressions, and perceptions of appropriateness. The perceived appropriateness of negative emotion experience and expression were lower among Japanese-American couples than Euro-American couples. Interesting relationships between emotion expression and relationship satisfaction were also found. The expression of Euro-American men's emotions—whether positive or negative—was related to their own and their partners' relationship satisfaction. However neither the positive nor the negative emotion expressions of Euro-American women were associated with their own or their partners' relationship satisfaction.

Negative emotion expression by Japanese-American women and men was not related to their own or their partners' relationship satisfaction. Positive emotion expression by Japanese-American women was related to their partners' relationship satisfaction but not to their own satisfaction. Positive emotion expression by Japanese-American men was not related to their own or their partners' relationship satisfaction.

It is interesting that expressiveness among Euro-American men was associated with the most positive outcomes. This may be due to an added complexity that Euro-American men face regarding emotion expression that Japanese Americans may not face. As already noted, expressiveness is encouraged among members of individualistic cultures; however, emotion expression by Euro-American men is generally less supported than is emotion expression by Euro-American women. Nevertheless, Aune and Kim's study found that Euro-American women who have partners who are, in fact, more expressive of their feelings—whether positive or negative—are relatively more satisfied than those with less expressive partners. It may be that more emotion expressiveness among Euro-American men is indicative of a general tendency to be more open and communicative with their partners. Since Euro-American women place a high value on communication in their relationships, and Euro-American men are not encouraged to be very expressive, having a partner who is more open and willing to communicate may constitute a rather pleasant violation of expectations for Euro-American women.

In general, the findings may reflect the greater value that members of individualistic cultures place on open and direct communication, even regarding one's emotion state. Those in collectivistic cultures do not place as high a value on explicit communication; rather, they believe "let nature take its course."

Cultural Influences on Emotion Management

Cross-cultural research has proposed that the way people see themselves as individuals in relation to others in one's group—self-construal—can alter the effects of culture on their behavior. A growing number of cross-cultural researchers are making use of individual-level versions of the culture-level variables of individualism and collectivism. These researchers examine independent and interdependent self-construals instead of assessing whether an individual is from an individualistic or collectivistic culture. In this manner, researchers can identify a person as being more independent or interdependent, which are dimensions of personality that are similar to the culture-level dimensions of individualism and collectivism. Persons with a more independent construal of the self would be more likely to focus on their own goals and individuality, similar to people from an individualistic culture. People with a more interdependent construal of the self would be more concerned with maintaining harmonious relationships with others, as do people from collectivistic cultures.

Aune and Aune (1997b) examined the usefulness of self-construals in predicting motivations for engaging in emotion management. They found that the more independent one's self-construal, the less likely one is motivated to manage emotions in service of any identity, interpersonal, or instrumental goals. Conversely, the more interdependent types reported more motivation to engage in emotion management to satisfy identity and interpersonal goals. It seems clear that even within cultures there is a fair amount of variance in the extent to which individuals are motivated to engage in emotion management. On the other hand, if these findings are generalized to cross-cultural research, members of more collectivist cultures would be expected to find more motivations to manage their emotions than would members of individualist cultures.

Conclusion

Research on emotion in relationships is flourishing. However considerable work is still needed in order to understand the complexities of feeling and display rule development. The cultural context and the context of intimacy are intricately intertwined, and both influence emotion behavior. As the world becomes a smaller place—a global village—interactions with a greater variety of the world's peoples will be more frequent than at any time in history. These interactions will run the gamut from formal business activities to interpersonal and even romantic engagements. The study of emotion experience and expression offers a depth of understanding of interpersonal interaction that is in keeping with the magnitude of changes in people's personal, social, and cultural lives.

See also: BODY MOVEMENT, GESTURE, AND DISPLAY; CULTURE; EMOTION SUPPRESSION; FACIAL EXPRESSION; GENDER AND EMOTIONS; RELATIONSHIPS; UNIVERSALITY OF EMOTIONAL EXPRESSION

Bibliography

Aune, Krystyna S. (1997). "Participant and Partner Perceptions of Appropriateness of Emotions." *Communication Reports* 10:133–142.

Aune, Krystyna S., and Aune, R. Kelly. (1996). "Cultural Differences in the Self-Reported Experience and Expression of Emotions in Relationships." *Journal of Cross-Cultural Psychology* 27:67–81.

Aune, Krystyna S., and Aune, R. Kelly. (1997a). "Effects of Relationship Level and Biological Sex on Motives for Emotion Management." Paper presented at the May meeting of the International Communication Association, Montreal.

Aune, Krystyna S., and Aune, R. Kelly. (1997b). "The Relationship between Self-Construals and Motivations for Emotion Management." Paper presented at the November meeting of the National Communication Association, Chicago.

Aune, Krystyna S.; Aune, R. Kelly; and Buller, David B. (1994). "The Experience, Expression, and Perceived Appropriateness of Emotions across Levels of Relationship Development." *Journal of Social Psychology* 134:141–150.

Aune, Krystyna S.; Buller, David B.; and Aune, R. Kelly. (1996). "Display Rule Development in Romantic Relationships: Emotion Management and Perceived Appropriateness of Emotions across Relationship Stages." *Human Communication Research* 23:115–145.

Aune, Krystyna S., and Kim, Min-Sun. (1995). "The Effect of Emotion Experience and Expression on Relationship Satisfaction: A Comparison between Ethnically Homogeneous and Heterogeneous Couples." Paper presented at the May meeting of the International Communication Association, Albuquerque, NM.

Berscheid, Ellen. (1987). "Emotion and Interpersonal Communication." In *Interpersonal Processes: New Directions in Communication Research*, ed. Michael E. Roloff and Gerald R. Miller. Beverly Hills: Sage Publications.

Buck, Ross. (1989). "Emotional Communication in Personal Relationships: A Developmental-Interactionist View." In *Close Relationships*, ed. Clyde Hendrick. Newbury Park, CA: Sage Publications.

Clark, Ruth Ann, and Delia, Jesse G. (1979). "Topoi and Rhetorical Competence." *Quarterly Journal of Speech* 65:187–206.

Cloven, Denise H., and Roloff, Michael E. (1994). "A Developmental Model of Decisions to Withhold Relational Irritations in Romantic Relationships." *Personal Relationships* 1:143–164.

Ekman, Paul, and Friesen, Wallace V. (1975). *Unmasking the Face.* Englewood Cliffs, NJ: Prentice-Hall.

Gaelick, Lisa; Bodenhausen, Galen V.; and Wyer, Robert S. (1985). "Emotional Communication in Close Relationships." *Journal of Personality and Social Psychology* 49:1246–1265.

Hochschild, Arlie R. (1979). "Emotion Work, Feeling Rules, and Social Structure." *American Journal of Sociology* 85:551–575.

Hofstede, Geert. (1980). *Culture's Consequences: International Differences in Work-Related Values.* Beverly Hills, CA: Sage Publications.

Markus, Hazel R., and Kitayama, Shinobu. (1991). "Culture and the Self: Implications for Cognition, Emotion, and Motivation." *Psychological Review* 98:224–253.

Matsumoto, David. (1991). "Cultural Influences on Facial Expressions of Emotion." *Southern Communication Journal* 56:128–137.

Notarius, Clifford I., and Johnson, Jennifer S. (1982). "Emotional Expression in Husbands and Wives." *Journal of Marriage and the Family* 44:483–489.

Shimanoff, Susan B. (1985). "Rules Governing the Verbal Expression of Emotions between Married Couples." *Western Journal of Speech Communication* 49:147–165.

Krystyna Strzyzewski Aune
R. Kelly Aune

EMOTION SUPPRESSION

Emotions provide time-tested solutions to the adaptive problems people face. They do this by rapidly coordinating behavioral, experiential, autonomic, and neuroendocrine systems, helping individuals to respond effectively to perceived challenges and opportunities. Thus, when people are afraid, their senses are sharpened, their muscles are primed to move them quickly out of harm's way, and their cardiovascular systems are tuned to provide increased oxygen and energy to large muscle groups that will be called upon when they flee.

However, emotions do not *compel* people to respond in any one specific way. Unlike reflexes, emotions are flexible. This flexibility permits people to regulate their emotions, often by decreasing them. Thus, when neighbors criticize a person's parenting skills, he or she can discount the criticism by thinking, "What do they know, they've never spent time with children." When students are worried about an impending exam, they can try to decrease their feelings of anxiety. When an executive is worked up about being stuck in a frustrating meeting, he or she can breathe deeply to slow a racing heart. And when one driver becomes angry with another driver who almost causes an accident, the first driver usually can keep from chasing after the other driver to teach him or her a lesson.

These examples illustrate some of the ways people regulate emotions. The concern of this entry is emotion suppression, defined as the inhibition of ongoing emotion-expressive behavior. To distinguish between emotion suppression and other forms of emotion regulation, it is useful to refer to a consensual model of emotion that highlights two major classes of emotion regulation. The emotion-generative process begins with an evaluation of either internal or external emotion cues through antecedent-focused emotion regulation (e.g., reappraisal). The resulting evaluation then generates a coordinated set of behavioral, experiential, and physiological response tendencies. These response tendencies may then be modulated by response-focused emotion regulation (e.g., suppression), with this modulation producing the final emotional response.

As this description of the consensual model of emotion indicates, emotions may be regulated at two points in the emotion-generative process. Antecedent-focused emotion regulation is the regulation of emotions by changing either the input to the emotion system or the evaluation of this input. Thus, in the example given above, a parent may re-evaluate the neighbors' criticism of child-rearing techniques in light of their lack of knowledge about children. Response-focused emotion regulation is the regulation of emotions by modulating emotion response tendencies once they have already been generated. Thus, in the examples given above, individuals may deny feelings of anxiety, decrease their physiological arousal in a meeting, or inhibit their aggressive impulses. Finer distinctions may be made among various forms of emotion regulation, but these distinctions are sufficient for the purposes of this entry.

The Development of Emotion Suppression

From an early age, parents teach children not to show their disappointment when relatives give them disappointing presents, such as knitted socks, for their birthdays. With their parents' help, children learn display rules, cultural rules regarding which emotions to express, when to express them, and how to do so. The ability to suppress emotional expression is vital for carrying out many such display rules. Indeed, children's skill at emotion suppression has been demonstrated in several research studies. In one study, Carolyn Saarni (1984) found that children between the ages of six and ten were able to keep from expressing negative emotion when given an unattractive present and often tried to put on a smile (although young boys did tend to show some negative emotion). In a second study, Pamela Cole (1986) found that children as young as three or four years of age were able to suppress their negative facial expressions when given an unattractive present in the presence of an experimenter.

As Paul Harris (1989) points out, however, there may be an important difference between the three-year-old children and the ten-year-old children in these studies. When the three-year-old children in Cole's study were asked to describe how the adult experimenter thought they felt about the present, they said that the experimenter knew that they were disappointed. This finding suggests that the younger children were unable to distinguish between their experience of the emotion and their expression of it. Harris's own work shows that children between the ages of six and ten begin to understand that

emotions have multiple components and that emotion experience can be different from emotion expression. Understanding this distinction is vital for understanding that one's feelings can be effectively hidden from others, via suppression. It is during this period, then, that children truly begin to understand the display rules they have been practicing for many years.

Emotion Suppression and Gender

Apart from age, one of the most important predictors of emotion suppression is gender. In Great Britain and the United States, display rules against open emotion expression generally are stronger for men than for women. One emotion for which this is particularly true is sadness. Cultural stereotypes assert that "real men do not cry" and that boys who cry are "sissies." Research generally confirms these stereotypes. Men report weeping less frequently and with lesser intensity than women, and men are seven times less likely to cry during a sad film than are women. Note that differences in expressivity are not simply the result of men experiencing less emotion than women. One study showed that men were less expressive than women during a sad film even though they reported feeling comparable levels of sadness.

One indicator of the level of a child's development is the ability to suppress negative facial expressions in public situations, such as when a child is opening gifts in the presence of others. (Corbis/Jennie Woodcock; Reflections Photolibrary)

Sex differences in emotion expression are not limited to sadness; there have also been documented sex differences in happiness and fear expressive behavior. The findings in this area suggest that men generally may be somewhat more likely to suppress emotion than women. There may, however, be emotions for which the typical sex difference is absent or even reversed. For example, women seem to be called upon to suppress anger to a greater degree than men. The evidence on this point is somewhat mixed, but research on emotion expressivity suggests than men in Western cultures suppress their emotions to a greater degree than do women. Consistent with this general notion, men report masking their emotions for the purposes of self-presentation more than women.

Emotion Suppression and Culture

Gender differences illustrate how emotion suppression can vary for individuals within one culture. Of even greater import, perhaps, are cultural differences, which illustrate how emotion suppression can vary for individuals from different cultures. Indeed, the very concept of *cultural* display rules makes explicit the notion that culture determines the expression of emotion. One example of how cultures differ concerns anger. Aggression and the expression of anger are carefully regulated in American culture and many others. However, this is not always the case. Among the Ilongot, a tribe of hunters in northern Lozan in the Philippines, the display of the emotion of anger, or liget as it is called, plays a very important part in the culture. Harris (1989, p. 128) describes liget in the following way: "[L]iget, roughly translated as energy/anger/passion, . . . can rouse men to kill, not simply as an act of vengeance, but as a means of emotional expression and as a means of emulating the feats of their fathers and elders." The pressure on young men is to express liget, not to suppress it.

There also are more pervasive differences among cultures that are important to an understanding of emotion suppression. For example, cultural psychologists Hazel Markus and Shinobu Kitayama (1991) have suggested that one important difference among cultures is that of independence versus interdependence. In independent cultures such as the United States, the self is seen as independent from others, and behavior is organized and understood through relations to one's own internal states (e.g., thoughts and feelings). Thus, individual expression, including emotion expression, is encouraged. In interdependent cultures such as Japan, by contrast, the self is seen as intertwined with others. The focus is on the relationship between the self and others, and a great premium is placed on maintaining group harmony. In such cultures, emotions are shaped and directed through the consideration of the reactions of others.

These cultural differences lead to different rules governing the expression of certain emotions, such as disgust, anger, and sadness, that might adversely effect group harmony if they were expressed. For example, David Matsumoto (1990) has shown that Americans find it more acceptable to display sadness and disgust to friends and relatives than do the Japanese. Likewise, Paul Ekman (1973) has shown that although there are no differences in the expressions of Japanese and American participants watching a disgusting film alone in the semi-darkness, Japanese participants are far less expressive than the Americans when answering questions about their feelings while watching a disgusting film in the presence of a member of their own culture. Other research shows that Japanese children are taught not to show emotions such as anger and sadness early on, highlighting the important role played by culture in emotion suppression.

The Immediate Effects of Emotion Suppression

Does inhibiting emotion-expressive behavior decrease emotion? Or, on the contrary, does inhibiting emotion-expressive behavior increase the emotional response? These questions have been much debated by psychologists, and two relevant literatures make opposing predictions. The internalizer-externalizer literature shows that individuals who are typically emotionally inexpressive (i.e., internalizers) are more physiologically reactive than those who are expressive (i.e., externalizers). These findings have been interpreted in terms of a "hydraulic model" that suggests that the inhibition of emotion expression leads to greater responses in other channels such as the autonomic nervous system. The facial feedback literature, in contrast, is based on the notion that emotion-expressive behavior has positive feedback effects. This literature suggests that decreased expressiveness through emotion suppression should decrease emotion experience.

Several studies addressing this debate suggest that emotion suppression leads to findings consistent with *both* sets of predictions. James Gross and Robert Levenson (1993, 1997) asked individuals to suppress their expressions of disgust, sadness, or amusement during a series of emotionally evocative films. Participants asked to suppress their emotions exhibited diminished behavioral responding across emotion conditions, and their heart rates generally followed the changes in their bodily movements. At the same time, however, participants asked to suppress their emotions showed *greater* sympathetic nervous system activation, which is a key component of the stress response system and prepares the body for vigorous action. Despite these pronounced physiological changes, emotion suppression had little effect on the subjective experience of emotion. One exception was the suppression of amusement, which led to decreased self-reports of amusement experience.

The Long-Term Effects of Emotion Suppression

Over the long term, emotion suppression appears to play an important role in psychological health. This is because it is often vitally important to restrain emotional impulses. For example, depressed individuals must suppress negative responses to others if they are to avoid alienating themselves from loved ones. Chronically angry men must suppress their urges to strike their wives or children. And social phobics must suppress anxious feelings that compromise their functioning at work. At other times, however, emotion suppression actually may be detrimental to one's psychological health, particularly when suppression is chronic and inflexible. As research has shown, suppression does not decrease the experience of negative emotions, and it may make it difficult for a person's social partners to be aware of and respond to his or her needs. If one's partner does something that makes one angry, but one suppresses the emotion, then the partner may be oblivious to the problem and do nothing to change the behavior. In this case, one is likely to have even more negative feelings, perhaps at even greater intensity levels. In support of this idea, a study by David Spiegel and his colleagues (1983) found that women who felt that they could be open with their families about their feelings experienced less mood disturbance than women who did not feel this way.

Emotion suppression may also affect long-term physical health, especially if the transient increases in sympathetic activation associated with emotion suppression are repeated frequently over a long period of time. This is particularly likely if emotion suppression prevents the people one is interacting with from adjusting their behavior to meet one's needs, as this increases the frequency of one's emotional responses.

The result would be both more frequent and more pronounced physiological responses, which potentially could have consequences for physical health. Although the evidence linking emotion suppression with long-term physical health outcomes is far from conclusive, there are hints that emotion suppression may negatively affect long-term physical health. James Pennebaker (1989) found that college students who disclosed the most traumatic, stressful experience of their lives and their feelings about it had fewer visits to the student health center in the six months following the study than did students writing either only about the facts of the trauma or only about their feelings. Emotion suppression has also been linked with more serious health conditions. Research on cardiovascular disease has shown that a pattern of behavior, called Type A behavior pattern (TABP), is a significant risk factor for disease, and the suppression of hostility may play a key role in the relationship between TABP and cardiovascular disease. For example, a study by Carol Malatesta-Magai and her colleagues (1992) found that the group of individuals who are most at risk for cardiovascular disease (i.e., men under the age of fifty who exhibited TABP) reported suppressing the expression of anger more than other individuals. Emotion suppression may also play a role in cancer onset and progression. For example, Spiegel (1992) has shown that women with metastatic breast cancer who were involved in a support group emphasizing direct confrontation of fears and expression of affect (especially negative affect) lived longer than otherwise equivalent women who were not involved in a support group. Together, these findings raise more questions than they answer, but they also suggest that emotion suppression may indeed play a role in long-term health and illness.

See also: BODY MOVEMENT, GESTURE, AND DISPLAY; EMOTION EXPERIENCE AND EXPRESSION; FACIAL EXPRESSION; HEALTH AND ILLNESS; UNIVERSALITY OF EMOTIONAL EXPRESSION

Bibliography

Averill, James R. (1982). *Anger and Aggression: An Essay on Emotion.* New York: Springer-Verlag.

Buck, Ross W. (1979). "Individual Differences in Non-Verbal Sending Accuracy and Electrodermal Responding: The Externalizing-Internalizing Dimension." In *Skill in Non-Verbal Communication,* ed. Robert Rosenthal. Cambridge, MA: Oelgeschlager, Gunn & Hain.

Cole, Pamela M. (1986). "Children's Spontaneous Control of Facial Expression." *Child Development* 57:1309–1321.

Ekman, Paul. (1973). "Cross-Cultural Studies of Facial Expression." In *Darwin and Facial Expression,* ed. Paul Ekman. New York: Academic Press.

Ekman, Paul, and Friesen, Wallace V. (1969). "The Repertoire

> *Anton Chekhov's "A Doctor's Visit" (1898) describes a young physician who is making a house call out in the country to see what is ailing the factory owner's daughter, who suffers from heart palpitations. Although he finds nothing physically wrong with the girl, the physician realizes that the loneliness, isolation, and prison-like quality of her life prevent the girl from having an emotional outlet.*

of Nonverbal Behavior: Categories, Origin, Usage, and Coding." *Semiotica* 1:49–98.

Gross, James J. (1989). "Emotional Expression in Cancer Onset and Progression." *Social Science and Medicine* 28:1239–1248.

Gross, James J. (1998a). "Antecedent- and Response-Focused Emotion Regulation: Divergent Consequences for Experience, Expression, and Physiology." *Journal of Personality and Social Psychology* 74:224–237.

Gross, James J. (1998b). "The Emerging Field of Emotion Regulation: An Integrative Review." *Review of General Psychology* 2:217–299.

Gross, James J.; Fredrickson, Barbara L.; and Levenson, Robert W. (1994). "The Psychophysiology of Crying." *Psychophysiology* 31:460–468.

Gross, James J., and John, Oliver P. (1998). "Mapping the Domain of Expressivity: Multimethod Evidence for a Hierarchical Model." *Journal of Personality and Social Psychology* 74:170–191.

Gross, James J., and Levenson, Robert W. (1993). "Emotional Suppression: Physiology, Self-Report, and Expressive Behavior." *Journal of Personality and Social Psychology* 64:970–986.

Gross, James J., and Levenson, Robert W. (1997). "Hiding Feelings: The Acute Effects of Inhibiting Negative and Positive Emotion." *Journal of Abnormal Psychology* 106:95–103.

Harris, Paul L. (1989). *Children and Emotion: The Development of Psychological Understanding.* Cambridge, MA: Basil Blackwell.

Kring, Ann M., and Gordon, Albert H. (1998). "Sex Differences in Emotion: Expression, Experience, and Physiology." *Journal of Personality and Social Psychology* 74:686–703.

Malatesta-Magai, Carol; Jonas, Ruth; Shepard, Beth; and Culver, L. C. (1992). "Type A Behavior Pattern and Emotion Expression in Younger and Older Adults." *Psychology and Aging* 7:551–561.

Markus, Hazel R., and Kitayama, Shinobu. (1991). "Culture and the Self: Implications for Cognition, Emotion, and Motivation." *Psychological Review* 98:224–253.

Matsumoto, David. (1990). "Cultural Similarities and Differences in Display Rules." *Motivation and Emotion* 14:195–214.

Pennebaker, James W. (1989). "Confession, Inhibition, and Disease." In *Advances in Experimental Social Psychology, Vol. 22,* ed. Leonard Berkowitz. San Diego, CA: Academic Press.

Saarni, Carolyn. (1984). "An Observational Study of Children's Attempts to Monitor Their Expressive Behavior." *Child Development* 55:1504–1513.

Sapolsky, Robert M. (1998). *Why Zebras Don't Get Ulcers: An Updated Guide to Stress, Stress-Related Diseases, and Coping.* New York: W. H. Freeman.

Spiegel, David. (1992). "Effects of Psychosocial Support on Patients with Metastatic Breast Cancer." *Journal of Psychosocial Oncology* 10:113–133.

Spiegel, David; Bloom, Joan R.; and Gottheil, Ellen. (1983). "Family Environment as a Predictor of Adjustment to Metastatic Breast Carcinoma." *Journal of Psychosocial Oncology* 1:33–44.

Tooby, John, and Cosmides, Leda. (1990). "The Past Explains the Present: Emotional Adaptations and the Structure of Ancestral Environments." *Ethnology and Sociobiology* 11:375–424.

Williams, D. G. (1982). "Weeping by Adults: Personality Correlates and Sex Differences." *Journal of Psychology* 110:217–226.

Heather J. Miles
James J. Gross

EMPATHIC ACCURACY

Empathic *inference* is the "everyday mind reading" that people do whenever they attempt to infer other people's thoughts and feelings. Empathic *accuracy* is the extent to which such attempts are successful. When Sara's roommate Joanne is the only one who understands that Sara is embarrassed, rather than pleased, that her neighbors have thrown a surprise birthday party for her, Joanne has achieved better empathic accuracy than any of Sara's neighbors have. Similarly, when Carlos is the only person in the office who understands the meaning of the look that passes between the boss and his secretary, Carlos has achieved better empathic accuracy than any of his fellow salespersons. On the other hand, when Frieda is the only person in the classroom who fails to understand that Sam has been mimicking the speech of their teacher, Mr. Yardley, her relative lack of empathic accuracy becomes evident to all of the other students.

Empathic accuracy has long been recognized as one of the most fundamental aspects of human social intelligence. Carl Rogers, the American clinical psychologist, used the term *accurate empathy* in 1957 to describe an important attribute of the ideal counselor or psychotherapist. More recently, science writer Daniel Goleman (1995) summarized a large body of research on emotional intelligence and concluded that the ability to accurately "read" other people's thoughts and feelings is an important skill that affects people's social adjustment in all phases of their life: as students in the classroom, as playmates and platonic friends, as dating and marriage partners, as parents, as members of the workforce, and as members of the larger community.

Measurement and Theoretical Background

As important as empathic accuracy is acknowledged to be, it has also proved to be a difficult concept to study. How, for example, can one measure the degree to which one person accurately infers the specific content of another person's thoughts and feelings? The work of Carl Rogers suggested that an ideal measure of empathic accuracy would be one that (1) could be used to track the accuracy of the therapist's inferences over the course of the client-therapist interaction and (2) would be objective in defining accuracy in terms of the degree to which the perceiver's inferences matched the client's actual reported thoughts and feelings. Many attempts to develop such a measure were made over the next four decades by researchers in areas such as clinical and counseling psychology, communication studies, marriage and family studies, psychiatry, and personality and social psychology. It was not until the 1990s, however, that researchers developed measurement procedures that satisfied the criteria suggested by Rogers.

In 1990, William Ickes, Linda Stinson, Victor Bissonnette, and Stella Garcia reported a technique for measuring empathic accuracy as the degree to which each of a perceiver's inferences matches the actual reported content of a target's person's successive thoughts and feelings. In 1992, Robert Levenson and Anna Ruef reported a technique for measuring empathic accuracy as the degree to which each of a perceiver's inferences matches the actual reported valence and intensity of a target person's changing emotional states. In both techniques, perceivers attempt to infer aspects of a target person's actual subjective experience "on line" while viewing a videotape of the target person in conversation with either a therapist or another interaction partner. Empathic accuracy is objectively defined in terms of the degree to which the perceiver's inference matches the target's actual reported experience at each of the target-defined tape stops. The accuracy scores for the individual inferences can then be collected across time or across targets for subsequent analysis.

The measurement technique developed by Ickes and his colleagues tends to emphasize the cognitive-inferential aspect of empathic accuracy, whereas the technique developed by Levenson and Ruef tends to emphasize the emotional resonance aspect. Various writers have proposed that the emotional resonance aspect of empathic accuracy is based largely on the physiological synchrony between the perceiver and the target person (i.e., the degree to which certain of the perceiver's physiological responses covary with those of the target). In contrast, writers who have focused on the cognitive-inferential aspect of empathic accuracy have proposed that it depends on factors such as cognitive perspective taking, "theory of mind," socialization and enculturation, and general information processing ability.

Whereas accuracy in decoding another person's changing emotional state appears to be relatively automatic and to depend less on prior knowledge of the other person, accuracy in inferring the specific content of another's thoughts and feelings appears to be more deliberate and to require the types of knowledge structures that are acquired during the course of an acquaintanceship. Not surprisingly, research has revealed that friends are generally more accurate in "reading" each other's thoughts and feelings than strangers are. However, as Geoff Thomas and Garth Fletcher (1997) have noted, empathic accuracy is determined not only by the knowledge structures developed within the relationship but by those developed outside the relationship as well. They have argued for the relevance of several types of knowledge structures that include idealizations or models of hypothetical relationships, theories about specific relationships and specific partners, general and partner-specific stereotypes, and heuristic cognitive strategies such as assumed similarity (i.e., "projection").

Research Findings and Implications

For decades, researchers have found it difficult to identify personality variables that reliably distinguish "good" from "poor" perceivers. Surveying the available research conducted since 1955, Mark Davis and Linda Kraus (1997) concluded that self-report measures of social sensitivity have consistently failed to predict individual differences in accuracy on various social inference tasks. Plausible reasons for this failure are that (1) evolutionary pressures have operated to create a relatively narrow range of individual differences in empathic ability and (2) individuals cannot easily discern these subtle individual differences and therefore lack valid observational knowledge about their own empathic ability.

What about gender as a basis for individual differences in empathic ability? Contrary to the social stereotype regarding the presumed superiority of "women's intuition," a review by Tiffany Graham and Ickes (1997) of the relevant literature yielded no compelling evidence that women, on average, have more ability than men to infer accurately the specific content of other people's thoughts and feelings. Instead, the findings suggested that situational factors can evoke more motivation in women to do well on empathic inference tasks and that women will outperform men only to the extent that this differential motivation is engaged. Given equal opportunities to develop their empathic skills and equal motivation to apply them, men seem to be able to close the gap between their performance and that of their female counterparts.

Individuals seem to benefit from receiving immediate feedback about the accuracy of their empathic inferences. In a clinically relevant study conducted by Carol Marangoni and her colleagues (1995), perceivers attempted to infer the actual thoughts and feelings reported by three female clients who appeared in videotaped psychotherapy sessions. Some perceivers were able to see the client's actual thought or feeling following each of their empathic inferences (feedback condition); other perceivers were not (control condition). Perceivers in the feedback condition subsequently displayed greater empathic accuracy than those in the control condition, and this effect was greater when the client was relatively easy to "read" than when the client was relatively difficult to "read."

This finding suggests that empathic accuracy is, to some degree, a trainable skill.

Contrary to the commonsense intuition that better understanding always contributes to better relationships, research findings suggest that satisfaction and stability in close relationships are not always enhanced by high levels of empathic accuracy. Under certain circumstances, motivated *inaccuracy* appears to be adaptive in helping individuals preserve their close relationships in situations in which accurate knowledge of the partner's thoughts and feelings would have a highly threatening and destabilizing effect. Indeed, there is evidence that much of the distress experienced by anxious-ambivalent individuals in dating relationships can be attributed to their apparently strong need to infer accurately their partner's relationship-threatening thoughts and feelings.

Although the research on empathic accuracy is still in its infancy, the topic has already proved to be of considerable theoretical and applied interest. As a fundamental dimension of social intelligence, empathic accuracy is of interest to communication researchers, evolutionary theorists, clinical and counseling psychologists, developmental and social psychologists, and psychiatrists and social workers. From an applied perspective, it is of interest not only to clinical practitioners but also to professionals in fields such as education, diplomacy, bargaining and negotiation, personnel management, and direct sales and marketing. Because empathic accuracy is important in practical as well as theoretical terms, it should increasingly become an important focus of psychological research.

See also: EMOTIONAL INTELLIGENCE; EMPATHY; ROGERS, CARL RANSOM; SYMPATHY

Bibliography

Colvin, C. Randall; Ickes, William; and Vogt, Dawn. (1997). "Why Do Friends Understand Each Other Better Than Strangers Do?" *Empathic Accuracy,* ed. William Ickes. New York: Guilford.

Davis, Mark H., and Kraus, Linda A. (1997). "Personality and Empathic Accuracy." In *Empathic Accuracy,* ed. William Ickes. New York: Guilford.

Eisenberg, Nancy; Murphy, Bridget C.; and Shepard, Stephanie. (1997). "The Development of Empathic Accuracy." In *Empathic Accuracy,* ed. William Ickes. New York: Guilford.

Goleman, Daniel. (1995). *Emotional Intelligence.* New York: Bantam Books.

Graham, Tiffany, and Ickes, William. (1997). "When Women's Intuition Isn't Greater Than Men's." In *Empathic Accuracy,* ed. William Ickes. New York: Guilford.

Ickes, William. (1993). "Empathic Accuracy." *Journal of Personality* 61:587–610.

Ickes, William, ed. (1997). *Empathic Accuracy.* New York: Guilford.

Ickes, William; Stinson, Linda; Bissonnette, Victor; and Garcia, Stella. (1990). "Naturalistic Social Cognition: Empathic Accuracy in Mixed-Sex Dyads." *Journal of Personality and Social Psychology* 59:730–742.

Levenson, Robert W., and Ruef, Anna M. (1992). "Empathy: A Physiological Substrate." *Journal of Personality and Social Psychology* 63:234–246.

Levenson, Robert W., and Ruef, Anna M. (1997). "Physiological Aspects of Emotional Knowledge and Rapport." In *Empathic Accuracy,* ed. William Ickes. New York: Guilford.

Marangoni, Carol; Garcia, Stella; Ickes, William; and Teng, Gary. (1995). "Empathic Accuracy in a Clinically Relevant Setting." *Journal of Personality and Social Psychology* 68:854–869.

Rogers, Carl R. (1957). "The Necessary and Sufficient Conditions of Therapeutic Personality Change." *Journal of Consulting Psychology* 21:95–103.

Simpson, Jeffry A.; Ickes, William; and Blackstone, Tami. (1995). "When the Head Protects the Heart: Empathic Accuracy in Dating Relationships." *Journal of Personality and Social Psychology* 69:629–641.

Thomas, Geoff, and Fletcher, Garth J. O. (1997). "Empathic Accuracy in Close Relationships." In *Empathic Accuracy,* ed. William Ickes. New York: Guilford.

William Ickes

EMPATHY

Empathy has been a topic of interest to philosophers and scientists for several centuries, but only since the 1950s has empathy been the topic of research by social scientists interested in understanding empathy as an emotional reaction. Some researchers have defined empathy as an emotional reaction that is congruent with the emotional reactions of a target, whereas other researchers have argued that empathy is an other-oriented feeling of concern and compassion that results from witnessing the suffering of another person.

The most comprehensive and inclusive definition is offered by Mark Davis (1994) in an organizational model of empathy that seeks to capture all of the facets of this important human phenomenon. He defines empathy as "a set of constructs having to do with the responses of one individual to the experiences of another. These constructs specifically include the processes taking place within the observer and the affective and non-affective outcomes which result from those processes" (p. 12). The model takes into account the importance of what the person brings to the situation, the thoughts that accompany and contribute to empathy, the emotions that are experienced during an empathetic episode, as well as the behaviors that are likely to result from the experience of empathy.

Basic Components of Empathy

Using Davis's multidimensional approach to empathy facilitates the understanding of the components of empathy. The antecedents to empathy involve both aspects of the person and the situation. Person variables include whether or not a person has the intellectual capacity for empathy, the person's exposure to opportunities to learn about empathy, and the extent to which the person has internalized those empathic values, as well as individual differences in perspective taking and emotionality. Situational variables include the strength of the situation, such as how obvious the needs of targets are, as well as the degree of similarity between the observer and the target.

The processes that generate empathic outcomes include noncognitive processes, such as the innate tendency to respond to a baby's cry and the tendency to mimic the reactions of others, as well as simple cognitive processes that are shaped by classical conditioning and direct association, and advanced cognitive processes that depend on language and interpretation. The outcomes of empathy can be both intrapersonal and interpersonal. The intrapersonal outcomes consist of the emotional reactions that are experienced by the observer in response to the other. These can include either the reproduction of the other's feelings, the reactive emotions such as compassion or personal distress, or nonaffective outcomes such as empathic accuracy, which is the successful estimation of other people's thoughts, feelings, and characteristics. Finally, interpersonal outcomes involve the behaviors that empathy elicits from observers toward targets, such as helping, aggression, and relationship building.

Empathy and Other Emotions

The difficulty with Davis's broad definition of empathy is that it does not contribute to distinguishing empathy from related, but separate, emotions. Daniel Batson (1991), for example, argues that people can experience two kinds of emotional reactions upon witnessing the suffering of another person: empathy and personal distress. Empathy is composed of other-oriented feelings, such as compassion and warmth, whereas personal distress is composed of self-focused negative feelings such as anxiety and fear. In a series of carefully controlled experiments, Batson found that when a person focuses on the well-being of the other, or when empathy is elicited, helping occurs. But when a person focuses on his or her own well-being or when feelings of personal distress are elicited, helping is reduced or avoided.

The Origins of Empathy

There are thee levels of analysis in understanding the origins of empathy. The first considers empathy in the context of the evolution of altruism (i.e., unselfish regard for or devotion to the welfare of others). Given that survival is a strong motive, why is it that members of some groups act in ways that benefit others, even to the detriment of themselves? An evolutionary interpretation suggests that the fitness of an organism may be advanced by altruism in two ways: through kin selection altruism (by helping others with high genetic similarity) and through reciprocal altruism (by promoting mutually beneficial exchange relations among non-kin). One mechanism to encourage such forms of altruism is empathy. The tendency of infants to cry in response to the cries of other infants has been cited by Abraham Sagi and Martin Hoffman (1976) as evidence of an innate affective response to the distress of others. Such affective responses can serve as motivation for the development and performance of helping behavior. Research on emotional intelligence by Daniel Goleman (1996) and John Mayer and Peter Salovey (1997) also suggests the importance of empathy as a valuable skill for surviving in an increasingly complicated social world.

A second level of analysis in the origin of empathy focuses on empathy as a stable individual disposition that varies across people. Twin studies conducted by Robert Plomin (1986) indicate that many personality traits, such as extroversion and emotional reactivity involve heritability coefficients of 0.40 to 0.50. Empathic concern, as studied by Davis and his colleagues (1994) seems to be heritable at comparable or higher levels. Other studies, such as those conducted by Albert Mehrabian and his colleagues (1988), have shown that temperament qualities, such as emotionality, are an important aspect of the heritability of empathy.

The third level of analysis in examining the origins of empathy focuses on the situational variables that promote or discourage empathetic responses. Most of this work centers around the importance of family relationships and patterns of parental discipline in the development of empathy. Roberta Kestenbaum and her colleagues (1989) have found that securely attached children exhibit more empathetic behaviors, such as patting a peer who is distressed, than do insecurely attached children. In addition, Carolyn Henry and her colleagues (1996) have found that family cohesion and emotional expressiveness also predict adult empathic reactions to others in distress.

Research on parenting style found that parents who use inductive child-rearing methods, such as appealing to a child's guilt by stressing the consequences of the misbehavior for others, are more likely to produce children who care about and defend others at school and offer sympathy and help to victims. Thus, how children are raised affects their levels of expressed empathy.

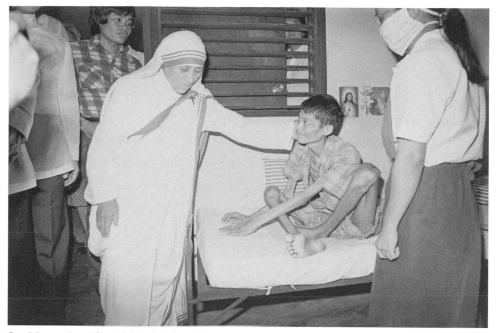

On November 27, 1982, Mother Teresa provides compassionate comfort to a polio victim at a home for the destitute in Manila, Philippines. (Corbis/Bettmann)

Variability in Experience and Expression of Empathy

There may be wide variability in the experience and expression of empathy among humans. Some research has explored whether or not differences exist between men and women. The meta-analysis conducted by Nancy Eisenberg and Randy Lennon (1983) of a number of studies found no substantial differences between girls and boys. They did find, however, that adult women surpassed men in decoding of both visual and auditory cues of others and that women were more likely to score higher on self-report measures of affective tendencies than men. It should be noted that questions have been raised about the validity of self-report findings that mirror sex-role stereotypes.

Effects of Empathy on Targets

There is a growing literature about the development of empathy and its relationship to important human behaviors such as helping, aggression, and relationship formation and maintenance.

The research about altruism has found a complex link between emotional aspects of empathy and helping. For example, the paradoxical finding that negative mood sometimes increases helping can be explained by the relation of guilt and sadness to feelings of empathy. Michael Cunningham and his colleagues (1980, 1990) reported that negative mood may decrease or increase helping behavior, depending on the helper's focus of attention and feelings of personal responsibility to help. Anita Barbee and Cunningham (1995) have found that high empathy induces individuals to employ more helpful forms of social support with their friends and romantic partners. There is also some evidence that empathy suppresses aggressive tendencies, although more research is needed to fully understand the relationship between these two variables.

Much of the research since the mid-1980s has focused on the effect of empathy on the maintenance of close relationships. Studies conducted by Tom Bradbury and Frank Fincham (1988) of married couples suggest that those individuals who have better perspective-taking skills and emotional empathy respond in more positive ways toward their partners in conflict situations and are more likely to give their partner the benefit of the doubt when they act bad. Furthermore, Davis and Linda Kraus (1991) found that having a partner who is high on dispositional empathy is associated with greater relationship satisfaction.

Conclusion

Empathy is a complex, socially relevant emotion. While evolutionary forces have led to a situation in which the majority of humans possess the ability to understand the thoughts and feelings of others and to respond affectively to the experience of those others, there are large individual differences in the degree to which these abilities are employed. Genetic, cognitive, and environmental factors influence the experience and expression of empathy in a variety of interpersonal contexts. Thus, empathy will continue to be a topic of interest to scientists and the general public for some time to come.

See also: ATTACHMENT; EMOTIONAL INTELLIGENCE; EMPATHIC ACCURACY; GENETICS; GUILT; MOOD; RELATIONSHIPS; SADNESS; SYMPATHY; TEMPERAMENT

Bibliography

Barbee, Anita P., and Cunningham, Michael R. (1995). "An Experimental Approach to Social Support: Interactive Coping in Close Relationships." *Communication Yearbook* 18:381–413.

Batson, C. Daniel. (1991). *The Altruism Question: Toward a Social-Psychological Answer.* Hillsdale, NJ: Lawrence Erlbaum.

Bradbury, Thomas, and Fincham, Frank. (1988). "Individual Difference Variables in Close Relationships: A Contextual Model of Marriage As an Integrative Framework." *Journal of Personality and Social Psychology* 54:1–9.

Cunningham, Michael R.; Steinberg, Jeff; and Grev, Rita. (1980). "Wanting to and Having to Help: Separate Motivations for Positive Mood and Guilt-Induced Helping." *Journal of Personality and Social Psychology* 38:181–192.

Cunningham, Michael R.; Shaffer, David R.; Barbee, Anita P.; Wolff, Patricia L.; and Kelly, David J. (1990). "Separate Processes in the Relation of Elation and Depression to Helping: Social Versus Personal Concerns." *Journal of Experimental Social Psychology* 26:13–33.

Davis, Mark H. (1994). *Empathy: A Social Psychological Approach.* Madison, WI: Brown and Benchmark.

Davis, Mark H., and Kraus, Linda A. (1991). "Dispositional Empathy and Social Relationships." In *Advances in Personal Relationships, Vol. 3,* ed. Warren H. Jones and Daniel Perlman. London: Jessica Kingsley.

Davis, Mark H.; Luce, Carol; and Kraus, Stephen J. (1994). "The Heritability of Characteristics Associated with Dispositional Empathy." *Journal of Personality* 62:369–391.

Eisenberg, Nancy, and Lennon, Randy. (1983). "Sex Differences in Empathy and Related Capacities." *Psychological Bulletin* 94:100–131.

Goleman, Daniel. (1996). *Emotional Intelligence.* London: Bloomsbury.

Henry, Carolyn; Sager, David W.; and Plunkett, Scott W. (1996). "Adolescents' Perceptions of Family System Characteristics, Parent-Adolescent Dyadic Behaviors, Adolescent Qualities, and Adolescent Empathy." *Family Relations* 45:283–292.

Ickes, William. (1997). *Empathic Accuracy.* New York: Guilford.

Kestenbaum, Roberta; Farber, Ellen A.; and Sroufe, L. Alan. (1989). "Individual Differences in Empathy among Preschoolers: Relation to Attachment History." *New Directions for Child Development* 44:51–64.

Mayer, John D., and Salovey, Peter. (1997). "What Is Emotional Intelligence?" In *Emotional Development and Emotional Intelligence: Educational Implications,* ed. Peter Salovey. New York: Basic Books.

Mehrabian, Albert; Young, Andrew; Sato, Sharon. (1988). "Emotional Empathy and Associated Individual Differences." *Current Psychology: Research and Reviews* 7:221–240.

Plomin, Robert. (1986). "Behavioral Genetic Methods." *Journal of Personality* 54:226–261.

Rosenstein, Paula. (1995). "Parental Levels of Empathy As Related to Risk Assessment in Child Protective Services." *Child Abuse and Neglect* 19:1349–1360.

Sagi, Abraham, and Hoffman, Martin. (1976). "Empathic Distress in Newborns." *Developmental Psychology* 12:175–176.

Anita P. Barbee

ENTHUSIASM

See Happiness; Motivation; Pleasure; Sports

ENVY

Envy is experienced when people compare themselves to other individuals and begrudge them their superior achievements, possessions, personality traits, or whatever else happens to be of value at the time of the comparison. Accompanying this mental assessment of inferiority is the desire to possess the superior qualities or the wish that the object of the comparison did not possess them. There is the tendency to use the word *jealousy* in place of the word *envy.* Jealousy refers to the fear of losing something of value to a rival, perhaps one's job or, more common in romantic relationships, one's partner.

Approximately 20 percent of the world's languages have only one word for envy and the related emotion of jealousy. Even when languages identify the emotions with two separate terms, they differ in how carefully the distinction is observed in everyday usage. For example, the terms are not used interchangeably in Russian. On the other hand, Richard Smith and his colleagues (1988) found that in the United States the term *jealousy* has broader meaning for the general public than does the term *envy.* That is, the term *jealousy* can refer either to jealousy or envy predicaments, whereas the term *envy* refers only to envy predicaments. The public is not alone in its lackadaisical application of the two terms. Some researchers, such as Peter Salovey and Judith Rodin (1984), also view envy and jealousy as synonymous. However, Gerrod Parrott and Richard Smith (1993) found that envy and jealousy are in fact two distinct experiences. Envy involves feeling inferior in comparison to another individual, longing for what the other one has, resentment, and (perhaps because of the Christian view of envy as one of the seven deadly sins) disapproval of one's envy. In contrast, romantic jealousy involves distrust, anxiety, anger, and the fear of losing one's partner to a rival. In short, jealousy is experienced as a threat, while envy is experienced as a feeling of mortification and ill will by both men and women.

Causes of Envy

The Dutch have a proverb, "If envy were a fever, all the world would be ill." Perhaps this pessimistic view stems from the recognition of the pervasive and automatic tendency of human beings to evaluate. Nevertheless, many of the triggers of envy are learned. They are products of the culture. Most assuredly, biological needs required for survival can trigger envy, as when hunger may elicit envy at the sight of others eating food. But as Susan Isaacs (1970) noted, few achievements, possessions, personality traits, and so on have an absolute and intrinsic value. What may be valued and envied in competitive and individualistic societies may not be valued in cooperative societies. Each society teaches what is important and thereby sets the occasion for envy. For example, if a society places no value on power, wealth, or status, then they are less likely to be sources of envy than in a society where such achievements provide many rewards. No empirical research is available about how cultural variables affect the level of envy in societies, but the likelihood of them having an effect can be illustrated by ethnographic reports of societies.

Charles Lindholm (1982) reports that betrayal, mistrust, treachery, the desire for wealth, resentment of the good fortune of others, deliberate attempts to arouse the envy of others, and taking pride that others are envious of one's superior fortune are major themes in the life of the Swat Pukhtun, a tribe in northern Pakistan. Contrast this with a society committed to peacefulness and cooperative behavior, such as the Amish of the United States and Canada. Bruce Bonta (1997) reports that the emphasis in Amish schools is on group excellence, not on individualism. Thus, the Amish students support and encourage each other to perform well so that the whole class succeeds. In place of competition, the Amish believe in humility and self-denial. Logic dictates that the Swat Pukhtan and Amish experience different frequencies, most likely even different causes, of envy due to the nature of their cultural values. Envy, then, may not be inevitable and the frequency of envy is to some degree affected by social constructions, such as cultural values, economic opportunities, disparities in wealth, and so on.

But more is involved in the arousal of envy than social constructions. What is envied tends to change over a lifetime; few envy in old age what they envied while young. Therefore, as the goals in life and the ideas of who one is and who one wants to be change, so do the conditions that elicit envy. That choice is to some extent involved in what is envied throughout the life span is succinctly expressed in the Russian proverb, "Envy can see the ship well enough, but not the

In a mid-nineteenth-century drawing by Louis Boilly, one cook whose creation has been ruined displays envy when another cook's creation remains perfect. (Corbis/Historical Picture Archive)

leak." As Helmut Schoeck (1969) observed, the proverb expresses the thought that people experiencing envy see only what is enviable, not the countervailing handicaps in what is being envied.

Contentment in life tends to dampen envy. Smith and his colleagues (1990) found that people are less likely to feel envious of the superior fortunes of others when they are satisfied and happy with their own lot. Alternatively, dissatisfaction with one's lot generates much envy. Therefore, it helps to be successful in at least some domains. Envy is less likely, observed the Smith research team, if individuals have achievements in some domains that neutralize failure in areas where others have been successful. In this situation, the high standing in an alternative domain important to the individual counters the unflattering comparison with others and enables him or her to focus on a comparative success.

A somewhat similar factor in the arousal of envy is the relevance of the superior fortunes of others to one's self-concept. Salovey and Rodin (1984) found envy to be most likely when individuals compare themselves unfavorably with others on dimensions that are important to their self-concept. For example, a tinge of envy may be aroused if a person's friends are accepted into graduate school but the individual in question is not. This presupposes, however, that the individual's self-worth is based on the goal of getting into graduate school. Envy would be unlikely if, instead of entering graduate school, the individual was looking forward to taking over the lucrative family business.

Consequences of Envy

Envy breeds hostile feelings, at least to some degree, in the person experiencing the emotion. The ill will, according to Smith and his colleagues (1994), is due to the belief that the advantages belonging to the person being envied are unfair and undeserved. The research team speculated that the injustice beliefs (e.g., "I've been dealt an unfair hand by life" and "It's unfair that others start out in life with advantages over me") originate because the individuals experiencing the envy perceive themselves to be undeserving of such uncontrollable disadvantages. However, comparing oneself to the superiority of others may not always breed ill will. Smith and his colleagues found that unfavorable comparisons can cause depression when people focus on their inferiority and disadvantage rather than on unfairness and justice concerns.

Schadenfreude refers to gloating, the feeling of malicious satisfaction at another's suffering. Smith and his colleagues (1996) suggest that envy creates the conditions under which schadenfreude occurs. To test their idea, they aroused envy in university students by having them watch a videotaped interview of a student who was portrayed as superior. An epilogue made it known that the student had suffered a setback. The envy aroused in the students did indeed enhance the likelihood of them feeling schadenfreude upon learning of the setback. The research team speculated that one explanation why envy might spawn schadenfreude is that the misfortune lessens or might even eliminate the reason for the initial envy.

Cynthia Ozick's "The Shawl" (1980) takes place during the Holocaust in World War II. Rosa, her infant daughter Magda, and her twelve-year-old niece Stella all struggle to survive in a concentration camp. Magda has a special shawl, something like a security blanket, that she hides in and sucks on. Stella, who is envious of that special comfort, takes Magda's shawl and wraps herself up in it. The toddler, searching for the shawl, stumbles out into the yard and is thrown against the electrified barbed wire by a Nazi prison guard.

Regarding the consequence of the envy of others, George Foster (1972), who draws most of his examples from ethnographic reports of peasant societies, writes that people fear the envy of others and that they take steps to neutralize the danger. According to Foster, concealment, denial, symbolic sharing, and true sharing are ways of coping with the fear of the envy of others in peasant societies. Strategies for concealing potential envy-eliciting possessions include not boasting, not appearing enviable, pretending to be poor or ill, and surrounding one's home with dilapidated walls to make it more difficult to tell who is actually poor and who simulates poverty. Denial of reasons to be envied may also take the form of verbal protestations and symbolic acts. Thus, successful individuals deny their success to forestall envy in others. Admiring a new possession causes the owner in some Mexican villages to assert that the possession is ugly. Symbolic ways in Egyptian and Moroccoan villages to deny others cause for envy is to dress children poorly and to allow them to remain dirty and unkempt so that no one would want them. Even in the United States, the statement, "I was just lucky," in response to a compliment from the loser of a much-coveted promotion could well be motivated by the recognition, perhaps also fear, of the envy behind the compliment. Attributing the promotion to luck rather than superior performance makes it easier for the loser to accept the situation. Likewise, a loved one assuring a dying individual that he or she will soon follow may be motivated by the wish to counteract the possibility of envy on the part of the dying with regard to the good fortune of those who will continue to live.

Symbolic sharing to assuage the envy of others includes customs, according to Foster, such as a new father passing out cigars to male friends upon the birth of a child, the groom sharing his good fortune by throwing the bride's garter, and the bride kissing the groom's friends in a symbolic gesture of sharing her favors with them. When traveling, people feel compelled to bring home presents for relatives who remained at home. Foster suggests that this is also a symbolic sharing of the joys of the trip with the less fortunate.

True sharing is another method to deflect the envy of others. By true sharing Foster cites customs such as the practice among Arabs of inviting anyone who observes them eating to partake of the food to avert the danger of the suspect's covetous eye. The Nyakyusa of Malawi have flimsy houses that are built close together, making it difficult to conceal that food is being cooked. Witchcraft and sorcery, much feared among the Nyakyusa, is believed to be bred by the neighbors' envy, particularly for the possession of milk and meat. To solve the food envy, the Nyakyusa evolved the custom of never eating alone. Men and boys are expected to eat with age-mates. This is accomplished by the mates taking turns eating in each other's homes. Thus, no one gains or loses, observes Foster, and the ill will of envy is forestalled.

The effect of envy on societies can be negative and, paradoxically, possibly positive at the same time. Foster proposed that societies with wide disparities in wealth, where the wealth and power of some people is visible and resented by those with little, are characterized by the belief in the "image of limited good." That is, the belief that one person's gain is at the expense of someone else. All of the good things in life are viewed as a closed system, finite in quantity, and incapable of growth. Hence, any increase in wealth by one individual is regarded as a loss to the others. The goal in such societies, observes Foster, is shared poverty, the maintenance of a delicate equilibrium in which relative positions are changed as little as possible. Progress is unlikely in such societies because of the fear that neighbors may convert their envy into aggression. Envy serves as a policing agent.

In the opinion of Schoeck (1969), envy not only makes possible social control but also, by forcing inventors to leave their native locality to avoid the envy of neighbors, promotes civilization. Inventions, innovations, and new ideas are more likely to be conveyed to distant people when innovators meet with prejudice at home. New ideas are more readily accepted, writes Schoeck, from strangers than fellow villagers because the superiority of strangers can be attributed to them having had opportunities unavailable to the local villagers. Envy remains thus dormant and the innovation is more likely to be adopted.

Conclusion

No encompassing theory of envy has yet been proposed. Some researchers approach the study of envy from the perspective of social comparison. Others explore the influence of cultural values, beliefs, and economic conditions on the level of envy in societies. Whatever the approach, the realization that few achievements, possessions, and so on have absolute and intrinsic value shows how much envy is generated by individuals and, therefore, is under their control.

See also: HATE; JEALOUSY

Bibliography

Bonta, Bruce D. (1997). "Cooperation and Competition in Peaceful Societies." *Psychological Bulletin* 121:299–320.

Foster, George M. (1972). "The Anatomy of Envy: A Study in Symbolic Behavior." *Current Anthropology* 13:165–201.

Isaacs, Susan. ([1948] 1970). *Childhood and After: Some Essays and Clinical Studies.* New York: Agathon.

Lindholm, Charles. (1982). *Generosity and Jealousy.* New York: Columbia University Press.

Parrott, W. Gerrod. (1991). "The Emotional Experiences of Envy and Jealousy." In *The Psychology of Jealousy and Envy,* ed. Peter Salovey. New York: Guilford.

Parrott, W. Gerrod, and Smith, Richard H. (1993). "Distinguishing the Experiences of Envy and Jealousy." *Journal of Personality and Social Psychology* 64:906–920.

Salovey, Peter, and Rodin, Judith. (1984). "Some Antecedents and Consequences of Social-Comparison Jealousy." *Journal of Personality and Social Psychology* 47:780–792.

Schoeck, Helmut. (1969). *Envy: A Theory of Social Behaviour.* New York: Harcourt, Brace & World.

Silver, Maury, and Sabini, John. (1978). "The Social Construction of Envy." *Journal of Theory and Social Behaviour* 8:313–332.

Smith, Richard H. (1991). "Envy and the Sense of Injustice." In *The Psychology of Jealousy and Envy,* ed. Peter Salovey. New York: Guilford.

Smith, Richard H.; Diener, Ed; and Garonzik, Ron. (1990). "The Roles of Outcome Satisfaction and Comparison Alternatives in Envy." *British Journal of Social Psychology* 29:247–255.

Smith, Richard H.; Kim, Sung Hee; and Parrott, W. Gerrod. (1988). "Envy and Jealousy: Semantic Problems and Experiential Distinctions." *Personality and Social Psychology Bulletin* 14:401–409.

Smith, Richard H.; Parrott, W. Gerrod; Ozer, Daniel; and Moniz, Andrew. (1994). "Subjective Injustice and Inferiority as Predictors of Hostile and Depressive Feelings in Envy." *Personality and Social Psychology Bulletin* 20:705–711.

Smith, Richard H.; Turner, Terence J.; Garonzik, Ron; Leach, Colin W.; Urch-Druskat, Vanessa; and Weston, Christine M. (1996). "Envy and *Schadenfreude.*" *Personality and Social Psychology Bulletin* 22:158–168.

Weinbrot, Howard D. (1985). "An Ambition to Excell: The Aesthetics of Emulation in the Seventeenth and Eighteenth Centuries. *Huntington Library Quarterly* 48:121–139.

Ralph B. Hupka

ERIKSON, ERIK HOMBURGER

b. Frankfurt, Germany, June 15, 1902; *d.* Harwich, Massachusetts, May 12, 1994; *human development, personality, psychoanalysis.*

Erik Homburger Erikson was a German-born Danish-American psychoanalyst whose ideas and writings on social psychology, individual identity, human psychological development, and the interactions of psychology with history, politics, and culture have influenced psychology, psychiatry, anthropology, sociology, and history. An only child whose parents separated before his birth, he was officially named Erik Homburger (Homburger being the surname of his stepfather, whom Erikson was led to believe was his natural father). When his mother and stepfather eventually told him the truth, he changed his name to Erikson, keeping "H" as a middle initial to show respect to his stepfather. Erikson attended art school before traveling around Europe, eventually gaining a teaching position

Erik H. Erikson. (Corbis/Ted Streshinsky)

stage theory of human development that, though criticized for lacking scientific support, has been widely influential in psychology and education. The eight stages, which all people move through over the course of a lifetime, are trust versus mistrust (during the first year of life); autonomy versus shame and doubt (in years one through three); initiative versus guilt (in years four through six); industry versus inferiority (in the early school years); identity versus identity confusion (in adolescence); intimacy versus isolation (in early adulthood); generativity or helping younger generations versus stagnation (in middle adulthood); and integrity versus despair (in late adulthood). From Erikson's point of view, as each conflict is resolved in the favor of the first of the paired items, the personality develops along a healthy path. Erikson's study of psychohistory is set forth in works such as *Young Man Luther* (1958) and *Gandhi's Truth* (1969). He examined modern ethical and political problems in a collection of essays, *Life History and the Historical Moment* (1975), linking psychoanalysis to history, political science, philosophy, and theology.

Erickson has been described by some people as being a "literary American hero" who developed such now familiar concepts as "life cycle," "identity crisis," "inner space," and "psychohistory" through his work in psychology and psychoanalysis.

See also: FREUD, ANNA; FREUD, SIGMUND; HUMAN DEVELOPMENT; PERSONALITY; PSYCHOANALYTIC PERSPECTIVE

in Vienna at a school that was attended by many American children whose parents were in Vienna to be psychoanalyzed by Sigmund Freud and his associates. Erickson met Freud, was friendly with his daughter Anna, and underwent analysis with her. He later graduated from the Vienna Psychoanalytical Institute in 1933. Like Anna Freud, Erikson's interest was in children, a topic that would occupy him, along with numerous others, until the end of his life.

When the Nazis under Adolf Hitler gained power in Germany in 1933, Erickson moved to the United States with his wife and two children and gained a position at Harvard University. He also opened a practice specializing in child psychoanalysis, a novel specialty at the time. Later appointments took him to the University of California at Berkeley, the Austin Riggs Center in western Massachusetts, and then back to Harvard before his formal retirement as a professor emeritus in 1970. Erikson was a curious and creative thinker, and his research involved cultural influences on psychological development, Sioux Indian children at the Pine Ridge Reservation in South Dakota, personality development, an individual's sense of identity, group identity, and African Americans.

Erikson is best known for his theory of personality development and his work that helped to create the new field of psychohistory. Erikson proposed an eight-

Bibliography

Coles, Robert. (1970). *Erik H. Erikson: The Growth of His Work.* Boston: Little, Brown.

Erikson, Erik H. (1950). *Childhood and Society.* New York: W. W. Norton.

Erikson, Erik H. (1958). *Young Man Luther: A Study in Psychoanalysis and History.* New York: W. W. Norton.

Erikson, Erik H. (1968). *Identity: Youth and Crisis.* New York: W. W. Norton.

Erikson, Erik H. (1969). *Gandhi's Truth: On the Origins of Militant Nonviolence.* New York: W. W. Norton.

Erikson, Erik H. (1982). *The Life Cycle Completed: A Review.* New York: W. W. Norton.

Erikson, Erik H. (1975). *Life History and the Historical Moment.* New York: W. W. Norton.

Evans, Richard L., ed. (1995). *Dialogue with Erik Erikson.* Northvale, NJ: Jason Aronson.

Roazen, Paul. (1997). *Erik H. Erikson: The Power and Limits of a Vision.* North Vale, NJ: Jason Aronson.

Wallerstein, Robert S., and Goldberger, Leo, eds. (1998). *Ideas and Identities: The Life and Work of Erik Erikson.* Madison, CT: International Universities Press.

Ben Manning
David Levinson

ETHICS

See Philosophy; Sin

EXPRESSION OF EMOTIONS

See Body Movement, Gesture, and Display; Communication; Emotion Experience and Expression; Facial Expression; Universality of Emotional Expression

EYSENCK, HANS JURGEN

b. Berlin, Germany, March 4, 1916; *d.* London, England, September 4, 1997; *psychology.*

Hans Eysenck was a German-born psychologist who received his training and spent his career in London. He was one of the best-known, most-widely cited, and most controversial academic psychologists of the twentieth century.

Eysenck was the only child of Eduard and Ruth (Werner) Eysenck. Both parents were actors, and when they divorced when Eysenck was two years old, he was placed in the care of his father's mother. Educated at public schools in Berlin, Eysenck was rejected by the University of Berlin (at which he had hoped to study physics) in 1934 because he refused to join the Nazi Party. Because he had no future in Germany and because he was an opponent of both Adolf Hitler and Nazism, Eysenck left Germany to study at the University of Dijon in France and the University College of Exeter in England before settling in London. When he was denied admission to the physics program at the University of London because of gaps in his German education, he selected psychology instead and studied under Sir Cyril Burt, the most prominent British psychologist of the mid-twentieth century. Burt stressed a scientific, statistical approach to psychology, and Eysenck remained within that tradition throughout his career. Despite this scientific background, the first positions Eysenck held (after obtaining his B.A. in 1938 and his Ph.D. in 1940) were at London psychiatric institutes including the world famous Maudsley Hospital, where he was exposed to the diagnosis and treatment of emotional disorders. At Maudsley, Eysenck founded a department of psychology and remained its director until his retirement in 1983. In 1950, he also joined the faculty of the University of London, becoming a professor in 1955. Except for visiting professorships at the University of Pennsylvania (1949–1950) and the University of California at Berkeley (1954), his academic career remained rooted in the psychology department at the University of Lon-

don until his retirement. Eysenck was a productive scholar, and during his career, he wrote or edited some sixty books, wrote more than six hundred articles for professional journals, edited the journal *Personality and Individual Differences* and founded the journal *Behaviour Research and Therapy.*

Eysenck is best known for his theory of personality and his harsh and persistent criticism of psychoanalysis as a form of treatment. Eysenck applied statistics to psychological information about individuals to develop his trait theory of personality. He suggested that the human personality can be conceptualized along two primary dimensions (i.e., extraversion-introversion and neuroticism-stability) and constructed various personality tests to measure these dimensions. His work has been substantially extended by other psychologists, and most experts now accept both extraversion-introversion and neuroticism-stability to be among the basic dimensions of the human personality. Eysenck also suggested that these personality dimensions and variations in them across individuals are caused by biological processes, which in turn are genetically determined. His ideas about genetic determinism were not as readily accepted by the scientific community, especially in the 1960s and 1970s when there was more interest in the relationship between personality and society, but they were revived in the 1990s with the shift back to the study of biological and genetic factors in personality and emotional expression. Eysenck's public criticism of psychoanalysis is dated to 1952 when he published a journal article that reviewed the effectiveness of psychoanalytic treatment and concluded that it had no more value than no treatment at all. Eysenck's skepticism about analysis began in his student days at the University of London, where he was unimpressed by the psychoanalytic lectures, and was supported by his observations in the clinical hospital settings, which suggested that over time many people recovered without intervention. For the remainder of his life, Eysenck remained a strong and vocal critic of analysis and a supporter of the scientific study of treatment effectiveness, a practice that is rejected by many psychoanalysts. Eysenck's insistence on the importance of the objective study of treatment effectiveness was several decades ahead of its time, but it has now become accepted practice in psychological research. In place of analysis and other forms of psychodynamic therapy, Eysenck advocated and established a program in learning or behavioral therapy that focused on the "here and now" and people's actual behavior with little or no consideration of the underlying psychological processes. His advocacy of behavioral therapy placed him at odds not just with the analysts but with psychologists who favored cognitive-based therapies. He was especially criticized for not being a therapist or an analyst himself and therefore, at least according to his critics, lacking in first-hand knowledge of the therapeutic situation. His position remained, however, that problematic behavior was learned and therefore could be unlearned by focusing on actual behaviors.

Eysenck also studied and wrote about many topics other than personality and treatment, including intelligence (a focus of work late in his life), crime, racism, politics, and even the relationship between smoking and cancer. His views on some of these matters have been controversial, especially his belief that genetics plays a major role in intelligence and his belief that the scientific evidence is not sufficient to support the conclusion that cigarette smoking causes cancer. Because of his willingness to attack accepted views and his strong advocacy for his own ideas, which were often innovative and perhaps ahead of their time, he is remembered as one of the most controversial psychologists of the twentieth century. Eysenck was also a gifted teacher and trained many students for careers in academic and clinical psychology. That his work remains in the forefront of psychology is in part due to their efforts.

In addition to writing and editing many works for his psychology colleagues, Eysenck wrote several books, all published by Penguin in Britain, for the general public. Some of the better known publications are *Uses and Abuses of Psychology* (1953), *Know Your Own IQ* (1964), and *I DO: How to Choose Your Mate and Have a Happy Marriage* (1985). Eysenck himself was married twice, in 1939 to Margaret Davies (they later divorced) and in 1950 to Sybille Bianca Guilietaa Rostal, a former student and later collaborator. He had five children from the two marriages, and his son Michael (the sole child from the first marriage) is a psychologist who has applied his father's ideas to the study of cognition and memory.

See also: HUMAN DEVELOPMENT; PERSONALITY; PSYCHOLOGY OF EMOTIONS

Bibliography

Eysenck, Hans J. (1952). "The Effects of Psychotherapy: An Evaluation." *Journal of Consulting Psychology* 16:319–324.

Eysenck, Hans J., ed. (1960). *Behaviour Therapy and Neuroses: Readings in Modern Methods of Treatment Derived from Learning Theory.* New York: Pergamon.

Eysenck, Hans J. (1964). *Crime and Personality.* London: Routledge and Kegan Paul.

Eysenck, Hans J. (1967). *The Biological Basis of Personality.* Springfield, IL: C.C. Thomas.

Eysenck, Hans J., and Eysenck, Michael. (1997). *Mindwatching: Why We Behave the Way We Do.* London: Trafalgar.

Eysenck, Hans J., and Kamin, Leon J. (1981). *The Intelligence Controversy.* New York: Wiley.

Gibson, Hamilton B. (1981). *Hans Eysenck: The Man and His Work.* London: Peter Owen.

Modgil, Sohan, and Modgil, Celia, eds. (1986). *Hans Eysenck: Consensus and Controversy.* Philadelphia: Falmer Press.

David Levinson

F

FACIAL EXPRESSION

Most people rely on facial expressions as the main source of information about a conversational partner's emotions. When a contradiction arises between a person's self-report of emotion and his or her facial expressions, people most often turn to the latter as the more reliable source of the true emotional state. While body posture, vocal tones, and other nonverbal behaviors provide cues to a person's emotional state, they are often used primarily to determine the intensity of the emotion dictated by the facial expression.

Why do people rely on facial expressions so much? The simplest reason is that they are the most observable element of the emotion (a concept known as visual primacy). Although people can and do detect more subtle cues, they tend to believe those things they "see" with their eyes. Also, people learn from the time they are babies that the face is a main provider of emotional information. Babies tend to focus on their mother's face or on other objects that have a face-like appearance. Long before children learn language, they depend on nonverbal cues for information. In many instances, these "concrete" pictures of faces may convey emotional sentiments better than the use of language could.

In addition to being a focal point in interactions with others, the face is endowed with numerous muscles that can make slight movements, allowing the face to be one of the most adaptable tools people have for communicating nonverbally. Paul Ekman (1982), one of the leading scholars in the area of emotions and facial displays, notes that the face can send numerous signals simultaneously and sequentially. Contrast the ability to modify facial expressions on a moment to moment basis with the ability to modify posture or the use of space in an interaction. Although one can modify these latter features quite easily, the face can undergo a greater change and a quicker change. In addition, the changes in the face are capable of encompassing more unique combinations of behaviors than are changes in posture and space.

Encoding and Decoding Emotion

A child's dependence on nonverbal cues to communicate raises the following questions: From where do facial expressions come? Are they innate, or do we learn them? Convincing cross-cultural evidence, drawn from several literate and pre-literate societies and presented by Ekman (1973), Carroll Izard (1994), and Nico Frijda and Anna Tcherkassof (1997), shows that several facial expressions are universal. In particular, these expressions are related to the six emotions of happiness, sadness, fear, anger, disgust, and surprise.

Studies involving blind-deaf children suggest that some facial expressions are innate. Irenäus Eibl-Eibesfeldt (1973) found that children who were born deaf and blind (and therefore could not learn facial expressions through imitation) still exhibited the "universal" facial expressions for happiness, sadness, fear, anger, pouting, and surprise. Another line of research with infants suggests that they develop facial expression displays with regularity. For example, distress, disgust, and interest are seen with newborns. Anger and surprise typically appear at three to four months, and fear and joy appear at five to seven months. Tiffany Field and her colleagues (1982) found that two-day-old babies could imitate the happy, sad, and surprised expressions of an adult. The infants' tendency to imitate facial expressions of their caregivers also may indicate that facial responsiveness has an important social function for babies and caregivers alike.

Identifying emotions by their corresponding facial display is the categorical approach to coding emotions. For the purpose of discerning emotions and facial displays, the face is "categorized" according to behaviors in three facial areas: the eyebrows and forehead; eyes, eyelids, and bridge of nose; and cheeks, nose, mouth, chin, and jaw. The six basic emotions can be distinguished according to the different variations of the features. Happiness is expressed by an upward turn of the corners of the mouth, raised cheeks, and crow's feet wrinkles at the edge of the eyes, among other finer details. Sadness is expressed by a downturn of the lips and an upward turn of the inner corners of the eyebrows. Anger is exhibited through vertical lines between the eyebrows, lip tension, and hard staring eyes. A fearful expression is one where the eyebrows are raised and drawn together, the eyelids are raised, the mouth is open, and there is tension in the lips.

Les Grimaces, *a lithograph from the early nineteenth century, depicts anger, disgust, happiness, sadness, and surprise—five of the six basic facial expressions.* (Corbis)

Surprise is similar to fear in that the eyebrows are raised, the eyes are wide open, the eyelids are raised, and the mouth is open. Surprise differs from fear in that there is no tension in the mouth and lips when the jaw drops open and the eyelids are not raised as much. Disgust is expressed by raising the lower lip with the corners pulled back, turning the cheek, and lowering the eyebrows.

With these physical representations in mind, it is possible to conclude that there may be physiological reasons why people display similar expressions. For example, when people are surprised, they are caught off guard and need to survey their environment to discern the cause of the startle. It makes sense that people would open their eyes wide to take in peripheral information and open their mouths to take a gasp of air so that they have the energy to respond with "fight or flight."

In contrast to the categorical approach, the dimensional approach to coding and classifying facial displays suggests that people do not have certain facial expressions that match their emotions. Instead, facial expressions can be classified according to where they fall in relation to the underlying dimensions of pleasantness, activity, and intensity. For example, rage may be very unpleasant, highly active, and highly intense, whereas frustration may be moderately unpleasant, moderately active, and low to moderately intense. Emotions that are located near each other when plotted in this three-dimensional space may be expressed in more similar ways than emotions that are dissimilar with regard to these underlying dimensions. The dimensional approach is able to handle emotion blends and varied experiences of "pure" emotions better than the categorical approach. Emotions can also be compared according to a two-dimensional model that recognizes only the pleasantness and activity dimensions.

But is the *experience* of emotion necessarily reflected in people's facial *expression* of emotion? John T. Lanzetta's research, as reviewed by Gregory McHugo and Craig Smith (1996), suggests that regulating facial expressions may help people to regulate their experience of emotions. This view explores a mutual influence process between experience and expression. That is, if a person masks or neutralizes an emotional expression, he or she may be more likely to experience it less intensely than if a full facial expression is allowed. Similarly, a person may experience a positive emotion more fully if he or she exaggerates a positive facial expression intensely. The facial feedback hypothesis also suggests that a facial expression may evoke feelings consistent with the facial display, but there is conflicting evidence about how much and in what way the face influences felt emotions. For example, there is some evidence that if a person is feeling negative, putting on the happy face can make him or her feel more positive. And yet, others such as Paul Robbins and Roland Tanck (1997) have found that inhibiting expressions of anger was related to feeling more depressed, suggesting that people need to release their feelings rather than suppressing them and having them "build up."

Emotion Blends

Although people express the "pure" emotions similarly, particularly when prompted to express the emotion without moderation, people more often experience and express emotion "blends," which are combinations of several emotions. The term *blend*, however, is somewhat misleading in that the emotions do not necessarily commingle to form new emotions like a new drink is formed by pouring different beverages into a punch bowl. At times, the emotions remain distinct, yet they form a pattern like colored threads in a fabric. Each emotion is responsible for activating a particular cognition and action; its presence and interdependence with all other experienced emotions affects the nature of the overall pattern. For example, a young mother entering the kitchen finds her little daughter covered in pudding and spreading the yellow dessert in artful swirls across the floor. The incident evokes the emotions of surprise, disgust, anger, and humor. Thus, the emotion of anger is regulated by, or must adjust to, the presence of humor. The "blend" of emotions calls for various facial expressions. A lowered brow suddenly raises and a frown transitions into a smile as anger must allow for the presence of humor that now activates other cognitions and actions.

Other emotions do not have a "set expression." For example, a respectful look is one that "fits" the situation. A proud father's respect for his graduating daughter is reflected in his smile and gleeful cheer as she crosses the stage, yet that same respect is later shown in his look of intense interest as she shares her dreams and plans for the future. Similarly, other emotions, such as love and jealousy, are expressed in many ways. One interesting finding is that facial displays for love often resemble the facial displays for sadness. Love and sadness may, therefore, both have the underlying kernel of "longing" that produces similar displays.

Display Rules

Culture often influences when, where, how, and to whom emotions are expressed. That is, people abide by the display rules for their particular culture or sub-culture. Japanese display rules, for example, tend to neutralize negative emotional displays (or mask them with positive ones) in order to allow interactional partners to "save face." These rules are consistent with a collectivistic culture that values harmony and consensus. Consider the culture-bound display rules of a simple smile. An American attending a Japanese funeral may be surprised to find the widow hiding her sorrow with a smile. Many international students in the United States are surprised by the American display rule that allows such liberal expression of the smile. Laray Barna (1991) reported that an Arabian student was disturbed by the many smiles he received walking on campus; he felt "very embarrassed and rushed to see if [he had] made a mistake with [his] clothes." A Japanese student soon realized that the smiles were only friendly greetings and that the smilers had "no interest." A Korean student had a similar reaction to American smiles and explained that in her country they "never talk or smile at strangers." A female American student recounted smiling at the sight of a foreign man holding a baby. The student's smile was interpreted as a flirtation, and the man responded by saying, "Are you waiting for me? You meet me later?" Without realizing it, she had acted as a prostitute would in his country.

In addition to varying between cultures, these display rules often vary within given cultures. In the United States, it is more socially acceptable for men to express anger than for women, whereas it is more acceptable for women to show fear than for men. Stereotypes and social pressures indicate that men are supposed to "be strong," so some men, when they are discouraged, frightened, or sad, may express anger, humor, or ambivalence rather than their true emotions, which would make them seem "weak."

Although culture influences how men and women express their emotions, childhood and adolescent experiences within the family also have an effect. A man raised in an emotionally expressive, warm, and accepting family environment may not conform as stringently to male emotional display rules. Similarly, reactions to emotional expressions by friends may affect how (and if) men and women express their emotions according to these gender-related display rules. That is, culture sets one level of display rules, while the numerous subcultures that people are raised in (e.g., family, region, religion) may further enhance, restrict, or override the larger cultural norms.

The main forms of display rules are masking, intensification, deintensification, and neutralizing. All of these modify the expression of felt emotion. Masking is the substitution of a different emotional expression for the one experienced in an attempt to conceal one's true emotional state. The first runner up in a beauty pageant might display expressions of joy at the announcement of the winner's name yet inwardly experience acute sorrow at not gaining the title. The second-string football player's looks of concern for his teammate's serious injury might hide his jubilance as he straps on his helmet to replace his fallen comrade.

Similar to masking, intensification involves some falsification in the display of felt emotions. However, intensification does not involve substituting facial expressions, but rather exaggerating the display of the emotion one is actually experiencing. Someone who opens his or her apartment door knowing that a surprise birthday party is waiting on the other side might exaggerate genuine surprise and joy with a look of absolute shock, bewilderment, and elation.

Conversely, deintensification is decreasing the amount of the emotional display from what one is actually experiencing. The winner of the beauty pageant might be overjoyed and ecstatic at the announcement of her victory but decide to maintain composure by displaying a smile that expresses less intensity of the emotion. The injured football player sitting on the sidelines in extreme pain and feeling heartsick that he is unable to play in the final season game may merely register discomfort and disappointment to his teammates and coaches.

Neutralizing refers to showing no emotional expression. The frightened boy atop the high dive platform neutralizes any expressions of fear as his taunting friends watch from the pool below. The elementary school teacher keeps a straight face while suppressing the urge to laugh when an innocent child unexpectedly burps to the delight of the other children.

Even when display rules are operating, however, research indicates that a micro-momentary "flash" of the real emotional-facial response will occur before people are able to gain control over their facial expressions. Although viewers may not be able to discern the "leakage," they may notice that the person's response was different in some unidentifiable way. Take the runner up in the beauty pageant. Her first response of disappointment and sadness most likely flashed across her face. A videotaped recording of the reaction, played in slow motion, may be able to detect her initial "disappointed" facial display. Consequently, the runner-up's contrived happiness facial display will be more exaggerated and stiff than if she were truly happy, and she would probably not think to raise her cheeks up and her forehead down a slight bit toward her eyes—muscular reactions that are part of the facial expression of one who is experiencing joy. These micro-momentary flashes and failure to display the "harder to control" facial actions can be used as leakage cues when detecting emotional deceit.

Interpreting Facial Expressions

Just how accurate are people in decoding (interpreting) facial expressions? In general, people are fairly accurate in identifying or "recognizing" the six basic emotions based on facial expression, even when the culture involved has explicit taboos against expressing some of these facial displays.

Andrew Young and his colleagues (1997) provide evidence for categorical perception of these facial expressions. The more pure the form of the facial expression (as opposed to emotion blends created by morphing a facial expression), the less time it took to judge the emotion and the more accurate people were in their judgments. When facial expressions were misjudged, the errors followed a common pattern. That is, if fear was misjudged, it was most likely recognized as anger because of similarities in facial expression. Disgust proved more difficult to interpret than happiness or sadness. Research indicates that there is a slight tendency for women to be more accurate decoders than men. This finding is not surprising given that women are often better encoders and decoders of nonverbal (social) information. Most scholars suggest that women are socialized to attend to social and relational information more than men, rather than attributing the advantage to an innate/genetic decoding superiority.

Several methodological criticisms of emotional recognition experiments are worth noting. Early studies used photographs or slides of facial expressions that subjects then labeled (decoded). Although these studies were conducted in various cultures and found relatively high decoding accuracy, they were criticized because the unnatural (posed) facial expressions ignored context (i.e., the situational events that surround facial movement) and other features that would be present in real-life situations. Other scholars have shown films (which include contextual features) and other more "realistic" stimuli for the subjects to decode. The accuracy remained relatively high in these studies but not as high as was demonstrated with the posed photographs.

James Russell (1994) argues that the universality of emotional expression and recognition is not as solidly supported as it could be. In addition to methodological criticisms, he suggests several alternative explanations to the universal recognition of facial expressions. Russell suggests that people may perceive emotions in different categories than those traditionally used in research, they may interpret them along dimensions rather than categorically, or perhaps they interpret them situationally.

To explore how situational information may affect the decoding of facial displays, consider the following story. Kristen walks in late to a basketball game. As she takes a seat in the stands, her attention turns to a young player seated on the bench. His lips are tightly pressed, tears fall down his cheeks, and his facial features contract. From his expression, Kristin infers sadness, concluding that his team must be losing, but a quick glance at the scoreboard reveals a six-point lead for his team. Kristin looks back at the player and notices the sweaty jersey, damp hair, and flushed face, a clear sign he was playing only moments ago. With this additional information, Kristin now concludes that the player must have been pulled from the game and is angry at either the coach or himself. The man seated next to Kristin suddenly informs her that the team just pulled ahead after being behind by ten points. Having ruled out sadness and anger, Kristin decides that the expression must be one of fear. She determines that the stress of being in the finals after working so hard all season must be taking its toll; the pressure is just too much. But Kristin is surprised when the man next to her says that the player was in a serious accident a year earlier and was not expected ever to play again —only his hard work and determination brought him back. Furthermore, the man informs Kristin that the crowd just gave the player a standing ovation when he walked off the court. As Kristin watches the player's teammates pat him on the back and smile, she finally solves the puzzle—not sadness, not fear, and not anger, but intense happiness underlies the player's expression.

As this story underscores, context plays an important role in interpreting facial displays and creating emotional messages. Kristin's initial inference (that the player was sad) was drawn almost exclusively from information she decoded from examining the player's face—his eyes, lips, the wincing of the face. Traditional research in the area of facial expressions presupposes that this information is sufficient for Kristin to accurately decode the emotional message. In other words, Kristin should have successfully interpreted the specific meaning of the facial displays independent of the context because a facial expression is (according to the traditionalists) fixed by nature and consistent across changes in context. Research on emotions and facial displays, however, is increasingly examining the role that context plays in generating meaning, challenging this traditional assumption.

Although Kristin's initial inference was certainly feasible and might have been correct under a different set of circumstances, the meaning behind an expression cannot always be determined without reference to its context. Kristin arrives at a more accurate judgment of the player's emotional state only after she combines facial information with contextual information (e.g., the posted basketball scores, the sweaty jersey, the story of the accident, the standing ovation, and the smiles of his teammates). Obviously, facial displays do not take place in a vacuum; they occur in a certain time and place. As such, the meaning of a facial display is inextricably connected to the context of the situation and offers no determinate meaning independent of that context.

Facial Expressions and Communication

Not all facial expressions are indicative of emotion. People use facial expressions to transmit interest, displeasure, and a host of other messages. A mother, for example, may shake her head and make an angry facial expression to communicate that her child should not touch a vase. In conversations, people use facial expressions to provide feedback to the speaker. If someone tells an incredible story, the listener's mouth may drop open as if he or she were "surprised." If someone tells about a horrible accident, the listener may grimace in pain. These facial expressions often exaggerate the one or two facial features that best represent the emotion in order to signal understanding, empathy, and attentive listening.

Nicole Chovil (1991) and Alan Fridlund (1991) found that people are more facially expressive when they are being observed. If people are watching a movie or listening to tape-recorded conversations in the presence of others, they will be more facially expressive than if they were doing these same things alone. The mere presence of others causes people to be more facially responsive if that display is socially acceptable in that culture. Conversely, if an emotional response is "taboo" in that culture, there may be an inhibition of the facial display in the presence of others.

Facial expressions are particularly important in signaling interactional availability and interest. In particular, eye contact and smiling signal interest and liking, especially when coupled with proximity and direct facial and body orientation. As a result, people may try to increase their attractiveness by smiling, laughing, making eye contact, and exhibiting other related verbal and nonverbal behaviors. Joseph Cappella (1991) has suggested that mimicry of facial expressions as well as other nonverbal behaviors (such as posture and gestures) may function to signal rapport, increase bonding and affiliation, facilitate social interaction, and regulate emotional communication.

In addition to these somewhat intentional signaling systems, some scholars suggest that emotions are "catching." According to this theory of emotional contagion, people often feel their conversational partner's mood or adopt their behavior pattern during interactions. Elaine Hatfield and her colleagues (1994) suggest that people automatically mimic facial expressions as well as other nonverbal behaviors during interactions. These responses occur spontaneously, which suggests that they may be innate empathic responses. Mother-infant interactions are particularly full of facial mimicry by both the mother and the infant.

Conclusion

Facial expressions of emotion are as varied as the people who make them. Emotional expressions are influenced by cultural rules, situational context, gender, and competing emotional experiences. And yet, there seem to be some universals in the encoding and decoding of a few basic emotions. Besides an emotional transmitter, the face is a multifunctional tool in social interactions. People use facial expressions to communicate interest, signal availability, provide feedback, and make connections with others through slight variations in facial movements such as eye contact, smiling, and eyebrow scrunching.

See also: BODY MOVEMENT, GESTURE, AND DISPLAY; COMMUNICATION; CULTURE; EMOTION SUPPRESSION; UNIVERSALITY OF EMOTIONAL EXPRESSION

Bibliography

Barna, Laray M. (1991). "Stumbling Blocks in Intercultural Communication." In *Intercultural Communication: A Reader,* 6th ed., ed. Larry Samovar and Richard E. Porter. Belmont, CA: Wadsworth.

Bavelas, Janet Beavin, and Chovil, Nicole. (1997). "Faces in Dialogue." In *The Psychology of Facial Expression,* ed. James A Russell and José-Miguel Fernandez-Dols. New York: Cambridge University Press.

Cappella, Joseph N. (1991). "The Biological Origins of Automated Patterns of Human Interaction." *Communication Theory* 1:4–35.

Carroll, James M., and Russell, James A. (1996). "Do Facial Expressions Signal Specific Emotions? Judging Emotion from the Face in Context." *Journal of Personality and Social Psychology* 70:205–218.

Chovil, Nicole. (1991). "Social Determinants of Facial Displays." *Journal of Nonverbal Behavior* 15:141–154.

Eibl-Eibesfeldt, Irenäus. (1973). "The Expressive Behavior of the Deaf-and-Blind Born." In *Social Communication and Movement: Studies of Interaction and Expression in Man and Chimpanzee,* ed. Mario von Cranach and Ian Vine. New York: Academic Press.

Ekman, Paul. (1973). "Cross Cultural Studies of Facial Expression." In *Darwin and Facial Expression,* ed. Paul Ekman. New York: Academic Press.

Ekman, Paul. (1982). "Methods for Measuring Facial Action." In *Handbook of Methods in Nonverbal Behavioral Research,* ed. Klaus R. Scherer and Paul Ekman. New York: Cambridge University Press.

Ekman, Paul, and Friesen, Wallace V. (1969). "The Repertoire of Nonverbal Behavior: Categories, Origins, Usage, and Coding." *Semiotica* 1:49–98.

Ekman, Paul, and Friesen, Wallace V. (1971). "Constants across Cultures in the Face and Emotion." *Journal of Personality and Social Psychology* 17:124–129.

Fernandez-Dols, José-Miguel, and Carroll, James M. (1997). "Is the Meaning Perceived in Facial Expression Independent of Its Context?" In *The Psychology of Facial Expression,* ed. James A. Russell and José-Miguel Fernandez-Dols. New York: Cambridge University Press.

Field, Tiffany M.; Woodson, Robert; Greenberg, Reena; and Cohen, Debra. (1982). "Discrimination and Imitation of Facial Expressions by Neonates." *Science* 218:179–181.

Fridlund, Alan J. (1991). "Sociality of Solitary Smiling: Potentiation by an Implicit Audience." *Journal of Personality and Social Psychology* 60:229–240.

Fridlund, Alan J.; Ekman, Paul; and Oster, Harriet. (1987). "Facial Expressions of Emotion." In *Nonverbal Behavior and Communication,* 2nd ed., ed. Aron W. Siegman and Stanley Feldstein. Hillsdale, NJ: Lawrence Erlbaum.

Frijda, Nico H., and Tcherkassof, Anna. (1997). "Facial Expressions As Modes of Action Readiness." In *The Psychology of Facial Expression,* ed. James A. Russell and José-Miguel Fernandez-Dols. New York: Cambridge University Press.

Hatfield, Elaine; Cacioppo, John T.; and Rapson, Richard L. (1994). *Emotional Contagion.* Cambridge, Eng.: Cambridge University Press.

Izard, Carroll E. (1994). "The Innate and Universal Facial Expressions: Evidence from Developmental and Cross-Cultural Research." *Psychological Bulletin* 115:288–299.

McHugo, Gregory J., and Smith, Craig A. (1996). "The Power of Faces: A Review of John T. Lanzetta's Research on Facial Expression and Emotion." *Motivation and Emotion* 20: 85–120.

Robbins, Paul R., and Tanck, Roland H. (1997). "Anger and Depressed Affect: Interindividual and Intraindividual Perspectives." *Journal of Psychology* 131:489–500.

Rosenberg, Erika L., and Ekman, Paul. (1995). "Conceptual and Methodological Issues in the Judgment of Facial Expressions of Emotion." *Motivation and Emotion* 19:111–138.

Russell, James A. (1994). "Is There Universal Recognition of Emotion from Facial Expressions? A Review of Cross-Cultural Studies." *Psychological Bulletin* 115:102–141.

Young, Andrew W.; Rowland, Duncan; Calder, Andrew; and Etcoff, Nancy L. (1997). "Facial Expression Magamix: Tests of Dimensional and Category Accounts of Emotion Recognition." *Cognition* 63:271–313.

Lesa A. Stern
Mark A. Callister

FEAR AND PHOBIAS

Fear is a normal emotion exhibited in potentially dangerous situations. In contrast to anxiety, fear is intense and occurs when danger is physically present. Walter Cannon described in 1927 the basic processes of fear as being the fight-or-flight response. Upon noticing a threat, the sympathetic branch of the autonomic nervous system is triggered, which in turn elicits mental, behavioral, and physiological responses. Mentally, the person becomes preoccupied with the threat and ways to ensure safety. Behaviorally, the person could freeze, attempt to flee, or stand and fight. Physiologically, a set of changes occurs that prepares the body to flee or fight so that the potential physical danger can be survived. Epinephrine is released to stimulate the body to action, pupils dilate to attend to threat, breathing rate increases, and heart rate and blood pressure increase to ensure an adequate supply of oxygen. Blood is diverted to the muscles (which tense up to be ready for action), the temporarily unnecessary immune and digestive functions are inhibited, the liver releases glucose to provide quick energy, and sweating is initiated to cool the body. This fight-or-flight reaction is a normal response to danger that increases the probability that an individual will be able to cope with a threat. Similar reactions are observable in non-humans, although the particular manifestations differ across species (e.g., an opossum will "play dead" and a porcupine will raise its spines).

Phobias share much in common with fears. People with phobias demonstrate the fight-or-flight reaction regularly and reliably in response to an object or situation that they perceive to be threatening. However, there are differences. People with phobias recognize their fear is out of proportion to the danger, and many avoid the phobic stimulus. In severe cases, the fear and avoidance come to interfere significantly with the person's life and functioning.

The experience of a phobia can be hard to appreciate. The individual may fearfully anticipate harm from an object or situation that others consider innocuous. They may be plagued by worries about losing control, panicking, and fainting, all of which are concerns that do not preoccupy the non-phobic individual. The experience of a phobia is illustrated by A. H., a thirty-five-year-old woman who complained about a phobia of birds. For as long as she could remember, she was terrified whenever birds were present. She would even experience fear when she thought about birds, when someone mentioned them in conversation, or if she watched nature shows or went to places where a bird could be. If a bird were close by, she would start to sweat, her heart would pound, her legs would feel as if they were made of jelly, she would shake all over, and she would need to run to safety.

Graham Greene's "The End of the Party" (1947) tells the story of Francis, a young boy, who is literally scared to death at a party that he did not want to attend. He is panicked at playing hide and seek with the lights turned out, but he is shamed into playing by the teasing of the other children. Although his twin brother tries to help him, Francis dies of his terror.

She was deeply embarrassed by fleeing and her need to wildly flap her hands to scare off any birds. When not around birds she was immensely frustrated by the experience. She commented that she was bigger than the sparrows she feared and that while they might fly into her, they could not really harm her. Notwithstanding her knowledge that the birds she feared were generally harmless, her fear had caused her to give up a job because she was scared to walk from her car to the office. At the time of treatment she was virtually housebound.

Types of Phobias

Phobias can be classified into three major groupings. First, there are specific phobias, in which a person demonstrates debilitating, excessive, and unreasonable fear in response to particular stimuli. Specific phobias have been labeled by attaching the appropriate Greek prefix to the root word *phobia* (e.g., arachnophobia, a fear of spiders, and xenophobia, a fear of strangers). The resulting alphabetical listing obscures an important attribute of specific phobias. The feared objects and situations are not random, but can be grouped into animals (e.g., spiders, insects, dogs), aspects of the natural environment (e.g., storms, heights, water), blood-injury-injections, and specific situations (e.g., flying, driving, enclosed places). Specific phobias are found in 10 percent of the population, are reported more often by females, and vary across cultures. An example of this variation is the fact that the fear of witchcraft is more common among non-Western societies; its occurrence would not be considered a phobia until the level of fear for an individual was out of proportion to that experienced by others in the society. The age of onset of a phobia varies depending on the fear. Phobias of specific situations tend to have one peak age of onset in childhood and a second in the mid-twenties, whereas phobias about the natural environment, animals, and blood-injury-injections begin in childhood. People with phobias of blood, injury, and injections also demonstrate a phenomenon unique among the phobias, namely, they can lose consciousness and faint. Just as fight-or-flight may be an adaptive reaction to threat, fainting could be an adaptive response to injury. The drop in blood pressure occurring during fainting could stem blood flow. Alternatively, the appearance of being dead could dissuade a predator, providing an opportunity to flee.

In addition to specific phobias, there is a second clustering called social phobia. In social phobia there is a marked and persistent fear of social or performance situations in which embarrassment may occur. People suffering from this phobia fear others will judge them to be anxious, weak, "crazy," or stupid. Public speaking is feared because of worries that others will notice signs of anxiety, such as trembling. People with social phobia may avoid writing in public in case others see their hands shake. They may avoid eating or drinking in public for fear that they may choke and cause embarrassment. Estimates of the prevalence of social phobia range from 3 percent to 13 percent, extending as high as 20 percent when fear of public speaking is included. Social phobia is more common among females. Since many social demands are culture specific, social phobia can have different manifestations across cultures. While individuals with social phobia in the United States may fear bringing embarrassment upon themselves in social situations, those in Japan and Korea may fear offending or causing embarrassment to others. Social phobia changes as a person progresses from childhood to adulthood. Children may express fear as tantrums, freezing, and clinging or staying close to a familiar people. They appear timid, preferring to stay on the edge of social activities and group play. Adolescents may avoid dating and

A Palestinian child, who suffers from social phobia as a result of the outbreaks of violence in her hometown of Hebron, Israel, clutches her mother's hand when she sees a stranger near her house. (Corbis/David Turnley)

class presentations. Adults may avoid social and work situations that involve interactions with others and possible scrutiny. Thus, schooling, work, and leisure can all be severely handicapped by social phobia.

The final type of phobia is agoraphobia. This involves fear of being in places or situations from which escape might be difficult or embarrassing and may not be available. Typical situations that are avoided include being alone outside the home, being in a crowd, standing in a line, being on a bridge, and traveling by bus, train, or car. People with agoraphobia often experience attacks of panic. These are unpredictable attacks of intense fear. Thus, while standing in a shopping line, a person may experience, out of the blue, the same fear that another may experience when confronted by an armed assailant. To the individual having such an attack, the feelings are inexplicable, but the person still worries that he or she is about to die, go crazy, or lose control. Agoraphobia is often called a fear of open spaces, but this is incorrect. The name *agoraphobia* literally means "fear of the market place." While people with the disorder do avoid supermarkets, they typically avoid places because they are afraid of having a panic attack. Fearing they might die, go crazy, or lose control, they flee to situations where these events may be less likely to happen or more easily managed if they do happen (e.g., a hospital emergency room). Agoraphobia afflicts around 3 percent of the population and begins between late adolescence and the mid-thirties. It usually has its onset after an unexpected and unpredicted panic attack. While panic attacks afflict males and females equally, females are more likely to exhibit the agoraphobic avoidances.

Theories of Phobias

The diversity of phobias has presented a challenge for the creation of theories that attempt to explain the core factors responsible for the origin and maintenance of these intense and unreasonable fears. In one of the earliest theories of phobias, Sigmund Freud (1909) proposed that phobias arise from unresolved sexual urges toward the opposite sex parent. Freud argued that a boy, known as Little Hans, developed a horse phobia because of his unresolved Oedipal complex (i.e., he desired his mother and resented his father for possessing her). As a consequence of his jealousy, the boy wished to kill his father. Realizing these sexual and murderous wishes were abhorrent, Little Hans tried to keep them out of his consciousness by repressing them. However, the repression was imperfect and the wishes emerged into consciousness in a symbolic form. According to Freud, the horse symbolized the boy's father and Little Hans projected his fear onto it.

Freud's theory was later replaced by an account that said that the origin of phobias lay in Pavlovian conditioning. Joseph Wolpe and Stanley Rachman (1960) re-analyzed the case of Little Hans, and they noted that Little Hans had been present when a horse and cart had fallen down and the horse flailed wildly in front of the boy. The experience of terror would thus have been paired with a previously neutral stimulus (the horse). Therefore, on future occasions a horse would re-elicit the terror in the same way that a light elicited salivation in Ivan Pavlov's dogs, once the light had been paired with food. To explain the persistence of fears, it was argued that each time a person avoided a feared object or situation there was a decrease in anxiety. The relief would be rewarding, thereby raising the probability of future avoidance.

These ideas were extended by Susan Mineka (1988), who showed that actual injury is not needed to generate phobic behavior. Working with rhesus monkeys, she showed that laboratory-reared monkeys (who have never seen a snake and have no fear of snakes), developed enduring fear of snakes following a single exposure to a wild-reared monkey reacting fearfully to a snake. Such observational learning is also possible among humans, but people can also acquire fears by being given information about how dangerous some object or situation is.

The chief problems with the conditioning, observational, and informational theories of the origins of phobias is the inequitable distribution of phobias. The number of stimuli that one could fear is exceedingly large, but the number of stimuli that people actually are phobic about is relatively small. Phobias about spiders and enclosed spaces are common, but fear of flowers and vegetables are rare. Martin Seligman (1971) proposed that the inequitable distribution of phobias arises because some stimuli are more easily associated with aversive events than others. Human ancestors who possessed a capacity to learn quickly that animals such as snakes were potentially fatal were more likely to survive and pass on the genes responsible for this learning.

Ross Menzies and Chris Clarke (1995) have offered an alternative to the preparedness theory to account for the inequitable distribution of phobias. They suggest that people inherit a predisposition to fear stimuli that have evolutionary significance because they represented a danger to human ancestors (e.g., heights). These fears emerge in a predictable sequence as part of normal child development. Children acquire a fear of heights as they learn to crawl, a fear of strangers as they learn to walk (and wander from familiar people), and so on. Children are then taught to recognize the bounds of safety and these fears are overcome. How-

ever, some fail to learn to overcome their fears, and the fears are easily re-aroused during periods of stress.

Evidence from genetic studies is consistent with these theories that assume a heritable component to phobias. These studies indicate that phobias cluster in families, but to date there is little strong evidence that individual anxiety disorders are inherited. Rather, the tendency to be a nervous person seems to be inherited. This tendency makes the person vulnerable to the development of a phobia or other anxiety disorder at some time.

The variety of explanations reflects the fact that researchers are continuing to refine their understanding of the causes of phobias, but it also reflects the variety of possible pathways to the acquisition of a phobia. However, regardless of the paths people take to develop phobias, once a person has a phobia, the effects can be substantial. Individuals who fear injections may avoid necessary medical care. People with agoraphobia can become housebound and completely dependent upon others for support. Individuals with social phobia can end up avoiding virtually all social relationships, seeking employment in solitary occupations, or refusing promotions to maintain minimal social contact. Constant worry can accompany the phobia, and depression and drug addiction are found all too frequently among individuals suffering from fear and phobias.

Treatment of Phobias

Fortunately, effective treatments for phobias are available. The most effective psychological therapy for phobic fear involves exposure and response prevention. The sufferer is encouraged to confront the phobic object or situation under circumstances that ensure that the feared outcome does not occur. Since continuous exposure to a stimulus weakens the responses triggered by it, confronting the feared stimulus reduces the fear response.

Since confronting phobic stimuli can be terrifying, the way exposure is conducted varies. One format is flooding, in which the person with a phobia confronts his or her most feared object or situation and remains until anxiety dissipates. A variant on this process is graded exposure, in which the feared objects and situations are ordered in a hierarchy according to the amount of fear they trigger. Exposure begins with the least fear-provoking step in the hierarchy. Once fear is no longer triggered, the focus of exposure moves to the next most fear-provoking stimulus in the hierarchy. This process continues until the person has mastered the most feared situation. A further variant is systematic desensitization, in which people are first taught progressive muscle relaxation so that they can produce the relaxation response during graded exposure. It is reasoned that, because experiencing the relaxation response is incompatible with experiencing fight-or-flight, the phobia will be overcome since the once-feared stimulus is now paired with relaxation.

The second component of exposure-based treatments is response prevention. Response prevention is used to counter the usual tendency of people with phobias to flee their phobic objects and situations. Exposure triggers the intense and unpleasant fight-or-flight response. Fleeing will cause this unpleasant state to be replaced by the pleasant experience of relief. However, avoidance means that the person cannot learn that the phobic stimulus is not truly dangerous, and the relief is so rewarding that avoidance is reinforced. To counter this tendency, when the person is undergoing exposure, the usual avoidance responses are prevented.

Exposure and response prevention treatments that focus on the person's behavior are often supplemented with therapy that focuses on the person's thoughts (or cognitions). These cognitive-behavior therapies seek to change the catastrophic thoughts that the person has about the feared objects and situations. Since worries that feared objects and situations are truly dangerous will increase fear, being able to replace these thoughts with more appropriate and helpful cognitions will reduce fear.

In addition to psychological treatments, fears and phobias can be treated with certain pharmacological treatments. Anti-anxiety medications can reduce the frequency and intensity of panic attacks and levels of general fear and anxiety. These medications include benzodiazepines, tricyclic antidepressants, and selective serotonin reuptake inhibitors. By acting on the systems in the brain that give rise to fear, these medications have the capacity to reduce fear and panic.

See also: ANXIETY DISORDERS; FREUD, SIGMUND; MOOD DISORDERS; POST-TRAUMATIC STRESS DISORDER

Bibliography

Andrews, Gavin; Crino, Rocco; Hunt, Caroline; Lampe, Lisa; and Page, Andrew. (1994). *The Treatment of Anxiety Disorders: Clinician's Guide and Patient Manuals.* New York: Cambridge University Press.

Barlow, David H. (1988). *Anxiety and Its Disorders: The Nature and Treatment of Panic and Anxiety.* New York: Guilford.

Cannon, Walter B. (1927). *Bodily Changes in Pain, Hunger, Fear, and Rage.* New York: Appleton-Century-Crofts.

Freud, Sigmund. ([1909] 1977). *Case Histories, Vol. 1: "Dora" and "Little Hans."* Middlesex, Eng.: Penguin.

Menzies, Ross G., and Clarke, J. Chistopher. (1995). "The Etiology of Phobias: A Nonassociative Account." *Clinical Psychology Review* 15:23–48.

Mineka, Susan. (1988). "A Primate Model of Phobic Fears." In *Theoretical Foundations of Behavior Therapy,* ed. Hans J. Eysenck and Irene Martin. New York: Plenum.

Rachman, Stanley J. (1990). *Fear and Courage,* 2nd ed. W. H. Freeman.

Seligman, Martin E. P. (1971). "Phobias and Preparedness." *Behavior Therapy* 2:307–320.

Wolpe, Joseph, and Rachman, Stanley J. (1960). "Psychoanalytic Evidence: A Critique Based on Freud's Case of Little Hans." *Journal of Nervous and Mental Disease* 131:135–145.

Andrew C. Page

FLIRTATION

What does it mean to flirt? The *American Heritage Dictionary* definition of flirtation includes "to amuse oneself in playful amorousness; to play lightly or mockingly at courtship; to deal playfully, triflingly, or coyly; to toy." Central to this definition is the notion that flirtation is not serious and that it reflects a positive, carefree emotional state. Frequently, flirtation is meant to be fun; engaging in flirtatious banter is a way to show one's wittiness and pass time at a social function. At other times, serious feelings for the other person are behind the flirtation. By acting as if one's sexual innuendos are all in fun, flirting can be a self-presentational strategy used to avoid the embarrassment of showing that one cares and learning that one's companion does not.

Social scientists Sandra Metts and Brian Spitzberg (1996, p. 50) have defined flirtation as "the signaling of sexual interest." From the perspective of the recipient, Matthew Abrahams (1994, p. 283) writes that "flirtatious communications are messages and behaviors . . . purposefully attempting to gain . . . attention and stimulate . . . interest in the sender."

Why Do People Flirt?

Flirting is the start of a courtship ritual; it provides a method of indicating that an individual has more than a platonic interest in his or her companion. Flirtation may culminate in a sexual relationship, or it may end quickly if one's partner does not signal return interest.

Flirtation is often considered to be a "game" that involves the use of subtlety, innuendo, and ambiguous cues that hint at sexuality without being direct. By keeping the conversation light and using humor, one can test one's partner's degree of sexual attraction without being overt. Flirtation often involves making jokes about potential sexual behaviors, such as giving someone a massage or taking a shower together. If one's partner laughs, it is easy to pretend it was just a joke and laugh along. If one's partner agrees, then one has a sexual opportunity.

How Is Flirtation Conveyed?

Many researchers have identified cues that are used to express liking, affection, attraction, and sexual interest. Common verbal cues include asking questions, giving compliments, keeping the conversation flowing, and expressing shared interests. Common nonverbal cues include touching, maintaining eye contact, smiling, leaning forward, creating close physical proximity, and presenting a relaxed posture. Paraverbal cues such as laughter and an animated tone of voice can also be important signs of attraction. Determining when a cue is intended to signify friendliness as opposed to flirtation can be difficult because many of the same cues are used to convey both platonic friendliness and sexual attraction. In general, flirtation is associated with a moderate amount of a given cue. For example, a little smiling or a handshake might be perceived as friendliness, a moderate amount of smiling or a pat on the knee may be perceived as flirtation, and a great deal of smiling or kisses may be perceived as seduction. Although such distinctions seem reasonable, the line between mild and moderate cue usage is easy to confuse. Antonia Abbey and Christian Melby (1986) have found that men tend to perceive women's friendly cues as conveying more sexuality than the woman intended. As a result, women's attempts to be friendly are often misperceived by men as flirtation.

Another approach to assessing how individuals flirt is to observe women and men in natural settings. Monica Moore (1995) describes a study she conducted that involved observing adult women in public settings such as bars, restaurants, and parties. She identified a large number of cues that were used to elicit the attention of men including glancing around the room, looking specifically at one man, head tossing, hair flipping, makeup application, gesturing, laughing, and smiling. Moore's follow-up study with adolescent girls found that they used many of the same strategies although less subtly. Deborah Walsh and Jay Hewitt (1985) had women specifically vary how they acted in a bar to determine which responses were most likely to lead a man to approach the woman. Men were most

likely to talk to the woman when she repeatedly looked at him and smiled. It is noteworthy that all of these studies focus on women's flirtatious cues and men's responses to them. As noted below, there is some debate about which gender typically initiates flirtatious behavior.

What Are the Stages in Flirtation?

Psychologists use the term *script* to describe individuals' expectations for situations. For example, people have a general script that reflects the expected order of events and possible outcomes when one enters a restaurant, but they also have more specific scripts that include details about fast food versus four star establishments. Members of the same society tend to have similar scripts, which simplifies expectations and communication. There are unique aspects of scripts, however, and misperceptions can occur when individuals' scripts differ (e.g., one individual's first date script includes sexual behavior but the companion's first date script does not). Sexual involvements require negotiation. Although individuals can rely on the basic cultural script, it is vague and continually changing (e.g., After how many dates is sexual intercourse appropriate? When is recreational sex acceptable? For whom?), so communication, either overt or covert, is necessary to negotiate through the situation with one's partner. Flirtation provides a relatively nonthreatening way to communicate one's desires and learn about one's partner's interests.

Scripts about how to meet people and assess their degree of sexual interest include flirting as a central element. Metts and Spitzberg (1996) have indicated that flirtation with a stranger typically includes five stages: recognition, conversation and small talk, immediacy and responsiveness, physical contact, and declaration of intentions. Recognition involves gaining others' attention through strategies such as looking at them, standing near them, smiling, or gesturing to them. The conversation stage involves initiating conversation, often with a pick up line (e.g., "Haven't I seen you here before?"). Then the individuals begin to talk, usually about mundane issues (e.g., weather, sports). As the conversation continues, it becomes more personal, there is more self-disclosure and more joking about sexual topics. If the interaction continues, one individual may touch the other (e.g., a pat on the arm or knee). A sequence may end with partners' exchanging telephone numbers or leaving together.

There is some debate about who initiates flirtatious encounters. In American society, men are expected to be the initiators of sexual interactions, whereas women are responsible for setting the limits on sexual activity. Although men may make the first overt move

---

Sherwood Anderson, in "Sophistication" (1919), portrays two teenagers who are both keenly aware that they are growing out of childhood and into adulthood. Both care about each other but cannot find the right words to say that. They kiss, but they are embarrassed by their awkwardness and soon revert to "the animalism of youth," laughing and chasing after each other.

A man and a woman make flirtatious eye contact as they pass each other on a road in Colombia. (Corbis/ Jeremy Horner)

in the initiation of a flirtation, women often signal their willingness to be approached. Timothy Perper (1989) gives the example of a woman positioning herself near a man who interests her at a party. She may leave it to him to start a conversation, but she has signaled her readiness to talk by moving close to him.

Regardless of who initiates the flirtation, the process disintegrates if one of the two individuals does not reciprocate. If one person looks and smiles at another person across the room and receives absolutely no acknowledgment, the first person is unlikely to take additional steps. If one person tries a pick up line and is given a withering look, the first person is likely to walk away. Each response requires a positive return response for the flirtation to continue. Of course, people vary in their persistence—some people give up quickly and others ignore repeated messages that their attentions are unwanted. Sometimes when individuals persist despite their partner's lack of interest, it is due to misperception; the initiators do not comprehend the message and mistakenly think their companions are sexually attracted to them. This is one of the disadvantages of the use of subtle, ambiguous messages in flirting; these messages are not always understood. At other times, an individual knowingly continues to force sexual attention on someone who has expressed disinterest. Thus, unwanted flirtation can culminate in sexual harassment or date rape. In general, however,

people are sensitive to companions' responses and want to avoid rejection (to protect their ego), so the flirtatious encounter ends if one's partner is not encouraging.

Depictions of Flirting

Fiction reflects the beliefs, attitudes, and cultural norms of the society in which it is written. People's conceptions of flirtation are influenced by the way it is portrayed in fictional interactions, such as those in novels, television shows, and songs. Because fiction both reflects and influences real-world interaction, it is not surprising that fictional accounts often correspond to the models of flirtation described by social scientists.

Literature

Descriptions of flirtation appear in literature from every age. In William Shakespeare's *As You Like It,* Rosalind argues,

Your brother and my sister no sooner met but looked;
no sooner looked but they loved;
no sooner sighed but they asked one another the
   reason;
no sooner knew the reason but they sought the remedy.

Rosalind portrays an evolving relationship using stages similar to those described by Metts and Spitzberg. The two characters gain each other's attention by looking, display immediacy and responsiveness by sighing, and declare their intentions by asking one another the meaning behind their sighs.

An excerpt from a poem written by Robert Herrick in the mid-1600s provides another example of flirting in literature:

> Anthea bade me tie her shoe;
> I did and kist the instep, too;
> And would have kist unto her knee
> Had not her blush rebuked me.

By asking her companion to tie her shoe, Anthea provides an opportunity for the two to touch, which is a well-documented sign of attraction. By asking her companion for his assistance, Anthea also signals her willingness to be approached. The narrator responds by kissing Anthea's foot. His response is comparable to those found in modern observational studies in which men make an overtly flirtatious move only after the woman has signaled her willingness to be touched. The narrator considers kissing Anthea's knee, but decides not to escalate the flirtation when she blushes in response to his first kiss. Escalation does not typically occur unless a positive response has been received.

Modern Fiction, Television, and Music

Romance novels provide a rich source of examples of flirtation. J. K. Alberts (1986) has analyzed the stages of relationship development in Harlequin romance novels. The standard script includes the initial use of indirect, ambiguous cues to assess the other's degree of interest. One indirect technique involves denying the possibility of a relationship. Alberts provides the following example from Charlotte Lamb's novel *Possession* (1979, p. 135),

> Dan: The fellow in Geneva. The unhappy Max . . .
>   whom you handed over to your flatmate with such
>   calm unconcern, as though he were a doll you no
>   longer wanted.
> Laura: I'm very fond of Max, as it happens.
> Dan: Never be fond of me sweetheart, I might get very
>   nasty.

Dan brings up the subject of a relationship with Laura but protects himself from possible rejection by warning her not to get involved with him. This cautious testing of the other's interest corresponds to the early stages of involvement described by Metts and Spitzberg.

Examples of flirtatious behavior are extremely common in television shows. The popular television programs *Cheers, Moonlighting*, and *Northern Exposure* included in their central story lines a developing romantic relationship between the two main charac-

ters. In each of these shows, the main characters' interactions were characterized by witty banter. Their humorous conversations exemplified the use of flirtation to show one's wittiness and social skill, as well as flirtation's playful nature. Flirtatious interactions in television programs follow the familiar script of beginning with indirect, ambiguous cues of interest and then building to more direct, intense exchanges between the characters. The escalating nature of flirtation works well as a plot device because it keeps viewers wondering if and when a romantic relationship will develop, which keeps them tuned in to the show in order to find out.

Love and romance are staples of modern song lyrics. In the song "Something to Talk About," popularized by Bonnie Raitt in the 1980s, the singer is beginning to think that a friendship may be developing into a sexual attraction. The following cues are taken as signs of flirtation,

> We laugh just a little too loud
> We stand just a little too close
> We stare just a little too long.

As noted earlier, research demonstrates that these nonverbal cues can be difficult to interpret accurately because they are used to express both platonic friendliness and sexual attraction. Therefore, it is not surprising that the characters in the song are unsure about how to interpret these cues.

Advice Books

Almost every large bookstore has an entire section of books devoted to the topic of flirting and dating. Most of these books are "how to" books, giving advice on how to flirt, how to perceive and interpret others' flirting, and how to use flirting as a strategy for starting or maintaining a relationship. The information contained in these books on the mechanics of flirting, such as maintaining eye contact and use of touch, largely agrees with the literature on interpersonal attraction.

Most flirtation advice books are oriented toward women. An underlying assumption of many of these books is that men and women do not always have the same goals in interactions with the opposite sex. These books assume that a woman's goal is to develop a committed relationship. One best-selling dating book, *The Rules* (1995) by Ellen Fein and Sherrie Schneider, purports to contain "Time Tested Secrets for Capturing the Heart of Mr. Right," as stated in the subtitle of the book. In contrast, Marty Westerman (1992, p. 90) upholds the view that "flirting isn't about hunting," and Susan Rabin and Barbara Lagowski (1997, p. 10) recommend that readers "think of flirting as a playful, unpredictable adventure, rather than a ticket to commitment."

Conclusion

Overall, the themes that social scientists have investigated regarding flirtation correspond to depictions of flirtation in literature, the mass media, and advice books. Flirting is meant to be fun, although feelings can be hurt when one individual's intentions are more serious than the other's. Courtship is depicted as a game in which subtle, ambiguous cues are used to signal sexual interest. Although such indirect strategies can reduce embarrassment, they also guarantee that motives are frequently miscommunicated.

See also: ATTRACTIVENESS; COMMUNICATION; DESIRE; FRIENDSHIP; INFATUATION; LUST; SMILING

Bibliography

Abbey, Antonia. (1982). "Sex Differences in Attributions for Friendly Behavior: Do Males Misperceive Females' Friendliness?" *Journal of Personality and Social Psychology* 42:830–838.

Abbey, Antonia. (1987). "Misperception of Friendly Behavior As Sexual Interest: A Survey of Naturally Occurring Incidents." *Psychology of Women Quarterly* 11:173–194.

Abbey, Antonia, and Melby, Christian. (1986). "The Effects of Non-Verbal Cues on Gender Differences in Perceptions of Sexual Intent." *Sex Roles* 15:283–298.

Abbey, Antonia; McAuslan, Pam; and Thomson-Ross, Lisa. (1998). "Sexual Assault Perpetration by College Men: The Role of Alcohol, Misperception of Sexual Intent, and Sexual Beliefs and Experiences." *Journal of Social and Clinical Psychology* 17:167–195.

Abrahams, Matthew F. (1994). "Perceiving Flirtatious Communication: An Exploration of the Perceptual Dimensions Underlying Judgements of Flirtatiousness." *Journal of Sex Research* 31:283–292.

Alberts, J. K. (1986). "The Role of Couples' Conversations in Relational Development: A Content Analysis of Courtship Talk in Harlequin Romance Novels." *Communication Quarterly* 34:127–142.

Burgoon, Judee K.; Buller, David B.; Hale, Jerold L.; and deTurck, Mark A. (1984). "Relational Messages Associated with Nonverbal Behaviors." *Human Communication Research* 10:351–378.

Coker, Deborah A., and Burgoon, Judee K. (1987). "The Nature of Conversational and Nonverbal Encoding Patterns." *Human Communication Research* 13:463–494.

Fein, Ellen, and Schneider, Sherrie. (1995). *The Rules: Time-Tested Secrets for Capturing the Heart of Mr. Right.* New York: Warner Books.

Grauerholz, Elizabeth, and Serpe, Richard T. (1985). "Initiation and Response: The Dynamics of Sexual Interaction." *Sex Roles* 12:1041–1059.

Greer, Arlette, and Buss, David M. (1994). "Tactics for Promoting Sexual Encounters." *Journal of Sex Research* 31:185–201.

Koeppel, Liana B.; Montagne-Miller, Yvette; O'Hair, Dan; and Cody, Michael J. (1993). "Friendly? Flirting? Wrong?" In *Interpersonal Communication: Evolving Interpersonal Relationships,* ed. Pamela J. Kalbfleisch. Hillsdale, NJ: Lawrence Erlbaum.

Metts, Sandra, and Spitzberg, Brian H. (1996). "Sexual Communication in Interpersonal Contexts: A Script Based Approach." *Communication Yearbook* 19:49–91.

Moore, Monica M. (1995). "Courtship Signaling and Adolescents: 'Girls Just Wanna Have Fun'?" *Journal of Sex Research* 32(4):319–328.

Perper, Timothy. (1989). "Theories and Observations on Sexual Selection and Female Choice in Human Beings." *Medical Anthropology* 2:409–454.

Rabin, Susan, and Lagowski, Barbara. (1997). *101 Ways to Flirt.* New York: Penguin.

Stockdale, Margaret S. (1993). "The Role of Sexual Misperceptions of Women's Friendliness in an Emerging Theory of Sexual Harassment." *Journal of Vocational Behavior* 42:84–101.

Turner, E. S. (1955). *A History of Courting.* New York: E. P. Dutton.

Walsh, Debra G., and Hewitt, Jay. (1985). "Giving Men the Come-On: Effect of Eye Contact and Smiling in a Bar Environment." *Perceptual and Motor Skills* 61:873–874.

Westerman, Marty. (1992). *How to Flirt: A Practical Guide.* Los Angeles: Price Stern Sloan.

Antonia Abbey
Tina Zawacki

FOLK THEORIES OF EMOTION

Since the late 1970s, there has been an increasing emphasis on the study of folk theories of psychological concepts, such as intelligence, ability, motivation, and personality. This line of research is based on two assumptions: (a) people, in their attempt to understand and control their mind, generate hypotheses and develop theories about "what things are" and (b) these folk theories are implicit in the development of motives, goals, and actions. In this context, scientific efforts have been devoted to the description of the meanings and attributes that people attach to emotional experiences.

Theoretical Basis

The idea that people hold theories about the attributes of emotions is based on the fact that emotional arousal leads people to generate, test, and evaluate alternative hypotheses in order to understand the changing sensations that affect them. Like other psychological processes, these hypotheses, derived from personal experiences and cultural knowledge, may create some thoughts and ideas about the attributes of emotions. It is important to recognize that "emotion" is an ill-defined category that cannot be identified precisely in terms of necessary and sufficient criteria and that its meanings may vary somewhat from person to person. These individual variations in the attributes attached to emotions are not surprising because *emotion* is an abstract term that summarizes the unique experiences of a person and the particular beliefs he or she internalizes over the life span.

The profusion of attributes related to emotional experiences is notable in both psychological and folk theories. Historically, emotional experiences have been alternatively conceptualized as adaptational devices and as primary sources of human problems. Accordingly, some authors, such as Carroll Izard (1977), have related emotion to the adaptive organization of perception, memory, and behavior, whereas others, such as David Rapaport (1942), have taken the position that emotion plays a main role in the development of psychopathology. In folk theories, romanticism assumes that emotion is one of the most important and challenging human experiences, whereas the tendency of Western civilization to connect emotion to intellect links emotion to cognitive and behavioral problems.

The Contents of Folk Theories of Emotions

Few studies have been designed to study folk theories of emotion. For example, Craig Smith and Phoebe Ellsworth (1985) asked subjects to recall personal experiences related to fifteen emotional states (e.g., guilt, shame, happiness) and to answer questions that tap eight potential attributes of emotional experiences (e.g., control, certainty, pleasantness). Six cognitive dimensions were recovered following statistical analyses, and the fifteen emotions were found to lie systematically along them. Phillip Shaver, Judith Schwartz, Donald Kirson, and Cary O'Connor (1987) examined individuals' knowledge of emotions by asking them to recall particular emotional states and to describe their feelings, thoughts, and behaviors in those states. John Mayer and Yvonne Gaschke (1988) also dealt with the way people appraise emotions and developed a "meta-mood" scale encompassing five mood attributes: control, clarity, acceptance, stability, and typicality. Along this line of research, Elisheva Ben-Artzi and Mario Mikulincer (1996a) asked people to report attributes of emotions, content analyzed their answers, and developed a forty-item self-report scale. The findings revealed that people spontaneously appraise emotions in terms of eight categorical attributes, which are structured around two global folk theories of emotions.

One folk theory reflects a "benefit" appraisal of emotion. In this appraisal, emotion is regarded as having three attributes—intensity, motivational power, and experiential significance. This appraisal emphasizes the conviction that emotion shapes personal goals and actions and gives meaning to individual experiences. It focuses on the central role emotion plays in motivating and organizing behavior and in facilitating achievement of a meaningful existence.

The second folk theory reflects a "threat" appraisal of emotion in that it focuses on the threatening and disturbing aspects of emotional experiences. This appraisal encompasses three attributes—bizarreness, uncontrollability/unpredictability, and unstability—that reflect the belief that emotions are not subject to the laws of logic and reason. It also includes two other attributes—cognitive interference and disturbance—that emphasize the danger emotion poses to clear thinking and personal well-being. In this appraisal, the world of emotions is alien and even a threat to the cognitive world. In general, people who adopt a threat appraisal of emotions seem to believe that emotions belong to the dark side of the mind and are a source of problems.

The various attributes people attach to emotion are also found in formal psychological theories of emotion. For example, the motivational and experiential significance of emotion has been emphasized by a high number of theorists who suggest that emotion constitutes a basic motivational system and that emotion plays an important role in organizing attention, memory, and action. The various components of the threat appraisal also are found in psychological theories. For example, the belief that emotion is disturbing can be found in theories that describe adjustment problems related to emotions. The belief that emotions interfere with cognition appears in cognitive theories of emotions. Because emotional experiences, according to George Mandler (1980, p. 222), reflect the "confluence of experiences of autonomic activity, cognitive analysis of the current state of the world, and interactions with other cognitive processes," they demand cognitive resources and deplete the resources available for the processing of information.

The belief that emotions are bizarre and irrational can be found in classical psychological theories, which view emotions as inferior or more animal-like than the higher mental processes of logic and reason. This belief about emotions is also found in classic psychoanalytic writings, which view emotions, like dreams, as primitive psychological processes. The belief in the uncontrollability and unpredictability of emotion also has parallels in formal theories, which argue that emotions fascinate people, are difficult to control, have no essential rhythm, and have freedom of duration. Finally, the belief in the instability of emotion has been noted by Herbert Spencer (1890, p. 172), who argued that "[emotions'] beginnings and endings in time are comparatively indefinite. . . . That is to say, they are not limited by preceding and succeeding states of consciousness with any precision." In these terms, emotions seem to be constantly changing, appearing without any anticipatory signal and vanishing into a different emotion.

In general, the two folk theories of emotion emphasize two classic views of emotions. The benefit appraisal seems to emphasize the view that emotions are one of the principal organizing forces of the organism. As Jeffrey Gray (1973, pp. 8–9) wrote, emotions "pick up and organize cognitive elements into . . . an emotional-cognitive structure, and it is the repetition of this process . . . that constitutes the development of mind." The threat appraisal corresponds to the view that emotions can be overwhelming, burdening, and disturbing experiences.

The two folk theories also reflect a basic paradox of emotion. In Joseph DeRivera's (1977) terms, emotion involves two basic contradictory features: passivity and the sense of actively doing things that seem to be coming from within. People also perceive this basic contradiction and emphasize both the motivational and overwhelming qualities of emotions. The question remains whether the two folk theories (threat appraisal and benefit appraisal) are opposing or independent, unrelated appraisals. Although one can conceptualize the two folk theories as the negative and positive poles of a single dimension, Ben-Artzi and Mikulincer (1996a) found that some persons emphasize both the importance and disturbing aspects of emotion, whereas other people emphasize one aspect at the expense of the other.

Folk Theories of Particular Emotional States

Beyond holding global theories about the emotional world, people also seem to have specific beliefs about particular emotional states. For example, people may regard fear, hope, and surprise as more unpredictable than other emotions, and they may feel that they have more control over guilt than over sadness. People may also consider happiness and disgust as more intense than pleasantness, and they may be more likely to approve positive emotions than to approve negative emotions.

People also have some basic common knowledge of the particularities and similarities of momentary emotional states. For example, people may regard positive emotions as beneficial and negative emotions as threatening. Accordingly, people may believe that happiness and anxiety are generally experienced more intensely and with less control than calmness and sadness. In addition, people may consider anxiety as a source of cognitive and behavioral problems and joy as a source of motivation.

Ben-Artzi and Mikulincer (1996b) found that particular emotional states varied across the benefit and threat folk theories of emotions. Among negative emotions, people tended to appraise both anger and anxiety as disturbing or interfering with cognitive activity

and having motivational power. Although sadness is also generally regarded as a negative emotion, people appraised it in less threatening terms than anxiety and anger. In addition, they tended to appraise sadness as having more experiential significance than other negative emotions. Such an appraisal seems to reflect existential and humanistic ideas that sadness allows people to understand their existence in a meaningful way.

Among positive emotions, people tended to appraise both joy and love as having motivational and experiential significance. However, they also appraised love as a threatening emotion, whereas they believed that joy can be experienced in harmony with motivational and cognitive systems and can give meaning to life. People tended to appraise both sadness and joy as sources of personal meaning.

People tended to appraise love in beneficial and threatening terms. On the one hand, they tended to appraise love as a strong experience that shapes their goals and gives meaning to life. On the other hand, they tended to appraise love as a bizarre, unstable, and uncontrollable experience that disturbs the life course and interferes with logical reasoning. This ambivalent appraisal reflects centuries of literary and philosophical arguments that persons who fall in love cannot choose the object of their love in a rational way, cannot control the onset and course of their love, and are unable to think of anything else, as well as the conviction that their aspirations, thoughts, and behaviors are directed toward the object of love. It also reflects the romantic view of love as both the highest human experience and a source of problem.

Psychological Repercussions

Folk theories of emotion seem to make an important contribution to the understanding of cognitions and behaviors in emotional episodes. According to Carol Dweck and Ellen Leggett's (1988) theory, different appraisals of the self and the world generate different concerns, orient people toward different goals, and thus foster different response patterns. In illustrating their theoretical approach, Dweck and Leggett show that people tend to hold different folk theories of intelligence, which influences their aspirations, goals, and responses in achievement settings. In the same way, the appraisal of the emotional world may be a consistent predictor of a person's goals and responses during and after emotional episodes. That is, folk theories of emotions may lead people to pursue particular goals in emotional episodes, which, in turn, may guide their behavior.

In a series of seven studies, Ben-Artzi and Mikulincer (1997) found interesting associations between folk theories of emotions and responses to emotional episodes. People who appraise emotions in threatening terms tended to react to negative emotional states with negative self-evaluation (e.g., "I'm a failure!"), negative thoughts, and less constructive responses aimed at ending the negative episode. In addition, they tended to react to positive emotional episodes with thoughts about the legitimacy and causes of the aroused emotion (e.g., "Why do I feel in that way?") and less active attempts to conserve the positive emotional state. It seems that a threat appraisal of emotion leads people to adopt what Dweck and Leggett called an "evaluation goal." This goal seems to be manifested in thoughts about the nature of the emotional state, self-evaluative responses, and lack of active constructive responses.

People with high threat appraisal seem to be convinced that they can neither end negative emotions nor maintain positive emotions because they believe that emotions are bizarre, uncontrollable, unpredictable, and unstable. That is, they believe that they do not have sufficient external or internal resources to manipulate and control the course and consequences of emotions. As a result, they may feel passively overwhelmed and may perceive that the goal of learning better ways of dealing with emotions is futile. Instead, they may prefer to document the emotional state passively and to engage in self-evaluation. This orientation may be manifested in self-focused worries, passivity, and lack of active constructive responses.

With regard to the benefit appraisal of emotion, Ben-Artzi and Mikulincer (1997) found that people holding such a folk theory tended to attempt to end the negative emotional episode and to express their inner tension. In positive emotional episodes, these people tended to experience their feelings in a meaningful way, to externalize them, to share them with others, and to generalize them to related behavioral and cognitive areas. This generalization was manifested in increases of altruistic behavior, optimistic judgments, and creative thinking following the experience of a positive emotion. It seems that a benefit appraisal of emotions leads people to experience emotions intensely, to be attuned to them, and to use them as important cues in shaping behavior.

People who hold a benefit appraisal stance seem to perceive emotions as central, harmonious components of their mental lives and thus may be oriented toward experiencing emotions in a strong, overt way and toward using emotions to shape their cognitions and behaviors. Those people who hold a threat appraisal view seem to feel overwhelmed by emotions without having suitable responses for dealing with them, and thus they may be oriented toward documenting emotions without making any attempt to change or conserve them. In this way, a benefit ap-

praisal of emotion may reflect the extent to which individuals emphasize and attend to emotional experiences, whereas a threat appraisal of emotion may reflect the extent to which they fail to enhance their mastery over emotions and instead passively document their emotional state.

See also: COGNITIVE PERSPECTIVE; EMOTIONAL INTELLIGENCE; PERSONALITY; PSYCHOANALYTIC PERSPECTIVE; SOCIOLOGY OF EMOTIONS

Bibliography

Arnold, Magda B. (1960). *Emotion and Personality.* New York: Columbia University Press.

Ben-Artzi, Elisheva, and Mikulincer, Mario. (1996a). "Lay Theories of Emotion: 1. Conceptualization and Measurement." *Imagination, Cognition, and Personality* 15:249–271.

Ben-Artzi, Elisheva, and Mikulincer, Mario. (1996b). "Lay Theories of Emotion: 2. Interindividual and Intraindividual Variance in the Appraisal of Emotions." *Imagination, Cognition, and Personality* 15:273–294.

Ben-Artzi, Elisheva, and Mikulincer, Mario. (1997). "Lay Theories of Emotion: 4. Reactions to Negative and Positive Emotional Episodes." *Imagination, Cognition, and Personality* 16:89–113.

DeRivera, Joseph. (1977). *A Structural Theory of Emotions.* New York: International Universities Press.

Dweck, Carol S., and Leggett, Ellen L. (1988). "A Social-Cognitive Approach to Motivation and Personality." *Psychological Review* 95:256–273.

Frijda, Nico H. (1986). *The Emotions.* New York: Cambridge University Press.

Furnham, Adrian F. (1988). *Lay Theories: Everyday Understanding of Problems in the Social Sciences.* New York: Pergamon.

Gray, Jeffrey A. (1973). "Emotional-Cognitive Structuring: A New Theory of Mind." *FORUM for Correspondence and Contact* 5:1–6.

Izard, Carroll E. (1977). *Human Emotions.* New York: Plenum.

Mandler, George. (1980). "The Generation of Emotion: A Psychological Theory." In *Emotion: Theory, Research, and Experience, Vol. 1: Theories of Emotion,* ed. Robert Plutchik and Harold Kellerman. New York: Academic Press.

Mayer, John D., and Gaschke, Yvonne N. (1988). "The Experience and Meta-Experience of Mood." *Journal of Personality and Social Psychology* 55:102–111.

Plutchik, Robert. (1980). "A General Psychoevolutionary Theory of Emotion." In *Emotion: Theory, Research, and Experience, Vol. 1: Theories of Emotion,* ed. Robert Plutchik and Harold Kellerman. New York: Academic Press.

Rapaport, David. (1942). *Emotions and Memory.* Baltimore, MD: Williams & Wilkins.

Shaver, Phillip; Schwartz, Judith; Kirson, Donald; and O'Connor, Cary. (1987). "Emotion Knowledge: Further Exploration of a Prototype Approach." *Journal of Personality and Social Psychology* 52:1061–1086.

Smith, Craig A., and Ellsworth, Phoebe C. (1985). "Patterns of Cognitive Appraisal in Emotion." *Journal of Personality and Social Psychology* 48:813–838.

Spencer, Herbert. (1890). *The Principles of Psychology.* New York: Appleton.

Mario Mikulincer

FOOD AND EATING

Obtaining, preparing, and eating food are major waking activities for humans, and throughout the world, more money is spent on food than on any other category of expenses. The choice of foods to consume may be the major selective force in animal evolution, accounting for major differences in physical shape, behavior, and brain functioning. In human cultural evolution, food and matters pertaining to it are and have been the basis of many technologies, rituals and religions, social exchange entities, and metaphors. Many phrases in common use are based on food terms (e.g., "That person has bad taste" or "I cannot digest that argument"). *Bitter* and *sweet* are two examples of words that are derived from the food domain and have a particularly strong affective (emotional) tone.

Food and eating (along with beverages and drinking) are fundamental in themselves, but they also provide a foundation for other activities. This foundation role can be described by the process of preadaptation, the idea that something that evolved for one purpose becomes used for another. The mouth is a fine example of this—as a route of entry for food (and air), it included adaptations such as teeth and the tongue for handling food, adaptations that later became fundamental in the expression of speech.

For every individual, the world can be divided into two categories: the self and everything else. Eating involves taking matter from outside the self and putting it inside the self, a very intimate act. It is not surprising that people feel strongly about what they eat. The costs in terms of toxins, micro-organisms, or imbalanced nutrients are high, but the benefits are at least as high—survival is at stake.

Humans are omnivores or, more critically, generalists (as are rats, raccoons, cockroaches, and many other animals). They eat a wide range of foods; virtually anything that can fit into the mouth is potential food. Generalists have few innate determinants of food choice, simply because it is not easy to predict, based on sensory grounds alone, the nutrient and toxic properties of a potential food source. Usually, one must try it and see what happens, costly as this might be. There are, however, three documented innate biases in human food choice. First, there are innate taste preferences. There is an innate tendency to like sweet tastes, which, in nature, are predictive of calorie sources. The long history of sweetness in human culture, from fruit preferences, to cultivation of fruits, to extraction of sugar from fruits, to colonization of the Americas partly to get a source of sugar, to the development of sugar substitutes, is all driven by the innate liking for sweets. There are also innate tendencies to dislike bitter tastes and to reject very strong tastes (e.g., highly salty or sour foods). There may also be innate tendencies to like fatty textures and to dislike oral irritation (as from peppers). Second, there is a suspicion about trying new foods (because of potential toxicity), as well as a conflicting interest in them (because of their potential as a new nutrient source). Third, there is a special learning mechanism that allows learning about the consequences of ingestion, even when these may occur hours after ingestion.

Mammals have a unique first food: milk. All mammals make a transition from this first food to an adult diet. For humans and other mammalian omnivores, the transition is from a single food to a very wide range of foods. Weaning is therefore a very challenging event that involves forsaking a very special food in favor of a wide range of unknown foods. To ease the transition, which is made under the guidance of parents and other caretakers, a process is usually adopted that consists of a scheduled and graduated introduction of new foods.

Basic Determinants of Food Choice and Intake

The factors that regulate humans' food choice and intake fall into three major categories: biological, cultural, and psychological (related to individual experience).

All animals have some biological means of regulating their food intake. There are costs to both consuming too little and too much. For humans and virtually all other non-grazing animals, eating (and drinking) occurs principally in regular meals. The major focus of research in this area is the determination of what controls how much is eaten. The relevance of food intake with regard to emotion and affect is that hunger is a substantial predictor of whether an individual will eat and how much will be eaten. There is reason to believe that the pleasure of eating relates to an individual's biological state. Michel Cabanac (1971) has shown experimentally, for example, that sweet tastes become less pleasant the more satiated an individual becomes; he points out that one way the body regulates intake is to modulate the pleasure of eating as a function of needed nutrients. Cabanac calls this process alliesthesia.

Although biological factors may be the most basic, cultural factors are the most powerful. The most reliable means of predicting an individual's food preferences and attitudes is to ask the questions "What is your culture or ethnic group?" Culture operates to determine human food choice in ways that have little psychological interest or emotional relevance. Availability is a major condition for consumption of foods, and the consequent exposure is a major determinant of liking. Cultural and economic forces determine to what foods a person is exposed. These same forces determine the cost of foods, which also influences exposure and consumption.

Cost and availability aside, it is the psychological factors represented in the individual (though, of course, heavily influenced by culture) that principally determine food choice. Human preferences and food attitudes can be framed by the psychological (as opposed to nutritional) taxonomy of foods developed by Paul Rozin and April Fallon (1987). There appear to be three types of reasons for rejecting or accepting a food: sensory affective, that is, how pleasant a food tastes and smells; anticipated consequences, what the expected consequences are of eating a food; and ideation, what is known about a food (e.g., where it comes from, what the nature of it is).

Food rejections, which can be understood in terms of the selection and interplay of these three reasons, fall into four categories: distaste, danger, inappropriate, and disgust. Distaste involves the entities that are rejected because of negative sensory-affective properties, such as (for some people) lima beans, broccoli, beer, or chili peppers. Danger involves things that are rejected primarily because they are believed to be harmful and have acute or long-term negative consequences. The emotion of fear is often associated with the consumption of these danger items. Inappropriate—the largest category—involves things that the culture labels as inedible, such as pencils, grass, paper, or cloth. These items might taste good and be harmless, but they are rejected for ideational reasons. The fourth category, disgust, is also based on culturally transmitted information, but unlike elements in the inappropriate category, there is a strong belief that elements in the disgust category taste bad and are harmful. Unlike the neutral response to inappropriate items, the response to disgust items is strongly negative and emotional. Disgust is the most powerful reaction people have to food. Such entities are so powerful that if they touch an otherwise acceptable food, they render it undesirable, disgusting, and inedible (the principle of contamination or contagion).

There are four comparable categories for food acceptance: good taste (items accepted principally because of sensory properties), beneficial (items accepted largely because of consequences), appropriate (items accepted because they are culturally designated as food), and transvalued (items whose value as food has been enhanced by their prior history). The transvalued category, in most cultures, is much weaker and smaller than the corresponding disgust category. In Hindu India, *prasad,* food that has been "shared" with the Gods (i.e., donated to the priests in the temple and then returned in part), is an example of a transvalued item. As this demonstrates, some foods can be positively contaminated. Unlike the rejection categories, there is little differentiation of associated emotions or affect on the acceptance side—the accompanying psychological state is either pleasure or rather neutral, though a sense of "participation" or elevation may accompany ingestion of transvalued foods.

Acquisition of Food Preferences

For newborn infants, the only functioning categories of the above psychological taxonomy of foods are good taste (e.g., sweet) and distaste (e.g., bitter). Full functioning of the taxonomy is not generally in place until an individual is roughly five to eight years of age.

The greatest amount of research information is related to the distinction between distaste and danger. When ingestion of a food is followed by nausea, the food tends to become disliked (i.e., placed in the distaste category). However, if ingestion of a food is followed by most other negative symptoms (e.g., stomach pain, skin rash, respiratory distress), the food is typically placed in the danger category. Although people reject a food that has caused such symptoms, it does not usually become a disliked taste. This distinction has also been demonstrated in the laboratory with rats. With respect to affect and emotion, it is notable that items in the distaste and danger categories have very different properties, although the outcome (rejection) is the same. It is not at all clear why nausea should produce one type of response (distaste) and most other negative consequences should produce the other type of response (danger). The nausea-based acquired distaste (often called a conditioned taste aversion), unlike danger classification, is not based on a legitimate sense of danger. Even if a person knows that the nausea/illness was not produced by the food, the aversion remains. Thus, people who get nauseous and vomit after a meal usually develop an aversion to some food in the meal, even if they know that the illness was simply the onset of influenza.

The acquisition of good tastes is more complex and less understood. Mere exposure to a food, in itself, often seems sufficient to produce an acquired liking. In addition, the pairing of a food with an already positive event (e.g., an already liked food mixed with the new food, positive regard by a respected person, a pleasant environment), by a process called evaluative conditioning, can lead to acquired likes (or acquired dislikes, if the paired events are negative, as in conditioned taste aversion). Leann Birch and her colleagues (1996) have demonstrated that indications of liking by a significant other (e.g., peer, sibling, teacher, parent) may cause acquisition of liking. The process at work here is not clearly understood. It could be a form of evaluative conditioning, but it also may involve an important instance of communication of affect or emotion. The expressed pleasure by a significant other, on consuming a food, may directly induce a pleasant state in an observer, or it may induce a mimicked positive facial expression. Either of these responses may cause enhancement of liking. Birch has demonstrated, in the laboratory, that efforts by adults to promote liking by emphasizing the beneficial consequences (e.g., better health, a specific reward for eating) seem to block the acquisition of liking for the food. It seems that when a child observes respected others enjoying a food, liking is promoted; when a reward is given for consuming food, the acquisition of liking is blocked.

The acquisition of knowledge of appropriate and inappropriate foods seems to be largely cognitive and affect free. The affect-laden acquisition of disgust and transvaluation contrasts with this. Some communication (facial and other) of affect is almost certainly involved, but there are also important cognitive aspects; it is the nature of the foods and their history that is central to this category. Disgusting foods, and at least some transvalued foods, have contamination properties. This property requires a realization that appearance does not equal reality—a contaminated food looks like any other food, but it is distinguished by its history. Young children have difficulty making the appearance-reality distinction, and it is not until they are four to seven years of age that they begin to exhibit the ability to appreciate contamination, and hence disgust.

Generally, an infant will place anything in his or her mouth if it fits, including feces and potentially toxic foods. Rejections are made only on the basis of sensory properties. Gradually, the infant will acquire distastes or good tastes and learn about danger and beneficial foods. It is much later that the full manifestations of disgust appear.

Acquired Preferences for Innately Unpalatable Substances

Around the world, individuals in specific cultures develop likings for some foods that are innately unpalatable (e.g., bitter, very strong tasting, irritating). Innately unpalatable foods are typically among the favorite foods: chili peppers, black pepper, ginger and other irritant spices, coffee, bitter chocolate, tobacco, alcohol, burnt foods, and highly salted foods. Such reversals of innate aversions are common in humans, but they are rare in other animals. This reversal of an innate aversion is striking, particularly because people of non-participant cultures cannot comprehend why some of these foods are liked (although they almost always have similar situations in their own culture). It

A worker displays a tray of food in front of Groppi's Dessert Shop in Cairo, Egypt, but cultural influences can determine whether or not an individual will have a preference for or aversion to the items. (Corbis/Robert Holmes)

is not known how these preference reversals occur. In part, it may be through the same processes involved in the development of normal likes: mere exposure, evaluative conditioning, and social approval.

For the case of chili peppers, two other affect-related mechanisms have been proposed by Rozin (1990b). The first is that innately negative foods produce the secretion of endorphins, chemicals secreted in the brain in response to pain and irritation. These modulate the displeasure and in high levels can produce pleasure. Normally, one ceases to interact with a bad-tasting food. However, cultural forces continually reintroduce innately unpalatable foods to the child. It may be that with repeated exposures the body endorphin response becomes stronger and eventually cancels and then overwhelms the displeasure. The second account, again related to affect and emotion, is that it is the very displeasure that is the source of the pleasure. This places liking for innately unpalatable foods in the same category as thrill-seeking activities such as riding a roller coaster. That is, humans get pleasure out of situations in which innate aversions or fears are stimulated, but in which there is no real danger. Roller coasters are safe, and so are chili peppers. This may be a case of pleasure derived from "mind-over-matter." One's body responds negatively, but one's mind knows there is no real danger.

Family Influences

Common sense dictates that the principal influence on preference formation should be the family, particularly the traditional mother. It is widely believed that lifetime food preferences and attitudes are generally established in the first years of life, when the child is under maximum parental influence. However, the research literature does not suggest that food experiences in the first six years of life are more important than those in the next six years in determining preferences as an adult. This is a matter of great importance because in the second six years of life, peer and teacher influences become at least as important as parental influence.

Whether or not there is a special early period of imprinting or special influence on food habits, there are strong arguments for high parent-child resemblance in food habits. There is the common genetic heritage, the fact that parents control access (and hence exposure) to foods, and the fact that parents provide the principal affective signals about foods. Yet, it is now a well-established fact that parent-child correlations in liking for foods are very low, in comparison to parent-child correlations in values (such as attitudes about abortion), temperament, or abilities. The low parent-child correlations with regard to liking for specific foods appear whether the children studied are four-year-olds or college students. This "family paradox" is yet deeper, since mother-child correlations are not higher than father-child correlations and children are not more likely to resemble their same sex, as opposed to opposite-sex, parent. The paradox raises many problems for the understanding of the acquisition of preferences, and there are not yet any answers.

Conclusion

With the modern surplus of food in the developed world and the conquest of most infectious diseases, a new set of concerns about food has emerged. Rather than focusing on the fear of an inadequate supply of calories or nutrients, concern has shifted to overnutrition, obesity, and diets that purportedly promote degenerative diseases. As a result, the earlier unalloyed pleasure of eating has become, for many people, an ambivalence, or even an outright fear. This is most well developed in American women, who often fear food as much as savor it. In some, there is now embarrassment and guilt about consuming high-fat foods, an emphasis on thinness, and great concern about the healthiness of every bite of food. This fear of food contrasts with the pleasure of food experienced in developing nations (and indeed in many other developed nations). But it is a fact of the modern world that the older fears of acute harm from foods have been transformed, to a great extent, into fears of fatness and the long-term effects of food.

See also: DISGUST; HEALTH AND ILLNESS; SELF-ESTEEM

Bibliography

Barker, Lewis M., ed. (1982). *The Psychobiology of Human Food Selection.* Westport, CT: AVI Publishing.

Birch, Leann L.; Fisher, Jennifer O.; and Grimm-Thomas, Karen. (1996). "The Development of Children's Eating Habits." In *Food Choice, Acceptance, and Consumption,* ed. Halliday MacFie and Herbert Meiselman. Glasgow, Scotland: Blackie Academic.

Booth, David A. (1994). *Psychology of Nutrition.* London: Taylor & Francis.

Cabanac, Michel. (1971). "The Physiological Role of Pleasure." *Science* 173:1103–1107.

Fischler, Claud. (1990). *L'homnivore.* Paris: Editions Odile Jacob.

Kass, Leon. (1994). *The Hungry Soul.* New York: Free Press.

Logue, Alexandra. (1991). *The Psychology of Eating and Drinking,* 2nd ed. New York: W. H. Freeman.

MacFie, Halliday, and Meiselman, Herbert, eds. (1996). *Food Choice, Acceptance, and Consumption.* Glasgow, Scotland: Blackie Academic.

Rozin, Paul. (1982). "Human Food Selection." In *The Psychobiology of Human Food Selection,* ed. Lewis M. Barker. Westport, CT: AVI Publishing.

Rozin, Paul. (1990a). "The Acquisition of Stable Food Preferences." *Nutrition Reviews* 48:106–113.

Rozin, Paul. (1990b). "Getting to Like the Burn of Chili Pepper: Biological, Psychological, and Cultural Perspectives." In *Chemical Senses, Vol. 2: Irritation,* ed. Barry S. Green, J. Russell Mason, and Morley R. Kare. New York: Marcel Dekker.

Rozin, Paul. (1998). *Towards a Psychology of Food Choice,* Danone chair monograph. Brussels, Belgium: Danone Institute.

Rozin, Paul, and Fallon, April E. (1987). "A Perspective on Disgust." *Psychological Review* 94:23–41.

Shepherd, Richard, and Raats, Monique M. (1996). "Attitudes and Beliefs in Food Habits." In *Food Choice, Acceptance, and Consumption,* ed. Halliday MacFie and Herbert Meiselman. Glasgow, Scotland: Blackie Academic.

Paul Rozin

FORGIVENESS

"[My father] never made it as a ballplayer, so he tried to get his son to make it for him. By the time I was ten, playing baseball got to be like eating vegetables or taking out the garbage. So, when I was fourteen, I started to refuse. Can you believe that, an American boy refusing to have a catch with his father? ... Anyway, when I was seventeen, I packed my things, said something awful, and left. After a while I wanted to come home, but I didn't know how." This speech given by the character Ray Kinsella in the film *Field of Dreams* (1989) illustrates the pains people can inflict on one another. At the movie's end, Ray and his father are playing catch, reunited. Ray overcame the resentment of being pressed into baseball service, and his father, John, overcame the insults and abandonment. Both learned to forgive.

Definition

Forgiveness always occurs in the context of injustice, in which one person is treated unfairly by another. In forgiving, the person abandons resentment, anger, and related emotions and instead responds to the wrongdoer with empathy and the moral qualities of compassion and love. Forgiveness is a process that can take time.

Forgiveness is different from condoning or excusing, forgetting, and reconciling. When people condone or excuse, they are basically saying that what happened was not so bad, perhaps because of the circumstances. When people forgive, they know that what happened was and always will be unfair. When people forget, they put the past behind themselves to such an extent that there is no memory of the event. When people forgive, they do not forget what happened primarily because people rarely eliminate from their memories the deep hurts of life. When two or more people reconcile, they come together again in mutual trust. The offending person recognizes his or her transgression and strives to do better. When people forgive, it is their own choice to offer the gift of mercy to an offending person. A person might choose to forgive but then not reconcile if the offending individual refuses to change abusive behavior. Reconciliation is conditional on the offender's change of behavior. Forgiveness can be unconditional and starts whenever the forgiver wishes.

When a person has been treated unfairly, a typical response is anger and resentment. In other words, without realizing it, people are taking Mark Twain's advice from *The Tragedy of Pudd'nhead Wilson* (1894): "When angry, count four; when very angry, swear." In essence, the offended person is saying, "I will not stand for this!" The initial resentment is a sign of self-respect as the person defends his or her rights. Forgiveness is sometimes misunderstood as a process that short-circuits this time of resentment and anger; however, therapeutic and educational programs centered on forgiveness provide time for this emotional reaction. Forgiveness is sometimes misunderstood as doing away with self-respect as the forgiver abandons resentment, but when a person forgives, he or she acknowledges that both the offender and the self are worthy of respect. Forgivers respect themselves by acknowledging that they do not have to live as angry, bitter people. Forgiveness is sometimes misunderstood as sidestepping justice, but it is possible to forgive and seek justice. In the film drama *The Scarlet and the Black* (1983), Gregory Peck, playing Monsignor Hugh O'Flaherty, forgives and visits regularly a Nazi SS officer who was cruel and dishonest. However, the monsignor, in his forgiving, does not try to work for the officer's prison release. Forgiveness is intermingled with justice in this case.

Process of Forgiveness

Once a person confronts injustice and experiences resentment, he or she makes a decision to forgive or not. This is a free choice offered by the offended to the offender. Of course, there are many different options people have for dealing with the emotional pains when wronged. People can deny what happened, talk to a friend, seek counseling, decide to forgive, or engage in any number of other responses.

Once the person decides to forgive, he or she begins thinking about the offending person in a new way (i.e., reframing). In reframing, the forgiver begins to see the offending person in a context larger than the original offense. The forgiver realizes that the offender is a vulnerable person, worthy of respect, not because of the offense, but because the wrongdoer is a human being (and all people are worthy of respect).

These cognitive insights can lead to a sense of compassion toward the offender. Again, the compassion, which is a feeling of suffering along with the other person, is not offered because of the offense, but in spite of it. Such compassion is illustrated in Charles Dickens's *A Christmas Carol* (1843). Scrooge's nephew, Fred, knowing his uncle's bitterness and loneliness, joyfully asks him to Christmas dinner. Fred is met with one of the most memorable insults in all of literature as Scrooge says, "[E]very idiot who goes about with 'Merry Christmas' on his lips should be boiled with his own pudding, and buried with a stake of holly through his heart." When Scrooge surprisingly does show up at the party, after his transformation, Fred welcomes him: "It is a mercy he didn't shake his arm off. He was at home in five minutes. Nothing could be heartier." Of course, people do not necessarily respond as quickly as Fred just because the offending one has changed. Related to compassion is the feeling of empathy.

The Return of the Prodigal Son, *an eighteenth-century Austrian print, depicts a father bestowing his forgiveness on his errant son who has returned to the family.* (Corbis/Gianni Dagli Orti)

When empathizing with an offender, an offended person, in a manner of speaking, "steps inside the shoes" of the other person to experience, to feel, his or her qualities of vulnerability, confusion, and humanness. The emotions of compassion and empathy for an offender develop slowly, especially if the injustice was serious. A forgiver does not will these feelings into existence; they must emerge. Reframing can aid in the development of compassion and empathy, but reframing itself does not automatically lead to them.

Along with empathy and compassion, a forgiver may show moral love for an offender. Aristotle distinguished different qualities of love, such as brotherly love (i.e., love for a sibling), romantic love (i.e., love for a man or a woman), and moral love (i.e., love centered on helping the other be the best person he or she can be). Moral love shows a deep concern for the welfare of the other person. In forgiving someone, the forgiver is helping the other person have that second (or third or fourth) chance to begin anew. It is a gift of mercy, whether deserved or not.

Compassion and empathy in a forgiveness context do not exist in isolation. They coexist with a clear sense of who did the wrong and specifically what that wrong was. They coexist with reframing. Unfortunately, compassion and empathy by themselves may blind a person to the offending person's weaknesses, making the one who empathizes vulnerable to continuing abuse.

Age, Gender, and Forgiveness

Children understand forgiveness in a different way than do adults. The younger the child, the greater the likelihood that he or she will confuse forgiveness with justice-seeking. For example, a fourth grader who is hit on the arm by a classmate may believe that all will be forgiven and forgotten when he or she can hit the offender back. With advancing age and experience, adolescents see the merciful quality of forgiveness but sometimes are hesitant to extend it to offenders unless there is peer or family encouragement to do so. Understanding the moral quality of forgiveness, its compassionate, loving, and giftlike nature, develops slowly in adolescence, and that development continues on into adulthood.

Studies find no gender-based differences in the ability of males and females to understand forgiveness or to forgive people successfully in therapeutic and educational programs. Cross-cultural studies have shown far more similarities than differences in the degree of forgiveness exhibited by adolescents and adults toward an offending person. These studies have included samples from Austria, Brazil, Israel, Korea, Taiwan, and the United States.

Conclusion

Research has shown that a person who takes the time to forgive can experience a release from high levels of anxiety, psychological depression, low self-esteem, and hopelessness. However, shorter therapeutic and educational programs (lasting a few hours) are not as effective in inducing forgiveness as are longer programs (lasting up to fourteen months). When people take the time, they can exxperience what Portia knew in William Shakespeare's *Merchant of Venice:*

> The quality of mercy is not strain'd,
> It droppeth as the gentle rain from heaven
> Upon the place beneath; it is twice blest;
> It blesseth him that gives and him that takes.

When it is properly understood, forgiveness, in other words, provides genuine human benefits. Perhaps even Mark Twain would have amended his own advice on anger to add "when very, very angry, forgive."

See also: ANGER; EMPATHY; SYMPATHY

Bibliography

Al-Mabuk, Radhi; Enright, Robert D.; and Cardis, Paul. (1995). "Forgiveness Education with Parentally Love-Deprived College Students." *Journal of Moral Education* 24:427–444.

DiBlasio, Frederick A. (1998). "The Use of a Decision-Based Forgiveness Intervention within Inter-Generational Family Therapy." *Journal of Family Therapy* 20:77–94.

Enright, Robert D., and The Human Development Study Group. (1991). "The Moral Development of Forgiveness." In *Handbook of Moral Behavior and Development, Vol. 1,* ed. William Kurtines and Jacob Gewirtz. Hillsdale, NJ: Lawrence Erlbaum.

Enright, Robert D., and North, Joanna, eds. (1998). *Exploring Forgiveness.* Madison: University of Wisconsin Press.

Enright, Robert D.; Santos, Maria J. O.; and Al-Mabuk, Radhi. (1989). "The Adolescent as Forgiver." *Journal of Adolescence* 12:95–110.

Fitzgibbons, Richard P. (1986). "The Cognitive and Emotional Uses of Forgiveness in the Treatment of Anger." *Psychotherapy* 23:629–633.

Freedman, Suzanne R., and Enright, Robert D. (1996). "Forgiveness as an Intervention Goal with Incest Survivors." *Journal of Consulting and Clinical Psychology* 64:983–992.

Haber, Joram. (1991). *Forgiveness.* Savage, MD: Rowman & Littlefield.

Holmgren, Margaret R. (1993). "Forgiveness and the Intrinsic Value of Persons." *American Philosophical Quarterly* 30:341–352.

McCullough, Michael E., and Worthington, Everett L., Jr. (1995). "Promoting Forgiveness." *Counseling and Values* 40:55–68.

North, Joanna. (1987). "Wrongdoing and Forgiveness." *Philosophy* 62:499–508.

Smedes, Lewis B. (1984). *Forgive and Forget: Healing the Hurts We Don't Deserve.* New York: Harper & Row.

Robert D. Enright

FREUD, ANNA

b. Vienna, Austria, December 3, 1895; *d.* London, England, October 8, 1982; *child development, psychoanalysis.*

Anna Freud was a Jewish-Austrian psychoanalyst who was a major figure in the psychoanalytic movement from the 1920s until her death in 1982. Her influence derived both from her status as the daughter of and assistant to Sigmund Freud, the founder of psychoanalysis, as well as her own contributions to the field in developing child psychoanalysis and writing about the mechanisms of defense used by the ego to control feelings of anxiety. She was the sixth and youngest child of Sigmund and Martha Freud and grew up in Freud household in Vienna during the time when her father and his associates were developing the psychoanalytic theory. Although she had no formal higher education, she received training in psychoanalysis, was analyzed by her father (a practice now considered inappropriate), wrote several books and more than one hundred scholarly papers, and served as chairman of the Vienna Psychoanalytic Society from 1925 to 1938. She also analyzed and trained a number of leading analysts, most notably Erik Erikson. Freud became involved in psychoanalysis in 1918 when she began attending meetings of the Vienna Psychoanalytic Society with her father. By 1920, she was serving as his secretary, and from then on she became fully involved in the field. Freud served her father as assistant and then collaborator, and for the last fifteen years of his life, she nursed him through dozens of operations for cancer of the jaw. In the 1930s, she began helping Jewish psychoanalysts to escape from Europe, and in 1938 she helped arrange for her own family to move to London, where she lived with her father until his death in 1939.

Although Freud never married and had no children of her own, one of her major contributions to

Anna Freud speaks at the Sorbonne in a debate regarding psychoanalysis. (Corbis/Bettmann)

psychoanalysis and psychology were her study of children and the central role she played in developing the field of child psychoanalysis. Her information about children came from her experiences as an elementary school teacher, from observing and interacting with the children of friends, and from her work at the Hampstead War Nursery in London during World War II, and as director of the Hampstead Child-Therapy Course and Clinic (which she founded in 1947). Freud developed what came to be called the "Continental" approach to child psychoanalysis. While she relied on the psychoanalytic principles and methods of her father and his followers, Freud also recognized that children were different from adults and therefore modified some practices to meet the needs of children. For example, the rigid barrier between patient and analyst interaction was relaxed some to allow appropriate non-analytic communication between the two. Her "Continental" approach differed from the "British" approach of Melanie Klein, another Austrian psychoanalyst who was instrumental in the establishment of child psychoanalysis in London. Klein retained more of the traditional approach to analysis and also revised Freudian

thinking about emotional development during the first year of life. The two approaches each drew their supporters and critics, creating a breach in the European psychoanalytic community that has continued past the deaths of both women.

In addition to her work on the analysis of children, Freud also played a role in developing psychoanalytic theory during the 1930s by focusing on the role of the ego in controlling the drives of the id. Her most significant work was on the psychological mechanisms of defense used by the ego to control anxiety. Her ideas were set forth in the *Ego and the Mechanisms of Defense* (1937), which has been considered by subsequent generations of psychologists to be her most important work. It remains the basic statement about psychological defense mechanisms, although her work has been much revised by psychiatrists and psychologists since the book was first published.

Freud also had a strong interest in the legal rights of children and worked toward that end in both Great Britain and the United States (where she worked at Yale University during the 1960s). Many of her ideas were set forth in 1973 in *Beyond the Best Interests of the Child,* which was written with two Yale colleagues. Among other things, Freud and her colleagues advocated legal counsel of children in divorce and adoption cases and stressed the role of the psychological parent in a child's well-being. Beyond her contributions to treatment and theory, Freud also played a leading role in popularizing psychoanalysis. A clear and vivid writer and an effective public speaker, she made the often technical and obscure ideas of psychoanalysis available to the general public. Freud remained active in the field almost to the end of her life. For her work, she received numerous honors, including honorary degrees from Yale and the University of Chicago and The Grand Decoration of Honor in Gold from Austria. She also served as editor for many years of the *Psychoanalytic Study of the Child,* the most important annual publication in the field.

See also: DEFENSE MECHANISMS; FREUD, SIGMUND; PSYCHOANALYTIC PERSPECTIVE

Bibliography

Appignanesi, Lisa. (1993). *Freud's Women.* New York: Basic Books.

Coles, Robert. (1992). *Anna Freud: The Dream of Psychoanalysis.* Reading, MA: Addison-Wesley.

Freud, Anna. (1937). *The Ego and the Mechanisms of Defense.* London: Hogarth Press.

Freud, Anna; Goldstein, Joseph; and Solnit, Albert. (1973). *Beyond the Best Interests of the Child.* New York: Free Press.

Sayers, Janet. (1991). *Mothers of Psychoanalysis.* New York: W. W. Norton.

David Levinson

FREUD, SIGMUND

b. Frieber, Moravia, May 6, 1856; *d.* London, England, September 23, 1939; *neurology, psychoanalysis.*

Sigmund Freud, the developer of psychoanalytic theory and the psychoanalytic method of treatment, is generally considered to be one of the four men (the other three being British naturalist Charles Darwin, German political philosopher Karl Marx, and German-American physicist Albert Einstein) whose ideas have most influenced life in the twentieth century. Freud's many ideas about the structure and function of the mind, human emotional development, and human interaction have, for better or worse (depending upon one's point of view), changed how people view themselves, raise their children, and relate to one another.

Freud's father, Jacob, was a wool merchant, and Sigmund was the first child of Amalia Nathansohn Freud, Jacob's second. In order to escape anti-Semitism, the family moved from Moravia to Vienna, Austria, when Sigmund was four years of age. Young Freud was a gifted student and graduated with a degree in medicine in 1881 from the prestigious University of Vienna. Freud sought a career in neurology, but because of anti-Semitism, he switched to psychiatry. Throughout his career, Freud continued to see himself as a scientist and view psychoanalysis as a science. His initial interest was in hysterias—physical disorders such as paralyzed limbs that had no physical cause—and through his work with Austrian physician Josef Breuer and French neurologist Jean-Martin Charcot, he was introduced to the "talking cure" and hypnosis as possible methods of treatment. In 1886, Freud married Martha Bernays, and the couple had six children—three sons and three daughters (the youngest of which was Anna, who followed her father into the psychoanalytic field and became a prominent analyst herself). In 1891, Freud moved to Berggasse 19 in Vienna and opened his private practice, beginning his search for the psychological cause and treatment of hysteria and other disorders.

Freud developed his initial theories and method of treatment, which he began calling "psychoanalysis" in 1896, through a combination of self-analysis and dream interpretation conducted between 1897 and 1900, analysis of several key patients (Dora, Little Hans, the Rat Man, Daniel Schreber, and the Wolf Man), and discussions in his home with a small circle of fellow analysts who in 1909 formed the Vienna Psychoanalytic Society. Such localized societies have been the model that psychoanalysts in Europe, Great Britain, and the United States have used to organize themselves ever since. Many of the basic principles of psychoanalysis—including the role of the unconscious in human emotion and action, dreams as the pathway to the unconscious, the role of sexuality in human psychological development, and the sexual desire of the child for the parent of the opposite sex (the Oedipus Complex)—emerged during this early period. Over the course of his lifetime, Freud and his colleagues amplified, revised, and added to these initial insights and extended psychoanalytic theory to encompass virtually all elements of the human experience, including jokes, accidents, religion, creativity, and even civilization itself. Thus, Freud came to see psychoanalysis as the ultimate explanation for all of the human situation, a view that has been widely and loudly criticized by later opponents of psychoanalysis. The development of psychoanalysis as a method of treatment for neuroses (Freud came to believe it was not useful for psychotic disorders) followed the development of the initial theories and largely took place between 1911 and 1915. Freud set forth numerous guidelines and instructions for the proper conduct of analysis. His approach to analysis has been much revised over the years, and most modern analysis is different in important ways from Freud's approach. Now, for example, there is often more patient-analyst interaction, the relationship is more formal, and practices such as having patients to dinner or analyzing one's family members are considered inappropriate.

Freud was a prolific lecturer, author, and letter-writer, and his collected written works fill twenty-four volumes. Most of Freud's writings were quickly translated into English, bringing psychoanalysis to Great Britain and the United States, and some works were eventually translated into as many as twelve languages. This rich collection of writings has given both his supporters, biographers, and critics much ammunition to use in either defending or attacking Freud's ideas and Freud himself. As a major figure of the twentieth century, Freud and his ideas were controversial. His ideas about sexuality shocked Victorian Europe, and his theory and method were rejected at first by the medical establishment. They only really gained popularity in the second decade of the century when American, British, and continental intellectuals were drawn to analysis, with some even moving to Vienna to undergo analysis with Freud or his associates. Psychoanalysis was brought to America through translations by Freudian follower A. A. Brill. Although the United States remains a center for psychoanalytic study, Freud visited America only once—when he gave five well-received lectures at Clark University in Massachusetts in 1909. It is impossible to list all of Freud's works, but many experts consider his first major book, *The Interpretation of Dreams* (1900), to be the most insightful and significant.

In 1923, Freud, a lifelong cigar smoker who was once quoted as saying "Sometimes a cigar is just cigar," was diagnosed with cancer of the jaw. Over the next sixteen years, he endured dozens of operations and radiation treatments and had to wear a prosthetic device that made it difficult for him to speak clearly. Through much of this period, he was nursed by his daughter Anna, who also took over much of the secretarial work and later assisted with his theoretical work as well. Throughout this period, Freud continued to develop his psychoanalytic theory and method and became a famous figure in Europe and the Americas. His fame protected him and his family from attacks by the Nazis, who had come to power in Germany and then annexed Austria, but as threats grew greater, Freud, Martha, and their children fled to London in 1938. Freud died on September 23 of the following year in his home at Marshfield Gardens. Both the home in London and the home in Vienna are now museums, with the famous couch preserved in the former.

Especially since the 1950s, Freudian theory and method and Freud himself have been subject to numerous severe criticisms. Of these, two general lines of criticism are perhaps most important. First, psychoanalysis has been criticized as being unscientific and unsupported (or even being unsupportable) by scientific research and thus has been rejected by many scientifically-oriented psychologists. Psychoanalysis no longer plays a role in many theories about emotion, motivation, personality, or behavior and has been replaced by behavioral and cognitive approaches. At the same time, its influence has also waned in psychiatry as psychodynamic theories, short-term forms of therapy, and the use of drugs have proven far more useful, effective, quicker, and less costly than analysis. Analysis is now used most often as a vehicle for self-exploration by people largely free of major emotional problems. In response to these criticisms, some supporters of Freud point out that he always viewed psychoanalysis as an evolving theory subject to change and also saw it as a theory that would eventually be replaced by biological theories of the mind, a prediction that seems to becoming true. The second major line of criticism comes from women who view Freud's theories as being male-centered ideas that reflect minimal insight into women's lives. Thus, psychoanalysis has been rejected by many feminists since the 1960s. Defenders of Freud accept that his ideas about women seem dated by late-twentieth-century standards but note that they reflect Victorian values and also that several women (Anna Freud, Melanie Klein, Helen Deutsch, and Karen Horney) were involved in the psychoanalytic movement in its early years. In addition to attacks on his ideas, Freud has also been criticized personally. These include charges that he misrepresented data to support his ideas, had an unhappy family life (or at least a less happy one than he claimed), that he had an adulterous relationship with his wife's sister, that he was cold and distant, and that he was authoritarian and could not accept criticism from colleagues. All of the professional and personal criticisms continue to be debated by his supporters and opponents. One public manifestation of these debates was the controversy surrounding the October 1998 exhibit at the Library of Congress about Freud's influence. The exhibit was delayed for several years by critics who wanted to see criticisms as well as praise exhibited.

Despite the continuous discussion of Freud and his work, psychoanalysis remains an important influence in contemporary life. Perhaps Paul Kline came closest to indicating why Freud's ideas remain popular when he noted that Freud's ideas about many matters ring true for many people because they fit with people's own experiences and insights. In addition, the use of many concepts and terms from psychoanalysis—unconscious, ego, superego, id, castration anxiety, penis envy, talking cure, Freudian slip—suggests that psychoanalysis continues to inform daily life. Perhaps his

Sigmund Freud. (Corbis)

influence was best summed up by British poet W. H. Auden, who asserted that Freud has become a "whole climate of opinion" that influences how people conduct their lives rather than a mere person.

See also: DEFENSE MECHANISMS; EYNSENCK, HANS JURGEN; FREUD, ANNA; HORNEY, KAREN; PSYCHOANALYTIC PERSPECTIVE; SULLIVAN, HARRY STACK

Bibliography

Fancher, Raymond. (1973). *Psychoanalytic Psychology: The Development of Freud's Thought.* New York: W. W. Norton.

Fisher, Seymour, and Greenberg, Roger P. (1977). *The Scientific Credibility of Freud's Theories and Therapy.* New York: Basic Books.

Flanagan, Owen, Jr. (1984). *The Science of the Mind.* Cambridge: Massachusetts Institute of Technology Press.

Gay, Peter. (1988). *Freud: A Life for Our Time.* New York: W. W. Norton.

Jones, Ernest. (1953–1957). *The Life and Work of Sigmund Freud,* 3 vols. New York: Basic Books.

Kline, Paul. (1981). *Fact and Fantasy in Freudian Theory.* London: Routledge.

Roth, Michael S., ed. (1998). *Freud: Conflict and Culture.* New York: Knopf.

Strachey, James, ed. (1953–1974). *Standard Edition of the Complete Psychological Works of Sigmund Freud,* 24 vols. London: Hogarth Press.

Sulloway, Frank. (1979). *Freud: The Biologist of the Mind.* New York: Basic Books.

David Levinson

FRIENDSHIP

The term *friendship* describes a broad category of positively disposed interpersonal relationships in Western culture with emotional textures ranging from casually superficial to profoundly involved. People may use the word *friend* to refer to someone they recently met at school or work, a long-standing professional associate, a family member, a dating partner, or an irreplaceable individual they have known, enjoyed, and depended on for years. Friendship can also complement, fuse with, compete with, or substitute for other personal and social relationships. For people who teach together, for example, friendship can complement an otherwise professional relationship, whereas becoming friends might compete with the demands of a superior/subordinate association. Friendship can fuse so completely with spousal or sibling bonds that it becomes difficult to decide when persons are acting as spouses or siblings and when as friends. Finally, when kin are absent, friends may substitute for one's family. The highly variable use of the word in Western culture makes general definitions vulnerable to situational applications. Even so, these diverse uses draw on the benign connotations of friendship: good will, pleasure, assistance and moral comportment (celebrated ideals in Western culture that date back at least as far as ancient Greece).

Formation of Friendships

In Western societies, friendship is defined by five characteristics—voluntary, personal, equal, mutual, and affective—that are accomplished to varying degrees in specific relationships. First, friendships are voluntary relationships. Nothing can compel persons to be friends. People choose each other and continue as friends because they are treated the way they want to be treated. This voluntary attribute of friendship contrasts with blood ties to kin that persist whether a person desires them or not. Individuals can purposefully avoid disliked siblings, for example, but they remain related. Similar avoidance of friends could announce the end of the friendship. Likewise, marital bonds are sanctioned legally and religiously. A person might simply drift or move away from a friend, but this is not possible with a spouse; it requires legal measures such as a divorce and, in some cases, religious procedures to end a marriage. Work relationships and partnerships are also governed by economic contracts and external obligations rather than the choice of the parties involved. In contrast to relationships sustained primarily by their connections to the social structure, this voluntary basis makes the continuance of friendships highly dependent upon their emotional dynamics. Second, friendships are personal relationships that are privately negotiated between particular individuals. People typically choose others as friends because of their unique and intrinsic qualities as individuals, not because they are members of a category or occupy a particular role. Third, a spirit of equality pervades friendship. Although friendship may develop between individuals of different status, ability, attractiveness, or age, friends tend to find facets of their relationship that function as levelers, allowing the individuals to view and deal with each other as equals. Fourth, friendships are collaborative achievements involving mutual good will, understanding, trust, support, and acceptance. Over time there are fairly symmetrical inputs into the relationship and to each other's welfare. Finally, friends feel and express abiding affection. Positive feeling, caring, and concern exist between friends. While friends may feel profound love for each other, the love of friendship is usually distinguished from sexual or romantic loving, which have overtones of possessiveness and exclusivity. However, relationships that are primarily defined by these latter forms of loving may include or aspire to the attributes of friendship as well.

Though every friendship arises from the interaction of specific individuals and their social contexts (which allows for limitless variation), forming friendships typically involves certain conditions. Persons need to have the opportunity to meet and spend time with each other, so physical proximity and corresponding schedules facilitate making friends. Potential friends often share similar points in the life course or at least a similar cluster of roles, which finds them doing some of the same things at the same times. The possibility of exposure to others—at school, work, in the neighborhood or nursing home, in sports teams, clubs or civic organizations, in car pools or parenting activities—largely depends on how individuals organize their time around the most salient priorities of their lives. In these situations, would-be friends announce their interest through recognizing and talking with others in personalized ways. Then they gradually allow these others to know them in ways that transcend the specific situation where they routinely meet.

Encountering other persons in this fashion, though important, is not enough for friendships to develop. The term *acquaintances* is usually reserved for ongoing affiliations that may be upbeat but basically persist because people are required to see each other on a regular basis, such as in class, the neighborhood, or at work. In contrast, friendship typically involves singling someone out or being invited oneself to do something together outside of situations where role requirements compel the persons to interact. Thus, along with the excitement of possibly finding a new friend, there is risk of rejection and anxiety about how well things will go in trying to make new friends. Consequently, people are often reluctant to take this chance. One of the worries individuals of all ages feel about moving is the ordeal of making new friends and the sadness of leaving proven friendships behind.

Existence of Tension

Contextual and interactional tensions shape and reflect the range of emotions experienced in established friendships. Contextual tensions between the ideal and the real as well as the public and the private derive from the distinctive place of friendship in Western culture. The first tension describes the ideals and high expectations that people associate with friendship and the troublesome realities or unexpected rewards of actual relationships with friends. Friendship has positive connotations in Western culture, and people want to feel that their friends will always be there for them in times of need or celebration. Meanwhile, friends have their own pressures, unforeseen demands or opportunities, and choices to make about how or with whom to spend their time. When friends do not behave as

Huck Finn and Tom Sawyer are classic best friends in Mark Twain's novels The Adventures of Tom Sawyer *(1876) and* The Adventures of Huckleberry Finn *(1881). While the first work emphasizes the boys' resourcefulness and their distrust of the adult world, which seems full of lies and hypocrisy, the second book takes Huck into an intense moral conflict with that adult world of slavery and racism. Huck finds his true friend and surrogate father in Jim, an escaped slave.*

expected, confusion, disappointment, and hurt feelings can arise. Further, some of life's most despairing and angry moments can arise from perceived or actual betrayal by a (now former) friend. In contrast, friends who are loyal in trying times or who share generously during successful times produce great happiness and personal confirmation. The most pronounced emotional reactions regularly occasioned by friendship tend to occur during adolescence, when young people's emotions are generally more labile (i.e., continually changing) and their expectations of friends are still highly idealized. Later in life, people tend to temper their expectations and thereby experience less extreme reactions to friends' behaviors. The exception to this rule is betrayal, which remains the cardinal sin against a friend. Professional and personal betrayals between friends during adulthood can literally break hearts and ruin lives.

The tension between the public and the private involves the cognitive and emotional tensions produced as friends' activities and decisions weave in and out of public and private situations. Because friendships are privately negotiated between individuals, people can voice matters and know and feel things about each other that would be inhibited in more publicly performed relationships. Strains can occur, however, when either friend's private activities must answer to the larger society or when the friends' public actions impinge on their private domain of friendship. Picture the ambivalence felt by a young person whose friend cheated on an exam, resulting in a prestigious scholarship sponsored by the club in which they both serve as officers. What happens when a person confides in a friend concerning a decision about a course of action that potentially could harm him- or herself or others? How does one react to a friend who publicly opposes an important initiative he or she is developing at work? How does a search committee member ethically evaluate a friend who is competing with other applicants identified in a publicly advertised job search? Friendship is a double-edged sword in its capacity to transcend public and private contexts. Sometimes, knowing a friend can personalize and provide comfort in an otherwise cold-hearted and bureaucratic situation. In other circumstances, caring for someone can produce wrenching conflicts between the private morality and affections of the friendship and the public morality and expectations for impartial decisions of the social system.

Four interactional tensions develop between friends due in part to the distinctive characteristics of friendship: the tension between the freedom to be independent and the freedom to be dependent, the tension between affection and instrumentality, the tension between judgment and acceptance, and the tension between expressiveness and protectiveness. Many of the positive and negative emotions occurring within ongoing friendships involve these interactional tensions.

The tension between the freedom to be independent and the freedom to be dependent arises from the patterns of availability, obligation, separation, and time together characterizing friendships in light of their voluntary basis. In forming a friendship, friends recognize each other's liberty to pursue a separate life and individual interests without the friend's interference or help. But they also tacitly or explicitly offer the privilege of calling upon or relying on one another in times of need. Exercising these freedoms gives friendship both liberating and dependable qualities but can cause friction and resentment as well. For example, if one friend innocently plans a vacation at a time when the other needs assistance, their options collide. Some pairs value the privilege of depending upon each other so much that either person's independent behavior is infrequent and resented. Conversely, other friendships are characterized by a pattern of such mutual independence that dependence is ritually enacted by "touching base" or actualized only when there is serious need. Despite the practices established in a friendship, the contradictory and ambiguous nature of these freedoms can make it difficult to know for certain whether a given pattern is affirming or weakening the friendship. An overly dependent relationship may constrain the friends' independent action and breed ill will. Independent friends may need to renew contact to be sure that they are still involved in a friendship. Perhaps one of them has changed careers or fundamental values and now views encounters with the other as too limiting and/or undesirable. While these freedoms negotiated in friendships allow for flexibility and individual choice, they can also result in uncertainty and anxiety about obligations or the extent of the friends' connection or concerns about being smothered by the relationship.

The tension between affection and instrumentality involves the ambiguities between caring for a friend as an end-in-itself and caring for a friend as a means-to-an-end. Throughout life, friends periodically rely on each other for emotional and practical assistance. People like to do things for their friends because they care for them. Older adults, for example, experience significantly enhanced morale and self-esteem from helping others, especially their friends. It can be frustrating and off-putting for people of all ages when friends do not allow them to help or share with them. People also have fond feelings for friends who come through for them by listening, by providing physical and material aid, or by helping to solve a problem. As the saying goes, "A friend in need is a friend indeed." Even so, people do not want to feel too indebted or exploited in friendships. The feelings produced by a relationship sustained primarily because of what the individuals can do for each other are quite different from the feelings produced by a relationship where it is clear that giving and receiving instrumental aid expresses mutual affection.

On numerous occasions people ask their friends for opinions on issues ranging from a song they have heard to career or marital matters. The tension between judgment and acceptance describes the dilemmas between providing objective appraisals of a friend's actions or thoughts and giving unconditional acceptance and support. People expect acceptance and encouragement from their friends for most of their conduct and decisions; this is part of the rich personal validation experienced in friendships. But persons also employ certain standards in choosing friends and look to them for tough truths and wise counsel. Even though individuals do not enjoy being evaluated by their friends, sincerely judging a person's actions or words can uphold the values shaping the friendship as well as communicate that one cares enough to criticize the friend. Frequently, the emotional pinch is determining whether a friend is basically asking for support or a true opinion no matter what. In certain instances, persons may feel compelled to give their true judgment regardless of its immediate emotional effect on the friend.

The tension between expressiveness and protectiveness refers to the conflict between the tendency to speak openly with a friend and relate private thoughts and feelings and the tendency to restrain disclosures to preserve privacy and avoid burdening the friend. Developing and maintaining a friendship conversationally involves revealing personal thoughts and feelings and responding to one's friend. As relationships become more personal, participants are more relaxed and expressive with each other, disclosing private concerns and exposing areas of personal vulnerability to various degrees. In developing awareness of sensitive topics for each other, friends learn to communicate in protective ways. They try to limit self-disclosures that make themselves too vulnerable or that impose unnecessary or unwanted responsibilities on the friend, to preserve each other's confidences, and to exercise restraint in commenting on touchy issues. Trust develops within friendships to the extent that the tension between expressiveness and protectiveness is appropriately managed. That is, each person limits his or her own vulnerability and strives to protect the other's sensitivities while still expressing personally crucial thoughts and feelings.

Gender and Friendships

The tensions and benefits of friendship are patterned in gender-linked ways across the life course although scholars disagree on the precise nature and extent of the differences. First, it may be that the modal (i.e., customary) emotional attachments identified with male and female friendships are comparably intense with the genders merely differing in their practices for expressing commitment and emotional involvement. Or there may in fact be meaningful differences in the potential experiences and emotional benefits of the modes of friendship commonly documented by gender alignments in research results. Second, these are general and modal patterns; individual friendships involving members of either gender may deviate considerably from the norms discussed here. Depending on their particular friendship style and practices and their embracing life structures, men's friendships may resemble the modal patterns associated with women and vice versa. Third, in women's and men's closer friendships the differences diminish. The closer friendships of both genders approach the practices and ideals of communal friendships, which are emotionally involved relationships that include shared activities but center on talking together and emphasize intimacy. Finally, these patterns are based on social scientific research that has primarily addressed white, North American middle-class participants. Little comprehensive work on cross-cultural and ethnic variations of friendship exists (with the notable exception of Robert Brain's 1976 anthropological survey, *Friends and Lovers*) even though anthropologists have routinely described friendships in non-Western cultures. Among the patterns suggested by these descriptions are a strong preference for same-sex friendships, a belief that men and women cannot be friends, a tendency to view friendship as a lifetime commitment, the use of physical contact as a sign of friendship, and the observance in some cultures of ceremonies to formalize friendships.

In managing the tension between the freedom to be independent and the freedom to be dependent, women friends tend to interweave their lives extensively and to value interdependence. Men expect and enact more independence in their friendships; they do not like to feel dependent upon their friends. In a related matter, women experience a dynamic tension between affection and instrumentality in their friendships. Women describe themselves as more affectionate and report more emotional involvement with their friends than do men. Meanwhile, in juggling multiple household, professional, and recreational activities, women place high demands on each other for instrumental help. The persistent requirements of caring and mutual reliance can be a source of strain in women's friendships. In contrast, men's friendships do not seem as emotionally charged in these areas as women's. Men do not demonstrate affection for each other in the ways and to the degree that women do, but men do offer and receive instrumental assistance with various projects while striving to maintain their independent stances through appropriate reciprocation. Standing ready to help without excessive sentiment is a feature of many men's friendships.

Women's friendships are energized by the potentially volatile interplay between judgment and acceptance. Because women seem to care about and expect so much of their friends, they are more inclined to communicate their evaluations when friends disappoint them. By comparison, men seem less concerned about and therefore more accepting of their friends' behaviors. A situation causing notable irritation between two female friends may be regarded by males as insignificant. Females may not understand how males are able to put up with certain actions by their friends. Finally, one of the most robust patterns in research on friendships is the tendency for women to be more expressive with their friends and to discuss and trust each other with emotionally trying matters. Men are more reserved and protective with their friends, seemingly less willing to make themselves vulnerable or burden their friends with personal concerns and doubts.

Overall, patterns identified across developmental periods suggest two major modes of friendship. As stated above, communal friendships are emotionally involved relationships that include shared activities but center on talking together and emphasize intimacy. These are commonly associated with females. Agentic friendships are instrumentally oriented, organized mainly around doing things together, and emphasize sociability. These are commonly associated with males.

Other consistent findings complement this discussion of gender and friendship. Females repeatedly rate their same-sex friendships higher than their friendships with males. In contrast, males typically rate their cross-sex friendships higher than their same-sex friendships. A married man will typically report that his wife is his best friend, but a married woman typically views her husband as a good friend while having a woman friend whom she considers to be as close as

Three friends engage in a discussion about their common interest at the Deal Island shipjack race in Chesapeake Bay, Maryland. (Corbis/James L. Amos)

the husband or closer. Several studies indicate that in later life women have more friends overall, a greater variety of friends, and closer friends than men. Finally, many men depend on their wives for close friendship in later life and retreat from wider participation or initiatives in making new friends.

People pursue varying degrees of closeness in their friendships. Some individuals prefer a limited number of exclusive relationships that are carefully chosen, deeply validating, and sorely missed when they end. Others like more easy-going and superficial connections with a number of people, readily making and relinquishing such friends wherever they go. Still other persons pursue a combination of these involvements with others. It is not clear whether a specific style of friendship is a better facilitator of emotional well-being. Older adults, for example, differ in their preference for multiple companions versus select, intimate friends. It may be that in favorable cases persons have practiced and become accustomed to a style of friendship that best suits their emotional needs. There is still considerable work to be done on the relative merits of different modes of friendship.

Ending Friendships

Friendships decline and end for multiple reasons. They are essentially fragile due to their voluntary nature and minimal support from the social structure. Thus, persons can leave friendships with negligible societal repercussions. This ease of termination makes mutually satisfactory management of the expectations and tensions within friendships especially important. Inappropriate demands, unbalanced reciprocity, and insensitive remarks or actions plant the seeds of friendship dissolution, but they do not necessarily mean the end of the friendship. However, significant negative relational events such as major dishonesty, violation of trust, adultery, or betrayal virtually assure the demise of a friendship.

Moreover, opportunities for friendship are usually contingent upon the friends' clusters of socially sanctioned relationships, such as marriage, family, and work. Throughout life, changes in friends' physical, temporal, and emotional availability to each other markedly affect the viability of friendships. Shifting schedules, changing jobs, getting married or divorced, having children, moving to another neighborhood, and developing new interests—all present practical and emotional contingencies to be managed by affected friends. Some friends make the time or effort to address such altered circumstances to sustain their relationship; others, consciously or unconsciously, allow their contact to lapse and the friendship to fade.

Conclusion

Beginning in later adolescence, when individuals typically develop mature conceptions of friendship, people report similar expectations of friends across the life course. Even though the gravity of life choices increases and the circumstances of their achievement may change markedly, people expect their close friends to be people with whom they can talk, people on whom they can depend, and people with whom they enjoy spending time. Despite tensions, ambiguities and occasional ambivalence, friendships are hopeful, benevolent relationships that contribute significantly to personal validation and enjoyment of life. They also serve social functions. Developmentally, friendships cultivate ethical sensibilities as children and their friends learn the practices of cooperation, caring, good will, commitment, and loyalty that enhance their abilities to get along with others later in life. Connections with friends also lure persons into broader social participation, community association, and political activity.

Friendships pose many riddles. Throughout life, friends may foster selectivity, coalitions, and bitter rejections, generate volatile predicaments, create unspoken obligations, and burden others with things they wish they did not know. But friends can also be cherished sharers of assistance, wisdom, laughter, pain, and joy. For many people friendships make life worth living.

See also: ATTACHMENT; ATTRACTIVENESS; COMMUNICATION; INTIMACY; JEALOUSY; LONELINESS; LOVE; RELATIONSHIPS; TRUST

Bibliography

Adams, Rebecca G. (1986). "Secondary Friendship Networks and Psychological Well-Being among Elderly Women." *Activities, Adaptation and Aging* 8:59–72.

Adams, Rebecca G., and Blieszner, Rosemary. (1992). *Adult Friendship.* Newbury Park, CA: Sage Publications.

Allan, Graham. (1989). *Friendship.* New York: Harvester Wheatsheaf.

Aristotle. (1980). *The Nichomachean Ethics,* tr. David Ross. Oxford, Eng.: Oxford University Press.

Babchuk, Nicholas, and Anderson, Trudy B. (1989). "Older Widows and Married Women: Their Intimates and Confidants." *International Journal of Aging and Human Development* 28:21–35.

Berndt, Thomas J. (1982). "The Features and Effects of Friendship in Early Adolescence." *Child Development* 53:1447–1460.

Brain, Robert. (1976). *Friends and Lovers.* New York: Basic Books.

Broude, Gwen. (1994). *Marriage, Family, and Relationships: A Cross-Cultural Encyclopedia.* Santa Barbara: ABC-CLIO.

Davidson, Lynne R., and Duberman, Lucille. (1982). "Friendship: Communication and Interactional Patterns in Same-Sex Dyads." *Sex Roles* 8:809–826.

Douvan, Elizabeth, and Adelson, Joseph. (1966). *The Adolescent Experience.* New York: Wiley.

Fehr, Beverly. (1996). *Friendship Processes.* Thousand Oaks, CA: Sage Publications.

Fox, Margery; Gibbs, Margaret; and Auerback, Doris. (1985). "Age and Gender Dimensions of Friendship." *Psychology of Women Quarterly* 9:489–502.

Hays, Robert B. (1984). "The Development and Maintenance of Friendship." *Journal of Social and Personal Relationships* 1:75–98.

Helgeson, Vicki S.; Shaver, Phillip; and Dyer, Margaret. (1987). "Prototypes of Intimacy and Distance in Same-Sex and Opposite-Sex Relationships." *Journal of Social and Personal Relationships* 4:195–233.

Hess, Beth B. (1979). "Sex Roles, Friendships, and the Life Course." *Research on Aging* 1:494–515.

Lopata, Helena Z. (1988). "Support Systems of American Urban Widowhood." *Journal of Social Issues* 44:113–128.

Matthews, Sarah H. (1986). *Friendships Through the Life Course: Oral Biographies in Old Age.* Beverly Hills: Sage Publications.

Oliker, Stacey J. (1989). *Best Friends and Marriage: Exchange among Women.* Berkeley: University of California Press.

Paine, Robert. (1969). "In Search of Friendship: An Exploratory Analysis in 'Middle-Class' Culture." *Man* 4:505–524.

Peters, George R., and Kaiser, Marvin A. (1985). "The Role of Friends and Neighbors in Providing Social Support." In *Social Support Networks and the Care of the Elderly,* ed. William J. Sauer and Raymond T. Coward. New York: Springer.

Rawlins, William K. (1982). "Cross-Sex Friendship and the Communicative Management of Sex-Role Expectations." *Communication Quarterly* 30:343–352.

Rawlins, William K. (1989). "A Dialectical Analysis of the Tensions, Functions, and Strategic Challenges of Communication in Young Adult Friendships." In *Communication Yearbook, Vol. 12,* ed. James A. Anderson. Newbury Park, CA: Sage Publications.

Rawlins, William K. (1992). *Friendship Matters: Communication, Dialectics, and the Life Course.* Hawthorne, NY: Aldine de Gruyter.

Rose, Suzanna M. (1984). "How Friendships End: Patterns among Young Adults." *Journal of Social and Personal Relationships* 1:267–277.

Rose, Suzanna M., and Serafica, Felicisima C. (1986). "Keeping and Ending Casual, Close, and Best Friendships." *Journal of Social and Personal Relationships* 3:275–288.

Werking, Kathy J. (1997). *We're Just Good Friends: Women and Men in Nonromantic Relationships.* New York: Guilford.

Wright, Paul H. (1982). "Men's Friendships, Women's Friendships, and the Alleged Inferiority of the Latter." *Sex Roles* 8:1–20.

Wright, Paul H. (1989). "Gender Differences in Adults' Same- and Cross-Gender Friendships." In *Older Adult Friendship,* ed. Rebecca G. Adams and Rosemary Blieszner. Newbury Park, CA: Sage Publications.

William K. Rawlins

G

GENDER AND EMOTIONS

Although there are a great many stereotypes about gender and emotions, there are also many factual differences in the ways males and females differ in their emotional functioning. These differences include the extent to which they recognize emotions in others and express their own emotions through facial and vocal expressions, words, physiological arousal, and behaviors such as aggression. These gender differences vary according to the particular situation involved and the cultural background of the participants.

Stereotypes about Gender and Emotions

People's stereotypes about gender differences in emotional functioning are pervasive, overly general, and exaggerated. Briefly, women are stereotyped to be the more emotional sex across many diverse cultures, especially in sending and recognizing nonverbal cues and in the extent to which they are believed to laugh, smile, and express sadness and fear. Men are believed to express more anger and aggression than women and to be less expressive of other emotions. The two sexes are believed to differ more in the extent to which they express emotions than in the extent to which they experience them.

These stereotypes ignore the fact that differences between the emotional functioning of men and women vary depending on the particular situation in which the emotion is being expressed, the cultural backgrounds of the participants, their ages, and their individual personality characteristics. Moreover, gender differences in emotional functioning vary a great deal depending on which emotion is being expressed and how it is being expressed (e.g., using words or using changes in facial or vocal expressions). Perhaps the biggest danger of stereotypes is that in ignoring the importance of the social context, they lead to the erroneous conclusion that gender differences in emotional functioning are exclusively biological in origin.

People's stereotypes about gender and emotional functioning may actually influence gender differences in emotional functioning in two ways. First, stereotypes may cause people to expect certain behaviors from their same and opposite sex partners, and these beliefs may elicit particular behaviors and emotional expressions from the partners, thereby becoming self-fulfilling prophecies. Second, people are motivated to adhere to stereotypes in their own emotional functioning (as in men should not cry), since failing to conform to stereotypes can lead to negative social consequences such as social rejection, reduced attractiveness to potential sexual partners, and even occupational discrimination.

The power and pervasiveness of stereotypes should lead to cautious interpretations of the research on gender differences in emotional functioning, since researchers may be biased (even unconsciously) to see their research participants' emotional behaviors in stereotypic ways. Stereotypes can also affect research participants, who may distort their reports of emotional functioning in order to present themselves in ways that are socially acceptable.

Questionnaires and the Use of Words

Researchers such as Frank Fujita, Ed Diener, and Ed Sandvik (1991) and James Gross and Oliver John (1998) have found that when men and women are asked to complete questionnaires describing how "emotional" they are, or how expressive they are of particular emotions, women rate themselves to be more expressive than men and more intensely expressive than men. Women rate themselves as expressing more intense positive and negative emotions than men across a wide variety of age groups and cultures, in response to questions such as "When I'm happy I feel very energetic" or "When I talk in front of a group for the first time my voice gets shaky and my heart races."

As to specific feelings, women report more intense or frequent positive feelings, such as joy, love, affection, warmth, and feelings of well-being, than do men, especially in intimate interpersonal relationships. Women also generally report more negative feelings, such as empathy, sympathy, distress, fear, hurt, shame, embarrassment, and disgust, than do men. Sadness, depression, and dysphoria are also reported to be of longer duration by women than by men.

Although men express more anger through vocal, facial, and behavioral means than do women, Leslie Brody (1997) has shown that, on questionnaires, women report either more anger than men or levels of anger equal to those that men report. Women also report more enduring experiences of anger than men do. They are also more likely than men to report hurt or disappointment in response to anger-inducing situations.

According to Brody and Judith Hall (1993), the only emotions that males report or are reported to express more frequently or more intensely than females are contempt, loneliness, guilt, pride, and confidence. However, gender differences in contempt, guilt, and loneliness have been inconsistent across studies, depending on situational circumstances and the characteristics of the particular samples assessed.

Some research indicates that these findings hold across diverse cultures: that is, women express more intense positive and negative emotions than men do using global self-report measures. Other studies suggest that the extent of gender differences varies across different cultures. For example, Wendy Silverman, Annette La Greca, and Shari Wasserstein (1995) found that there were no gender differences in the amount of worry reported by African-American boys and girls, even though European-American and Hispanic school-aged girls reported more anxiety and worry than boys as measured via interviews and self-report. Using the cross-cultural database of the International Survey on Emotion Antecedents and Reactions, which was initiated by Klaus Scherer at the University of Geneva, Agneta Fischer and Antony Manstead (2000) compared gender differences in cultures that emphasize the importance of individual achievement (i.e., individualistic cultures, such as the United States) to gender differences in cultures that emphasize the importance of group solidarity and cohesiveness (i.e., collectivistic cultures, such as most Asian countries). Gender differences in the intensity of joy, shame, disgust, and guilt and in the nonverbal behaviors (e.g., laughing and smiling) associated with those same emotions were greater in individualistic than in collectivistic countries.

Gender differences on questionnaires that ask people how they are feeling at a particular point in time are less apt to emerge consistently than gender differences on measures that ask people how intensely they feel overall, or how intensely they have felt in the past. In work by Larry Seidlitz and Diener (1998), men actually reported positive events in their lives to be *more* intense than did women when using daily rating forms, but not when subsequently recalling those same events on other questionnaires. Similarly, Lisa Barrett and her colleagues (1998) found that women and men rated their specific emotional experiences to be equal in intensity immediately after a social interaction, even though women rated their *global* emotional intensity and expressiveness higher than did men.

Several explanations are possible for these discrepancies. Men and women may attempt to conform to sex-role stereotypes when responding to global questionnaires but not when responding to questions about their specific emotional experiences. Or perhaps women's memories of their emotional experiences are more vivid than men's, contributing to their reports of greater emotional intensity on global measures. It is also possible that women may ruminate over, or repeatedly think about, emotional events even after they occur, which retriggers emotional experiences and makes them relatively more intense at a later time. Global self-report measures may tap into "emotionality," a mixture of both emotional experience and emotional expressiveness. In contrast, asking about ongoing experiences may tap into a different dimension of emotional functioning—either experience or expressiveness.

However, the gender differences that appear on global self-report measures, with females reporting a wide range of both more frequent and more intense emotions than men, are unlikely to be solely determined by stereotypes, self presentation biases, or even memory differences between males and females. Gender differences appear on many other measures of emotional expressiveness, including observations of interactions, the verbalization of emotion, facial expressions, and nonverbal measures. For example, consistent with questionnaire data, Susan Girdler and her colleagues (1990) found that women refer more to positive and negative emotions (such as warmth, happy, glad, hopeless, and worthless) than men in both conversations with others and in their writing samples. Observations and self-descriptions of marriages corroborate that women express more emotion words, especially more negative emotions in interpersonal interactions than men, including more distress and anger. Wives are also more willing to tell their husbands when they are feeling tense, they are more apt to disclose their feelings, and they are more apt to try to explain their feelings than are husbands.

Facial Expressions

Women, according to Hall (1984), are more facially and gesturally expressive than men, including nodding, gazing, and smiling more. Women are also more facially expressive of most emotions, with the possible exception of anger, than are men in both natural situations and situations in which they are asked to pose different expressions. This has been found to be true using both measures of facial muscle reactivity, in which women's facial movements are more reactive than men, and judge's ratings of facial expressivity according to gender. Some evidence suggests that this gender difference is cross-cultural. For example, female university students (between eighteen and fifty-three years of age) in a wide variety of cultures reported more nonverbal emotional reactions than did males, including facial reactions, vocal reactions, body movements, laughing, smiling, and movements toward other people. Klaus Scherer, Harald Wallbott, and Angela Summerfield (1986) reported that these gender differences in nonverbal behaviors held true for several emotions, including joy, sadness, fear, and anger. Participants in a six-nation study conducted by Michael Biehl and his colleagues (1997) judged the emotions depicted by females more accurately than those depicted by males. However, inconsistent gender differences in facial expressivity across some cultures and for some emotions have also been reported.

Naomi and George Rotter (1988) found that men convey anger more clearly in their facial expressions than women, and Ulf Dimberg and Lars Lundquist (1990) found that men show more facial reactivity in response to angry stimuli than women. Similarly, Erik Coats and Robert Feldman (1996) showed that men's facial displays of anger are more accurately identified than women's by college student judges when men and women discuss angry, sad, and happy emotional memories. However, some of these studies have relied on judges who make global assessments of the emotions being conveyed and who may be biased to see men as more angry or intense than women.

Vocal Expressiveness

Research on gender differences in vocal expressiveness is quite inconsistent, with some suggestions in the literature that men may convey emotions more clearly using their voices than women. For example, a study by Terri Bonebright, Jeri Thompson, and Daniel Leger (1996) found men to be superior at expressing fear and anger through the voice, while other studies, including that by Renee van Bezooyen (1984), showed gender differences in specific vocal characteristics, such as men conveying more "harshness" (a rough and rasping quality associated with anger and joy) than women, as well as more laxness (a sonorous and resonant voice quality associated with shame, interest, and neutral speech).

Men have also been found by Hall (1984) to speak more loudly and more quickly than women. For both men and women, loud volume is associated with anger, and a slow speech rate is associated with sadness. Gender differences in vocal volume and speed may underlie perceived gender differences in anger and sadness, with men perceived as expressing relatively more anger and less sadness than women.

However, other studies indicate no gender differences in the patterns of vocal characteristics, such as the loudness, pitch level, timbre, and rate used to express emotion, or in the clarity with which males and females convey emotional expressions.

Behaviors

Emotions can be expressed through a wide variety of behaviors, including aggression, withdrawal, or crying. Women have been observed to cry more frequently than men across a wide variety of studies and are especially more likely to cry when angry.

In neutral situations, males are moderately more verbally and physically aggressive than females. However, B. Ann Bettencourt and Norman Miller (1996) point out that in situations involving provocation, such as having their progress on a task impeded or being verbally insulted or physically attacked, women become as verbally aggressive as men but still not as physically aggressive. By age nine, according to Nicki Crick and Jennifer Grotpeter (1995), girls in several different cultures (including America and Finland) are more likely to use "indirect" or relational aggression than are boys. Indirect or relational aggression involves social manipulation in which the aggressor uses social relationships to harm the target person without being personally involved. Gender differences in relational aggression have not been found to be as pronounced as gender differences in physical aggression.

It is also important to note that based on ethnographic reports for thirty-one societies, the differences in aggression between cultures have been found by Ronald Rohner (1976) to be greater than sex differences within the same culture. These data indicate that cultural influences play a strong role in the development of aggression in both sexes.

The two sexes use withdrawal in different types of emotional situations. Males withdraw, or distract themselves, when confronted with sad feelings and loss. They also withdraw from criticism and conflict, especially marital conflict, by "stonewalling" more than their wives do, which involves inhibiting facial action and minimizing listening and eye contact. Females withdraw in the face of potential aggression and conflict. For example, Bridget Murphy and Nancy Eisenberg (1996) found that, in the face of peer conflicts, young girls withdraw (by hiding, complying, avoiding, acting shy, or breaking off an interaction) more than do boys.

Situational Specificity

It is important to note that the meaning of a situation for the two sexes affects patterns of emotional expressiveness a great deal. One clear example of the specificity of gender differences comes from a study by Reed Larson, Maryse Richards, and Maureen Perry-Jenkins (1994) in which participants recorded their emotions as they were randomly beeped by pagers for a one-week period. Women were found to report more positive affect states (i.e., happy; cheerful, and friendly as opposed to unhappy, irritable, and angry) while at work than while at home. The opposite was true of men. They reported more positive affect states while at home.

Different situations have also been found to make men and women angry. The violation of interpersonal relationships is more likely to cause anger among women than among men. According to Mary Biaggio (1989), women report that they become angry when someone's behavior "is not in keeping with the kind of relationship" they would like to have or would expect to have. Women also report becoming angry when they have unwillingly passively consented to something, a demonstration of powerlessness.

In contrast, Biaggio (1989) and Bettencourt and Miller (1996) found that men and boys cite issues related to control as causes for their anger. Boys cite that they get angry when they are told what to do or are not allowed to do what they want to do. Adult men's anger is reported to be caused by violations of their autonomy or self-esteem, including situations in which they are either physically or verbally antagonized, their intelligence is insulted, or they are condescended to by women.

A critical aspect of the situation is who the participants in the interaction are. The intimacy of their relationship, their power and status with respect to each other, and their respective genders may each influence the types of emotions they express. Both men and women express more emotions to people they know intimately than to those they do not, and both men and women express more emotions to women than they do to men. Anger may be the only feeling that is verbally disclosed or directed more (using behaviors such as aggression) toward men than toward women, especially in situations in which no provocation is involved. Bernard Rimé and his colleagues (1991) found that women from a wide variety of cultures express emotions to a greater number of people than do men, who tend to limit themselves to expressing emotions only to intimate partners.

Physiological Arousal

Emotional situations stimulate both the sympathetic nervous system and the pituitary-adrenal cortical system. Heart rate, blood pressure, skin conductance, and levels of catecholamines (epinephrine and norepinephrine) may each become elevated under some stressful or emotional conditions. Although much literature indicates that men become more physiologically aroused in response to emotional stimuli than do women, especially on cardiovascular measures, the bulk of the research suggests that gender differences are specific to particular physiological measures and to particular tasks and circumstances. For example, Karen Matthews and Catherine Stoney (1988) reported that in many stressful situations, even when some measures of arousal (such as neuroendocrine functioning or blood pressure) show men to be more aroused than women, women still have higher heart rates than men.

Some previous reviews of gender differences in the patterns of relationships among physiological arousal and other modes of emotional expression have suggested that men are more often internalizers (i.e., showing physiological arousal with no overt facial or verbal emotional expressions), whereas women are more often externalizers (i.e., showing overt emotional expressions with no corresponding physiological arousal). For example, Ross Buck (1977) showed a negative relationship between facial expressiveness and physiological arousal in preschool boys that did not hold true for preschool girls.

A review of the literature suggests the alternative interpretation that males may indeed be internalizers but that women appear to be generalizers, expressing emotions in many forms simultaneously. When the definition of generalizers is broadened to include not only a correspondence between physiological arousal and facial expressiveness but between all forms of emotional expression, females especially conform to a generalizing pattern. For example, a wide variety of studies have shown that women and school-aged girls express feelings of sympathy and distress concurrently using facial expressions, behaviors, words, and physiological arousal more than boys do.

Recognizing Emotional Expressions in Others

Hall (1978, 1984) reports that females are superior to males at identifying or decoding affect from nonverbal cues of face, body, and voice. This gender difference is relatively constant across the gender of the stimulus person, tasks, different ages of the subjects being tests, and cultures, with the strongest female advantage being for facial cues. The one exception to women's superior decoding of cues may be when expressions of anger are concerned. For example, Rotter and Rotter (1988) have found that women may read angry facial cues less accurately than men do, especially when the encoder is male.

Emotions and Gender Roles

Many theorists hypothesize that expressing different emotions may help the two sexes to adapt to or perform their differing gender roles (including caregiving versus provider and protector roles). For example, expressing less vulnerability may enable men to be competitive with others more easily, a role consistent with being a provider. Expressing more warmth may enable women to affiliate with others more easily, enabling them to be better family caregivers.

Differing patterns of emotional expression may also help the two sexes to adapt to the power and status imbalances between men and women that exist in most cultures. For example, expressing contempt, but not vulnerability, may enable men to maintain relatively high status positions, whereas expressing low levels of aggression, pride, and confidence may help to maintain women's relatively low status positions.

Further, expressing different emotions is consistent with the differing views the two sexes may have of themselves (i.e., self-schemas), including being individualistic for men and interdependent or affiliative for women. Even gender differences in the patterns through which emotions are expressed can be seen as being adaptive for gender roles—internalization, or not expressing emotions outwardly, may enable males to maintain individualism and control, while women's style of generalization may be adaptive for a more in-terdependent style in which boundaries between self and others are more open.

The question of why men and women differ in their emotional experience and expression is complex and involves multiple interrelated factors, including biological, cultural, social, interpersonal, and intrapersonal levels of analysis.

Developmental Perspective of Gender Differences

Brody (1999), has proposed a feedback loop in which differing characteristics of male and female infants elicit differential responses from caregivers and peers and are molded in accordance with cultural values surrounding gender roles. Moreover, males and females may identify with and imitate same-sex caregivers and peers and de-identify, or attempt to become different from, their opposite-sex caregivers and peers.

Male and female infants differ from each other in four domains: activity and arousal levels, self-control processes, language development, and sociability. Female infants have lower activity levels than males; lower arousal levels in reaction to stimulation; higher sociability and empathy; faster maturation rates for the ability to regulate and inhibit inappropriate behaviors; and faster rates of language development. Some evidence indicates that activity levels and empathy are partly genetic, with higher rates of similarity in identical twins as compared to fraternal twins, as shown by Kim Saudino and her colleagues (1996) and Carolyn Zahn-Waxler and her colleagues (1992). Some aspects of emotionality may also be genetic. For example, H. Hill Goldsmith and his colleagues (1997) have found that contentment, social fearfulness, and anger-proneness are more similar in identical twins than in fraternal twins, and David Lykken and Auke Tellegen (1996) have found that genetic factors contribute more than social factors (such as family income or marital status) to individual differences in levels of contentment. However, it is important to remember that biological development itself is always shaped in interaction with social inputs. Differing biological development for the two sexes may be the result, not the cause, of the differing environmental stimulation that the two sexes receive.

Parents may respond differently to their sons and daughters partly because of early differences in their functioning. For example, parents may feel that their sons need to learn to constrain or regulate their feelings because of their sons' high arousal and activity levels. Analyses by Robyn Fivush (1993) of conversations between preschoolers and their parents have shown that mothers elaborate the causes and consequences of feelings more with sons than with daughters, thus teaching them the importance of controlling feelings. Phyllis Bronstein (1988) has shown that fathers also emphasize explanations and understanding events for their sons, even when the assigned task is not set up to be about feelings.

Perhaps in response to their daughters' perceived and actual expressive language abilities, parents discuss emotional reactions and experiences more with daughters than with sons and respond more positively (or with more warmth) to their daughters than to their sons. Further, perhaps in response to their daughters' abilities to regulate their own behaviors, parents focus and elaborate on the emotion state itself, thus teaching their daughters to be sensitive to the emotional experience and minimizing the importance of control. They also tend to minimize the facial expressions of fear they make to their daughters as opposed to their sons, perhaps because their daughters pay more attention to emotional signals than do their sons, not requiring as much emphasis.

Parents' responses to their infant sons and daughters are influenced by the children's characteristics, by the parents' cultural values surrounding gender, and by the characteristics of the family system (including the temperament of the parents, the quality of the marital relationship, the cultural and socioeconomic background, and the particular gender constellation of the children in the family).

Parents also socialize their children in accordance with stereotypic social norms for emotional expression. Children who conform to such norms are more popular and socially competent. For example, parents of preschool and young-school-aged daughters emphasize the expression of sadness and fear but not anger, whereas they emphasize the expression of anger but not other feelings to their sons. This is characteristic of parent-child interactions when parents are asked to create stories for their children using wordless illustrations, when parents and children reconstruct memories for actual events that occurred in their lives, and when parents discuss pictures of facial expressions with their children.

The structure of the family and the roles that each parent plays in the family also influence the socialization of emotional expression. Brody (1999) has shown that when fathers are involved in family life, daughters and sons become less gender stereotypic in how they express emotions. Sons whose fathers are more involved in child care express more intense feelings of vulnerability, such as warmth and fear, and less aggression in stories than sons with less involved fathers. They also describe themselves to be more interpersonally oriented than other sons. Daughters with involved fathers express more aggression, competition, and less intense fear and sadness than girls with less involved fathers. There is also some evidence that sons become different from their mothers in emotional expressiveness, perhaps in an effort to develop a masculine gender identity.

Boys and girls tend to interact in sex-segregated peer groups with distinct patterns of play that result in the socialization of different types of emotional expression. Boy's play tends to involve large organized groups, to take up large amounts of space, and to involve control and competition goals. This type of play would result in maximizing expressions of aggression, pride, anger, and contempt (including insults) and in minimizing expressions of fear, warmth, guilt, and vulnerability. For example, boys tend to express anger and insults directly to each other and are often publicly shamed if they express vulnerability. Boys who are seen as being vulnerable, weak, or sissies are socially rejected; those who display moderate amounts of aggression and are "tough" are the ones who are more popular. The expression of aggression, the direct expression of verbal anger, and the suppression of vulnerability would enable boys to win competitive games, engage in risk-taking activities, and gain status within their peer group.

Girls tend to play in intimate, small groups, and their goals are focused on affiliation, intimacy, and equality in their relationships rather than competition and control. They also emphasize not getting into trouble with adults more than boys do, and they tend to avoid direct confrontation and risk-taking behaviors. Girls express warmth, vulnerability, weakness, and humility in their peer groups, which helps them to accomplish their goals of affiliation. Popular girls are those who are not aggressive and who are socially sensitive and verbally expressive. In addition, girls do not express their anger directly to each other; they instead act mean, socially ostracize their former friends, or express hostility about their former friends behind their backs.

There are other socialization agents, including teachers, schools, and the media, that affect the emergence of gender differences in emotion. The evidence suggests that these influences also present children with same-sex gender-stereotypic models that they imitate and opposite-sex models with which they de-identify.

See also: AGGRESSION; ANGER; BODY MOVEMENT, GESTURE, AND DISPLAY; CROSS-CULTURAL PATTERNS; CULTURE; EMOTION EXPERIENCE AND EXPRESSION; HUMAN DEVELOPMENT; PERSONALITY; UNIVERSALITY OF EMOTIONAL EXPRESSION

Bibliography

Barrett, Lisa Feldman; Robin, Lucy; Pietromonaco, Paul; and Eyssell, Kristen. (1998). "Are Women the More Emotional Sex? Evidence from Emotional Experiences in Social Context." *Cognition and Emotion* 12:555–578.

Bettencourt, B. Ann, and Miller, Norman. (1996). "Gender Differences in Aggression as a Function of Provocation: A Meta-Analysis." *Psychological Bulletin* 119:422–447.

Bezooyen, Renee van. (1984). *Characteristics of Vocal Expressions of Emotion*. Dordrecht, The Netherlands: Foris Publication.

Biaggio, Mary. (1989). "Sex Differences in Behavioral Reactions to Provocation of Anger." *Psychological Reports* 64:23–26.

Biehl, Michael; Matsumoto, David; Ekman, Paul; Hearn, Valerie; Heider, Karl; Kudoh, Tsutomu; and Ton, Veronica. (1997). "Matsumoto and Ekman's Japanese and Caucasian Facial Expressions of Emotion (JACFEE): Reliability Data and Cross-National Differences." *Journal of Nonverbal Behavior* 21:3–21.

Bonebright, Terri; Thompson, Jeri; and Leger, Daniel. (1996). "Gender Stereotypes in the Expression and Perception of Vocal Affect." *Sex Roles* 34:429–445.

Brody, Leslie. (1997). "Beyond Stereotypes: Gender and Emotion." *Journal of Social Issues* 53:369–393.

Brody, Leslie. (1999). *Gender, Emotion, and the Family*. Cambridge, MA: Harvard University Press.

Brody, Leslie, and Hall, Judith. (1993). "Gender and Emotion." In *Handbook of Emotions*, ed. Michael Lewis and Jeannette M. Haviland. New York: Guilford.

Bronstein, Phyllis. (1988). "Father Child Interaction: Implications for Gender Role Socialization." In *Fatherhood Today: Men's Changing Role in the Family*, ed. Phyllis Bronstein and Carolyn P. Cowan. New York: Wiley.

Buck, Ross. (1977). "Nonverbal Communication Accuracy in Preschool Children: Relationships with Personality and Skin Conductance." *Journal of Personality and Social Psychology* 33:225–236.

Coats, Erik, and Feldman, Robert. (1996). "Gender Differences in Nonverbal Correlates of Social Status." *Personality and Social Psychology Bulletin* 22:1014–1022.

Crick, Nicki, and Grotpeter, Jennifer. (1995). "Relational Aggression, Gender, and Social-Psychological Adjustment." *Child Development* 66:710–722.

Dimberg, Ulf, and Lundquist, Lars. (1990). "Gender Differences in Facial Reactions to Facial Expressions." *Biological Psychology* 30:151–159.

Fischer, Agneta, and Manstead, Antony. (2000). "Culture, Gender, and Emotion." In *Gender and Emotion*, ed. Agneta Fischer. Cambridge, Eng.: Cambridge University Press.

Fivush, Robyn. (1993). "Emotional Content of Parent-Child Conversations about the Past." In *Memory and Affect in Development*, ed. Charles A. Nelson. Hillsdale, NJ: Lawrence Erlbaum.

Fujita, Frank; Diener, Ed; and Sandvik, Ed. (1991). "Gender Differences in Negative Affect and Well-Being: The Case for Emotional Intensity." *Journal of Personality and Social Psychology* 61:427–434.

Girdler, Susan; Turner, J. Rick; Sherwood, Andrew; and Light, Kathleen. (1990). "Gender Differences in Blood Pressure Control during a Variety of Behavioral Stressors." *Psychosomatic Medicine* 52:571–591.

Goldsmith, H. Hill; Buss, Kristin; and Lemery, Kathryn. (1997). "Toddler and Childhood Temperament: Expanded Content, Stronger Genetic Evidence, New Evidence for the Importance of Environment." *Developmental Psychology* 33:891–905.

Gross, James, and John, Oliver. (1998). "Mapping the Domain of Expressivity: Multimethod Evidence for a Hierarchical Model." *Journal of Personality and Social Psychology* 74:170–191.

Hall, Judith. (1978). "Gender Effects in Decoding Nonverbal Cues." *Psychological Bulletin* 85:845–857.

Hall, Judith. (1984). *Nonverbal Sex Differences: Communication Accuracy and Expressive Style*. Baltimore, MD: Johns Hopkins University Press.

Larson, Reed; Richards, Maryse; and Perry-Jenkins, Maureen. (1994). "Divergent Worlds: The Daily Emotional Experience of Mothers and Fathers in the Domestic and Public Spheres." *Journal of Personality and Social Psychology* 67:1034–1046.

Lykken, David, and Tellegen, Auke. (1996). "Happiness Is a Stochastic Phenomenon." *Psychological Science* 7:186–189.

Maccoby, Eleanor. (1998). *The Two Sexes*. Cambridge, MA: Harvard University Press.

Matthews, Karen, and Stoney, Catherine. (1988). "Influences of Sex and Age on Cardiovascular Responses during Stress." *Psychosomatic Medicine* 50:46–56.

Murphy, Bridget, and Eisenberg, Nancy. (1996). "Provoked by a Peer: Children's Anger Related Responses and Their Relations to Social Functioning." *Merrill-Palmer Quarterly* 42:103–124.

Rimé, Bernard; Mesquita, Batja; Philippot, Pierre; and Boca, Stefano. (1991). "Beyond the Emotional Event: Six Studies on the Social Sharing of Emotion." *Cognition and Emotion* 5:435–465.

Rohner, Ronald P. (1976). "Sex Differences in Aggression: Phylogenetic and Enculturation Perspectives." *Ethos* 4:57–72.

Rotter, Naomi, and Rotter, George. (1988). "Sex Differences in the Encoding and Decoding of Negative Facial Emotions." *Journal of Nonverbal Behavior* 12:139–148.

Saudino, Kimberly; Plomin, Robert; and DeFries, John. (1996). "Tester-Rated Temperament at 14, 20, and 24 Months: Environmental Change and Genetic Continuity." *British Journal of Developmental Psychology* 14:129–144.

Scherer, Klaus; Wallbott, Harold; and Summerfield, Angela. (1986). *Experiencing Emotion: A Cross-Cultural Study*. Cambridge, Eng.: Cambridge University Press.

Seidlitz, Larry, and Diener, Ed. (1998). "Sex Differences in the Recall of Affective Experiences." *Journal of Personality and Social Psychology* 74:262–271.

Silverman, Wendy; La Greca, Annette; and Wasserstein, Shari. (1995). "What Do Children Worry About? Worries and Their Relation to Anxiety." *Child Development* 66:671–686.

Tannen, Deborah. (1994). *Gender and Discourse*. New York: Oxford University Press.

Zahn-Waxler, Carolyn; Robinson, JoAnn; and Emde, Robert. (1992). "The Development of Empathy in Twins." *Developmental Psychology* 28:1038–1047.

Leslie R. Brody

GENETICS

In 1872, Charles Darwin observed the continuities of emotion across different species and inferred that the emotions represent adaptive solutions to prehistoric problems. More than one hundred years later, David Buss (1991, p. 483) elaborated on this view, describing "emotions, mood states, preferences, and desires [as] . . . products of natural selection." This view encourages studies of the biological bases of emotion, including studies of the role of genetics. Until the 1990s, however, the genetic analysis of individual differences in emotion was limited.

Experimental studies of emotion have focused on species-typical, or normative, behaviors. Such research often has involved eliciting emotions in the laboratory to examine, for example, the underlying physiology of emotion and the relationship between cognition and emotion. In contrast, the genetic analysis of emotion has focused on individual differences in temperament and personality, which may be thought of as inclinations to respond to emotional stimuli. This research often relies on self-report, or questionnaire, methods of measurement. A complete understanding of emotion awaits a synthesis of these approaches. The growing emphasis on individual differences in laboratory studies of emotion, along with sophisticated developments in quantitative and molecular genetics, suggest the time is ripe for such a synthesis.

Genetic Bases of Emotion

There are many studies that concern the genetic bases of emotion. Animal studies have examined the genetic bases of emotionality; human studies have explored differences in the general tendency to experience positive and negative emotion, as well as the effect of genetic differences on specific emotions such as sadness and fear. This research suggests that genetic factors contribute to individual differences in emotionality and, further, that variability in the tendency to experience distinct emotions also may be influenced by genetic differences.

Animal Studies of Emotionality

Genetic analysis of emotion began early in the twentieth century, when selective breeding was used to establish lines of rats that differed in measures of emotionality. Successful modification of a trait through selective breeding implies (although does not confirm) a genetic influence on that trait. That is, if selective breeding successfully establishes two lines that differ reliably in the phenotype, or trait, of interest, it is more likely that the phenotypic differences arise from genetic factors. The Maudsley selective breeding study of emotionality in rats, begun in the early 1950s by Peter Broadhurst (1960), represents the longest-standing and most extensive investigation of this type. Maudsley Reactive and Maudsley Nonreactive strains were selectively bred for high and low open-field defecation, which is considered a measure of emotion in rats. Thus, the establishment of the two distinct lines provided evidence of a genetic effect on emotionality.

A second long-standing selective breeding experiment began in the 1960s. It was conducted by William Reese (1979) and his colleagues and has resulted in the development of a strain of pointer dogs that has maintained nervous characteristics for more than eight generations. These characteristics include excessive timidity, reduced exploratory behavior, hyper-startle, avoidance of humans, catatonic freezing or immobility, cardiovascular changes, urination, and defecation. For these dogs, "the most potent stimulus for maladaptive nervous behavior . . . is man, [and this effect] cannot be vitiated by increase of friendly human contact during development, nor by foster-parent rearing by normal mothers" (p. 1171). On the contrary, a number of studies have found that these nervous behaviors are most pronounced when the dogs are exposed to humans or novel environments. This suggests that, in addition to an inherited tendency toward emotionality that is conceptually similar to that exhibited by the Maudsley Reactive rats, these dogs are predisposed to react fearfully to a particular stimulus (i.e., humans).

Temperament and Personality

Twin and family studies provided the first evidence of the importance of genetic factors in humans. For a given phenotype, if family members are more similar to one another than randomly selected members of the general population, it is likely that genetic factors affect that phenotype. However, because family members generally share aspects of the environment as well as genes, family studies cannot demonstrate genetic effects unequivocally. Twin and adoption methods permit genetic and environmental contributions to familial resemblance to be estimated. Monozygotic (MZ) twins have identical genotypes, while dizygotic (DZ) twins share, on the average, 50 percent of their genes. Thus, if identical, or MZ, twins are more similar phenotypically than fraternal, or DZ, twins, genetic factors may contribute to trait variance. In adoption studies, to assess the contribution of genes and environment to individual differences in a trait, adopted individuals are compared to their biological relatives (from whom they received their genes) and to their adoptive relatives (with whom they shared an environment). If adoptees are more similar to their biological relatives (even though they were not raised with those relatives) than they are to their adoptive relatives, genetic factors may be important.

The clearest demonstration of the importance of genetic factors in human emotion is provided by twin and adoption studies in childhood temperament. Emotionality, one of three temperament dimensions described by Arnold Buss and Robert Plomin (1984), has been the subject of many twin and adoption studies. In general, these studies provide evidence of moderate genetic effects on emotionality.

H. Hill Goldsmith and Joseph Campos (1982) distinguished among the various emotions, defining temperament as individual differences in tendencies to

Because of their genetic make-up, identical (monozygotic) twins are often used in studies that seek to determine the connection between genetics and emotion. (Corbis/Vince Streano)

express the primary emotions (e.g., fear, anger, pleasure). Moreover, Goldsmith and Mary Rothbart (1988) developed a method of quantifying temperament that involves measuring fear, anger, pleasure, interest, and activity in multiple, controlled situations in the laboratory. Using this method in a twin study, Goldsmith and Campos (1986) found that different combinations of genetic and environmental factors operate in different situations (e.g., in the presence of a visual cliff versus a stranger). Further, the nature of the emotional response (e.g., bodily avoidance of a stranger versus aversion of gaze from a stranger) may be affected by genetic factors.

The concept of emotion also has been incorporated into theories of adult personality. For example, Auke Tellegen and his colleagues (1988, p. 1033) found that high scorers on a psychometric, or questionnaire, measure of positive affect describe themselves as being "engaged in active, pleasurable, and efficacious trans-

actions with their environment and as being ready to experience the positive emotions congruent with these involvements. Low scorers report few of these pleasurable transactions." In contrast, high scorers on a measure of negative affect describe themselves as being "unpleasurably engaged, stressed and harassed, prone to experiencing strong negative emotions such as anger and anxiety," while low scorers "have a higher threshold for negative affect" or are less likely to experience negative emotions. In a unique sample that included twins who were raised apart as well as twins who were raised together, Tellegen and his colleagues found strong evidence for heritable dimensions in personality that affect the inclinations of individuals to experience positive and negative emotion.

In selective breeding studies, when biobehavioral correlates of strain differences in emotionality are characterized, hypotheses about causality can be tested. The Maudsley Reactive and Nonreactive strains have been characterized and compared on a wide variety of behavioral, cardiovascular, endocrinological, and neurochemical measures. For example, as David Blizard (1981) and his colleagues have reported, relative to nonreactive rats, reactive rats have been found to perform active avoidance conditioning less efficiently, to develop more pronounced conditioned emotional responses, and to show lower basal sympathetic tone and a greater sympathetic nervous system response to stress. Research on the nervous pointer dogs has provided further evidence of differences in nervous system function that are related to the behavioral differences in emotionality for which the strains were bred.

In light of the strain differences in stress reactivity, it is interesting to note that several twin and twin-family studies suggest that there are genetic influences on individual differences in cardiovascular response to stress in the laboratory. Harold Sneider and his colleagues (1993), for example, found that the role of genetic factors in systolic and diastolic blood pressure responses was greater for a more stressful speeded mental arithmetic task than for a simple reaction time task, suggesting that the genes that are involved may operate specifically in response to a stressful, or emotion eliciting, task, rather than simply affecting overall cardiovascular function.

Thus, selective breeding studies suggest that there is a genetically influenced trait, emotionality, that describes reactivity to environmental stressors; other selective breeding studies suggest that autonomic correlates of emotionality are affected by the same genes that influence the behavioral measures of emotionality. In humans, there are temperament and personality dimensions that are conceptually similar to emotionality in animals (i.e., that index an individual's tendency to experience emotion), and those dimensions appear to be genetically influenced. In humans, as in animals, genetic factors also play a role in autonomic responsivity to the environment. The link between psychometric measures of emotionality and autonomic responsivity, however, has not been well established in humans.

Sadness and Depression

In addition to the genetic effect on emotionality, there is also evidence, mostly from twin and twin-family studies, of a genetic effect on specific emotions. The relationship between normal variation in emotion, such as sadness and fear, to clinical disorders, such as depression and phobias, is not well understood. Nevertheless, there is evidence that studies bearing on disordered emotion also may contribute to an understanding of normal emotional behavior and its biogenetic bases.

Several studies show that symptoms of depression and anxiety are heritable in the general population. In a study of 3,810 Australian twin pairs, Kenneth Kendler and his colleagues (1986) found strong evidence that genetic factors account for variability in symptoms of anxiety and depression, while, contrary to popular belief, evidence for familial environmental factors was much weaker. Suggesting that these findings are relevant to normal variation in emotion, Tellegen and his colleagues (1988) found that a psychometric measure of negative affect, itself under moderate genetic control, was correlated with clinical diagnoses of depressive and anxiety disorders. Similarly, they reported that a measure of positive affect, also genetically influenced, was inversely correlated with diagnoses of depression.

For many years, the anxiety associated with thoughts of being separated from a loved one, called separation anxiety, was attributed to traumatic events in early childhood. Moreover, the role of early separation in inducing depression has been well demonstrated, and mother-infant separation has been used extensively to create an animal model of depression. Derrick Silove and Vijaya Manicavasagar (1993) studied the role of genetic factors in the development of separation anxiety in normal twins, as measured by a self-report inventory. They found that there were individual differences in the extent to which people are vulnerable to separation anxiety and that those individual differences were, in part, genetically determined. In a laboratory study of the genetics of infant-caregiver attachment in twins, Deborah Finkel and her colleagues (1998) also found differential reactions to separation from the caregiver that were partially genetically influenced.

Fears and Phobias

Throughout the twentieth century, it was thought that fears and phobias were learned—as a result of a frightening experience, stimuli that were associated with that experience would come to elicit a conditioned fear response. As early as 1897, however, G. Stanley Hall observed that certain fears might be more easily conditioned than others; years later, Martin Seligman (1971) elaborated on this observation.

In fact, studies conducted by Richard Rose and W. Blaine Ditto (1983) of twins and their families have found genetic contributions to variability in many self-reported fears, and the magnitude of those genetic influences varies strikingly across fears. This not only provides evidence of a genetic influence on a specific emotion (fear) but suggests that stimuli vary in their fear-eliciting potency and that genes may affect individual differences in that potency.

Application of Genetic Strategies to the Study of Emotion

The above evidence indicates that there are substantial genetic contributions to the dimensions of temperament and personality (which reflect individual differences in the tendency to experience emotion). The body of research that addresses genetic contributions to specific emotions is more limited. Developments in quantitative genetics now offer the potential to elaborate on these findings and address the enduring questions in the field of emotion, such as questions about the interrelationships of the components of emotion (i.e., physiology, behavior, and cognition). Moreover, rapid advances in molecular genetics present the opportunity to specify the locations of the genes that affect emotion.

Quantitative Genetics

In the early years of behavior-genetic research, the primary outcome of twin and family studies was an estimate of heritability, or the proportion of variance in a trait that is accounted for by genetic factors. More sophisticated approaches, some of which have been used in the study of emotion, are reflected in the more recent literature. Kinship data are used to formulate and test models that include estimates of the proportion of variance that is accounted for by additive genetic factors, by interactions among genes at two (dominance) or more (epistatic) loci, by shared family environment, by unique environmental effects that are experienced by individuals, by gene-environment covariance, and by gene-environment interactions. Moreover, multivariate analysis is used increasingly to examine the genetic bases of relationships between multiple traits.

The goal of most of the studies that have been described here has been to estimate the genetic and environmental contributions to the covariance of a single characteristic, such as cardiovascular reactivity or negative affect, in pairs of related individuals. The same approach can be taken to examine the phenotypic correlation between two traits. If two characteristics, X and Y, are associated in a population (i.e., phenotypically correlated), that correlation may arise from environmental or genetic causes. By examining the cross-covariance of traits in pairs of related individuals (e.g., the cross-covariance of trait X in parents with trait Y in offspring), the genetic and environmental contributions to that phenotypic association can be estimated. Richard Davidson (1992) and his colleagues, for example, have examined the relationship between hemispheric asymmetries in the electroencephalogram and affective, or emotional, response. By assessing these two variables in strategically chosen family members, it would be possible to test the hypothesis that common genetic effects underlie the relationship between these asymmetries and affective response. Multivariate genetic designs also could address the nature of the relationships between emotion and cognition, between autonomic patterns and emotional expression, and between personality and laboratory-based assessment of emotion.

Repeated measures genetic analysis is a multivariate technique in which repeated measurements on the same measure are collected for pairs of related individuals, permitting the genetic contribution to change (or stability) over the repeated measurements to be estimated. This method has obvious implications for the study of the development of emotions, but it would also be useful in laboratory studies of emotion. That is, a repeated measures genetic analysis could be used to test the hypothesis that the genes that affect the cardiovascular response to an emotional stimulus, for example, are distinct from those that determine baseline cardiovascular activity.

A variant of the twin design involves comparing the kinship derived from identical twin mothers with that derived from identical twin fathers. Because their twin parents have identical genes, children of MZ twins are genetically related to one another as half-siblings; socially, they are reared as cousins in separate homes. By comparing the groups of maternal half-siblings (in which the mothers are identical twins) and groups of paternal half-siblings (in which the fathers are identical twins), the design permits hypotheses of maternal effects to be tested. Such effects may result from X-linkage, intrauterine, or maternal rearing effects and are of particular interest in the study of emotion.

The potential importance of maternal effects to the study of emotion is exemplified by their role in the open-field activity of Maudsley Reactive and Nonreactive rats. John Jinks and Broadhurst (1974) found that the open field activity of the reciprocal F1 generations (Nonreactive female/Reactive male versus Nonreactive male/Reactive female), while both falling between that of the parental lines, differ significantly from one another. Offspring of the second cross (in which the mother is Reactive) show less open field activity (i.e., more emotionality) than the offspring of the cross in which the mother is Nonreactive. The difference between the two F1 generations is increased when the mother is chronically stressed prior to mating. These findings suggest that the MZ half-sibling design should be used to study maternal effects on emotionality in humans and that special care should be taken to document the mothers' life stresses.

Molecular Genetics

Molecular genetics continues to capture attention as the human genome is mapped and as linkage studies identify the genes that are involved with various medical disorders (even though linkage studies are capable only of detecting genes that have a relatively large effect on the phenotype). Behaviors and other traits that are relevant to emotion are most likely to be quantitative, or continuously varying (versus qualitative, or categorical). Such traits are more likely to be affected by sets of genes, each of which exerts a small influence, rather than by a single major gene; thus, linkage studies may be of limited value in the study of emotion. Association studies, however, which are capable of detecting genes that have a very small effect, have been used to identify genes that contribute to individual differences in continuously varying traits (i.e., quantitative trait loci). In one such study, conducted by Kimberly Saudino and her colleagues (1993), maternal ratings of temperament were used to select children in the top or bottom 25 percent of the distribution of emotionality scores. A comparison of these two groups of children revealed significant genetic differences. By examining the chromosomal locations of these genetic differences, researchers may be able to identify genes that affect emotionality in humans.

A "molecular twist" on the twin method, employed by Walter Nance and Michael Neale (1989), provides a means of estimating the contribution of candidate loci to variation in a trait. MZ twins always have two alleles in common at any locus; at any polymorphic locus, DZ twins may have zero, one, or two alleles in common. Thus, one can ask whether phenotypic similarity increases as the number of shared alleles at the candidate locus varies from zero to two. Increased phenotypic similarity with increased genetic similarity suggests that the marker gene (and/or the adjacent chromosomal area) has an effect on variation in that trait. This method has been employed successfully in the study of risk factors for cardiovascular disease and promises to provide important information with regard to the genetic variability that is relevant to emotion.

The effective use of molecular genetic techniques in the study of emotion awaits the development of adequate definitions of the phenotypes that are relevant to emotion. That is, complex behavioral phenotypes must be dissected into units that are more likely to be associated with genetic variation. The development of more restrictive phenotypes will facilitate the identification of genes that are relevant to emotion, and it will promote an understanding of the affective, behavioral, and cognitive components of emotion.

See also: ANXIETY; ATTACHMENT; DARWIN, CHARLES ROBERT; FEAR AND PHOBIAS; HUMAN DEVELOPMENT; PERSONALITY; TEMPERAMENT

Bibliography

Blizard, David A. (1981). "Maudsley Reactive and Non-Reactive Strains: A North American Perspective." *Behavior Genetics* 11:469–489.

Broadhurst, Peter L. (1960). "Experiments in Psychogenetics." In *Experiments in Personality, Psychogenetics, and Psychopharmacology, Vol. 1,* ed. Hans J. Eysenck. London: Routledge and Kegan Paul.

Buss, Arnold H., and Plomin, Robert. (1984). *Temperament: Early Developing Personality Traits.* Hillsdale, NJ: Lawrence Erlbaum.

Buss, David. (1991). "Evolutionary Personality Psychology." *Annual Review of Psychology* 42:459–491.

Darwin, Charles. ([1872] 1979). *The Expression of the Emotions in Man and Animals.* London: Julian Friedmann.

Davidson, Richard J. (1992). "Anterior Cerebral Asymmetry and the Nature of Emotion." *Brain and Cognition* 20:125–151.

Eaves, Lindon J. (1978). "Twins As a Basis for the Causal Analysis of Human Personality." In *Twin Research: Psychology and Methodology,* ed. Walter Nance, Gordon Allen, and Paolo Parisi. New York: Alan R. Liss.

Finkel, Deborah; Wille, Diane; and Matheny, Adam P., Jr. (1998). "Preliminary Results from a Twin Study of Infant-Caregiver Attachment." *Behavior Genetics* 28:1.

Goldsmith, H. Hill, and Campos, Joseph. (1982). "Toward a Theory of Infant Temperament." In *The Development of Attachment and Affiliative Systems,* ed. Robert N. Emde and Robert J. Harmon. New York: Plenum.

Goldsmith, H. Hill, and Campos, Joseph. (1986). "Fundamental Issues in the Study of Early Temperament: The Denver Twin Temperament Study." In *Advances in Developmental Psychology, Vol. 4,* ed. Michael E. Lamb, Ann L. Brown, and Barbara Rogoff. Hillsdale, NJ: Lawrence Erlbaum.

Goldsmith, H. Hill, and Rothbart, Mary. (1988). "The Laboratory Temperament Assessment Battery (LAB-TAB): Locomotor Version (edition 1.2)." Oregon Center for the Study of Emotion Technical Report #88–01.

Hall, G. Stanley. (1897). "A Study of Fears." *American Journal of Psychology* 8:147–249.

Jinks, John L., and Broadhurst, Peter L. (1974). "How to Analyse the Inheritance of Behaviour of Animals: The Biometrical

Approach." In *The Genetics of Behaviour,* ed. J. H. F. van Abeelen. Amsterdam: North Holland.

Kendler, Kenneth S.; Heath, Andrew; Martin, Nicholas G.; and Eaves, Lindon J. (1986). "Symptoms of Anxiety and Depression in a Volunteer Twin Population: The Etiologic Role of Genetic and Environmental Factors." *Archives of General Psychiatry* 43:213–221.

McGuffin, Peter; Owen, Michael J.; O'Donovan, Michael C.; Thapar, Anita; and Gottesman, Irving I. (1994). *Seminars in Psychiatric Genetics.* London: Royal College of Psychiatrists.

Nance, Walter E., and Neale, Michael C. (1989). "Partitioned Twin Analysis: A Power Study." *Behavior Genetics* 19:143–150.

Plomin, Robert, ed. (1986). *Development, Genetics, and Psychology.* Hillsdale NJ: Lawrence Erlbaum.

Plomin, Robert. (1990). "The Role of Inheritance in Behavior." *Science* 248:183–248.

Reese, William G. (1979). "A Dog Model for Human Psychopathology." *American Journal of Psychiatry* 136:1168–1172.

Rose, Richard J., and Ditto, W. Blaine. (1983). "A Developmental-Genetic Analysis of Common Fears from Early Adolescence to Early Adulthood." *Child Development* 54:361–368.

Saudino, Kimberly J.; Chorney, Michael; McClearn, Gerald E.; McGuffin, Peter; Owen, Michael; Smith, Deborah; Letterman, Douglas; Thompson, Lee; and Plomin, Robert. (1993). "Applying a QTL Association Approach to Temperament." *Behavior Genetics* 23:564.

Seligman, Martin E. P. (1971). "Phobias and Preparedness." *Behavior Therapy* 2:307–320.

Silove, Derrick, and Manicavasagar, Vijaya. (1993). "The Contribution of Genetic Factors to the Development of Early Separation Anxiety." *Behavior Genetics* 23:566.

Snieder, Harold; Boomsma, Dooret I.; and van Doornen, Lorenz J. P. (1993). "Stability of Genetic Influences on Blood Pressure Response to Psychological Stress." *Behavior Genetics* 23:567.

Tellegen, Auke; Lykken, David; Bouchard, Thomas; Wilcox, Kimerly; Segal, Nancy; and Rich, Stephen. (1988). "Personality Similarity in Twins Reared Apart and Together." *Journal of Personality and Social Psychology* 54:1031–1039.

Frances H. Gabbay

GESTURE

See Body Movement, Gesture, and Display; Emotion Experience and Expression; Facial Expression; Universality of Emotional Expression

GIFT GIVING

Giving and receiving gifts is a practice common to all cultures in the world. It is part and parcel of everybody's life, although the extent to which this is the case may vary. For many people, life is considered to be the first "gift." Next, people receive food, care, and shelter from their parents. Childhood birthdays are often celebrated with sweets and presents, as are other ritual gift-giving occasions such as Christmas or Valentine's Day. In adult life, gift giving is pursued and extended.

Numerous other ritual occasions for gift giving are added: weddings, births, funerals, exams, promotions, welcoming or farewell-parties, and so on. People give when they are invited to dine with other people or when they visit an ill friend. They give to beggars, to the church, and to charity. In fact, gift giving is so normal that most people are not aware of its fulfilling important psychological and social functions: gift exchange carries a range of psychological meanings and is the cement of social relationships. When one party always gives and never receives, the relationship will have very low chances for survival. Never giving any gift probably means, in the end, the discontinuation of a relationship. Breaking off an engagement was, and perhaps in some cases is, traditionally accompanied by the returning of the gifts received from family members, removing the symbols of past ties.

Gifts and social relations are fundamentally tied to each other. This becomes clear from an interesting observation made by Barry Schwartz (1967) in his classic article about the social psychology of the gift. According to Schwartz, psychological selves and identities are created and reinforced by the social act of gift. Gifts reveal something about the identity of the giver, about his or her personal taste, financial or cultural resources, or special character traits. But a gift also imposes an identity on the recipient, in the sense that the ideas that the recipient's needs and desires evoke in the giver's imagination—ideas about typical characteristics and peculiarities—are exposed to a certain extent in the gift. Because the gift defines both the giver and the recipient, it might be considered to be a social looking glass. In the same vein, the Canadian sociologist David Cheal (1987, 1988) considers gift exchange as a "moral economy" in which symbolic meanings are conveyed to significant others, making possible the extended reproduction of social relations. Gifts offer the precious symbolic nourishment that keeps interpersonal relationships alive.

What motivates the giving of gifts? Is gift giving mainly a sign of altruistic feelings or may more negative, even selfish, motives be involved? These questions pertain to the psychological meanings of gift giving. Everywhere in society, gift exchange seems to follow the rule of reciprocity (i.e., receiving a gift obliges the recipient to give a gift in return in due time). Gift giving seems to be based on expectations of return, and these expectations form the impetus for social interaction. The social and cultural meanings of the gift are reflected in the principle of reciprocity.

Psychological Meanings of Gift Giving

A whole range of emotions and motivations seems to be involved in gift giving. The most well-known motivations underlying gift giving are positive feelings: friendship, love, sympathy, gratitude, respect, loyalty, solidarity, and so on. But even gifts motivated by such good feelings may be accompanied (consciously or unconsciously) by some strategic aims. The giver may wish to compensate for some wrong done, to make a good impression, to get special attention, or to ensure a place in the recipient's memory. The distinction between when a gift is given out of purely positive feelings and when it is an attempt to flatter or manipulate is not always quite clear.

A gift may also be given because of fear, anxiety, or uncertainty. For example, the giver may fear losing an important relationship. Anxiety can be a powerful motive to give in an attempt to divert possible danger by showing an enemy that there are no bad intentions. Also, uncertainty, powerlessness, dependency, or a need for approval may be incentives for gift giving.

Furthermore, gifts may be inspired by conscious or unconscious needs of power and prestige. The anthropologist Claude Lévi-Strauss (1965) analyzed the habit of showing Christmas cards on the mantelpiece as a manifestation of status and prestige: the more cards, the more the individual is esteemed and loved by others. He compared this ritual with the "potlatch" in some non-Western cultures, a ceremonial contest in generosity (where the more one gives, the greater is one's prestige) that culminates in the public destruction of wealth. Gift exchange may be regarded as a continuous contest of honor. The giver's honor is at stake when he or she does not give a gift with the appropriate value or the gift is not given at the right moment. Because a gift causes the recipient to be indebted to the giver, the recipient's honor is in danger when the occurred "debt" is not cleared with an appropriate gift given in return. As the sociologist/ethnologist Marcel Mauss (1923) has pointed out, giving is placing oneself in a superior position in relation to the recipient. An overly generous gift may be an expression of power if it becomes very difficult or even impossible for the recipient to return, forcing him or her to remain in a dependent position.

Gifts may convey unfriendly feelings as well. Gifts may be given out of hostile feelings such as revenge or the desire to offend, punish, or harm someone. The etymology of the term *gift* illustrates its agonistic origin. The German word *gift* originated from the Greek-Latin *dosis,* which, in its turn, had replaced *venenum* (or poison), because of the need for a euphemism. Snow White's poisoned apple is but one of the many examples of hostile gifts that can be found in fairy tales. The Trojan horse is an example from Greek history. In the psychoanalytical literature, certain forms of excessive altruism or generosity have been interpreted as a defense against anxiety or aggressive impulses. Generosity may also be a sign of either a desire to assert oneself or guilt feelings.

Tlinglets arrived in large numbers to attend an 1895 potlatch (a gift-giving ceremony) in Kok-wol-too, near the Chilkat River in Alaska. (Corbis)

Social Meanings of Gift Giving

Mauss (1923) argued that (conscious or unconscious) expectations of return underlie every gift and that gifts form the basis of a shared culture. In his opinion, the principle of *do ut des* (i.e., "I give so that you give in return") characterizes gift exchange in Western as well as non-Western cultures. If this pattern of giving and giving-in-return (the principle of reciprocity) is indeed universally valid, what are its functional and structural meanings?

On the basis of his study of the ceremonial gift exchange among the Trobriand Islanders, Bronislaw Malinowski (1922) showed how the principle of give and take was the basis of a shared culture. Reciprocal gift giving allowed the inhabitants of the Trobriand archipelago to create the groundwork for other kinds of exchange (e.g., food, services, information) and to lay the foundation for shared meanings and interests.

Malinowski emphasized the functionalist aspect of the ceremony of gift exchange (i.e., its function of creating and sustaining a common culture), but this practice may also be regarded from a structuralist point of view. Lévi-Strauss (1949), an exponent of structuralist thinking within social science, considered reciprocity to be a fundamental structure underlying the development of stabilized relationships and a common culture. To a great extent, this structure determines

gift-giving behaviors. For example, patterns of gift exchange such as the exchange of women in some non-Western cultures are determined by this underlying structure of reciprocity, as are kinship relationships in some cultures.

What exactly makes the principle of reciprocity work? Sociologist Georg Simmel (1908) argued that feelings of faithfulness and gratitude play a crucial role in sustaining reciprocity in human relationships and establishing social cohesion. Gratitude is, in Simmel's words, "the moral memory of mankind," and the motivation it creates to give gifts in return is essential for establishing and maintaining social relations. Another sociologist, Alvin Gouldner (1960), explored the meaning of reciprocity as a mechanism to start and sustain social relationships. Because reciprocity is based on strong normative feelings and social expectations, it reduces one's hesitancy to be the first to give in a relationship and thus enables the creation of social interaction and the development of the exchange process.

See also: SOCIOLOGY OF EMOTIONS; SYMPATHY

Bibliography

Cheal, David. (1988). *The Gift Economy*. Cambridge, Eng.: Cambridge University Press.

Cheal, David. ([1987] 1996). "Showing Them You Love Them: Gift Giving and the Dialectic of Intimacy." In *The Gift: An*

Interdisciplinary Perspective, ed. Aafke Komter. Amsterdam: Amsterdam University Press.

Ekstein, Rudolf. (1978). "Psychoanalysis, Sympathy and Altruism." In *Altruism, Sympathy, and Helping*, ed. Lauren Wispé. New York: Academic Press.

Freud, Anna. ([1936] 1946). *The Ego and the Mechanisms of Defence*, tr. Cecil Baines. New York: International Universities Press.

Gouldner, Alvin W. ([1960] 1996). "The Norm of Reciprocity: A Preliminary Statement." In *The Gift: An Interdisciplinary Perspective*, ed. Aafke Komter. Amsterdam: Amsterdam University Press.

Komter, Aafke, ed. (1996). *The Gift: An Interdisciplinary Perspective*. Amsterdam: Amsterdam University Press.

Lévi-Strauss, Claude. ([1949] 1969). *The Elementary Structures of Kinship*, tr. James Harle Bell, John Richard von Sturmer, and Rodney Needham. Boston: Beacon Press.

Lévi-Strauss, Claude. ([1965] 1996). "The Principle of Reciprocity." In *The Gift: An Interdisciplinary Perspective*, ed. Aafke Komter. Amsterdam: Amsterdam University Press.

Malinowski, Bronislaw. ([1922] 1950). *Argonauts of the Western Pacific: An Account of the Native Enterprise and Adventure in the Archipelagoes of Melanesian New Guinea*. London: Routledge.

Mauss, Marccl. ([1923] 1990). *The Gift: The Form and Reason for Exchange in Archaic Societies*, tr. W. D. Halls. London: Routledge.

Schwartz, Barry. ([1967] 1996). "The Social Psychology of the Gift." In *The Gift: An Interdisciplinary Perspective*, ed. Aafke Komter. Amsterdam: Amsterdam University Press.

Simmel, Georg. ([1908] 1996). "Faithfulness and Gratitude." In *The Gift: An Interdisciplinary Perspective*, ed. Aafke Komter. Amsterdam: Amsterdam University Press.

Aafke Elisabeth Komter

GRIEF

Grief may be defined as the sorrow, mental distress, emotional agitation, sadness, suffering, and awareness of loss that follows a death or other loss. This definition is a start toward understanding grief, but it is important to remember that there are enormous differences among people in how they feel, what they think, and how they behave following a loss. The differences are related to the relationship ended by the loss, how the loss came about, the bereaved person's culture, gender, and social situation, previous experience with loss, and much more. In addition, grief is not only not the same from person to person, it is often not the same for a grieving person from one time to another.

The list of feelings commonly experienced in grief would certainly include depression, sorrow, loneliness, anxiety, guilt, anger, and fear. Many people feel spiritual feelings. In fact, a grieving person may experience almost any conceivable emotion. For example, some people in certain contexts laugh at major losses, and people who find comfort in sexual contact may experience sexual feelings during a time of loss. Therefore,

trying to understand grief by listing feelings that are common following a loss is not very helpful in understanding any specific grieving person.

Trying to understand grief by listing feelings that are common is also misleading because grieving people often feel their feelings as blends—not sorrow but perhaps sorrow/anger, not depression but perhaps depression/loneliness/searching. Also, any list of feelings comes out of a specific culture and language. Yet cultures differ enormously in how grieving people are likely to behave, think, and feel, and languages differ enormously in the terms used to describe feelings of grief. In fact, the words used in one language to describe grief feelings do not necessarily translate into another language. Personal languages and experiences may get in the way when an individual tries to understand grief in another culture. For example, trying to understand a bereaved Iranian's feelings of martyrdom and of identification with religious martyrs may be harder if the observer keeps trying to fit those feelings into the framework of feelings from a non-Iranian culture.

It is also important, in understanding grief, not to think that there is a clear line between feelings and thoughts. The line between feelings and thoughts is rarely clear. Grieving people may experience confusion as both an emotional feeling and as a state of mind. They may be preoccupied with thoughts about what they have lost or with how the loss could have been prevented, and with those thoughts can come aching grief or many other feelings or feeling blends. Grieving people may think they are in contact with someone close to them who died, and with that belief may come feelings ranging from reassurance to terror.

The long list of behaviors that are common in grief includes restlessness, keeping others at a distance, avoiding or seeking out reminders of the deceased, sighing, crying, eating and sleeping more than (or less than) before the loss, and using alcohol or other "medicators" of emotional discomfort.

It is also important to be cautious about using someone's experience of loss as a way of defining what she

---

Donald Hall has written a poetic chronicle of his wife's dying of leukemia and of his grieving for a year after she died. The poetry collection, Without *(1998), has two main sections: the intense caring for her in the knowledge that her death was immanent, and the grieving after she was gone. Hall vividly describes the emptiness that was caused by her loss and the many sudden "up shorts" he experiences when she is not in her habitual places.*

or he is grieving. People are not always aware that something is a loss for them, and yet it may affect them as a loss. For example, there are losses that are defined for a person as a good thing—things like graduation or having a baby—but they are still losses. A person may not recognize the losses that come with graduating (and leaving home, friends, family, and familiar routine) or having a baby (who may be adored but who certainly changes every aspect of daily life), and yet with those gains come losses. Those losses may be grieved in ways not recognized as grief by the person doing the grieving or the people around that person. Or if the grief is recognized and acknowledged, it may puzzle the person and others who do not understand why there should be grief when something defined as good has occurred.

Also, what is a loss for one person is not always a loss for another. Or even if a loss is a loss for everyone, it may have very different meanings from one person to another. So one person may not experience a given situation as a loss while someone else may experience the same situation as an intense loss. For example, in some heterosexual couples a miscarriage might be grieved intensely by the female partner and not at all by the male. And even if both individuals grieve the loss, it may have very different meanings for the female than for the male. For example, a miscarriage might be seen by the man as the loss of a planned future, but a future that may be easily adjusted to accommodate new plans. Whereas for the woman, it might be seen as the death of a known and loved child, a loss that might be grieved for a lifetime.

In addition, there are areas of oppression and hardship that many people may not think of as matters of grief, but it is easy to see the losses if one looks for them. And with the losses there is the likelihood of grieving. Oppression-based losses include losses due to discrimination, racism, homophobia, sexism, ageism, classism, or ethnocentrism. Hardship-based losses include the loss of a job, the loss of a home, poor performance in school, or the end of a love relationship. The remainder of this entry focuses primarily on grief resulting from a death, but what is said about grief applies to losses of all sorts, including losses that might not be widely recognized as losses.

Basic Components

One way to think about an emotion is that it is essentially biological or that it is so built into the human species that most humans will feel it the same way. Thirst, if thirst can be considered an emotion, is like that. There is a physiology to thirst, so with rare exceptions almost all humans will feel thirst in the same way. There are basic components to thirst: dryness in the mouth, longing for water, aversion to salt, and so on.

Some people may think that grief is like thirst. They may view grief as being essentially biological and built into humans so that most people will feel it. And yet there is an enormous range of human grief feelings. There are cultural, social, family, religious, and other differences in what counts as a loss and what feelings are expressed and presumably felt following a loss.

In making the biological case for grief, people can point to obvious physical changes in grief, such as changes in neuroendocrine and immune function. They can also say that humans are a social species. Human connections are so important that the end, or possible end, of a connection produces what could be called a biological reaction that at one level seems designed to try to restore the connection—people grieve in order to reconnect. At another level grief represents how important the closest connections are to people. Humans also are biological organisms in valuing what meets biological needs, and humans can be said to grieve being deprived of what meets those needs. In fact, something like grief can be seen in many nonhuman mammals. In this way, a case can be made that there is a strong biological element in grieving.

In making the case against a biology of grief, people can say that there are enormous cultural differences. A grieving person from the culture of Bali in Indonesia is likely to maintain a happy exterior following a major loss and will be encouraged to do this by friends and relatives. A Balinese will be encouraged to minimize or shrug off the death of a lover, close relative, or close friend. That Balinese do not fully succeed, that internally they may be hurting enormously, gets back to the biological nature of loss. But that they ordinarily succeed very well at maintaining a smooth exterior says a lot about the power of culture and the mind to shape grief.

Grief Distinguished from Related Emotions

With grief so much a blend of feelings and of different feelings from person to person, culture to culture, and situation to situation, it is difficult to distinguish grief from related emotions. Grief is not a feeling with distinct boundaries. For many people in many situations there is no clear boundary or no boundary at all between grief and pain, sadness, mourning, depression, sorrow, longing, rage, disappointment, frustration, anxiety, fear, guilt, self-reproach, or other feelings. But some distinctions are recognized by many who study grief or who counsel bereaved people. In understanding grief it is particularly useful to explore the distinctions between grief on the one hand and pain, mourning, and depression on the other. The distinctions are important to some who write about grief, and understanding the ways in which the distinctions are difficult is educational.

People sometimes use the word *pain* in talking about feelings of grief. This is sometimes a way of saying that the grief is like physical pain, but it is emotional. Emotional pain is as unpleasant as physical pain, is something one wants to medicate and stop, heals slowly, and leaves a scar. But in grief, people often literally feel pain—headache, stomachache, an aching jaw, aching muscles—so the distinction between emotional pain and physical pain is blurred.

People sometimes use the word *mourning* in talking about grief. But some scholars try to draw a distinction between grief and mourning. They would say that mourning is what is required by culture and custom after a death or other major loss. These outward signs of mourning might include wearing mourning clothing or staying away from joyous events for a specific length of time. Grief, in contrast, is the feeling not coerced by culture and custom.

Depression is another term that sometimes is used interchangeably with the term *grief*. But depression can come from many sources other than loss, and it does not necessarily involve the sadness that comes with grief. Depression is a feeling of being emotionally down and flat, of having no energy and little interest in things. Grieving people sometimes are given prescription antidepressants, and the antidepressant medication seems to make the grieving less intense. Although many people who are grieving say that they feel depressed and seem to others to be depressed, there are other grieving people who show no signs of depression.

How Grief is Experienced and Expressed

There is an enormous literature communicating people's written or spoken words about their experiences of grief. The literature includes many powerful and moving statements that eloquently and poignantly describe the pain, devastation, and power of grief. For example, Rafael Karsten (1935, p. 457) recorded the following grief experience of a woman who was a member of a South American Indian group called the Jivaro:

O my dear husband, why have you left me alone, why have you abandoned me? How happily we have passed the years together in harmony, until cruel fate and the *tunchi* of the treacherous enemy separated us! You will never again wake me in the morning with your speech, when you were cooking your tobacco water and guayusa at the fire! . . . Now you lie here mute and lifeless. Your mouth

has ceased speaking, your arm is paralyzed for ever. O, dear me, what will become of me?

Another version of mourning for a lost husband comes from the June 26, 1822, entry in the diary of Susan Mansfield Huntington:

Have been reading over some of my old letters to my beloved husband, & been ready to long that the bond may be sundered wh. holds me to earth, & detains me from *him*. . . . Reading these letters (a thing wh. I have never trusted myself to do before) seems to have revived all the exclusiveness & intenseness of my love for him I once called *husband*. I am so filled with a sense of the fearfulness of my loss & the awful chasm made in my heart & affections that all on earth seems a void without him. 'I sit alone as a swallow upon the house top.' My heart turns away from all human helpers. Oh how bitter was that cup of trembling wh. God put into my hands!

In one of the most famous and influential personal descriptions of grief in the English language, C. S. Lewis described in *A Grief Observed* (1961, p. 30) his reaction to the loss of his wife, who had died from cancer:

It's not true that I'm always thinking of H. Work and conversation make that impossible. But the times when I'm not are perhaps my worst. For then, though I have forgotten the reason, there is spread over everything a vague sense of wrongness, of something amiss. Like in those dreams where nothing terrible occurs . . . but the atmosphere, the taste, of the whole thing is deadly. . . . I hear a clock strike and some quality it always had before has gone out of the sound. What's wrong with the world to make it so flat, shabby, worn-out looking? Then I remember.

The literature on grief, however, is not limited to the loss of a spouse. Paul C. Rosenblatt (1990, p. 105) reported the grief experienced by a woman whose Minnesota family had lost its farm:

I totally fell apart, just totally, completely, physically, mentally, totally. . . . I cried all the time. I mean we would sit down at lunch with the kids and I would cry. And we would go to church and the tears would just roll. I would go to extension meetings and I would cry. . . . It meant so much to us, and we worked so hard. All of our goals and all of our dreams were out the window. That was really hard; that was the hard thing of it. It seemed so unfair.

These are but four examples of the countless descriptions of grief that are available in the literature. But throughout the various accounts of grief, there is a sense of human commonality, with people from very different cultures, time periods, and walks of life expressing feelings that ring true to most if not all humans. That literature also provides a sense of how different grief can be from person to person, culture to culture, and time period to time period.

Theories of Grieving

Sigmund Freud, in his essay "Mourning and Melancholia" (1917), wrote that when someone dies people begin to withdraw emotional attachment from that person, but they struggle because it is difficult and painful to back away from an emotional attachment and yet realistically the person is no longer available to them. The pulling away, Freud said, is done bit by bit, over considerable time and with much energy. During this period, individuals think repeatedly about the person who died. The emotional detachment goes slowly because people must deal with each memory and hope connected to the person who died, and that cannot possibly be done all at once. Eventually, perhaps after months, perhaps after years, people become free to invest their thinking and emotional attachment elsewhere.

John Bowlby, in *Attachment and Loss* (1980), offered the image of the crying infant separated from its mother as a model for how to understand grief. For an infant, crying often succeeds in restoring the attachment. And grief, Bowlby argues, has that same quality, with grieving entangled in a process of longing for, searching for, and attempting to restore contact with the person who has died.

J. William Worden, in *Grief Counseling and Grief Therapy* (1991), lays out what he considers to be the four tasks for a grieving person. These are to accept the reality of the loss, to experience the pain of grief, to adjust to an environment in which the deceased is missing, and to withdraw emotional energy and reinvest it in another relationship. These four tasks encompass what Worden considers to be normal grieving and are a guide to what sorts of help a bereaved person might need who is having difficulty in dealing with a death.

There are many theories of stages in grieving. Colin Murray Parkes, in *Bereavement* (1972), is perhaps the most influential stage theorist of grieving. Stage theories say that in grief for a major loss there is usually an initial period of numbness or disbelief, followed by a period of intense grieving, followed by one or more stages in what might be called a recovery process, followed by a stage of resolving (or fully coming to terms) with the loss. Experts disagree about stages. Some say that the stage idea can cause trouble because grief is often a back and forth thing rather than an orderly progression through stages. And for major losses, many people never fully come to the end of grieving. The pain will come back again and again. (Parkes uses the term *pangs* to refer to this return of strong feelings of grief.)

Grieving can be thought of as the development of a narrative. Many grieving people think repeatedly of the person who died, their relationship with the person, the death, their feelings, and what to make of their life now. Often they talk over important aspects of these things again and again with others. In the process, they develop a story or set of stories. A story gives meaning to all that has happened, defining the person who died, the cause of death, the bereaved person, and the bereaved person's past and present relationship with the person who died. Until the story comes together, a grieving person remains confused, disoriented, and unconfident. Having a story can be thought of as something like healing. However, the story a person comes to is never the final word; the story may change often. But still, having a story is a kind of coming to terms with the death.

Various grief therapists and grief researchers—for example, Therese Rando, in *Grief, Dying, and Death: Clinical Interventions for Caregivers* (1984)—have written about pathologies of grief. These include grieving too little, grieving for too long, delayed grieving, denial that the loss happened, grieving to the point of feeling suicidal, and grieving too much for what most people would experience as an insignificant loss. The idea of grief pathologies can be helpful in deciding who would benefit from clinical intervention. But some grief experts have strong reservations about the idea of grief pathology. They argue that pathologizing certain kinds of grieving overlooks how much personal, ethnic, and cultural diversity there is in the world. What is pathology by one culture's standards may be perfectly normal, even desirable, by the standards of another. What is pathological given one person's circumstances may be perfectly normal given another person's circumstances. They also argue that the idea of pathology can mislead individuals into thinking that they know what is best for others when they do not. In fact, grief researchers learn more every year about how extreme normal grief can be for major losses. For example, there once was a rule of thumb that a person should be close to being finished with grieving a year after a major loss, and now it is known that the rule of thumb fits very few people. In fact, for major losses, strong feelings of grief can return repeatedly for years, perhaps even for a lifetime. Similarly, grief scholars once thought there was something very wrong with people who did very little outward grieving or who did not talk about a major loss, and now it is clear that a very large percentage of Americans and Europeans (men more than women) grieve that way. Clinical work with grieving people—grief therapy—can be of immense value. And many of the leading clinicians hold firmly to ideas of grief pathology, but effective grief therapy can occur without com-

In the Haktong-ni area of Korea on August 28, 1950, a grief-stricken American infantryman, whose friend has been killed in action, is comforted by another soldier, while a corpsman methodically fills out casualty tags in the background. (Corbis)

paring a person's way of grieving to some standard of what is healthy or not and what is good or bad.

Grief is often thought of as an individual phenomenon. After all, it is the individual's internal feelings, facial expressions, words, and actions that are looked at in deciding that he or she is grieving. But now many grief researchers say that grief must be understood in terms of how it plays out in families and other social contexts. It is in these contexts that meanings are made about the person who died, about the death, and about each person's grieving. Social relationships regulate how and when emotions are expressed.

Families must often wrestle with the task of whether or how to replace the emotional and practical roles the person who died carried out in the family. Grieving family members can be simultaneously very needy and not in a good position to meet the needs of other family members. That means that when a death occurs in the family, family members can feel that they have lost each other as well as the person who died. Looking at a grieving person in isolation from the family, much will be missed that would aid in understanding how the person is grieving.

Family members who are grieving must work hard to understand, tolerate, and accommodate their differences in the timing, pattern, nature, and intensity of grieving. People always differ in grieving. For example, following the death of a parent, one offspring may feel that the death is a great disaster and that the parent who died was a saint. Another offspring may feel relief that a long illness and decline had finally ended and see the parent who died as someone who was often hurtful. A family task in grieving is to live with and support one another despite the differences. In coming to terms with a loss and developing meanings about it, family members would do well to understand and accept their differences in meanings.

The family perspective on grieving shades into theories of the social construction of reality. From the perspective of these theories, all of reality is constantly being created, recreated, and modified in social interactions. That reality involves everything with which a person deals, including the person's sense of self, the person's feelings and moods, the past, the present, the future, what is good and what is not, the meaning of work, the meaning of family, and the meaning of every relationship. For a bereaved person, the construction of reality includes the meaning of the death, the meaning of grief, the relationship the person had with the person who died, the meaning of human mortality, and much more. Related to the notion of reality being different in different social settings, Janice Winchester Nadeau, in *Families Making Sense of Death* (1997), showed that people may give rather different meanings to a family death when they are with other family members than when they are away from other family members.

There are enormous differences across cultures in grieving, though in every culture most people obviously have feelings of grief over the deaths of people close to them. Understanding cultural differences in grieving begins with the realization that deaths have meanings that differ from culture to culture. For example, in one culture a child's dying may be considered a blessing from God and a cause for prayerful thanks, in another a martyrdom caused by an enemy and requiring revenge, and in another a sign that the child lacked sufficient will to live. Also, there are enormous cultural differences in how much mourning is elaborated and required. At one extreme, many cultures in the United States simply acknowledge the loss immediately after it occurs and have a single funeral ritual. At the other extreme, there are cultural groups that hold a series of funeral ceremonies over a period of a year or more. During the time in which these ceremonies occur, the principle mourners may be expected to dress differently from other people, to limit their activities and contact with others, and to express their feelings of loss. They may also receive considerable emotional, material, and spiritual support from others during this time.

There are many theories of grief that detail how people deal with specific kinds of loss. For example, there are theories about disenfranchised grief (when the culture does not recognize that the grieving person has a right to grieve), grief after divorce, grief following losses resulting from a natural disaster like a flood or hurricane, grief following an AIDS death, and grief resulting from experiencing infertility. Although there may be common feelings involved with all of these kinds of loss, there are also unique feelings and thoughts and social issues to deal with.

Effects of Grief

In the depths of grief, the individual is dominated by grief. Thoughts of the loss swamp other thoughts. Social relationships, work, sexuality, eating, sleeping, everything becomes pervaded by grief. In that sense, grief is one of the most powerful of emotions. Consequently, grief can cause a great amount of trouble for a person. The person may lose social support partly because of the feelings and actions of bereavement (though it is also true that many people draw away from somebody who is grieving). A grieving person may be sleep deprived, eat poorly, get in trouble at work or in school, and having many other problems.

How to interact with a grieving person is very well defined in some cultures, but for many people in the

United States it is not. Consequently many bereaved Americans find that others pull away from them immediately or soon after the first expressions of sympathy. If the others do not pull away, they often act like nothing has happened, that after the first days following the loss they expect a grieving person to be back to "normal." Such expectations do not fit the grief process and can cause trouble for a bereaved person.

In America, tens of millions of people are grieving at any given time. Their grief makes them less available to others, less productive on the job, and less able to be attentive to parents, siblings, children, lovers, or spouses. The neediness of a grieving person can be a call to others to try to provide support, and many grieving people find support among family and friends. But in America there is so much professionalization of help that many bereaved people turn to professionals (particularly counselors, physicians, and clergy) for help. Professionals differ enormously in their competence to support a grieving person, and all too often grief is dealt with in the medical model (grief as an illness to be cured) or with some other approach that is insensitive to the long-term process of normal grief. American society also puts enormous pressure on grieving people to return quickly to acting like they are not grieving and to keep their feelings to themselves. A critic might say that such pressures make all Americans insensitive, ignorant, and ill prepared to deal with personal losses or the losses of others.

What can a person do to be supportive of another who is grieving? The first thing to do is to acknowledge the loss and to express sympathy. In expressing sympathy, it is much better to say something like, "I'm sorry this happened." Do not say, "I know how you feel," because that is not the case. A person who also had a relationship with the deceased might usefully express sympathy by saying what the person who died meant to him or her, "He was a good person. I had good times with him. I'll never forget him making home movies about us when we were kids." Do not be surprised or put off if a grieving individual is not tactful in responding to social contact. Grief does not make a person socially graceful. Do not expect a griev-

> *Anton Chekhov's "Misery" (1921) describes an elderly cab driver, Iona, who has just lost his son to a sudden illness. Every time he tries to talk about his son's death with his passengers, they turn away from him and refuse to hear his story. Finally, since he cannot find anyone to whom he can tell his grief, Iona goes to the barn and talks to his little mare, who gives him at least some animal warmth and sympathy.*

ing person to share a lot, and do not expect the person to be over the grief quickly. Even if a person's grief makes you feel uncomfortable, do not pressure the person to get over grief. And even if a person's not expressing grief makes you feel uncomfortable, do not pressure the person to grieve more openly. Do not assume that if grief is not visible it is not there or will not occur later. It is quite appropriate to ask, "How are you doing?" Do not be put off by tears or anger or extreme statements (for example, rage at God). A grieving person may have a lot to say, so be prepared to be a good listener—using the heart and soul as well as the ears. Sometimes, people who do not drop away from a person who is grieving when others do may find themselves more important in the bereaved person's life than they were before. The opportunity to say a few words (or to hear a few words from someone else) may be enormously supportive to the bereaved. Support can also be demonstrated by something as simple as a touch or a hug.

In American society, death is often understood in religious terms. For many Americans (and for many people in other societies), death is not the end of a person but a time when the person moves to another plane of existence. Consequently, many people continue to have some sort of relationship with the deceased or feel that there is real hope of reunion in Heaven. That does not mean grief goes away, but it does affect the grieving process. For some people, prayer becomes a part of grief. Others may change how they act or begin to observe religious practices in an attempt to increase their chances of a reunion in Heaven.

People who are grieving should be patient and gentle with themselves. They should let the process happen. Bereaved people do not have to talk about things, but many, at some point, find it healing to talk with someone they trust.

See also: ABANDONMENT; ATTACHMENT; BOWLBY, JOHN; EMPATHY; FREUD, SIGMUND; HOPELESSNESS; LONELINESS; PAIN; SADNESS; SYMPATHY

Bibliography

Bowlby, John. (1980). *Attachment and Loss, Vol. 3: Loss.* New York: Basic Books.

Cochran, Larry, and Claspell, Emily. (1987). *The Meaning of Grief.* Westport, CT: Greenwood.

Corr, Charles A., and Balk, David E., eds. (1996). *Handbook of Adolescent Death and Bereavement.* New York: Springer.

Counts, David R., and Counts, Dorothy, eds. (1991). *Coping with the Final Tragedy: Cultural Variation in Dying and Grieving.* Amityville, NY: Baywood.

Doka, Kenneth J., ed. (1995). *Children Mourning, Mourning Children.* Washington, DC: Hospice Foundation of America.

Freud, Sigmund. ([1917] 1959). "Mourning and Melancholia." In *Collected Papers of Sigmund Freud, Vol. 4: Papers on Metapsy-*

chology, Papers on Applied Psychoanalysis. New York: Basic Books.

Gilbert, Kathleen R., and Smart, Laura S. (1992). *Coping with Infant or Fetal Loss: The Couple's Healing Process.* New York: Brunner/Mazel.

Good, Byron J.; DelVecchio Good, Mary-Jo; and Moradi, Robert. (1985). "The Interpretation of Iranian Depressive Illness and Dysphoric Affect." In *Culture and Depression,* ed. Arthur Kleinman and Byron J. Good. Berkeley: University of California Press.

Harvey, John H. (1996). *Embracing Their Memory: Loss and the Social Psychology of Storytelling.* Boston: Allyn & Bacon.

Karsten, Rafael. (1935). *The Head-Hunters of Western Amazonas: The Life and Culture of the Jibaro Indians of Eastern Ecuador and Peru.* Helsinki: Finska Vetenskaps-Societeten.

Klass, Dennis; Silverman, Phyllis R.; and Nickman, Steven L., eds. (1996). *Continuing Bonds: New Understandings of Grief.* Washington, DC: Taylor & Francis.

Lewis, C. S. (1961). *A Grief Observed.* New York: Seabury Press.

Lopata, Helena Z. (1996). *Current Widowhood: Myths and Realities.* Thousand Oaks, CA: Sage Publications.

Mansfield Huntington, Susan. (1822). Unpublished diary manuscript, Sterling Memorial Library, Yale University.

Nadeau, Janice Winchester. (1997). *Families Making Sense of Death.* Thousand Oaks, CA: Sage Publications.

Parkes, Colin Murray. (1972). *Bereavement: Studies in Grief in Adult Life.* London: Tavistock.

Parkes, Colin Murray; Laungani, Pittu; and Young, Bill, eds. (1997). *Death and Bereavement across Cultures.* London: Routledge.

Rando, Therese A. (1984). *Grief, Dying, and Death: Clinical Interventions for Caregivers.* Champaign, IL: Research Press.

Rosenblatt, Paul C. (1990). *Farming Is in Our Blood: Farm Families in Economic Crisis.* Ames, IA: Iowa State University Press.

Rosenblatt, Paul C.; Walsh, R. Patricia; and Jackson, Douglas A. (1976). *Grief and Mourning in Cross-Cultural Perspective.* New Haven, CT: Human Relations Area Files.

Stroebe, Margaret; Gergen, Mary M.; Gergen, Kenneth J.; and Stroebe, Wolfgang. (1992). "Broken Hearts or Broken Bonds: Love and Death in Historical Perspective." *American Psychologist* 47:1205–1212.

Stroebe, Margaret S.; Stroebe, Wolfgang; and Hansson, Robert O., eds. (1993). *Handbook of Bereavement.* New York: Cambridge University Press.

Wikan, Unni. (1990). *Managing Turbulent Hearts: A Balinese Formula for Living.* Chicago: University of Chicago Press.

Worden, J. William. (1991). *Grief Counseling and Grief Therapy: A Handbook for the Mental Health Practitioner.* New York: Springer.

Paul C. Rosenblatt

GUILT

Dictionaries are relatively devoid of references to guilty *feelings* or to guilt as an *emotion.* In fact, they never discuss guilt as an emotion, and they bury references to guilty feelings deep down in their long lists that contemplate meanings of the word *guilt.* Instead, dictionaries emphasize definitions of the state of *being* guilty.

What does the state of guilt involve? The Old English word *gylt* (a primary sense of debt) has a dubious historical connection to the modern English word *guilt*, even though the two words appear similar. The modern term *guilt* seems to derive, instead, from the Old English *scyld* (debt). In his book *On the Genealogy of Morals* (1887), the philosopher Friedrich Nietzsche points out that the German word *schuld* (guilt) derived from the word *schulden* (debts). The *state* of being guilty conveys a sense of indebtedness because of a person's culpability for a failure, offense, crime, or sin.

Contemporary Western society often attaches negative *feelings* to the state of guilt. In everyday language, guilty feelings refer to one's sense of regret, remorse, tension, and anxiety about being culpable and punishable for an offense, a failure of duty, or conscience. People who *feel* guilty experience a need to repay society or individuals for their debts—be these debts merely psychological or more tangible offenses. It is important to remember, however, that a person can "be guilty" without necessarily "feeling guilty." Conversely, individuals can "feel guilty" without really being so. This lack of strict equivalence between "I am guilty" and "I feel guilty" may be an important determinant of the function that guilt serves in individuals' daily existence.

Differentiating Guilt from Related Emotions

Guilt clearly can be a negative emotion. But, how exactly does the emotion of guilt differ from other negative emotions, such as anger, fear, sadness, shame, or embarrassment? All of these negative emotions indicate that perceivers appraise an action (e.g., hitting the "delete" key on their computer) or outcome (e.g., losing an important computer file) as being inconsistent with their goals or values in a situation. Shame, embarrassment, and guilt differ qualitatively from the emotions of anger, sadness, or fear, however. Specifically, shame, embarrassment, and guilt are social, self-reflexive, self-conscious, or self-evaluative emotions. All three of these emotions involve an appraisal that the self has failed in some important respect (e.g., physical, relational, athletic, or academic competence). The elicitors, appraisals, and subjective experiences involved in shame, embarrassment, or guilt do nonetheless differ significantly.

Embarrassment is a very public reaction to specific, often uncontrollable, events. People who are embarrassed blush, feel awkward, and are extremely concerned about what others think of them. Like embarrassment, shame can be a public reaction, but it certainly is not always felt in an audience's presence. More critically, shame is a devastating experience in which people appraise the global self as being person-ally responsible for violating an important ideal, sometimes feel immoral, and invariably feel that there is something fundamentally defective, inferior, or bad about them as a person. People who are ashamed manifest one of two distinct reactions. Either they feel helpless, shrink away from contact, and hide, or they lash out at the environment with rage or what Helen Block Lewis (1971) called "humiliated fury." Some social scientists (although certainly not all), in fact, differentiate shame from guilt by invoking the "globally bad self" versus "specifically bad deed" distinction. In these scientists' views, people feel ashamed about who they are but guilty about what they think they did or failed to do.

Functions of Guilt

Why do people even have the capacity to experience a negative emotion such as guilt? From a functionalist perspective, emotions help regulate one's own and others' behaviors. Each emotion communicates its own distinct message to the individual and society about valued standards and goals, likes and dislikes, as well as views of the self, others, and the situations they encounter. The capacity to experience and express guilt thus serves several vital individual and social functions. Guilt signals an awareness of appropriate standards of behavior. Guilt can prevent undesirable actions from occurring. It can be used as a power ploy by less influential members in a relationship. Guilt can actually help victims feel better because the emotional distress is now shared by the perpetrator, and expressions of guilt can reaffirm one's worthiness as a relationship partner or member of society at large.

The moral and social control functions of guilt are so crucial that it is terrifying to imagine a world devoid of this emotion. Fortunately, guilt is not a rare emotional commodity in daily life. In point of fact, Susan Shimanoff (1984) reports that regret (which includes guilt) makes the "top two list" of the emotions that are most often talked about by married couples. Although people report guilt less frequently than other emotions, Roy Baumeister and his associates (1994, 1995) found that individuals spend about two hours of each waking day "feeling" guilty. One college student described her most recent experience of guilt as follows:

> My boyfriend and I meet after classes for lunch. Last week when he came, a guy from my psychology class had seen me sitting here and sat down to ask me how I had done on my last test. My boyfriend walked in and saw us talking and laughing. When I introduced him to the guy in my class, I didn't say he was my boyfriend. After introducing the two of them, the guy from class left and my boyfriend made some lame excuse and left also. My boyfriend was

pretty upset and made me feel very guilty. Told me I should date others if I wanted and he was unsure about me and my feelings for him. I felt like I had almost betrayed him. He always introduces me as his girlfriend, and if he had done what I did to him to me, I would have been hurt. I feel better now 'cause we have since talked things out and both apologized. It was a good learning experience.

This description illustrates the commonplace nature of guilty feelings, as well as the important functions they serve.

Elicitors of Guilt

What kinds of events elicit guilt? People typically think that guilt results from a *serious* moral breach, such as lying, cheating, stealing, or outright attempts to hurt another person. In fact, individuals actually report feeling guilty about a much wider array of standard violations (including failures in the academic, spiritual, and social realms).

The above narrative of a college student's guilty feelings reveals that many guilt-eliciting standard violations center on how actions or inactions negatively affect other people. There are countless ways in which people can disadvantage others. They may reap disproportionate benefits, act inconsiderately or selfishly, fail to provide assistance, take unfair advantage, wield excess power, or hurt others' feelings or not spend enough time with them. In fact, Kristin Sommer and Baumeister (1997) report that neglect of a relationship partner frequently elicits feelings of guilt.

Appraisals and Actions Involved in Guilt

Certain appraisals are known to arouse feelings of guilt. Most important, guilty feelings involve perceptions that one can or should prevent or control a standard violation and will be *held* responsible (even though the person might not be *objectively* responsible). Feelings of guilt can thus be experienced in anticipation of committing an act, such as cheating on a test. Individuals feel anticipatory guilt because they perceive themselves to be capable of avoiding, being morally obligated to avoid, and being punishable for failing to avoid a wrongdoing. These types of appraisals can thus prevent one from ever succumbing to a temptation. Individuals do not, however, always withstand temptation, and they sometimes accidentally perpetrate a wrong. In these cases, guilt is associated with various action tendencies that reflect concerns with the victims' welfare, preserving relationships, and avoiding severe punishment or reprisals. When a transgression has occurred (sometimes unwittingly), post-transgression guilt frequently promotes behaviors that involve confession, repair, apology, or avowals to avoid committing the same mistake in the future. In essence, people reestablish parity—that is, they reduce their sense of indebtedness—in relationships by reparation, physical punishment, or the emotional punishment of guilt itself. The desire to set things right indicates that guilt involves a kind of "moral or emotional bookkeeping." It is not surprising that Gerold Mikula and his colleagues (1998) demonstrated that people perceive guilty feelings to be much more justified than other feelings, such as anger, disgust, fear, or sadness.

Expressive or Physiological Aspects of Guilt

Exactly how outsiders know when people feel guilty (apart from a confession or observers' projecting their feelings onto the situation) is a good question. A handful of studies nonetheless indicate that observers can reliably discern when someone actually feels guilty, although the cues they use to detect guilt are unclear. Charles Darwin (1872) observed in his survey of experts around the world that the eyes were almost always referred to in descriptions of guilt—the guilty person was said to avoid looking at the accuser or to give the accuser stolen looks, while the eyes of the guilty person wavered from side to side and the eyelids were lowered.

Few social scientists have studied the expressive features of guilt, and many question whether there are expressive or physiological characteristics unique to this emotion. However, consistent with the idea that guilt shares an affinity with anxiety and thereby involves physiological activation, Karen Barrett (1995) points out that heart rate and skin conductance are elevated when a person feels guilt, and these signs are accompanied by irregular respiration and a narrow, tense, but relatively full voice. Donald Nathanson (1992) notes that although psychopharmacological studies of guilt have been undertaken only since the 1980s, they already offer intriguing discoveries. For example, one study showed that depriving patients of tryptophan can exacerbate a variety of symptoms, including feelings of guilt.

Guilt-Trips

While outsiders can be sensitive to whether or not a person feels guilty, they can also be adept at inducing guilt. People try to make others feel guilty (i.e., guilt-trip) for various reasons: to persuade them to behave in specific ways, to gain compliance with a certain wish, to restore emotional balance in the dyad, and to achieve power. Guilt-tripping others is thus a powerful tool for exerting influence. Guilt appeals are used not

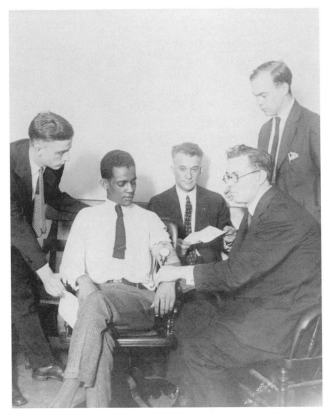

A murder suspect in the 1920s undertakes a lie detector test, or as it was called then a truth detector test. Like a modern-day polygraph, this sphygmomanometer, measured changes in human arterial blood pressure, which some people believe to be physiological evidence of psychological guilt or panic. The accuracy of these measurements in determining guilt is often called into question because feeling guilty does not always mean being guilty and being guilty does not always mean feeling guilty. (Corbis/Bettmann)

only in close relationships but by industry, government, politicians, and religious organizations. Bruce Huhmann and Timothy Brotherton (1997) demonstrate that verbal and visual guilt appeals are prevalent in television commercials, newspaper or magazine advertisements, public service announcements, health pamphlets, mailings from charitable organizations, telemarketing programs, and sales pitches for various products and services.

Anita Vangelisti and her colleagues (1991), Mica Estrada-Hollenbeck and Todd Heatherton (1998), Sommer and Baumeister (1997), as well as Maria Miceli (1992), have analyzed the various shapes that guilt-trips can take. Using Miceli's classification of guilt induction tactics, Tamara Ferguson and Heidi Eyre (1998) demonstrated that some guilt-trips are more effective or at least induce longer lasting feelings of

guilt than others. In Miceli's view, a very assertive and intentional form of guilt induction involves tactics that directly accuse or verbally reproach a person for some mistake (e.g., "How dare you treat me this way?!"). People typically use direct, assertive methods to thwart the culprit's own conscious (or possibly unconscious) avoidance of guilty feelings. Using direct, assertive guilt induction is known to arouse short-lived feelings of guilt. The guilt dissipates relatively quickly, partly because direct assertion often gets the perpetrator to apologize or make amends. Using direct, assertive methods to arouse guilt is, however, somewhat risky because they attack the perpetrators' self-image and may cause them to respond defensively (e.g., denying the accusation; lashing out in anger).

A second type of guilt induction involves indirectly confronting perpetrators with the injury done. The inducer's own nonverbal cues (e.g., a sad look, crying, turning away) or another's overheard but supposedly "private" remarks (e.g., "Did you hear what Merrell said about Lynch?") suggest that the perpetrator's actions caused misfortune for the inducer. Although indirect messages effectively avoid implying that the inducer is being manipulative, they may not arouse strong or long-lasting feelings of guilt because they can fail to communicate just how much the inducer has suffered *or* how responsible the perpetrator really is. Because they are so indirect, these strategies may also invoke self-defensive coping efforts (e.g., denying or downplaying) rather than active attempts to rectify the misdeed.

The third (and very treacherous) form of guilt induction, which is referred to as the adoptive method, involves people actually adopting the perpetrator's perspective (which, of course, is to not feel guilty!). Thus, inducers act as though perpetrators are not really guilty or at least not *all that* guilty. They do so by, for example, forgiving recipients or turning the other cheek (e.g., "That's okay; don't sweat it."), offering justifications (e.g., "Maybe I deserved what you did."), or excuses (e.g., "Well, maybe you're just too tired to go out tonight."). There are various reasons for believing that adoptive strategies may be extremely effective in promoting long-lasting feelings of guilt. Adoptive strategies prevent perpetrators from making benign appraisals of their "guiltworthiness." The very acts of forgiveness, reinterpretation of perpetrators' actions, or turning the other cheek presuppose perpetrators' culpability and affirm inducers' morally superior status. Adoptive strategies also prevent perpetrators from effectively coping with the guilt. By forgiving and turning the other cheek, inducers maintain a psychological grip on perpetrators by disallowing execution of the normal action tendency of guilt, which is to atone, make amends, or repay the emotional debt. Of course, using adoptive methods sometimes backfires in making others feel guilty. Perpetrators may catch on to the inducer's manipulative intentions, or they may think that they really have been forgiven. Ferguson, Eyre, and their colleagues (1998), in fact, demonstrated that eighth- and especially sixth-grade children literally interpret acts of forgiveness to be letting them off the hook. They do not, therefore, report much guilt after being forgiven for a wrongdoing.

Emergence of Guilt in Development

In order for these guilt appeals to successfully meet their mark, people need to be "capable" of feeling guilty. This raises questions concerning when, how, and why guilt develops.

Sigmund Freud (1905), the father of classic psychoanalytic theory, believed that individuals are born with certain instincts or drives, including eros or libido (a desire for sexual pleasure) and thanatos (the death instinct or drive to aggress). Children experience anxiety arising from conflicts between their id impulses (e.g., a desire to masturbate or aggress against the same-sex parent) and the knowledge that others might reject or severely harm them for acting on these impulses. Their fears become internalized as a kind of moral anxiety or guilt (the superego or conscience). Freud initially saw guilt as being a kind of anxiety (motivated by fears of abandonment or punishment) that did not arise until children had resolved parentally-oriented *sexual* conflicts and thereby developed superegos. Jeffery Binder (1970) notes that Freud subsequently changed his tune on the sexual origins of guilt and came to emphasize that any behavior sanctioned by the superego could arouse "guilt-like anxiety." Freud's de-emphasis on the sexual origins of guilt actually agrees with neo-psychoanalytic theories, which highlighted guilt's social-cultural antecedents in terms of meeting various life tasks and prohibitions during the toddlerhood years. In all, these theories suggest that guilt could appear in late toddlerhood but might not fully emerge until around the age of five years.

There are similar disagreements among cognitive theorists about when guilt emerges. Some cognitivists argue that feelings of guilt are not possible until children understand that they really can *choose* between different ways of behaving. Jerome Kagan (1984) maintains that this occurs at around four years of age, but Michael Lewis (1992) places the emergence of guilt somewhat earlier, at around three years of age. Important cognitive achievements that must precede feelings of guilt include perceiving the self as a unique entity that is distinct from others; knowing that standards, rules, and goals guide behavior; being able to evaluate the self in light of these norms, and being capable of attributing a norm violation to global (shame) versus more specific (guilt) aspects of the self.

In Barrett's (1995) developmental account, guilt does not necessarily build on specific cognitive requirements. She argues instead that guilt serves certain functions in the individual's commerce with the environment (signaling that harm is undesirable and that the person wishes to make repair). What develops, according to this functionalist perspective on emotion, is the child's emotional responsiveness to the growing *number* of contexts in which guilt is a warranted response to signal to others. Barrett's research reveals behaviors that are consistent with these functions in extremely young toddlers.

Martin Hoffman (1983) emphasizes the important connections between guilt and empathy. From about two years of age onward, children begin to differentiate the self from others; show awareness of which behaviors are—or are not—appropriate; begin to evaluate outcomes in terms of standards, rules, and goals; and realize that others have feelings that their behavior can affect. The capacity to experience empathy develops first in response to a victim's distress, whether caused directly or simply witnessed by the child. In this view, the experience of guilt results from the conjunction of an empathic response to the other's distress and the juxtaposition of several realizations by children: (1) that they can be agents of harm, (2) that they can control their behavior and choose to behave in harmful or nonharmful ways, (3) that there are moral prescriptions and prohibitions regarding how people treat each other and their property, and (4) that their behavior can differ from these dictates.

The consensus of the literature on guilt seems to be that children experience at least rudimentary forms of guilt in early childhood. Although observational studies suggest that children experience guilt when they are about two to three years of age, one must also consider the age at which individuals provide reliable reports of their guilty experiences or understand components of this emotion. Ferguson and Hedy Stegge (1995, 1998) and June Tangney (1998) have noted that the word *guilt* is not part of people's active lexicon until they are about five and a half to six years of age, but many children who are seven to eight years of age can reliably differentiate guilt from shame in tasks that do not rely heavily on productive language skills.

Gender Differences in Guilt

The weight that some scientists attach to connections between empathy and guilt naturally leads to the question of whether there are gender differences in people's tendency to experience or express this emotion. Many have noted the implication of Freud's early work that females are the weaker "moral sex," which suggests that females would experience and express less guilt than males. Yet, extremely diverse and sizable literatures reveal that girls and women, much more so than boys or men, are encouraged to both feel and express guilt, especially in Western cultures.

In reviewing these literatures, Ferguson and Eyre (2000) note that it has become almost a myth that females actually experience and express greater feelings of guilt than males, particularly in adolescence and adulthood. Although stereotypes about gender-related differences in guilt are rampant, women appear to be more guilt-prone than men only on certain measures—those that portray women as violating standards of behavior that are extremely inconsistent with a feminine identity. The conditions promoting gender differences and similarities in guilt, and the consequences of gender-inconsistent expressions of guilt, desperately need further scientific scrutiny.

Cultural Differences in Guilt

In *The Chrysanthemum and the Sword* (1946), the anthropologist Ruth Benedict cataloged her World War II studies of Japanese culture, studies that had been commissioned by the U.S. government. Millie Creighton (1990) notes that Benedict was aptly criticized on various grounds but points out that she often is misinterpreted as claiming that the Japanese typified a "shame" culture in contrast to the "guilt" culture embodied by Western societies (including the United States). Several authors, including Takie Lebra (1983), have taken great pains to debunk the inaccurate cultural myths spawned by Benedict's work. The Japanese are very sensitive to feeling guilty for the plight of others. They report guilt even when they are not responsible for the suffering—even on impulse of hurting a close other and because of strong identification with and sense of obligation to the group's welfare. Although guilt is systematically found in Japanese culture, the culture *appears* to be more integrated or motivated by shame because of its collectivistic, group-oriented values, a greater desire for unity, belonging-ness, and interdependence, as opposed to Americans' zeal for greater individuality, autonomy, and defeating competitors. The Chinese also exhibit a strong social orientation in which the sense of self is firmly rooted in the group's welfare. Deborah Stipek (1998) found that Chinese participants reported feeling much guiltier (and ashamed) about someone else's untoward behavior (e.g., cheating by their brothers) than did American participants. Some cultures appear to be devoid of guilt in its more moral, obligatory sense. Michelle Rosaldo (1983) reports that the Ilongots (a

tribe in Northern Luzon of the Philippines) espouse kinship and a sense of "fellow humans" to be important values. These values appear to guide their behavior rather than any dictated, internalized, punitive *moralized* sense of conscience, guilt, ought, or obligation. In this respect, it is interesting to note that a 1983 report by the World Health Organization shows that a sense of *moral* guilt is involved in depression more in Western (e.g., Canada and Switzerland; 68%) than Eastern (e.g., Iran; 32%) societies.

Guilt appears to be experienced differently in collectivistic compared to individualistic cultures. Collectivistic societies look after larger units in the community in exchange for loyalty. A collectivist orientation is presumably represented by the cultures of Brazil, Chile, Greece, Hong Kong, and Mexico. Individualistic societies look after the self and the immediate family and, supposedly, are represented by countries such as Australia, France, Italy, the Netherlands, and the United States. In a study of twenty-four cultures, Harald Wallbott and Klaus Scherer (1995) found that collectivistic cultures (in comparison with individualistic cultures) rated guilt as lasting longer, as involving greater degrees of immorality, and as evoking greater symptoms (e.g., stomach troubles or crying/sobbing). In the same study, Wallbott and Scherer identified cultures that were high or medium in uncertainty avoidance (the degree to which cultures create relatively rigid belief systems and institutions, such as organized religion, to cope with threatening or ambiguous situations). Chile, France, Greece, Japan, Mexico, Portugal, and Spain had relatively high scores in uncertainty avoidance, while Hong Kong, India, the Netherlands, Sweden, and the United States had low uncertainty avoidance scores. Cultures that were high or medium in uncertainty avoidance (as compared to those with low scores) rated guilt as lasting longer, as being more unpleasant, and as producing certain physical symptoms or certain types of arousal to a greater extent. Clearly much more work is needed with regard to cultural appreciation of, and attitudes toward, guilt and other related emotions.

Western Evaluation of Guilt

The results of the study conducted by Wallbott and Scherer could be construed to mean that Westerners value guilt and thus feel much less threatened by it than do individuals from other cultures. In reality, Westerners manifest an ambivalent attitude toward the value of guilt. Friedrich Nietzsche stated that "guilt is the most terrible sickness that has ever raged in man," which is echoed by Nicholas Rowe's comment that "guilt is the source of sorrows, the avenging friend that follows us behind with whips and strings." In contrast,

Nadezhda Mandelstam proclaimed that "a sense of guilt is a man's greatest asset," which is echoed in the Jewish proverb that "guilt is the gift that keeps on giving."

Some of these quotes reveal that feeling guilty has received an undeservedly bad reputation, especially in Western, individualistic cultures. Western society's aversion to guilt is tellingly revealed in the titles of popular self-help books and magazine articles. Guilt is also a prevailing theme in Western philosophy, the visual artists, world literature, and film. These media tend to center on the devastating consequences of guilt, especially survivor or existential guilt.

In *The Brothers Karamazov* (1879–1880), the Russian novelist Fyodor Dostoyevsky dramatizes the guilt suffered by four brothers because of their father's murder. Dostoyevsky focuses on parallels between the emotional consequences of children defying their earthly father versus their heavenly father. He also explores how guilt arouses a need for punishment or expiation in his novel *Crime and Punishment* (1866). The central character, Raskolinov, robs and kills an elderly woman. He ultimately pays for this crime by falling in love with a young prostitute, who herself suffers from intense remorse for her way of life. Playwrights such as William Shakespeare plumb the depths of guilty despair, survivor guilt, or existential guilt in many plays. For example, Macbeth murdered his king, Duncan, thereby assuming power over the kingdom. However, Macbeth's remorse ultimately undermines his ability to lead the country in a courageous and rational fashion.

Depressive and existential forms of guilt are central refrains in the works of many Western poets. Many poets themselves have been known to suffer excruciating feelings of guilt, which are portrayed in their profound literary contributions about this emotion. The romantic poet Lord Byron was hounded by feelings of guilt over his sexual passion for his half sister, which he attempted to expiate in the drama *Manfred* (1817), and John Berryman, famous for his *77 Dream Songs* (1964), was hounded by feelings of guilt about his father's suicide. The confessional poet Anne Sexton felt guilt because of the accumulated emotional wounds suffered throughout her life, as reflected in *The Awful Rowing Toward God* (1975). Historical figures, too, suffered the weight of unbearable guilty feelings, including Tsar Alexander (for being indirectly involved in the successful conspiracy to murder his father, Paul I), Mahatma Gandhi (for his boyhood mistakes), and Thomas Jefferson (for sexual indiscretions).

Themes of excessive guilt pervade countless films. The young high school student Conrad Jared in *Ordinary People* (1980) wrestles with guilt, and almost succeeds in committing suicide, because he survived while his older brother drowned during a boating accident. Will Hunting, in the movie *Good Will Hunting* (1997), displays various self-, relational-, and societally-destructive behaviors. While he obviously expresses shame-rage in this film, he also displays perplexing and persistent feelings of guilt about the tremendous abuse and rejection he suffered as a child. In *Unforgiven* (1992), Clint Eastwood disturbingly portrays the callous violence of America's "wild west" and, through the complex character of William Munny, essentially apologizes to America for the role that his own film career played in simplistically glorifying such violence.

Modern science exhibits a conflicted attitude toward guilt. This ambivalence is fueled by contradictory findings and beliefs regarding the role that guilt plays in healthy and unhealthy human functioning. Possessing inappropriate feelings of guilt is one of several criteria that are use to diagnosis depression as defined by the American Psychiatric Association's *Diagnostic and Statistical Manual of Mental Disorders* (DSM-IV, 1994). Several authors, as reviewed by David Harder (1995) or Carolyn Zahn-Waxler and JoAnn Robinson (1995), point out how loving and caring for others can result in irrational or exaggerated experiences of guilt (such as survivor guilt) in psychotherapy patients. These feelings of guilt—when unresolved—often activate repetitive restorative and/or self-punitive actions.

Evidence in the psychological literature connects what has been labeled as guilt to a long list of clinical symptoms, disorders, or full-blown syndromes. A short-list of the problems in which guilt is presumably implicated in actual studies includes anxiety-based problems (such as obsessive-compulsive disorder); various types of depressive disorders (excluding borderline depression); depressive episodes associated with early child death, parental death, or placing an elderly parent in residential care; the suicide of a child or loved one; a child or loved one afflicted with a physical disability or disease (including traumatic brain injury and Alzheimer's); infertility; premature birth, abortions, or miscarriages; relinquishing a child

Edgar Allan Poe's "The Tell-Tale Heart" (1850) describes a madman who kills an old man because he could not stand the sight of the old man's eye. The madman dismembers the body and hides it under the floor boards. When the police arrive, he acts as if nothing had happened, but his guilty conscience convinces him that he hears the dead man's heart beating louder and louder until finally he is driven to confess the murder.

for adoption; neurotic perfectionism; binge eating; post-traumatic stress disorder (such as survivor guilt elicited by child and spousal abuse, transportation disasters, war, or terrorism); suicidal ideation; schizotypal, avoidance, dependent personality or dissociative identity disorders; and having an alcoholic parent.

There is an important flip side to the coin, however. The DSM-IV also treats the absence of guilt as one feature of societally-threatening disorders that are often diagnosed in adult criminal populations or children at risk for becoming criminals (e.g., antisocial personality disorder, conduct disorder). Adults diagnosed with antisocial personality disorder differ from "normal" comparison groups in their attributions of emotion. Psychopaths actually declare happiness or indifference about wrongdoings, whereas comparison groups report elevated feelings of guilt.

Several researchers are understandably skeptical of the view that guilt is involved in psychopathology. Tangney and her colleagues (1995) assert instead that guilt is debilitating only when it is fused with shame. Several authors have convincingly shown that purely guilt-prone individuals are more empathic, helpful, better at taking the perspective of others, endorse a religion-as-quest orientation, constructively deal with anger, and perform better in the social and academic realms. Adults, adolescents, and older children who score high on certain measures of guilt show few antisocial tendencies and appear well adjusted on various indices of psychological health. People who score high in shame, in contrast, manifest the kinds of psychological, social, and academic problems that traditionally have been attributed to guilt. Considered as a whole, these results support the conclusion that guilt, unlike shame, is strongly related to indices of well-being and adjustment across a wide age range.

Ferguson and Stegge (1998) urge caution in accepting these findings as the "full story," however. They emphasize that the studies verifying the adaptive (i.e., positive) value of guilt have assessed this emotion using measures that represent unambiguous standard violations about which most individuals probably *should* feel guilty and in which it is easy to repair the wrongs done. In essence, the *feelings* of guilt in these studies are equivalent to really *being* guilty. There are other measures that reveal the close association between unjustified guilty *feelings* and maladaptive (i.e., negative) tendencies. These measures include certain behavioral observations, parental reports, reports by friends, or unstructured reports. Each of these measures allows the expression of painful experiences following real or perceived transgressions. In other words, the person may *feel* guilty while not *actually* being so. Using these types of assessments, Zahn-Waxler, Kochanska, Ferguson, and their colleagues (as reviewed by Ferguson and Stegge, 1998) show that pre-school-age and older children (especially girls) exhibit unhealthy guilt-related beliefs and behaviors. These include heightened levels of empathy, a misplaced sense of responsibility, and unrealistic ideas about their own ability to produce or reduce another person's plight. The guilt-behavior links shown in these studies and others do not bode well for the children's future adjustment.

Conclusion

Is guilt adaptive? Yes. Is guilt maladaptive? Yes. Both assertions align neatly with the warning by Lee Anna Clark and David Watson (1994) that emotions in *themselves* (including guilt) are never dysfunctional; they simply "are." There are various contexts in which people feel guilt and walk away having successfully absolved themselves of this feeling because certain conditions promote this very attitude and outcome. These conditions include a person's recognition that it is *really* wrong to unnecessarily hurt another person. They also include environments or cultures that teach people that guilt can genuinely be relieved through apology, reparation, or avoidance of similar situations in the future and that allow them to settle their guilty debts in a *sincere* manner. Obviously, however, not everybody subscribes to these attitudes or is subjected to such understanding reactions. Certain victims are masters at maintaining the illusion of indebtedness, and some victims are no longer around to forgive or forget one's trespasses. Moreover, certain individuals have learned from their culture, subculture, institutions, or families that mistakes are *always* avoidable and that one *never* does wrong. In all of these instances, the individuals will probably suffer from feelings of guilt long after the circumstance that caused the feeling is past and—more important—far in excess of their true state of guiltworthiness. Undue feelings of guilt can, in turn, bode poorly for people's ability to sustain healthy intrapersonal or interpersonal functioning.

See also: ANGER; ANXIETY; COMMUNICATION; DARWIN, CHARLES ROBERT; EMBARRASSMENT; EMPATHY; FEAR AND PHOBIAS; FORGIVENESS; FREUD, SIGMUND; GRIEF; HELPLESSNESS; NIETZSCHE, FRIEDRICH WILHELM; SELF-ESTEEM; SHAME; SIN

Bibliography

American Psychiatric Association. (1994). *Diagnostic and Statistical Manual of Mental Disorders,* 4th ed. Washington, DC: American Psychiatric Association.

Barrett, Karen C. (1995). "A Functionalist Approach to Shame and Guilt." In *Self-Conscious Emotions: The Psychology of Shame, Guilt, Embarrassment, and Pride,* ed. June P. Tangney and Kurt W. Fischer. New York: Guilford.

Baumeister, Roy F.; Reis, Harry T.; and Delespaul, Philippe A. E. G. (1995). "Subjective and Experiential Correlates of

Guilt in Daily Life." *Personality and Social Psychology Bulletin* 21:1256–1268.

Baumeister, Roy F.; Stillwell, Arlene M.; and Heatherton, Todd F. (1994). "Guilt: An Interpersonal Approach." *Psychological Bulletin,* 115:243–267.

Benedict, Ruth. (1946). *The Chrysanthemum and the Sword: Patterns of Japanese Culture.* Boston: Houghton Mifflin.

Binder, Jeffery L. (1970). "The Relative Proneness to Shame or Guilt As a Dimension of Character Style." Ph.D. diss. University of Michigan, Ann Arbor.

Clark, David, and Watson, Lee Anna. (1994). "The Vicissitudes of Mood: A Schematic Model." In *The Nature of Emotion,* ed. Paul Ekman and Richard J. Davidson. New York: Oxford University Press.

Creighton, Millie R. (1990). "Revisiting Shame and Guilt Cultures: A Forty-Year Pilgrimage." *Ethos* 18:279–307.

Darwin, Charles. ([1872] 1998). *The Expression of the Emotions in Man and Animals,* 3rd ed. New York: Oxford University Press.

Estrada-Hollenbeck, Mica, and Heatherton, Todd F. (1998). "Avoiding and Alleviating Guilt through Prosocial Behavior." In *Guilt and Children,* ed. Jane Bybee. San Diego, CA: Academic Press.

Eyre, Heidi L.; Ferguson, Tamara J.; Ives, Dune E.; Vollmer, Russell L.; Petersen, Dane; Alberico, Stephanie; and Abbruzzese, Dawn. (1998). "The Socialization of Conscience by Peers: Exactly How Do Children Make Each Other Feel Guilty." Poster presented at the July meeting of the International Society for the Study of Behavioural Development. Bern, Switzerland.

Ferguson, Tamara J., and Eyre, Heidi L. (1998). "The Interpersonal (Mal)functions of Guilt." In *Guilt and Shame As Interpersonal Communications and Regulators,* chaired by Tamara J. Ferguson. Symposium presented at the August meeting of the American Psychological Association. San Francisco.

Ferguson, Tamara J., and Eyre, Heidi L. (2000). "Engendering Gender Differences in Shame and Guilt: Stereotypes, Socialization, and Situational Pressures." In *Gender and Emotion,* ed. Agneta Fischer. Cambridge, Eng.: Cambridge University Press.

Ferguson, Tamara J., and Stegge, Hedy. (1995). "Emotional States and Traits in Children: The Case of Guilt and Shame." In *Self-Conscious Emotions: The Psychology of Shame, Guilt, Embarrassment, and Pride,* ed. June P. Tangney and Kurt W. Fischer. New York: Guilford.

Ferguson, Tamara J., and Stegge, Hedy. (1998). "Measuring Guilt in Children: A Rose by Any Other Name Still Has Thorns." In *Guilt and Children,* ed. Jane Bybee. San Diego, CA: Academic Press.

Freud, Sigmund. ([1905] 1953). "Three Essays on the Theory of Sexuality." In *The Standard Edition of the Complete Psychological Works of Sigmund Freud, Vol. 7,* ed. James Strachey. London: Hogarth Press.

Harder, David W. (1995). "Shame and Guilt Assessment, and Relationships of Shame- and Guilt-Proneness to Psychopathology." In *Self-Conscious Emotions: The Psychology of Shame, Guilt, Embarrassment, and Pride,* ed. June P. Tangney and Kurt W. Fischer. New York: Guilford.

Hoffman, Martin L. (1983). "Affective and Cognitive Processes in Moral Internalization." In *Social Cognition and Social Development,* ed. E. Tory Higgins, Diane N. Ruble, and Willard W. Hartup. New York: Cambridge University Press.

Huhmann, Bruce A., and Brotherton, Timothy P. (1997). "A Content Analysis of Guilt Appeals in Popular Magazine Advertisements." *Journal of Advertising* 26(2):35–45.

Kagan, Jerome. (1984). *The Nature of the Child.* New York: Basic Books.

Lebra, Takie S. (1983). "Shame and Guilt: A Psychocultural View of the Japanese Self." *Ethos* 11:192–209.

Lewis, Helen B. (1971). *Shame and Guilt in Neurosis.* New York: International Universities Press.

Lewis, Michael. (1992). *Shame, the Exposed Self.* New York: Free Press.

Miceli, Maria. (1992). "How to Make Someone Feel Guilty: Strategies of Guilt Inducement and Their Goals." *Journal for the Theory of Social Behavior* 22:81–103.

Mikula, Gerold; Scherer, Klaus R.; and Athenstaedt, Ursula. (1998). "The Role of Injustice in the Elicitation of Differential Emotional Reactions." *Personality and Social Psychology Bulletin* 24:769–783.

Nathanson, Donald L. (1992). *Shame and Pride: Affect, Sex, and the Birth of the Self.* New York: W. W. Norton.

Nietzsche, Friedrich. ([1887] 1967). *On the Genealogy of Morals,* tr. Walter Kaufmann and R. J. Hollingdale. New York: Vintage Press.

Rosaldo, Michelle Z. (1983). "The Shame of Headhunters and the Autonomy of Self." *Ethos* 11:135–151.

Shimanoff, Susan B. (1984). "Commonly Named Emotions in Everyday Conversations." *Perceptual and Motor Skills* 58:514.

Sommer, Kristin L., and Baumeister, Roy F. (1997). "Making Someone Feel Guilty: Causes, Strategies, and Consequences." In *Aversive Interpersonal Behaviors,* ed. Robin M. Kowalski. New York: Plenum.

Stipek, Deborah. (1998). "Differences between American and Chinese in the Circumstances Evoking Pride, Shame, and Guilt." *Journal of Cross Cultural Psychology* 29:616–629.

Tangney, June P. (1998). "How Does Guilt Differ from Shame." In *Guilt and Children,* ed. Jane Bybee. San Diego, CA: Academic Press.

Tangney, June P.; Burggraf, Susan A.; and Wagner, Patricia E. (1995). "Shame-Proneness, Guilt-Proneness, and Psychological Symptoms." In *Self-Conscious Emotions: The Psychology of Shame, Guilt, Embarrassment, and Pride,* ed. June P. Tangney and Kurt W. Fischer. New York: Guilford.

Vangelisti, Anita L.; Daly, John; and Rudnick, Janine R. (1991). "Making People Feel Guilty in Conversations: Techniques and Correlates." *Human Communication Research* 18:3–39.

Wallbott, Harald G., and Scherer, Klaus R. (1995). "Cultural Determinants in Experiencing Shame and Guilt." In *Self-Conscious Emotions: The Psychology of Shame, Guilt, Embarrassment, and Pride,* ed. June P. Tangney and Kurt W. Fischer. New York: Guilford.

World Health Organization. (1983). *Depressive Disorders in Different Cultures.* Geneva, Switzerland: World Health Organization.

Zahn-Waxler, Carolyn, and Kochanska, Grazyna. (1990). "The Origins of Guilt." In *Nebraska Symposium on Motivation, Vol. 36: Sociometric Development,* ed. Ross A. Thompson. Lincoln: University of Nebraska Press.

Zahn-Waxler, Carolyn; Kochanska, Grazyna; Krupnick, Janice; and Mcknew, Donald. (1990). "Patterns of Guilt in Children of Depressed and Well Mothers." *Developmental Psychology* 26:51–59.

Zahn-Waxler, Carolyn, and Robinson, JoAnn. (1995). "Empathy and Guilt: Early Origins of Feelings of Responsibility." In *Self-Conscious Emotions: The Psychology of Shame, Guilt, Embarrassment, and Pride,* ed. June P. Tangney and Kurt W. Fischer. New York: Guilford.

Tamara J. Ferguson

H

HAPPINESS

In *An Essay on Man* (1744), Alexander Pope wrote,

Oh Happiness! Our being's end and aim!
Good, Pleasure, Ease, Content! Whate'er thy name:
That something still which prompts the'eternal sigh,
For which we bear to live, or dare to die.

Happiness and its close cousin joy remain an enigma. On the one hand, most people maintain, when surveyed, that they are happy and feel that way much of the time. Yet, on the other hand, poets and writers, among others, have for ages described happiness as an elusive goal.

Two not atypical examples of the latter can be seen in revelations by Jean-Jacques Rousseau and Ivan Turgenev. Rousseau identified but two times in his life when he was truly happy: one that began with his seduction at age fifteen by a voluptuous patroness who was twenty-nine years of age; a second later in life when, over the course of a month, he immersed himself in a firsthand study of botany on a small island in the middle of a Swiss lake. Likewise, Turgenev recounted that happiness for him occurred only once, perhaps twice, in the entire course of his life.

What accounts for the different outlooks about personal happiness? One theory is that the points of view stem from a focus on different aspects of happiness and that happiness is a complex phenomenon whose scope transcends emotional as well as moral concerns. At least five perspectives on happiness deserve scrutiny: happiness as a response to a specific adaptational encounter, happiness as a facilitator of thought and initiator of action, happiness as a product of absorption in a creative activity or life project, happiness as a quality of life as a whole, and happiness as a manifestation of love and religious or spiritual experience.

Adaptational Response

A common interpretation of happiness is that it is an emotional response to something pleasant or wonderful. In this regard, appraisal theories provide perhaps the fullest account of happiness.

The idea behind appraisal theories is that happiness is the result of one's evaluation of an event or situation that has produced a positive outcome. The core of the appraisal is the comparison of an actual state to a desired state. A necessary condition for the experience of happiness is that one recognizes his or her motives as being appetitive (i.e., it entails a reward one seeks) and that the circumstances facilitate or promote its realization. Richard Lazarus (1991) uses the terms *goal relevance* and *goal congruence,* respectively, to refer to these conditions.

Broadly speaking, happiness occurs in response to three classes of positive outcomes: an unanticipated good fortune or pleasant happening, the achievement of a goal, or the beneficial consequences accruing as one pursues a goal. Theorists differ about which ones lead to happiness construed broadly and which ones lead to different positive emotions that are distinct from happiness.

Ira Roseman (1991) is typical of many appraisal theorists who limit happiness to positive outcomes that are produced by external circumstances. For example, people become happy when positive personal meanings happen: a paper long under review is accepted for publication, a child takes his or her first steps, or a friend responds to assistance with genuine gratitude. When an outcome has not yet occurred but is still expected as a result of circumstance, the positive emotion being experienced is labeled hope. Lazarus limits hope to unpleasant states and defines it as a "yearning for amelioration of a dreaded outcome," although he allows, as does Roseman, that hope also occurs infrequently and in anticipation of a positive outcome for an event that has a low perceived chance of occurrence.

When positive outcomes happen and are attributed to actions or attributes of the self rather than to circumstance, the emotion being experienced is defined as pride instead of happiness. Likewise, when positive outcomes result from the actions of another person or persons rather than the circumstances, the resulting emotion is liking (or something similar, such as caring, or love, depending on the situation).

Happiness as a response is closely tied to personal goals under the communicative theory of Keith Oatley and Philip Johnson-Laird (1987). In their view, happiness (and indeed all emotions) function within the individual to coordinate parts of one's cognitive system so as to manage responses to events with an aim either to change from ongoing activities to new activities or to maintain desired states or activities. According to Oatley (1992, p. 50), self-regulation of goals is believed to be the main function of emotions:

> Each goal and plan has a monitoring mechanism that evaluates events relevant to it. When a substantial change in probability occurs of achieving an important goal or subgoal, the monitoring mechanism broadcasts to the whole cognitive system a signal that can set it into readiness to respond to this change. Humans experience these signals and the states of readiness they induce as emotions.

Unlike Roseman and Lazarus, who limit happiness to circumstance-caused positive outcomes, Oatley emphasizes four cases under which self-caused and circumstance-caused outcomes (or a combination of the two) can lead to happiness: (1) when a goal is achieved, (2) when a plan is progressing well, (3) when subgoals are being achieved, and (4) when the probability of a main goal being achieved is increased. Just as Aristotle believed that making progress in the pursuit of goal attainment is more conducive to happiness than is goal attainment itself, Oatley and Johnson-Laird conclude that happiness is triggered most frequently when subgoals are achieved; the experience of happiness then serves to promote and guide striving toward a goal.

It should be noted that happiness is often accompanied by other emotions; it rarely occurs alone. Thus, happiness and pride, happiness and love, or happiness and hope are frequently yoked together in pairs. On occasion, happiness is coupled with negative emotions, such as when one struggles before solving a problem, triumphs over turmoil, or experiences frustration and pain in personal relationships as a prelude to reconciliation. Even guilt or anxiety can combine with happiness if one's good fortune is resented by others who are filled with envy or jealousy.

Up to this point, there has been no differentiation between happiness and joy. On the basis of categorizations performed by respondents, Phillip Shaver and his colleagues (1987) concluded that emotions are prototypes that people hold in memory and that there are five basic emotion categories: love, anger, sadness, fear, and joy. Joy was found to subsume such instances of positive emotions as happiness, gladness, elation, satisfaction, excitement, pleasure, pride, hope, contentment, and relief. In a similar way, Lazarus and Roseman equate happiness with joy.

An argument can be made for regarding happiness and joy as synonyms because both are governed by the same combination of appraisal alternatives—namely, both are motive-consistent appetitive emotions that are produced by external circumstances under conditions of high outcome certainty. But this interpretation is limited to the adaptational response model of happiness. For the other models of happiness, happiness and joy do not coincide fully—indeed, joy seems more delimited, perhaps restricted to an outcome of appraisal processes. Happiness, in contrast, is broader and more complex in meaning and implications.

Happiness and arousal have frequently been portrayed as orthogonal (i.e., independent) dimensions of emotions. With this in mind, researchers have shown that most emotions can be arranged in a circumplex (or bipolar) pattern with regard to the dimensions of pleasantness-unpleasantness and high arousal-low arousal. Proponents of the circumplex model of emotions categorize happiness in terms of the intensity determined by different combinations of pleasantness (which is a special case of happiness) and arousal. Intense forms of happiness—for example, euphoric, gleeful, enthusiastic, excited, joyous, elated, ecstatic, and exultant—occur when pleasantness is combined with high arousal. Middle forms of happiness—for example, glad, content, serene, quietude of mind (the Greek *ataraxia*), and amused—occur when pleasantness is combined with low arousal. Two other orthogonal dimensions that can be used in the circumplex model are high positive affect-low positive affect and high negative affect-low negative affect.

The bipolar conceptualization of emotions brings into question the relationship between positive and negative emotions. What is the relationship between happiness and sadness, for example? Can one be both happy and sad at the same time, or must one be either happy or sad? A related issue is whether the experience of happiness is accentuated by feelings of sadness occurring immediately prior to happiness. Perhaps negative emotional experiences help people to better appreciate happiness when it does occur and provide contrasting color in their lives. Alternatively, negative emotions might interfere with one's ability to have, sense, or savor one's happiness. These issues are in need of further study.

Facilitator and Initiator

Happiness, under appraisal theories, is seen as being a by-product of favorable goal pursuit, goal attainment, or encounters with the environment or other people. But happiness also has implications for thought processes and, more generally, for action.

Consider the effects of happiness on cognitive processes as reported by Norbert Schwarz and Herbert Bless (1991). Happiness facilitates the recall of positive information. Happiness also induces optimism and decreases judgments that unpleasant events will occur. Further, happiness widens one's field of attention. A happy person tends to be less self-centered and more other-centered than a sad person and frequently expands his or her attention to multiple objects. To the extent that decision making is a function of information processing, happy states can shape the outcome of decision making by influencing the nature and scope of the processed information.

There are only a few studies of this sort, but a number of their findings are of note. In both judgment and persuasive communication research, happy subjects use heuristic, as opposed to analytical, processing strategies more than those subjects who are in neutral or negative moods. Heuristic strategies entail the use of simple rules, intuition, or focus upon peripheral cues (e.g., attractiveness of a spokesperson). Analytical strategies include focus upon central cues (e.g., argument quality) and greater cognitive elaboration of information. Happy individuals also experience higher levels of physiological arousal and exhibit more physical activity than did sad individuals.

Happiness has consequences for one's relationships with other people. Mark Schaller and Robert B. Cialdini (1990) report that happy individuals are friendlier, convey more liking, and view others more positively than sad individuals. In addition, happiness increases the chances that one will help others, even strangers.

The motivation to act arising from happiness seems to be different from the motivation to act stemming from negative emotions. When individuals experience a negative emotion (e.g., anger, sadness, fear), they are in disequilibrium and wish to return to their normal state. Lazarus (1991) points out that one or both of the following two coping processes are used to achieve this: problem-focused coping, where individuals attempt to alleviate the source of distress, and emotion-focused coping, where individuals either change the meaning of the source of distress (e.g., deny that a threat exists) or avoid thinking about a problem.

In contrast, when individuals are happy, helping or altruistic actions are often energized. Why? Schaller and Cialdini (1990, pp. 284–285) offer two explanations: "positive mood leads to enhanced helping via the more positive outlook and enhanced activity that appear to spring automatically from the experience of happiness" and "happiness is associated with a motivation toward disequilibrium—toward the possible attainment of additional personal rewards that transcend the basic concern over one's mood." The personal rewards referred to here concern such self-enrichment motives as affiliation, achievement, competence, and esteem.

Another way that happiness affects others is through emotional contagion, which, according to Elaine Hatfield and her colleagues (1992, p. 153), is based on "the tendency to 'catch' (experience/express) another person's emotions (his or her emotional appraisals, subjective feelings, expressions, patterned physiological processes, action tendencies, and instrumental behaviors)." Nuances in individuals' facial expressions, vocalizations, and body posture induce emotional responses in people as the individuals interact with them such that the people (often unconsciously) mimic the individuals' emotions. Thus one's own happiness can become infectious, whether intended or not.

In sum, happiness makes one more expansive, friendly, outgoing, generous, empathetic, open to new experiences, and able to appreciate the beauty in things and others. Some theorists, such as Nico Frijda (1986), emphasize that happiness is not merely an appraisal and emotional response to an event. Happiness includes action tendencies, which Frijda and his colleagues (1989, p. 213) define as "a readiness to engage in or disengage from interaction with some goal object." Action tendencies include the impulse to move toward, move away from, or move against the object. When people are happy, they often feel the urge to approach, make contact with, or reach out to another person; to attend to things in their immediate environment with openness and interest; to enjoy or ap-

Sprinter Michael Johnson raises his arms in a triumphant expression of his happiness at breaking the world record in the men's 200-meter sprint at the 1996 Olympic Trials in Atlanta, Georgia. (Corbis/Wally McNamee)

preciate what they are experiencing or doing; to celebrate and release energy; and to share with and give of themselves to others.

Many of the consequences of happiness are more or less automatic reactions and "end" with the behavioral responses they produce. However, a class of more purposive consequences has received attention from Richard Bagozzi, Hans Baumgartner, and Rik Pieters (1998), who have shown that happiness (as well as other positive and negative emotions) stimulates goal-directed behaviors. The idea is that people contemplate the consequences of achieving and failing to achieve a possible goal and form positive and negative emotions toward anticipated goal achievement and failure, respectively. The result of the emotional responses then elicits reactions in the form of implementation intentions, plans, and impulses to expend effort in goal pursuit. These reactions, in turn, energize instrumental acts in the service of goal attainment. Anticipated happiness is a key instigator of goal striving in this sense.

Consider the decision and effort to control body weight. Images of achieving one's weight goal lead to anticipated positive emotions (e.g., happiness, delight, pride), while images of failing to achieve one's weight goal engenders negative emotions (e.g., disappointment, worry, shame). The push and pull of these feelings stimulate a desire and intention to do what it takes to regulate one's body weight. Various forms of exercising and dieting may be used to accomplish weight control. Subsequent success or failure in goal achievement will be appraised, and happiness (as well as other positive and negative emotions) will reinforce one's ongoing efforts in this regard. Indeed, happiness will be a key regulator of goal striving, as one makes progress in goal pursuit.

Absorption in a Creative Activity

Sometimes happiness is neither an effect nor a cause, per se, but rather an ongoing immersion in some activity. Oatley (1992, p. 348) asserts that to be "creatively, wholeheartedly, doing what one is doing is to be happy." Three aspects of happiness in this regard deserve scrutiny.

First, happiness is an active emotion in the sense that it springs from one's own striving to attain understanding about things and oneself, including self-actualization. A somewhat similar idea was expressed by Baruch Spinoza, who wrote in his *Ethics* (1677) about the power or freedom expressed through the exercise of one's "active" emotions. Spinoza contrasted this with the enslavement characterized by "passive" emotions, where people act out of compulsion (e.g., in envy, jealousy, greed, hatred, frustration, pain), and he believed that ultimate knowledge or salvation is reached through "intellectual love of God."

Second, striving for understanding occurs in relation to a particular creative activity or life project. Here one finds happiness through personal expressiveness in the furtherance of skills and talents. The activity serves as intrinsic motivation, and happiness will be sustained to the extent that the activity is rich or challenging and one is able to grow intellectually and emotionally while doing it. People often think that happiness through absorption in a creative activity is reserved for artists or people in certain "creative" professions. Yet, Mihaly Csikszentmihalyi (1991) describes instances where laborers and others achieved this happiness in everyday life through a process he termed *flow*. Nevertheless, happiness, as a manifestation of personal expressiveness, probably occurs most frequently, if it occurs at all, as involvement in one's life work or in dedication to a personal ideal or service to others. Two qualities seem to promote such a realization. One is a sense of personal freedom, control, and responsibility. Another is an attitude or personal policy that happiness resides more in the striving or doing than in any specific outcome. This perspective, too, was recognized early on by Aristotle and can be found in words from the *Bhagavad Gita* (II, 48): "On action alone be thy interest; never on its fruits . . . abiding in discipline perform actions, abandoning attachment . . . being indifferent to success or failure."

A third aspect of happiness through absorption is that it occurs earnestly and in the here and now. A person engaged wholeheartedly in an activity is neither concerned nostalgically with the past nor anticipating joy in the future. Rather, he or she is engrossed in the present, perhaps to the extent of losing track of time altogether. At the same time, absorption in a creative activity is often marked by a conspicuous unselfconsciousness and single-minded commitment. A good example of happiness through experience of the present and the exercise and power of active emotions can be seen in Norman Cousins's (1979, pp. 72–73) account of his meeting with Pablo Casals on the eve of Casals's ninetieth birthday:

> His various infirmities made it difficult for him to dress himself. Judging from his difficulty in walking and from the way he held his arms, I guessed he was suffering from rheumatoid arthritis. His emphysema was evident in his labored breathing. . . . He was badly stooped. His head was pitched forward and he walked with a shuffle. His hands were swollen and his fingers were clenched. . . . Don Pablo went to the piano . . . arranged himself with some difficulty on the piano bench, then with discernible effort raised his swollen and clenched fingers above the keyboard.
>
> I was not prepared for the miracle that was about to happen. The fingers slowly unlocked and reached toward the keys like buds of a plant toward the sunlight. His back straightened. He seemed to breathe more freely. Now his fingers settled on the keys. Then came the opening bars of Bach's *Wohltemperierte Klavier*, played with great sensitivity and control. . . . His entire body seemed fused with the music; it was no longer stiff and shrunken but supple and graceful and completely freed of its arthritic coils. . . . He hummed as he played, then said that Bach spoke to him here—and he placed his hand over his heart.

A Quality of Life As a Whole

The happiness discussed so far has been episodic and acute. Moreover, the adaptational response and facilitator/instigator forms of happiness are hedonic (i.e., characterized by pleasure) in the sense that a person believes, as Richard Kraut (1979, p. 178) puts it, that "one is getting the important things one wants, as well as certain pleasant affects that normally go along with this belief." Absorption in a creative activity can be driven by, or degenerate into, hedonism but it also can be motivated by higher aims (e.g., non-hedonical moral principles).

In contrast to the above forms of happiness, happiness can be a chronic quality of one's life as a whole. At least two ways exist for viewing life as a whole: one predicated on a moral philosophy of utilitarianism and one expressed in actions that fulfill one's potential in accordance with objective criteria for the good life (or living well).

John Stuart Mill, in *Utilitarianism* (1863), asserted that happiness is the *summum bonum*, the highest good, to which human actions are directed and by which actions are judged morally right or wrong (i.e., actions are morally right to the extent that they produce happiness for oneself or for all people affected by the actions). Mill defined happiness as being the attainment of pleasure and the absence of pain. To achieve happiness, one must take into account the amount and quality of pleasure and pain generated by an action. This is done by some method of calculation where alternative courses of action are evaluated in terms of the pleasure and pain expected and the pleasure and pain are weighed and integrated according to some rule. Pleasure is construed broadly to include higher pleasures of the intellect, emotions, and moral sentiments, as well as lower sensational pleasures. Pain might also be conceived of in "lower" and "higher" forms, but less thought has been given to this by utilitarianists.

A fundamentally different way of thinking about one's life as a whole was formulated early on by Aristotle. He thought of happiness as *eudaimonia,* by which he meant a type of personal flourishing that results when one lives a life marked by the cultivation and exercise of virtue. Each person is believed to have a set of potentials shared with humankind, as well as a set that is unique to him- or herself. To the extent that one's strivings fulfill these potentials, one will be happy. Happiness is sought for its own sake and is achieved through the exercise of such activities as intellectual contemplation and performance of virtuous acts, which, in turn, depend on a virtuous character. A key to living well is choosing and doing morally right actions in the right way. Activities are to be guided by the exercise of practical reason and theoretical activity.

Eudaimonic happiness is somewhat similar to emotional well-being, as studied by psychologists. Researchers who study emotional well-being focus on the relationship of pleasant to unpleasant emotions, and, although this is measured most frequently by self-reports, Ed Diener and Randy Larsen (1993, p. 408) advocate measuring "physiological, facial, nonverbal, cognitive, behavioral, and experiential components" as well. An attempt is made to include subjective and objective aspects of happiness, and in this sense, the quality of one's life as a whole is approached.

On the other hand, eudaimonia is different from emotional well-being (and its more cognitive cousin, subjective well-being) in that it focuses on the objective character of a person's life. Moreover, eudaimonia emphasizes activity in pursuit, and ongoing experience of, living well, whereas emotional well-being is an affective summary of, or reaction to, one's life as a whole. In other words, the former is a doing, whereas the latter is more akin to a sentiment or trait. Finally, emotional well-being researchers maintain that it is the frequency of pleasant affect, and not affect intensity, that determines well-being, whereas eudaimonia is more directly tied to the activity executed in pursuit of living well and the strength or importance of the virtues involved therein (i.e., virtues can be arranged from the lowest to the highest). Emotional well-being research finds that most people say they are happy, echoing the famous statement in Aldous Huxley's *Brave New World* (1932): "Everybody is happy nowadays." But eudaimonia is more of a striving or journey, and one suspects few individuals reach the pinnacle of living well—even fewer sustain it.

Love, Religion, and Spirituality

It is important to recognize that happiness is more than an intrapersonal experience centered on what one does or feels. Happiness is also an interpersonal experience and a larger social happening that reflects qualities embedded in shared understandings, reciprocal affect, and joint activities that are not easy, or perhaps are even impossible, to reduce to the intrapersonal level.

In literature and everyday life, happiness is often fused with love or religious experience, or with both love and religious experience. This aspect of happiness gives it a universal, communal, and timeless quality, in contrast to the "scientific" and "philosophical" perspectives discussed above.

One of the earliest recorded recognitions of the many facets of love and its effects on one's emotions was provided by the poet Sappho (c. 600 B.C.E.), who represented one aspect of love, the excitement of sexual attraction, with descriptions of intimate attention, enticing laughter, a fast heart beat, an inability to speak, a drumming in the ears, dripping with sweat, and turning paler than dry grass. These physical reactions concerning the author's romantic love for another person, which is a special case of love in the tradition of *eros,* contrast with love in the sense of *agape* (e.g., God's love for people, a person's love of God, Christian neighbor-love, and the love between parent and child or grandchild). A brief definition of love that captures much of its essence has been given by Erich Fromm (1956, p. 24): "Love is the active concern for the life and the growth of that which we love." Eros is differentiated from agape largely by its erotic component. Lazarus (1991, p. 276) points out that both forms of love reflect a core theme marked by "desiring or participating in affection, usually but not necessarily reciprocated."

Happiness has a complex relationship with love. Oatley (1992, p. 370) characterizes love as an "interpersonal form of happiness" and asserts that "the state of being in love is, in our society, the very paradigm of happiness." But what is this state of being in love, and how is it related to happiness? Love and happiness seem to exist in a symbiotic alliance that occurs at two interconnected levels. At the individual level, love is experienced acutely as a positive emotional experience signified by feelings of happiness. The feelings of happiness occur intermittently and have a periodic rhythm to them. Yet, continuity is provided through the three ways in which a person subjectively interprets and feels the happiness: nostalgically or sentimentally, when one relives past moments of happiness with a loved one; experientially, as one is actually engaged in mutual affection and physical and intellectual intimacy with a loved one; and prospectively, as one anticipates or longs for contact with a loved one. The cycle of happiness that occurs while one is in a state of love is frequently interrupted, yet often ultimately enriched, by setbacks and bittersweet experiences. Even heartbreaks can lead to personal growth after a period of time.

The experience of love and happiness at the individual level always occurs within a larger social and cultural context. To take but one specific example, James Averill (1985) suggests thinking of romantic love as a social construction. In many Western cultures, and increasingly in some Eastern cultures, falling in love begins with an initial receptivity on the part of two people, which is based on some complex mixture of biological needs, sexual fantasies, cognitive schemas governing individual and societal goals, standards of conduct, and a willingness or desire to "fall in love." Next, the two people come into contact, either by accident or by plan, and some excitement and interest emerges in one or both persons. This then begins an interpersonal exchange that might lead to either disinterest and rejection or mutual desire to pursue a relationship. Typically, the initial encounter proceeds only so far, and then the parties separate, whereupon a period of time passes where fantasies about the other person build up in both individuals. If the level of arousal and interest becomes sufficiently great, one person will make contact and attempt to continue the relationship. A period of courtship will follow, characterized by frequent interactions and sharing of experiences. Some point may be reached, as both people develop favorable idealizations and come to common understandings, where the parties embark on a series of mutual plans and commitments, perhaps culminating in marriage and evolving to new levels of intimacy. At all stages of romantic love, the process is punctuated with, and indeed sustained by, different forms and intensities of happiness.

For many people, happiness and love are entangled with religious or spiritual beliefs and the enactment of their faith. Indeed, most religions emphasize love and happiness (or joy) as central parts of their theology and practice. Hinduism, for example, maintains in the Bhagavata Purana that people seek joy as an ultimate goal and that the way to God is through love: "[As] the waters of the Ganges flow incessantly toward the ocean, so do the minds of the *bhakta* [*yoga*] move constantly toward Me, the Supreme Person residing in every heart, immediately they hear about My qualities." And it is not only the love one has for God, but the love that God has for the individual, that often gives one happiness, as this passage from the Koran (93:1–8), the sacred book of Islam, emphasizes:

By the noonday brightness, and by the night when it darkens, your Lord has not forsaken you, neither has He been displeased. Surely the Hereafter shall be better for you than the past; and in the end He will be bounteous to you, and you will be satisfied. Did He not find you an orphan, and give you a home; erring, and guided you; needy, and enriched you?

Two qualities of early Christians impressed outsiders. One was their love for humankind—Christians and non-Christians alike—and their disregard for social status. Indeed, Christianity took root among the afflicted, poor, and oppressed; also Christians took seriously Jesus's example and directives to "love the Lord, your God, with all your heart, with all your soul, and with all your mind" and "love your neighbor as yourself" (Matthew 22:37, 39). A second quality that moved non-Christians was their perception of an unusually strong inner calm and peace of mind in Christians, even under the most dire conditions. Paul of Tarsus, a Jew, early in his life zealously persecuted Christians in an attempt to suppress the movement. But after watching St. Stephen calmly kneel and pray for the forgiveness of those who were stoning him to death, Paul was convinced of the authenticity of Jesus and began a life-long mission to spread the word, eventually becoming one of Christiandom's most influential Apostles.

The relationship between happiness and love in Christianity can be seen in Jesus's explanation of his teachings to his followers: "As the Father loves me, so I also love you" and "I have told you this so that my joy might be in you and your joy might be complete" (John 15:9, 11). It is significant that Christian love was not limited to the love between God and the worshiper but radiated out from worshipers to reach others and resulted in an inner peace, expression of joy, and overall feeling of happiness.

Conclusion

Is happiness—a complex emotional, philosophical, and spiritual phenomenon—a universal phenomenon? Unfortunately, this question remains unanswered. This is due in part to the fact that great variations in the language of emotions can be found across cultures. Happiness has about forty subtypes or subtle variations in English, but many other languages have only a few close substitutes. At the same time, some cultures have words for emotions that are not easily translated into English or other languages. Furthermore, cultural influences may affect the experience and expression of happiness. As these and other issues concerning happiness continue to be researched, it is important that people not forget the wisdom already residing in the arts and literature, as exemplified by John Dryden's poem "Happy the Man" (1685):

Happy the man, and happy he alone,
He who can call today his own:
He who, secure within, can say,
Tomorrow do thy worst, for I have lived today.
Be fair or foul or rain or shine
The joys I have possessed, in spite of fate, are mine.
Not Heaven itself upon the past has power,
But what has been, has been, and I have had my hour.

See also: ACHIEVEMENT MOTIVATION; ATTRIBUTION; CREATIVITY; CULTURE; HOPE; LOVE; PLEASURE; SADNESS; SATISFACTION; SPINOZA, BARUCH; UNIVERSALITY OF EMOTIONAL EXPRESSION

Bibliography

Aristotle. (1985). *Nicomachen Ethics,* tr. Terence Irwin. Indianapolis, IN: Hackett.

Averill, James R. (1985). "The Social Construction of Emotion: With Special Reference to Love." In *The Social Construction of the Person,* ed. Kenneth J. Gergen and Keith E. Davis. New York: Springer.

Bagozzi, Richard P.; Baumgartner, Hans; and Pieters, Rik. (1998). "Goal-Directed Emotions." *Cognition and Emotion* 12:1–26.

Barnard, Mary. (1958). *Sappho: A New Translation.* Berkeley: University of California Press.

Bennett, Jonathan Francis. (1984). *A Study of Spinoza's Ethics.* Indianapolis, IN: Hackett.

Brakel, Jaap van. (1994). "Emotions: A Cross-Cultural Perspective on Forms of Life." In *Social Perspectives on Emotion, Vol. 2,* ed. William M. Wentworth and John Ryan. Greenwich, CT: JAI Press.

Campbell, Angus; Converse, Philip E.; and Rodgers, Willard L. (1976). *The Quality of American Life.* New York: Russell Sage Foundation.

Cousins, Norman. (1979). *Anatomy of an Illness as Perceived by the Patient.* New York: W. W. Norton.

Csikszentmihalyi, Mihaly. (1991). *Flow: The Psychology of Optimal Experience.* New York: HarperCollins.

Diener, Ed, and Larsen, Randy J. (1993). "The Experience of Emotional Well-Being." In *Handbook of Emotions,* ed. Michael Lewis and Jeannette M. Haviland. New York: Guilford.

Frijda, Nico H. (1986). *The Emotions.* Cambridge, Eng.: Cambridge University Press.

Frijda, Nico H.; Kuipers, Peter; and Schure, Elisabeth ter. (1989). "Relations among Emotion, Appraisal, and Emotional Action Readiness." *Journal of Personality and Social Psychology* 57:212–228.

Fromm, Erich. (1956). *The Art of Loving.* New York: Harper & Row.

Hatfield, Elaine; Cacioppo, John T.; and Rapson, Richard L. (1992). "Primitive Emotional Contagion." In *Review of Personality and Social Psychology, Vol. 14: Emotions and Social Behavior,* ed. Margaret S. Clark. Newbury Park, CA: Sage Publications.

Kraut, Richard. (1979). "Two Conceptions of Happiness." *Philosophical Review* 88:167–197.

Larsen, Randy J., and Diener, Ed. (1992). "Promises and Problems with the Circumplex Model of Emotion." In *Review of Personality and Social Psychology, Vol. 14: Emotional and Social Behavior,* ed. Margaret S. Clark. Newbury Park, CA: Sage Publications.

Lazarus, Richard S. (1991). *Emotion and Adaptation.* Oxford, Eng.: Oxford University Press.

Mill, John Stuart. ([1863] 1998). *Utilitarianism.* Oxford, Eng.: Oxford University Press.

Oatley, Keith. (1992). *Best Laid Schemes: The Psychology of Emotions.* Cambridge, Eng.: Cambridge University Press.

Oatley, Keith, and Johnson-Laird, Philip N. (1987). "Towards a Cognitive Theory of Emotions." *Cognition and Emotion* 1:29–50.

Ortony, Andrew; Clore, Gerald L.; and Collins, Allan. (1988). *The Cognitive Structure of Emotions.* New York: Cambridge University Press.

Quennell, Peter. (1988). *The Pursuit of Happiness.* London: Constable.

Roseman, Ira J. (1991). "Appraisal Determinants of Discrete Emotions." *Cognition and Emotion* 5:161–200.

Russell, James A. (1980). "A Circumplex Model of Affect." *Journal of Personality and Social Psychology* 39:1161–1178.

Russell, James A., and Yik, Michelle S. M. (1996). "Emotions among the Chinese." In *Handbook of Chinese Psychology,* ed. Michael H. Bond. New York: Oxford University Press.

Schaller, Mark, and Cialdini, Robert B. (1990). "Happiness, Sadness, and Helping: A Motivational Integration." In *Handbook of Motivation and Cognition, Vol. 2,* ed. E. Tory Higgins and Robert M. Sorrentino. New York: Guilford.

Schwarz, Norbert, and Bless, Herbert. (1991). "Happy and Mindless, but Sad and Smart? The Impact of Affective States on Analytic Reasoning." In *Emotion and Social Judgments,* ed. Joseph P. Forgas. Oxford, Eng.: Pergamon.

Shaver, Phillip; Schwartz, Judith; Kirson, Donald; and O'Connor, Cary. (1987). "Emotion Knowledge: Further Exploration of a Prototype Approach." *Journal of Personality and Social Psychology* 52:1061–1086.

Smith, Craig A., and Ellsworth, Phoebe C. (1985). "Patterns of Cognitive Appraisal in Emotion." *Journal of Personality and Social Psychology* 48:813–838.

Smith, Houston. (1991). *The World's Religions.* San Francisco: Harper.

Soble, Alan. (1990). *The Structure of Love.* New Haven, CT: Yale University Press.

Spinoza, Baruch. ([1677] 1982). *The Ethics and Selected Letters,* tr. Samuel Shirley. Indianapolis, IN: Hackett.

Waterman, Alan S. (1993). "Two Conceptions of Happiness: Contrasts of Personal Expressiveness (Eudaimonia) and Hedonic Enjoyment." *Journal of Personality and Social Psychology* 64:678–691.

Watson, David, and Tellegen, Auke. (1985). "Toward a Consensual Structure of Mood." *Psychological Bulletin* 98:219–235.

Wierzbicka, Anna. (1994). "Emotion, Language, and Cultural Scripts." In *Emotion and Culture,* ed. Shinobu Kitayama and Hazel Rose Markus. Washington, DC: American Psychological Association.

Richard P. Bagozzi

HATE

The term *hate* was used generically in the past to refer to any intense dislike or hostility, whatever its object.

Hate could, according to this use of the term, be directed at a person, a group, an idea, some other abstraction, or an inanimate object.

Hate As Bigotry

Beginning in the mid-1980s, the term *hate* became increasingly used, in a much more restricted sense, to characterize an individual's negative feelings toward the members of some other group of people—because of their race, religious identity, ethnic origin, gender, sexual orientation, age, or disability status. With regard to hate crimes, this use overlaps with terms such as *prejudice, bias, ethnocentrism,* or *ethnoviolence* (which is used for more specific forms of hate crimes related to racism, sexism, ageism, homophobia, and xenophobia).

Among the concepts in the vocabulary of bigotry, *hate* is not alone in having undergone a significant shift of meaning. A parallel transition has occurred with the term *prejudice,* the original definition of which has shifted from "any prejudgment" to "a hostile attitude directed specifically toward the members of another group."

Although there is some overlap, there are important differences between hate and prejudice. Hate tends to be based less on cognition (i.e., stereotyping) and more on the emotional or affective component of bigotry. Prejudice tends to be based more on cognition and less on the affective component of bigotry. Indeed, until hate became associated with intergroup hostility, researchers focused almost exclusively on the cognitive dimension of prejudice. As a result, sociologists and psychologists have offered many more insights into the nature of prejudice than they have into the nature of hate.

Hate frequently has a cultural basis that finds expression in the popular arts. Much of the "culture of hate" is directed particularly at youths through popular music and motion pictures. Since the mid-1980s, a significant proportion of the lyrics in rap and metal music have been sexist, racist, homophobic, and violent. Standup comics have, to an increasing extent, aimed their savage barbs at blacks, Latinos, gays,

"Hop Frog" (1840), Edgar Allan Poe's story about a mistreated dwarf, demonstrates how insult and abuse can gradually turn a court jester into a bitter person who hates the source of his torment. After years of suffering and of seeing another dwarf also mistreated, Hop Frog finally figures out a way to get revenge—he turns his hatred of the king and his counselors into a murderous plot.

Asians, and women. In addition, R-rated films have frequently depicted women being brutalized at will as though they are deserving victims.

The continuing influence of hate in the lives of Americans is illustrated by the wide—perhaps widening—gap between black and white Americans with respect to their worldviews. On both sides of the racial ledger, there are Americans who tend to be pessimistic about the future of the United States as a multicultural nation. Some even predict civil war. Before blowing up the federal building in Oklahoma City, Timothy McVeigh had secured the "blueprint" for his mass murder from Andrew Macdonald's novel *The Turner Diaries* (1978), in which Americans battle the forces of evil represented by Jews, blacks, and a communist-inspired federal government.

The cultural gap between whites and blacks can be seen in survey data that examine racial differences in Americans' explanations for inequality. Howard Schuman and his colleagues (1997) have found that respondents from both racial groups tend to reject the idea that blacks have less innate ability than whites; both whites and blacks stress the need to equalize educational opportunities. But when asked to account for continuing black disadvantage, the majority of whites blame lack of motivation—in other words, they believe that blacks do not make enough of an effort on their own behalf to crawl out of the gutters of America. In sharp contrast, the majority of blacks explain their own economic disadvantage as a result of persistent white discrimination or racism, something which many white Americans deny.

According to Patricia Turner (1993), the collective thinking of many black Americans assumes the status of urban legends in which white Americans are seen as conspirators against them. Whereas most white Americans saw O. J. Simpson as his wife's murderer, the majority of black Americans believed Simpson to be not a perpetrator but an innocent victim of racist police officers who conspired to plant incriminating evidence against him. Many blacks similarly believe that nationwide restaurant chains add a secret ingredient to sterilize black men, that soft drink companies are owned by the Ku Klux Klan, that the U.S. government's so-called war against drugs was actually waged as an excuse to incarcerate large numbers of young black men, and that the U.S. military conspired to infect people in Africa with HIV.

The pessimism of black America has been channeled into predictions of an impending civil war. The distinguished journalist Carl T. Rowan, who is not otherwise prone to hyperbole, wrote a book entitled *The Coming Race War in America: A Wake-Up Call* (1996). The national television commentator Tony Brown, in his book *Black Lies, White Lies* (1995), suggested that blacks must give up on efforts by whites to provide opportunities and seek their own solutions within the black community—they must "stop waiting for white people to solve their problems."

Some of the racial skepticism of black Americans has been translated into hate directed toward whites —especially Catholics and Jews. A 1998 rally of thousands of black youths in New York City was organized by Khallid Mohammed (a former spokesperson for the Nation of Islam), who has repeatedly referred to Jews as "bloodsuckers" and to the Pope as "a cracker."

A Typology of Hate

To some extent, hate thrives on ignorance, so that those individuals who are poorly educated also tend to be most prejudiced. Yet information or moral persuasion alone does not always reduce bigotry. What may be more important—if less understood—is the fact that numerous Americans actually benefit from being intolerant and hate-filled, or at least they *believe* that they benefit. The gains may be short term or long term, imagined or real, economic or psychological, but Jack Levin and William Levin (1982) have found that such individuals depend to a considerable extent on hate to give them a sense of well-being and adequacy, to reduce uncomfortable ambiguities in their everyday lives, and to sustain their socioeconomic advantages.

Metaphorically, there is a tendency to regard hate as though it imitates the switch on a lamp—the light is either totally on or it is totally off. However, a more apt parallel might be found in a dimmer switch, by which the illumination is varied from dark to bright. It is not merely hardened hatemongers at the margins of America who benefit from bigotry; there is an entire spectrum along which individuals can be located with respect to their propensity for hate and violence as a result of their stake in preserving the status quo. In addition to hatemongers, there are dabblers, sympathizers, and spectators—individuals who may not always stand out as active and consistent bigots but who, by their very indifference, occasional violence, or verbal encouragement, contribute to preserving intergroup tensions and conflict. Moreover, at the other extreme from hatemongers are rebels who defy conventional wisdom, regardless of how costly it is to them in psychological or economic terms, in order to express their respect and tolerance for diversity. In a cultural sense, such individuals can be regarded as "deviants" who may be stigmatized by friends, coworkers, and family members.

Hatemongers

When a sadistic offense is committed because a victim is different, there seems to be much reason to sug-

On January 25, 1999, John William "Bill" King (center) was led from the Jasper County Courthouse in Jasper, Texas, following the first day of jury selection in his murder trial. The jury ultimately returned a guilty of capital murder verdict after only two and a half hours of deliberation on February 23. Two days later, King was given a sentence of death for his role in the 1998 dragging death of James Byrd, Jr. (Corbis/AFP)

gest that the motivation contains important elements of hate. Sadism is essentially designed to give the perpetrator a sense of power, control, and dominance, but at the expense of a set of victims. The white supremacists who were implicated in James Byrd's murder in Jasper, Texas, beat the black hitchhiker until he was unconscious, chained him to their pickup truck, and then dragged him down the road for more than two miles. Investigators discovered a Ku Klux Klan manual among the possessions carried by one of the perpetrators; a second perpetrator wore white supremacist body tattoos depicting the Confederate Knights of America. All three were definitely ardent admirers of the Klan who used white supremacist propaganda and enjoyed being identified with white supremacy symbols of power.

Although no more than 5 percent of all hate crimes nationwide are committed by members of organizations such as the Ku Klux Klan, Aryan Nations, or the White Aryan Resistance, Jack Levin and Jack McDevitt (1993) point out that groups of white supremacists continue behind the scenes to inspire vandalism, assault, and murder. In doing so, these individuals encourage and support larger numbers of violent offenses committed by non-members who may be totally unsophisticated with respect to the ideology of hate—racist skinheads, alienated teenagers, or hate-filled young men looking to have a good time at someone else's expense.

The murder in Jasper was not the first to incriminate white supremacy from a distance. In 1990, Tom and John Metzger of the White Aryan Resistance lost a major lawsuit implicating them in the skinhead murder of an Ethiopian man, Mulugeta Seraw, on the streets of Portland, Oregon. Awarding the victim's family nine million dollars, the jury concluded that the Metzgers, operating from their headquarters a thousand miles away, had orchestrated the Portland murder by their coaching of skinheads in the use of weapons and in how to assault blacks with impunity by claiming self-defense.

While serving time behind bars for burglary convictions, two of the suspects in Jasper apparently had links with the Aryan Brotherhood, a prison hate group whose members are often recruited by white supremacists after they have been released. Established in many states around the country, the Aryan Brotherhood introduces inmates to the theology of the Identity Church, according to which Jews are the children of Satan and blacks are subhuman "mud people." Prison may be a school for crime, but it is also a crash course in hatred and a training ground for leaders of the most dangerous white supremacy groups in America.

Hatemongers often retaliate in an organized fashion. These individuals want more than just to stop a particular event from happening or a particular individual from intruding; they believe that the very presence of certain groups of people in *their* town, *their* state, *their* country represents an intolerable threat to their personal well-being and to the survival of their group's way of life. They provide propaganda to individuals looking to justify their own hateful behavior. They train youths in the art of bashing minorities. They recruit on college campuses, at prisons, and in the workplace. They operate cable-access television programs featuring interviews with one another. They are the individuals who join Posse Comitatus, the Identity Church, the White Aryan Resistance, the Ku Klux Klan, the American Nazi Party, and similar organizations. Hatemongers, although they may be relatively few in number (between twenty thousand and fifty thousand), are responsible for some of the most vicious acts of violence.

Many members of organized hate groups are marginal and alienated; they are poorly educated and financially troubled. In order to locate the source of their problems and feel morally superior, they engage in "protest by proxy." That is, they scapegoat on a collective level by constructing an evil force, an enemy, that becomes the perceived source of their predicament and the object of their animosity.

The deep recession of the early 1980s had already convinced some destitute and out-of-work automobile workers, farmers, ranchers, miners, and individuals in the timber industry that Jews, Asians, and blacks were responsible for all of their *economic* woes. But since this was still during the Cold War era, many Americans traced their *personal* problems to the conspiratorial activities of the "evil empire" located in the vast and powerful republics under the control of the Soviet Union. With the demise of Eastern European Communism at the end of the 1980s, however, the enemy had to be reconstructed. Rather than locate evil in Europe, more and more Americans found it in Washington, D.C., New York City, and Hollywood. Since the 1970s, the credibility of all leadership positions in the United States—government, science, medicine, education, business, and even religion—has seriously eroded. Fewer and fewer Americans believe that people in positions of power represent the interests of the average citizen. In fact, some people are convinced that communists have taken over the White House, the Supreme Court, and Congress.

Protest by proxy gives a sense of satisfaction that is not possible if one attacks vague and abstract economic and social forces. Thus, rather than blame global competition, corporate downsizing, and automation for putting them out of work, some Americans prefer putting a human (or subhuman) face on the enemy—communists in the White House, the Satanic Jewish lobby, blacks and Latinos who unjustly demanded special treatment and privilege, or the menace of immigration. Protest by proxy is not a new phenomenon; there is a long history of violence being perpetrated, during periods of economic turmoil, against vulnerable and marginalized groups. Between 1800 and 1930, whenever the cotton crops failed in the South, blacks were lynched. At low points in the business cycle, Ku Klux Klan membership rose. During the Great Depression of the 1930s, there were 114 organizations whose purpose was to spread anti-Semitism, not to mention the numerous nativist organizations that attempted to reduce the flow of immigrants to zero. It is hard to bash an abstraction; it is much more satisfying psychologically for hatemongers to burn a black church, blow up a federal building, or bludgeon someone to death with a baseball bat.

Dabblers

For hatemongers, hate becomes the basis for a full-time preoccupation, almost a career. Yet, in everyday life, not all such incidents are so clearly full of hate.

Certain individuals dabble in bigotry (i.e., they convert their prejudices into behavior, but only on a part-time basis as a hobby)—for example, by going out on a Saturday night with their buddies to assault someone, to burn crosses, or to spray-paint graffiti. Dabblers are typically young people—usually teenaged boys—who are not getting along at home, in school, or on the job. They may hate themselves as much as they hate their victims. Most hate crimes against blacks, gays, Latinos, Asians, and Jews are committed by dabblers who gain "bragging rights" with their friends at the same time that they fill the idle hours with excitement. In 1990, for example, three skinheads literally hammered to death Julio Rivera, a twenty-nine-year-old gay man who was on his way home from a job as a local bartender. Bored and idle, the three assailants walked the streets of Queens, New York, in the early morning hours until they located "the enemy." The 1998 murder of Matthew Shepard, a gay student at the University of Wyoming, seems to have contained similar elements of thrill motivation because of the "overkill" involved in his death.

Dabblers typically do not limit their attacks to any particular group. The interesting thing theoretically, as pointed out by Paul Sniderman and Thomas Piazza (1993), is that a dabbler who hates someone because he or she is black is also likely to hate someone who is Latino or gay or Asian or Jewish or disabled. Prejudice is part of American culture, but it also serves an important psychological need for self-esteem and respectability. The target of prejudice is selected because he or she has been widely stereotyped as inferior—as dirty or lazy or stupid or immoral or alcoholic or sly or treacherous or whatever. Through a process of social comparison, the perpetrator is able to gain a sense of personal superiority (e.g., being beautiful, smart, or moral) only to the extent that the victim is placed in an inferior position. This zero-sum definition of respectability can be found in early conceptions of the authoritarian personality theory suggested by Theodor Adorno and his colleagues (1950). According to this theory, prejudice has its roots in harsh and threatening child-rearing practices. Because of mistreatment at an early age, the bigoted youth grows up feeling a profound sense of powerlessness. As an adult, he or she identifies with the powerful elements of society

and maintains distances from the groups that are stereotyped as being inferior, weak, and powerless.

According to Levin and McDevitt (1995), some dabblers are motivated to commit hate crimes because they believe the event to be a *defensive* action. Such attacks are typically precipitated by a threatening episode—a gay rights parade, blacks moving into a previously all-white neighborhood, the first Latino or Asian student on a campus. Failing to elicit the desired response (e.g., the immediate withdrawal of the threat), there may be an escalation of violence. A verbal attack by telephone may become a personal visit with a firearm; vandalism and harassment may turn deadly.

Sympathizers

Most people are not completely tolerant and accepting of differences, but they are not raving bigots either—with respect to their personal prejudices, they fall somewhere in between. Millions of Americans may not be active hatemongers or even dabblers, but they agree in principle with those who are. Such individuals can be regarded as being sympathizers—their prejudiced attitudes are generally at a verbal level only. They may repeat a joke to their like-minded associates, and that is as far as they are willing to go. However, their voices give encouragement and comfort to those who express their hatred in discrimination or violence. Moreover, because of their refusal to cooperate with those who seek to bring bigots to justice, sympathizers also share responsibility for the acts that their sympathetic stance makes possible.

Although they are hardly represented among violent bigots, sympathizers play an especially important role in perpetuating institutionalized forms of discrimination against underrepresented groups in society. In the atmosphere of an executive boardroom, a real estate agency, or a university admissions office, verbal bigotry is just what it takes to stifle the ambitions of individuals who seek jobs, homes, or a place in the classroom. The individual hatred of powerful decision makers can easily be transformed into company policy. This was demonstrated when it was disclosed that certain Texaco directors, while meeting to formulate company procedures, had voiced racist feelings about their black employees. Some observers connected directors' attitudes with the fact that few black workers had attained executive positions in the Texaco hierarchy.

Sympathizers can, given the appropriate conditions, be moved to dabble in bigotry or even to become a hatemonger. According to Daniel Goldhagen (1996), tens of thousands of German citizens during the Nazi era of the 1930s, reacting to Adolf Hitler's interpretation of a terrible economic situation, trans-

---

Iago, in William Shakespeare's Othello *(1604), expresses his hatred of the Moor by lying and by tricking him into believing that his wife, Desdemona, is unfaithful. Othello, in a rage of jealousy, kills her before discovering Iago's hateful deception.*

lated their sympathy for anti-Semitism into mass murder.

When a particular hatred becomes part of the culture—the way of life—of a group of people, sympathy for that hatred may become a widely shared and enduring element in the normal state of affairs for that society. As such, sympathizers (through reinforcing contact with parents, friends, teachers, and the mass media) develop their hate from an early age. Stereotyping also seems to have a cultural basis, but it depends on the cognitive development of the individual. As a result, the particular cultural images (i.e., stereotypes) of a group of people may not be accepted, or even understood, by a child until long after he or she has already developed an intense hatred toward its members. Education seems to be effective in reducing stereotyped thinking, and legislation can, within limits, reduce discriminatory behavior. Yet hate may persevere over the course of a lifetime, regardless of attempts to modify it. Beginning so early in life, hate may become a "passion" for the individual who acquires it, and passions are much more difficult to modify than are stereotypes and the tendency to discriminate.

The cultural aspects of hate can be seen in its amazing ability to sweep across broad geographical areas. Individuals separated by region, age, social class, and ethnic background all tend to share roughly the same stereotyped images of various groups. In the United States, for example, some degree of antiblack racism can be found among substantial segments of the population—males and females, young and old, rich and poor—from New York to California, from North Dakota to Texas. At the same time, the emotional character of racial or religious hatred is reflected collectively in laws and norms that prohibit intimate contact between different groups of people. In the South, Jim Crow laws created separate public facilities—"colored" and "white" restrooms, waiting rooms, water fountains, and sections on public buses. Under apartheid in South Africa, blacks were restricted to living in segregated communities and could work among whites only under the strictest supervision.

In his analysis of race relations in the United States, psychiatrist James Comer (1972) recounts the story of a white teenager who was scolded by her father for putting a coin in her mouth. "Get that money out of your mouth," he yelled, "it might have been in a nigger's hand!" At the time, being black was seen by many white Americans as a contagious disease in need of being quarantined. Nazi-era Germany provides an example of the same sort of enduring sympathy for hate (with regard to anti-Semitism). Goldhagen (1996), in explaining the particular stronghold of Hitler's "final solution," argues that an "eliminationist anti-Semi-

tism" was a centuries-old feature of German culture. The vast majority of ordinary German citizens believed that the Jews, ostensibly being responsible for all of their country's economic woes, had to be eliminated at any cost. Thus, rather than being some dark and repulsive secret, gruesome stories about the Nazi's brutal anti-Jewish policies—the death camps, gas chambers, hideous experiments, and mass murders—were told and retold proudly across the land to ordinary German citizens who were eager to hear them. What is more, Meredith Watts (1997), in an analysis of anti-Jewish attitudes in Germany, found that strong feelings of anti-Semitism remained even after "four decades of re-education . . . and a nearly total taboo on public expressions of anti-Semitism" (p. 219).

Spectators

Spectators, who make up the largest of the four typology divisions, appear to be indifferent or apathetic rather than hateful because they do little if anything to stop a hate incident from occurring. As a matter of abstract principle, spectators may support equal treatment of blacks and whites in the major public areas of everyday life—in schools, neighborhoods, workplaces, and public accommodations. In the context of everyday decision making, however, they stand idly by, hoping not to get personally involved.

In survey after survey, the majority of Americans claim to be accepting of racial integration, at least as a matter of principle. For example, only 7 percent of all Americans think that "blacks and whites should go to separate schools," and only 4 percent now characterize blacks as "lazy" (compared to 26 percent in 1967 and 75 percent in 1933). When it comes to government efforts to implement equal treatment, however, there is considerably less support. In fact, Schuman and his colleagues (1997) report that public support for government intervention to integrate schools and provide equal treatment in the use of public accommodations has actually decreased since the 1970s. The continuing weakness of white support for the implementation of racial integration is demonstrated also by variations in willingness to participate personally in integrated settings. Very few white Americans object to neighborhood or school integration when it involves only a small number of blacks. When blacks promise to become anything like a majority, however, white support dwindles.

How does one explain these bystanders to bigotry? Spectators benefit from whatever advantages their group receives as a result of the perpetuation of the bigotry, even if they believe in the principles of democracy and equality of opportunity. As a result, they laugh along with their friends at the most bigoted jokes, they walk right by teenagers painting hateful graffiti, they make no effort to stop any scheme aimed at harassing black neighbors, and they would never attend the wedding of an interracial couple. Rather than participate actively and put their beliefs into practice, they just "go along" as spectators to a situation over which they may feel powerless. Of course, spectators' very inactivity—the failure to act on their convictions—tends to give license to hatemongers.

Before the American Civil War, slavery was widely viewed in the South as being a necessary aspect of the southern economic order. Slave owners were not the only southerners who benefited from slavery. Many more were spectators who never made money but enjoyed being members of a "superior" caste.

In Northern Ireland, middle-class residents can avoid the most dangerous aspects of the religious conflict and terrorism by remaining spectators. This position also allows the most tolerant of citizens to benefit economically from the religious differences.

During the Nazi era, many otherwise decent German citizens benefited in a material sense from the confiscation of Jewish property. Personal belongings and furniture were auctioned to the highest bidder, and tens of thousands of Jewish apartments were taken over. Moreover, the expulsion of Jews from prestigious or lucrative occupations seriously reduced the competition for well-paying and high-status jobs. On the other side, citizens of Germany and Nazi-occupied European countries who aided Jews by concealing them from German soldiers exposed themselves to the possibility of paying the ultimate price. In one Ukrainian village, for example, an entire family—husband, wife, and three children—were shot to death for sheltering a Jewish woman.

During periods of economic downturn in the 1980s and 1990s, Asian Americans often became the targets of hate. Just as Jews had been blamed for Germany's economic woes during the Nazi era, Asians were held responsible for America's declining position in the global economy. In 1982, during the deepest recession since World War II, two out-of-job automobile workers in Detroit killed Vincent Chin, a Chinese-American man who was celebrating just prior to his wedding day. The two men blamed the Japanese for their financial problems and failed to distinguish Chinese from Japanese or Asian Americans from Asians. Ten years later, just as an epidemic of corporate downsizing hit the American economy, the Los Angeles office of the Japanese American Citizens League received a bomb threat in which the caller warned, "I'll show you a year of remembrance, you dirty Japs. What we remember is Pearl Harbor." During the same period, an Asian American from Sacramento was stabbed to death by someone who sought to "defend our country" from the onslaught of Asian newcomers. In a study by Levin

and McDevitt (1995) of hate crimes reported to the Boston police in 1992, it was found that Asians and Latinos were the two groups at greatest risk for victimization. These are the "new kids on the block," the newcomers who are seen as being a threat to the economic well-being of groups of Americans who have been in the United States longer and who now feel they must protect their stake in the country.

Reducing Hate and Producing Rebels

The cultural, structural, and psychological bases for inspiring hate give it a resistance to change that may be difficult (albeit not impossible) to overcome. Culture is, to some extent, self-perpetuating, especially when it serves important psychological and economic functions for the individuals and specific groups in a society. At the individual level, however, Thomas Pettigrew (1997) suggests that the emotional component of intergroup hostility can be reduced by the encouragement of intimacy and friendship between the members of different groups.

At the group level, the key to producing rebels—individuals who defy conventional standards of bigotry in order to express tolerance and respect for diversity—may be to provide society's members with functional alternatives to hate and violence. One might speculate that hate declines to the extent that hatemongers, dabblers, sympathizers, and spectators are given structured opportunities to feel good about themselves, have some hope for the future, and gain a sense of belonging—without hating and hurting other people. If this is so, then anything less than a major structural change will, in all likelihood, be ineffective.

See also: AGGRESSION; ANGER; ANNOYANCE; ENVY; FEAR AND PHOBIAS; HATE CRIMES; JEALOUSY; PREJUDICE; XENOPHOBIA

Bibliography

Adorno, Theodor W.; Frankel-Brunswik, Else; Levinson, Daniel J.; and Sanford, R. Nevitt. (1950). *The Authoritarian Personality.* New York: Harper & Row.

Ancheta, Angelo N. (1998). *Race, Rights, and the Asian American Experience.* New Brunswick, NJ: Rutgers University Press.

Brown, Tony. (1995). *Black Lies, White Lies: The Truth According to Tony Brown.* New York: William Morrow.

Browning, Christopher R. (1992). *Ordinary Men: Reserve Police Battalion 101 and the Final Solution in Poland.* New York: HarperCollins.

Comer, James P. (1972). *Beyond Black and White.* Chicago: Quadrangle Books.

Ezekiel, Raphael S. (1995). *The Racist Mind: Portraits of American Neo-Nazis and Klansmen.* New York: Viking Press.

Fox, James, and Levin, Jack. (1996). *Overkill: Mass Murder and Serial Killing Exposed.* New York: Dell.

Goldhagen, Daniel Jonah. (1996). *Hitler's Willing Executioners: Ordinary Germans and the Holocaust.* New York: Basic Books.

Halpern, Thomas, and Levin, Brian. (1996). *The Limits of Dissent: The Constitutional Status of Armed Civilian Militias.* Amherst, MA: Aletheia Press.

Jacobs, James B., and Potter, Kimberly A. (1998). *Hate Crimes: Criminal Law and Identity Politics.* New York: Oxford University Press.

Jenness, Valerie, and Broad, Kendal. (1997). *Hate Crimes: New Social Movements and the Politics of Violence.* New York: Aldine De Gruyter.

Karl, Jonathan. (1995). *The Right to Bear Arms: The Rise of America's New Militias.* New York: HarperPaperbacks.

Keough, William. (1990). *Punchlines: The Violence of American Humor.* New York: Paragon House.

Levin, Jack, and Levin, William J. (1982). *The Functions of Discrimination and Prejudice.* New York: Harper & Row.

Levin, Jack, and McDevitt, Jack. (1993). *Hate Crimes: The Rising Tide of Bigotry and Bloodshed.* New York: Plenum.

Levin, Jack, and McDevitt, Jack. (1995). "Landmark Study Reveals Hate Crimes Vary Significantly by Offender Motivation." *Klanwatch Intelligence Report,* August, pp. 7–9.

Macdonald, Andrew. (1978). *The Turner Diaries.* New York: Barricade Books.

Pettigrew, Thomas F. (1997). "The Affective Component of Prejudice: Empirical Support for the New View." In *Racial Attitudes in the 1990s: Continuity and Change,* ed. Steven A. Tuch and Jack K. Martin. Westport, CT: Praeger.

Rowan, Carl T. (1996). *The Coming Race War in America.* Boston: Little, Brown.

Schuman, Howard; Steeh, Charlotte; Bobo, Lawrence; and Krysan, Maria. (1997). *Racial Attitudes in America: Trends and Interpretations,* rev. ed. Cambridge, MA: Harvard University Press.

Selznick, Gertrude J., and Steinberg, Stephen. (1969). *The Tenacity of Prejudice: Anti-Semitism in Contemporary America.* New York: Harper & Row.

Sniderman, Paul M., and Piazza, Thomas. (1993). *The Scar of Race.* Cambridge, MA: Belknap Press.

Turner, Patricia A. (1993). *I Heard It Through the Grapevine: Rumor in African-American Culture.* Berkeley: University of California Press.

Watts, Meredith. (1997). *Xenophobia in United Germany: Generations, Modernization, and Ideology.* New York: St. Martin's Press.

Jack Levin
Monte Paulsen

HATE CRIMES

People across the United States were shocked in June 1998 by the vicious murder of James Byrd, Jr., a twenty-nine-year-old African-American man who was dragged to his death on a back road of Jasper, Texas. Three men with ties to white supremacist groups had apparently beaten the African-American hitchhiker until he was unconscious, chained him to their pickup truck, and then dragged him down the road for more than two miles. Just three months later, twenty-one-year-old

Matthew Shepard, a gay student at the University of Wyoming, was repeatedly beaten until dead, allegedly by two of homophobic schoolmates. Many people regarded the murders of Byrd and Shepard as "hate crimes." Both men had been slain because they were different—Byrd because of the color of his skin and Shepard because of his sexual orientation.

As a matter of law, the particular groups protected under hate crime statutes vary from state to state. At present, forty-nine states have some form of anti–hate crime legislation—most jurisdictions cover offenses against individuals who are targeted because of their race, religion, or ethnicity. However, only twenty states include sexual orientation and disability, and even fewer states cover gender and age. In some states, a separate statute exists that prohibits hate crime behavior, while in other states, the hate crime statute is a "penalty enhancement." This means that if an existing crime is committed and is motivated by bias, the penalty on the existing crime may be increased.

Why Treat Hate Crimes Differently?

Since hate crimes by definition involve behavior that is already prohibited by state or federal statutes (e.g., assault, threats, vandalism), the question is frequently posed as to why there is a need for additional penalties. Are these crimes truly different?

In fact, a number of the characteristics of hate incidents make them different from other types of offenses. First, hate crimes are directed at large groups of people. What distinguishes hate crimes (or bias crimes) from other sorts of offenses and makes them so terrifying to so many citizens is that hate crimes are motivated either entirely or in part by the fact or perception that a victim is different from the perpetrator. In a sense, Byrd's murder was not against a person; it was against an entire race. It was not *what* Byrd happened to say or do that made him a target; it was not even *where* he happened to be at the time he was attacked. The motivation for the victimization of Byrd was *who* he happened to be. In short, the target of a hate crime is defined by the perpetrators as the "enemy"—as lacking in human qualities and therefore exempt from the rules that govern civilized society.

If someone is murdered in the course of a burglary, the offenders typically have no desire to communicate anything in particular to the property owner; in fact, they frequently do not know anything about the victim they have targeted and have little interest in changing his or her behavior. Very simply, they seek only to perform the burglary and make a clean get away. By contrast, hate crimes are about sending and receiving messages. Offenders use a criminal event to put the members of an entire group on notice, by example, that they are not welcome in a community, in a workplace, on a college campus, or at school. Their intention is to send a message not just to that victim but to every member of the group—all African Americans, all Latinos, all Asians, all gays, all whites—informing them that their presence will not be tolerated.

Another characteristic that differentiates hate crimes from most other offenses is that the victim characteristic motivating the attack (e.g., race or ethnicity) is in most cases ascribed and immutable. A person cannot change his or her race, ethnicity, age, gender, or disability status. Even a religious identity cannot be modified without causing an individual to make dramatic and difficult changes in lifestyle. Characteristics such as religion, political affiliation, and sexual orientation are civil rights protected by the American Constitution. Consequently, if an individual is attacked because he or she is Asian, there is nothing that individual can do to become "de-Asianized" and thus reduce the likelihood of future victimization. This is also true of perceived characteristics. If an individual becomes a hate-crime victim because he or she is perceived by a group of youths to be gay, that individual is also powerless to change the offenders' perceptions. The feeling on the part of victims that they lack control over the characteristic that motivated their victimization causes most hate crime victims to feel extremely vulnerable to future bias-motivated attacks.

A third characteristic of hate crimes that makes them different from many other offenses is that the individual victim typically did nothing to provoke the attack and is therefore interchangeable, at least from the perpetrator's standpoint. To a group of youths waiting outside a gay bar to attack someone whom they believe might be gay, it does not matter which particular individual comes through the door next. The individual who happens to come out first is likely to become the victim because all patrons of a gay bar are identical in the minds of the perpetrators.

Indeed, the interchangeability of victims tends to apply as well across groups of victims. In general, youths who commit hate crimes do not specialize with respect to their targets. For example, if they cannot locate someone to bash who is African American, they might instead target a Latino or an Asian. If they cannot find someone who is gay, they might search out someone who is Jewish or Muslim. This aspect of hate crimes suggests that they are often motivated by an offender's psychological need to feel superiority at the expense of the victim.

Finally, hate-motivated attacks tend to be more vicious than comparable attacks. In fact, some research suggests that hate-motivated assaults against individuals can be incredibly violent. In Boston, for example,

Jack Levin and Jack McDevitt (1993) found that victims of hate-motivated assaults were three times more likely to need hospital treatment than other assault victims. Moreover, research by Gregory Herek and Kevin Berrill (1992) indicates that victims of anti-gay attacks experienced more trauma than victims of non-bias motivated attacks and that this trauma had longer lasting effects for the hate crime victims. The especially brutal nature of hate violence may be due to the depersonalization that many hate crime offenders employ in justifying their offenses. Hatemongers frequently view members of targeted groups as less than human. They reason, therefore, that it is appropriate to treat their victims in the manner they might treat a wild animal or a demon rather than a human being.

A Typology of Hate Crimes

The term *hate crime* was first used during the mid-1980s by journalists and politicians, but it quickly became employed by scholarly researchers as well. In a sense, the term is somewhat misleading in its emphasis on "hate" as a defining basis for choosing and attacking a particular victim. The level of brutality in the Jasper, Texas, murder does suggest the presence of intense hostility or anger (i.e., hatred) in the motivation of the assailants. In the more typical hate crime, however, the perpetrators may be motivated more by a desire for belonging or profit than by hatred for a particular victim. They may go along simply because their friends do. They may even simply act out of a need to feel important or to protect their territory. In many crimes, hatred toward the victim may be present but the motivation for the crime was not bias—these crimes can confound the definition of hate crimes.

In fact, hate crimes can be classified (in terms of their motivational bases) into three major types: thrill, defensive, and mission. The majority of hate crimes seem to be thrill hate crimes—recreational offenses committed by youths (usually teenaged boys operating in groups) who seek excitement at someone else's expense. They are more than willing to travel to another neighborhood or some other part of town where they believe that the members of a targeted group congregate. Such attacks provide the offenders with "bragging rights" that allow them to impress their friends who regard hate as cool. They achieve a sense of belonging, as well as a feeling of their own importance. For a teenager who is not getting along at home, is not successful at school, and has little hope for the future, the benefits of committing a hate crime—a sense of power and kinship—may seem considerable.

Many of the hate crimes that are directed against property—acts of desecration and vandalism—can be included in the thrill seeking category. In an incident in Wellesley, Massachusetts, for example, two alienated white youths looking for excitement went on a spree of destruction and defacement that resulted in attacks on twenty-three properties in three different communities. The two went out at night when "there was nothing else to do" and defaced walls, driveways, and automobiles with slurs against Jews, African Americans, Greeks, and even skinheads. After their arrest, the two young men claimed that they had not intended to hurt anyone and that it happened because they were drunk. The selection of victims in the Wellesley incident is typical of thrill hate crimes in general—particular victims are chosen more or less on a random basis. Thus, interchangeability occurs not only within a target group—for example, among African Americans, Jews, or Asians—but across groups as well. Indeed, almost any vulnerable and easily-identified victim will do.

Defensive hate crimes are designed to protect an individual's neighborhood, workplace, school, or cohorts from those who are considered to be outsiders or intruders. This type of hate crime often occurs when a family from a different racial group moves into a previously all-white neighborhood, dormitory, or school. Even the unexplained presence of "outsiders" who walk through "the wrong neighborhood" has, in the past, been enough reason to commit a hate offense. In December 1986, in the infamous Howard Beach case in New York, a young African-American man was killed crossing a highway as he attempted to flee from a mob of white teenagers hurling racial epithets. What was his "crime"? Attempting to phone for help after his car had broken down. Wherever it occurs, a defensive attack is often an act of domestic terrorism because it is designed to send a message to every member of the victim's group—that they had better watch their step or they could easily be next. It sends a signal, loud and clear, for those who come from the victim's group to back off, to get lost, or to stay in their place. Do not come to this school, do not move into this community, do not take this job . . . stay out of Howard Beach!

Following the December 1986 death of Michael Griffith, more than five hundred demonstrators marched through Howard Beach, New York, chanting antiracist slogans and carrying placards. Additional demonstrations occurred in December 1987 when one white teenager was cleared of all charges in Griffith's death and three other white teenagers were convicted of manslaughter rather than murder. (Corbis/Bettmann)

The third type of hate crime is the mission offense, usually committed by the members of an organized hate group. Actually, no more than 5 percent of all hate crimes nationwide are committed by the members of organizations like the Ku Klux Klan, Aryan Nations, or the White Aryan Resistance. But organized hate groups continue behind the scenes to inspire murder, assault, and vandalism. They encourage and support much larger numbers of violent offenses committed by non-members who may be totally unsophisticated with respect to the ideology of hate—racist skinheads, alienated teenagers, or hate-filled young men looking to have a good time at someone else's expense.

Byrd's murder in Jasper, Texas, is not the first to incriminate white supremacy from a distance. In 1990, Tom and John Metzger of the White Aryan Resistance lost a major lawsuit implicating them in the skinhead murder of an Ethiopian man on the streets of Portland, Oregon. Awarding the victim's family nine million dollars, the jury concluded that the Metzgers, operating from their headquarters a thousand miles away, had orchestrated the Portland murder by their coaching of skinheads in the use of weapons and in how to assault African Americans by provoking them first and then claiming self-defense. In Byrd's murder, investigators discovered a Klan manual among the possessions carried by one of the suspects, and two of the suspects wore white supremacist tattoos depicting the Confederate Knights of America. The three defendants may not have been active members of any white supremacy group at the time of the murder, but they were definitely ardent admirers who used white supremacist propaganda and enjoyed being associated with white supremacist symbols of power.

Organized hate groups are also active in penitentiaries around the country. While serving time behind bars for burglary convictions, two of the suspects in Jasper apparently had links with the Aryan Brotherhood, a prison hate group whose members are often recruited by white supremacists after they have been released. Established in many states, the Aryan Brotherhood introduces inmates to the theology of the Identity Church, according to which Jews are the children of Satan and African Americans are subhuman "mud people." Prisons, which in the past had been known to be schools for crime, are now operating as places in which a crash course in hatred can be obtained.

According to the Anti-Defamation League (1997), there are some 3,500 racist skinheads in the United States, most of whom probably lack connections to white supremacy groups. "Two Years After" (1997), a report by the Southern Poverty Law Center's Klanwatch project, indicates that there may be more than 20,000 (but almost certainly no more than 50,000) people who are members of white supremacist groups across the United States, which has a total population of 265,000,000. The report indicates also that there are approximately 370 basic citizens' militia groups, which are only loosely connected to one another. Membership in these militia groups has been estimated by Jonathan Karl (1995) to be between 15,000 and 100,000. It should also be pointed out that the militia movement in the United States is diverse. Some members are clearly racist in their beliefs, but there are also Jewish and African-American militia members.

Very rarely is a mission hate crime committed by a single individual, and the few perpetrators of mission hate crimes who operate alone typically suffer from a profound mental illness that may cause hallucinations, impaired ability to reason, and withdrawal from contact with other people. The mission of such individuals is to get even for the horrific problems that they have suffered. In their paranoid and delusional way of thinking, they see a conspiracy of some kind for which they seek revenge. Their mission is in part suicidal. Before actually committing suicide, however, they must attempt to eliminate the *entire category* of people that is responsible (at least as they see it) for their personal frustrations.

In January 1989, twenty-four-year old Patrick Purdy put on his military flak jacket, picked up a handgun and an AK-47 semiautomatic assault rifle, and drove his 1977 Chevrolet station wagon a couple of miles to the Cleveland Elementary School in Stockton, California—the same elementary school he had attended from kindergarten to third grade. When he had lived there as a child, the neighborhood was white, but now it was predominantly Asian. Purdy blamed the newcomers in his community for taking his job and destroying his educational opportunities. Through a gap in the fence surrounding the building, Purdy walked into the crowded school grounds and opened fire. For a period of two minutes, Purdy sprayed sixty rounds of bullets from his AK-47 at screaming children in a sweeping motion across the blacktop. He then took the handgun from his belt and shot himself in the head. Five children, all from Southeast Asia, were killed, and thirty more were wounded.

Are Hate Crimes on the Rise?

Due to the inadequacy of hate crime data, it is difficult to determine with certainty whether the number of hate crimes has increased, decreased, or remained stable over time. Because legal definitions are in flux and additional law enforcement agencies are constantly being added to those who report to the Federal Bureau of Investigations, the data frequently is not comparable from one year to the next. In addition, some of the data collected on an annual basis has been reported by advocacy groups such as the Anti-Defamation League and the National Gay and Lesbian Task-Force, making the results subject to the criticism that such organizations have a vested interest in generating inflated figures. Indeed, some observers such as James Jacobs and Kimberly Potter (1997, 1998) have even suggested that those who support anti–hate crime legislation are creating a "social construction" without any basis in reality.

With such limitations in mind, however, it is still possible to gain some perspective as to changes in the prevalence of hate crimes over time. Based on data collected by various advocacy groups such as the Anti-Defamation League, the Southern Poverty Law Center, and the Gay and Lesbian Alliance, it is likely that hate crimes increased beginning in the early 1980s, a trend that perhaps continued into the early 1990s. First, this conclusion is in agreement with evidence gathered by independent research organizations, such as the National Institute Against Prejudice and Violence, that are interested in a more general way in hate crimes. Moreover, anti-government militias and survivalists—groups almost totally unheard of before 1980—have made their presence increasingly known throughout the 1980s and into the 1990s. Although many militia members disavow any connection with hatemongers, there is at least some overlap between militia groups and white supremacists.

Although claims as to the increasing presence of hate crimes in the United States may be controversial, reports of escalating violence directed against Jews and immigrant groups in the early 1990s remains essentially undisputed for many European countries, including France, Germany, England, Poland, Italy, Russia, and Hungary. In these countries during the early 1990s, there were, according to Meredith Watts (1997), dramatic increases in violent skinhead and neo-Nazi demonstrations and in the prevalence of political bigotry.

Those such as Susan Olzak and her colleagues (1996) who argue that hate crimes have been increasing also note that intergroup competition has been on the rise. Whether or not this competition is economically based, the perception of growing threats to the advantaged majority group may have inspired a rising tide of hate incidents directed against members of challenging groups. Since the mid-1980s, there have been dramatic increases in interfaith and interracial dating and marriage; immigration (especially from Latin America and Asia); integration of neighborhoods, schools, college dormitories, and workplaces; and gay men and lesbians coming out (and, in many cases, organizing on behalf of their shared interests).

It is not surprising that hate crimes occur most frequently in "defended" white neighborhoods—that is, in predominantly white areas that have experienced these kinds of change.

As for the contention that advocacy groups inflate their estimates of hate crimes, it is interesting to note that the Anti-Defamation League (1997) reported decreases in skinhead activity and in the overall level of hate crimes between 1994 and 1997. Their conclusions concerning the downward trend in hate offenses is consistent with evidence collected by the Federal Bureau of Investigations that indicates crime in general has declined in the United States since 1992.

Conclusion

Whether or not hate-motivated offenses are on the rise, the murders of Byrd and Shepard show that hate is alive and well. Most people would not think of committing a sadistic murder just because someone is from a different race. But there are many individuals who do share the attitudes of white supremacy. There are people who resent policies and programs designed to equalize opportunities for African Americans and Latino Americans. There are people who despise immigrants from eastern Europe, Asia, and Latin America who have relocated to the United States in order to escape oppression or impoverishment in their homelands. And there are people who feel threatened by the increasing presence of African Americans in their workplaces, neighborhoods, and schools. To treat the murder of Byrd as an aberration or as something peculiar to Jasper, Texas or to the South for that matter—would be to miss the point. Hate crimes have an underlying basis in a culture of prejudice that transcends the boundaries that divide Americans by region, social class, or ethnic background. Hate is indeed as American as the success ethic, apple pie, and violence.

See also: AGGRESSION; ANGER; FEAR AND PHOBIAS; HATE; PREJUDICE; XENOPHOBIA

Bibliography

Anti-Defamation League. (1997). *Vigilante Justice: Militias and Common Law Courts Wage War Against the Government.* New York: Anti-Defamation League.

Ehrlich, Howard. (1990). *Ethno-Violence on College Campuses.* Baltimore, MD: National Institute Against Prejudice and Violence.

Fox, James, and Levin, Jack. (1996). *Overkill: Mass Murder and Serial Killing Exposed.* New York: Dell.

Green, Donald P.; Strolovitch, Dara Z.; and Wong, Janelle S. (1997). "Defended Neighborhoods, Integration, and Hate Crime," unpublished manuscript, Institution for Social and Policy Studies, Yale University.

Halpern, Thomas, and Levin, Brian. (1996). *The Limits of Dissent: The Constitutional Status of Armed Civilian Militias.* Amherst, MA: Aletheia Press.

Herek, Gregory M., and Berrill, Kevin T. (1992). *Hate Crimes: Confronting Violence against Lesbians and Gay Men.* Newbury Park, CA: Sage Publications.

Jacobs, James B., and Henry, Jessica S. (1996). "The Social Construction of a Hate Crime Epidemic." *Journal of Criminal Law and Criminology,* Winter:366–391.

Jacobs, James B., and Potter, Kimberly A. (1997). "Hate Crimes: A Critical Perspective." In *Crime and Justice,* ed. Michael Tonry. Chicago: University of Chicago Press.

Jacobs, James B., and Potter, Kimberly A. (1998). *Hate Crimes: Criminal Law and Identity Politics.* New York: Oxford University Press.

Karl, Jonathan. (1995). *The Right to Bear Arms.* New York: HarperCollins.

Levin, Jack. (1997). "Visit to a Patriot Potluck." *USA Today,* March 1, p. 6A.

Levin, Jack, and McDevitt, Jack. (1993). *Hate Crimes: The Rising Tide of Bigotry and Bloodshed.* New York: Plenum.

Levin, Jack, and McDevitt, Jack. (1995). "Landmark Study Reveals Hate Crimes Vary Significantly by Offender Motivation." *Klanwatch Intelligence Report,* August, pp. 7–9.

Martin, Susan. (1995). "A Cross-Burning Is Not Just an Arson: Police Social Construction of Hate Crimes in Baltimore County." *Criminology* 33(3):303–330.

Olzak, Susan; Shanahan, Suzanne; and McEneaney, Elizabeth H. (1996). "Poverty, Segregation, and Race Riots: 1960 to 1993." *American Sociological Review* 61(4):590–613.

"Two Years After: The Patriot Movement Since Oklahoma City." (1997). *Klanwatch Intelligence Report,* Spring:18–20.

Watts, Meredith. (1997). *Xenophobia in United Germany.* New York: St. Martin's Press.

Jack Levin
Jack McDevitt

HEALTH AND ILLNESS

Emotions have long captured the interest of people from different generations, cultures, and scientific disciplines. They have been examined by psychologists, philosophers, playwrights, and poets. As far back as Aristotle, emotions have been addressed in terms of definition, characteristics, causality, expression, meaning, structure, and function as reflected in social relationships and individual experience. Because of the strong emphasis on behaviorism during most of the twentieth century, however, it has only been since the 1980s that there has been any extensive study concerning the biological and medical aspects of emotions.

Emotions play a central role in how people think and act and how they relate to others as they adapt to various events in their environment. Furthermore, how people respond emotionally to ongoing situations, as well as to traumatic events, can influence their physical and mental health and their general sense of well-being. People are holistic beings with multiple interacting subsystems that function together as a whole unit in dynamic interaction with a constantly changing environment. From this perspective, the body, mind, emotions, and spirit influence and control each other in a creative whole that is greater than the sum of the individual components. Thus, emotional arousal and agitation may be associated with such descriptions as having one's "bowels in an uproar." Health, then, may be defined as a state of physical, mental, emotional, social, and spiritual well-being; it is more than just the absence of disease or disability.

Characteristics of Emotion

Although there are differing views about what constitutes an emotion and how various emotional states are manifested, most people would probably agree that an emotion is a distinct feeling or quality of consciousness, such as joy, sorrow, anger, or fear, that reflects the personal meaning of an emotion-arousing event. Emotions affect the basic processes of perception and creativity and thus influence the ways in which individuals interpret the world within and around them.

Individuals tend over time to develop patterns of responses to various stimuli. A particular emotional response at a specific point in time, however, is temporary and serves as an evaluative state that is focused on a particular person, event, or situation. Richard Lazarus (1994) describes emotions as organized psychophysiological reactions to some received information that has personal significance about one's relationships with either the environment or, most often, another person.

Lazarus makes the case that the quality and intensity of emotions depend on individuals' subjective evaluations of how they are doing in relation to their desired goals, as well as their individual propensities to act on those interpretations. In other words, emotions are essentially outcomes of a cognitive process of appraisal that is concerned with the loss or gain of something that one wants from an investment in a relationship with the environment or a significant other person. Because emotions depend on particular situations or context, they are subject to constant change, as are the relationships between a person and the environment that generate the emotions initially.

How an individual responds depends on his or her assessment of the circumstances. Appraisals of threatened loss or harm generate perceptions of stress and negative emotions such as fear, anger, anxiety, shame, and jealousy. Positive emotions, such as happiness, love, and gratitude, on the other hand, arise in response to anticipated opportunity for personal gain. These positive emotions can help replenish damaged or depleted resources, restore energy, and provide opportunity for emotional healing.

Neuroendocrine Responses to Perceived Threat

Stress, as defined by Shelley Taylor (1999, p. 168), is a "negative emotional experience accompanied by predictable biochemical, physiological, cognitive, and behavioral changes that are directed either toward altering the stressful event or accommodating to its effects." When someone perceives a threat, the body reacts with arousal and motivation to action via the sympathetic nervous system and the endocrine system. This physiological response, initially described by Walter Cannon (1932) as the fight-or-flight response, mobilizes the individual to attack the threat or to flee.

The fight-or-flight response could be considered adaptive in that it facilitates fast action in the face of danger; however, it may also be harmful because it disrupts emotional and physiological functioning, which can lead to potential medical problems over time. When a person is exposed to prolonged stress and is unable to fight or flee, he or she may remain in a state of physiological arousal trying to cope with the unrealized threat over an extended period of time, developing a maladaptive pattern of physiological responses that establishes a basis for disease.

Regardless of the cause of the threat, Hans Selye (1956) found that an individual tends to respond with the same physiological reaction pattern that eventually wears the system down. If the person is unable to overcome the threat, he or she may deplete physiological resources and become exhausted. Selye identified these reactions as the general adaptation syndrome, which consists of three phases: alarm, resistance, and exhaustion. Selye's work had a substantial effect on the understanding of stress and disease and is still widely accepted. His perspective has been criticized, however, because of his limited recognition of psychological factors such as event appraisal and his assumption that stress responses are always the same in people, regardless of the situation.

Emotional reactions tend to vary greatly and may include anxiety, denial, excitement, embarrassment, fear, anger, depression, and more. Medical disorders such as arthritis, cardiovascular disease, and immune system deficiencies have been linked to prolonged or repeated stress exposure. However, not all people who are exposed to the same situations develop one of these conditions; rather, their individual perceptions, personalities, and biological make-up greatly influence how they will respond. Since emotions play such an important role in stress appraisal and reaction, much of the knowledge based on stress research is critical to understanding how emotions influence health and illness.

There is an elaborate chain of psychophysiological events that occur when a person's brain interprets a situation as threatening or harmful and generates a bodily response. Specifically, the cerebral cortex identifies the threat and sends a message to the hypothalamus, which performs two important functions. First, it arouses the sympathetic nervous system, initiating the fight-or-flight response. This state of arousal stimulates the medulla of the adrenal glands to secrete the catecholamines, epinephrine and norepinephrine. Once this occurs, the person starts to feel alarmed. The heart rate and blood pressure go up in response to constriction of peripheral blood vessels, and the body starts to sweat. Second, the hypothalamus secretes a substance (corticotropin releasing factor) that causes the pituitary gland to secrete a hormone (adrenocorticotropic hormone) that stimulates the cortex of the adrenal glands to release corticosteroids. These secretions, especially cortisol, let the brain know to start storing carbohydrates for energy and to initiate the inflammatory response in case of injury. Other responses include an increased production of growth hormone and beta-endorphins, which block pain in case of injury.

Relationship of Physiological Stress Responses to Health

These multiple arousal responses would be appropriate enough if the person experiencing them actually needed to deal with a potentially life-threatening situation. That is seldom the case, however, and if the excess energy that is created is not discharged in some physically demanding activity, then the person is left with excessive amounts of epinephrine and norepinephrine in the circulatory system. These hormonal excesses are thought to produce cardiovascular changes that elevate heart rate and blood pressure, alter cholesterol and free fatty acid levels, and cause abnormal heart rhythms that may lead to a sudden death event. Additionally, the oversupply of these hormones could potentially suppress immune system function at the cellular level and produce neurochemical changes that may contribute to developing psychiatric disorders. Taylor (1999) asserts that any of these outcomes are more likely to occur if events are perceived to be negative and are repetitive, unpredictable, or uncontrollable in nature because they generate feelings of loss of control, mastery, and self-esteem.

Advances in immunology and increased physiological research on human subjects have lead to vast in-

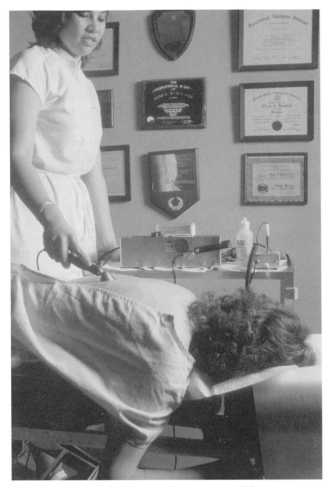

Headaches, which can result from stressful events or sustained negative emotions, can often be reduced or eliminated with the use of medical treatment, such as that being received by this patient at a medical clinic. (Corbis/Shelley Gazin)

creases in knowledge about the relationships between emotional distress and disease. Even though there is increasing evidence that chronic stress states are associated with decreased immune system efficiency, the mechanisms by which some of the cellular changes occur in human subjects seem less clear. For example, William Lovallo (1997) has reported that most human ulcers are caused by the recurrence of a chronic bacterial infection, although the causal link with emotional distress is not firmly established.

Prolonged secretion of cortisol, which is directed toward conserving energy, has been associated with storage of excess fatty tissue around the abdominal organs, decreased effectiveness of lymphocytes in warding off disease, and destruction of neurons in the brain of the elderly, leading to memory and concentration problems. Taylor (1999) states that cortisol secretion has also been noted more often and for greater periods of time in people who are considered to be depressed as compared with those who are not depressed.

There is some debate in the literature about which physiological stress responses have greater implications for disease processes. Richard Dienstbier (1989) is among a number of investigators who consider that activities that produce only sympathetic adrenal arousal, such as exercise, tend to serve a protective function; whereas, as Taylor has pointed out, activation of the hypothalamus, pituitary gland, and adrenal cortex can create more serious health outcomes. Dienstbier has described a pattern of physiological toughness that is associated with emotional stability, complex task achievement, and immune system enhancement. Clearly, individual reactivity to stress may vary from minimal to high. That is, some people display little change in their neuroendocrine, autonomic, or immune systems, whereas other people show greater sympathetic arousal.

Lovallo (1997) surmised after reviewing the literature that even though many stressors pose little threat themselves, a person's sense of control may serve as a significant mediator on mood and health outcomes. Whether people show large or small reactions to perceived threat, their individual patterns may to some extent be genetically determined.

Individual Differences in Responses and Outcomes

Certain people are more prone to interpret events as being stressful by virtue of their personalities, and their reaction could influence the development of symptoms or rates of illness. For example, some individuals show a general tendency toward negative mood states, that is, frequent anger, anxiety, depression, and hostility. They are often distressed and may drink heavily, feel depressed, and act out suicidal feelings. These negative emotional states predict short-term decreases in immune function and negative health effects over the long run.

Negativity has long been linked to poor health outcomes such as asthma, arthritis, ulcers, coronary artery disease, and headaches. However, in their meta-analysis of the literature focusing on correlates of these five diseases with several emotional aspects of personality, Howard Friedman and Stephanie Booth-Kewley (1987) found only weak evidence to support the construct of a disease-prone personality. Stronger associations were noted in relation to coronary heart disease (CHD). These researchers concluded that chronic negative emotional states are more characteristic of coronary proneness than previously thought. They found strong associations between CHD and de-

Leo Tolstoy wrote his "Death of Ivan Ilyich" in 1886, but the story remains pertinent today as a picture of suffering and dying, especially of one who lives his life in an ordinary, unthinking way. As Ivan grows gravely ill, his family grows more remote and even blames him for his illness. Only his peasant servant gives him any recognizable care and comfort.

pression and between CHD and anxiety, anger, hostility, and aggression.

There is some evidence of a genetic predisposition to higher reactivity in stressful situations. Vincent DeQuattro and Debora Lee (1991) suggested that reactivity could be an inherited predisposition toward elevated sympathetic nervous system activity in response to stressful events. William Gerin and Thomas Pickering (1995) found that people who are at risk for hypertension but are not yet diagnosed, and have a family history of hypertension, show reliably greater cardiovascular reactivity in response to stressful events and a slower recovery afterward than people without hypertension who have no family history of the disorder.

Inability to recover quickly from a stressful occurrence appears to be a marker for unfavorable physiological changes. The secretion of cortisol normally helps decrease the inflammatory response to injury and the release of carbohydrate stores for energy, assisting the body's return to equilibrium or a state of balance. However, in situations of high or prolonged stress and continuing cortisol secretion, individuals may be more vulnerable to disease or injury.

Taylor (1999) cites several studies that provide support for the hypothesis that differences in reactivity may contribute to the development of hypertension and coronary artery disease in particular. In studies of preschool children, for example, W. Thomas Boyce and his colleagues (1995) found that stress was associated with increased rates of illness only among children who had previously demonstrated strong immune or cardiovascular reactivity to a stressful event, in contrast to less reactive children who showed no change in illness after stress exposure.

Other factors that have been implicated in the development of hypertension are hostility, suppressed anger and rage, defensiveness, and high stress environment. It is unclear what role the early family environment may play in development of the disease, but it has been suggested by Craig Ewart (1991) and others that negative verbal and nonverbal family communication may lead to chronic anger or the tendency to excessive sympathetic nervous system reactivity.

Elizabeth Semenchuk and Kevin Larkin (1993) noted negative verbal and nonverbal interactive styles among people who were at risk for hypertension. Although there has been long-standing debate about the role of hostility in cardiovascular reactivity, research findings increasingly link the trait of inappropriate competitiveness, rather than general hostility, with hypertension.

Some people respond to threatening events with avoidance behaviors. Avoidance responders, who may worry and focus attention on their negative emotions, seem to manage pretty well for short periods of time. If the threat is repetitive or continues over an extended period of time, however, they may have problems dealing well with the situation. Conversely, those who cope with threat by confronting a situation head on may manage well over the long haul, but they may feel anxious and distressed about things initially.

Relationship of Emotional Disclosure and Health

Under normal circumstances, it seems that people talk about their emotionally significant experiences with friends or family soon after an event occurs. In fact, James Pennebaker (1995) is among a growing number of investigators who suggest that individuals have a need to disclose intense emotional experiences by talking or writing about them and that such disclosures can have positive effects on their psychological and physical health. It may be that the ability and willingness to face up to one's feelings or to share them with others decreases the adrenocortical activity that is associated with threatening or traumatic events. Brian Esterling and his colleagues (1994) found that when people talk or write about traumatic incidents, their immune and cardiovascular systems function more effectively, they have fewer visits to the doctor, and they perform better at school and work.

Conversely, the more that people feel compelled to inhibit their thoughts, emotions, and behaviors, the more activity is likely to increase in the adrenocortical system. Bernard Rimé and his colleagues (1991) found that when people do not acknowledge or talk about emotionally significant events, they may experience increased autonomic nervous system activity, rumination, and health problems. Additionally, these pent-up feelings may fester for many years, potentially creating problems at a later time.

Pennebaker (1995) observes that talking about personal experiences, which has been the basis of most psychotherapies regardless of theoretical perspective, may ultimately be as important as any particular feedback that a client might receive from a therapist, just because the process helps individuals translate their experiences into words. Certainly the uses of confession and acknowledgment of secrets and wrongdoing have been integral to some religious and cultural healing practices around the world for centuries.

Eugenia Georges (1995) examines the meanings of confession in cultures that use it explicitly for healing and to maintain health. Medical anthropologists view confession as a form of symbolic healing—that is, as a therapy based on the use of words and symbols in ritual. Even though the links between the symbolic and physiologic states are not well understood, Georges points out that healing is facilitated when symbolic therapies are used to cause changes in emotional and physiological states. Historically derived cultural values and social processes attribute meaning to symbolic therapy and facilitate its ability to effect healing within a given context.

Comparisons of the public and private confession practices of various cultures that have been described by Georges and others reveal vast cross-cultural differences in perception, expectation, and tradition. Unacculturated Ojibwa, living in Canada in the 1930s and 1940s, for example, considered serious illness to be a penalty for violating social norms and moral codes. Developing a serious illness generated fear and anxiety and mandated ritual public confessions. In contrast, public confession among the Ndembu of West Africa involved the healer in listening to confessions of the whole social group in order for the sick person to get well.

Public disclosure of emotions by many Asians and Pacific Islanders, however, is linked to ill health and misfortune. For example, Unni Wikan (1990) describes Balinese children who are socialized from infancy not to disclose such negative emotions as anger and sadness even to family or close friends. They are taught to present a happy face to others, to laugh and joke even in serious situations, and to forget their bad feelings in order to stay healthy and keep sadness from spreading to others.

Coping Styles, Emotional Disclosure, and Health Outcomes

The fact that emotional disclosure can have beneficial effects presumes that people are motivated and able to share their feelings and experiences. If there are cultural prohibitions, as in the Balinese example, or if a person is defensive, repressive, or has limited emotional awareness or vocabulary with which to express feelings, then any potential positive effects may be limited as well. For example, if a person is unconsciously excluding awareness of the painful or undesirable aspects of a situation, as is the case with repression, talking things over with someone else may not reveal the emotionally charged material.

Keith Petrie and his colleagues (1995) state that enough data exist now to suggest that people who actively inhibit emotional expression show immunological changes that are consistent with poor health outcomes. For example, the use of a repressive coping style has been associated by James Gross (1989) with the onset or progression of cancer. Studies by Steven Greer and Marianne Brady (1988) and Keith W. Pettingale and his colleagues (1985) have implicated repressive coping with poor natural killer cell activity, diagnosis of malignancy, and subsequent death from cancer. Patients with better cancer survival rates have been shown to have greater emotional expressiveness, including explosions of anger and rage, and willingness to confront the situation. Difficulty expressing emotions and an attitude of resignation or feelings of helplessness and hopelessness in combination with particular personality traits have consistently been associated with a diagnosis of cancer and a grim prognostic outlook.

Some research has shown associations between anxiety levels and immunity in healthy college students who had previously been exposed to the Epstein-Barr virus. Esterling and his colleagues (1993) found that higher blood levels of antibodies against the virus were associated with higher anxiety levels, indicating students with high anxiety levels had weaker immune control over the latent virus than in students with low anxiety levels. Subjects who were higher in defensiveness also had higher antibody levels than low-defensive subjects, suggesting that emotional nondisclosure may be an important variable in moderating these results. An increasing number of studies that show related findings adds tentative support for the hypothesis that defensiveness, or inhibition, while important in promoting the appearance of mental and emotional health, may ultimately increase vulnerability to disease.

Inhibition has been characterized as consisting of low levels of thinking and communicating about emotions, dissociation between personal feelings and bodily complaints, and conflicting tendencies to repress or confide emotional experience. The precise mechanisms that are involved in these processes are not entirely clear, but George Schwartz (1983) has proposed that some form of disconnection may occur where natural substances such as beta-endorphins tend to override physiological distress signals. According to this hypothesis, people with this disconnectivity would be less likely to focus on internal symptoms, thus delaying medical treatment.

Excessive Anxiety and Related Disorders

Anxiety is a normal emotion that is experienced as a state of physical or emotional uneasiness of varying intensity. Sometimes, however, anxiety becomes excessive, either in response to an actual or anticipated event or as a pathological state. Disorders that involve excessive anxiety are common conditions that may affect up to one-fourth of the population and can occur at any point in a person's life. In addition to a generalized anxiety disorder, the major anxiety disorders include panic disorder, phobias, obsessive-compulsive disorder (OCD), and post-traumatic stress disorder (PTSD). Symptoms of anxiety and of these anxiety-related disorders are many and varied. Some of the physiologic symptoms include elevated blood pressure and heart rate, palpitations, chest pain or tightness, difficulty breathing, sneezing, headache, and gastrointestinal and sleep disturbances. Emotional and mood disturbances include irritability, anger, and feelings of hopelessness, helplessness, worthlessness, and depression.

Doreen Cawley (1998) has reported that an estimated 16 percent of adult Americans will experience a panic attack at some point during their lifetime. A panic attack consists of a specific episode of sudden, intense fear or discomfort that is associated with several other symptoms such as heart palpitations, sweating, a feeling of choking, chest pain, nausea, or feeling dizzy. Panic attacks may appear unexpectedly and repeatedly over time, eventually being diagnosed as panic disorder.

Some people may develop phobias—that is, symptoms of severe anxiety when exposed to certain situations or objects, such as snakes, or when in places from which escape would be difficult, such as an airplane. Often these individuals do not seek help for these fears but try to adapt by limiting their activities and exposure. Whether learned or genetic, phobias tend to run in families and are more common in women. Desensitization therapy and helping people to confront their fears and substitute healthier thoughts can be useful.

OCD is twice as common as schizophrenia and has been ignored or misdiagnosed for many years. Obsessions are persistent thoughts or impulses that are considered to be intrusive and inappropriate and cause marked anxiety or distress. To control these disruptions and reduce the distress, individuals develop behaviors that may not be appropriate but that they feel compelled to perform. It is a reasonable behavior, for example, to double check if the door is locked or if the stove is turned off; however, this behavior is problematic when it becomes repetitive and time consuming, interfering with daily activities. As with phobias, many people suffering from OCD, adjust their lives around the ritualistic behavior to keep the phobia secret, and they do not seek the help they need, although both antidepressant medications and cognitive-behavioral therapies can be effective.

Preliminary results of a study by Susan Swedo and her colleagues (1997) have revealed an antibody in children who developed OCD after they were exposed to streptococcal infections. These early findings suggest that this form of OCD could be an autoimmune response triggered by antibodies. Instead of warding off the infection, the antibodies attack the basal ganglia of the brain, leading to ritualistic behaviors such as checking, hoarding, and handwashing. Compared to healthy children, 85 percent of those individuals with this type of OCD have been found to have the identifiable antibody. Discovery of a biological marker for this form of OCD may lead to early detection and treatment using both pharmacological and nonpharmacological therapies.

Somatoform disorders are disorders in which a person may report physical symptoms such as a headache, pain, or gastrointestinal distress that suggest a physical disorder even though no medical diagnosis can be made on the basis of the evidence. Such disorders involve the use of physical symptoms to express emotional problems and psychosocial stress. There are various hypothetical causes, including early childhood abuse or neglect, deficient communication between the right and left cerebral hemispheres of the brain, and faulty regulation of sensory information by the central nervous system.

PTSD and dissociative disorders occur when individuals endure one or more events that are so dreadful that the experience is beyond that of most people. Some months or years later, an individual may develop intense fear, hyperarousal, helplessness, and avoidance behaviors when a stressful event occurs that triggers memories of the earlier incident. PTSD is more likely to occur with people who have been exposed to severe violence, war, or torture. It is also likely to develop in those individuals who experienced abuse as children. Antidepressant medications have been somewhat effective in treating PTSD; however, there is little information available on their use in dissociative disorders.

Emotions and Chronic Illness

Anxiety is a common response to the overwhelming amount of potential change that people often face after the initial diagnosis of a chronic illness as well as during the course of the disease process. Learning that one is HIV-positive, for example, can lead to frightening and intense feelings that can be totally overwhelming and intolerable. According to Gary Grossman (1996), the degree to which an HIV-infected gay man can come to grips with any internal anxieties about being gay will significantly affect his emotional response to having HIV. Although some people will do their best to avoid experiencing their feelings,

When Anatole Broyard realized that he was danger-
ously ill with cancer, he wrote about his experiences
in a series of essays and a short story that were collected after his death in Intoxicated by My Illness and
Other Writings on Life and Death (1992). The work
shows that Broyard was interested in the style of his
illness and the meanings of it that emerged as he
wrote.

others may be unable to control their emotions and
respond explosively or become immobilized with anxiety. Cutting oneself off from experiencing emotional
reactions can interfere with effective coping, including gaining the benefits of social, therapeutic, and
financial support.

Pennebaker (1997) cites numerous examples of
detrimental physiological effects for people who are
unable to talk about their personal feelings and experiences in contrast with the positive changes in
health status that often follow writing or talking about
the feelings and experiences. For example, in a study
of disease risk over time in gay men who were not
infected with the AIDS virus, Steve Cole and his colleagues (1996) found that those men who tended to
conceal their homosexual status from others were
three times as likely as men who were more open
about their sexuality to experience cancer, pneumonia, and tuberculosis and to die faster from complications of AIDS. Pennebaker notes that there are not
enough data yet to know if psychotherapy or expressive writing can really prolong the lives of AIDS patients, but he suggests the potential for this outcome
since AIDS is an immunological disorder where stress
is associated with symptom exacerbation and remis-
sion.

For people who have experienced a heart attack,
every twinge of chest pain or increase in other symptoms raises anxiety and concern about having another
heart attack. Similarly, for cancer survivors, any experience of pain or discovery of an enlarged lymph node
signals a potential recurrence of cancer. Anxious cancer patients, in fact, may be so affected by their emotional distress that they cope poorly with radiation
therapy and experience less benefit from behavioral
therapies that are aimed at decreasing chemotherapy-
related distress. Even recovery from surgical treatment
can be complicated by preoperative anxiety and depression.

Depression is also a common and frequently debilitating reaction to chronic illness. While depression
may affect between 10 and 20 percent of the general
adult population, a much greater number of people
who are coping with a medical condition may have the

symptoms of depression. Gary Rodin and Karen Voshart (1986) report that approximately one-third of all
patients who are hospitalized with a chronic disease
report moderate symptoms of depression, while up to
one-fourth of these patients may suffer from severe
depression. Taylor and Lisa Aspinwall (1990) cite numerous studies where depression has been documented in different phases of the disease process with
patients who have experienced heart disease, stroke,
cancer, and numerous other chronic diseases.

The fourth edition of the American Psychiatric Association's *Diagnostic and Statistical Manual of Mental
Disorders* (DSM-IV, 1994) identifies eleven types of psychiatric disorders (including depression and other
mood disorders) that are due to general medical conditions. However, making the diagnosis of depression
in the chronically ill can be somewhat problematic because fatigue, sleep difficulties, and other physical indicators of depression can also be symptoms of medical disease or side effects of treatment.

Although there is no single objective or laboratory
test to detect major depression or other mood disorders, awareness of depression is important because of
the effect it has on recovery or rehabilitation, as well
as because of the distress it brings. One study by
Kenneth Wells and his colleagues (1989) found that
patients with arthritis, diabetes, hypertension, and
gastrointestinal disorders in addition to a depressive
disorder had significantly greater impairment of physical and social functioning than patients who had other
types of chronic general medical disorders. Furthermore, some depressed people who have chronic conditions, such as those who are recovering from a
stroke, have longer hospital stays and show less motivation to participate in rehabilitation programs. Illnesses and treatments that are related to depression
have also been linked, by Taylor (1999), to suicide in
chronically ill elderly individuals, including those who
have cancer, AIDS, or are dependent on dialysis. The
significant morbidity that is associated with depressive
disorders emphasizes the importance of accurate diagnosis and appropriate treatment.

Failure to diagnose depression in people who have
a chronic illness is common because of the belief that
it is a normal response to the diagnosis and the related
disability. Unfortunately, the lack of recognition leads
to a lack of intervention, despite the availability of
beneficial treatments. The most common treatment
for depression is antidepressant medication. Adjunc-
tive cognitive-behavioral therapies, however, may help
people lower their arousal state and adapt in healthier
ways to their situation, thereby also relieving some of
their depressed affect. These interventions include
biofeedback, exercise, massage, nutritional supple-
mentation, support groups, relaxation, meditation,
hypnosis, and psychotherapy.

See also: ANXIETY DISORDERS; EMOTIONAL ABUSE; EMOTION SUPPRESSION; FEAR AND PHOBIAS; FOOD AND EATING; HUMAN DEVELOPMENT; MIND-BODY DICHOTOMY; MOOD DISORDERS; POST-TRAUMATIC STRESS DISORDER; STRESS

Bibliography

American Psychiatric Association. (1994). *Diagnostic and Statistical Manual of Mental Disorders,* 4th ed. Washington, DC: American Psychiatric Association.

Boyce, W. Thomas; Alkon, Abbey; Tschann, Jeanne M.; and Chesney, Margaret A. (1995). "Dimensions of Psychobiologic Reactivity: Cardiovascular Responses to Laboratory Stressors in Preschool Children." *Annals of Behavioral Medicine* 17:315–323.

Cannon, Walter. (1932). *The Wisdom of the Body.* New York: W. W. Norton.

Cawley, Doreen. (1998). "Anxiety Disorders." In *Contemporary Psychiatric Mental Health Nursing: The Brain-Behavior Connection,* ed. Carol A. Glod. Philadelphia: F. A. Davis.

Cole, Steve W.; Kemeny, Margaret E.; Taylor, Shelley E.; and Visscher, Barbara R. (1996). "Elevated Physical Health Risk among Gay Men Who Conceal Their Homosexual Identity." *Health Psychology* 15:243–251.

DeQuattro, Vincent, and Lee, Debora D. (1991). "Blood Pressure Reactivity and Sympathetic Hyperactivity." *American Journal of Hypertension* 4:624S-628S.

Dienstbier, Richard A. (1989). "Arousal and Physiological Toughness: Implications for Mental and Physical Health." *Psychological Review* 96:84–100.

Esterling, Brian A.; Antoni, Michael H.; Fletcher, Mary A.; Margulies, Scott; and Schneiderman, Neil. (1994). "Emotional Disclosure through Writing or Speaking Modulates Latent Epstein-Barr Virus Reactivation." *Journal of Consulting and Clinical Psychology* 62:130–140.

Esterling, Brian A.; Antoni, Michael H.; Kumar, Mahendra; and Schneiderman, Neil. (1993). "Defensiveness, Trait Anxiety, and Epstein-Barr Viral Capsid Antigen Antibody Titers in Healthy College Students. *Health Psychology* 12:132–139.

Ewart, Craig K. (1991). "Familial Transmission of Essential Hypertension: Genes, Environments, and Chronic Anger." *Annals of Behavioral Medicine* 13:40–47.

Friedman, Howard S., and Booth-Kewley, Stephanie. (1987). "The 'Disease-prone Personality': A Meta-Analytic View of the Construct." *American Psychologist* 42:539–555.

Georges, Eugenia. (1995). "A Cultural and Historical Perspective on Confession." In *Emotion, Disclosure, & Health,* ed. James W. Pennebaker. Washington, DC: American Psychological Association.

Gerin, William, and Pickering, Thomas G. (1995). "Association between Delayed Recovery of Blood Pressure after Acute Mental and Parental History of Hypertension." *Journal of Hypertension* 13:603–610.

Greer, Steven, and Brady, Marianne. (1988). "Natural Killer Cells: One Possible Link between Cancer and the Mind." *Stress Medicine* 4:105–111.

Gross, James. (1989). "Emotional Expression in Cancer Onset and Progression." *Social Science and Medicine* 28:1239–1248.

Grossman, Gary. (1996). "Psychotherapy with HIV-Infected Gay Men." In *Handbook of Diversity Issues in Health Psychology,* ed. Pamela M. Kato and Traci Mann. New York: Plenum.

Lazarus, Richard S. (1994). "Why We Should Think of Stress As a Subset of Emotion." In *Handbook of Stress: Theoretical and Clinical Aspects,* 2nd ed., ed. Leo Goldberger and Shlomo Breznitz. New York: Free Press.

Lovallo, William R. (1997). *Stress & Health: Biological and Psychological Interactions.* Thousand Oaks, CA: Sage Publications.

Pennebaker, James W., ed. (1995). *Emotion, Disclosure, & Health.* Washington, DC: American Psychological Association.

Pennebaker, James W. (1997). *Opening Up: The Healing Power of Expressing Emotions.* New York: Guilford.

Petrie, Keith J.; Booth, Roger J.; and Davison, Kathryn P. (1995). "Repression, Disclosure, and Immune Function: Recent Findings and Methodological Issues." In *Emotion, Disclosure, & Health,* ed. James W. Pennebaker. Washington, DC: American Psychological Association.

Pettingale, Keith W.; Morris, Tina; Greer, Steven; and Haybittle, J. L. (1985). "Mental Attitudes to Cancer: An Additional Prognostic Factor." *Lancet* 1:750.

Rimé, Bernard; Mesquita, Batja; Philippot, Pierre; and Boca, Stefano. (1991). "Beyond the Emotional Event: Six Studies on the Social Sharing of Emotion." *Cognition and Emotion* 5:435–465.

Rodin, Gary, and Voshart, Karen. (1986). "Depression in the Medically Ill: An Overview." *American Journal of Psychiatry* 143:696–705.

Schwartz, George. (1983). "Disregulation Theory and Disease: Applications to the Repression/Cerebral Disconnection/Cardiovascular Disorder Hypothesis." *International Review of Applied Psychology* 32:95–118.

Selye, Hans. (1956). *The Stress of Life.* New York: McGraw-Hill.

Semenchuk, Elizabeth M., and Larkin, Kevin T. (1993). "Behavioral and Cardiovascular Responses to Interpersonal Challenges among Male Offspring of Essential Hypertensives." *Health Psychology* 12:416–419.

Swedo, Susan E.; Leonard, Henrietta L.; Mittleman, Barbara B.; Allen, Albert J.; Rapoport, Judith L.; Dow, Sara P.; Kanter, Melissa E.; Chapman, Floresta; and Zabriskie, John. (1997). "Identification of Children with Pediatric Autoimmune Neuropsychiatric Disorders Associated with Streptoccal Infections by a Marker Associated with Rheumatic Fever." *American Journal of Psychiatry* 154:110–112.

Taylor, Shelley E. (1999). *Health Psychology,* 4th ed. Boston: McGraw-Hill.

Taylor, Shelley E., and Aspinwall, Lisa G. (1990). "Psychological Aspects of Chronic Illness." In *Psychological Aspects of Serious Illness: Chronic Conditions, Fatal Diseases, and Clinical Care,* ed. Paul T. Costa, Jr., and Gary R. VandenBos. Washington, DC: American Psychological Association.

Wells, Kenneth B; Stuart, Anita; Hays, Ron D.; Burnam, M. Audrey; Rogers, William; Daniels, Marcia; Berry, Sandra; Greenfield, Sheldon; and Ware, John. (1989). "The Functioning and Well-Being of Depressed Patients." *Journal of American Medical Association* 262:914–919.

Wikan, Unni. (1990). *Managing Turbulent Hearts: A Balinese Formula for Living.* Chicago: University of Chicago Press.

Barbara L. Irvin

HELPLESSNESS

Psychology's interest in most emotions probably originated in everyday experience. Certain emotions—anger, envy, fear, greed, lust, pride, and so on—are widely recognized as real phenomena that affect how people behave. The tasks of psychologists who are interested in these emotional states include determining the situations that trigger them, their consequences, and ways to help curb their excesses. Helplessness has a different history, one that reverses what has just been described. In the 1960s, animal learning researchers used the term *helpless* to describe the striking passivity displayed by dogs after experiencing uncontrollable aversive events (e.g., electric shocks). The causes and consequences of this helplessness have been extensively investigated in both animals and people. Ways to combat helplessness have been developed. What remains is to describe the experience of helplessness and explain why helplessness, in contrast to other emotions, entails passivity rather than activity.

Learned Helplessness

As noted, learned helplessness was first described by psychologists studying animal learning. Researchers immobilized a dog and exposed it to electric shocks that could be neither avoided nor escaped. Twenty-four hours later, the dog was placed in a situation in which shocks could be terminated by a simple response. However, the dog did not make this response, instead sitting and simply enduring the shocks. This behavior was in marked contrast to dogs in a control group that reacted vigorously to shock and learned readily how to turn it off. These investigators proposed that when originally exposed to uncontrollable shocks, the first dog learned that nothing it did mattered. This learning of response-outcome independence was represented cognitively as an expectation of helplessness that was generalized to new situations to produce motivational, cognitive, and emotional deficits. The passivity of helpless animals could be reversed by forcibly exposing them to the relationship between their responses and outcomes: shocking them and then literally dragging them to safety. And helplessness could be prevented by first giving animals experience with aversive events they could control.

The deficits that follow in the wake of uncontrollability have come to be known as the learned helplessness phenomenon, and their cognitive explanation is the learned helplessness model. Psychologists interested in human problems were quick to see the parallels between learned helplessness as produced by uncontrollable events in the laboratory and maladaptive passivity as it exists in the real world. Consider Bruno Bettelheim's description in *The Informed Heart* (1960, pp. 151–152) of the helplessness shown by some inmates of the Nazi concentration camps:

Events that are beyond an individual's control, such as the political events that led to this young Kurdish girl becoming a refugee on the Turkish border in 1991, can result in a feeling of helplessness than can then be generalized to other areas of life. (Corbis/ Francoise de Mulder)

People who came to believe the repeated statements of the guards—that there was no hope for them, that they would never leave the camp except as a corpse—who came to feel that their environment was one over which they could exercise no influence whatsoever, these prisoners were in a literal sense, walking corpses. . . . They were people so deprived of affect, self-esteem, and every form of stimulation, so totally exhausted, both physically and emotionally, that they had given the environment total power over them. These individuals stopped eating, stopped moving, and soon died.

So began several lines of research looking at learned helplessness in people. In one line of work, helplessness in people was produced in the laboratory as it had been in animals, by exposing them to uncontrollable events and seeing the effects on motivation, cognition, and emotion. Unsolvable problems were usually substituted for uncontrollable shocks, but the critical aspects of the phenomenon remained: Following uncontrollability, people show a variety of deficits. Other studies further attested to the similarity between the animal phenomenon and what was produced in the human laboratory. Forcible exposure to outcome options reverses helplessness deficits, and previous exposure to controllable events immunizes against learned helplessness.

In another line of work, researchers proposed various failures of adaptation as analogous to learned helplessness and investigated the hypothesized similarity. Especially popular was Martin Seligman's (1975) proposal that reactive depression and learned helplessness shared critical features: causes, symptoms, consequences, treatments, and preventions.

Attributional Reformulation

It soon became clear that the original learned helplessness explanation was an oversimplification when applied to people because it failed to account for the range of reactions that people display in response to uncontrollable events. Some people show learned helplessness, as the model hypothesized, that is general across time and situation, but others do not. Further, failures of adaptation that the learned helplessness model was supposed to explain, such as depression, are sometimes characterized by a striking loss of self-esteem, about which the model was silent.

In an attempt to resolve these discrepancies, Lyn Abramson, Martin Seligman, and John Teasdale (1978) reformulated the helplessness model as it applied to people. The contrary findings could be explained by proposing that when people encounter an uncontrollable aversive event they ask themselves why it happened. The nature of their answer sets the parameters for the helplessness that follows. If their causal attribution is stable ("It's going to last forever"), then induced helplessness is long lasting; if this causal attribution is unstable, then learned helplessness is transient. If their causal attribution is global ("It's going to undermine everything"), then subsequent helplessness is manifest across a variety of situations; if their causal attribution is specific, then learned helplessness is limited to that particular event. Finally, if their causal attribution is internal ("It's all my fault"), then the individual's self-esteem drops following uncontrollability; if their causal attribution is external, then self-esteem is left intact.

These hypotheses comprise the attributional reformulation of helplessness theory. This new theory left intact the original model, because uncontrollable aversive events were still hypothesized to produce deficits when they gave rise to an expectation of response-outcome independence. However, the nature of these deficits was now said to be influenced by the causal attribution offered by the individual. In some cases, the situation itself provides the explanation made by the person. In other cases, the person relies on his or her habitual way of making sense of events that occur, what is called one's explanatory style. All things being equal, people tend to offer similar sorts of explanations for different bad events. Accordingly, explanatory style influences helplessness and the failures of adaptation that involve helplessness. According to the attributional reformulation, explanatory style itself is not a cause of problems but rather a risk factor. Given uncontrollable events and the lack of a clear situational demand on the proffered attribution for uncontrollability, explanatory style should influence how the person responds. Helplessness will be long lasting or transient, widespread or circumscribed, damaging to self-esteem or not, all in accordance with the individual's explanatory style.

Explanatory style has since been extensively studied in its own right. Explanatory style seems to take form as a coherent individual difference around eight years of age, when children's cognitive abilities allow them to think in cause-and-effect terms. Twin studies suggest that explanatory style is moderately heritable (i.e., genetic), but there is no reason to believe that there is a specific explanatory style gene. Rather, such characteristics as intelligence, physical prowess, and attractiveness—which are themselves heritable—set the stage for success or failure in a variety of domains, and these experiences lead the individual to entertain optimistic or pessimistic causal explanations for important outcomes. Early loss, such as the death of a parent, or early trauma, such as sexual abuse, makes an individual more pessimistic. Early success makes an individual more optimistic. Social learning is also involved in the origins of explanatory style. Studies show relationships between the explanatory styles of parents and their children, although the fine detail of how explanatory style is transmitted from parent to child has yet to be explored. Messages from teachers, peers, and the media may also be critical. However explanatory style is forged, it can be highly stable, sometimes over decades. The self-fulfilling nature of

Raymond Carver, in "A Small, Good Thing" (1989), portrays two parents who watch helplessly as their son dies as a result of a brain injury that was sustained in an accident. The medical professionals do not seem to understand how this patient should be treated, and their inability to communicate effectively with the parents makes them all the more isolated and helpless.

explanatory style—and helplessness per se—explains this stability. Helplessness leads to failure, which strengthens helplessness; control leads to success, which strengthens control. At the same time, explanatory style can and does change in response to ongoing life events. Cognitive therapy, for example, can move explanatory style in an optimistic direction.

Applications

Learned helplessness has become a popular line of investigation in part because the phenomenon seems similar to various human ills involving passivity. Helplessness theory and attributional reformulation suggest a ready explanation of such instances of passivity as well as interventions to prevent or remedy them. However, there is a downside to the availability of powerful theory: Some applications have been glib, overstating the similarity between learned helplessness and a given failure of adaptation.

Learned helplessness ideas are best applied to situations where the following three conditions are present:

1. *Objective noncontingency.* One must take into account the relationships between a person's actions and the outcomes. Learned helplessness is only present when there is no contingency. Learned helplessness must be distinguished from extinction (where responses once leading to reinforcement no longer do so) and from learned passivity (where active responses are contingently punished and/or passive responses are contingently reinforced).

2. *Cognitive mediation.* Learned helplessness involves a characteristic way of perceiving, explaining, and extrapolating the contingencies between responses and outcomes. The attributional reformulation specifies cognitive processes that make helplessness more (versus less) likely following uncontrollable aversive events. If these processes are not implicated in particular instances of passivity, then learned helplessness is not present.

3. *Cross-situational generality of passive behavior.* Finally, learned helplessness is shown by passivity in a situation different from the one in which uncontrollability was first encountered. Does the individual give up and fail to initiate actions that might allow him or her to control this situation? It is impossible to argue that learned helplessness is present without the demonstration of passivity in new situations.

With these ideas in mind, consider two lines of work that represent the best applications to date of helplessness ideas to complex failures of human adaptation: depression and physical illness. In each case, researchers have demonstrated the critical features of learned helplessness: contingency, cognition, and generality of passivity.

How does depression satisfy the three criteria? To start, depression involves passivity; this is part of its very definition. Depression also follows bad events, particularly those that people judge to be uncontrollable. And depression is mediated by cognitions of helplessness, hopelessness, and pessimism. Explanatory style is a consistent correlate of depressive symptoms, as well as a demonstrable risk factor. Cognitive therapy for depression, which is highly effective, explicitly targets helpless expectations and pessimistic attributions, and research suggests that cognitive therapy may work precisely because it changes these. Improvement in depression is directly related to changes in attributions for bad events from internal, stable, and global to external, unstable, and specific. An intriguing possibility is that the encouragement of an optimistic explanatory style might prevent depression.

Another popular application of helplessness ideas is to physical illness. Again, How are the three criteria of learned helplessness satisfied? First, passivity refers not to behavior but to the individual's ability to maintain physical health. Second, research with both animals and people shows that uncontrollable stress foreshadows poor health. Third, explanatory style has been found to be related to such indices of health as duration of symptoms, physician exams, medical tests, longevity, and survival time with diseases such as cancer. Pessimistic people have worse health than their optimistic counterparts.

Why does learned helplessness influence health (mental and physical)? Several processes have been implicated. There may be an immunological pathway, because animal studies imply that uncontrollable stress can suppress aspects of immune functioning. However, it should be noted that these findings are complex, and one should be cautious about offering broad generalizations about immune functioning. Another pathway may be emotional. As described, learned helplessness is involved in depression, and epidemiologists have shown that depressed individuals are at increased risk for morbidity and mortality. Perhaps learned helplessness influences health in part because of its role in depression. A number of studies attest to a behavioral pathway, and behavior may be the most important route between helplessness and physical illness. People with a pessimistic explanatory style tend to neglect the basics of health care, and when they fall ill, they tend not to do the sorts of things that might speed recovery. As these failures to promote health through one's actions accumulate, the observed link between explanatory style and illness results. Furthermore, a pessimistic explanatory style puts individuals at risk for untimely death due to accidents or violence, implying the role of a lifestyle that puts the individual in the wrong place at the wrong time. A final possibility is that helpless people fall ill because they are socially estranged. Rich and supportive relationships with others are related to good health. When helpless people do not partake of social support, poor health is often an unsurprising result.

Conclusion

Depression and physical illness are obviously overdetermined. For example, women are more likely to be depressed than men, and men are more likely to die early than women, yet there is no evidence that helplessness or explanatory style differs across gender. Other considerations must be relevant. Nonetheless, the case has been made for at least some involvement of the three features of learned helplessness in many instances of these phenomena.

An ongoing puzzle is why learned helplessness ideas appear so applicable. This entry has focused on the examples of depression and physical illness, but it could have discussed academic failure, unemployment, mental retardation, chronic pain, epilepsy, or crowding. What determines whether a given individual who has experienced uncontrollable bad events and thinks about them in pessimistic ways shows any of the possible consequences attributed to helplessness? It might be that all of these outcomes occur to the same individuals, in which case their problems probably exacerbate one another. Or it might be that other considerations—biological, psychological, and/or social—lead an individual in one disastrous direction or another once a state of helplessness is present.

In its most extreme version, helplessness entails an emotional deficit, the profound absence of feelings that Bettelheim described. Less extreme versions of helplessness involve depression, as already described, as well as feelings of anxiety. Helplessness may also be entwined with frustration, anger, and guilt. Further research is of course needed, but it appears that helplessness, at least as studied within the learned helplessness tradition, is not a discrete emotion. Rather, it is linked to a variety of other emotional states (or their absence) in ways presumably determined by the extent of uncontrollable events and perhaps by cultural scripts that specify legitimate emotional responses to such events.

Why do animals and people have the capacity to be depressed? Why should experience with uncontrollable aversive events result in passivity rather than activity? Some have speculated that helplessness—in the short term—is adaptive because it disengages individuals from fruitless pursuits and allows them to conserve resources until such time as renewed efforts to control outcomes will succeed. As studied in the laboratory, the learned helplessness phenomenon has a time course. The passivity following uncontrollability only lasts for a relatively short period unless uncontrollability is repeated; then chronic helplessness is produced.

See also: ACCEPTANCE AND REJECTION; ATTRIBUTION; HEALTH AND ILLNESS; HOPE; HOPELESSNESS; MOTIVATION; SELF-ESTEEM; STRESS

Bibliography

Abramson, Lyn Y.; Seligman, Martin E. P.; and Teasdale, John D. (1978). "Learned Helplessness in Humans: Critique and Reformulation." *Journal of Abnormal Psychology* 87:49–74.

Bettelheim, Bruno. (1960). *The Informed Heart—Autonomy in a Mass Age.* New York: Free Press.

Buchanan, Gregory M., and Seligman, Martin E. P., eds. (1995). *Explanatory Style.* Hillsdale, NJ: Lawrence Erlbaum.

Maier, Steven F., and Seligman, Martin E. P. (1976). "Learned Helplessness: Theory and Evidence." *Journal of Experimental Psychology: General* 105:3–46.

Mikulincer, Mario, and Caspy, Tamir. (1986). "The Conceptualization of Helplessness." *Motivation and Emotion* 10:264–294.

Peterson, Christopher, and Bossio, Lisa M. (1991). *Health and Optimism.* New York: Free Press.

Peterson, Christopher; Maier, Steven F.; and Seligman, Martin E. P. (1993). *Learned Helplessness: A Theory for the Age of Personal Control.* New York: Oxford University Press.

Seligman, Martin E. P. (1975). *Helplessness: On Depression, Development, and Death.* San Francisco: W. H. Freeman.

Seligman, Martin E. P. (1990). *Learned Optimism.* New York: Knopf.

Christopher Peterson

HISTORICAL STUDY OF EMOTIONS

Historical research has become a significant contributor to the exploration of emotion and the role of emotion in larger social interactions. Although there are a number of different approaches to emotions history, and several different rationales, historians have particularly concentrated on *changes* in emotional standards and experience. They seek to chart what the changes were, granting that explicit standards (i.e., emotional culture or emotionology) are easier to delineate than actual individual or collective experiences. They also try to explain what the *causes* of change were, which helps connect emotions to larger social developments. And they are eager to show what the *results* were, not just in individual perceptions of emotions and capacities for display but in other institutions and interactions. Change, causation, and effect, then, particularly focus what historians contribute to the understanding of how emotions work.

Examples of this analysis are numerous. American parents in the early nineteenth century increasingly turned away from using shame in disciplining children—the common eighteenth-century mode—in favor of new forms that used guilt. In the same time period, the French middle class developed a powerful new disgust reaction that occurred when encountering certain bodily odors, including the smell of urine, that had previously seemed perfectly normal. American Catholics began to reject traditional religious uses of fear in the 1950s as part of a larger adjustment to increased prosperity and the mainstream features of American culture, which had attacked invocations of fear with growing vigor from the 1920s onward. An elaborate culture of grief, actively urged in the nineteenth century, was assailed for its excesses in twentieth-century American emotionology, as people were encouraged to recover from grief quickly in order not to bother others with emotional demands. Causes included changes in death rates and the wider, pleasure-seeking promptings of a consumer culture. This change in the approach to dealing with grief led to major shifts in death rituals, new therapy for extensive grief, and the rise of collaborative grief groups in which strangers supported each other in an otherwise hostile cultural environment. Change and emotion are not constant companions, but their encounters produce significant individual and social outcomes.

The Origins of the Field

Historians have been dealing with emotional issues and expressions for centuries. Even before the rise of psychohistory—the application of psychological theories, particularly Freudian psychoanalytic concepts, to historical data—biographers often referred to the emotional characteristics of their subjects. Classic attempts to convey the larger spirit of a historical period, such as Jacob Burckhardt's characterizations of Italian Renaissance city-states, often included emotional dynamics. So did descriptions of reactions to wars or crowd behavior. With all this, however, the principal focus was not on emotion per se but on emotion as a component of some other phenomenon.

Emotions history received a considerable boost in the 1930s. The rise of social history in France, seeking to understand the experience of ordinary people in the past, involved exploring topics that were not previously part of the historical repertoire. Innovators

such as Lucien Febvre specifically called for research on emotions as part of the larger social history effort. At about the same time, German sociologist Norbert Elias sketched his theory of a "civilizing process," arguing that standards of self-control became more rigorous in Europe's upper classes in the seventeenth and eighteenth centuries. His primary focus involved physical behavior, such as eating habits, but his attention to more refined manners involved discipline over emotions as well. Neither Febvre nor Elias generated an immediate response; indeed, Elias's theories were more widely used in the 1990s than ever before.

The development of psychohistory in the 1970s certainly called new attention to historical exploration of emotion. Historians of childhood such as Philip Greven and David Hunt thus explored using psychoanalytic theory the emotional effect of characteristic styles of child rearing in the seventeenth and eighteenth centuries. Most psychohistorians, however, concentrated primarily on biography, as in Erik Erikson's classic study of Young Man Luther; while emotional repertoires figured prominently, they were not easily generalized to other aspects of history. Further, the primary reliance on psychoanalytic concepts risked conveying a static quality to past emotional life, since fundamental dynamics, while varying among individuals, were seen as largely immune to historical change. (The past thus illustrated durable emotional constructs rather than exemplifying differentiation and change—a key distinction.) Still, historians influenced by Freudianism have continued to contribute to the study of emotions, particularly when they have turned to larger cultural standards and individual experiences around these standards. For example, details of the emotions experienced as a result of generational experience in World War I have been used in some explanations of the rise of German Nazism (including the effect of father absence). On a broader scale, Peter Gay sketched a large array of emotional characteristics common to the nineteenth-century North American and West European middle classes, in facets such as love and anger, by combining psychoanalytic assumptions with cultural evidence.

The most explicit attention to emotions history, however, resulted from a slightly different set of developments (in social history and related social sciences) that occurred as the framework established in the 1970s was translated into explicit research during and after the mid-1980s. Social historians, dominant in many areas of historical research, widened their exploration of how ordinary people functioned in the past. A major extension of these inquiries, launched in France but which spread more widely, argued for inquiry into deep-held values and assumptions—*mentalités*—concerning subjects such as death, community, or the forces of nature. Not surprisingly, attitudes about emotion quickly became involved. English and American historians, for their part, broadened the investigation of family patterns into qualitative relationships among family members. In this vein they explored shifts in the definition and valuation of love (both marital and parental), as well as changes in the ways anger was viewed in family life. Mentalities and family historians alike painted a distinctive picture of emotional standards in sixteenth- and seventeenth-century (early modern) European and American societies, as compared to more modern norms. They also paid explicit attention to processes of change, particularly those that occurred by the eighteenth century. New definitions of love began to figure into the selection of marital partners during this period, for example, and love itself became a more powerful argument for accepting a partner or, where laws permitted, dissolving a union. In addition, traditional peasant ideas about fear, often incorporated into popular Christianity, began to yield during the eighteenth century to a greater sense of control over nature.

Two related strands of social history inquiry thus produced a new understanding of the extent to which past cultures (and institutions like the peasant village or the family) could not be grasped without assessing the emotional dynamics involved. The same inquiry underlined the extent to which emotional dynamics varied over time—with the historical period—and were therefore subject to explainable change.

Concurrently, various social scientists who were exploring emotion began to probe the historical record as well, and their primary, though not exclusive, attention was given to more recent developments. As service-sector jobs expanded in the twentieth century, American sociologists and social psychologists began to look at new emotional standards in the workplace. They also investigated changing definitions of family-related emotions. While most anthropologists concentrated on painting rich but fairly static pictures of emotional standards in various societies, others began to pay attention to change. Thus Robert Levy dealt with the effect of Western colonialism on Tahitian emotional culture, while Catherine Lutz (relying heavily on contemporary fieldwork descriptions for her basic categories) looked at shifts in emotion over time. A number of European sociologists, some strongly influenced by Elias's theories, began to examine changes, particularly in the twentieth century but in some cases over a longer sweep of time, in "emotion management," with a focus on the ways emotional impulses were to be controlled. A Dutch group, in particular, studied the emotional standards that accompanied the more informal manners and relationships that are characteristic of the twentieth century.

These initial inquiries began to generate explicit historical work on emotions by the mid-1980s, including the expanding efforts of historically-minded sociologists of emotion. Mentalities studies, for example, formed the context for elaborate treatments of fear in European peasant and religious culture from the Middle Ages to the late eighteenth century. These ambitious surveys covered a mass of data concerned with the role of fear in daily community life and festival ritual, but they also traced the bases of a redefinition of fear on the eve of the nineteenth century. Other studies focused on familial emotions and called attention to patterns and changes from the seventeenth century to the twentieth century. Emotions historians thus initially concentrated on family-related emotions such as love and jealousy, with attention to anger spilling over into wider public contexts as well. These studies also emphasized gender differentiation through emotion, and change in these formulas in such areas as intensified reliance on maternal love and public versus familial repertoires of acceptable anger.

The Amplification of Historical Research on Emotion

Once launched, emotions history inevitably gained additional vantage points and emphases. The list of emotions historically explored now includes envy, disgust, joy (tentatively), grief, shame, and guilt, as well as the initial roster of love, fear, and anger.

Historical study of emotions has also widened in terms of place and time—a crucial indication of a project's significance. Thus several studies have dealt with changes and continuities in emotional standards and expressions in Chinese history. Historians addressing medieval Europe have generated an impressive literature, including an important set of studies on anger and projects on wonder and empathy. Classicists are also dealing with love in the context of further exploration of family history, but the growing range still begs for expansion and connection. Changes within the Middle Ages need to be linked more explicitly to the patterns noted in the early modern centuries, while relevant study of the Renaissance period has been minimal at best. (One previous sociological study did, to be sure, attempt to trace the history of love from its troubadour formulations to more modern times. However, the more extensive inquiries now available have not been put to the same ambitious survey scrutiny; even the systematic treatment of fear ended with the year 1800, casting only a brief, evocative look at different patterns of this emotion in more modern times.) Geographical gaps are at least as obvious as the challenges in chronology and linkage. Specialists dealing with a number of key areas—

Eastern Europe, Africa, Latin America, and additional parts of Asia—have yet to generate focused histories of emotion, as opposed to more haphazard overlaps and connections with other histories such as that of family life. In fact, key theories about emotional change—such as the civilizing process idea—have yet to be seriously tested beyond the Western context, so despite some speculation there is no consensus about possible applicability. Nevertheless, it is fair to say that the process of moving emotions history toward inclusion in a full historical canvass is underway.

The Focus on Major Change

The most elaborate work, however, emphasizes developments in the United States and Western Europe. Here, in addition to broadening the varieties of emotions considered and the contexts in which they operate, historians and kindred social scientists have particularly emphasized two points of revealing transformation. An important set of changes redefined emotional culture between the late seventeenth and early nineteenth centuries, with timing of the redefinition varying somewhat with the emotional configuration involved. A subsequent turning point intervened in the second quarter of the twentieth century, possibly a bit earlier in the United States than in Western Europe. Within this periodization framework, a host of questions remain disputed or unanswered, but the framework itself has proven widely useful in explaining significant recastings of emotional guidelines and experience and in the amassing of evidence about why emotions change and with what larger results.

The early modern emotionological transformation continues to refine changes in the roles and definitions of love. Two factors propelled change. First, growing commercialization helped place new value on the family as communities became somewhat more competitive. Family ties were alternatives to older, now frayed communitarian bonds. Same-sex friendships, by the same token, declined. Along with this, Protestantism, attacking the idea of special credit for celibacy, greatly improved the religious status of marriage (and, in destroying convents, made marriage more essential for women). By the seventeenth century, Protestant writers urged emotional sharing in marriage. From these twin bases, actual emphasis on love as a key ingredient in forming and evaluating marriage measurably expanded by the mid-eighteenth century. There was also, by this point, a more systematic attack on anger in the family, as contradictory to love and to the greater equality in human relationships being promoted by Enlightenment ideology. Growing emphasis on parent-child love, combined with further erosion of community controls, helped generate the growing

reliance on guilt over shame in child rearing. Techniques such as isolation increasingly supplanted both shaming and physical punishments, convincing children that love was temporarily interrupted and could be restored only by sincere repentance—often establishing guilt as a durable emotional enforcer of character standards. Grief, though more fully amplified in the nineteenth century, also followed from greater emphasis on love, along with new beliefs that deaths should be brought under greater control. The apparatus available to commemorate death changed in order to accommodate growing grief needs. Jealousy, finally, was increasingly narrowed to focus on love relationships (rather than wider affairs of honor); and it was increasingly reproved, as incompatible with true devotion.

Emotional change also developed outside the family. The acceptability of sadness and melancholy declined, with people (initially men in particular) urged to present a cheerful demeanor. More broadly, emotions were increasingly seen as operating under individual control rather than sweeping through the body as an outgrowth of physical humors. Correspondingly, responsibility for personal emotion management increased. Words such as *temper* began to suggest a type of anger that should be controlled, while outright neologisms, such as *tantrums*, indicated a childish level of rage that could disqualify an adult from serious consideration. The rise of new standards for disgust followed from cultural redefinitions of emanations from the body and from growing social inequality, with disgust used to mark and justify boundary lines between respectable and unrespectable people and situations.

During the 1700s and the 1800s, West Europeans and North Americans, particularly in the rising middle class, developed a rather new emotional repertoire built on factors that were already in existence. Historians are still working out some of the implications of these changes, how they alter the context of family life and spill over into wider public arenas. The transformation of criminal justice, shifting from shaming to imprisonment, clearly reflected the new commitment to guilt, for example, along with growing disgust at crowd reactions to public punishments. Ramifications of emotional change could reach into a wide spectrum.

Redirections in emotional culture between 1900 and 1950 were also extensive. Here, the dominant motifs are greater control over intensity plus growing informality in social relationships. Some historians also add the motif of an increasing democratization of emotional standards, with fewer systematic social divisions between respectable groups and others. Suspicion of intensity showed in several arenas. Anger, previously approved for men as a motivation for busi-

The nineteenth-century movement away from the public shaming depicted in W. H. Pyne's 1808 illustration of a pillory and toward imprisonment and private punishment is an important event in the historical study of emotion. (Corbis/Historical Picture Archive)

ness and professional life (though dangerous in the home), was now more systematically reproved, with new techniques designed to defuse it. Grief, as has been seen, was increasingly disallowed. Even more revealing attacks on intensity turned against too much stress on guilt, which might damage children's self-confidence. Maternal love, praised without major qualification in the nineteenth century, now fell victim to extensive criticism because of its overpowering qualities; it was felt that mothers should keep their affection under tighter bounds. Romantic love, which had evolved toward increasingly idealistic statements in the nineteenth century, seemed excessive as well by contemporary standards; many prescriptive writers urged more limited, realistic emotional connections while freeing sexuality from some of the emotional commitment promoted in nineteenth-century advice literature.

The new concern about intensity was no accident, and it had some of the same range of effects noted in the earlier Western transformation. Causes centered on changes in economic structure, and therefore emotional functions, along with the rise of a new, psychologically informed expertise. Growing consumerism urged investment in acquisition and goods rather than the emotional investments that figured powerfully in the eighteenth and nineteenth centuries. Corporate and service employment required higher levels of emotional self-manipulation; workers needed to be able to turn on a friendly smile and avoid bureaucratic confrontations. "Impersonal, yet friendly" became a literal catchphrase in business training programs, with considerable emotional implications. At the same time, experts now referred to their psychological, rather than moral, credentials, creating a picture of a more fragile mental structure than had previously prevailed.

The consequences of change involved, as with earlier redirections, both personal and social features. Americans became more nervous about emotional display, convinced that intensity reflected immaturity on their part; hence, one study emphasizes a proclivity to check with others about onsets of jealousy in order to provide a peer-mirror to guard against lack of restraint. Other studies show how rigorous emotional control on the job can result in the distortion of responses, even in private relationships. Legal changes, including the rise of no-fault divorce, incorporated the growing belief that modern individuals should be able to keep anger and grief in check, even in the most trying circumstances. Changes in protest rates—the marked decline of labor strikes after 1958—also derived in part from successful efforts to persuade workers that anger was childish, the reflection of a personal flaw rather than a valid emotional response to objective problems. The reach of this new change in basic emotional style, in sum, was considerable.

Additional vantage points on twentieth-century change feature the growth of informality. Rigorous manners unquestionably declined. People were expected to display some flexibility, in matching emotions to the situation. Increasing contact between men and women, in schools and on the job, reduced emphasis on gender differences in emotional characteristics—typified by the abandonment of the nineteenth-century claim that respectable women should not become angry. Finally, amid growing constraints on certain emotional expressions, a recreational culture arose that provided some symbolic contrasts. Intense spectatorship at theatrical and sporting events, for example, balanced normal emotion management. Athletes and actors were allowed to display the anger, grief, or vivid camaraderie that were not usually countenanced in daily life. This spectatorship provided, in other words, what has been described as a compensatory surrogate culture where people could watch others expressing the emotions that they were not allowed to express themselves.

Issues and Challenges

The success of historical work has added considerably to the available information about the varieties of emotional formulations and the ways values and emotions interact. It thus has amplified the constructionist approach to research on emotion, arguing that a significant part of emotional codes and responses depends upon the context—the time as well as the place. The exploration of change and causation builds a further ingredient into constructionism (one that is often missing from anthropological studies) by showing how one emotion variant may transform into another in response to factors in the wider economic, political, and cultural structure.

In addition to these questions about the relationships between time, place, and types of emotions, the historical agenda raises other problems that are still open to analytical inquiry. The relationship between widely prescribed cultural standards and other aspects of emotional experience—aspects that usually leave less explicit past records—is an obvious example. Standards are an important consideration because they affect social rules and practices that are based on

expected emotional behavior, they color evaluations of others and of the self, and they unquestionably shape actual experience. Thus a culture that discourages romantic love—a common pattern in premodern peasant societies—almost certainly has less of it. But there are disjunctures as well, and historians must be sensitive to these. Among other things, emotional experience may vary somewhat less than standards do. For example, historians who initially assumed that the absence of explicit encouragement (indeed, there was considerable explicit hostility) to marital love in prescriptive materials before the seventeenth century meant that there was little marital love during that period were assuming too much. More recent researchers have generated more nuanced statements of contrast and change.

A related issue, now beginning to gain constructive attention, involves subcultures. Most previous emotions history has focused on mainstream standards issuing from dominant social groups. However, various social classes, religious contingents, and age groups form emotional cultures of their own. Research in American history, particularly, is beginning to reveal patterns of emotionology in various religious and racial groups, as well as in the working class. These patterns sometimes link to mainstream trends (albeit occasionally with a certain chronological lag), but at other times they deliberately run counter (as demonstrated by the enthusiastic religious sects that arose around 1900 as an antidote to growing mainstream hostility to emotional intensity).

Comparison deserves more attention as well. The extensive focus on large transformations invites finetuning. Most research on both the early modern and the twentieth-century turning points has either been strictly national (i.e., just the United States or just France) or has assumed larger transatlantic, Western trends. Yet it is known that, in key particulars, regional patterns vary—the French get angry when jealous, the Dutch sad. Historical comparisons are need to determine when and, above all, why these distinctions emerged.

Based on the accumulation of cases, history can also generate middle-level hypotheses about emotional change. Partial models can be constructed about the factors most likely to cause change, as well as the length of time normally required between the introduction of widely shared new standards and the actual changes in social arrangements and behaviors. It took about a century, for example, for warnings against scaring children with bogeymen stories to gain sufficient acceptance after the 1920s that the prescriptive emphasis could be cut back. Thirty years elapsed between new strictures against anger in the workplace, and incorporation of the same standards in parenting advice. And almost forty years elapsed between the new culture's inception and clear implementation in laws and protest levels. These cases emphasize the importance of more systematic statements about timing.

The most obvious challenge to the study of emotions is interdisciplinary. Historians have found a ready audience among anthropologists, sociologists, and some social psychologists, but actual interdisciplinary projects that would deal with change and effect in relation to current emotional manifestations have yet to emerge. The collaboration necessary for using historical analysis to help test the boundary lines between inherent emotional components and the role of cultural standards is lacking, yet precisely this collaboration constitutes the vital next step in the historical study of emotions.

Conclusion

History contributes not only to an understanding of emotion but to a wider assessment of emotion's effect on behaviors and social institutions. Too often, emotions research focuses on individual experience, but even in the short time that explicit emotions topics have commanded attention, historians have advanced the exploration of why particular emotional articulations matter. Researchers have seen how emotional articulations affect the experience of family life and friendship, how they connect to regimens at work, and even how they can help shape the political arena. Historians will continue to probe the emotional characteristics of the past (particularly cases of significant change), but they will also be eager to incorporate the study of emotion into their larger understandings of how societies function.

See also: ANTHROPOLOGY OF EMOTIONS; PHILOSOPHY; SOCIOLOGY OF EMOTIONS

Bibliography

Burckhardt, Jacob. ([1860] 1995). *Civilization of the Renaissance in Italy.* Boise, ID: Boise State University Press.

Corbin, Alain. (1986). *The Foul and the Fragrant.* Cambridge, MA: Harvard University Press.

Delumeau, Jean. (1978). *La peur en Occident, XIVe-XVIIe siècles: Une cité assiégée.* Paris: Fayard.

Elias, Norbert. ([1939] 1994). *The Civilizing Process,* tr. Edmund Jephcott. Oxford, Eng.: Blackwell.

Elvin, Mark. (1989). "Tales of the Shen and Xien: Body-Personal and Heart-Mind in China during the Last 150 Years." *Zone* 4:266–349.

Febvre, Lucien. ([1933] 1973). *A New Kind of History.* New York: Harper & Row.

Gay, Peter. (1984–1986). *The Bourgeois Experience: Victoria to Freud,* 2 vols. New York: Oxford University Press.

Gillis, John R. (1985). *For Better, For Worse: British Marriages, 1600 to the Present.* New York: Oxford University Press.

Greven, Philip J., Jr. (1977). *The Protestant Temperament: Patterns of Child Rearing, Religious Experience and the Self in Early America.* New York: Knopf.

Harré, Rom, and Stearns, Peter N., eds. (1995). *Discursive Psychology in Practice.* London: Sage Publications.

Hunt, David. (1970). *Parents and Children in History: The Psychology of Family Life in Early Modern France.* New York: Basic Books.

Kofler, Angelika, ed. (1997). "Emotion and Culture." *Innovation: The European Journal of Social Sciences* 10:Special Issue.

Lantz, Herman R. (1982). "Romantic Love in the Pre-Modern Period: A Social Commentary." *Journal of Social History* 15:349–370.

Levy, Robert I. (1973). *Tahitians: Mind and Experience in the Society Islands.* Chicago: University of Chicago Press.

Lutz, Catherine A. (1988). *Unnatural Emotions: Everyday Sentiments on a Micronesian Atoll and Their Challenge to Western Theory.* Chicago: University of Chicago Press.

Lystra, Karen. (1989). *Searching the Heart: Women, Men, and Romantic Love in Nineteenth-Century America.* New York: Oxford University Press.

Pfister, Joel, and Schnog, Nancy, eds. (1997). *Inventing the Psychological: Toward a Cultural History of Emotional Life in America.* New Haven: Yale University Press.

Rosenblatt, Paul C. (1983). *Bitter, Bitter Tears: Nineteenth Century Diarists and Twentieth-Century Grief Theories.* Minneapolis: University of Minnesota Press.

Rosenwein, Barbara. (1998). *Anger's Past: The Social Uses of an Emotion in the Middle Ages.* New York: Cornell University Press.

Seidman, Steven. (1991). *Romantic Longings: Love in America, 1830–1980.* New York: Routledge.

Stearns, Carol Z., and Stearns, Peter N. (1986). *Anger: The Struggle for Emotional Control in America's History.* Chicago: University of Chicago Press.

Stearns, Carol Z., and Stearns, Peter N., eds. (1988). *Emotion and Social Change: Toward a New Psychohistory.* New York: Holmes & Meier.

Stearns, Peter N. (1994). *American Cool: Constructing a Twentieth-Century Emotional Style.* New York: New York University Press.

Stearns, Peter N., and Lewis, Jan, eds. (1998). *Emotional History of the United States.* New York: New York University Press.

Wouters, Cas. (1992). "On Status Competition and Emotion Management: The Study of Emotions as a New Field." *Theory, Culture and Society* 9:229–52.

Peter N. Stearns

HOPE

Since the time of the ancient Greeks, the emotional purpose of hope has been ambiguous. The myth of Pandora has become a paramount example of this ambiguity in the Greek philosophical traditions. As retribution for Prometheus stealing fire from the gods and giving it to humans, Zeus sent Pandora as a "gift" to Prometheus' brother, Epithemeus, along with a jar containing all the evils of the world. When Pandora opened the jar, all of its contents escaped, except for hope. If Zeus had intended for the contents of Pandora's jar to bring misery to humans, was hope considered to be an evil in the same way as the others? Did Zeus hide hope away from humans so that they would not have protection against the evils? The nature and purpose of hope in this tale is unclear. However, one accepted interpretation is that hope was a means of prolonging humans' suffering by giving them the desire to continue living, despite the evils running rampant in the world. This focus on the negative consequences of hope was echoed by Greek philosophers and playwrights such as Aeschylus who characterized hope as "the food of the exiles" and Euripides who called hope "man's curse."

Contrary to this view of the ancient Greeks, the Judeo-Christian tradition has embraced hope as one of three cardinal virtues, the others being charity and faith. Currently, the Western philosophical view of hope is inspired by this tradition—viewing hope as a positive emotion—but certain ambiguities remain as to its nature and utility. What characterizes hope as an emotion, separate from other emotions? Is hope a positive or negative emotion? How is emotion experienced and what functions does it serve?

Defining Hope

Despite its seeming importance in human functioning, early theories of emotion rarely included hope as a discrete emotion perhaps because it lacks a unique facial and behavioral expression. Since the advent of cognitive theories of emotion, however, the classification of hope as an emotion has begun to receive more attention. These cognitive theories propose that emotional experience occurs in response to an appraisal of one's environment as it relates to personal values and goals, rather than as a direct behavioral reaction to a specific type of situation. This appraisal process accounts for hope's distinctiveness from other emotions by differentiating between those that involve a retrospective assessment of an individual's situation in relation to his or her goals (e.g., happiness, sadness) and those that involve a prospective assessment (e.g., hope, fear). Thus, according to most cognitive theorists, hope is considered to be a discrete emotion.

Although there is no absolute standard by which hope is defined, Kenneth Nunn (1996) has suggested that three components of the appraisal process are associated with hope and appear to be common to most models: temporality, desirability, and expectancy. The first component—temporality—captures hope's prospective orientation. In contrast to emotions that rely on a retrospective assessment of goal attainment —such as happiness—hope is experienced under conditions where a goal has not yet been obtained (and may or may not be obtained in the future).

The second component of hope—desirability— focuses on the person's motivation to attain a goal. Emotion researchers, such as Ira Roseman (1984), believe that hope is intimately linked with the object, event, or state that is hoped for. In order to experience hope, a person must *want* to attain the goal. Furthermore, as this desire for the goal increases, so does the intensity of hope. Outcomes considered undesirable or those met with indifference result in the experience of fear or the absence of emotion, respectively.

The third, and perhaps most controversial of the three components—expectancy—refers to the perceived likelihood that the desired outcome will occur. The meaning of the "perceived likelihood" aspect of expectation has been the subject of much debate among hope researchers. Beatrice Wright and Franklin Shontz (1968) have suggested that expectation is the result of a reality-based assessment process used to determine the likelihood of the desired event occurring. Others have proposed that expectation is an assessment of what is possible and *subjectively* probable, even if its realistic or objective probability is low. For example, according to Ezra Stotland (1969), positive affect (hope) is experienced by individuals seeking a desired goal when perceived probability is high, whereas anxiety is experienced when perceived probability is low. A related view supported by Linda Levine's (1996) study is that expectation is a necessary component of hope but that the experience of hope is not necessarily related to the degree of perceived probability as Stotland suggests—the slightest subjective possibility of attaining a goal or desired state is sufficient to elicit hope, even when faced with an objective probability of zero. According to this view, the intensity of hope depends primarily on the importance of the goal.

As mentioned earlier, hope has historically been an emotion to which it has been difficult to assign a positive or negative valence, and this difficulty persists. For the most part, the modern conception of hope is as a positive emotion. Richard Lazarus (1991), however, considers hope to be a negative emotion, albeit for different reasons than did the ancient Greeks. According to Lazarus, an emotion is considered to be positive or negative depending on the current situation's congruence with the person's goals. Hope, by his definition, is a goal-incongruent emotion because it reflects a state of mind in which the individual is "yearning for amelioration of a dreaded outcome" (p. 282). It can be argued, however, that this yearning that Lazarus considers to be the core of hope is actually a blending of two different emotions: fear and hope. Fear is the most viable candidate for hope's negatively-valenced counterpart. Like hope, fear is comprised of a future orientation and the perceived probability of the feared event occurring. But unlike hope, fear involves an

Children watch in anticipation as U.S. and international forces enter Somalia in 1992 as part of "Operation Restore Hope," which was created to bring aid to the Somalians who had been suffering through an extended period of famine and civil war. (Corbis/Peter Turnley)

undesirable event. Simply put, Andrew Ortony and his colleagues (1988, p. 110) describe hope as being "pleased about the prospect of a desirable event" and fear as being "displeased about the prospect of an undesirable event." Returning to Lazarus' description of hope, it can be seen that elements of both fear and hope are involved. Awareness of a dreaded outcome assumes that a person has appraised his or her situation and assessed the probability of an undesirable result; this appraisal would elicit fear. Yearning for amelioration, however, suggests that the person has assessed the likelihood that there may be an alternative, more desirable outcome in the future; this appraisal would elicit hope. Because hope and fear differ in their experience and in the appraisals that elicit them, it is difficult to accept this view as a plausible explanation for viewing hope as a negative emotion.

Hope As a Trait Characteristic

Researchers have examined hope as a dispositional trait, sometimes referred to as personal hopefulness or optimism, although some consider these to be operationally distinct from one another. In contrast to emotion or state hope, C. R. Snyder and his colleagues (1996) suggest that trait hope implies a relatively stable mosaic of personality characteristics that are underscored by the belief that the person's goals can be met and that the person has the ability to plan the appropriate steps to reach these goals. Individuals with trait hope tend to place themselves in situations that are conducive to experiencing goal-attainment, and they tend to view setbacks along the way as temporary obstacles that can be overcome.

The Utility of Hope

One of hope's unique characteristics is its ability to serve as a protective factor for individuals facing adverse situations. Hope provides a way of appraising stressful events such that stressors are seen in a different, less threatening, light. This positive appraisal may then facilitate the person's use of adaptive coping strategies. Hellen Lewis and Wendy Kliewer (1996) have found that hope's relationship to positive adjustment in the face of adverse situations is moderated by the type of coping strategy used by the person. In their study on coping and adjustment among children with sickle-cell anemia, Lewis and Kliewer found that children who coped with their disorder by dealing directly with the stressor, by using support from other sources, or by distracting themselves through physical release of their emotions benefited more from high levels of hope than those who used avoidance to cope with their disorder. Therefore, it may be that hope works reciprocally with existing coping styles to produce its buffering effect.

An increasing amount of empirical and anecdotal evidence has shown a link between hope's beneficial role in coping with severe illnesses and the positive health outcomes that result. Treatment for severe illnesses are often long and unpleasant, and hope provides motivation for maintaining patience with such treatments, even when faced with the possibility of not recovering from the illness. Additionally, Shelley Taylor (1983) has found that hope is associated with the process of creating positive illusions to buffer individuals from the stark reality of a serious condition. Other evidence of the role of hope in illness comes from accounts of chronically and terminally ill patients who maintain a positive outlook on life despite their impending fate. Barring self-deception, the perceived probability of full recovery from the illness is zero, making hope a seemingly logical impossibility. Yet, according to Ron Leifer (1996), some individuals are able to construct new hopes that fall within the restrictions of the illness. These hopes can range from simple goals, such as looking forward to visits from friends, to more extensive goals, such as the hope that one's experience with the disease will inspire others.

In contrast, hopelessness has been implicated in negative health outcomes. Lyn Abramson and her colleagues (1989) have linked hopelessness to depression, in which individuals maintain a negative appraisal strategy for interpreting new information. Physiologically, a depressive or hopeless mind-set can impair the functioning of the immune system, thereby increasing the person's physical vulnerability to certain illnesses. With the evidence of the protective benefits of hope and the dangers of hopelessness, it seems appropriate that the old colloquialism, "Where there's life, there's hope," be rephrased as C. David Jenkins (1996) has suggested: "Where there's hope, there's life."

Just as hope has implications for positive health outcomes, it also has been linked with positive psychological outcomes. Hope's connection with achievement provides one argument for its psychological benefits. For example, research by Lewis Curry and his colleagues (1997) provides convincing evidence of hope's adaptive role in academic and athletic achievement, which seems to be distinct from the effects of other achievement-enhancing factors such as self-esteem

and general positive affect. Hope maintains a goal-oriented way of thinking that results in setting positive goals for success and a mind-set conducive to achieving these goals.

Based on the evidence presented thus far about the utility of hope, one might characterize hope as a dependable protective factor. There are times, however, when hope can be maladaptive. Such is the case when a gambler in Las Vegas puts his or her last dollar in the slot machine with the hopes that *this* pull of the lever will bring the fortune of a lifetime—only to come out with nothing. This is an example of what Haim Omer and Robert Rosenbaum (1997) call "diseases of hope," whose victims cling mercilessly to hopes of "singing tomorrows" that never come. Omer and Rosenbaum suggest that hope can be considered a "disease" when it leads an individual to (a) adopt a disparaging attitude toward the present, (b) be mindless of the sacrifices made by oneself and by others, and (c) have decreased behavioral flexibility.

The Cross-Cultural Experience of Hope

One interest of emotion researchers is how emotions are experienced in different cultures. Cognitive theories of emotion hold that emotions are elicited through situational appraisals using one's values and belief systems as guides. These values and belief systems in part are based upon one's cultural and religious background. Thus, cultures with different philosophical and cultural traditions would be expected to give rise to some differences in the expression and understanding of emotions.

As part of a multifaceted investigation of hope, James Averill, George Catlin, and Kyum Chon (1990) compared the experience and expression of hope of Americans and Koreans. They found that Americans tended to view hope as a transitory state, often related to faith and prayer, whereas Koreans tended to see hope as a more stable component of one's personality, influenced by one's own ambition and effort. Furthermore, Americans reported having more specific, materialistic, or person-oriented hopes (e.g., "I hoped my sister would have a healthy baby") than did Koreans,

> In George Bernard Shaw's St. Joan (1925), Joan of Arc demonstrates confident hope that she will succeed in restoring the Dauphin to the throne of France. Buoyed by her faith and hope, she is able to overcome formidable opposition both on and off the battlefield, although once she has accomplished her mission, the powers that be see fit to burn her at the stake.

who reported having general, altruistic, or achievement-related hopes (e.g., "I hoped to be the most humanistic person").

Averill and his colleagues explain the difference between the two experiences of hope in terms of the religious and philosophical traditions of the two countries. They argue that the American view of hope is influenced by Judeo-Christian philosophy, which teaches that in times of helplessness, one must look toward a higher power for salvation. Hence, hope tends to be seen as something to rely upon when one's own actions cannot achieve the goals that one desires. Koreans, however, are influenced by Confucianism; a religion without a central deity, which emphasizes the ideal of establishing one's own humanity and establishing balance between oneself and others. This ideal is reflected in the Korean conception of hope as an enduring personality characteristic that is derived from one's own efforts. These findings thus illustrate how the appraisals that elicit emotional experiences draw upon cultural traditions such as religion and philosophy.

Hope in Philosophy and Literature

From the Greeks to modern-day philosophers and theorists, hope has been conceptualized as both a positive and negative emotion. Mirroring its ambiguous nature, the arts also have had a tradition of expressing hope with either celebration or slander. Whereas William Shakespeare describes hope as a cure for misery: "The miserable have no other medicine but only hope" (*Measure for Measure;* Act III, Scene i), for some later philosophers, hope seems to embody that misery. Immanuel Kant (1800, p. 122) writes: "For the mind gives itself over completely to hope, as an affect when the prospect of immeasurable good fortune opens unexpectedly, so that the affect tends to rise to the point of suffocating us." Or, stated more bluntly, Friedrich Nietzsche (quoted in Menninger, 1959, p. 483) writes: "Hope is the worst of all evils, for it prolongs the torment of man."

One of the most intriguing metaphors for hope in literature is its association with flight, as seen in this stanza of an Emily Dickinson poem (included in Linscott, 1959, p. 79):

> Hope is the thing with feathers
> That perches in the soul,
> And sings the tune without the words
> And never stops at all.

Similarly, Shakespeare equates hope with flight in *King Richard III* (Act V, Scene ii): "True hope is swift and flies with swallow's wings; Kings it makes gods, and meaner creatures kings." Averill and his colleagues (1990) point out that a large proportion of colloquial sayings for hope also involve an "elevation" or "flight" theme (e.g., "pie in the sky," "on the wings of hope"). This tendency for people in Western culture to use perceptual space when conceptualizing positive versus negative states (e.g., being "high as a kite" versus "having a sinking feeling") may be related to the spatial distinction between Heaven above and Hell below in the Judeo-Christian tradition. Averill and his colleagues assert that the relation of hope with elevation and flight most likely follows from its association with prayer, that is typically directed upward toward Heaven.

Perhaps the most poignant use of hope in art is its use to inspire others. Messages of perseverance and inspiration run throughout the music people listen to and throughout the television commercials they watch—even if the only purpose is to get them to buy a particular brand of athletic shoe. Stories of success despite all odds turn up in books, magazines, news programs, movies, and theater, and they inspire others to achieve the same.

See also: ACHIEVEMENT MOTIVATION; DESIRE; HAPPINESS; HELPLESSNESS; HOPELESSNESS; TRUST

Bibliography

Abramson, Lyn Y.; Metalsky, Gerald I.; and Alloy, Lauren B. (1989). "Hopelessness Depression: A Theory-Based Subtype of Depression." *Psychological Review* 96(2):358–372.

Averill, James R.; Catlin, George; and Chon, Kyum K. (1990). *Rules of Hope.* New York: Springer-Verlag.

Curry, Lewis A.; Snyder, C. R.; Cook, David L.; Ruby, Brent C.; and Rehm, Michael. (1997). "Role of Hope in Academic and Sport Achievement." *Journal of Personality and Social Psychology* 73(6):1257–1267.

Jenkins, C. David. (1996). " . . . While There's Hope, There's Life." *Psychosomatic Medicine* 58:122–124.

Kant, Immanuel. ([1800] 1974). *Anthropology from a Pragmatic Point of View,* tr. Mary J. Gregor. The Hague: Martinus Nijhoff.

Lazarus, Richard S. (1991). *Emotion and Adaptation.* New York: Oxford University Press.

Leifer, Ron. (1996). "Psychological and Spiritual Factors in Chronic Illness." *American Behavioral Scientist* 39(6):752–766.

Levine, Linda J. (1996). "The Anatomy of Disappointment: A Naturalistic Test of Appraisal Models of Sadness, Anger, and Hope." *Cognition and Emotion* 10(4):337–359.

Lewis, Hellen A., and Kliewer, Wendy. (1996). "Hope, Coping, and Adjustment among Children with Sickle Cell Disease: Test of Mediator and Moderator Models." *Journal of Pediatric Psychology* 21(1):25–41.

Linscott, Robert N., ed. (1959). *Selected Poems and Letters of Emily Dickinson.* Garden City, NY: Doubleday.

Menninger, Karl. (1959). "Hope." *American Journal of Psychiatry* 116:481–491.

Nunn, Kenneth P. (1996). "Personal Hopefulness." *British Journal of Medical Psychology* 69:227–245.

Omer, Haim, and Rosenbaum, Robert. (1997). "Diseases of Hope and the Work of Despair." *Psychotherapy* 34(3):225–232.

Ortony, Andrew; Clore, Gerald L.; and Collins, Allan. (1988). *The Cognitive Structure of Emotions.* New York: Cambridge University Press.

Roseman, Ira J. (1984). "Cognitive Determinants of Emotion: A Structural Theory." *Review of Personality and Social Psychology* 5:11–36.

Seligman, Martin E. P. (1990). *Learned Optimism.* New York: Knopf.

Snyder, C. R.; Sympson, Susie C.; Ybasco, Florence C.; Borders, Tyrone F.; Babyak, Michael A.; and Higgins, Raymond L. (1996). "Development and Validation of the State Hope Scale." *Journal of Personality and Social Psychology* 70(2):321–335.

Stotland, Ezra. (1969). *The Psychology of Hope.* San Francisco: Jossey-Bass.

Taylor, Shelley E. (1983). "Adjustment to Threatening Events: A Theory of Cognitive Adaptation." *American Psychologist* 38:1161–1173.

Wright, Beatrice A., and Shontz, Franklin C. (1968). "Process and Tasks in Hoping." *Rehabilitation Literature* 29(11):322–331.

Kimberley A. Babb
Linda J. Levine

HOPELESSNESS

Hopelessness has been most commonly characterized as an overwhelming feeling of despair or discouragement, a sense that all is forever lost or that life is not worth living. This emotional state is accompanied by characteristic ways of thinking and behaving. Hopeless people typically feel trapped by their situation with no perceivable means of escape, and thus they have difficulty developing and finalizing their plans and realizing alternative methods of resolving issues. They believe that, in their isolation, help in solving their problems is inaccessible or unavailable and therefore expect little from themselves and others. They consequently will tend to lack supportive friends and families as well as personal and environmental resources.

Hopelessness has been further described as being accompanied by feelings of paralysis and the inability to act. Because of the thoughts and feelings that are associated with hopelessness, people who feel hopeless tend to have difficulty articulating their desires and often set goals that are unattainable, inflexible, and unrealistic. Hopelessness may be normally experienced following encounters with repeated stressors and disappointments, when life becomes extremely difficult and unbearable, or when one's goals have not been met. A diminished level of physical functioning, mental and emotional well-being, and quality of life will typically result. Specific thoughts or feelings that are associated with hopelessness have included actual or threatened losses, unresolved issues, and changes in physical health.

Perhaps the most basic experiences of hopelessness are associated with captivity and suffering. Hopelessness in a religious context has been described as a spiritual and existential crisis that is experienced when life is perceived to have no meaning or when one believes him- or herself to be forsaken by God. The many components of the hopelessness experience are evident in the following excerpt from an interview conducted by Carol Farran and her colleagues (1995, p. 23). The woman being interviewed had recently experienced a number of tragic events—her husband had had both of his legs amputated and was diagnosed with clinical depression; her sister, grandson, and daughter had all died within the previous six months; and another grandson was still in a coma nine months after he had had a motorcycle accident. The woman related her feelings with regard to her circumstances: "Sometimes I don't have enough energy to keep going. I come every day and try and be cheerful and make [my husband] laugh. I don't tell him how much I hurt inside. I don't want him to have to go to a nursing home, but I am getting so tired I don't know if I can take care of him anymore. I said to God, 'I'm mad, I'm mad.' Why do some people have to suffer so?"

The Experience of Hopelessness

Hopelessness can be experienced to different degrees and on different levels. It may be viewed as either a transitory state (lasting for a period of a few days to weeks), or it can resemble a personality trait (existing across the life span of the individual). At its most basic and least damaging level, a person can feel hopelessness in reaction to the experience of a loss, such as the death of someone who was close, or when the person is simply worn down to exhaustion by life's stresses. In most cases, these feelings are temporary and can be reduced when the individual copes with the situation by using social resources and support. Short bouts of hopelessness can be further combated with rest and relaxation and a reassessment of life goals and priorities. At a more serious and detrimental level, people who have experienced repeated losses or who have emotionally succumbed to the challenges of life by giving up tend to experience a more pathological form of hopelessness that is associated with mental illness, feelings of depression, and even suicide ideation (i.e., the seriousness of intent in unsuccessful suicidal attempts and completed suicides). What appears to be fundamental in preventing the progression of hopelessness to such a point is the presence of optimism and the motivation to keep trying to find positive aspects in a seemingly hopeless and impossible situation.

For example, in cases of terminal diseases such as cancer, patients who try to find meaning in their predicament and look to identify ways for personal growth manage to avoid feeling hopeless, even when they know that there are no treatments or cures available.

There has been limited research that specifically addresses whether hopelessness is experienced differently by men and women or by different cultures and ethnicities. In regard to gender differences, it is clear that women are indeed more likely than men to experience hopelessness, although this finding has not been consistent across all studies (some studies show no differences, but none suggest that men are more likely to experience hopelessness). Given that hopelessness is a construct that is closely related to depression, it is not surprising that women, who are more likely to report and experience feeling depressed, are also more likely to report higher levels of hopelessness. It is interesting to note that the effects of hopelessness on depression seem to differ across genders. Whereas hopelessness has been found to be a predictor of severity of future depression for men, it has not been found to be a significant predictor for women.

Some studies have also demonstrated that ethnic differences exist, although these findings are closely related to socioeconomic factors such as lower education, lower income, and unemployment. For example, being African American and having a lower family income have been shown to be associated with significantly higher psychological distress as measured by reports of hopelessness, depression, and life dissatisfaction. John Chiles and his colleagues (1989) found evidence in their cross-cultural studies of hopelessness that suggests that significant differences between Western (e.g., American) and Eastern (e.g., Chinese) populations do in fact exist. A significant relationship was found between hopelessness and suicidal ideation for Americans, yet not for Chinese participants. In contrast, it was depression that was significantly related to suicide ideation for the Chinese. On an absolute level, Asian individuals have been found to have lower levels of suicidal intent. Yet despite this report, it is agreed that the Chinese had higher rates of depression and hopelessness. It is likely that cultural differences in the growth of individuality and personal boundaries may predispose individuals to psychiatric problems such as hopelessness, depression, and anxiety. Excessive individualism (as shown within the modern Western societies) with privacy but without intimacy, may drive frustrated adults to helplessness and hopelessness, whereas excessive family control (as shown within the Eastern or other older societies), with intrafamilial dependency but without two-way intimacy, may make frustrated adults prone to hopelessness.

Portrayals of Hopelessness

The degree to which the concept of hopelessness is generally understood (i.e., as a feeling of despair and discouragement) is relatively frequently experienced, and its importance in the range of human emotion can be seen within its pervasive depiction in both literary and cinematic mediums. English literature, in particular, is full of characters who are engulfed in the throes of hopelessness. For many, periods of despair and hopelessness serve as an instigation for new beginnings, with despair pushing characters, readers, and authors toward new hope. For example, Eugene O'Neill's *The Emperor Jones* (1921) tells the story of Brutus Jones, a man who lives life with greed and avarice, and it is in such pursuits that he ultimately seals his fate by succumbing to hopelessness, removing all potential of escape. Paralleling research on learned helplessness and hopelessness, Jones can be viewed as being forever oppressed, regardless of the situation. Similarly, Tennessee Williams's *Streetcar Named Desire* (1947) features Stella Kowalski, a woman who is stuck in an abusive marriage, and her hardened sister, Blanche DuBois, who desperately tries (ultimately without success) to open Stella's eyes to her plight. Stella's weakness and thus her hopelessness are apparent from the start, for she never summons the

Two teenagers attempt to comfort a distraught friend.
(Corbis/Jennie Woodcock; Reflections Photolibrary)

strength, let alone the will, to regain her independence.

Hopelessness has been vividly portrayed in a variety of movies across the ages. The 1995 feature film *Leaving Las Vegas* is a wonderful case in point. Director Mike Figgis adapted the autobiographical novel by John O'Brien to tell what is arguably the prototypical experience of hopelessness. It is the story of Ben Sanders, who, following a separation from his wife and son, decides to start upon a suicidal path of alcoholism and self-destruction. He burns all of his worldly possessions and flees to Las Vegas to wallow in his misery and ultimately end it all. The movie illustrates all of the components of hopelessness, particularly a suicidal idealization that results from a belief that there is nothing Ben can do that will make any difference—he sees no reason to make plans for any type of future. The movie also illustrates one of the primary behaviors that is associated with hopelessness: alcohol and drug abuse, a theme that is found in many other movies that compellingly depict characters who are experiencing hopelessness. These movies include Orson Welles's *Touch of Evil* (1958) and Billy Wilder's *The Lost Weekend* (1945).

Origins and Theories of Hopelessness

There have been different explanations to account for the sources of hopelessness. Arthur Schmale (1964), using a psychoanalytic perspective, suggested that hopelessness arises in early childhood when a child's emotional needs are not gratified. One of the foremost theories of hopelessness actually derives from work on the construct of hope. In 1969, Ezra Stotland theorized that "a sense of the possible" was a prerequisite of hope (an action-oriented motivational force) and that hopelessness was its polar opposite, a "negative expectancy toward oneself and the future." Stotland suggested that the roots of hopelessness lie in personal experiences or attitudes, similar to the work on learned helplessness. Clinical psychologist Martin Seligman's (1975) work on the closely related construct of helplessness documents that when people are faced with events that they perceive to be outside of their control, their motivation to initiate responses to control other events is undermined. Seligman theorized that this loss of control and the belief that success and failure are no longer contingent upon one's own actions can result in the experience of hopelessness. This feeling of having no control and making no attempt to better one's situation is so powerful that it has been found to cause death in animals, who give up and die in response to uncontrollable laboratory stressors such as electric shocks, immersion in cold water, or loud noises.

A related theory that focuses on the type of thoughts that people have was developed by Aaron Beck and his colleagues (1974). They hold that negative feelings and moods like those that are associated with hopelessness are a result of an irrational and distorted thought process. Individuals who experience hopelessness are believed to have "automatic thoughts" that are pessimistic in their content and that the individuals have little control over. It is the repeated occurrence of these thoughts that shapes the experience of hopelessness. Most contemporary work on hopelessness focuses on irrational thought patterns. Other theories suggest that a focus on a hopeless environment might facilitate an individual experience of a broader scale "social ill." Erich Fromm (1968) postulated that an individual's hopelessness is largely linked to the hopelessness that exists within his or her class or society, while Frederick Melges and John Bowlby (1969) suggested that hopelessness is associated with feelings of alienation from society.

In their extensive treatment of hopelessness, Farran and her colleagues (1995) document that people arrive at hopelessness in different ways. Based on clinical work, they report that some people have never learned to hope or have never had reason to hope. This uninterrupted pattern of hopelessness might be seen in persons who have a basic personality trait of hopelessness or those who are characterized as being chronically ill. Other people might appear to be focused primarily on specific occurrences, such as the meaninglessness that has been experienced in the past and that is therefore anticipated in the future. These people exist only for the present and experience a type of hopelessness that is characteristic of alcoholics and drug addicts. Still others experience hopelessness only in the context of the present while remaining hopeful about the future and having been hopeful in the past. This situation was often reported by people who had been in concentration camps whose survival was associated with the ability to maintain hope and the will to live in the future in the face of the absolute misery

John Steinbeck's The Grapes of Wrath *(1939) depicts the Joad family, which is forced off of their Oklahoma farm and then further degraded by the migrant labor camp conditions in California during the Great Depression. Out of money, unemployed, and homeless, the family moves into an empty boxcar where the daughter gives birth to a dead baby as torrential rains cause flooding. Although apparently hopeless, some of these people do survive.*

of the present. This type of hopelessness might also exist in situations of traumatic loss and grief.

Unlike other negative emotional states, such as depression, no physiological theories or mechanisms have been suggested to account for the experience of hopelessness in humans. A psychobiological approach to hopelessness in animals suggests that hopelessness, defined as an emotional reaction to persistent restraint, results in an over-activity of the parasympathetic nervous system (i.e., the branch of the nervous system that is responsible for returning the body to a relaxed state after a stressful experience). Advances in biological measurement and the physiological study of emotions will undoubtedly provide a better understanding of the chemical basis of the experience of hopelessness.

Hopelessness and Related Constructs

Most research studies of hopelessness examine the experience of this emotion in the context of the related constructs of helplessness, anxiety, and depression. A large number of these studies now provide consensus that hopelessness can be viewed as a continuum, incorporating and leading to many of these other emotions and often culminating, in extreme cases, in suicide. Illustrative of these associations is the helplessness-hopelessness theory of anxiety and depression that has been developed by the psychologist Lauren Alloy and her colleagues (1990). This theory is perhaps the most specific psychological theory to date to attempt to explain the associations of these emotions and the patterns of relationship. The theory states that once negative life events occur, an individual attempts to determine the degree to which the event is within his or her control, whether the cause of the event is due to the self (i.e., internal), the event's endurance over time (i.e., stable), and the likelihood of the event influencing outcomes in different areas of life (i.e., global). Anxiety and depression are both characterized by helplessness (i.e., the expectation that future negative outcomes, should they happen, would be uncontrollable), yet they differ in that only depression is characterized by hopelessness (i.e., the expectation that future negative outcomes will occur and be stable and global). Helplessness (caused by anxiety) can occur without hopelessness or depression. However, hopelessness cannot occur without the prerequisite helplessness, so, consequently, depressive symptoms commonly have significant anxiety symptoms. The progression from anxiety to depression is also explained by a move from helplessness to hopelessness, such that the inference of negative characteristics about the self from negative life events coupled with the experience of these neg-

ative life events contributes to the development of depression through hopelessness. This theory and sequence of events has received substantial empirical support.

It is interesting to note that the previously described relationships between hopelessness, anxiety, and depression seem to hold true primarily for adult samples. Hopelessness has not been a potent predictor of suicide-related behavior in adolescents. Depression has been found to be a better predictor than hopelessness in high school adolescents, and both were relatively weak predictors in studies of nonclinical adolescents and male juvenile delinquents.

Measurement and Treatment

Hopelessness was originally regarded more as a subcomponent of depression and did not receive any direct attention until the early 1970s. The facts that hopelessness constitutes many different experiences and that it was considered too vague and diffuse an experience limited the construction of objective measures of it, retarding its clinical assessment and treatment. The first measures correspondingly grew out of a clinical need to measure the concept, driven by the work of Beck and his colleagues (1974). His scale, the Beck Hopelessness Scale, is the most widely used measure of hopelessness and was constructed from two different sources. Nine items were gathered from a test on future attitudes, and eleven were gathered from well known pessimistic statements by psychiatric patients. Hopelessness, as measured by this scale, is conceptualized as the perceptual experience of anticipation of undesirable situations or consequences that are largely beyond one's control. The Beck Hopelessness Scale measures three specific dimensions of hopelessness—affective (e.g., lack of hope, enthusiasm, faith), motivational (e.g., giving up, not trying), and cognitive (e.g., lack of future expectations)—and is the only instrument reported to give a reliable measurement of hopelessness in old, frail, multiply impaired nursing home residents. Separate scales based on the Beck Hopelessness Scale have since been designed to measure hopelessness in young children and the elderly.

The ability to transcend the immediate situation, to use rational approaches for confronting daily challenges, and to call upon supportive relationships to help one through the experience of hopelessness appear to be critical to combating hopelessness. Accordingly, most clinical treatments of hopelessness attempt to ensure that patients set realistic goals, have adequate resources, take appropriate action, cope actively, and exercise control over the situation. It should also be noted that, whereas hopelessness is primarily studied in the areas of clinical and counseling psychology, most social and personality psychologists do not consider hopelessness to be an emotion in the truest sense of the word.

Effects of Hopelessness

The experience of hopelessness can seriously affect the individual in that it is related to a range of negative outcomes from physical and mental illness to premature death. Research has shown that hopelessness is associated with conflict in relationships and dissolution and divorce, as well as an increase in the incidence of physical illness, particularly cancer. For example, Susan Everson and her colleagues (1996) examined the relationship between hopelessness, causes of death, heart disease, and cancer in a sample of 2,438 men. Their findings demonstrated that both moderately and highly hopeless men were at significantly increased risk of death from heart attacks and cancer, and these same men (compared to men who were not experiencing hopelessness) were more than three times as likely to die from violence or injury. The most compelling aspect of hopelessness is its relationship to depression and suicide.

Hopelessness has special clinical implications because it is one of the strongest and most consistently found predictors of suicidal ideation. For example, high clinician-ratings of hopelessness in patients who have major depressive disorder shortly after admission to hospital were characteristic of those who later committed suicide. Although it is closely related to depression, hopelessness is a unique predictor of suicide and has emerged as a modulating emotion that links depression and suicidal intent. Hopelessness has been shown to be as much as 1.5 times more important than depression in explaining suicidal ideation and suicidal intent. Whereas depression was thought to be the key predictor of suicide in the past, it is now clear that hopelessness is the important underlying variable. Statistically controlling for or knowing an individual's level of depression does not lessen the strong relationship between hopelessness and suicide ideation. Conversely, knowing an individual's level of hopelessness and statistically controlling for it in the prediction of suicidal ideation makes the level of depression a nonsignificant factor.

The experience of hopelessness can also have important consequences for individuals' immediate social environment, their family and friends. Hopelessness that has environmental origins is often referred to as a form of sociopathy and is marked in adolescents by truancy, expulsion, delinquency, lying, theft, vandalism, repeated drunkenness, or substance abuse. In adults, hopelessness could also be manifested in the form of poor work patterns, bad parenting, poor re-

lationships, irritability, aggressiveness, and a disregard for the law. The most common consequence of hopelessness tends to be alcohol and drug abuse, which as has been mentioned above, is the feature most commonly seen in literary and cinematic descriptions of hopelessness.

Conclusion

There is no single symptom or single consequence of hopelessness. It has cognitive, emotional, and behavioral antecedents and consequences, and although people who experience it can and do improve, treatments and theories for hopelessness still warrant further research attention.

See also: ABANDONMENT; AMBIVALENCE; ANXIETY; ATTACHMENT; BOWLBY, JOHN; GRIEF; HELPLESSNESS; HOPE; LONELINESS; MOOD DISORDERS; PAIN

Bibliography

Alloy, Lauren B.; Kelly, Kelly; Mineka, Susan; and Clements, Caroline. (1990). "Comorbidity of Anxiety and Depressive Disorders: A Helplessness-Hopelessness Perspective." In *Comorbidity of Mood and Anxiety Disorders,* ed. Jack D. Maser and Robert C. Cloninger. Washington DC: American Psychiatric Press.

Beck, Aaron T.; Weissman, Arlene; Lester, David; and Trexler, Larry. (1974). "The Measurement of Pessimism: The Hopelessness Scale." *Journal of Consulting and Clinical Psychology* 42:861–865.

Chiles, John A.; Strosahl, Kirk D.; Ping, Zheng Yan; Michael, Mark C.; Hall, K.; Jemelka, R.; Senn, B.; and Reto, C. (1989). "Depression, Hopelessness, and Suicidal Behavior in Chinese and American Psychiatric Inpatients." *American Journal of Psychiatry* 146:339–344.

Engel, George L. (1968). "A Life Setting Conducive to Illness: The Giving Up-Given Up Complex." *Annuals of Internal Medicine* 11:330–340.

Everson, Susan A.; Goldberg, Debbie E.; Kaplan, George A.; Cohen, Richard D.; Pakkala, E.; Tuomilehto, J.; and Salonen, J. T. (1996). "Hopelessness and Risk of Mortality and Incidence of Myocardial Infarction and Cancer." *Psychosomatic Medicine* 58:113–121.

Farran, Carol J.; Herth, Kaye A.; and Popovich, Judith A. (1995). *Hope And Hopelessness: Critical Clinical Constructs.* Thousand Oaks, CA: Sage Publications.

Fromm, Erich. (1968). *The Revolution of Hope: Toward a Humanized Technology.* New York: Harper & Row.

Melges, Frederick T., and Bowlby, John. (1969). "Types of Hopelessness in Psycho-Pathological Process." *Archives of General Psychiatry* 20:690–699.

Schmale, Arthur H. (1964). "A Genetic View of Affects: With Special Reference to the Genesis of Helplessness and Hopelessness." *Psychoanalytic Study of the Child* 19:287–310.

Seligman, Martin E. P. (1975). *Helplessness: On Depression, Development, and Death.* San Francisco: W. H. Freeman.

Stotland, Ezra. (1969). *The Psychology of Hope.* San Francisco: Jossey-Bass.

Swendsen, Joel D. (1998). "The Helplessness-Hopelessness Theory and Daily Mood Experience: An Idiographic and Cross-

Situational Perspective." *Journal of Personality and Social Psychology* 74:1398–1408.

Regan A. R. Gurung

HORNEY, KAREN

b. Eilbek, Germany, September 16, 1885; *d.* New York City, United States, December 4, 1952; *human development, psychiatry, psychoanalysis.*

Karen Horney was a German-American psychiatrist, teacher, and writer on psychoanalytical theory and practice. Born Karen Danielson in Eilbek, just outside of Hamburg, she married political scientist and corporate executive Oskar Horney when she was twenty-four years of age. After she received her medical degree from the University of Berlin in 1911, Horney choose to specialize in psychiatry in Berlin, where she performed outpatient and clinical work for five years, taking on her first patient in 1912. Her experiences as a wife, physician, and later as a mother played a major role in guiding her interest in and writings about the role and status of women in society. They also led her to propose ideas that contradicted those of the leading male psychiatrists of her time, including Sigmund Freud.

Unlike most of her male colleagues, Horney took an optimistic view of the human experience and saw people as progressing through a series of life stages, each providing new potentials for happiness and self-actualization. She did not see people as being typically overburdened by powerful internal sexual and aggressive drives that might cause emotional and other problems. Thus, she saw psychoanalysis as a method for personal growth, as well as a technique for treating emotional problems, and later in her career became a strong advocate of self-analysis. Horney also broke with her Freudian colleagues over their male-centered explanations for human emotional development and emotional problems. This break came early in her career and became public in 1917 when, during a talk before the Berlin Medical Society for Sexology, Horney openly criticized some of Freud's ideas while he was present in the room. She questioned Freud's ideas about penis envy and its role in female emotional development and argued that if females were envious of anything, it was the higher status afforded men. Contemporary feminists recognized Horney as being an early, leading feminist thinker. Although Freud, who was not tolerant of critics, is said to have described Horney as being "malicious and mean," he never questioned her abilities as an analyst. Quite the opposite, Freud complimented her on many occasions. Horney went on to become the only woman among the six founders of the Berlin Psychoanalytical Institute, and she was the first woman to hold a teaching position there.

Horney's revisionist ideas, later referred to as neo-Freudianism, and the fact that she was a woman in a world dominated by men, caused her to be viewed with suspicion by some people in the field. Although her first book, *The Neurotic Personality of Our Time* (1937), which traced the neurotic personality back to a lack of parental affection and a need for love, received reasonable reviews and was considered by many reviewers to be particularly suited to the general public, her second work, *New Ways in Psychoanalysis* (1939), was condemned by many analysts, and much of her subsequent work was routinely ignored by the psychoanalytic establishment. Despite this, sociologists and anthropologists on the whole praised her work. Support from these disciplines was not surprising since Horney's ideas about the social origin of neuroses placed her firmly in the camp of neo-Freudians, who considered social and cultural factors as well as internal psychological processes in studying emotional development and emotional problems.

In 1932, Horney moved to New York, feeling that America provided a more open intellectual climate for

Karen Horney. (Corbis/Bettmann)

the continuing exploration of her "feminine" psychology. Nonetheless, resistance to her ideas continued. Although she was involved in founding the New York Psychoanalytic Institute, Horney was prevented from teaching upper-level courses. As a result, she did much of her teaching at the New School for Social Research. Horney later began to concentrate her time on writing rather than teaching and practice. She produced, during this period, a series of books, some revising her older ideas and others presenting new ideas on the causes of emotional problems, the uses of analysis, and a female-oriented psychology. While these books were well received by people outside of the field of psychoanalysis and even by the general reading public, they continued to be ignored by most people within the establishment. Her works were later collected by Harold Kelman and published (along with colleagues' comments on Horney's works or their own related writings) under the title, *Perspectives in Psychoanalysis: Contributions to Karen Horney's Holistic Approach* (1965). The previously unpublished lectures, papers, and notes that Horney produced in the last years of her life were later made available under the collective title *Final Lectures* (1987).

Horney's greatest fame came in the decades after her death, particularly in the 1960s and 1970s, when her ideas were embraced by feminists who at the same time harshly attacked many of the ideas of traditional psychoanalysis. Her ideas about the need for somewhat distinct explanations for female and male emotional development, her optimistic view of human potential, her willingness to accept new ideas and revise her own, and her use of analysis to better people's lives all made her attractive to both feminists and humanistic psychologists. Horney's wish to make psychoanalysis readily available to all people was fulfilled with the founding of the Karen Horney Clinic in New York City.

See also: FREUD, SIGMUND; HUMAN DEVELOPMENT; PSYCHOANALYTIC PERSPECTIVE

Bibliography

Horney, Karen. (1937). *The Neurotic Personality of Our Time.* New York: W. W. Norton.
Horney, Karen. (1939). *New Ways in Psychoanalysis.* New York: W. W. Norton.
Horney, Karen. (1942). *Self-Analysis.* New York: W. W. Norton.
Horney, Karen. (1945). *Our Inner Conflicts.* New York: W. W. Norton.
Horney, Karen. (1950). *Neurosis and Human Growth.* New York: W. W. Norton.
Ingram, Douglas H., ed. (1987). *Final Lectures.* New York: W. W. Norton.
Kelman, Harold, ed. (1965). *New Perspectives in Psychoanalysis: Contributions to Karen Horney's Holistic Approach.* New York: W. W. Norton.
Paris, Bernard J. (1994). *Karen Horney: A Psychoanalyst's Search for Self-Understanding.* New Haven: Yale University Press.
Sayers, Janet. (1991). *Mothers of Psychoanalysis.* New York: W. W. Norton.

Ben Manning
David Levinson

HORROR

The object or cause of horror is death. William James, in *The Varieties of Religious Experience* (1902), suggests that religious motivations arise from horror: "Back of everything is that great spectre of universal death, the all encompassing blackness." In the *Powers of Horror* (1982, p. 4), Julia Kristeva describes horror from a psychoanalytic perspective: "It is no longer I who expel [as in sickening wastes]. 'I' is expelled [as in a corpse]."

Definition

Terror management theory, as described by Jamie Arndt and his colleagues (1997), suggests that it is the awareness that there is but a temporary fragile line that separates being from non-being, and physical vitality from rotting flesh, that creates the potential for paralyzing terror. The macabre images and experiences of dismemberment and torture, mental confusion and helplessness, and death and dying elicit both terror and horror. Yet there is a subtle difference. James Averill (1993) offers the useful distinction that the physiological response is a *feeling* and the cognitive appraisal of that response is the *emotion*. Terror is the primal autonomic physiological sensation, and horror is the cognitive appraisal of revulsion to the object or cause of terror: "I feel [sensation: terror]"; "I feel as if I am [cognitive appraisal: horrified]." Therefore, horror may be defined as the cognitive awareness and appraisal of the physiological feelings of terror and helplessness, associated with imminent or imagined loss of physical or mental integrity, as socially constructed by culture. This definition specifies four necessary conditions for the emotion of horror.

The first condition is self-awareness, which is the recognition of personal relevance and vulnerability. Research findings, such as those by Tom Pyszczynski and his colleagues (1990), suggest that level of self-awareness is positively correlated with level of experienced terror.

The second condition for horror is helplessness, loss of control, and unpredictability. Horror is accentuated by the inability to stop, manage, or control a sequence of events that are leading to a physical trauma. Indeed, the way individuals manage paralyz-

Joseph Conrad, in Heart of Darkness *(1899), speaks through his narrator, Marlow, who travels up the Congo River to find Kurtz—a charismatic company hero who has brought huge amounts of ivory out of the middle of Africa. But Kurtz has gotten sick, literally and figuratively. He has turned into a depraved man who has recreated himself as a god whom the natives must worship. Kurtz recognizes the heart of darkness in himself when he whispers, "the horror, the horror," just before he dies.*

ing terror and horror is to take action, resume control, and re-establish routine and stability.

The third condition for horror is feared loss of physical or mental integrity, such as physical deformity, mental depravity, and death. Physical deformity is associated with death of the body, and mental depravity is associated with death of the mind or soul. Physical trauma represents the uselessness of the body and the reduction of self to waste (e.g., bloody limbs or slimy organs), and mental loss corresponds to fears of the meaningless of life and existence. Horror is an emotional response to the recognition of ultimate helplessness in maintaining physical and mental integrity; therefore, people fear aging, dementia, corpses, disease, accidents, terrorism, and control of the mind by conspiracies, governments, corporations, or cultures.

The final condition for horror is the social construction of meaning. While terror of impending death is universal and is manifested in the common drive for self preservation, what is cognitively appraised as horrific varies by culture. What would be considered a traumatic event by some can be imbued with social meaning as a cultural ritual by others (e.g., the Kuru tradition of eating the brains of ancestors); what is socially constructed as horrifying is that which is outside the values and boundaries of the culture.

Response Management

Terror management theory posits that people manage terror (and horror) by investing in the values, religion, traditions, posterity, history, and relationships that provide personal meaning, affirm existence, and ensure the continuation of culture.

People construct "safety zones" through an ordered society that involves people who identify with each other and who share their vulnerabilities, helping them to calm their fears as they realize that even though they are mortal, they are not alone in their mortality. Horror exists in the circumstances surrounding the breakdown of moral order and society —values are challenged, people no longer behave in predictable ways, and things that should never happen occur suddenly and without warning or reason. Because people, as a society, construct what is moral and right, they also determine what is horrifying—that which reminds them of the vulnerability that was to be eliminated by the creation of ordered social lives.

According to Naomi Breslau and Glenn Davis (1991), 40 percent of adults have experienced terror and horror as a result of witnessing or experiencing a sudden serious injury accident or physical assault or of observing the death of another. Acute stress disorder or psychological trauma may also be elicited by war, physical and/or sexual abuse, violent crime, political terrorism, and random shootings or bombings. The experience of terror and horror may include autonomic (reflex), somatic (behavioral), and/or semantic (mental) processes, and different parts of the brain are involved in each response. Context determines which takes precedence. A real-life disaster may be first experienced as an autonomic sensation, whereas a horror movie or roller coaster may be primarily experienced somatically, and reading a newspaper account of a disaster or heinous crime may be evaluated against judgments of morality and therefore processed semantically.

Horror often begins with the primal autonomic sensations of terror: "Fear came upon me, and trembling; . . . the hair of my flesh stood up" (Job 4:14–15). Autonomic responses reflect emotional and cognitive disengagement, such as numbing, absence of emotional responsiveness, reduced awareness of surroundings, slow motion de-realization, and dissociative amnesia. Sheer terror may lead to freezing, like animal prey. Any negative autonomic reaction, according to Leonard Berkowitz (1993), leads to an initial flight/fight response. The flooding of neurotransmitters may lead to freezing and physical withdrawal or a block of cognition and rush of adrenaline that promotes superhuman strength in crisis.

Somatic responses to terror and horror vary by individual and situation. The experience is by definition outside cultural norms and expectations; people have no place to store the horror in memory and no schema for processing the horrifying object or cause. Rebeka Moscarello (1991) describes two opposite responses to horror: expressed horror characterized by agitation, emotional instability, and disorganized behavior; and controlled horror characterized by automaton-like calmness, detachment, and coherent verbal narratives. Moscarello notes that expressed horror is often labeled *hysteria* by the culture, and controlled horror likely reflects a massive psychological regression.

Semantic appraisal of horror involves constructions of narratives that create assessments of responsibility and control and thresholds for experiencing feelings and emotions. People must construct a story of the experience of horror to create meaning out of a trauma that threatens the meaning of the essential "self." They must reconcile their horror with their self-identity by constructing assessments of their responsibility in the trauma and their ability to control future trauma. Constructions of responsibility and control that are discrepant with one's self-identity may lead to anxiety, fear, depression, guilt, shame, and alienation. Narratives may also reflect defense mechanisms—such as denial, suppression, projection, and sublimation—to inhibit the experience of feelings and emotions associated with the trauma. Less critical constructions of one's responsibility and control may evoke the expression of grief and anger, absolution of self, a reaffirmation of cultural values and self-esteem, and reinvestment in relationships with community. The semantic resolution of horror can be seen in community rebuilding efforts, interpersonal and community bonding and support, survivor support groups, and community prayer vigils.

Experiencing terror and horror can result in long-term effects. Symptoms such as avoidance of stimuli associated with the trauma, anxiety and arousal, and impairment of social or occupational functioning that last less than four weeks may constitute acute stress disorder. These symptoms lasting more than one month and accompanied by re-experiencing of the trauma may constitute post-traumatic stress disorder. Dreams, flashbacks, and intrusive images and thoughts may activate physiological feelings of terror, somatic responses (manifested in sleep disorders, irritability, lack of concentration, hypervigilance, and exaggerated startle responses), and disquieting constructions of responsibility and lack of control. Repeated physiological sensations are tied to neurobiological changes in brain metabolism. Lawrence Kolb (1993) explains that just as an explosive sound may cause permanent nerve damage to the ear, excessive stimulation resulting from terror and horror may cause permanent neural changes. Persons diagnosed with post-traumatic stress disorder exhibit heightened levels of adrenaline (which may induce panic responses), cortisol releasing factor stress hormones (which may induce exaggerated perceptions of danger), and opioids (which may induce detachment, apathy, and emotional blunting). At a physiological level, the resolution of horror is tied to the ability of the brain to regulate the release and reception of neurotransmitters associated with autonomic stress responses. At a somatic and semantic level, the resolution of horror is encumbered by the inability to store the horror experience in long-term memory. If horror, by definition, contradicts core beliefs and values, the experience of horror may be kept in active memory until the emotion can be reconciled with existing beliefs.

Media Representation

Although horror is elicited by that which threatens society and social meanings, it has in many ways been embraced by society in the popularity of violent films, television programs, and video games. Box office successes attest to a desire to experience terror and horror vicariously. As society changes, so too do individual fears and the genre of horror media that embody those fears. A closer look at the horror genre and its devotees reveals that people may no longer fear fear itself; instead, that which they fear is themselves.

Gothic novels and early twentieth-century horror films reflected an emerging scientific society that feared the barbarous and the unknown—a monster lurking in the swamp or a madman scientifically creating a beast to destroy a village. This genre reminded people of their individual helplessness and promoted community togetherness and values through the monster's defeat at the hands of the village. Trouble may come, but it comes from outside the structure and safety of society, appears only under extreme circumstances, and can be successfully defeated by logic, reason, and order. The modernistic seed that science will prevail was neatly planted.

The postmodern horror film continues the tradition of threatening a safe and ordered society, but circumstances and resolutions have changed. The boundaries that were previously erected (e.g., education, religion, and family) are no longer impenetrable defenses against evil. Society is suddenly being deconstructed from the inside out—the old rules and solutions no longer apply. Wes Craven's 1997 thriller *Scream* mocks the classic characteristics of the horror genre; characters discuss their actions in relation to the "rules" of horror but find there are new twists to the old rules. Modernity's faith in science, knowledge, and community are mocked. The "monster" is no longer something or someone outside the constructed limits of society like an escaped psychopath or a human-eating blob. In the postmodern horror film, everyone is suspect. Those who seem virtuous and safe can no longer be ruled out. The killer could be the school principal or a family member. Terror no longer strikes on nights with a full moon or on the anniversary of murdered girls' deaths; Valentine's Day, Christmas, family vacations, innocent dates, and suburbs are all being used as backdrops for bloodshed—nothing is sacred, and no one is safe. Nor can it be assumed

Alfred Hitchcock's 1960 film Psycho, *with the famous scene of Janet Leigh being murdered in her shower at the Bates Motel, was one of the first horror movies to have a character who seemed virtuous and safe— Norman Bates—be the source of the horror.* (Corbis/ Bettmann)

that the killer has a good reason, or any reason, for killing. Team efforts to defeat the terror have been rendered ineffective. The isolation of the victim is emphasized, and postmodern society is depicted as one in which altruism is dead and people are saving only themselves. In a society that values knowing why and how things happen, inexplicable violence enhances horror.

The stylized horror genre is being replaced in popularity by the superviolence genre. This genre focuses on realism and exaggerates the horror films' irreverence for death and body. These films focus on realistic homicide; psychological profiles of serial killers; graphic flesh mutilation; a juxtaposition of humor, sex, and fear; and a greater demographic pool of victims. The films elaborate the perspective of the killer, who is less superhuman and relies on intellect, cunning, and sophisticated creative sadism to enact what Jonathan Crane (1997, p. 167) calls "choreographed deaths." It is the presentation of body as waste that is more horrific than death itself.

Crane theorizes that changes in horror films are a response to the terror of everyday life. Watching horror is a reality check in a society that attempts to deny epidemic random violence. There is a sort of nihilistic arrogance associated with media violence. The viewer assumes a perspective of foreknowledge: "We're all going to die, but at least I see it coming." Media horror mocks the do-gooders, the optimists, the altruistic, and the naïve; they will meet an early demise. The classic line of the television series *South Park* is the casual remark "Oh my god, they've killed Kenny!" Kenny is killed in every episode, and the third-grade characters see this as being natural.

The focus on the gory presentation of mutilated bodies in contemporary media may represent the use of special effects and images to mock the manufactured image-based reality of postmodern society. This subversion of symbols forces the audience to confront the nihilism that the culture wishes to deny. The mind can be seduced by false images, but bodily pain and torture is the last bastion of authentic feeling.

There are also gender messages in contemporary media violence. Carol Clover (1992) has pointed out that there is a symbolic annihilation of traditional gender roles. In particular, contemporary horror emasculates males—they are increasingly portrayed as victims and ineffective rescuers. Females, however, are empowered—they are increasingly portrayed as active fighters rather than passive victims. Still, the brute force of the monster wins, both sexes lose, and anarchy reigns. There is an antifeminist theme in the nihilism resulting from the loss of the masculine defender and in the killing of sexually active women. Though confounded with sanctions for sexual activity, Gloria Cowan and Margaret O'Brien (1990) have found some support for female intelligence: stupid sexually provocative women die and smart virginal (or at least monogamous) women may live to be victimized in the sequel.

Social Effects

Although contemporary horror media paint a bleak picture of life and death in postmodern society, many are attracted to the terror- and horror-inducing viewing experience, especially adolescents. Deirdre Johnston (1995) reports four adolescent viewing profiles for slasher films: gore-watchers, characterized by low fear and low empathy; thrill-watchers, characterized by high sensation seeking; independent-watchers, characterized by a need to master fear; and problem-watchers, characterized by social delinquency and generalized anger. Her study suggests that people have different motivations for viewing and exposure to media violence will affect people in different ways. Dolf

Zillmann and James Weaver (1997) have also found a link between attraction to graphic horror media, psychoticism, and violent beliefs. Psychoticism, characterized by a hostile disposition, low empathy, and contempt for risk and danger, is similar to the gore-watcher profile. Whereas one might expect viewing-related aggression from gore-watchers, it is less likely that thrill-watchers will enact violence, and thrill-watchers represent the majority of adolescent viewers. Building on Crane's theory of the terror of everyday life, adolescents may be so over-stimulated with the horror of modern society that they seek violent media to experience the cognitive and emotional numbing effects of terror, or adolescents' attraction to horror may be a counter-phobic response to an increasingly violent society.

Another individual difference in the experience of horror is the tendency to blunt or monitor neurophysiological responses. Glenn Sparks's (1986) activation-arousal theory suggests that some people minimize or verbally and mentally transform threatening stimuli while others focus externally and experience more arousal and negative affect.

Although there is little evidence that the experience of real-life terror and horror varies by gender, there are gender differences in the horror media viewing experience. Zillmann and Cantor (1997) found that those viewers who identify with the victim (typically females) may experience hostility, anxiety and depression, whereas those who identify with the killer (typically males) may experience aggression, power, and even delight. Ron Tamborini, James Stiff, and Zillmann (1987) found that males are attracted to horror films to see destruction, and females are attracted to films providing a just resolution. They have also found evidence that males with traditional attitudes toward female sexuality and males who enjoy pornography are more likely to be attracted to violent horror media, harbor misogynist beliefs, enjoy female victimization, and engage in aggressive behavior.

Conclusion

Horror is fear of individual mortality and the death of social posterity. In a postmodern society plagued by increased violence, social uncertainty, nuclear war, germ warfare, AIDS, and environmental threats, humans are faced with potential individual and social annihilation. The attraction of horror media celebrating murder and alien invasion may reflect a hope that someone or something else will be responsible for that ultimate destruction.

See also: FEAR AND PHOBIAS; HELPLESSNESS; JAMES, WILLIAM; POST-TRAUMATIC STRESS DISORDER

Bibliography

American Psychiatric Association. (1994). *Diagnostic and Statistical Manual of Mental Disorders,* 4th ed. Washington, DC: American Psychiatric Association.

Arndt, Jamie; Greenberg, Jeff; Solomon, Sheldon; Pyszczynski, Tom; and Simon, Linda. (1997). "Suppression, Accessibility of Death-Related Thoughts, and Cultural Worldview Defense: Exploring the Psychodynamics of Terror Management." *Journal of Personality and Social Psychology* 73:5–18.

Averill, James R. (1993). "Putting the Social in Social Cognition, With Reference to Emotion." In *Advances in Social Cognition, Vol. 6: Perspectives on Anger and Emotion,* ed. Robert S. Wyer, Jr., and Thomas K. Srull. Hillsdale, NJ: Lawrence Erlbaum.

Berkowitz, Leonard. (1993). "Towards a General Theory of Anger and Emotional Aggression: Implications of the Cognitive-Neoassociationistic Perspective for the Analysis of Anger and Other Emotions." In *Advances in Social Cognition, Vol. 6: Perspectives on Anger and Emotion,* ed. Robert S. Wyer, Jr., and Thomas K. Srull. Hillsdale, NJ: Lawrence Erlbaum.

Breslau, Naomi, and Davis, Glenn C. (1991). "Traumatic Events and Posttraumatic Stress Disorder in an Urban Population of Young Adults." *Archives of General Psychiatry* 48:216–222.

Clover, Carol J. (1992). *Men, Women, and Chainsaws: Gender in the Modern Horror Film.* Princeton, NJ: Princeton University Press.

Cowan, Gloria, and O'Brien, Margaret. (1990). "Gender and Survival vs. Death in Slasher Films: A Content Analysis." *Sex Roles* 23:187–196.

Crane, Jonathan. (1997). *Terror and Everyday Life.* Thousand Oaks, CA: Sage Publications.

Goleman, Daniel. (1992). "Wounds: How Trauma Changes Your Brain." *Psychology Today* 88:62–66.

Horowitz, Mardi J. (1978). *Stress Response Syndromes.* New York: Jason Aronson.

James, William. ([1902] 1985). *The Varieties of Religious Experience.* Cambridge, MA: Harvard University Press.

Johnston, Deirdre. (1995). "Adolescents' Motivations for Viewing Graphic Horror." *Human Communication Research* 21:522–552.

Kristeva, Julia. (1982). *Powers of Horror.* New York: Columbia University Press.

Kolb, Lawrence C. (1993). "The Psychobiology of PTSD: Perspectives and Reflections on the Past, Present, and Future." *Journal of Traumatic Stress* 6:293–304.

Moscarello, Rebeka. (1991). "Posttraumatic Stress Disorder after Sexual Assault: Its Psychodynamics and Treatment." *Journal of the American Academy of Psychoanalysis* 19:235–253.

Oliver, Mary Beth. (1993). "Adolescents' Enjoyment of Graphic Horror." *Communication Research* 20:30–50.

Pyszczynski, Tom; Greenberg, Jeff; Solomon, Sheldon; Hamilton, James. (1990). "A Terror Management Analysis of Self-Awareness and Anxiety: The Hierarchy of Terror." *Anxiety Research* 2:177–195.

Simpson, Ruth. (1996). "Neither Clear Nor Present: The Social Construction of Safety and Danger." *Sociological Forum* 11:549–562.

Sparks, Glenn. (1986). "Developing a Scale to Assess Cognitive Responses to Frightening Films." *Journal of Broadcasting and Electronic Media* 30:65–73.

Tamborini, Ron; Stiff, James; and Zillmann, Dolf. (1987). "Preference for Graphic Horror Featuring Male Versus Female Victimization." *Human Communication Research* 13:529–552.

Wyer, Robert S., and Srull, Thomas K., eds. (1993). *Advances in*

Social Cognition, Vol. 6: Perspectives on Anger and Emotion. Hillsdale, NJ: Lawrence Erlbaum.

Zillmann, Dolf, and Cantor, Joanne. (1977). "Affective Responses to the Emotions of a Progagonist." *Journal of Experimental Social Psychology* 13:155–165.

Zillmann, Dolf, and Weaver, James B. (1997). "Psychoticism in the Effect of Prolonged Exposure to Gratuitous Media Violence on the Acceptance of Violence as a Preferred Means of Conflict Resolution." *Personality and Individual Differences* 22:613–627.

Deirdre D. Johnston
Elissa M. Wickmann

HUMAN DEVELOPMENT

This entry consists of the following six subentries: Overview; Infancy; Childhood; Adolescence; Adulthood; Old Age.

OVERVIEW

The expression and regulation of emotions have been the topics of a growing body of research since the late 1980s. There is evidence that the ways that individuals express and control their emotions are related to a variety of social outcomes (e.g., social competence, popularity, emotional health). Thus, it is important to consider the development of emotions and emotion regulation across the life span.

The expression of emotions is particularly important in infancy, as it is the primary way that infants can communicate their needs to their caregivers. Research on the normative development of emotions has demonstrated that some emotional expressions are present at birth (e.g., distress, disgust, rudimentary smiles), whereas others appear somewhat later. For example, expressions of anger have been observed in infants as young as two months of age. Moreover, the emergence of fear has been found to occur between eight and nine months of age. These changes in emotional expressions are thought to be related to cognitive developments (e.g., in memory and recognition) and maturation of the nervous system.

The ability to regulate emotions also begins in infancy. According to Ross Thompson (1994), emotion regulation encompasses initiating and modulating or maintaining the occurrence or intensity of emotions and involves attentional, coping, and neurophysiological processes. Infants have some capacity to regulate their emotions at a very early age. Behaviors such as sucking, head turning, and orienting toward and away from objects are strategies that infants can use to control their emotional arousal. It is important to note that although infants have some emotion regulation abilities, caregivers play an essential role in infants'

emotion regulation. Early in life, caregivers help infants to maintain an optimal level of arousal and to relieve their distress.

As infants mature, significant developments in emotional responding, emotion regulation, and in the understanding of emotions occur as a result of changes in cognitive and language capacities. Around two years of age, self-conscious emotions, such as pride, shame, guilt, and embarrassment, emerge. These emotions, according to Michael Lewis and his colleagues (1989), depend on a concept of self and may require an understanding of rules of conduct. In addition, Judy Dunn and her colleagues (1987) have found that toddlers begin to talk about emotions between eighteen and twenty months of age, and they further increase their use of emotion language in their third year. The capacity of young children to label emotions, talk about past and future emotions, and discuss the causes and consequences of emotions demonstrates an understanding of emotions.

Emotion regulation skills also improve with age. For example, Sarah Mangelsdorf, Janet Shapiro, and Donald Marzolf (1995) have found that toddlers use more self-distraction (redirecting attention) and self-soothing strategies than do younger infants and are more likely to attempt to direct potentially stressful interactions than are younger infants. These findings are consistent with Claire Kopp's (1989) conceptual model, which suggests that during the second and third years of life, children gain more sophisticated and autonomous strategies to deal with their negative emotions.

In childhood, as cultural norms and rules are socialized, children come to understand display rules for emotion and start to regulate their emotional displays in accordance with cultural guidelines. For example, Carolyn Saarni and her colleagues (1998) report that older children are more likely than younger children to smile and inhibit the display of negative emotion when given an undesirable gift.

Over time, children begin to use more mentalistic types of emotion regulation strategies, including cognitive distraction, positive self-talk, and attention diversion. Nancy Eisenberg and her colleagues (1997) have found that as children age, there is an increase in their use of cognitive avoidance or distraction as opposed to complete avoidance of the stressor. As children learn to use these internal strategies to deal with their emotions, they seem to become more independent from their parents in terms of emotional support.

Adolescence has long been characterized by increased emotionality, mood swings, and extreme and intense emotions. Research findings, however, provide little support for this notion of emotional lability in adolescence. In one study by Reed Larson and Claudia

Lampman-Petraitis (1989), results demonstrated that adolescents did not report feeling more intense or more frequent emotions than did younger children, although they tended to report feeling lower in average mood than did younger children. Further, adolescents, in comparison to younger children, are more flexible in their use of emotion regulation strategies and are better able to chose context-specific emotion regulation strategies to deal with their emotions. Thus, adolescents are better than younger children at choosing the most effective strategy to use in particular situations. In addition, Wyndol Furman and Duane Buhrmester (1992) report that adolescents are more likely than younger children to rely on peers rather than adults for emotional support.

In brief, in infancy and childhood there appear to be several age-related trends in emotion-relevant regulation: (a) from socially-mediated strategies (i.e., parent-assisted strategies) to increased reliance on solitary or intra-individual strategies, (b) toward increased use of mentalistic strategies, and (c) toward increased ability to select appropriate strategies.

Research with adults suggests that there may be a decline in emotional intensity after the period of adolescence, and this decline seems to continue through old age. In one study by Ed Diener, Ed Sandvik, and Randy Larsen (1985), adults showed less extreme occasions of both positive and negative emotional states than did adolescents. There also is some evidence, as reported by M. Powell Lawton, Morton Kleban, Doris Rajagopal, and Jennifer Dean (1992), that people over sixty years of age have more emotional control and show more leveling of emotion than do younger adults.

The literature on emotions indicates that there are important developments across the life span. It is important to note that cross-sectional studies generally have been used to examine age trends in emotionality and regulation. Thus, there is a need for longitudinal work to examine the stability or change in emotional expressivity and regulation over the life span.

See also: ATTACHMENT; DEFENSE MECHANISMS; EMOTION EXPERIENCE AND EXPRESSION

Bibliography

Diener, Ed; Sandvik, Ed; and Larsen, Randy J. (1985). "Age and Sex Effects for Emotional Intensity." *Developmental Psychology* 21:542–546.

Dunn, Judy; Bretherton, Inge; and Munn, Penny. (1987). "Conversations about Feeling States between Mothers and Their Young Children." *Developmental Psychology* 23:132–139.

Eisenberg, Nancy; Fabes, Richard A.; and Guthrie, Ivanna K. (1997). "Coping with Stress. The Roles of Regulation and Development." In *Handbook of Children's Coping: Linking Theory and Intervention*, ed. Sharlene A. Wolchik and Irwin Sandler. New York: Plenum.

Furman, Wyndol, and Buhrmester, Duane. (1992). "Age and Sex Differences in Perceptions of Networks of Personal Relationships." *Child Development* 63:103–115.

Kopp, Claire B. (1989). "Regulation of Distress and Negative Emotions: A Developmental View." *Developmental Psychology* 25:343–354.

Larson, Reed, and Lampman-Petraitis, Claudia. (1989). "Daily Emotional States As Reported by Children and Adolescents." *Child Development* 60:1250–1260.

Lawton, M. Powell; Kleban, Morton H.; Rajagopal, Doris; and Dean, Jennifer. (1992). "Dimensions of Affective Experience in Three Age Groups." *Psychology and Aging* 7:171–184.

Lewis, Michael; Sullivan, Margaret Wolan; Stanger, Catherine; and Weiss, Maya. (1989). "Self Development and Self-Conscious Emotions." *Child Development* 60:146–156.

Mangelsdorf, Sarah C.; Shapiro, Janet R.; and Marzolf, Donald. (1995). "Developmental and Temperamental Influences in Emotion Regulation in Infancy." *Child Development* 66:1817–1828.

Saarni, Carolyn; Mumme, Donna L.; and Campos, Joseph J. (1998). "Emotional Development: Action, Communication, and Understanding." In *Handbook of Child Psychology, Vol. 3: Social, Emotional, and Personality Development*, 5th ed., ed. William Damon and Nancy Eisenberg. New York: Wiley.

Thompson, Ross A. (1994). "Emotional Regulation: A Theme in Search of Definition." *Child Development Monographs* 59: 25–52.

Tracy L. Spinrad
Nancy Eisenberg

INFANCY

For much of the twentieth century, infant emotional development has been a surprisingly neglected topic of scientific investigation. Certainly, psychiatrists and clinical psychologists have been concerned with infant emotions. However, because clinicians rely primarily on verbal communication, their theories (e.g., Sigmund Freud's theory of the psychosexual stages) have been developed chiefly through retrospective reconstruction. Academic psychologists have been even more negligent than clinicians, often denying the very existence of emotion as a meaningful independent construct.

Since 1970, however, the construct of emotion has been resurrected within the field of academic psychology. At the same time, under the influence of John Bowlby's (1969, 1973) influential attachment theory, clinically-oriented psychologists have turned to direct observation as a means of shedding light on infants' emotional lives. This confluence of events has produced a renaissance in infant emotion research and theory. While there is considerable theoretical divergence among investigators, there has also emerged a shared view about many aspects of emotional development during the first two years of life.

Constituents of Emotions and Their Development

Emotion researchers generally agree that there are several components of emotion and that emotion itself is embedded in the individual's transactions with the environment. These basic components include internal subjective feelings, goal-directed instrumental actions (e.g., fighting, fleeing), expressive behaviors (e.g., facial expressions, vocalizations, postures), and internal neurophysiological responses (e.g., patterns of cortical and subcortical activity, cardiac responses). Eliciting factors (i.e., emotion stimuli and emotion-producing interpretations thereof) and functional outcomes (i.e., changes in the relationship between the individual and the environment) are also typically included as part of the emotion process.

Types of Infant Emotion

Researchers concur that not all emotions are present at birth and that infants do not experience the same full range of emotions as adults. Furthermore, the various components of a specific emotion do not typically emerge simultaneously during development. Thus, infants may smile at birth during REM (rapid eye movement) sleep states but not in response to enjoyable stimuli. By six weeks of age, infants may smile at enjoyable stimuli (e.g., a human face), but they cannot produce any enjoyment-related instrumental behaviors (e.g., reaching and grasping a desirable object). Because researchers differ in the criteria they use to infer the presence of emotion, many different typologies and timetables for emotional development have been offered. Nevertheless, investigators agree (along with most parents) that newborn infants can experience negative emotion (i.e., distress) as well as states of calm. Within four to six weeks, positive emotion (i.e., enjoyment) is clearly in evidence. Between two and fifteen months, infants begin to show a variety of more specific discrete emotions (e.g., anger, fear, sadness, surprise). Depending upon which precise behaviors or combination of behaviors is measured, one may attribute these specific emotions to infants at earlier or later points within this twelve-month period. After fifteen months, infants begin to display embarrassment, an emotion that depends on their consciousness of being the object of others' attention. At around two years, infants begin to demonstrate the social emotions (e.g., shame, pride, guilt, envy) that depend upon an understanding of social standards and other people's expectations.

Internal Subjective Feelings

Although most people consider subjective experience to be the essence of emotion, feelings are not directly accessible by researchers who are studying nonverbal infants. Like other people, most psychologists assume that distinct emotions involve distinct feelings (directly perceivable internal sensations). However, emotional experience may include additional components, such as the conscious awareness of one's feelings and the situational context in which they are embedded. As such, the infant's experience of emotion changes with age. Until they are two to three months of age, infants experience emotions with little conscious awareness and virtually no understanding of their causes or consequences. During the next four to five months, infants develop a sense of their own physical coherence and agency (the core self). This brings an awareness of their own emotions along with some sense of the causes thereof. By the end of the first year, infants further understand that other people also have subjective states, and an emotion may now be experienced as a shared event. By the middle of their second year, infants achieve a new level of self-understanding, becoming aware that they are objective entities who are observable by others. This may be accompanied by a greater consciousness of their own emotions.

Functional Consequences

Emotional behaviors are highly variable; a fearful infant may cry, freeze, refuse to approach a person or object, reach toward its mother, crawl, or walk away. However, all of these behaviors seem to indicate that the infant wishes to distance itself from the feared object. That is, these behaviors seem directed toward a similar functional outcome (i.e., change in the relationship between the individual and the environment). Because functional consequences may be directly observed, many researchers define emotions to be response systems that promote a particular and significant type of relationship between the individual and the environment. For example, disgust promotes avoiding contamination, fear promotes avoidance of danger, and anger promotes removal of an impediment to one's goals.

Neurophysiological Constituents

While the emotion-related limbic system is well established at birth, cortical areas that regulate this system continue to develop during infancy. Thus, infant emotional responses become less labile and more modulated as development proceeds. Studies of infants have focused on electrical brain activity, heart rate, and adrenocortical activity, and they have begun to demonstrate both neurophysiological distinctions among the different emotions and differences among infants in their emotional responsiveness. Electroencephalogram studies of brain activity have shown that several negative emotions that are associated with behavioral withdrawal (e.g., disgust, fear) are accompanied by increased activity in the right cerebral hemisphere, while positive emotion is accompanied by greater activation of the left hemisphere. Furthermore, infants who tend to have more right hemisphere activation during rest periods may have a tendency to experience more negative emotion. Heart rate will increase in response to fear and surprise elicitors, but it will decrease when an infant appears attentive and interested in a stimulus. In addition, individual differences in several heart rate measures (e.g., variability, vagal tone) have been associated with differences in infants' distress reactivity, inhibition, and emotion regulation. Increased adrenocortical activity (indexed by salivary cortisol measures) is associated with both greater emotional reactivity and the infant's ability to modulate subsequently their emotional response.

Expressive Behaviors

Because infants cannot verbally convey their emotions, adults rely chiefly on expressive behavior to infer the infant's emotional state. Adults have little trouble identifying positive or negative emotion in infants on the basis of their smiles and cry faces. Beyond this, there is considerable debate as to whether one can identify more specific emotions (e.g., surprise, anger, sadness) solely from an infant's facial expression. Infants do produce a number of facial configurations that are morphologically similar (though not always identical) to universally identified adult expressions of discrete emotions. However, some of these expressions occur in situations in which their corresponding emotion is unlikely to be present (e.g., "surprise" expressions produced while mouthing a familiar object). Thus, other factors besides the facial expression itself must be considered in attempting to read the infant's emotion. This process is similar to the contextually-based interpretation process that people use when reading emotions in adults.

A second debate involves the differentiation of negative emotional expressions in infants. According to the position held by Carroll Izard and Carol Malatesta (1987), infants have specific expressions for specific negative affects (e.g., anger, sadness). However, some of these expressions actually occur in response to an extremely wide range of elicitors. Thus, other researchers, including Linda Camras (1992) and Harriet Oster and her colleagues (1992), have argued that these facial configurations should be considered expressions of general negative affect (distress) rather than more specific negative emotions. Inferences regarding the presence of a more specific, discrete emotion (e.g., anger) may be made, but they would be based on the presence of other indicators (e.g., an

The debate about identifying very specific emotions (i.e., more than just positive or negative emotions) is illustrated by the fact that although this child who is mouthing a star-shaped toy displays an expression that would be characterized as surprise in an adult, it is unlikely that the child is actually experiencing surprise. (Corbis/Henry Dilates)

anger-appropriate situation or instrumental behavior, such as hitting). Despite these disagreements, facial expressions are commonly acknowledged to be an effective and crucial means of infant emotion communication.

Perhaps even more than facial expression, crying effectively communicates infants' negative emotion. No other expressive signal so reliably elicits a solicitous response from others. As for facial expressions, researchers are currently debating the specificity of infant cries. According to one view, human infants have a repertoire of need-specific cries that adults can accurately interpret (e.g., the pain cry, hunger cry, mad cry). The alternative position is that infant cries vary along several dimensions (e.g., loudness, pitch, rhythm) that communicate information about distress intensity more than specific need. Caregivers use other cues to determine more precisely the source of infant distress. In either case, adults are usually (but not always) able to determine the source of and respond appropriately to the infant's negative emotion.

An important change in expressive behavior occurs as the individual develops the ability to exert voluntary control over his or her facial and vocal expressions. Most children and adults can inhibit their crying and facial behavior. They can also minimize, exaggerate, or completely falsify their expressions. Infants produce intentional nonfacial behaviors by the time they are about ten months of age, and they probably begin to exert voluntary control over their facial and vocal expressions by the end of the first year.

Eliciting Processes

During the first two months of life, emotional reactions primarily occur in direct response to the level and duration of arousal that is produced in the infant. For example, distress occurs in response to a high unmodulated level of arousal that may be caused by hunger, pain, physical restraint, or sudden, intense stimulation of any form. Arousal level depends solely upon the physical parameters of the stimulus rather than its interpretation or psychological meaning. In addition, some specific emotion-related behaviors may be shown in response to specific stimuli (e.g., disgust facial expressions to sour or bitter taste stimuli). These early emotion responses appear to be inborn.

During the next several months, emotional reactions may depend upon familiarity or accumulated experience with a particular stimulus event. Thus, a familiar, recognizable face may cause pleasure, while an unfamiliar face may cause wariness. Interference with a previously successful action routine may cause frustration. During the middle of the infant's first year, emotional reactions become based on goals as well as expectations. Thus, anger may occur when an intended action is thwarted, even if that action had never been successfully performed in the past. As infants get older, they develop new goals and desires that are based on their more advanced understanding of the world and of their own developing motor abilities. Thus, younger infants may be comforted by swaddling, while older infants may respond with distress because such swaddling obstructs their motor goals (e.g., prevents them from grasping desirable objects they see in the immediate environment).

By the end of the first year, emotions may be induced through social communication. For example, infants may learn to fear an object by observing their mother's fear response. Signs of approval or disapproval from their mother may cause infants to maintain or modify their own emotional responses. As development proceeds, emotions may be evoked by an ever-increasing range of stimuli as infants become increasingly able to interpret environmental events in terms that are associated with each emotion (e.g., "irrevocable loss" for sadness; "potential to harm" for fear).

Instrumental Behaviors

In comparison to children and adults, infants have limited means to accomplish the functional goals that are associated with each emotion (e.g., removing an obstacle for anger, withdrawing from a threat for fear). Nonetheless, considerable development occurs in infants' gross and fine motor skills during the first two years of life, and such newly developed skills can be recruited in the service of emotion. During the first three to five months, infants produce diffuse positive or negative reactions that involve the entire body (e.g., calm attentiveness or moderate body activity in response to positive stimuli, overall stiffening or flailing for negative stimuli). However, during the middle of the first year, infants become capable of producing more differentiated behaviors that are appropriate to the specific stimulus and the specific emotion (e.g., grasping hold of a desired object, striking at an offending object, moving away from a feared object). Such emotion-appropriate specific responses may be taken as evidence of discrete emotions in infants rather than states of less differentiated positive and negative affect. Beyond this, infants also gradually become capable of executing complex sequences of behavior in order to achieve their emotion-motivated goals (e.g., removing a series of obstacles in order to obtain a desired object).

Emotion Regulation

In order to serve effectively their adaptive function of motivating and organizing behavior, emotions must be regulated. One of the primary tasks of infancy is the transfer of regulatory control from the caregiver to the infant. During early infancy, a high level of arousal often occurs in conjunction with both positive and negative affect (e.g., during mother-infant face-to-face play or in response to physical pain). Such heightened arousal is difficult for infants to tolerate more than momentarily, and if prolonged to any degree, it will lead to uncontrolled distress. At first, infants have little ability to modulate their own arousal, so responsibility for preventing overarousal or for curtailing the infant's distress rests with the caregiver. Sensitive caregivers can often discern early signs of incipient overarousal in the infant or are aware of situations in which it is likely to occur. In these cases, the caregiver can sometimes act to prevent the buildup of arousal beyond tolerable levels. For example, during face-to-face play, sensitive mothers will recognize when their infant is becoming overexcited and will moderate the stimulation level of their own behavior until the infant's arousal level is reduced. In other cases (e.g., during routine infant inoculation procedures), overarousal cannot be prevented, but the caregiver can act to moderate the infant's distress through a variety of comforting techniques, including physical contact, providing an object to suck, and shifting the infant's attention away from the stress event (i.e., distraction).

During the course of the first year, infants begin to act on their own to both preclude overarousal and moderate their level of distress. At first, the infant's role is primarily to produce involuntary communicative signals to which the caregiver can respond (e.g., whimpering, crying). However, as early as three months, infants will shift their gaze away from a source of overstimulation. This includes averting their gaze from their mother momentarily during face-to-face play. Infants may also actively seek to suck their thumb or other objects or may rock themselves. As infants get older, they may distract themselves by engaging in alternative play activities or more explicitly (i.e., verbally) soliciting caregiver assistance. For example, in a delay of gratification procedure during which an eighteen-month-old infant must wait to obtain a snack reward, he or she may engage the parent in play with other toys in the room to prevent overarousal and distress. When exploring an unfamiliar (and potentially distress-producing) environment, the infant may periodically seek contact with the mother to reestablish a comfortable level of arousal. While the basic strategies of emotion regulation remain the same (e.g., distraction, comforting), the means by which they are enacted become more sophisticated as motor, cognitive, and linguistic skills develop.

Emotion Recognition and Social Referencing

Emotional development is commonly considered to include the development of emotion understanding. Indeed, observing others' emotional reactions is often crucial to establishing one's own patterns of affective response. By the time they are ten weeks of age, infants respond differentially to the combined facial and vocal displays of emotion that are produced by their mothers. For example, they may become distressed by displays of anger, sobered by displays of sadness, and attentive to displays of happiness. However, such responses may result from the stimulation levels provided by the mothers' affect expressions rather than any genuine understanding of the emotions being displayed (e.g., their motivational implications). By the time they are ten months of age, infants clearly demonstrate some understanding of these implications. When presented with a novel emotionally ambiguous object (e.g., a noisy robot toy), infants will look to their mothers for disambiguating information. If the mother smiles, the infant will be likely to approach the toy; if the mother shows a negative facial expression (i.e., fear or disgust), the infant will avoid the toy. This phenomenon, social referencing, demonstrates that infants understand at least the positive-versus-negative motivational dimension of these emotions. Older infants probably have a more differentiated understanding of other people's emotions, although this has not yet been systematically demonstrated for most negative affects. However, by eighteen months, some infants have been observed to respond to others' sadness displays with comforting behavior that is appropriate to that specific negative emotion.

Individual Differences

Individual differences in infant emotions are striking. Some infants tend to be fussy and irritable, while others are placid and calm. One infant may greet the mother with a smile after a brief separation, while another infant might show little emotion or even a negative response. Such differences in general emotionality or emotional responses to specific situations may derive from two sources: inherent temperament and environmental experience.

The concept of temperament includes more than emotionality. However, many theorists believe that infants differ in their propensity to experience some emotions due in part to differences in their inherited neurophysiology. For example, twin and adoption studies have found significant heritability for emotional characteristics such as fear, distress to limitations, irritability, and positive affect/extroversion. Jerome Kagan (1997) and his colleagues propose that variability in distress reactivity at sixteen weeks (i.e., in motor activity and distress response to mildly intrusive stimuli) reflects variability in the excitability of the amygdala and its projections to other parts of the

In A Portrait of the Artist as a Young Man *(1916), James Joyce opens with a charming sensual picture of the world as a toddler comes to know it through experience. From the taste of lemon candy and the texture of his father's beard to the nice way his mother smells and the sound of the story about the moo cow, "baby tuckoo" Stephen learns about his environment. He remembers that when one wets the bed, first it is warm and then it gets cold.*

brain. In one-year-old infants, these differences in excitability (limbic activation) produce differences in the tendency to be inhibited in the presence of unfamiliar stimuli (persons and situations) and later to develop fears. However, Kagan emphasizes that an inherent tendency toward inhibition and fearfulness is modifiable through intervening experience. Indeed, in his extensive longitudinal study, only 19 percent of the highly reactive infants developed into highly fearful and inhibited children. Kagan believes that many highly reactive infants learn to regulate their emotional response with the encouragement and guidance of their parents.

Initially, adults exert almost exclusive control over the environmental influences that their infants experience. However, gradually, infants make a greater contribution as they select their own activities and activity settings. The processes through which environment affects infant emotions and emotional development are themselves quite variable. Nonetheless, they share the common outcome of establishing expectations in infants that will influence their future emotional responses. Three of the most important processes are exposure, contingent responsiveness, and modeling. Exposure refers to the selection of environments and environmental events that the infant is allowed to experience. This may vary across families, across socioeconomic class, and across cultures. For example, some infants are frequently introduced to strangers, while other infants rarely see an unfamiliar face. More frequent experiences with sensitive strangers may produce adaptation by the infant, mitigating the tendency toward a fearful response. Contingent responsiveness refers to the reactions of other people to the infant and in particular to the infant's displays of emotion. For example, parents vary in their tendency to respond to infants' whimpering or other signals of mild distress. Thus, infants may be encouraged to minimize or maximize their expressions of distress. Modeling refers to adults' own emotional behavior. For example, adults themselves may demonstrate positive or negative affect in response to an environmental event (e.g., a stranger, a noisy robot), and this may influence the infant's response to that event through the infant's own social referencing behavior. While conceptually separable, these three processes often operate together in a single environmental event.

Within the family environment, parents clearly differ in their caregiving and nurturing practices. Consequently, they differ in the types of emotional experiences they provide for their infants. Attachment theorists have focused particularly on the effects of these differences on infant emotional development. According to attachment theory, infants develop internal working models of their attachment relationships that include expectations about the attachment figure's emotional responsiveness. For example, some mothers may often reject their infants, especially when the infant displays negative emotion. If this occurs consistently, the infant will come to expect such a response and develop its own emotional strategy for reducing the distress engendered by maternal rejection. This strategy may involve minimizing the infant's own display of negative affect so as to forestall further rejection.

Conclusion

Infants clearly lead rich emotional lives, as evidenced by their facial expressions, vocalizations, and other nonverbal behaviors. Within the first two years of life, substantial changes take place in the processes by which emotions are evoked, the types of emotion that infants experience, and in the nature of the infant's emotional reactions. These changes themselves set the stage for continuing affective development throughout the life span.

See also: ATTACHMENT; BOWLBY, JOHN; CRYING; FACIAL EXPRESSION; NEUROBIOLOGY OF EMOTIONS; TEMPERAMENT

Bibliography

Barrett, Karen C., and Campos, Joseph. (1987). "Perspectives on Emotional Development II: A Functionalist Approach to Emotions." In *Handbook of Infant Development,* 2nd ed., ed. Joy D. Osofsky. New York: Wiley.

Barrett, Karen C., and Nelson-Goens, G. Christina. (1997). "Emotion Communication and the Development of the Social Emotions." In *The Communication of Emotions: Current Research from Diverse Perspectives,* ed. Karen Caplovitz Barrett. San Francisco: Jossey-Bass.

Bowlby, John. (1969). *Attachment and Loss, Vol. 1: Attachment.* New York: Basic Books.

Bowlby, John. (1973). *Attachment and Loss, Vol. 2: Separation.* New York: Basic Books.

Bridges, Katharine M. B. (1932). "Emotional Development in Early Infancy." *Child Development* 3:324–341.

Camras, Linda A. (1992). "Expressive Development and Basic Emotions." *Cognition and Emotion* 6:269–284.

Camras, Linda A.; Lambrecht, Linda; and Michel, George F. (1996). "Infant 'Surprise' Expressions as Coordinative Motor Structures." *Journal of Nonverbal Behavior* 20:183–195.

Cassidy, Jude. (1994). "Emotion Regulation: Influence of Attachment Relationships." In *The Development of Emotion Regulation: Biological and Behavioral Considerations,* ed. Nathan A. Fox. Chicago: University of Chicago Press.

Fox, Nathan A., ed. (1994). *The Development of Emotion Regulation: Biological and Behavioral Considerations.* Chicago: University of Chicago Press.

Goldsmith, Hill. (1993). "Temperament: Variability in Developing Emotion Systems." In *Handbook of Emotions,* ed. Michael Lewis and Jeannette M. Haviland. New York: Guilford.

Haviland, Jeannette, and Lelwica, Mary. (1987). "The Induced Affect Response: 10-Week Old Infant's Responses to Three Emotion Expressions." *Developmental Psychology* 23:97–104.

Izard, Carroll; Fantauzzo, Christina; Castle, Janine; Haynes, Maurice; Rayias, Maria; and Putnam, Priscilla. (1995). "The Ontogeny and Significance of Infant's Facial Expressions in the First 9 Months of Life." *Developmental Psychology* 3:997–1015.

Izard, Carroll, and Malatesta, Carol. (1987). "Perspectives on Emotional Development I: Differential Emotions Theory of Early Emotional Development." In *Handbook of Infant Development*, 2nd ed., ed. Joy D. Osofsky. New York: Wiley.

Kagan, Jerome. (1997). "Temperament and Reactions to Unfamiliarity." *Child Development* 68:139–143.

Kopp, Clare. (1989). "Regulation of Distress and Negative Emotions: A Developmental View." *Developmental Psychology* 25:343–354.

Lazarus, Richard S. (1991). *Emotion and Adaptation*. New York: Oxford University Press.

Lester, Barry, and Boukydis, C. F. Zachariah. (1992). "No Language But a Cry." In *Nonverbal Communication: Comparative and Developmental Approaches*, ed. Hanus Papousek, Uwe Jurgens, and Mechthild Papousek. New York: Cambridge University Press.

Lewis, Michael. (1993). "The Emergence of Human Emotions." In *Handbook of Emotions*, ed. Michael Lewis and Jeannette M. Haviland. New York: Guilford.

Murray, Ann D. (1979). "Infant Crying As an Elicitor of Parental Behavior: An Examination of Two Models." *Psychological Bulletin* 86:191–215.

Oster, Harriet; Hegley, Douglas; and Nagel, Linda. (1992). "Adult Judgements and Fine-Grained Analysis of Infant Facial Expressions." *Developmental Psychology* 28:1115–1131.

Saarni, Carolyn; Mumme, Donna L.; and Campos, Joseph J. (1998). "Emotional Development: Action, Communication, and Understanding." In *Handbook of Child Psychology, Vol. 3: Social, Emotional, and Personality Development*, 5th ed., ed. William Damon and Nancy Eisenberg. New York: Wiley.

Schachter, Stanley, and Singer, Jerome E. (1992). "Cognitive, Social, and Physiological Determinants of Emotional State." *Psychological Review* 69:379–399.

Sroufe, L. Alan. (1996). *Emotional Development: The Organization of Emotional Life in the Early Years*. Cambridge, Eng.: Cambridge University Press.

Stern, Daniel N. (1985). *The Interpersonal World of the Infant: A View from Psychoanalysis and Developmental Psychology*. New York: Basic Books.

Thompson, Ross A. (1990). "Emotion and Self-Regulation." In *Nebraska Symposium on Motivation, Vol. 36: Socioemotional Development*, ed. Ross A. Thompson. Lincoln: University of Nebraska Press.

Tronick, Edward. (1989). "Emotions and Emotional Communication in Infants." *American Psychologist* 44:112–119.

Wolff, Peter H. (1987). *The Development of Behavioral States and the Expression of Emotions in Early Infancy*. Chicago: University of Chicago Press.

Zahn-Waxler, Carolyn, and Radke-Yarrow, Marian. (1990). "The Origins of Empathic Concern." *Motivation and Emotion* 14:107–130.

Linda A. Camras

CHILDHOOD

Emotions are a major force in children's lives, and they are central to how the children adapt to the world around them. This idea is reflected in the functionalist theory of emotion, which emphasizes the role emotions play in motivating individuals' behavior and helping them to achieve their goals. From this perspective, emotions are seen as forces that organize and regulate many aspects of life, including thought processes, social behaviors, and physical health. Children's emotions do not exist in isolation; they are part of the child's interactions with people and events in the world. As such, emotional development in childhood is a process of gaining understanding of emotional experience and developing abilities to regulate emotional states and expression so as to better adapt to the social and physical world. Daniel Goleman (1995) has suggested that aspects of emotional functioning, including self-awareness and impulse control, are crucial to success in life.

Understanding of children's emotional development involves understanding several different aspects of emotional experience that also relate to the child's cognitive and social development. Carolyn Saarni and her colleagues (1998) have identified several competencies that children need to develop in order to have effective emotional communication. These competencies include having awareness of the emotional state of oneself and others, becoming skilled in understanding emotion and using the emotional rules and concepts of one's culture, and developing practical knowledge about how to express emotions in social situations.

Children's understanding of emotions, awareness of their emotional state, and knowledge of cultural rules for displaying emotions are part of the "emotion regulation" process. Emotion regulation is not simply controlling emotion; it is the external and internal processes that people use to monitor, evaluate, and modify their emotional responses, particularly the length and intensity of the emotion, in order to achieve their goals. These processes are influenced by the child's age and gender as well as the social context, the child's expectations about the responses of others, and the specific emotion being experienced. Children who are able to regulate successfully their emotions tend to have more effective peer relationships and perform better on some cognitive tasks. In general, children's emotional abilities increase with age, in line with their cognitive ability to interpret emotional situations. However, the different aspects of emotional development tend to progress at different rates, influenced by such factors as gender and family environment.

Emotional Expression

Emotional expression is the outward appearance or manifestation of emotion; it is the information available to others about one's emotional state. It includes such aspects as facial expression, tone of voice, and body postures. Researchers who have examined the facial expressions of infants have determined that even babies express a range of basic emotions, including happiness, surprise, fear, anger, sadness, and disgust. Although it is difficult to assess whether infants are aware of their emotional states, by the time they are two to three years of age, children appear to be aware of and discuss their emotions. These young children also begin to exhibit a wider range of emotions, including "self-conscious" emotions (e.g., shame, embarrassment, guilt, envy, and pride), which begin to emerge some time after the child is two years of age. It is during this period that toddlers become more aware of their own behavior and begin to evaluate their behavior against social rules and standards. As a result, they may show shame or embarrassment when they fail to meet that standard. Emotions of pride, envy, and guilt are thought to emerge by the time a child is three years of age. Because self-conscious emotions are closely tied to evaluation in relation to culturally based rules for appropriate behavior, the situations in which a child feels such emotions will differ in different cultures. For example, in North American culture, pride is often associated with individual accomplishment, while in less individualistic cultures, pride is more closely tied to group successes. In addition to cultural differences, the events that are associated with self-conscious emotions tend to change with age. For example, a six-year-old child may feel guilty for any involvement in a negative event, even those that are out of the child's control, such as parental divorce. In contrast, older children are likely to focus more on the intent of their behavior and report feeling guilty only in situations where they see themselves as being to blame, such as lying or cheating.

In addition to differences with regard to when children develop different emotions, there are also developmental changes in how they express those emotions. Although some observational studies have suggested that children's facial expressiveness tends to decrease with age, Carol Malatesta-Magai and her colleagues (1994) suggest that development brings about increased flexibility in communicating and moderating emotion in response to the specific situation, rather than simple decreases in the use of specific types of emotional expression. For example, they observed that preschoolers' tended to increase their vocal expression of emotion with age, while the use of facial expressiveness did not change.

Rather than focusing on external observations of emotion, other researchers emphasize children's descriptions of internal emotional states. It is interesting to note that the connection between children's reports of internal emotional state and outward expression of emotion through facial expression is not always clear. By the time they reach their preschool years, children are able to create discrepancies between how they feel inside and their outward expression of emotion. The match between facial expression and children's reports of emotional state tends to be greatest for happiness. Negative emotions appear to be more likely to be associated with differences between appearance and reports. For example, children might exaggerate the intensity of their distress in order to gain attention. As children get older, they also develop the ability to minimize or decrease the intensity of their emotional responses, as well as the ability to mask or neutralize their expression of emotion, such as when a child attempts to look calm in a frightening situation. As these examples suggest, a lack of correspondence between the emotion experienced and the facial expression at times may serve a social purpose.

Gender also may influence reports of emotions, possibly because boys and girls learn some different rules for expressing and talking about emotions. When observed, it appears that both girls and boys have similar facial expressions in response to emotional situations, yet they often report feeling different emotions. For example, girls tend to be more likely to report sadness and fear, while boys are more likely to say they feel neutral or angry. Increasing the age of the children being studied does not necessarily appear to increase the correspondence between what is expressed and what children say they feel. This may be because children, like most adults, have some difficulty in identifying their emotions and may vary in accuracy. However, it is also possible that even children are able to engage in deliberate deception with their verbal reports to hide their actual emotions from others. It has been suggested that socialization processes may encourage the split between the emotion that is felt and the emotion that is displayed. Parents may focus on control of negative emotional displays rather than emphasizing accuracy of labels. This could increase the likelihood that there would be a mismatch between what children show and what they say they feel.

Being able to moderate the expression of emotion is involved with the child's growing ability to decide when and how to express emotions. "Display rules" are the cultural rules that exist concerning the expression of emotion. Even preschoolers realize that there are consequences that are associated with expressing emotions, particularly negative ones, and use rules for

A student in first grade in Esperanza, Puerto Rico, cries with frustration as he struggles with learning to read. (Corbis/Stephanie Maze)

emotional expression. Similar to their early level of moral development, children tend to obey display rules at first simply to avoid punishment or to gain approval. Later, they internalize the rules as they do other cultural standards for behavior. Children's ability to use display rules to regulate their emotions increases with age. As seen in a classic study by Saarni (1984), older elementary school children are better able to control their facial expressions so as to appear positive or happy even when they are receiving an undesirable gift. In contrast, younger children are more likely to show negative expressions in response to a gift that is not liked.

Children learn display rules and strategies for regulation of emotion through socialization processes, including direct parental instruction or warnings about emotional expression and more indirect instruction through parental modeling of emotional behaviors. Parents regulate their children's emotional behavior throughout childhood. However, the ways in which they do so vary somewhat with the age of the child and the type of emotion being experienced. For example, mothers may use more straightforward verbal inter-

ventions with older children in a situation that involves anger than they would use with younger children. Parents may also try to redirect children's attention as a way of helping them manage emotion. Younger children also make efforts to regulate their own emotions, often by trying to change the situation. In addition to these strategies, older children increasingly emphasize more cognitive and internal efforts to deal with emotions, such as distracting themselves or thinking about the situation in a different way. By mid-childhood, children's emotion regulation strategies are likely to be more internal and less likely to be influenced by others.

Part of regulating emotion involves making decisions (and using display rules) about the people to whom the child should express emotion and how much emotion to express. Children are aware of differing consequences for expressing emotions that depend on the type of emotion and the relationship. This knowledge is particularly important for their friendships. Children generally expect their peers to respond most positively to positive emotions and to sadness. In contrast, other negative emotions, such as anger, are expected to be met with negative responses. Some age-related changes have been reported. Younger children report more sadness and anger than do children in the older elementary school years. Children also realize that the intensity of emotion may influence the responses of others and that very intense emotions result in negative interactions. Children generally begin to vary the intensity of their emotions deliberately by the time they are six to eight years of age. Overall, children most openly express happiness and show the least intensity in their expressions of anger. In fact, school-age children are likely to hide or mask anger more than any other emotion. Age-related variations still occur, with younger elementary school children saying they would choose more honest expressions of happiness than would older children. Differences in expression of negative emotions have also been observed, but the research has been inconsistent. Throughout childhood, children control emotion more with their peers and are more likely to express negative emotion to parents or when alone. When asked why they control their emotions, children most often talk about expectations of negative reactions from others—in particular, they seem to expect peers to be less receptive than parents. In addition to seeking support for themselves, some children report having suppressed negative emotions in order to protect others. Patterns in expressing emotions to parents vary depending on the specific emotion, the age of the child, and which parent is present.

Children's Understanding of Emotion

Children's emotion regulation and experience is also influenced by their understanding of the emotions, including thoughts about causes. Researchers typically study children's understanding of emotion by conducting interviews and/or asking children to respond to stories about emotions. As such, the knowledge of children's understanding of emotion is limited by their awareness of the emotion and their ability to discuss it. In the preschool years, children are aware of causes of emotions, but they tend to focus on one external cause. By the time children are four to five years of age, their awareness of cause becomes more complex, and rather than just looking at the outcome of a situation, children consider the match between what outcome was desired or anticipated and what actually occurred. These connections become more sophisticated with age. For example, while a preschooler is likely to associate happiness with obtaining what is wanted, an eight-year-old child in the same situation might not feel happy if the success occurred through some kind of misbehavior. Instead, the result might be feelings of guilt or shame. Older children are also able

to consider many sources of information when they are interpreting the cause of someone's emotion, including information that is specific to that individual.

Another more sophisticated emotional skill concerns the ability to understand mixed or conflicted emotions. In general, children's reports of experiencing mixed emotions and their accuracy in identifying such emotions in others tends to increase with age. However, research results vary somewhat in terms of the age at which recognition of mixed emotions is attained. It is generally accepted that young children cannot understand mixed emotions. Instead, younger preschoolers usually report only one emotion (either positive or negative in tone) that may vary in intensity. At times, they recognize the possibility of having two different emotions in sequence, such as feeling sad and then happy, but they do not report having two separate emotions simultaneously. Still, some children who are six years age or younger may be able to understand conflicting emotions if they are given specific training, such as being taught to focus on the ambivalent aspects of the situation. By the time they are seven or eight years of age, children are able to report experiencing two emotions of the same general type, such as two positive emotions or two negative, in relation to one or more situations. It is in the later elementary school years (about eight to eleven years of age) that children's experience of mixed emotions is more similar to that of adults. They can discuss simultaneous mixed emotions of varying intensities, such as being both happy and sad. Typically, children first report feeling mixed emotions in regard to separate events or targets, such as feeling happy to be playing in the game but sad that it means missing the birthday party. Later, when they are closer to eleven years of age, children can recognize that these emotions may occur in response to one situation, such as happiness that school is over combined with sadness that they will not be seeing their friends.

Family experiences may increase children's ability to understand emotions, particularly family discussions about the causes of people's behaviors. In fam-

> *Initiation into the hard realities of adult life comes as a series of shocks and surprises to the boy in Robert Penn Warren's "Blackberry Winter" (1946). The freezing June weather and the drowned chicks contradict expectations. A mean tramp carrying a switchblade talks to the boy's mother in such rude language that the boy is stunned. He realizes also for the first time how desperately poor and hungry some of his neighbors are and how life is not always safe and good.*

ilies where anger and distress are often expressed, children tend to have more difficulty recognizing and understanding emotions. In contrast, in families where mothers discuss emotions with children, particularly when the children are expressing negative emotions, children are likely to do well on tests of emotional understanding. Unfortunately, this type of mother-child interaction is not typically seen in those families that express a lot of negative emotion. It may be that milder levels of negative emotion in the home may be adaptive for children if they lead to discussion of emotional states and conflict. In fact, in those homes where less negative emotion is expressed, children tend to expect a more understanding response from others when they are experiencing negative emotional states. In families where there are higher levels of emotional expressiveness, the children report less expectations of support or help and greater expectations of negative consequences for expressing negative emotions. Studies have also found that mothers in negatively expressive families tend to regulate positive emotions more than do those in less negative families. It seems that parents in highly negative expressive families may somehow encourage emotional behavior that is consistent with the family atmosphere. Therefore, it seems that exposure to negative emotions that are more controlled and are not overwhelming may help children practice their own emotion regulation skills. However, exposure that is too intense may overwhelm the child and hinder the learning of emotion skills.

In addition to awareness and control of their own emotions, children must develop an understanding of the emotions of others. Children's ability to understand the emotional expressions of others is related to success in relationships and may influence acceptance by peers. Popular and unpopular children tend to respond to the emotions of others in different ways. For example, when faced with anger or conflict from another child, a popular child is likely to respond assertively without escalating the conflict—an unpopular child is likely to respond in ways that increase the level of conflict. In order to respond in a socially appropriate manner, the child must first accurately identify the emotion of the other. The ability to identify emotional expressions is present in the preschool years and increases with age. In general, children are more skilled at recognizing expressions that are associated with positive emotions than those that are associated with negative emotions, with even preschoolers' recognition of happy emotions being similar to that of adults. In contrast, young children have difficulty identifying and interpreting negative emotions, and they confuse some emotions, such as anger and sadness.

A child's skill in identifying another person's emotion can greatly influence social relationships. Of particular concern are children who consistently misinterpret the emotions of others. Children who are rejected by their peers tend to be biased toward recognition of angry or hostile emotions in others; even accidental insults are interpreted to result from hostile intentions. This inaccuracy in assessing the emotions of others may result in withdrawal from peers or in conflicted peer relationships. Children who more accurately assess a peer's emotion are likely to have more interactions with others and thereby more opportunities to increase their ability to interpret social situations. In older children, the ability to recognize peers' emotions has been associated with social competence, self-esteem, and mental health, among other things. Similarly, preschoolers' ability to judge facial expression has also been associated with the possession of greater social skills.

As the ability to identify the emotional expressions of others increases, children also become able to make more sophisticated judgments about emotional expression, including awareness of possible differences between the emotions that other people show and the emotions that those people feel internally. Sensitivity to the emotions of others is related to the development of empathy, which involves both an awareness of another person's emotion and the ability to respond with a complementary emotion. The ability to make empathic responses increases throughout the grade school years as children understand a wider range of emotions and become more skilled in emotional communication.

See also: ACCEPTANCE AND REJECTION; BODY MOVEMENT, GESTURE, AND DISPLAY; EMOTION EXPERIENCE AND EXPRESSION; FACIAL EXPRESSION; FRIENDSHIP; GENDER AND EMOTIONS

Bibliography
Brown, Jane R., and Dunn, Judy. (1996). "Continuities in Emotion Understanding from Three to Six Years." *Child Development* 67:789–802.
Denham, Susanne A., and Couchoud, Elizabeth A. (1990). "Young Preschoolers' Understanding of Emotions." *Child Study Journal* 20:171–192.
Denham, Susanne A.; Renwick-DeBardi, Susan; and Hewes, Susan. (1994). "Emotional Communication between Mothers and Preschoolers: Relations with Emotional Competence." *Merrill-Palmer Quarterly* 40:488–508.
Dodge, Kenneth A., and Garber, Judy, eds. (1991). *The Development of Emotion Regulation and Dysregulation.* Cambridge: Cambridge University Press.
Dunn, Judy, and Brown, Jane. (1994). "Affect Expression in the Family, Children's Understanding of Emotions, and Their Interactions with Others." *Merrill-Palmer Quarterly* 40:120–137.
Fox, Nathan A., ed. (1994). *The Development of Emotion Regulation: Biological and Behavioral Considerations.* Chicago: University of Chicago Press.

Goleman, Daniel. (1995). *Emotional Intelligence*. New York: Bantam Books.

Harris, Paul L. (1989). *Children and Emotion: The Development of Psychological Understanding*. New York: Basil Blackwell.

Lazarus, Richard S. (1991). *Emotion and Adaptation*. New York: Oxford University Press.

Lewis, Michael, and Haviland, Jeannette M., eds. (1993). *Handbook of Emotions*. New York: Guilford.

Lewis, Michael, and Michalson, Linda. (1983). *Children's Emotions and Moods: Developmental Theory and Measurement*. New York: Plenum.

Malatesta-Magai, Carol; Leak, Sharon; Tesman, Johanna; Shepard, Beth; Culver, Clayton; and Smaggia, Beatrice. (1994). "Profiles of Emotional Development: Individual Differences in Facial and Vocal Expression of Emotion during the Second and Third Years of Life." *International Journal of Behavioral Development* 17:239–269.

Saarni, Carolyn. (1984). "An Observational Study of Children's Attempts to Monitor Their Expressive Behavior." *Child Development* 55:1504–1513.

Saarni, Carolyn, and Harris, Paul L., eds. (1989). *Children's Understanding of Emotion*. New York: Cambridge University Press.

Saarni, Carolyn; Mumme, Donna L.; and Campos, Joseph J. (1998). "Emotional Development: Action, Communication, and Understanding." In *Handbook of Child Psychology, Vol. 3: Social, Emotional, and Personality Development*, 5th ed., ed. William Damon and Nancy Eisenberg. New York: Wiley.

Strayer, Janet, and Roberts, William. (1997). "Facial and Verbal Measures of Children's Emotions and Empathy." *International Journal of Behavioral Development* 20:627–649.

Underwood, Marion K. (1997). "Peer Social Status and Children's Understanding of the Expression and Control of Positive and Negative Emotions." *Merrill-Palmer Quarterly* 43:610–634.

Wintre, Maxine Gallander, and Vallance, Denise D. (1994). "A Developmental Sequence in the Comprehension of Emotions: Intensity, Multiple Emotions, and Valence." *Developmental Psychology* 30:509–514.

Zeman, Janice, and Garber, Judy. (1996). "Display Rules for Anger, Sadness, and Pain: It Depends on Who is Watching." *Child Development* 67:957–973.

Zeman, Janice, and Shipman, Kimberly. (1996). "Children's Expression of Negative Affect: Reasons and Methods." *Developmental Psychology* 32:842–849.

Barbara Rybski Beaver

ADOLESCENCE

Adolescence has long been recognized as a period of increased turmoil for both teenagers and their parents. The increased emotionality of teenagers can best be understood in the context of the biological, social, and cognitive changes that characterize this period. In fact, much of adolescent emotion can be seen as serving the purpose of motivating behavior that allows teenagers to accomplish the following important tasks of adolescence: developing intimacy and self-disclosure with peers, beginning dating relationships, and moving toward increased autonomy within the family and peer group. Yet while emotions often facilitate adaptive behavior, they may also create problems for teenagers both in managing their own behavior and in their relationships with others. Failures to manage emotions may result in a variety of problem behaviors ranging from dysfunctional conflict with parents to delinquent behavior to unprotected sexual activity. These problem behaviors may produce long-term negative consequences for both the teenager and society. Close relationships with parents may serve as a protective base for teenagers as they seek to regulate emotions and cope with the developmental tasks of adolescence.

Researchers have long noted that adolescents are prone to emotional turmoil and negative affective states. Reed Larson and Maryse Richards (1994) found that young adolescents were twice as likely to report extreme negative feelings and five times more likely to report extreme positive feelings than were their parents. Larson and his colleagues (1980) found similar results among a sample of high school students and their parents. Although it is clear that adolescents experience a wide range of emotions, researchers have given a variety of explanations for the sources of increased emotionality.

Explanations for the emotionality of adolescence generally include biological changes that are associated with puberty, cognitive changes that are associated with new capacities for abstract thought, and social changes that involve increased intimacy with friends and romantic partners and increased autonomy with parents. Each of these changes has important implications for the emotional life of the teenager. For example, the hormonal changes that accompany puberty may result in girls experiencing increased depressive feelings and boys experiencing increased aggressive feelings. Similarly, the new capacity for abstract thinking often results in increased self-reflection and associated feelings of shame or embarrassment. Finally, both biological and cognitive change may disrupt social relationships. A teenager's physical and cognitive growth may result in increased challenge and renegotiation of family rules and routines, and these changes are often signaled by increased assertion or anger on the part of the teenager. At the same time, relationships with friends and romantic partners occupy a larger portion of teenagers' time and concern. Substantial positive feelings are directed toward developing increased intimacy with friends and romantic partners. However, these same relationships also leave the teenager vulnerable to feelings of betrayal or deep disappointment. Nowhere is the vacillation between intense positive feelings and negative feelings more evident than in teenagers' preoccupation with romantic relationships.

Emotions and Biological Change

The biological changes that are associated with puberty have often been seen as one of the major precipitants of increased negative affect among adolescents. Puberty leads to hormonal changes in the hypothalamic-pituitary-gonadal axis, which results in increased production of androgens. While Elizabeth Susman and her colleagues (1987) have found support for a link between androgens and aggressive affect for adolescent boys, Jeanne Brooks-Gunn and her colleagues (1994) have reported evidence that hormonal changes in estradiol, luteinizing hormone, and follicle-stimulating hormone are linked to increased depressive emotions in girls.

Despite the contribution of biological change to the increase in adolescents' emotionality, most researchers agree that these changes play at best a very limited role in explaining teenagers' emotions. Researchers consistently report that other factors such as changing cognitive abilities, challenging life events, and the transformation of family and peer relationships play a more immediate role in accounting for teenagers' emotions.

Emotions and Cognitive Change

New capacities for thinking about the self and parents are a hallmark of adolescent development, but there are both favorable and unfavorable manifestations of these new cognitive abilities. On the one hand, adolescents' access to an internal world may result in excessive self-preoccupation, ego-centrism, and a poignant disillusion with parents. These cognitive states are often accompanied by intense awareness of disappointments, sadness, and pining. On the other hand, these same new cognitive abilities may enhance mutuality in parent-teenager relationships, facilitate identity exploration, and increase teenagers' intimacy with their peers.

Self-reflection or the ability to take the self as an object of thought transforms the way that teenagers think about themselves and others. Robert Selman (1980) suggests that the acquisition of this kind of perspective-taking is essential for the development of self-reflection because one must first be aware that others are observing and evaluating the self. Whereas preadolescents generally have a style of thinking that is characterized by recognizing the self as the possible target of others' perspectives, adolescents become capable of thinking that is characterized by an increased awareness of mutual interests, allowing for greater coordination and cooperation between self and others. In interpersonal situations, this type of thinking allows the individual to step outside a two-person interaction to identify mutual interests or goals. This capacity for

taking an autonomous perspective on the self and others creates the possibility of evaluating and integrating conflicting aspects of the self.

True self-reflection requires that the teenager must access tacit experience to derive explicit and abstract descriptions of the self. This ability to distance from the immediacy of experience and to find accurate descriptions of the self increases with cognitive development. Studies of children and adolescents point to fundamental shifts in self-understanding. In her review of literature on the self-system, Susan Harter (1983) proposes a gradual transition from descriptions of the self based upon physical attributes (i.e., size, appearance, gender) to descriptions of the self based on actions to descriptions of the self based on psychological dimensions (i.e., moods, intentions, attitudes). Increasingly abstract self-descriptions allow individuals to integrate more concrete descriptions. For example, an abstract trait label such as *athletic* allows the child to integrate more concrete self-descriptions such as good in soccer, basketball, and gymnastics.

As adolescents' self-descriptions move from the concrete to the more abstract, they also shift from external action-oriented descriptions to internal emotional attributes. William Damon and Daniel Hart (1988) describe a developmental progression in self-understanding that moves from the physical self to the social self to the active self to the psychological self. Thus, most adolescents describe the self with psychological labels such as *tolerant, obnoxious, empathic,* or *sarcastic.* This move toward psychological and emotional descriptions signals new access to the internal world of experience. Increasingly, adolescents will integrate internal cues that involve feeling and memory in their self-descriptions. By articulating and differentiating internal cues, adolescents gain new access to information about themselves. Thus, the basic premises of the teenager's personality, which have guided emotional appraisals and behavior during childhood, become the object of the adolescent's attention. With their new thinking skills, many teenagers begin to represent and articulate these aspects of the self, making them available for review.

Adolescents' heightened self-consciousness can contribute to increased negative feelings such as shame, anxiety, and embarrassment. Larson and Richards (1994) found that young adolescents reported feeling "self-conscious" and "embarrassed" two to three times more often than their parents did. The increased self-awareness of the adolescent period coincides with teenagers increasing the amount of time they spend alone. In fact, Larson and Richards found dramatic increases in the time that adolescents spent in solitary activities, either in their own rooms or in relatively "private" parts of their homes. This time alone may serve as both a time for self-reflection and a time for letting down emotionally in ways that teenagers find restorative. Thus, it is clear that the intense social engagement with peers is also accompanied by increased time alone.

The disruptive features of formal operational thinking have received considerable attention in the literature on adolescence. Initially, when adolescents recognize that knowledge or belief is fallible, they may be prone to overextending this notion into generalized skepticism and doubt. For example, when teenagers first perceive the limitations of previously questioned assumptions and recognize a plurality of alternative possibilities, they may conclude that there are no simple criteria for arbitrating between different perspectives. Studies by William Overton and his colleagues (1987) of formal reasoning indicate that when adolescents first begin to recognize limitations in their ability to draw conclusions, they overextend their "can't tell" response to arguments that in fact offer a valid conclusion. As emerging skepticism and relativism destabilizes the world of the adolescents and their parents, teenagers may seek ways of regaining a sense of certainty. Michael Chandler (1975) suggests that adolescents may respond to this period of uncertainty with a variety of "regressive solutions." He views stereotypy, cliquishness, and pressures toward conformity in adolescent peer groups as attempts to escape from uncertainties that are created by formal operational thinking.

Emotions and Changes in Relationships

Emotions motivate teenagers' changing engagement in parent and peer relationships. As teenagers negotiate increased autonomy with parents and increased intimacy with friends and romantic partners, relationships become the focus of intense negative and positive feelings.

Parent-Teenager Relationships

Increased thinking capacities and the ability to recognize and evaluate alternative possibilities may pose new problems for an adolescent's relationship with his or her parents. In childhood, parents may appear to hold unquestionable truths and values, allowing them to hold also a position of unquestioned and unchallenged authority. As adolescents come to recognize that alternative possibilities exist for how to relate to parents and that their parents' own knowledge about the world is only partial, parental injunctions may no longer appear binding, and parental flaws and shortcomings become increasingly obvious. As a result, parents become "deidealized" and appear as more or less

ordinary people who possess the usual uncertainties, problems, and idiosyncrasies. This implies a true "widening of the world," as adolescents become able to grasp the existence of aspects of reality that are different from those they personally experience.

Changes in thinking about the self and parents may have a profound effect on behavior in parent-teenager interactions. Just as adolescents experience more negative emotions, emotions about their relationships with parents tend to become more negative and conflicted. Larson and Richards (1994) found that the emotions that children experienced with their parents changed dramatically from the fifth grade through early adolescence. Times when the children were "very happy" with mothers virtually disappeared, while the frequency of negative emotions when they were with their mothers increased dramatically.

As the adolescent recognizes the relativism of knowledge, parental authority loses its unquestioned status. Parental knowledge may be as fallible as a teenager's own knowledge. As a result, rules of conduct that were accepted in childhood lose much of their binding power. Judith Smetana's (1988) research on parent-teenager conflicts indicates a major shift in how adolescents reason about disagreement with their parents. Whereas preadolescents overwhelmingly accept parental rules as matters of convention, adolescents shift toward viewing rules as matters of personal jurisdiction to be arbitrated by the self. Thus, teenagers choose rules for personal conduct that are less in accord with parental authority and more in accord with the internal world of personal thoughts and feelings. Laurence Steinberg (1990) has found that this cognitive shift coincides with increased conflict between parents and teenagers during early adolescence.

Adolescents often identify values or criteria that allow them to arbitrate between their own perspective and the perspective of others. Many adolescents are faced with integrating positive and negative perceptions of themselves and their parents. In this process, they may come to recognize the importance of relationships with parents as potential sources of security and stability. By valuing family relationships, teenagers can reorder their priorities and limit the pursuit of purely "selfish" goals. During the later years of adolescence, this shift in perspective allows teenagers to decrease anger and frustration and gain new objectivity about themselves and their parents. The search for values or criteria that may resolve multiple or conflicting perspectives may form a hallmark of mid-adolescence. Studies of the self-system highlight how adolescents become increasingly concerned with criteria of *consistency* in evaluating different aspects of the self. Harter (1990) reports that middle adolescents (i.e., fourteen to fifteen years of age) not only detect inconsistencies across their various relationships with parents, friends, and romantic partners (i.e., their role-related selves) but are also extremely troubled and conflicted over these contradictions, much more so than younger or older adolescents.

Since the late 1970s, there has been a shift toward a more positive (and therefore less negative) depiction of adolescence. According to this new view, only a minority of adolescents experience *extreme* turmoil or emotional disengagement from their parents. Instead, the typical adolescent may experience only *momentary* disruptions with parents. Positive interactions and or connectedness predominate in parent-teenager encounters. In their studies of teenagers, Daniel Offer and his colleagues (1981) report that the vast majority of teenagers are likely to report admiring their parents, turning to their parents for advice and support and feeling loved and supported by them.

Friendships and Romantic Relationships

Adolescents experience the most positive emotions in the relationships with their friends. In part, teenagers' new self-perceptions allow them to share confidences with their friends and move friendships toward increased intimacy. However, Ritch Savin-Williams and Thomas Berndt (1990) have found that whereas boys tend to increase their contacts with friends through shared activities, girls tend to compare their private thoughts. Despite the new opportunities and the rewards provided by teenagers' friendships, these relationship may also be a source of distress. Larson and Richards (1994) report that peer relationships were second only to school as a source of negative emotions in young adolescents. Just as friends can be a source of comfort and enjoyment, friendships can also be a source of disappointment, envy, betrayal, and jealousy.

During adolescence, romantic relationships take on increasing emotional salience. In addition to the fact that teenagers report peak positive experiences after interacting with potential romantic partners, romantic relationship form a major topic for self-disclosure and sharing of confidence in friendships. During early and mid-adolescence, many romantic relationships occur at the level of fantasy. Larson and Richards (1994) report that some teenagers would report peak positive experiences after talking with an imagined romantic partner. Many romantic relationships during this period are short-lived and go through the cycle of romance and disillusionment in periods that do not even last one week. In romantic relationships that do last, many teenagers face challenges of negotiating sexual issues, and in many cases, females are burdened with setting the limits on sexual activity.

Being away from their family and peers, a young couple is able to concentrate on their one-on-one relationship as they relax on the Charles Bridge in Prague. (Corbis/Wolfgang Kaehler)

Functional and Dysfunctional Emotion Regulation

Despite the normal increase in negative feelings that is experienced by nearly all teenagers, a smaller number to teenagers may experience states of prolonged negative feelings that may result in more serious difficulties. For example, anger may serve an important function in helping teenagers' to assert themselves with parents in ways that eventually result in an increased autonomy in the parent-child relationship. However, anger may also serve to undermine trust and lead to defensive responses that exacerbate conflict and disengagement in the family. Similarly, self-consciousness that may facilitate reflection and the formation of a mature sense of identity can also become a source of withdrawal, self-doubt, and embarrassment for a teenager who is socially anxious. Sadness that may promote coping with disappointments in friendships and romantic relationships may become a chronic depressive mood that is accompanied by suicidal ideation. To the extent that teenagers are able to use emotions to enhance or facilitate their accomplishment, emotions may be considered functional. However, if emotions become problematic and interfere with the maintenance of successful relationships, they can be considered dysfunctional.

Dysfunctional expressions of emotions have often been associated with a number of problem behaviors. At a general level, delinquent behaviors are associated with problems in managing anger and aggression. Marion Forgatch and Gerald Stoolmiller (1994) have reported that in families in which contempt is expressed by both the mother and son, the son is likely to be engaged in higher levels of delinquent activity. Other studies, such as those by Joe Allen and his colleagues (1994) and Roger Kobak and his colleagues (1991), have found that the dysfunctional expression of emotion during mother-teenager conflict discussion results in higher levels of adolescent depression.

Researchers are beginning to identify the factors that distinguish between adolescents who manage to regulate emotion successfully and those who are likely to move toward more dysfunctional behaviors. Supportive parent-teenager relationships have been singled out as a critical resource for adolescents. When parents and teenagers successfully regulate emotions with each other, teenagers usually show more successful adaptation. Observational studies of parent-teenager interaction provide consistent evidence for this positive relationship between a supportive parent-teenager relationship and an adolescent's successful regulation of emotion. Allen and his colleagues (1994) have found that parent-adolescent relationships that are characterized by high levels of autonomous and supportive interactions are associated with higher levels of adolescent ego development and self-esteem. Similarly, Forgatch and Stoolmiller (1994) found that parent-teenager relationships that are marked by lax supervision are strongly associated with increased levels of delinquent activity.

Aspects of teenagers' personality may influence their pathway through adolescence. Jeannette Haviland and her colleagues (1994) found that adolescents who have contracted self-structures (i.e., those who are unable to think of the self in more than two or three social roles) identify conspicuously low levels of negative traits in the self-structure. In contrast, adolescents who have more advanced self-structures are able to integrate negative emotions into an overall balanced view of the self. This study points to important differences between adolescents in their ability to use and integrate negative emotions. Similarly, Stuart Hauser and Andrew Sayfer (1994) found that adolescents have higher levels of ego development exhibit

significantly higher levels of enthusiasm and affection and lower levels of sadness and anger. Attachment research has also highlighted the importance of teenagers' personality for managing emotion successfully. Using the Adult Attachment Interview, Kobak and his colleagues (1991, 1998) have found that teenagers who are judged to be autonomous demonstrate better emotion regulation as judged both by peers and by observers of parent-teenager interactions.

Conclusion

Adolescence is a time of increased emotionality. The significance of emotions can be best understood in the context of the major cognitive, biological, and relationship changes that are occurring during the teenage years. For most teenagers, emotions play an adaptive role in helping both to motivate and to cope with change. However, for a substantial minority of teenagers, emotions become dysfunctional and may lead to further difficulties and problem behaviors that can include delinquency, depression, unprotected sexual activity, and substance abuse. Successful emotion regulation results from supportive parent-teenager relationships and personality factors that include ego development and coherent thinking about the self.

See also: AGGRESSION; ANGER; EMOTION EXPERIENCE AND EXPRESSION; FRIENDSHIP; MOOD DISORDERS; PERSONALITY; RELATIONSHIPS; SADNESS; SELF-ESTEEM

Bibliography

Allen, Joe; Hauser, Stuart; Eickholt, Charlene; Bell, Kathy; and O'Connor, Tom. (1994). "Autonomy and Relatedness in Family Interactions As Predictors of Expression of Negative Adolescent Affect." *Journal of Research on Adolescence* 4:535–552.

Brooks-Gunn, Jeanne; Graber, Julia; and Paikoff, Roberta. (1994). "Studying Links between Hormones and Negative Affect: Models and Measures." *Journal of Research on Adolescence* 4:469–486.

Brooks-Gunn, Jeanne, and Warren, Michele. (1989). "Biological Contributions to Affective Expression in Young Adolescent Girls." *Child Development* 60:372–385.

Chandler, Michael. (1975). "Relativism and the Problem of Epistemological Loneliness." *Human Development* 18:171–180.

Cooper, Cathleen. (1988). "The Role of Conflict in Parent-Adolescent Relationships." In *Minnesota Symposium on Child Psychology, Vol. 21,* ed. Megan Gunnar and Andrew Collins. Hillsdale, NJ: Lawrence Erlbaum.

Damon, William, and Hart, Daniel. (1988). *Self-Understanding in Childhood and Adolescence.* New York: Cambridge University Press.

Elkind, David. (1967). "Egocentrism in Adolescence." *Child Development* 38:1025–1034.

Forgatch, Marion, and Stoolmiller, Gerald. (1994). "Emotions As Contexts for Adolescent Delinquency." *Journal of Research on Adolescence* 4:601–614.

Harter, Susan. (1983). "Developmental Perspectives on the Self-System." In *Handbook of Child Psychology, Vol. 4: Socialization, Personality, and Social Development,* ed. E. Mavis Hetherington. New York: Wiley.

Harter, Susan. (1990). "Self and Identity Development." In *At the Threshold: The Developing Adolescent,* ed. S. Shirley Feldman and Glen R. Elliott. Cambridge, MA: Harvard University Press.

Hauser, Stuart T., and Sayfer, Andrew. (1994). "Ego Development and Adolescent Emotions." *Journal of Research on Adolescence* 4:487–502.

Haviland, Jeannette; Davidson, Robin; Ruestsch, Charles; Gebelt, Janet; and Lancelot, Cynthia. (1994). "The Place of Emotion in Identity." *Journal of Research on Adolescence* 4:503–518.

Keating, David. (1990). "Adolescent Thinking." In *At the Threshold: The Developing Adolescent,* ed. S. Shirley Feldman and Glen R. Elliott. Cambridge, MA: Harvard University Press.

Kobak, Roger, and Sceery, Amy. (1988). "Attachment in Late Adolescence: Working Models, Affect Regulation, and Representations of Self and Others." *Child Development* 59:135–146.

Kobak, Roger; Sudler, Nanette; and Gamble, Wendy. (1991). "Attachment and Depressive Symptoms during Adolescence: A Developmental Pathways Analysis." *Development and Psychopathology* 3:461–474.

Lapsley, Daniel K. (1990). "Continuity and Discontinuity in Adolescent Social Cognitive Development." In *From Childhood to Adolescence: A Transitional Period?,* ed. Raymond Montemayor, Gerald R. Adams, and Thomas P. Gullotta. Newbury Park, CA: Sage Publications.

Larson, Reed; Csikszentmihalyi, Mihaly; and Graef, Roberta. (1980). "Mood Variability and the Psycho-Social Adjustment of Adolescents." *Journal of Youth and Adolescence* 9:469–490.

Larson, Reed, and Richards, Maryse H. (1994). *Divergent Realities: The Emotional Lives of Mothers, Fathers, and Adolescents.* New York: Basic Books.

Offer, Daniel; Ostrov, Eric; and Howard, Ken. (1981). *The Adolescent: A Psychological Self-Portrait.* New York: Basic Books.

Overton, William F.; Ward, S. L.; Noveck, I. A.; Black, J.; and O'Brien, D. P. (1987). "Form and Content in the Development of Deductive Reasoning." *Developmental Psychology* 23:22–30.

Savin-Williams, Ritch, and Berndt, Thomas. (1990). "Friendship and Peer Relations." In *At the Threshold: The Developing Adolescent,* ed. S. Shirley Feldman and Glen R. Elliott. Cambridge, MA: Harvard University Press.

Selman, Robert L. (1980). *The Growth of Interpersonal Understanding.* New York: Academic Press.

Smetana, Judith. (1988). "Concepts of Self and Social Convention: Adolescents' and Parents' Reasoning about Hypothetical and Actual Family Conflicts." In *Minnesota Symposium on Child Psychology, Vol. 21,* ed. Megan Gunnar and Andrew Collins. Hillsdale, NJ: Lawrence Erlbaum.

Steinberg, Laurence. (1990). "Autonomy, Conflict and Harmony in the Family Relationship." In *At the Threshold: The Developing Adolescent,* ed. S. Shirley Feldman and Glen R. Elliott. Cambridge, MA: Harvard University Press.

Steinberg, Laurence, and Silverberg, Susan. (1986). "The Vicissitudes of Autonomy in Early Adolescence." *Child Development* 57:841–851.

Susman, Elizabeth J.; Inoff-Germain, G. E.; Nottelmann, E. D.;

Cutler, G. G.; Lorizus, D.; and Chrousos, G. (1987). "Hormones, Emotional Dispositions, and Aggressive Attributes in Early Adolescents." *Child Development* 58:1114–1134.

Roger Kobak

ADULTHOOD

Research on emotional development in adulthood has lagged behind the renewed and widespread interest in the study of human emotions and feelings that began in the early 1980s. However, by the end of the 1980s and into the 1990s, the resurgent interest in the study of emotions had stimulated research in the emotional development during the latter half of the life span. Considerable progress has been made in multiple areas of adult emotional development, including emotional expression and communication, understanding the nature of emotions, individual differences in variables that affect the experience of emotions, the regulation of emotions, and the interface between emotion and cognition.

In contrast to emotional development, the developmental literature, in general, is replete with theory and research on cognitive development. In fact, cognition has been largely seen as being of primary importance in the development of the human organism. This is exemplified in the literature on childhood as well as the literature on adult development and aging. For example, research on adulthood has focused on the extent to which scientifically-observed age differences in cognitive functioning reflect performance-inhibiting emotional states such as anxiety—emotion has been considered only as a nuisance factor that interferes with the measure of cognitive change. Similarly, researchers on childhood development have relegated emotion to a secondary status in that they have explored the relationship between cognitive and emotional development, with cognition being a prerequisite to emotional functioning. For example, person and object permanence are viewed as prerequisites to stranger and separation anxiety, and the development of self-recognition is seen as a prerequisite for experiencing emotions such as pride and shame.

Although cognition-emotion relationships have not been abandoned in the 1990s, approaches to studying emotion development, especially in adulthood, have raised the status of emotion and placed it on equal grounds with cognition. This has been accomplished by taking a functional approach to the study of emotion in adulthood. In other words, instead of simply examining whether specific emotions or feeling states exist in adulthood, researchers go further and examine the degree to which emotions are goal-directed and change as a function of different environmental and psychological contexts. This leads to a concentration on the dynamic processes, strategies, and feeling states (emotions) that are involved in emotion regulation in adulthood rather than a concentration on emotions as static, invariant feeling states.

Two basic questions about emotions (one structural and the other functional) can be posed from an adult developmental perspective. The generic structural question is "Does development change the fundamental nature of emotion in adulthood, and if so, in what ways?" The generic functional question is "To what extent do age-related changes in emotion influence the effective functioning of the adult?" This functional question would be important even if it were the case that developmental processes in adulthood, for ex ample, had no effect on the fundamental structure of emotion. Regardless of developmental changes in the nature of emotion, the functional effectiveness of the individual can be enhanced or degraded by the kinds of emotions that are experienced as one grows older.

Structural Stability in the Nature of Emotions

From a structural perspective, the developmental focus has centered on two dimensions of emotions: (1) core feeling states and the expression of emotion and (2) whether they change with age. Differential emotion theory, which provides a framework for this line of research, suggests that emotions are the primary force for organizing human thought and behavior (and therefore give meaning and richness to the quality of one's life). In order to maintain a stable sense of self and personality, it follows that there should be continuity across adulthood as to what the core feeling states and expressions of emotions are. In fact, it appears that such core feeling states (i.e., anger, fear, sadness, joy, and interest, among others) and their motivational force (e.g., fear elicits protective behavior) remain relatively unchanging throughout adulthood and later life. In addition, studies that examine emotion from this perspective find that both the verbal and nonverbal expression of emotion do not change appreciably throughout adulthood. In par-

Ernest Hemingway, in "The Short Happy Life of Francis Macomber" (1927), tells the story of a rich thirty-five-year-old man who transforms from a "bloody coward" who is scorned by his wife into a fearless hunter who stands his ground to shoot at a rhinoceros that is charging straight at him. His newly discovered confidence and happy self-respect do not last long, however, because his wife "accidentally" shoots him in the head.

ticular, studies find that the frequency and intensity of emotional experience remain fairly stable across the adult life span.

However, a differential emotion theory perspective does suggest that developmental changes in emotion occur in the formation and continuous development of connections between emotion and personality, cognition, and behavior. Thus, when one shifts the attention from the core feeling states to a higher level of analysis, such as the examination of affective-cognitive relationships and the relationship between the situation (or elicitors of emotion) and the emotional response, one sees developmental changes. For example, the ability to appraise a situation in terms of the beliefs and desires of others and to anticipate their emotional response to an event increases with experience across adulthood. Similarly, as cognition becomes more complex with age, emotions will be activated by multiple sources instead of single sources (as is the case in early development). To illustrate, when infants are prevented from achieving a goal, the result is the primary sensation of anger. However, adults will appraise and interpret the situation, and how the situation is appraised will determine the extent to which anger is elicited. Such change introduces another body of research that examines emotion in terms of its social context and its relation to the development of thought and action. Rather than focusing only on core feeling states and expression, such approaches have examined other dimensions of emotion, including emotional understanding, subjective emotional experience, and the regulation of emotions.

Functional Change in the Nature of Emotions

For any study of emotional understanding, subjective emotional experience, and the regulation of emotions, the focus must be on the functionality of emotions across the life span. Again, this is prominent in the relational approach to studying emotions. Instead of examining simple relationships between a singular dimension of emotion and its outcome, this approach is more interested in the dynamics of the processes that are used in regulating the subjective experience of one's emotions. For example, marital satisfaction cannot be determined by a simple measurement of emotional intensity; the other dynamics of the emotional relationship must be considered, including the compatibility between the two partners and the content of their emotional reactions to an emotion response—in other words, their patterns of communication.

The role of behavioral communication in emotion is to signal to oneself and to others the extent of one's emotional response in order to achieve a desired outcome. In childhood, the development of communicative patterns includes conforming to display rules of emotions (e.g., appropriate emotions to display in public). In late adolescence and young adulthood, emotional communication is governed by the normative proscriptions defined by one's immediate culture. In adulthood, self-goals in emotional communication become important in that the inner self determines what emotions are appropriate to display in particular situations. Overall, changes in patterns of communicating emotions across adulthood are characterized by a gradual disinhibition in the expression of emotion (as dictated by the external culture).

A similar adult developmental pattern can be seen in progressive changes in one's understanding of the nature and causes of emotion. Gisela Labouvie-Vief (1997) has proposed a theory of emotional development that is strongly related to increases in cognitive complexity. Studies demonstrate that young adults tend to describe emotions in terms of the cultural rules and standards of emotional expression. Cognitively mature individuals question prevailing social conventions on emotions. Their descriptions involve a more differentiated or complex emotional experience that takes into consideration the inner subjective experience and one's mental processes. Labouvie-Vief's research suggests that this developmental progression peaks in middle age—both adolescents and older adults display lower-level, more concrete forms of emotional language description.

Labouvie-Vief suggests that there is a parallel progression in emotional control or regulation strategies. Youthful forms of emotional control involve repressive strategies such as controlling emotions through forgetting, ignoring, and redirecting negative emotions. The goal is to repress emotional tension and free oneself from emotional conflict. The mature adult is open to accepting periods of intense inner conflict and emotional experience. Owning one's emotions facilitates either taking action based on the emotion or accepting the situation.

However, it should be noted that age is not necessarily the key factor in these progressions in emotional complexity. In fact, Labouvie-Vief and others find that ego development is a better predictor of complexity in emotional understanding and emotional regulation than age. Ego development involves a move from external regulation of behavior (e.g., by powerful others, societal norms) to internal or self-regulation of behavior and the ability to see the multifaceted character of other people and situations. Thus, instead of being age-related, Labouvie-Vief's levels of emotional complexity and regulation represent a hierarchy of cognitive-emotional competencies that may or may not be manifested in different domains of functioning. With

an increase in cognitive development, one sees an increase in the link between cognitive and emotional systems.

Although the development of emotional understanding may change as a function of domain or context, other approaches have taken a more explicit contextual perspective and have examined adult emotional development within and across different social contexts. Laura Carstensen has proposed the socioemotional selectivity theory, which suggests that emotion regulation is a class of social motives (e.g., to feel good, to derive emotional meaning from life, to establish intimacy, and to validate self-representation) that remains important across the life span yet achieves greater importance relative to other social motives as one moves through the stages of adult development. For example, social motives that involve striving for knowledge are more important from late adolescence through young adulthood and early middle adulthood. During this period, the goal to attain knowledge is pursued at the cost of emotional satisfaction. The relationship is reversed in later adulthood. It should be noted that Carstensen also suggests that this relationship is not necessarily determined by age. It is possible that the change is driven by the perception of constraints in time or time limitations. When time is limited, as in the latter half of the adult life span, emotional goals (i.e., the need for emotionally meaningful experiences and deep feelings) rise to the forefront.

Another important component of Carstensen's approach is that she places emotion in a social context. Each culture socially constructs its members' emotional experience through the functions, rules, and social roles of the community. Childhood development involves the continual expansion of social worlds or contexts. In infancy and early childhood, emotional experience is embedded in the family context. In turn, children must seek knowledge regarding the meaning of the emotions that are expressed in this social context in relation to the larger cultural context. The primary goal in this phase of development is to attain emotional rewards that are derived from one's activities. In adolescence, the importance of the family context decreases, whereas the importance of peers increases. In turn, affect towards family becomes more negative, whereas affect toward peers becomes more positive. In late adolescence and early adulthood, knowledge seeking and the pursuit of future-oriented goals become the priorities, and the regulation of feeling states are subordinated. Emotional resilience in the face of failure or social rejection is valued over succumbing to emotional reactions such as escape or aggression. Early and middle adulthood may reflect the peak time for emotional sacrifice. By the time one

Graduation ceremonies are significant reminders of the diverging goals for individual family members; just as the child is going out into the world to pursue career goals at the possible expense of emotional sacrifice, the parents are likely to be at a place where their career goals have been attained and emotional connections to family and friends are becoming of greater importance. (Corbis/Annie Griffiths Belt)

is well into middle age, the world has been explored and one's identity has been established. At this point, emotional goals reemerge and again become influential in controlling one's activities. During early older adulthood, the importance of friends and family once again becomes paramount. Therefore, the focus of emotional experience shifts as a function of shifting relevant social contexts.

An Individual Difference Approach to Emotions in Adulthood

While most of the research literature reviewed up to this point has concentrated on the broad variable of age, there are other variables—individual variables—that must be considered as well when studying emotional change. From an individual difference perspective, age, like other background variables, is only one of the variables that are associated with changes in emotional functioning. Developmental differences in emotional functioning can be clarified further by understanding individual differences in relevant de-

velopmental constructs (e.g., cognitive abilities, ego level, cognitive appraisal). Thus, the individual differences approach makes it possible to evaluate the conditions under which adults of varying ages and of different personal and developmental characteristics are likely to exhibit change in emotional functioning.

There is a growing body of research that indicates that styles of emotional regulation are associated with individual differences in attachment style. According to John Bowlby (1969, 1973), attachment theory is concerned with the formation of a biologically-based, goal-corrected behavioral system that ensures the survival and emotional well-being of young and dependent offspring. This system results in an infant-mother bond or attachment. Although this process applies to all infants, the quality of the attachment bond varies from security and trust in relation to the caregiver to avoidance of the caregiver or ambivalence toward the caregiver. Research on adult attachment indicates that adults can also be characterized as secure, avoidant, or ambivalent in their close relationships. In turn, they display emotional and communicative patterns that are similar to those seen in comparably attached infants and children.

A secure attachment style in adulthood reflects trust and a general positive affect (i.e., cheerful, likable, well-adjusted). In turn, individuals with this style can express and manage negative affect constructively. An avoidant style reflects mistrust and a reluctance to display feelings. Restricting one's own emotional experience and distress in this way regulates negative affect. Hostility, anxiety, and a fear of intimacy characterize the demeanor of an adult with an avoidant style. Finally, an ambivalent style reflects the feeling that others are unpredictable and oneself is helpless. Thus, the emotional demeanor of an adult with an ambivalent style reflects high anxiety and low self-esteem, as well as excessive guardedness during times of distress and potential distress.

Research by Carol Magai and her colleagues (1995, 1997) indicates that facial expression patterns of emotions are consistent with the emotional traits and child-rearing experiences that are linked to different adult attachment styles. For example, facial expressions of joy predominate for adults with a secure attachment style, whereas facial expressions of shame predominate for adults with an avoidant style, and mixed emotional expressions predominate for adults with an ambivalent style. These findings emphasize that there are substantial individual differences in emotional communicative patterns within close relationships and that attachment and emotion systems are related.

Conclusion

Emotional expressivity appears to be preserved and remain stable over the adult life span. Change in emotional development is evident when the functional significance of emotions is taken into consideration. Thus, adulthood marks a maturity in the understanding of the nature and causes of emotion, an improvement in regulatory skills to maintain positive affect, a focus on self-regulated goals in the communication of emotions, and a resurgence in the primary importance of emotional goals.

See also: ATTACHMENT; BOWLBY, JOHN; EMOTION EXPERIENCE AND EXPRESSION; PERSONALITY; RELATIONSHIPS

Bibliography

Bowlby, John. (1969). *Attachment and Loss, Vol. 1: Attachment.* New York: Basic Books.

Bowlby, John. (1973). *Attachment and Loss, Vol. 2: Separation.* New York: Basic Books.

Campos, Joseph J.; Campos, Rosemary G.; and Barrett, Karen.
(1989). "Emergent Themes in the Study of Emotional Development and Emotion Regulation." *Developmental Psychology* 24:394–402.

Carstensen, Laura L.; Gross, James J.; and Fung, Helene H. (1997). "The Social Context of Emotional Experience." In *Annual Review of Gerontology and Geriatrics, Vol. 17: Focus on Emotion and Adult Development,* ed. K. Warner Schaie and M. Powell Lawton. New York: Springer.

Dougherty, Linda M.; Abe, Jo Ann; and Izard, Carroll E. (1996). "Differential Emotions Theory and Emotional Development in Adulthood and Later Life." In *Handbook of Emotion, Adult Development, and Aging,* ed. Carol Magai and Susan H. McFadden. San Diego, CA: Academic Press.

Labouvie-Vief, Gisela. (1997). "Cognitive-Emotional Integration in Adulthood." In *Annual Review of Gerontology and Geriatrics, Vol. 17: Focus on Emotion and Adult Development,* ed. K. Warner Schaie and M. Powell Lawton. New York: Springer.

Levenson, Robert W.; Carstensen, Laura L.; and Gottman, John M. (1994). "The Influence of Age and Gender on Affect, Physiology, and their Interrelations." *Journal of Personality and Social Psychology* 67:56–68.

Magai, Carol, and McFadden, Susan H. (1995). *The Role of Emotions in Social and Personality Development: History, Theory, and Research.* New York: Plenum.

Magai, Carol, and Passman, Vicki. (1997). "The Interpersonal Basis of Emotional Behavior and Emotion Regulation in Adulthood." In *Annual Review of Gerontology and Geriatrics, Vol. 17: Focus on Emotion and Adult Development,* ed. K. Warner Schaie and M. Powell Lawton. New York: Springer.

Fredda Blanchard-Fields

OLD AGE

Contrary to the widely held belief that aging brings decreased emotional intensity and greater negative affect and depression, the research points to little consistent change in later life and even suggests that emotions in very old age are more likely to be positive than negative. While the physiological underpinnings of emotions probably do change with age, cognitive strategies seem to operate to maintain stability in emotional experience and to encourage feelings that are more positive than negative. Further, there appears to be noticeable stability of personality over time—highly emotional individuals remain highly emotional and less highly emotional individuals remain less emotional.

Physiological Changes

Emotional experiences have been assumed to be related to physiological systems. Changes in the brain in later life include decreases in substances such as catecholamine, indoleamine, norepeniphrine, dopamine, and serotonin. Moreover, aging is also accompanied by decreased regulatory effectiveness of the central nervous system and thus decreased reliability of homeostatic mechanisms. Consequently, theorists have suggested that older individuals may take longer to react to stimuli, may reach higher levels of arousal, and may then take longer to return to baseline conditions afterward. Research with animals and humans does in fact show some decreasing emotional responsiveness and lowered affect intensity in old age. On the other hand, the emotional experiences of older adults may not reflect these changes in the structure and composition of the brain. Jaak Panksepp and Anesa Miller (1996) suggest that alterations in the brain in later life may not be associated with identifiable emotional or behavioral conditions in the same way that they are in early life. Rather, earlier learning and ingrained behavioral repertoires may sustain experiences in later life. As an example, they point out that a bulbectomy in a young adult rat destroys sexual functioning, whereas the same procedure in an older rat does not.

Furthermore, since there have been few longitudinal, let alone cross-sectional studies in this area, it is unknown at what ages psychophysiological changes are likely to occur. Older adults today may not experience changes at the same ages as earlier or future cohorts. It is also possible that psychophysiological changes in emotional experience take place prior to old age rather than during old age. For example, some studies show that psychophysiological responsiveness decreases in middle adulthood—that the difference is between young adults and middle adults and not between middle and older adults. A unique longitudinal study by Joan Tucker and Howard Friedman (1996) found that impulsive and cheerful children had lower survival to old age than did those who were more conscientious, which suggests that present-day aged people may no longer represent the same population as younger cohorts with whom they are compared. Alternately, different emotional experiences may be adaptive at different times of life. Panksepp and Miller suggest that strong emotions play a key role in an organism's early development but are not as useful in later life, when the ability to rely on past experience is more adaptive. Physiological issues constitute the least studied area of emotion in later life. Other areas of emotion have received greater attention, including: positive versus negative emotions, intensity of emotional experience, expression of emotion, emotion in social contexts, and emotional control.

Emotional Experience

Researchers have generally focused on two dimensions of emotional experience in later life: the direction of emotion (positive versus negative) and the intensity of emotional experience. Self-reports obtained by Colleen Johnson and Barbara Barer (1997) from very old people generally show that they feel they are more "mellow" than they used to be. In other studies, however, older adults report that their emotions have decreased in both frequency and intensity. When emotions have been induced in laboratory research by asking participants to recall particular experiences and talk about them, few age differences have been found. Cross-sectional research that involved multiple ethnic and cultural groups and was conducted by James Gross and his colleagues (1997) suggests that intensity and frequency of emotional experiences may decrease across adulthood. Older African Americans and older European Americans reported less intense and less frequent emotional feelings than their younger counterparts. There was, however, variation across ethnic groups. There were no age differences in reports of intensity of emotions for Chinese Americans.

Self-reports of decreased emotional intensity may reflect memory biases rather than actual age differences. A longitudinal study of emotional experiences conducted by Linda Levine and Susan Bluck (1997) revealed that older adults were as upset about a negative event as were younger adults at the time that it happened. When they were asked to compare their feelings about that event a year later, though, the older participants said they had been less upset than their self-reports at the time indicated.

Because there is wide age variance (e.g., older than eighty-five, between seventy and ninety-five, between sixty-five and eighty, older than sixty, and younger than sixty-eight) in the subjects of studies in this area, one must be cautious in making generalized predictions about age changes.

It is not clear whether the balance of positive and negative emotion changes across adulthood, although a consensus in the field suggests that negative affect decreases by very late life. Early cross-sectional national studies showed both positive and negative affect to be slightly lower among older respondents, yet the Berlin Aging Study, as reported by Jaqui Smith and Paul Baltes (1993), found that only positive affect decreased (slightly) with age, both in prevalence and intensity; that negative affect did not. These age differences may reflect differences in definitions of positive emotion. Compared to young adults, older people are less likely to need excitement and novelty and thus may experience less fun and jubilation.

At the same time, an emerging literature suggests that older adults experience less negative emotion too. Several explanations are available for why this may be the case. Older adults may have more experience dealing with problems, they may develop more adaptive coping mechanisms for handling the negative emotions that they do experience, or they may structure their day-to-day life to avoid things that might bother them. Finally, older people may become "habituated" to negative emotions, having experienced them so often during their lifetime that they are less affected by them.

Other studies suggest that there is a stability of positive and negative emotional experiences within individuals. Paul Costa and Robert McCrae (1996) have found that positive and negative emotions are related to the personality traits of extraversion and neuroticism, respectively. In fact, extraversion is sometimes referred to as positive emotionality. Findings from a longitudinal study of personality by Costa and McCrae (1994) suggest that affective traits are part of one's genetic makeup and are likely to be inherited and to remain stable over time, at least until the advent of mental deterioration. Accordingly, decreases in negative emotion in later life may reflect "survivor" factors; only those who have been low in negative emotionality throughout life may survive into very old age.

Emotion in Social Contexts

The role of emotions in social relationships has been widely investigated in the field of gerontology. Laura Carstensen and her colleagues (1997) have argued that older people tend to be more selective in their social contacts than do younger people. Older adults limit their relationships and concentrate their energy on those individuals from whom they tend to gain the greatest emotional rewards. These changes are not seen as wholly age-related, however. When individuals feel that they face a foreshortened future, they may seek such emotional rewards regardless of their chronological age.

In support of Carstensen's theory, studies of relationships show greater age discrepancies in reports of negative emotions than do studies of emotions in general. Older adults report few if any problems with their friends and family members. Attachment to close family members appears to remain over the lifetime. In fact, Johnson and Barer (1997) found that very old people have strong feelings toward their spouse and children and even toward their long-dead parents, although whether these feelings are as strong as they used to be cannot be determined without longitudinal data.

Social life is facilitated by the communication of feelings. If older people demonstrate less emotion or different emotions than they actually feel, this would have important consequences for their social relationships. Several studies show that facial expressions of emotion seem less intense among older people than among younger people. When a variety of emotions—happiness, anger, fear, sadness, and affection—were induced in young, middle-aged, and old women, Carol

An older couple devotes time to themselves as they enjoy skiing together near Leadville, Colorado. (Corbis/ Bob Winsett)

Malatesta and her colleagues (1987) found that those individuals who were in the oldest group exhibited fewer components of the emotions and that their facial expression was not as clear. Matched subjects who were "observers" in this study were less accurate in judging the emotions of the oldest group than they were in rating the two younger groups. Similarly, the emotional expressions of older subjects studied by Robert Levenson and his colleagues (1991) were rated as less discrete and distinctive. It has been suggested that age changes in appearance like wrinkles and sagging facial muscles made the emotions being expressed by the older subjects harder to assess, even by people their own age.

Emotional Control

Regulation of emotional experience appears to be particularly important to older people. Paul and Margaret Baltes (1990) suggest that successful aging is accompanied by "selective optimization with compensation." When it is no longer easy for older people to exert primary control over the events in their life (i.e., to attempt to shape their environment to fit their needs), they can and often do use more secondary control, turning to coping mechanisms such as distancing and reappraisal. As Sigrun-Heidi Filipp (1996, p. 222) notes, "If aged people sometimes appear to be 'less emotional' . . . this might be due in part to particular affect-regulation strategies they have learned to use." M. Powell Lawton and his colleagues (1992) found that their oldest respondents reported more self-regulation and greater emotional control than their younger ones did. The study by Gross and his colleagues (1997) of Norwegian older and younger adults suggested that it is control over emotions rather than intensity of emotional experiences that changes with age.

Cognitive strategies are particularly useful in the regulation of emotion in later life. Fredda Blanchard-Fields, Heather Casper Jahnke, and Cameron Camp (1995) found that older respondents used more avoidance and passive-dependence styles of problem solving than problem-focused styles when they were confronted with emotionally salient problems. They did not try to alter situations but to reinterpret them, a kind of energy conservation. There seemed to be no age differences in emotional salience, however. Alternatively, older adults may devalue and disengage from goals they cannot reach, readjusting their aspirations to fit their capacities. Instead of social comparisons, they tend to make comparisons to their own past, another way of conserving energy by limiting the range of their standards.

Well-Being and Morale

Gerontologists generally equate positive affect with successful aging, using outcome measures such as well-being, morale, or life satisfaction, as well as coping, self-esteem, and mastery. These measures are considered to be the opposite of depression and psychological dysfunction. The ways in which emotion relates to well-being in later life are complex. Ed Diener and his colleagues (1985) found that the relative frequency of positive over negative affect predicted well-being and happiness, while the intensity of these emotions did not. Carol Ryff (1995) argues that well-being is multidimensional. Aspects of well-being such as personal growth and purpose decrease from midlife to old age, but positive relations with others and self-acceptance show no age differences. Thus, to fully understand age differences in well-being, the source of the problems must be considered as well as the individuals' emotional reactions to them.

In The Gin Game (1979), D. L. Coburn presents two elderly people in a county nursing home who help and hurt each other. While they provide each other with companionship, they also force each other to face unpleasant truths about themselves. What starts out as a social game of gin rummy ends up escalating into verbal and physical violence.

Some evidence suggests that depression, as a pathological condition, is widespread in old age, but more recent data show the opposite. Costa and McCrae (1996), for example, found no correlation between depression and age and no change in depression over time. Epidemiological studies show that community dwelling older adults have very low rates of diagnosable major depression but very high rates of depressive symptoms when compared to middle-aged and younger adults. These findings may reflect cohort differences in the nature of depression, for example, with younger cohorts currently showing higher rates of depression than older cohorts did at a comparable age. Alternatively, there may be differences in the nature of depression in later life. One difficulty in diagnosing major depression in later life lies in the failure of older adults to report negative affect in the presence of other depression-related symptoms. Additional research is needed to differentiate aspects of well-being and mood disorders in later life.

See also: DEFENSE MECHANISMS; GRIEF; HEALTH AND ILLNESS; MOOD DISORDERS; RELATIONSHIPS

Bibliography

Baltes, Paul B., and Baltes, Margaret M. (1990). *Successful Aging.* Cambridge, Eng.: Cambridge University Press.

Blanchard-Fields, Fredda; Jahnke, Heather Casper; and Camp, Cameron. (1995). "Age Differences in Problem-Solving Style." *Psychology and Aging* 10:173–180.

Bowlby, John. (1988). "Developmental Psychiatry Comes of Age." *American Journal of Psychiatry* 145:1–10.

Carstensen, Laura L. (1995). "Evidence for a Life-Span Theory of Socioemotional Selectivity." *Current Directions in Psychological Science* 4:151–156.

Carstensen, Laura L.; Gross, James J.; and Fung, Helene H. (1997). "The Social Context of Emotional Experience." In *Annual Review of Gerontology and Geriatrics, Vol. 17: Focus on Emotion and Adult Development,* ed. K. Warner Schaie and M. Powell Lawton. New York: Springer.

Costa, Paul T., Jr., and McCrae, Robert R. (1994). "Stability and Change in Personality from Adolescence to Adulthood." In *The Developing Structure of Temperament and Personality from Infancy to Adulthood,* ed. Charles F. Halverson, Geldolph A. Kohnstamm, and Roy P. Martin. Hillsdale, NJ: Lawrence Erlbaum.

Costa, Paul T., Jr., and McCrae, Robert R. (1996). "Mood and Personality in Adulthood." In *Handbook of Emotion, Adult Development, and Aging,* ed. Carol Magai and Susan H. McFadden. San Diego, CA: Academic Press.

Diener, Ed; Sandvik, Ed; and Larsen, Randy J. (1985). "Age and Sex Effects for Emotional Intensity." *Developmental Psychology* 21(3):542–546.

Ekman, Paul. (1992). "An Argument for Basic Emotions." *Cognition and Emotion* 6:169–200.

Filipp, Sigrun-Heidi. (1996). "Motivation and Emotion." In *Handbook of Psychology of Aging,* 4th ed., ed. James E. Birren and K. Warner Schaie. San Diego, CA: Academic Press.

Gross, James J.; Carstensen, Laura L.; Pasupathi, Monisha; Tsai, Jeanne; Skorpen, Carina G.; and Hsu, Angie. (1997). "Emotion and Aging." *Psychology of Aging* 12:590–599.

Johnson, Colleen L., and Barer, Barbara M. (1997). *Life Beyond 85 Years: The Aura of Survivorship.* New York: Springer.

Lawton, M. Powell; Kleban, Morton H.; Rajagopal, Doris; and Dean, Jennifer. (1992). "Dimensions of Affective Experience in Three Age Groups." *Psychology and Aging* 7(2):171–184.

Levenson, Robert W.; Carstensen, Laura L.; Friesen, Wallace V.; and Ekman, Paul. (1991). "Emotion, Physiology, and Expression in Old Age. *Psychology and Aging* 6:28–35.

Levine, Linda J., and Bluck, Susan. (1997). "Experienced and Remembered Emotional Intensity in Older Adults." *Psychology and Aging* 12:514–523.

Malatesta, Carol Z.; Izard, Carroll E.; Culver, Clayton; and Nicolich, Mark. (1987). "Emotion Communication Skills in Young, Middle-Aged, and Older Women." *Psychology and Aging* 2:193–203.

Panksepp, Jaak, and Miller, Anesa. (1996). "Emotions and the Aging Brain." In *Handbook of Emotion, Adult Development, and Aging,* ed. Carol Magai and Susan H. McFadden. San Diego, CA: Academic Press.

Ryff, Carol D. (1995). *Psychological Well-Being in Adult Life.* Washington, DC: American Psychological Society.

Schulz, Richard. (1985). "Emotion and Affect." In *Handbook of the Psychology of Aging,* 2nd ed., ed. James E. Birren and K. Warner Schaie. New York: Van Nostrand Reinhold.

Smith, Jaqui, and Baltes, Paul B. (1993). "Differential Psychological Ageing: Profiles of the Old and Very Old." *Ageing and Society* 13:551–587.

Troll, Lillian E. (1994). "Family Connectedness of Old Women: Attachments in Later Life." In *Women Growing Older: Psychological Perspectives,* ed. Barbara F. Turner and Lillian E. Troll. Thousand Oaks, CA: Sage Publications.

Tucker, Joan S., and Friedman, Howard S. (1996). "Emotion, Personality, and Health." In *Handbook of Emotion, Adult Development, and Aging,* ed. Carol Magai and Susan H. McFadden. San Diego, CA: Academic Press.

Lillian E. Troll
Karen Fingerman

HUME, DAVID

b. Edinburgh, Scotland, April 26, 1711; *d.* Edinburgh, Scotland, August 25, 1776; *philosophy.*

David Hume was a leading philosopher of the eighteenth century and is considered by many scholars to have been the leading British philosopher of all time. Hume was born the second-oldest son of a Presbyterian family. Ardently anti-English and pro-Scot by the end of his life, Hume supported the colonists in the American Revolution and would very likely have rejected the title of leading British philosopher. Hume lived an unsettled life. Following study (in law and the classics) but not graduation from the University of Edinburgh, he suffered a nervous breakdown, found himself unsuited to the pressures of business, moved to France in 1734 (where he lived on a small inheritance), and wrote his most important work, *A Treatise of Human Nature* (1739). Much of the remainder of his philosophical career was devoted to expanding his ideas about knowledge and ethics, particularly in his *Philosophical Essays Concerning Human Understanding* (1748), later known as *An Enquiry Concerning Human Understanding,* and *An Enquiry Concerning the Principles of Morals* (1751). Upon his return to Britain, Hume worked as a tutor and government secretary and, having never married, lived a good part of his life with his unmarried sister. During his lifetime, Hume's most successful work was his six-volume *History of England* (1754–1762). His treatise on religion, *Dialogues Concerning Natural Religion,* was not published until three years after his death. Although written in 1750, Hume wisely withheld the manuscript from publication because he anticipated that it would cause a furor due

David Hume. (Corbis/Bettmann)

to his attacks on religion. He was correct since his rejection of miracles brought much discussion and criticism. Acceptance of his ideas and acclaim by his contemporaries mostly did not come until after his death. During his lifetime, Hume was known more as an economist (because of his support for the capitalist ideas of his friend Adam Smith) than as a philosopher.

Hume's reputation as a philosopher is based to a great extent on his writings about knowledge and ethics and his strong support for the Enlightenment, the European intellectual revolution that downplayed the importance of religion as a source of knowledge and instead stressed reason, rationality, and science. Hume, along with his friend the political economist Adam Smith, was also a strong advocate of capitalism, another influential idea of the time. Hume thought and wrote about a great range of topics, including logic, metaphysics, causation, reason and reasoning, the external world, individual identity, skepticism, the passions, morality, and religion. However, despite his pro-reason and anti-religion views, Hume, unlike many other contemporary philosophers, also considered the emotions, or what were called the passions or impressions in his time, to be as important as knowledge and ethics. In fact, one-third of his *Treatise* is devoted to his ideas about the role of emotions in human affairs, although he never further developed these ideas as he did his ideas about reason and morality. Consequently, his ideas about emotion have been generally ignored as scholars have chosen instead to focus on his more fully developed and influential ideas about reason and ethics.

Consideration of Hume's contribution to the study of emotion is guided by a basic contradiction. On the one hand, his ideas were largely ignored and had little effect on the scientific study of emotion in later centuries. On the other hand, Hume anticipated by hundreds of years several ideas (even though he made no direct contribution to the development of those ideas) that are now generally accepted in the study of emotion. Perhaps his most important contribution, or potential contribution, was the weight he initially afforded to the study of emotion. Beyond this, he anticipated the outlines of the cognitive perspective by linking emotion to ideas when he argued that ideas cause emotion (what he called impressions) and are in turn caused by emotion. Additionally, Hume, some 150 years before the emergence of the psychoanalytic perspective and the notions of the id, ego, and superego, linked emotion and morality and argued that there are good and bad emotions and that these are normal components of the human experience. Hume was especially interested in sympathy, which he classified as a good emotion. In particular, Hume felt that sympathy worked to balance unbridled self-interest and therefore helped to create a moral society.

See also: COGNITIVE PERSPECTIVE; PHILOSOPHY

Bibliography
Hume, David. ([1739] 1888). *A Treatise of Human Nature*, ed. L. A. Shelby-Bigge. Oxford: Oxford University Press.
Norton, David F. (1982). *David Hume: Common Sense Moralist, Skeptical Metaphysician*. Princeton, NJ: Princeton University Press.

Ben Manning
David Levinson

HURT

Although the term *hurt* is commonly used in everyday discourse by people (e.g., "My feelings were hurt") and by professionals who help clients with problems in living, hurt has rarely been defined in the literature. Hurt is defined here as a subjective state that occurs in response to frustration, threat, or injustice and that is accompanied by thoughts that attribute the cause of the provocation to oneself rather than to factors external to the individual (e.g., other individuals, the situation, "bad luck").

The key distinction between hurt and anger lies in the attribution regarding the cause of the provocation; hurt is experienced when the individual believes that he or she is the cause of the transgression, whereas anger is experienced when the individual believes that some factor external to him or her is the cause.

The emotion of hurt is of particular clinical importance. Not only does it represent a common emotional reaction to frustration, threat, or injustice, but it is a state that underlies sadness and depression. Even beyond its clinical importance, however, hurt affects daily living for large numbers of individuals who are not clinically depressed.

A Cognitive Perspective on Hurt

It helps to adopt a cognitive perspective in trying to understand the emotion of hurt. Cognitive theories of emotion posit that there are certain kinds of thoughts that must occur for a particular emotion to arise. For Aaron T. Beck (1976), sadness (which is not identical to hurt, but which is similar enough that Beck's analysis applies to hurt as well) or anger follow instances of downgrading, which involves the experience of being insulted or criticized. Beck maintains that the emotional response to downgrading, either anger or sadness, will depend upon whether the downgrading is perceived as unwarranted or unjust (anger) or as warranted or deserved (sadness). Thus, it is how the individual interprets the situation, more perhaps than the situation itself, that determines whether hurt or anger, some combination of hurt and anger, or even perhaps some other emotion, is experienced.

How Hurt is Experienced and Expressed

Hurt has been described in vivid ways in a variety of literatures. Victor Frankl (1984), in discussing his experiences in a concentration camp, recalled a time when he was beaten for no apparent reason. Referring to the sharp blows he received to his head, he wrote "it is not the physical pain which hurts the most . . . , it is the mental agony caused by the injustice; the unreasonableness of it all" (p. 36). The distress that hurt can evoke is exemplified in two quotes from esteemed literary figures. Jonathan Swift stated in *Journal to Stella* (1711), "One enemy can do more hurt than 10 friends can do good." Similarly, Samuel Johnson (1777) expressed a similar sentiment when he wrote, "[And] if I have said something to hurt a man once, I shall not get the better of this by saying many things to please him."

Thus, hurt can be experienced as a very unpleasant emotional experience. In what ways can it be expressed? There are probably as many ways to express hurt as there are different situations that evoke this emotion. However, there are four broad categories of ways that hurt can be expressed: with sadness and despair ("I must not be any good to be treated so poorly by others"); with anger ("How dare they not give me this promotion!"); with aggression ("I'll show you how it feels to be left out!"); and with avoidance and withdrawal ("If I withdraw from this group, no one can hurt me any more"). The particular way that hurt is expressed depends on a complex process involving the individual's unique characteristics and the context in which the hurt occurs.

Variability in the Experience and Expression of Hurt

There are individual differences in the extent to which people attribute provocations to justified or unjustified factors. Some individuals are prone to blaming themselves for being provoked and, thus, are more likely to experience hurt than anger. Some are more likely to blame others and are, thus, more likely to experience anger than hurt. It is quite important to realize that, because of these individual differences, different people are likely to interpret the same provocation quite differently. For example, some might experience hurt in response to being yelled at by another driver on the road, while others might

> *Katherine Anne Porter, in "The Jilting of Granny Weatherall" (1930), depicts two jiltings. In the first, some sixty years before the story takes place, the man she was to marry did not show up at the wedding. In the second, as Granny lies dying and expecting Christ to come get her to take her to heaven, "again no bridegroom" appears. She feels terribly hurt and abandoned.*

experience anger in response to the same treatment. Some studies have supported this cognitive perspective on how hurt is experienced. In a study that asked undergraduates to record thoughts and emotions whenever they felt angry, anxious, or sad, Cynthia Wickless and Irving Kirsch (1988) found that thoughts of loss were associated with sadness. Different types of thoughts, however, tended to occur in combination with each other and, consequently, individuals often felt both sad and angry at the same time.

Men and women tend to differ in their emotional responses to provocation, and several studies have found that women are more likely to experience hurt than men. Nevertheless, a caution is in order. It is possible that differing types of events evoke hurt in men than in women and that previous researchers have studied primarily the kinds of events that women find hurtful. Mary Biaggio (1988), for example, found that women reported greater hurt than men in response to a criticism scenario but that there were no gender differences for scenarios involving an annoying or ignorant person. Very few studies have looked at other individual differences in the experience and expression of hurt.

Effects of Experiencing Hurt

Although hurt is usually considered to be an unpleasant emotion to experience, it is important to recognize that it can have positive consequences. As Benjamin Franklin stated in *Poor Richard's Almanack* (1744), "The things which hurt, instruct." In addition to the educational benefits from experiencing hurt, the ability to experience and express hurt feelings is probably most important in the domain of close interpersonal relationships. Luciano L'Abate (1977) emphasized the critical role of the sharing of hurt feelings and fears in the development of intimacy, which, in turn, has been shown to be important in the prediction of healthy physical and psychological functioning. Further evidence supporting this hypothesis was provided by Jim McLennan, Gordon Gotts, and Mary Omodei (1988), who found that emotional vulnerability (they did not specifically assess hurt) was strongly related to feelings of well-being. In addition, Mark Fine and Kenneth Olson (1997) found a significant, although relatively small, positive relation between the tendency to report hurt feelings in response to hypothetical provocations and reported levels of intimacy for males and females.

If an individual experiences an excessive amount of self-blame, however, and consequently experiences considerable hurt, he or she may, because of a fear of rejection, feel powerless, be unassertive, and not take steps to resolve problems. Consistent with this claim, higher hurt scores for males (but not females) were associated with lower assertiveness in the Fine and Olson study. Perhaps because males experience hurt feelings less frequently than do females, males are more detrimentally affected by the sense of personal vulnerability that accompanies feeling hurt. As a result, males who have a tendency to experience hurt may be less assertive because they fear that being assertive will lead to further hurt-producing confrontations. Of course, it is also possible that men who are less assertive tend to be more sensitive and, therefore, are more easily hurt. In addition, Fine and Olson found that the tendency to experience hurt was associated with lower life satisfaction. Perhaps regularly anticipating and fearing that one may experience hurt negatively affects the course of daily living.

Conclusion

Based on knowledge about hurt and how it is experienced, three primary conclusions can be drawn. First, because hurt and anger are often experienced concurrently, one can expect that individuals who report experiencing one of these emotions are also, at some level of consciousness, experiencing the other. Practitioners who work with individuals with emotional problems can expect that clients showing emotional symptoms in one domain (i.e., hurt or anger) may also be experiencing the other emotion (i.e., anger or hurt) to a clinically significant degree. Thus, clinicians might help depressed clients become more aware of their possible feelings of anger. Similarly, clients with anger control problems might be encouraged to become more aware of their possible hurt feelings.

Second, there is enough empirical evidence to conclude tentatively that there are adjustment consequences—both positive and negative—that arise from experiencing the emotion of hurt. Thus, not only should practitioners assess the extent to which clients report hurt and anger, but they should also determine how individuals' tendencies to experience hurt are related to their psychological adjustment.

Finally, individuals who experience hurt quite often ("chronic" hurt) may benefit from examining their attributions about what causes the transgressions and provocations that they experience. These individuals are likely to have a tendency to blame themselves when they are provoked and may benefit from interventions designed to help them see that some of their unpleasant experiences are not caused by themselves, but rather by external conditions. Coming to have a more "balanced" set of attributions about the causes of unpleasant experiences may relieve hurt feelings and lead to greater satisfaction with life.

See also: AGGRESSION; ANGER; ANNOYANCE; ATTRIBUTION; COGNITIVE PERSPECTIVE; HATE; JEALOUSY

Bibliography

Atkinson, Carolyn, and Polivy, Janet. (1976). "Effects of Delay, Attack, and Retaliation on State Depression and Hostility." *Journal of Abnormal Psychology* 85:570–576.

Beck, Aaron T. (1976). *Cognitive Therapy and the Emotional Disorders.* New York: International Universities Press.

Biaggio, Mary K. (1988). "Sex Differences in Anger: Are They Real?" Paper presented at the American Psychological Association Convention, Atlanta, GA.

Biaggio, Mary K., and Maiuro, Roland D. (1985). "Recent Advances in Anger Assessment." In *Advances in Personality Assessment, Vol. 5,* ed. Charles D. Spielberger and James N. Butcher. Hillsdale, NJ: Lawrence Erlbaum.

Fine, Mark A., and Olson, Kenneth. (1997). "Hurt and Anger in Response to Provocation: Relations to Aspects of Adjustment." *Journal of Social Behavior and Personality* 12:325–344.

Frankl, Victor. (1984). *Man's Search for Meaning: An Introduction to Logotherapy,* 3rd ed. New York: Simon & Schuster.

Harris, Irving, and Howard, Kenneth. (1987). "Correlates of Depression and Anger in Adolescence." *Journal of Child and Adolescent Psychotherapy* 4:199–203.

L'Abate, Luciano. (1977). "Intimacy is Sharing Hurt Feelings: A Reply to David Mace." *Journal of Marriage and Family Counseling* 3:13–16.

Lazarus, Richard S. (1994). "Appraisal: The Long and Short of It." In *The Nature of Emotion: Fundamental Questions,* ed. Paul Ekman and Richard J. Davidson. New York: Oxford University Press.

McLennan, Jim; Gotts, Gordon; and Omodei, Mary. (1988). "Personality and Relationship Dispositions as Determinants of Subjective Well-Being." *Human Relations* 41:593–602.

Miller, Rickey S., and Lefcourt, Herbert M. (1982). "The Assessment of Social Intimacy." *Journal of Personality Assessment* 46:514–518.

Notarius, Clifford I.; Lashley, Samuel L.; and Sullivan, Debra J. (1997). "Angry at Your Partner?: Think Again." In *Satisfaction in Close Relationships,* ed. Robert J. Sternberg and Mahzad Hojjat. New York: Guilford.

Novaco, Raymond W. (1975). *Anger Control.* Lexington, MA: Lexington Books.

Wickless, Cynthia, and Kirsch, Irving. (1988). "Cognitive Correlates of Anger, Anxiety, and Sadness." *Cognitive Therapy and Research* 12:367–377.

Mark A. Fine
Adriana J. Umana